Flash Remoting
The Definitive Guide

Other resources from O'Reilly

Related titles Programming ColdFusion MX   ActionScript for Flash MX:
ActionScript for Flash MX   The Definitive Guide
Pocket Reference   ActionScript Cookbook

oreilly.com *oreilly.com* is more than a complete catalog of O'Reilly books. You'll also find links to news, events, articles, weblogs, sample chapters, and code examples.

oreillynet.com is the essential portal for developers interested in open and emerging technologies, including new platforms, programming languages, and operating systems.

Conferences O'Reilly & Associates brings diverse innovators together to nurture the ideas that spark revolutionary industries. We specialize in documenting the latest tools and systems, translating the innovator's knowledge into useful skills for those in the trenches. Visit *conferences.oreilly.com* for our upcoming events.

Safari Bookshelf (*safari.oreilly.com*) is the premier online reference library for programmers and IT professionals. Conduct searches across more than 1,000 books. Subscribers can zero in on answers to time-critical questions in a matter of seconds. Read the books on your Bookshelf from cover to cover or simply flip to the page you need. Try it today with a free trial.

Flash Remoting
The Definitive Guide

Tom Muck

Beijing · Cambridge · Farnham · Köln · Paris · Sebastopol · Taipei · Tokyo

Flash Remoting: The Definitive Guide
by Tom Muck

Published by O'Reilly & Associates, Inc., 1005 Gravenstein Highway North, Sebastopol, CA 95472.

O'Reilly & Associates books may be purchased for educational, business, or sales promotional use. Online editions are also available for most titles (*safari.oreilly.com*). For more information, contact our corporate/institutional sales department: (800) 998-9938 or *corporate@oreilly.com*.

Editor:	Bruce Epstein
Production Editor:	Genevieve d'Entremont
Cover Designer:	Emma Colby
Interior Designer:	David Futato

Printing History:

September 2003:   First Edition.

ISBN: 0-596-00401-X
[C]

Dedicated to the memory of my father-in-law,
Stanley S. Lee . . . a truly original man who
succeeded in living life on his own terms.
Dad, your character is an inspiration. It was a
privilege to have known you and I will miss you.

—Tom Muck

Table of Contents

Part III. Advanced Flash Remoting

Part IV. Appendixes

Preface

The Web has always been an expanding, changing medium. What was in vogue just a few years ago might be completely abandoned today, and what is in vogue today may be completely abandoned tomorrow. Java™ applets were considered a breakthrough technology that was going to revolutionize the Web when they first came out. Java applets failed to take hold for several reasons, chief among them the complexity of the Java language for nonprogrammers, the download size for anything more than a simple applet, and the security restrictions that effectively tied the hands of the applet. ASP was Microsoft's attempt to replace Java applets with server-side applications. JSP learned from the mistakes of ASP and provided a much more robust solution by offering compiled pages rather than interpreted pages. ASP.NET, in turn, learned from the mistakes of JSP by providing a framework that can be accessible to a variety of different languages using a common runtime environment.

And Flash has learned from the mistakes of those early Java applets. The Flash browser plugin is small, self-contained, and ubiquitous. Flash is attractive to designers as well as programmers, and it provides rich functionality that enhances the end user's experience. Also, a Flash movie looks essentially the same on a Windows machine as it does on a Macintosh.

Some things have not changed, however. The Web is still primarily based in HTML. Even though XHTML is coming into prominence, it is just a syntactically standardized version of HTML that conforms to XML specifications. Flash solves many of the deficiencies of HTML by improving on animation limitations of DHTML, allowing for true interactivity, offering greater cross-platform and cross-browser consistency, and allowing upgrades of the Flash Player without requiring the user to upgrade his browser. By making Flash consistent across platforms, Macromedia has ensured that the Flash designer can virtually eliminate the laborious trial-and-error work that HTML web page designers go through to keep their pages consistent across platforms and browser types.

Macromedia Flash Remoting MX, or simply *Flash Remoting*, first offered with Flash MX, allows sophisticated datatypes to be passed from the server to the client and back without the speed limitations, bulk, and manual serialization/deserialization required by the XML techniques in previous versions of Flash.

In a traditional HTML application, a typical user experience is like this:

1. The user comes to your site. He enters something into a search field and clicks the Submit button.

2. The user waits for a response from the server. His browser loads the page, allowing the user to view the search results.

3. If the results span more than one page and the user clicks the link for the next set of results, the search request is sent to the server again. The server conducts the search again and sends back the second page of results.

4. Again, a new page is loaded into the browser.

You can liken this experience to a very inefficient phone conversation with a friend. You ask a question and hang up the phone. Your friend calls back and answers the question, then hangs up. You call him back, add something to the conversation, and hang up again. Two tin cans with a taught string between them gives you a more advanced communication method. Yet this is similar to how the client/server communication with a browser operates, and it is the prevailing standard on the Web.

HTML can build primitive web applications, but its main advantage is its ubiquity. However, Flash Player 6, which plays back content authored in Flash MX (including Flash Remoting applications) has over 85% penetration and allows developers to deploy much more sophisticated web applications. Flash Player 7 is in public beta, and by the time you read this, the release version will be available. Flash Remoting offers seamless communication between the client browser and the remote server. Each revision of the Flash Player, whose uptake is much faster than browser updates, essentially upgrades the Web. Only minor changes have been made to Flash Remoting in Flash MX 2004 and Flash MX Professional 2004 (Flash Pro), although the latter offers enhanced support for SOAP-based web services. Regardless of whether you are using Flash MX, Flash MX 2004, or Flash Pro, the principles and examples shown throughout this book apply equally.

Singing the praises of Flash Remoting is not to say that HTML does not have its place—it clearly does—but Flash offers user interactivity closer to a desktop application than a traditional HTML web site. Also, because ActionScript's syntax is nearly identical to JavaScript, web scripters can easily transition to Flash. Flash MX also introduced Flash UI components, which are configurable and skinnable interface elements, such as checkboxes and list boxes. In previous versions of Flash, UI functionality had to be created for each new application. Components allow developers to concentrate on the application's functionality rather than worry about mundane aspects of buttons and form elements. Components share a common API that leverages easy-to-use methods. This brings rapid application development (RAD), familiar to Delphi and Visual Basic users, to Flash-based web applications. Components are also extremely flexible, allowing designers to skin the components to fit seamlessly with the site design.

Drumbeat 2000, a web development program from Elemental Software (later purchased by Macromedia), tried to abstract HTML into a visual interface by turning HTML elements into JavaScript objects. Strongly resembling Visual Basic, the interface of Drumbeat 2000 used drag-and-drop components that were thinly disguised HTML tags and server-side script objects. Unfortunately, HTML was not intended for a point-and-click environment or an event-based model. Drumbeat 2000 died a quick death because the HTML/JavaScript objects slowed down an already slow technology, although parts of it were rolled into UltraDev and Dreamweaver MX.

Flash, on the other hand, is designed around an event-based GUI that thrives on point-and-click interaction with efficient self-contained ActionScript objects. Flash allows designers to customize the user interface, limited only by their imagination. A Flash designer can utilize standard prebuilt interface objects or build his own to create the interaction between his application and the end user. The ActionScript programmer can use these components to call server-side methods through Flash Remoting. This allows the Flash movie to do what it does best—interact with the user—and allows the server-side application to do what it does best—process information.

Flash Remoting technology adds true client/server communication to browser-based applications because it is not page-based; it is based on a single interface that loads once for the entire application. The Flash movie creates a one-time connection to the server. The *application state* is maintained within the Flash Player. Gone is the click/wait/reload approach of HTML. As of Flash MX, you can build your web application as a unit with Flash as the front end and your application server on the back end. The communication with the server is handled by Flash behind the scenes. When you build an application with Flash Remoting, the user experience is similar to what you would expect from a desktop application.

Take, for example, an interaction with an online store. A typical HTML page can consist of dozens of files and be 20–100 KB or more. But what about subsequent pages? Even if a page is remarkably similar to the one that came before, each page is often loaded in its entirety from the server (unless that page is already cached locally, in which case it still has to be rerendered by the browser). Menus, headings, copyright notices, and so on might be identical on every page, yet they are reloaded each time. There has to be a more efficient means of downloading and rendering page content.

Enter the Flash Player and Flash Remoting. With Flash Remoting, the browser needs to download only the subset of information that has changed from page to page, which is typically fed from the application server. When you click a Search button in a Flash application that uses Flash Remoting, the request is sent to the server in a small ActionScript Message Format (AMF) packet, and another AMF packet is sent back to the browser. The Flash movie loads the information contained in the packet, such as a recordset, array, or other datatype, and utilizes it as needed.

If successive screens are highly similar, instead of loading each 25 KB page separately, Flash needs to download only the portion that differs—the information to be displayed instead of existing interface elements. If data is required, the AMF format ensures it can be downloaded efficiently in a mere few hundred bytes. There is no need to completely redraw the entire page as a new page loads in, because Flash Remoting is supplying only data from the server and the Flash movie uses the data as needed. Also, Flash can often download data in the background so it is ready when needed. In most cases, the user isn't even aware that the server was contacted.

You can picture poor old HTML just sitting there thinking, "now why didn't I think of that?" Developers are often slow to adapt, however. Many HTML developers are unwilling to admit that HTML, while apt for simple pages, was never designed for complex interactivity, animation, and sound. As such, it is not surprising that Flash is much more convenient for creating interactive sites. Nevertheless, Flash and Flash Remoting are bringing the same interactivity and usability to the Web that GUIs brought to the desktop a generation ago.

Remoting: More Than Just a Name

Flash Remoting is a technology that resides on the remote application server—hence the name. It acts as a *gateway* to the server and translates client calls from a Flash movie into calls that the server can understand. It is included with ColdFusion MX Server and JRun 4 and offered as an add-on for ASP.NET and J2EE-compatible servers, such as IBM WebSphere. Third-party developers have built versions for PHP and Perl as well.

Prior versions of Flash were able to communicate with a server in a limited fashion using name/value variable pairs or XML. Flash Remoting offers the following advantages over these methods:

- A Flash movie, through the server-side Flash Remoting gateway, can call server-side methods directly, not merely pass values or files back and forth.

- The client- and server-side XML or name/value parsing required for Flash 5 interaction is virtually eliminated with Flash Remoting, although it can still be used effectively in some situations.

- Because the server-side Flash Remoting gateway can communicate directly with the Flash movie, complex objects, such as arrays, structures, and recordsets, can be transferred without serialization/deserialization.

Also, because the server contains functionality that can be accessed directly (such as calling a server-side method by name from within the Flash movie), the Flash code can be more concise. Recordsets can be loaded into Flash movies using a *RecordSet* object, making it easy to sort and page through results directly from the client browser. In addition, the *DataGlue* class (part of the client components of Flash Remoting) offers a set of functions that allows you to bind Flash user interface elements to the data. Flash Remoting also offers debugging of client-side code and server communication using the *NetConnection debugger* and a *service browser* that allows you to introspect remote services from the Flash authoring environment. With all of these features, web programming has finally come of age.

 Throughout this book we refer to *recordsets* (data retrieved from a database on a server) and client-side *RecordSets* (the ActionScript class that is used in Flash Remoting). A third term—*resultset*—is used when talking about the *java.sql.resultset* class in Java.

Flash Remoting makes it a snap to connect to ColdFusion, J2EE, ASP.NET, and PHP applications and the back-end databases that these server technologies support, such as SQL Server, Oracle, DB2, Access, PostgreSQL, and MySQL. Using Flash Remoting, you can create sophisticated applications with a clear line drawn between the client-side interface (Flash) and the server-side logic (business logic). The Flash application can be deployed in the browser or on the desktop. Also, the server-side logic need not be tied to a Flash interface: your server-side code does not require any Flash-specific syntax. In addition to servicing the Flash client, the server-side methods of the application can be utilized by other server-side pages supplying HTML content, or even a .NET desktop application.

Flash Remoting, in conjunction with ColdFusion MX, JRun, and other technologies, also replaces much of the functionality of Macromedia's extinct Generator server-side Flash technology. Generator templates are no longer supported, but Macromedia offers a transition path to Flash Remoting. For more information on the transition, go to:

> *http://www.macromedia.com/software/generator/productinfo/faq/*

What Is Remoting Used For?

I've talked about the benefits of Flash Remoting, but what can you build with it? Here are some of the possible uses of Flash Remoting:

- Any application that requires a connection to a database, filesystem, or other server-side technology.
- Online stores that feature catalogs and shopping cart systems. The entire user experience can be consolidated into one central interface with no page reloads.

- Sound and video clip libraries. Using the streaming audio and video capabilities of Flash in conjunction with Flash Communication Server (FlashCom), along with the server-side capabilities of an application server, you can offer searchable, browsable clip libraries.

- Banner ads with built-in shopping carts, click-through tracking, and full-site search capabilities.

- New controls that can be used in place of HTML elements that leverage the server-side capabilities of ColdFusion, ASP.NET, or J2EE.

- Extensions to Flash, Dreamweaver, Fireworks, or other applications that provide instant access to a remote support site or reference material.

- An online auction interface that stores your own watched items locally and polls the remote web service for changes in bids.

- Front-ends to databases for administrators. You can give your client an administrative interface so that she can access tables and raw data without giving her the keys to the store, so to speak.

The architecture of Flash Remoting makes it easy for Flash programmers to develop Flash movies, knowing only the remote method names and functionality. They can access server-side functionality using familiar ActionScript syntax. Likewise, server-side coders can build functionality on the server without knowing how the Flash movie is going to interact with it. They merely have to provide an interface to the method and return a result. That result can be virtually anything, such as a record-set, string, number, array, or structure. Complex applications can be broken down into component parts, with designers building the Flash interfaces, ActionScript programmers coding the client-side Flash Remoting code, and server-side programmers (ColdFusion, PHP, Perl, Java, or ASP.NET) supplying the server-side functionality.

What This Book Contains

Flash development encompasses drawing, programming, animating, and working with sound, images, and video. You can be proficient at one or many of these technologies. There are numerous books that cover Flash, each with its own merits and approach. Knowledge of ActionScript is essential to understanding Flash Remoting. (However, the ActionScript gymnastics that Flash 5 developers had to employ to communicate with a server are virtually eliminated with Flash Remoting.)

This book teaches Flash Remoting for programmers, because it is a technology for programmers. I assume you are one of the following:

- A Flash (ActionScript) programmer who wants to use Flash Remoting to communicate with a server

- A server-side application developer who wants to expand his knowledge to Flash development

I discuss Flash Remoting using terminology that an experienced programmer will appreciate, but I try to keep the discussion within the reach of aspiring programmers as well. I also explain the best practices for working with Flash Remoting. Although best practices are often subjective, I try to be as objective as possible or offer consensus conclusions about best practices.

What This Book Is Not

Flash is traditionally an environment for designers, but the design aspects of Flash are not covered in this book. This book assumes you are familiar with the Flash authoring environment. When I mention the Actions panel, for example, I assume you know to find it under Window → Actions (F9). If not, go through the Flash tutorials under Help → Flash Tutorials, or read an overall tutorial book on the Flash MX environment and workflow, such as *Macromedia Flash MX Hands-On Training* (Peachpit Press).

Flash Remoting is not complex, but it helps to know the Flash authoring tool. If you are familiar with other programming environments, such as the Visual Basic or Delphi environments, learning the Flash interface is easy. Coming from a Visual Basic background, I felt right at home in Flash MX. Flash Pro extends the forms-based visual metaphor, making it even more accessible to Visual Basic developers.

This book assumes you know basic programming concepts—such as loops, variables, and arrays—and ActionScript programming techniques in particular. If you don't know ActionScript but are proficient in another language, such as JavaScript, C++, Java, or CFML, see *ActionScript for Flash MX: The Definitive Guide* by Colin Moock (O'Reilly). That book is recommended for ActionScript programmers of all levels, including those wanting to learn ActionScript (it too assumes familiarity with the Flash authoring environment's GUI).

Object-oriented programming (OOP) will play an important role in this book, but again, this isn't a book on OOP. I assume you have at least a passing knowledge of OOP; the book uses OOP techniques when they make sense, but it is not bound by them. There are some OOP purists who may scoff at some of the techniques, but it is my goal to show you the techniques you need to utilize Flash Remoting. OOP is, after all, only a methodology. It is most often the best tool for the job, but I don't want to burden the code with OOP for its own sake.

This book does not teach ColdFusion, C#, or Java; however, basic programming knowledge is sufficient to understand the examples even if you don't know much about server-side programming. Because Flash Remoting can be used in a variety of environments, examples are presented in different technologies. Wherever applicable, the server-side examples show ColdFusion (CFML), J2EE (Java), PHP, and ASP.NET (C# or VB) code. The Flash ActionScript, in most cases, remains essentially the same. Independence of the server-side server model is another cool benefit of Flash

Remoting. O'Reilly has a slew of excellent books on C#, Java, PHP, and ASP.NET. See Appendix B for some recommendations, or see the O'Reilly catalog page at *http:// www.oreilly.com/catalog* for a more complete list. For guidance on ColdFusion, see *Programming ColdFusion MX* by Rob Brooks-Bilson (O'Reilly).

The Book at a Glance

This is the first edition of *Flash Remoting: The Definitive Guide*. It covers new ground because Flash Remoting is a relatively new technology. Most of the examples in the book centralize the code on the first frame of the timeline or in an external include file.

Flash Remoting works with several different server-side technologies. You should skim the sections that cover alternative server models, as they contain useful nuggets applicable to other platforms. Each chapter may be read individually or as parts of a whole. The first three chapters will be crucial to understanding Flash Remoting and should be read sequentially.

The chapter breakdown is as follows.

Part I: Remoting Fundamentals

Part I covers the setup and installation of Flash Remoting and offers a basic introduction to its use. It also offers details on core concepts and Remoting internals.

Chapter 1, *Introduction to Flash Remoting*
> A general introduction to Flash Remoting and related technologies. It implements a sample "Hello World" application for all supported platforms, which demonstrates the simplicity of the technology.

Chapter 2, *Installing, Configuring, and Using Flash Remoting*
> Gives a complete rundown of what is needed to implement Flash Remoting and describes the basic installation processes for each component. The Flash authoring interface is described as it relates to Flash Remoting.

Chapter 3, *Client/Server Interaction, UI Components, and RecordSets*
> The Flash MX UI components are covered as they relate to Flash Remoting, along with several components released as commercial add-ons by Macromedia. In addition, techniques to build forms in Flash MX are described. Examples highlight each key point.

Chapter 4, *Flash Remoting Internals*
> Explains the Flash Remoting API by dissecting the various classes that are installed when you install the Flash Remoting components and methods of those classes. Again, each important point is shown using examples that you can run on your own system.

Part II: The Server-Side Languages

Part II covers the server-side environments that Flash can communicate with via Flash Remoting.

Chapter 5, *Flash Remoting and ColdFusion MX*
    ColdFusion is perhaps the easiest and most popular of the different server-side models available to Flash Remoting, and this chapter shows various techniques for using Flash Remoting with ColdFusion.

Chapter 6, *Server-Side ActionScript*
    Server-Side ActionScript (SSAS) allows Flash MX developers to develop server-side code using the familiar ActionScript syntax instead of ColdFusion or Java. ColdFusion and JRun servers can both execute Server-Side ActionScript using a built-in parser based on the open source Rhino implementation of JavaScript.

Chapter 7, *Flash Remoting and Java*
    Flash Remoting lets developers enhance any J2EE (i.e., Java) application. This chapter covers applications that run on supported J2EE servers, including Macromedia's JRun 4 server and IBM's WebSphere.

Chapter 8, *Flash Remoting and .NET*
    Microsoft's Active Server Pages (ASP) technology is being phased out in favor of ASP.NET. Flash Remoting works well with ASP.NET but does not support ASP. This chapter covers the idiosyncrasies of the ASP.NET implementation by building several real-world examples.

Chapter 9, *Flash Remoting and PHP*
    The PHP technology is an open source server platform that attracts many users. Macromedia did not release a version of Flash Remoting for PHP, but a group of developers have created an open source solution. This chapter covers the PHP implementation, AMFPHP.

Part III: Advanced Flash Remoting

Part III covers advanced Flash Remoting techniques.

Chapter 10, *Calling Web Services from Flash Remoting*
    Flash Remoting allows Flash to interface with SOAP-based web services, regardless of the server-side language with which the web service is implemented. This chapter covers both basic and advanced techniques for publishing and communicating with remote web services.

Chapter 11, *Extending Objects and UI Controls*
    Flash's built-in UI components and ActionScript objects can be extended to offer more functionality. This chapter examines several objects and components and explains how to extend functionality to enhance Flash Remoting.

Chapter 12, *Flash Remoting Best Practices*

Expands on earlier chapters by showing some common best practices that an ActionScript programmer can use with Flash Remoting, such as handling server-side results and errors, organizing code, and clearly separating the UI from the server-side functionality.

Chapter 13, *Testing and Debugging*

Flash supports important debugging tools for serious application development. This chapter explains the ActionScript and NetServices debuggers, as well as general techniques for both client-side and server-side debugging.

Chapter 14, *Real-World Application*

Demonstrates building a simple script repository, including the inserting, updating, deleting, and displaying of data from a database and the uploading, downloading, and storing of scripts.

Chapter 15, *Flash Remoting API*

A Flash Remoting API reference that you will refer to as you build your Flash Remoting applications.

Part IV: Appendixes

Appendix A, *ActionScript Datatype Conversion*

Covers datatype conversion from Flash Remoting to the different server-side languages.

Appendix B, *Books and Online Resources*

Lists other resources covering Flash Remoting or related technologies.

Appendix C, *Specification and Implementation for a Real-World Application*

Includes details of the user interface specification and implementation of the real-world script repository application demonstrated in Chapter 14.

Terminology Conventions

The word *Flash* has different meaning in different contexts, such as a browser plugin or the authoring environment. This book follows these naming conventions:

Flash

Refers generically to Flash movies and the Flash technology.

Flash MX

Refers to the Flash MX authoring environment.

Flash MX 2004 (Flash 2004)

Refers to the Flash 2004 authoring environment. Flash 2004, released in September 2003, is the sequel to Flash MX. Flash Remoting in Flash 2004 is the same as Flash Remoting in Flash MX.

Flash MX Professional 2004 (Flash Pro)

Refers to the Flash Pro authoring environment. Flash Pro offers all the features of Flash 2004, plus a forms-based UI and some additional components. Flash Remoting in Flash Pro is the same as Flash Remoting in Flash 2004 and Flash MX, although there is additional support for access to SOAP-based web services.

Flash Player 7, Flash Player 6, or Flash Player

Refers to the browser plugin that allows users play *.swf* files (movies). I use the term *plugin*, even though the Flash Player is an ActiveX control in Internet Explorer. If we use the generic term *Flash Player* in relation to Flash Remoting, you can assume we mean Flash Player 6 or later. Flash Player 7 has built-in support for SOAP-based web services without requiring a server-side installation.

Flash 5

Refers to the Flash 5 authoring environment. Flash 5 does not support Flash Remoting.

Flash Player 5

Refers to the earlier browser plugin. Flash Player 5 does not support Flash Remoting.

Standalone Player

Refers to the Flash Player that runs on the local system without needing the browser. The Standalone Player for Flash MX or later supports Flash Remoting, but earlier Standalone Players (i.e., Flash 5 and earlier) do not.

Flash Remoting

Refers generically to the technology that includes the ability to communicate between Flash and some server-side component, including the server-side software that supports Flash Remoting and the AMF message format.

Flash Remoting MX and Flash Remoting gateway

Both terms refer to the server-side modules needed for each server model. For ColdFusion, it is a native service (a Java servlet); in ASP.NET it's an assembly; in Java servers, it runs as a servlet; in PHP, it is a class.

Flash Remoting Components

Refers to the downloadable components from Macromedia that you have to install into the Flash authoring environment in order to work with Flash Remoting.

ColdFusion MX

Refers to the Macromedia ColdFusion MX application server.

ColdFusion Markup Language (CFML) and ColdFusion

Both terms refer to the ColdFusion programming language in which *.cfm* pages are implemented.

J2EE server

Refers to Java 2 Enterprise Edition servers, such as JRun 4 or IBM's WebSphere.

Java server

Refers to other implementations of Java servlet technologies, such as Tomcat, that don't necessarily support the J2EE specification.

Java

Refers to the programming language used to build J2EE and Java server applications.

Typographical Conventions

This book follows these typographical conventions:

Menu options

These are shown separated by the → character, such as File → New or Modify → Align → To Stage.

`Constant width`

Used for directives, variable names, property names, parameter names, ColdFusion markup tags, and code samples. It also denotes code within the text.

Italic

Italics indicate function names, object names, class names, directory names, commands, filenames, and file suffixes such as *.swf* or URLs such as *http://www.macromedia.com/index.html*. Italics are also used for emphasis, such as when introducing a new term to the reader. Functions or methods will usually be followed by parenthesis, like *myFunction()*.

`Constant width bold`

Indicates that the reader should enter something verbatim. It is sometimes used within code samples for emphasis.

`Constant width italic`

Indicates a placeholder that should be substituted with your own value, such as *`myServiceName`*. It can also be used for emphasis within code comments. Optional items are also sometimes shown in square brackets.

Some sections of text that require special attention will be set apart from the text with the following icons:

> This is a tip. A tip either reiterates an important point, offers a tidbit of information that relates to the current discussion, or brings to your attention an item that is crucial to understanding the topic at hand.

> This is a warning. A warning describes some aspect of the current topic that needs careful attention so that you can avoid possible problems down the road.

We'd Like to Hear from You

The book-writing process is long and arduous, and the examples have been tested and retested. However, mistakes do creep in from time to time. If you find any errors in the text or code examples, please write to:

O'Reilly & Associates, Inc.
1005 Gravenstein Highway North
Sebastopol, CA 95472
1-800-998-9938 (in the United States or Canada)
1-707-829-0515 (international/local)
1-707-829-0104 (fax)

We have a web page for the book, where we list any additional information. You can access this page at:

http://www.oreilly.com/catalog/flashremoting/

To comment or ask technical questions about this book, send email to:

bookquestions@oreilly.com

For more information about our books, conferences, software, Resource Centers, and the O'Reilly Network, see our web site at:

http://www.oreilly.com

In addition to the O'Reilly web site, the author maintains a web site that ties in with the book. There you will find articles, examples, and links to other resources. You can download working versions of most of the examples in the book from the online Code Depot on the author's web site, which is located at:

http://www.flash-remoting.com

You can reach the author at:

tom@flash-remoting.com

Future Versions of Flash

The examples in this book were tested most heavily in Flash Player 6 and Flash MX; however, Flash Player 7, Flash 2004, and Flash Pro were still in final beta at the time of this writing. Any discrepancies between Flash MX (and Flash Player 6) and later versions will be noted on the book's accompanying web site: *http://www.flash-remoting.com*.

Acknowledgments

Although I've written several books dealing with Macromedia tools, this has been the most difficult, due to the cutting-edge technologies being used. When we first began, Flash Remoting was available only for ColdFusion, with ASP.NET and Java versions in beta. Now, open source projects are springing up that utilize the AMF format and the Flash Remoting interface for PHP, Java, and Perl.

There are several people who have to be thanked for their generous contributions to the text and code contained in the book. First and foremost, my editor, Bruce Epstein, has gone above and beyond what is the norm for editing a book in this field. He seems to live and breathe for the sake of the books he edits, and has substantially improved the text through constant suggestions, comments, and revisions. Thanks Bruce!

Thanks are due to everyone at O'Reilly who contributed to the publication of this book, including the production editor, Genevieve d'Entremont; Brian Sawyer, who proofread the book; and Julie Hawks, who produced the final index. Likewise, my thanks to Rob Romano for creating the figures from my napkin sketches and for enhancing the screenshots.

The book was started by two of Macromedia's employees: Mike Chambers (Flash Community Manager) and Christian Cantrell (Server Community Manager). Parts of Mike's Chapter 1 still remain, as do parts of Christian's Chapter 5. They provided the seed that started the book.

Several other authors have greatly enhanced the book. Alon J. Salant, a Java expert at Carbon Five (*http://www.carbonfive.com*) who is known for the ASTranslator project, wrote Chapter 7. Joel Martinez wrote Chapter 8 covering ASP.NET based in part on a draft from Jason Michael Perry. Branden Hall, a well-known Flash guru and co-author of *Object-Oriented ActionScript* (New Riders), contributed Chapter 9. Devon H. O'Dell contributed PHP examples in Chapters 1 and 2. Thanks to all five of these gentlemen for making this a well-rounded book.

The book went through several rounds of technical editing to ensure the accuracy of the content. I'd like to thank all of the tech editors who added their comments and improved the book: Marc Garrett, Ray West, Massimo Foti, Sham Bhangal, Joel Martinez, Alon J. Salant, Devon H. O'Dell, Joey Lott, Chafic Kazoun, Jesse Warden, and Robin Debreuil. A special thanks to my usual writing partner Ray West, who was putting together Community MX and organizing several TODCON conferences while I wrote this book. Ray is a good guy and a great partner.

On a personal level, my family has always provided the inspiration for me to keep writing. My wife Janet is the best partner I could have. If this were a novel and I had written a character as a representation of my dream girl, she would be it. Her constant encouragement throughout the process kept me going even when the workload was overwhelming. My daughter Amber has taken a strong liking to Flash and helped with a lot of the visual aspects of Flash that would have completely escaped me had she not been there to help. Thanks Janet and Amber.

—Tom Muck
Fairfax, VA
July 2003

Remoting Fundamentals

Part I covers the setup and installation of Flash Remoting, as well as offering a basic introduction to its use. It also offers details on core concepts and Remoting internals. By the end of Part I, you will have a working knowledge of Flash Remoting, plus a deeper understanding that will act as a springboard for future development.

- Chapter 1, *Introduction to Flash Remoting*
- Chapter 2, *Installing, Configuring, and Using Flash Remoting*
- Chapter 3, *Client/Server Interaction, UI Components, and RecordSets*
- Chapter 4, *Flash Remoting Internals*

Introduction to Flash Remoting

When I was an 11-year-old kid, I thought I was pretty good on a bike. I could do wheelies around the neighborhood, drive on dirt hills, jump ramps. It wasn't enough, though. I wanted to make the transition to a minibike, which is basically a little bike with a lawn mower engine on it. If all I needed was my riding skills, I probably would have been set. Unfortunately, keeping my feet in one place, turning the throttle, and pressing the hand brakes on the minibike were unknown territories. My first time out I turned the throttle too far, lost my footing, and forgot how to hit the brake. I landed in a heap in the street.

If I had put a little forethought into it, I would have realized that riding a bike and riding a minibike were completely different things. Only some aspects were the same; by learning the new aspects and applying my prior knowledge of riding a bike, I eventually figured out how to stay put without falling on my butt.

Working with a new computer technology in a familiar environment is like that. In the case of Flash Remoting, everyone holding this book is probably familiar with Flash movies and ActionScript programming. Flash Remoting puts some new and exciting things into Flash that will require learning new ways to look at ActionScript and what it can accomplish. With Flash Remoting, Macromedia has put an engine on Flash.

What Is Flash Remoting?

These are exciting times. Macromedia is attempting to change the way application developers create web-based applications.

Flash Remoting constitutes a complete rethinking of how web applications are constructed. Using Flash Remoting, you can create complex client/server applications that more closely resemble desktop applications than traditional web pages. For those of you familiar with traditional Windows-style programming IDEs, Flash Remoting is roughly the web equivalent of a Visual Basic client/server application. This chapter presents a broad overview of Flash Remoting.

Flash Remoting technology is at the center of Macromedia's Studio MX product suite, linking the server platforms with the client-side tools. Flash Remoting is built into Macromedia's two application servers—ColdFusion MX and JRun 4. In addition, programmers using other technologies, such as ASP.NET or J2EE application servers, can purchase the Flash Remoting MX package so that Flash Remoting can be utilized on those servers. Although Macromedia doesn't officially support other languages, open source implementations are available for PHP (the AMFPHP project at *http://www.amfphp.org*) and Perl (the FLAP project at *http://www.simonf.com/flap*). There is also an open source Flash Remoting for Java implementation (OpenAMF at *http://www.openamf.org*).

The Flash authoring environment includes UI components, which form the basis of Macromedia's strategy of using a Flash movie as the client in a client/server atmosphere. This approach allows the application server to provide the programming power for the application. Using Flash Remoting, a Flash movie can act as the interface for diverse applications, including connections to databases, SMTP mailers, server components, web services, and much more. Flash Remoting ties together the Macromedia authoring tools and application server technologies to form a new approach to web application development and deployment.

Flash Remoting is a server-side technology that integrates with existing application servers to provide a gateway between the Flash Player and remote services deployed on the server. A *service* can be a simple ColdFusion page or ColdFusion Component (CFC), a PHP or Perl script, a Java class, or an ASP.NET page or DLL. Flash Remoting allows developers to access remote services and web services from within Flash through a simple ActionScript API that is similar to JavaScript. Flash Remoting also allows developers to integrate Flash with existing client/server applications with little modification, to provide a rich, robust user interface that can be deployed across browsers, platforms, and devices.

The Flash Remoting gateway on the server sits between the Flash Player on the client and the server-side tier of an application. It handles data serialization and procedure calls between the Flash Player and the server. *Serialization* is the translation of data to a format that can be easily transmitted over the Web. This translation is transparent to both client-side Flash developers and server-side developers. We'll discuss a client/server architecture using the Flash Player and the Flash Remoting gateway later in this chapter.

Using Flash Remoting, a Flash movie can connect to virtually any remote service deployed on the server. The remote services can be deployed using various languages and technologies, including:

- Java classes
- JavaBeans™
- Enterprise JavaBeans (EJB)

- Java Management Extensions (JMX MBeans)
- ColdFusion templates
- ColdFusion Components
- Server-Side ActionScript (SSAS)
- ASP.NET pages
- ASP.NET DLLs
- SOAP-based web services
- PHP pages

In other words, a remote service might be a ColdFusion page, a PHP page, or an ASP.NET DLL, among other things. Flash Remoting allows Flash to make remote procedure calls on existing server-side services; server-side developers do not have to implement any Flash-specific APIs or adjust their design patterns. Calling a service from a Flash movie is as easy as calling it by name. For example, if you have a server-side method named *getRecords( )* that you would typically call from another server-side page to feed an HTML page, Flash Remoting lets you call the *getRecords( )* method directly from the Flash movie. Gone are the page reloads associated with HTML pages. The communication with the server is seamless and invisible to the user. This means that the typical web experience is much more user friendly and performs more like a traditional desktop application.

How Does Flash Remoting Work?

The Flash Remoting gateway is installed on the application server and acts as an interface between the Flash Player and the server. The Flash Remoting software that implements the gateway is also called an *adapter*. It has three main tasks:

- Handle requests from the Flash Player to remote services. These services can be on the same server as the Flash Remoting gateway or can be external to the server in the form of web services.
- Translate requests and data from the Flash Player into server-side requests and datatypes.
- Translate responses and data from the server into native ActionScript datatypes.

Figure 1-1 depicts the Flash Player/Flash Remoting architecture.

Communication between the Flash Player and the Flash Remoting gateway is done via HTTP, which has a few implications:

Communication between the Flash Player and the Flash Remoting gateway is request-driven. The Flash Player must initiate all communication with the Flash Remoting gateway. The server cannot push data to Flash unless it is requested by the Flash Player. Use the ActionScript *XMLSocket* object, as discussed in

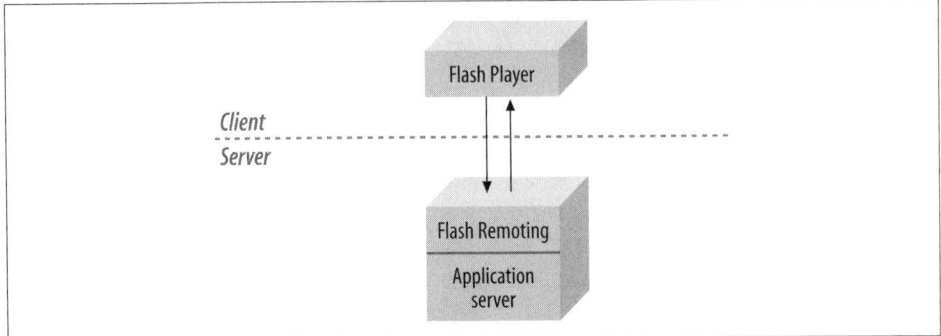

Figure 1-1. The Flash Player/Flash Remoting architecture

ActionScript for Flash MX: The Definitive Guide (O'Reilly), if you need to push data from the server to Flash, such as in a chat application. Another option is to use Macromedia's Flash Communication Server MX (FlashCom) for these types of applications.

HTTP is a stateless protocol, so each request from the Flash Player opens a new connection to the server. The Flash Remoting gateway automatically maintains state between requests through the use of cookies. If cookies are not available on the client, the session state is maintained through a header in the communication packets between the Flash Player and server.

Protocols that work with HTTP, such as SSL, also work with Flash Remoting.
As shown in Figure 1-2, the client/server architecture is the same when the Flash Player communicates with Flash Remoting via HTTPS or SSL as it is using HTTP. Support for HTTPS allows communication between the Flash Player and the server to be encrypted using SSL, provided that the Flash movie is delivered to the client over an SSL connection and displayed within an SSL-enabled browser. This gives a Flash application the same level of security that is available to the HTML application.

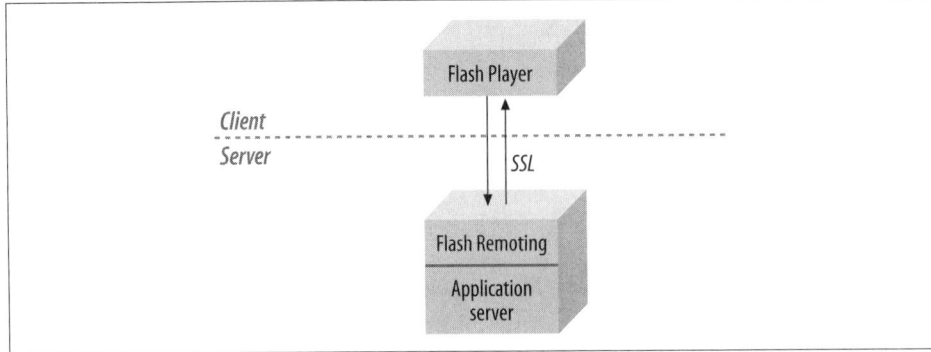

Figure 1-2. Flash Player/Flash Remoting architecture using SSL

Action Message Format

Flash 5 movies could send XML or name/value pairs across HTTP. Although these packets could be parsed automatically by Flash or manually by the developer using custom ActionScript, parsing could be slow because all XML data is sent as text strings encased by cumbersome tags. Flash Remoting is able to handle complex datatypes, such as objects, structures, arrays, and recordsets. A proprietary format was needed to transfer information back and forth between the Flash movie and the application server.

The protocol used for communication between the Flash Remoting gateway and the Flash Player is Action Message Format (AMF). AMF is a binary protocol designed by Macromedia to provide a lightweight, efficient means to serialize, deserialize, and transport data between the Flash Player and the Flash Remoting gateway, as shown in Figure 1-3.

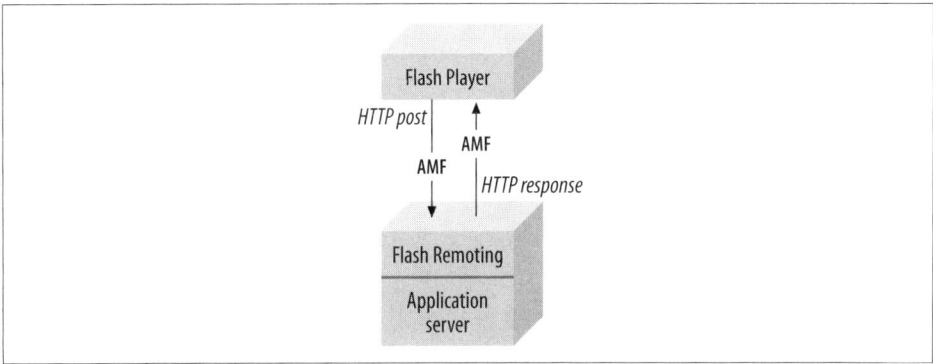

Figure 1-3. Flash Player/AMF/Flash Remoting

It is not necessary to understand AMF in detail to develop robust Flash applications that utilize Flash Remoting; however, it is useful to have a basic understanding of the protocol. Macromedia has not documented the protocol publicly, but the HTTP packets can be examined to gain insight into the format, which seems to be closely based on the format used in remote shared objects (RSOs). The developers of the AMFPHP project have partially documented the format at:

   http://amfphp.org/?g=amf_format

The Flash Player communicates with the Flash Remoting gateway via the AMF protocol sent via standard HTTP requests. An AMF packet is sent as a binary POST with the body of the request containing the binary data serialization and remote procedure call information.

 Flash Remoting requires browser support for binary POST. Because Netscape 6.x does not support binary POST, Flash Remoting does not work when the Flash Player is running within Netscape 6.x. The Flash Remoting call has no effect and no error is returned. This bug is fixed in Netscape 7. There are also issues with early versions of Safari and Chimera on the Macintosh. You can use a browser-detecting script to redirect users to an appropriate page that uses HTML or older Flash formats if the user's browser does not support your Flash Remoting application.

An AMF packet consists of the following:

- A *packet header*, which describes the AMF version information and includes HTTP headers
- A count of *context headers* in the array that follows
- The *context headers array*, which describes to the server the context in which the information should be processed (on calls from the client) or describes to the client what is coming from the server (a result or status) and its format (such as a recordset or a string)
- A count of the messages in the array that follows
- The *messages array*, which is typically a method call coming from the client or a status/result coming from the server

Following is the HTTP request and response generated by the Hello World examples shown later in this chapter. Because AMF is a binary format, the binary data is shown as periods (...). The ASCII text in the following excerpt, such as amf_server_ debug, is part of the literal message:

```
POST /flashservices/gateway HTTP/1.1
Referer: http://192.168.0.5:8500/flashservices/gateway
Content-Type: application/x-amf
User-Agent: Shockwave Flash
Host: 127.0.0.1
Content-Length: 198
Cache-Control: no-cache

.......amf_server_debug....pNetDebugConfig
coldfusion...
amfheaders....amf....
httpheaders....recordset....error....trace...m_debug.........
....*com.oreilly.helloworld.HelloWorld.sayHello.../1....
```

And the response from the server back to the Flash Player is as follows:

```
HTTP/1.0 200 OK
Date: Thu, 23 May 2002 02:53:09 GMT
Content-Type: application/x-amf
Content-Length: 69
Server: JRun Web Server
```

```
.....
/1/onResult...null.....
Hello World from ColdFusion Component
```

We can gain some insight into AMF by examining the request and response:

- The content type of AMF is `application/x-amf`.
- The AMF data is contained within the body of the request and response; it is primarily binary and is therefore difficult to show in print.
- There are human-readable strings within the AMF data.

The last point tells us that AMF is not entirely compressed. However, even uncompressed, the protocol is very efficient at serializing ActionScript data.

AMF has a number of advantages over traditional Flash data serialization techniques, such as XML and URL-encoded query strings, including:

- AMF is a binary format and thus creates serialized data that is smaller than using string-based encoding. This translates into lower bandwidth requirements and faster loading and response times.
- AMF was built specifically with Flash ActionScript datatypes in mind. Therefore, it can be serialized quickly and efficiently from ActionScript objects and deserialized into ActionScript objects within the Flash Player. In almost all cases, this leads to significant performance increases over string-based serialization.

Why does Flash Remoting use AMF instead of SOAP to communicate with the Flash Player? After all, SOAP was designed as a lightweight protocol for the exchange of information in a distributed environment, which sounds similar to the goals for AMF. Both SOAP and AMF can transfer data and make calls on remote services, and both work over standard HTTP and HTTPS. There are several reasons why Macromedia developed AMF instead of using SOAP:

- SOAP is implemented as XML and is therefore rather verbose compared to the binary AMF.
- AMF is designed and optimized to work with Flash ActionScript datatypes. Deserializing AMF in the Flash Player is much more efficient than parsing and deserializing SOAP, because AMF has direct support for ActionScript datatypes whereas SOAP is a general-purpose protocol. Even if SOAP messages were compressed, serialization in AMF would still be more efficient.
- Adding AMF support to Flash Player 6 required only a small increase in the Player size (about 4 KB compressed), maintaining its slim footprint.
- Integrating full SOAP support on the client side, with acceptable performance, requires an increase in Player size. Although Flash Player 6 includes XML support, it does not support some headers required by SOAP. Using Flash Remoting, Flash can access SOAP-based web services even though Flash Player 6 doesn't support SOAP directly. That is, the Flash Remoting gateway translates SOAP requests to and from AMF format on the server-side and then uses AMF

to communicate with the Flash Player. Flash Player 7 supports SOAP directly, but it will be late 2004 until Flash Player 7 is widely distributed.

The body of the AMF packet contains either an *onResult* event (i.e., *response* event) or an *onStatus* event (i.e., *error* event), which are both ActionScript objects. The Flash movie can then use the object directly, without any further parsing. Chapter 3 contains an in-depth discussion of the *onStatus* and *onResult* events.

Benefits

One of the key benefits of using Flash Remoting over XML or traditional HTML applications is that the application server no longer needs to handle any of the parsing or presentation of information. This frees resources on the server so that it can be better equipped to deal with more complex application logic and/or more users. In addition, session management can be handled on the client inside of the Flash movie rather than on the server. The server still keeps track of the session, but the developer doesn't have to jump through hoops to keep track of users who don't have cookies or track a user session across multiple pages. This equates to huge savings in development time and server resources.

Why Not XML?

I've talked about the benefits of Flash Remoting, but why not use XML? After all, using XML you could encapsulate all of the client/server communication within an ActionScript object and provide a simple API to transfer complex datatypes serialized with XML between Flash and the server. This would have the advantage of not requiring a server-side gateway and would work with Flash Player 5.

The main advantage of Flash Remoting over XML is that it relieves the developer from writing an entire layer of code on both the client and server. XML parsing is built into many of the popular server technologies, but it is cumbersome at best. However, Flash Remoting also has a number of additional advantages:

- It automatically handles all datatype conversions between ActionScript and the server.
- It can convert multiple complex datatypes.
- It seamlessly supports multiple server-side technologies and application servers.
- It allows remote services and web services to be called directly from Flash without requiring any additional server-side code to be written.
- It provides a simple and consistent API for calling remote services and web services from the Flash Player.
- It uses AMF to serialize data, which offers better performance than string-based serialization techniques (such as XML), even though AMF is not as widely supported as XML.

In a typical scenario involving an XML object being sent from a Flash 5 movie to a ColdFusion page, the Flash movie first has to create the XML string manually. Then it has to send the XML string to the ColdFusion page, which has to parse the XML before being able to utilize it. In addition, the server has to transform the result of any operation on the server back into XML to send the result to the Flash movie. The Flash movie then has to parse this XML once again to use the returned information. All of this parsing of data eats up valuable resources and bandwidth even before the application logic can be utilized.

In other words, a Flash 5 movie can't use the data directly from the application server, and the application server can't use the data directly from Flash 5.

Take a typical example of a username and password login. The ActionScript for the Flash movie could create a simple XML string and pass it to the ColdFusion page:

```
// Set up a new XML object.
var returnXML = new XML();
returnXML.ignoreWhite = true;

// Set the callback function for the response from the server.
returnXML.onLoad = handleReply;

// Create an XML string.
// Form field variables are replaced in the string.
var my_xml = '<?xml version="1.0" encoding="iso-8859-1"?>';
my_xml += '<myValidation>';
my_xml += '<username>' + username + '</username>';
my_xml += '<password>' + password + '</password>';
my_xml += '</myValidation>';
var flash_xml_object = new XML(my_xml)

// Send it to the server and then load it into the my_xml object.
flash_xml_object.sendAndLoad("http://192.168.0.4/myLogin.cfm", returnXML);

function handleReply (result) {
  if (result) {
    if (this.firstChild.attributes.logged == "1") {
      greeting = "Hello " + this.firstChild.attributes.username;
      greeting += ". Login was successful";
    } else {
      greeting = "Login failed";
    }
  } else {
      greeting = "There was a communication failure.";
  }
}
```

A ColdFusion page to handle the logic would look like this:

```
<!---Deserialize the username and password from the XML--->
<cfset logged="1">
<cfset my_xml = XMLParse(URLDecode(GetHttpRequestData().content))>
<cfset username = my_xml.myValidation.username.xmltext>
<cfset password = my_xml.myValidation.password.xmltext>
```

```
<!---Query the database for matching entries--->
<cfquery name="myLogin" datasource="myDatasource">
  SELECT username FROM Users
  WHERE username = '#username#' and password = '#password#'
</cfquery>

<!---Check whether a match was found--->
<cfif myLogin.RecordCount LT 1>
  <cfset logged = "0">
</cfif>

<!---Create an XML string to return to the Flash movie--->
<cfset returnXML = "<return username=""" & username>
<cfset returnXML = returnXML & """ logged=""" & logged & """ />">
<cfoutput>#returnXML#</cfoutput>
```

As you can see, the code is not intuitive—the XML is manually serialized into a string on both client and server, and the string has to be deserialized and turned into an XML object again on the Flash side. All of this code was created to send one simple XML object from the Flash movie to the server and back again. Imagine if this were something more complex, such as a recordset with 10 or 15 fields and 1,000 rows.

The Flash Remoting version of the previous code might look like this:

```
var myURL = "http://127.0.0.1/flashservices/gateway";
var myServer = NetServices.createGatewayConnection(myURL);
var myService = myServer.getService("com.oreilly.frdg.authentication", this);

myService.getLogin(username, password);

// The result handler for the getLogin() method invocation
function getLogin_Result (result_rs) {
  if (result_rs.getLength() < 1) {
    greeting = "Login failed";
  } else {
    greeting = "Hello " + result_rs.getItemAt(0).username;
    greeting += ". Login was successful";
  }
}
```

And the server-side code might look like this:

```
<cfcomponent displayName="login">
  <cffunction name="getLogin" returnType="query" access="remote">
    <cfargument name="username" type="string">
    <cfargument name="password" type="string">
    <cfquery name="myLogin" datasource="myDatasource">
      SELECT username FROM Users
      WHERE username = '#username#' and password = '#password#'
    </cfquery>
    <cfreturn myLogin>
  </cffunction>
</cfcomponent>
```

The Flash Remoting code in this version is more intuitive; it defines a component containing a function that accepts two arguments directly from Flash. There is no manual parsing; the arguments to the function are passed as strings and a recordset is returned. If the recordset contained 15 fields and 1,000 rows, the server-side code would not look much different.

Using Flash Remoting is much simpler because the Flash movie does not have to package the request in any special format such as XML. Likewise, the ColdFusion Server does not have to package the result for the Flash movie. The data is simply passed back and forth as is and put to use. It is the difference between having a pizza delivered and making the dough and baking the pizza yourself. If the pizza is delivered, the only action you have to take on the pizza is to eat it.

Manually serializing and deserializing data has the advantage of working with Flash Player 5. However, when you consider the amount of client- and server-side code that you have to write, debug, and maintain just to provide basic support for serializing one datatype, the advantages of Flash Remoting become clearer. Considering all the datatypes that Flash Remoting supports and the fact that you can call remote services by name without writing any extra server-side code, Flash Remoting becomes quite attractive.

HTML and Server-Side Code

A typical HTML/server-side template application has problems similar to those in our XML example. The server-side code does not simply perform logic and return information; in many cases, it formats the data as well. Take this simple ColdFusion snippet as an example:

```
<!---Query the database for matching entries--->
<cfquery name="rsGetSearchResults" datasource="bookstore">
SELECT Title, Category, Pub_No FROM Books
WHERE Title LIKE '%#form.searchfield#%'
</cfquery>
<!---Create an HTML table to display the matches--->
<table border="1">
  <tr>
    <td>Title</td>
    <td>Category</td>
    <td>Pub_No</td>
  </tr>
  <cfoutput query="rsGetSearchResults"
   startRow="#StartRow_rsGetSearchResults#"
   maxRows="#MaxRows_rsGetSearchResults#">
    <tr>
      <td>#rsGetSearchResults.Title#</td>
      <td>#rsGetSearchResults.Category#</td>
      <td>#rsGetSearchResults.Pub_No#</td>
    </tr>
  </cfoutput>
</table>
```

This example queries a database and outputs the results as a table in the browser. This type of mixture of HTML and server-side code is commonplace in web application development. Notice, however, that the presentation of the content is created entirely by the application server. The HTML table doesn't exist until the query is executed and the results are sent to the browser.

Using Flash Remoting, the application server code is utilized for the logic only—querying the database. The results of the query are returned to the Flash movie without any further parsing or manipulating. Using Flash Remoting, a ColdFusion component could be written as follows:

```
<cfcomponent displayName="searchBooks">
  <cffunction name="getTitles" returnType="query" access="remote">
    <cfargument name="search" type="string" default="%" />
    <cfquery name="rsGetSearchResults" datasource="bookstore">
     SELECT Title, Category, Pub_No FROM Books
     WHERE Title LIKE '%#form.searchfield#%'
    </cfquery>
    <cfreturn rsGetSearchResults />
  </cffunction>
</cfcomponent>
```

Notice the line in bold, `<cfreturn rsGetSearchResults />`, which returns the entire recordset to the Flash movie as an ActionScript *RecordSet* object. The Flash movie, in turn, can use the recordset without any further parsing. For example, to attach the recordset to a DataGrid component in Flash, you can simply use this result handler in ActionScript:

```
function rsGetSearchResults_Result (result_rs) {
  myGridComponent.setDataProvider(result_rs);
}
```

Again, the Flash movie is working with the recordset as it comes from the server. No further parsing is necessary. Also, the ActionScript programmer has at his disposal a series of highly complex and interactive interface elements, unlike HTML forms, which are limited in functionality.

Another advantage is that the Flash movie looks the same in all browsers. The HTML language is ubiquitous, but the implementation is not uniform. Typically, you have to rely on CSS implementation, JavaScript being enabled, and/or cookies being enabled, or you have to create even more client-side code to handle the many possible user configurations.

Session Management in Flash

HTTP is a stateless protocol. The web server treats each page request coming from a browser as coming from an entirely new user. To create the illusion of maintaining state, many application servers have *state management* (or *session management*) in place to create a seamless experience for the end user. Session management is a bit of an art form for the application developer, as there are no sure-fire, out-of-the-box methods to maintain state in most application servers.

Typically, in a web application, you use cookies in conjunction with session variables to maintain state. This method won't work if cookies are turned off on the client's browser; therefore, you must store the information in a database or text file for 100% reliability. Furthermore, session management and variables eat up server memory. In an ASP application, for example, each typical user session consumes at least 4.5 KB, unless sessions are explicitly turned off. Also, unless a server application is cluster-aware, managing session state across a cluster can become complicated (because different servers in the cluster might handle successive requests).

Flash Remoting handles session state through means that are invisible to both the user and the server. Session information is sent with each and every AMF packet between the client and the server. No manual session management is required. In a rich client implementation, the Flash movie is loaded into the user's browser only once, so session state is maintained automatically with every call to the server. In addition, because the session state is maintained within the Flash movie in the user's browser, it makes little difference if the application server is clustered.

Flash Remoting Requirements

To develop Flash applications that use Flash Remoting, you must have:

- Macromedia Flash MX or later
- The Macromedia Flash Remoting components
- A server that has the Flash Remoting gateway or the equivalent (such as AMFPHP, FLAP, or OpenAMF)

Macromedia Flash Authoring Tool

The Flash authoring environment is used to create Flash files (*.fla* and *.swf* files) and applications. Flash MX was a substantial upgrade to previous versions of Flash. In addition to cosmetic interface changes, the way in which Flash applications are developed has changed. Flash MX or later is required to develop Flash Remoting applications. A fully functional trial version is available from Macromedia at:

http://www.macromedia.com/software/flash/download/

You can find more information on Flash at:

http://www.macromedia.com/software/flash/

 As of Flash MX, Macromedia abandoned a consistent version-numbering scheme for the authoring tool, but the Flash Player is still assigned a numeric version. Flash Remoting requires that you publish your *.swf* files in Flash 6 format or later.

Director MX, a separate multimedia authoring tool sold by Macromedia, can access Flash Remoting using the Flash MX Asset Xtra (which is basically an embedded version of Flash Player 6). For simplicity, this book assumes you are running Flash in a browser or a standalone Projector.

Macromedia Flash Remoting Components

Flash MX does not come with the Flash Remoting components preinstalled. The Flash Remoting components add support for Flash Remoting to the Flash authoring environment and are required to create Flash files that take advantage of Flash Remoting. If you're using Director MX as the front end, you'll need the Flash MX Asset Xtra, which is compatible with Director MX or Shockwave 8.5.1 or later. The Flash MX Asset Xtra includes Flash Remoting support.

The Flash Remoting components are included with the Flash Remoting gateway and can be found on the Studio MX CD-ROM or downloaded for free from the Macromedia web site. If you're using versions from the Studio MX CD-ROM, make sure you get the latest updates from the Macromedia site as well. The components and other information about Flash Remoting can be found at:

> *http://www.macromedia.com/go/flashremoting*

The components make the following items available from within the Flash MX authoring environment:

- ActionScript code and classes necessary for Flash Remoting, including *NetServices.as*, *RecordSet.as*, *DataGlue.as*, and *NetDebugger.as*
- The Remote Service Browser, for examining remote services
- The NetConnection Debugger panel, for debugging Flash Remoting applications
- Flash MX ActionScript editor enhancements for Flash Remoting, and Reference panel documentation

All of these items are discussed in detail in this book, beginning in Chapter 2.

Macromedia Flash Remoting Gateway

The Flash Remoting gateway must be installed on the remote server to allow it to communicate with the Flash movie via Flash Remoting. If you are using an application server that comes with Flash Remoting preinstalled, such as ColdFusion MX or JRun 4, then this step is already taken care of.

Earlier versions of ColdFusion and JRun do not support Flash Remoting.

The Flash Remoting gateway is also sold separately for other application servers, including J2EE servers and Microsoft .NET, and must be installed and configured before it can be used. The trial version of the Flash Remoting gateway for J2EE and ASP.NET can also be downloaded from the Macromedia web site cited earlier.

There are several open source implementations of the Flash Remoting gateway, apart from the versions supported by Macromedia.

The AMFPHP project, discussed in Chapter 9, implements Flash Remoting for PHP application servers:

> *http://www.amfphp.org*

The FLAP project implements Flash Remoting for Perl:

> *http://www.simonf.com/flap*

The OpenAMF project is an open source alternative to Macromedia's Flash Remoting gateway for Java:

> *http://www.openamf.org*

Supported Platforms

This section is a quick summary of Flash Remoting capabilities and server-side services that can be exposed to Flash from supported application servers. For the latest list of supported application servers, platforms, and configurations, see:

> *http://www.macromedia.com/go/flashremoting*

Macromedia ColdFusion MX

The Flash Remoting gateway comes preinstalled with Macromedia ColdFusion MX and allows developers to deploy remote services as:

- ColdFusion pages
- ColdFusion Components
- Server-Side ActionScript (SSAS)
- SOAP-based web services

Flash Remoting is also included in the Macromedia ColdFusion MX for J2EE version for deployment on Java application servers, such as WebSphere and BEA WebLogic. It includes support for the remote services supported in ColdFusion MX in addition to those supported on a Java server that ColdFusion is installed on, as discussed below. For more information on ColdFusion MX, or to download a fully functional trial version, go to:

> *http://www.macromedia.com/software/coldfusion/*

See also *Programming ColdFusion MX*, by Rob Brooks-Bilson (O'Reilly), for information on ColdFusion. The trial/developer version of ColdFusion MX can be obtained together with Flash MX in the Macromedia Studio MX bundle.

J2EE Application Servers and Java Servlet Engines

The Flash Remoting gateway is available as a standalone product for any J2EE-compatible application server. It also works with a Java servlet engine that has been certified compatible with Sun's servlet 2.2 or 2.3 specifications, such as Tomcat. Flash Remoting for J2EE allows remote services to be deployed as:

- JavaBeans
- Java classes
- Enterprise JavaBeans

Macromedia has tested the functionality with J2EE servers such as JRun 4, IBM WebSphere AS 4, and Sun ONE Web Server, although they also mention reports of success with Tomcat and other servers. For the latest information on supported application servers, consult the Flash Remoting documentation at the Macromedia site.

Chapter 7 discusses Flash Remoting for J2EE servers in detail. The OpenAMF project, an alternative to Macromedia Flash Remoting gateway for J2EE, is also discussed briefly at the end of Chapter 7.

Macromedia JRun 4

JRun is Macromedia's J2EE-compliant Java application server. Flash Remoting comes preinstalled with Macromedia JRun 4 and allows developers to deploy remote services as:

- JavaBeans (stateful)
- Java classes (no state and no pool, new instance on every request)
- Enterprise JavaBeans (EJBHome and EJBObject)
- JMX MBeans
- Server-Side ActionScript (SSAS)
- SOAP-based web services

Because JRun 4 is a J2EE-based server, it supports access to the same services as other J2EE-compatible application servers mentioned earlier, as well as Server-Side ActionScript, JMX MBeans, and SOAP-based web services. For more information on JRun, or to download a fully functional trial version that will revert to a developer's version after 30 days, go to:

http://www.macromedia.com/software/jrun/

Microsoft ASP.NET Servers

Flash Remoting is available as a standalone product for Microsoft ASP.NET servers. It allows remote services to be deployed as:

- ASP.NET pages (*.aspx* pages)
- DLL libraries (in the local assembly cache)
- .NET executables
- SOAP-based web services

 Flash Remoting does not work with "classic" ASP pages. You must have the ASP.NET framework running on your server. To run the ASP.NET framework you need IIS 5.0 or later, running on Windows 2000 Professional, Windows 2000 Server, Windows XP Professional, or Windows Server 2003 (a.k.a. Windows .NET Server).

Hello World

An introduction to any technology would not be complete without a "Hello World" example. This will give you some hands-on experience with the client-side and server-side code before diving into details. It also provides a sound basis for exploring Flash Remoting on your own.

First, we will look at the Flash code necessary to call the remote service, which is virtually the same regardless of which server-side technology implements the service. We will then look at the server-side code implemented in ColdFusion, Server-Side ActionScript, Java, ASP.NET, PHP, and as a SOAP-based web service.

 The examples throughout the book assume that you have Flash Remoting installed and configured on your server, and that you have installed the Flash Remoting components for Flash MX. Chapter 2 covers Flash Remoting installation and configuration in more detail.

Flash ActionScript Code

The client-side ActionScript is virtually the same for each server-side service example. The only things that change are the path to the remote service when it is implemented as a web service and the path to the Flash Remoting gateway, which varies depending on the server implementation.

The client-side ActionScript code shown in Example 1-1 should be inserted on the first frame of the main timeline of a Flash movie, as shown in Figure 1-4.

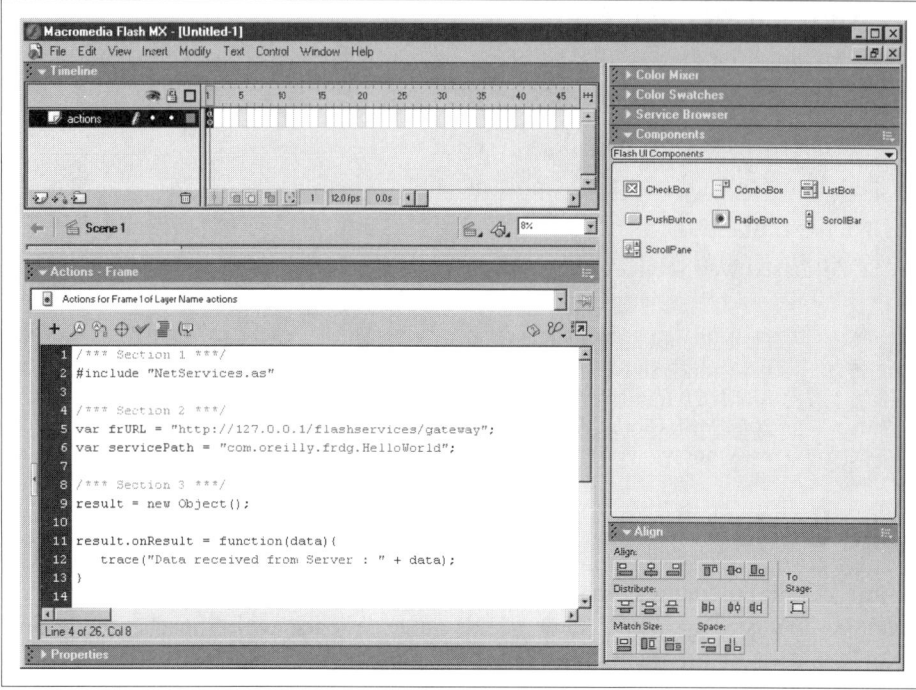

Figure 1-4. Flash timeline with attached client-side ActionScript

Example 1-1. Client-side ActionScript code (HelloWorld.fla)

```
/*** Section 1 ***/
#include "NetServices.as"

/*** Section 2 ***/
// Assign myURL so it points to your Flash Remoting installation.
var myURL = "http://localhost/flashservices/gateway";
var myServicePath = "com.oreilly.frdg.HelloWorld";

/*** Section 3 ***/
myResult = new Object( );

myResult.onResult = function (data) {
  trace("Data received from Server : " + data);
};

myResult.onStatus = function (info) {
  trace("An error occurred : " + info.description);
};

System.onStatus = myResult.onStatus;

/*** Section 4 ***/
var myServer = NetServices.createGatewayConnection(myURL);
```

Example 1-1. Client-side ActionScript code (HelloWorld.fla) (continued)

```
var myService = myServer.getService(myServicePath, myResult);

myService.sayHello();
```

Section 1 of Example 1-1 includes the *NetServices.as* library, which contains the code necessary to connect to a Flash Remoting–enabled server from Flash. If you do not include *NetServices.as*, the example will not work, but you will not receive any errors within the authoring environment.

Section 2 initializes two variables: myURL and myServicePath. The myURL variable will be used to create a *NetConnection* object that points to the server. The myServicePath variable will be used to create a *service object* that points to the service that will be called.

The myURL variable specifies the URL to the Flash Remoting gateway installed on the server. If the Flash Remoting gateway is installed on a Microsoft .NET server, the URL will point to the *.aspx* file for the gateway. Similarly, if you are using AMFPHP, the URL will point to a *gateway.php* file on your server.

The myServicePath variable specifies the path on the server to the remote service that will be called. The naming convention is similar to a Java package, with each section representing a directory on the server and the last section pointing to the actual service. If the remote service is a Microsoft .NET DLL, myServicePath should refer to the DLL's namespace and class name. Similarly, if the remote service is a Java class, the myServicePath variable will refer to the package name and class name of the Java class. If the remote service is a web service, myServicePath should contain the path to the web service's WSDL file.

Calls from the Flash Player to the application server via the Flash Remoting gateway are asynchronous. Code execution within the Flash Player continues while data is being loaded, which is similar to loading XML into the Flash Player. You must define callback functions, which will be called automatically when the data loads from the server.

> A *callback function* is a function that is called when a specific event occurs. For example, attaching a callback function to an object's onClick property causes the callback function to execute whenever the object is clicked. Similarly, a remote service call causes a specific event to occur, which can have a callback function associated with it.

In ActionScript, callback functions can be attached as properties to a generic object (instantiated from the *Object* class). The functions are used to catch data and messages sent back from the server.

Section 3 of Example 1-1 creates an object and attaches two callback functions to it. The *onResult( )* callback function is called when data is returned from the remote service, and the *onStatus( )* callback function is called if an error occurs. An object used to receive results from a remote service is called a *responder object* (or sometimes called a *response object*).

 Another way to trap events is to specify callback functions named the same as the service name with *_Result* and *_Status* appended to it. This technique, along with more information about callback functions and responder objects, is covered in Chapters 3 and 4.

The System.onStatus property specifies the function to be called if the Flash Player cannot connect to the server, as these types of errors are not handled by the *onStatus( )* callback function for the remote service call. Example 1-1 sets System.onStatus to execute our object's *onStatus( )* function. Once we have created an object and the callback functions to receive and process the data returned from the server, we are ready to call the remote service.

Section 4 of Example 1-1 makes a connection to the server by passing in myURL (initialized earlier) to the *NetServices.createGatewayConnection( )* function. The server connection information is stored in the myServer variable. The example then gets a reference to the remote service, which we store in the variable myService, by calling the *getService( )* method on the myServer variable initialized in the previous step. In the call to *getService( )*, we pass myServicePath to access the desired service and pass our myResult object to catch the data or status when the operation completes. We can then use myService (the reference to the remote service) to call methods on the service, such as the *sayHello( )* method.

 The path passed to *getService( )*, as specified by myServicePath, does not include a file extension for the remote service. Therefore, Flash can access a remote service without knowing its implementation details. One of the powerful aspects of Flash Remoting is that it makes almost all server-side services accessible in a uniform manner. However, you cannot automatically detect which remote services are available. That is, you need to know the remote service methods you intend to call. Flash Remoting has no mechanism in place to find unknown remote services on the fly.

Save the Flash movie as *HelloWorld.fla*. Before the movie can be tested, we need to create the server-side code that implements the *sayHello( )* function, as described in subsequent sections.

Example 1-1 utilizes the *trace( )* command to display the data in the Output window in the Flash authoring environment. Therefore, the output is visible only when the movie is tested in the authoring environment and not when tested in a browser.

Server-Side Code

In the next section, you'll create the remote service required by this simple Flash movie. Once you have created the remote service, you can test the Flash movie using Control → Test Movie. You should get the following output displayed in the Output window:

```
Data received from Server : Hello World from servertype
```

If you do not get this result:

- Set the Output window to verbose mode (Window → Output → Options → Debug Level → Verbose).
- Make sure that the server where the Flash Remoting gateway is installed is running and accessible.
- Make sure that there are no syntax errors in your client-side ActionScript code or server-side code.

ColdFusion MX

For the ColdFusion MX example, we will implement the remote service as a *ColdFusion Component* (CFC). CFCs are new to ColdFusion MX and provide an object-based approach to ColdFusion development. They are ideally suited to Flash Remoting. CFCs are discussed in depth in Chapter 5.

Create a file named *HelloWorld.cfc* and place it into the following directory, where *webroot* is the root of your web server and *com\oreilly\frdg* matches the service path specified by the initial portion of the `myServicePath` variable in Example 1-1:

webroot\com\oreilly\frdg

Example 1-2 shows the code that must be added to your *HelloWorld.cfc* component:

Example 1-2. ColdFusion code for HelloWorld.cfc

```
<cfcomponent>
  <cffunction name="sayHello" access="remote" returntype="string">
    <cfreturn "Hello World from ColdFusion Component" />
  </cffunction>
</cfcomponent>
```

This is a simple component that contains one function, *sayHello( )*, which returns a string. Notice that we set the `access` to `"remote"`, which is necessary to allow the component to be called remotely, either by Flash or as a web service.

Save the component. If you have access to the ColdFusion administrative interface (which you should if you have a local installation) browse to it through your browser with the following URL:

http://yourservername/com/oreilly/frdg/HelloWorld.cfc/

After entering your ColdFusion administrative password, you should see a description of the component, similar to Figure 1-5.

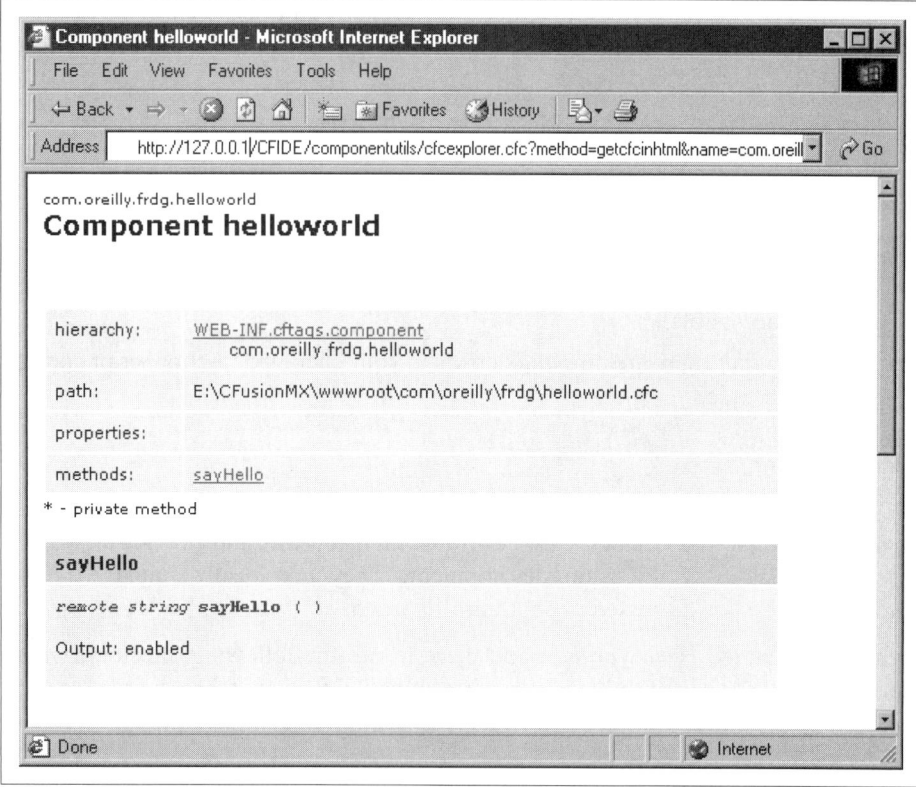

Figure 1-5. ColdFusion MX component description autogenerated by ColdFusion MX

If you do not see the description, or if you get an error, check and fix any syntax errors and try again.

Once you have verified that the ColdFusion component works via the browser, switch back to Flash and test the *HelloWorld.fla* movie created in Example 1-1. You should see "Hello World from ColdFusion Component" in Flash's Output window.

Server-Side ActionScript

ColdFusion MX and JRun 4 application servers allow developers to create remote services in Server-Side ActionScript (SSAS). *Server-Side ActionScript* is a scripting language that a Flash MX developer can use to create remote services without needing to know a server-side language such as ColdFusion Markup Language (CFML) or Java. Client-side JavaScript and ActionScript programmers may find SSAS easier than learning a new language. Using SSAS, simple services can be written that access databases or utilize the HTTP functionality of ColdFusion or JRun 4. Code written in

SSAS can be consumed by Flash via Flash Remoting only and cannot be used to create other types of output such as HTML.

The SSAS mechanism of ColdFusion MX and JRun 4 is actually a server-side implementation of the Rhino JavaScript parser, with some server-specific objects and methods added that allow the developer access to the functionality of <cfquery> and <cfhttp> tags of ColdFusion (found in the ActionScript *CF* object). Methods of the *CF* object can be accessed as CF.*methodName( )*. You can find a complete discussion of SSAS in Chapter 6. See *http://www.mozilla.org/rhino/* for details on the Rhino project.

To implement the Hello World example in SSAS, create a plain text file named *HelloWorld.asr* using any text editor, and place it into the following directory, where *webroot* is the root of your web server:

webroot/com/oreilly/frdg/

 The code in an SSAS (*.asr*) file is not compiled or encrypted. If a user browses to an *.asr* file, the browser displays the code as plain text unless you take steps to prevent it at the web server level. You should turn off read permissions for *.asr* files in your web server or keep the files in a secured directory.

Since ColdFusion can process CFCs, ColdFusion pages, and SSAS files, you need to make sure there are no name conflicts. If you created the ColdFusion component example file earlier, rename *HelloWorld.cfc* to *SomethingElse.cfc* to ensure that the SSAS (*.asr*) file, and not the ColdFusion file, is processed. You may also need to restart the ColdFusion MX server, as the *.cfc* file may have been cached. The exact order in which services are located varies with the application server on which the Flash Remoting gateway is installed. See the appropriate server chapters later in the book for details.

Example 1-3 shows the code that should be added to *HelloWorld.asr*; it creates a simple function called *sayHello( )* that returns a string to the client.

Example 1-3. Server-Side ActionScript code for HelloWorld.asr

```
function sayHello ( ) {
  return "Hello World from Server-Side ActionScript";
}
```

Save the file in plain text format and switch back to Flash. Test the Flash movie and you should see the output from the SSAS function.

If you get an error saying that the service cannot be found, check the service path, and make sure that there are no syntax errors in the *.asr* file.

Java using JRun 4 or other J2EE servers

For the Java example, we will implement our remote service as a simple Java class. Using Java as a remote service requires that the Flash Remoting gateway be installed on a Java application server such as Macromedia's JRun 4 or IBM's WebSphere. The Java version will not work with ColdFusion MX or Microsoft .NET servers.

Create a new plain text file in any text editor, name it *HelloWorld.java*, and enter the code shown in Example 1-4.

Example 1-4. Java code for HelloWorld.java

```
package com.oreilly.frdg;

public class HelloWorld {
  public String sayHello () {
    return "Hello World from Java";
  }
}
```

Compile the class into your web server's classpath. This may vary from server to server, but the server's *WEB-INF* (or *SERVER-INF* in the case of JRun) directory is usually included within the server's classpath. For example, to compile it using JRun 4, you would use (from a command prompt):

```
c:\jrun4\servers\myservername\server-inf\classes\com\oreilly\frdg\>javac
HelloWorld.java
```

If you are using JRun 4 and created the SSAS example earlier, rename *HelloWorld.asr* to *SomethingElse.asr* to ensure that the Java class is used instead.

Once the class has been successfully compiled, place it in the *classpath\com\oreilly\frdg* directory and switch to Flash and test your movie. You should see the output from the *sayHello( )* method of the *HelloWorld* Java class. If you get an error that the service cannot be found, make sure that you have compiled the class into the server's classpath.

Microsoft .NET server

ASP.NET services can be written in several languages, including VB.NET and C#. This Microsoft .NET service example is implemented as a .NET DLL written in C#.

Open Microsoft's Visual Studio .NET (VS.NET) and create a new project. From the Project Types window, select Visual C# Projects; then, from the Templates window, select Class Library. Set the name of the project to *HelloWorld*, as shown in Figure 1-6. Rename the class file that appears from *Class1.cs* to *HelloWorld.cs*. The code will work even if you do not rename the class file, but renaming it makes it easier to organize the files.

Example 1-5 shows the server-side C# code to implement the example as a Windows .NET service.

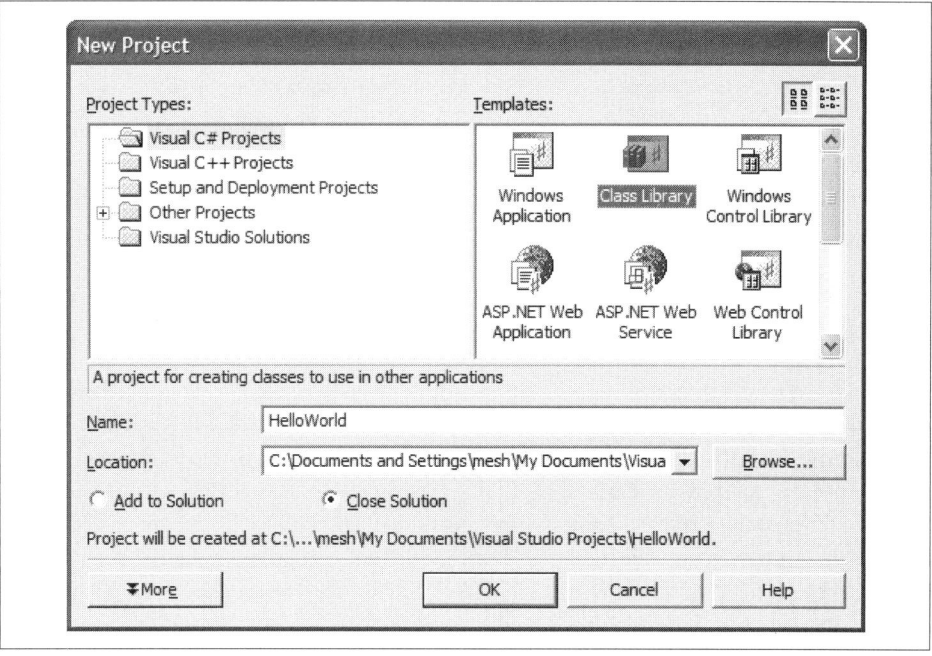

Figure 1-6. Visual Studio .NET project setup screen with settings for HelloWorld DLL

Example 1-5. C# code for HelloWorld.cs

```
using System;

namespace com.oreilly.frdg {
  public class HelloWorld {
    public String sayHello () {
      return "Hello World from ASP.NET DLL";
    }
  }
}
```

Enter the code shown in Example 1-5 and compile the DLL using VS.NET's Build →
Build Solution option, which creates *HelloWorld.dll* in the following directory:

   projectpath/bin/Debug

Copy *HelloWorld.dll* into the *flashservices/bin* directory on your .NET web server at:

   webroot/flashservices/bin/

The DLL contains a class with one function, *sayHello( )*, which returns a string. The
service path within Flash is determined by the DLL's namespace plus the class containing the method being called. By setting the namespace to the same as the directory structure for our other examples, we will not have to change the mySerivcePath
variable within our client-side ActionScript. Using a unique namespace also protects
your DLL from namespace collisions with other DLLs.

Switch back to the Flash movie and change the myURL variable in Example 1-1 to point to the .NET version of the Flash Remoting gateway, such as:

```
var myURL = "http://yourservername/flashremoting/gateway.aspx";
```

This is the only change that has to be made to the Flash movie. It is necessary because the .NET version of the Flash Remoting gateway is implemented differently than the Java and ColdFusion MX versions.

Save the Flash movie and test it. You should see the output from the DLL ("Hello World from ASP.NET DLL") in Flash's Output window.

PHP

The Hello World application (and other applications) must be set up a bit differently in PHP than in other environments. Flash Remoting with PHP is class-based, due to requirements of the AMFPHP library. That is to say, all Flash Remoting services must be written as classes in PHP. To install the AMFPHP library, simply download the source release package and copy its *flashservices* directory to your web server's document root (see Chapter 9 for additional details). Because the class is named *com.oreilly.frdg.HelloWorld*, AMFPHP searches in the services path for a *HelloWorld.php* file. The main *flashservices* directory resides under the web root, with the AMFPHP classes in that directory. The *services* directory resides in this *flashservices* directory as well.

When building PHP remote services, you should include a *gateway.php* file in your server-side application in the directory for your current project. This creates the Flash Remoting gateway and includes the necessary files. The *gateway.php* file (shown in Example 1-6) for the Hello World example should be saved in the *webroot\ com\oreilly\frdg* directory.

Example 1-6. PHP Remoting gateway.php file contents

```
<?php
  /* File: gateway.php
     Instantiates the Gateway for the HelloWorld Application */
  require_once '/app/Gateway.php';    /* Require files */
  $gateway = new Gateway();           /* Create the gateway */
  $gateway->setBaseClassPath('/services/com/oreilly/frdg');
                                      /* Set the path to where the service lives */
  $gateway->service();                /* Start the service */
?>
```

Create a file named *HelloWorld.php* and place it into the following directory, where *webroot* is the root of your web server and *com\oreilly\frdg* matches the service path specified by the initial portion of the myServicePath variable in Example 1-1:

> *webroot\flashservices\services\com\oreilly\frdg*

Add the code shown in Example 1-7 to your *HelloWorld.php* page.

Example 1-7. PHP code for HelloWorld.php

```php
<?php
  /* File: {SERVICES_CLASS_PATH}/com/oreilly/frdg/HelloWorld.php
     provides the HelloWorld class used in Chapter 1. */
  class HelloWorld {
    function HelloWorld () {
      $this->methodTable = array(
              'sayHello' => array(
                  'description' => 'Says Hello from PHP',
                  'access' => 'remote',
                  'arguments' => array ('arg1')
              )
          );
    }
    function sayHello () {
      return 'Hello World from PHP';
    }
  }
?>
```

Example 1-7 implements a simple class named *HelloWorld* that contains one method, *sayHello( )*, which returns a string. The class is named the same as the file. The methodTable array is used by AMFPHP to look up functions to invoke and to provide a pseudoimplementation of ColdFusion's CFCExplorer utility, which documents the class, methods, properties, arguments, return types, and so forth.

Switch back to the Flash movie and change the myURL variable in Example 1-1 to point to the AMFPHP gateway:

```
var myURL = "http://yourservername/com/oreilly/frdg/gateway.php";
```

This is the only change that has to be made to the Flash movie, and it is necessary because the PHP implementation utilizes PHP pages to handle the functionality of the gateway.

If you run the movie in the test environment, you should see the phrase "Hello World from PHP" in the Output window. If you don't see it, verify that you have correctly installed the AMFPHP classes and verify your code.

Web service

For the web service example, we will create a web service using ColdFusion MX. However, any web service containing a *sayHello( )* method that returns a string works just as well.

Creating a web service in ColdFusion MX is extremely simple; we simply pass the URL to our CFC, adding *?wsdl* to the query string, which tells ColdFusion to generate a web service from the component. We'll use the CFC that we created in Example 1-2, *HelloWorld.cfc*, saved in the directory specified earlier.

Browse to the component with a web browser, and add the *?wsdl* query string to the URL that points to the component:

http://localhost/com/oreilly/frdg/HelloWorld.cfc?wsdl

The browser should display the WSDL XML for the web service, as follows:

```
<?xml version="1.0" encoding="UTF-8"?>
<wsdl:definitions targetNamespace="http://frdg.oreilly.com"
xmlns:wsdl="http://schemas.xmlsoap.org/wsdl/"
xmlns:xsd="http://www.w3.org/2001/XMLSchema"
xmlns:wsdlsoap="http://schemas.xmlsoap.org/wsdl/soap/"
xmlns:intf="http://frdg.oreilly.com" xmlns:impl="http://frdg.oreilly.com-impl"
xmlns:SOAP-ENC="http://schemas.xmlsoap.org/soap/encoding/"
xmlns="http://schemas.xmlsoap.org/wsdl/">
  <wsdl:message name="CFCInvocationException">
  </wsdl:message>
  <wsdl:message name="sayHelloResponse">
    <wsdl:part name="return" type="SOAP-ENC:string"/>
  </wsdl:message>
  <wsdl:message name="sayHelloRequest">
    <wsdl:part name="username" type="SOAP-ENC:string"/>
  </wsdl:message>
  <wsdl:portType name="hellouser">
    <wsdl:operation name="sayHello" parameterOrder="username">
      <wsdl:input message="intf:sayHelloRequest"/>
      <wsdl:output message="intf:sayHelloResponse"/>
      <wsdl:fault name="CFCInvocationException"
message="intf:CFCInvocationException"/>
    </wsdl:operation>
  </wsdl:portType>
  <wsdl:binding name="hellouser.cfcSoapBinding" type="intf:hellouser">
    <wsdlsoap:binding style="rpc"
transport="http://schemas.xmlsoap.org/soap/http"/>
    <wsdl:operation name="sayHello">
      <wsdlsoap:operation soapAction=""/>
      <wsdl:input>
        <wsdlsoap:body use="encoded"
encodingStyle="http://schemas.xmlsoap.org/soap/encoding/"
namespace="http://frdg.oreilly.com"/>
      </wsdl:input>
      <wsdl:output>
        <wsdlsoap:body use="encoded" encodingStyle="http://schemas.xmlsoap.org/soap/
encoding/"
namespace="http://frdg.oreilly.com"/>
      </wsdl:output>
    </wsdl:operation>
  </wsdl:binding>
  <wsdl:service name="hellouserService">
    <wsdl:port name="hellouser.cfc" binding="intf:hellouser.cfcSoapBinding">
      <wsdlsoap:address
location="http://127.0.0.1/com/oreilly/frdg/hellouser.cfc"/>
    </wsdl:port>
  </wsdl:service>
</wsdl:definitions>
```

If you see only a blank screen, view the page's source in your browser (using View → Source in Internet Explorer, for example). If you receive an error, correct any errors identified by the error message and try again. Like any URL, the web service URL may be cached depending on the browser settings, so you should reload/refresh the page to make sure the browser isn't using the cached version. This web service can also be seen at the author's site at:

http://www.flash-remoting.com/oreilly/com/helloworld.cfc?wsdl

Switch to Flash and change the `myServicePath` variable to point to the web service's WSDL file. If you are using the CFC to create the web service, the path will be:

```
var myServicePath = "http://yourservername/com/oreilly/frdg/HelloWorld.cfc?wsdl";
```

Test your movie, and you should see the output from the *sayHello( )* method of the web service. Although our web service is on the same server as the Flash Remoting gateway, Flash Remoting is simply acting as a gateway when accessing an XML-based (SOAP-compliant) web service. The web service can be on any computer accessible via the network or the Internet.

When working with Flash Remoting and web services, you are not limited to ASP.NET, ColdFusion, PHP, and J2EE. Web services can be implemented in:

- Python or Perl
- C or C++
- Any other language that has a SOAP library implementation

More information on web services can be found at:

http://www.xml.com/webservices

Overview

The Hello World example, while simple, illustrates the power of using Flash Remoting. The core client-side ActionScript code is the same, regardless of the language or server model that the remote service is written in. At most, only the path to the Flash Remoting gateway or remote service is different.

Furthermore, none of the server-side code is Flash-specific. This means that you can create libraries of functions that work from the server-side languages, for use without Flash, which can also be called directly from Flash. In many cases, you will be able to integrate a Flash front end with existing server-side code and libraries with little or no changes on the server. (Details and exceptions are covered throughout the rest of the book.)

Isolation between server-side and client-side code allows for a clean division of labor. Server-side developers need not worry about what is calling their code; if there is a well-defined API on the server, Flash developers can seamlessly hook into the server-side code. Similarly, the Flash developer need not worry about the details of the server-side implementation. He need only know the API for the remote services he intends to call. If he is using web services, he can query the *.wsdl* file on the server to discover the methods. This allows both the server-side code and the Flash application to be developed simultaneously, reducing production time and making testing and debugging easier.

Even if one developer writes both the Flash and server-side code, the multitiered architecture is still advantageous. It allows you to define an API, implement it on the server, and then hook the Flash movie into it. This makes it possible to test each component on its own before connecting Flash to the server, ensuring that bugs are less frequent and easier to isolate.

Our example may seem simple, because we are only passing a string from the server to Flash. However, if you think of a string as just another type of object or datatype, you can begin to see the power of Flash Remoting. Try passing more complex datatypes, such as an array, from the server-side service to Flash, and see what is returned to the Flash movie. Modify the *onResult( )* callback function from Example 1-1 to do something more interesting with the data than display it in the Output window.

Workflow Example

Having discussed how the Flash Player and the Flash Remoting gateway communicate, now let's look at what occurs behind the scenes. We will examine each step of the earlier Hello World example. In Example 1-1, a remote service was called from Flash and received a "Hello World" string in response.

Here are the steps that occur:

1. Using the NetServices API within Flash, developer-written code makes a call for a remote service.
2. The NetServices library passes the remote service call, along with any arguments, to the *NetConnection* object within the Flash Player.
3. The *NetConnection* object serializes the request into AMF and sends it to server as an HTTP binary POST.
4. The Flash Remoting gateway on the server receives the request, deserializes it and determines the server-side service to which to pass the request.
5. The Flash Remoting gateway on the server invokes the server-side service, passing any arguments sent along with the request from the Flash Player.
6. The Flash Remoting gateway on the server receives any data returned from the service (in this case, the string "Hello World"), serializes it into AMF, and returns it to the client-side Flash Player as an HTTP response.

7. The Flash Player receives the AMF data from the server and deserializes it into a native ActionScript datatype (in this case a *String* object). Depending on the data sent back, the deserialization is done within the Flash Player or the NetServices code.

8. Finally, the string is returned to an ActionScript callback function specified by the developer to receive data loaded from the server.

Although a lot happens when a remote service is called from the Flash Player, most steps are abstracted away from the developer. The developer has only to write the client-side ActionScript that calls the remote service (Step 1) and receive the response from the remote service (Step 8). Of course, someone has to write the code for the remote service itself (Step 5), but that is often done by a different developer or independently of Flash, such as in the case where a Flash front end is being added to an existing web service.

Architecture for Flash Remoting Applications

We conclude this chapter with a general overview of a client/server architecture using the Flash Player and the Flash Remoting gateway. Generally, Flash/server applications follow an *n-tiered architecture*. Figure 1-7 depicts such an architecture, comprising a client/presentation tier (the Flash Player), a middle tier (Flash Remoting gateway running within an application server), and a data tier (a database, XML file, or other data source).

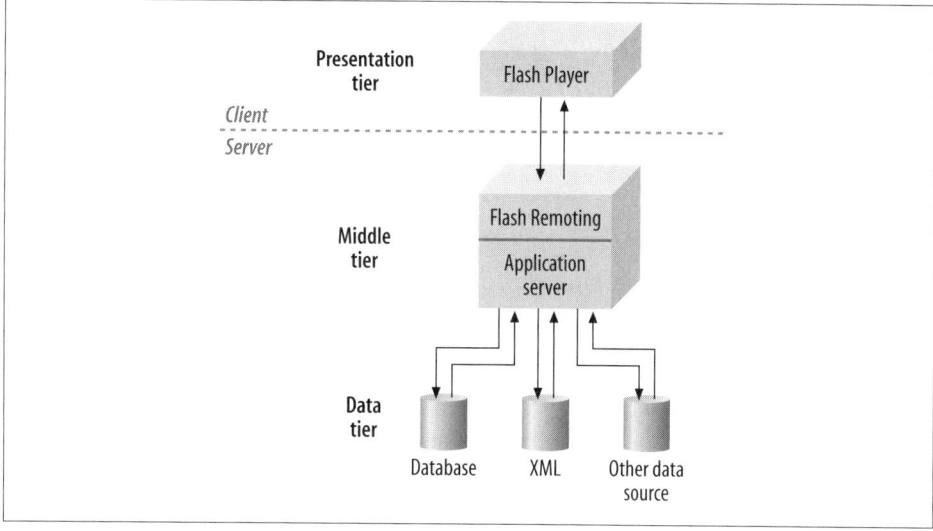

Figure 1-7. The Flash/server n-tiered application architecture

Presentation Tier

The presentation tier is responsible for the application's user interface (UI) and any client-side logic that is needed, such as client-side data validation. It communicates with the middle tier by sending and loading data on a request-driven basis. In most cases, the presentation layer consists of a Flash file embedded within an HTML page, but it can also be a Flash Standalone Projector running on the desktop, or even a Flash sprite within a Director Projector.

Middle Tier

The middle tier sits between the presentation layer and the data source. Its primary role is to separate the presentation tier from the data tier and provide access to the data tier from the Flash Player. The core application logic is also normally implemented in the middle tier. This frees the client to do what it does best—presentation—and frees the server to do what it does best—communicate with databases and manipulate data.

The middle tier resides on the server and can be implemented with various technologies, such as ColdFusion, ASP.NET, and Java. In addition, the middle tier can consist of multiple levels, each adding a layer of abstraction from those immediately above and below it.

In Flash 5, it was common to have a multitiered middle layer, with the uppermost layer serializing and deserializing data to and from the Flash Player, as shown in Figure 1-8.

However, using Flash Remoting and Flash Player 6 or later, this logic is handled by the Flash Remoting gateway, sitting on the server atop the middle tier, as shown in Figure 1-9. Flash Remoting eliminates the need to write Flash-specific code in the middle tier.

Data Tier

The data tier is the lowest level of the architecture and is responsible for managing the application's data, as well as the data's persistence. The data source resides on the server side and can be implemented as a database (such as SQL Server, DB2, MySQL, or Oracle), XML file, comma-separated file, and so forth. Client-specific data, such as user interface preferences, can be stored on the client side using cookies or ActionScript local shared objects (LSOs). Whether this data is stored on the client side or in the data tier on the server side depends primarily on the importance of the data to the functionality of the application, with application-critical data generally being stored on the server, which is considered more reliable.

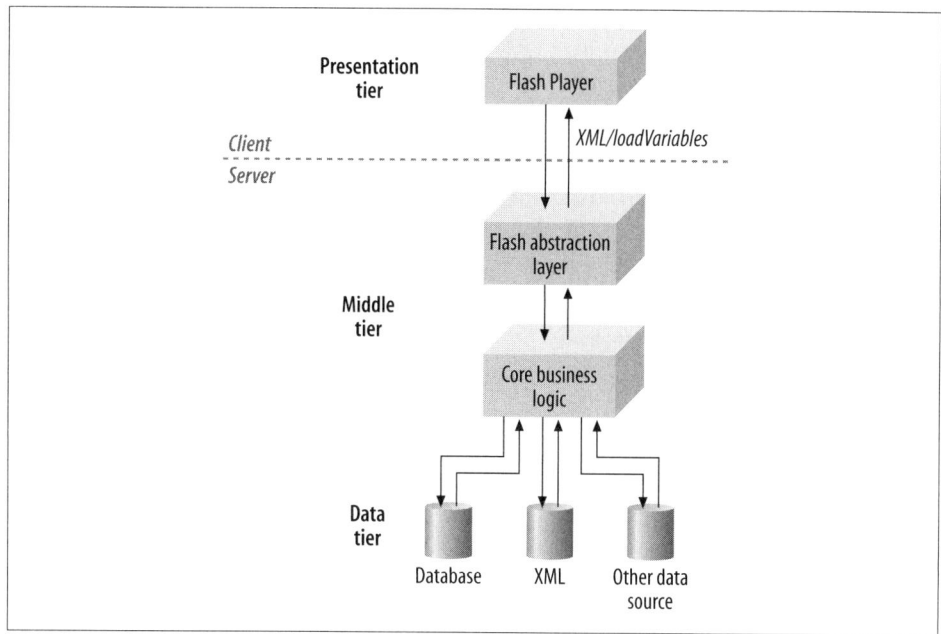

Figure 1-8. Flash 5 n-tiered application architecture with multilayered middle tier

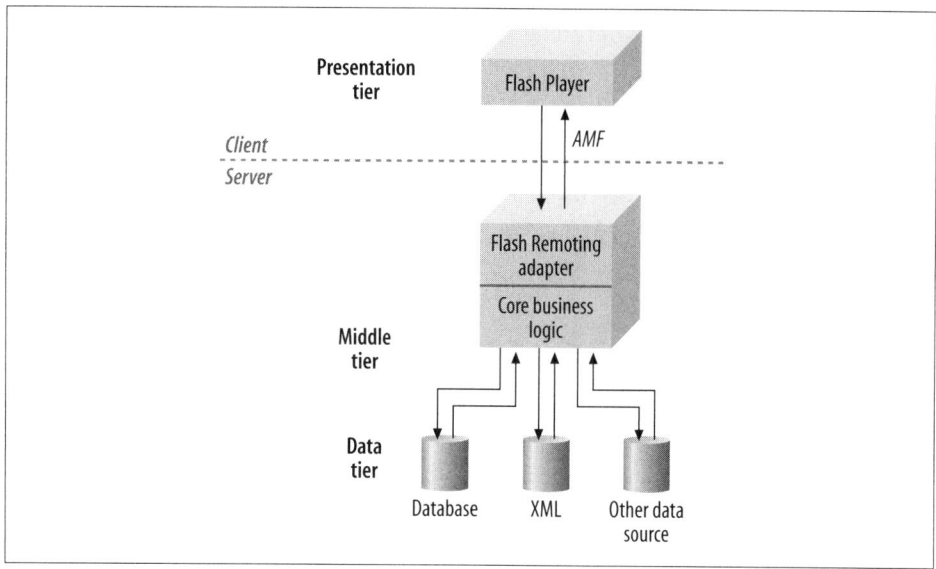

Figure 1-9. N-tiered application architecture with Flash Remoting gateway

This n-tiered architecture is similar to an n-tiered architecture that uses HTML within a web browser as the presentation tier. However, there are some important differences. When using Macromedia Flash, the presentation layer can be generated entirely on the client side, as the UI can be created dynamically at runtime on the client's machine. Furthermore, once the UI has been created or downloaded, only the updated data has to be sent back and forth to the server. This differs from dynamically generated HTML, which requires that the entire page be recreated on the server and served to the client each time the data or state of the application changes.

There are other advantages of using an n-tiered architecture with the Flash Player as the presentation layer. By abstracting the presentation layer away from the data source, you can completely change the data source or its format without affecting the interface or rewriting your Flash movie.

Changes to the data tier affect only the middle tier. Assuming that the API exposed by the middle tier to the presentation level does not change, the Flash movie will not be affected at all.

For example, the application's data source can be changed without affecting the Flash movie, as shown in Figure 1-10. Furthermore, because the middle tier might comprise multiple levels, only the middle tier's interface to the data tier needs to be adjusted.

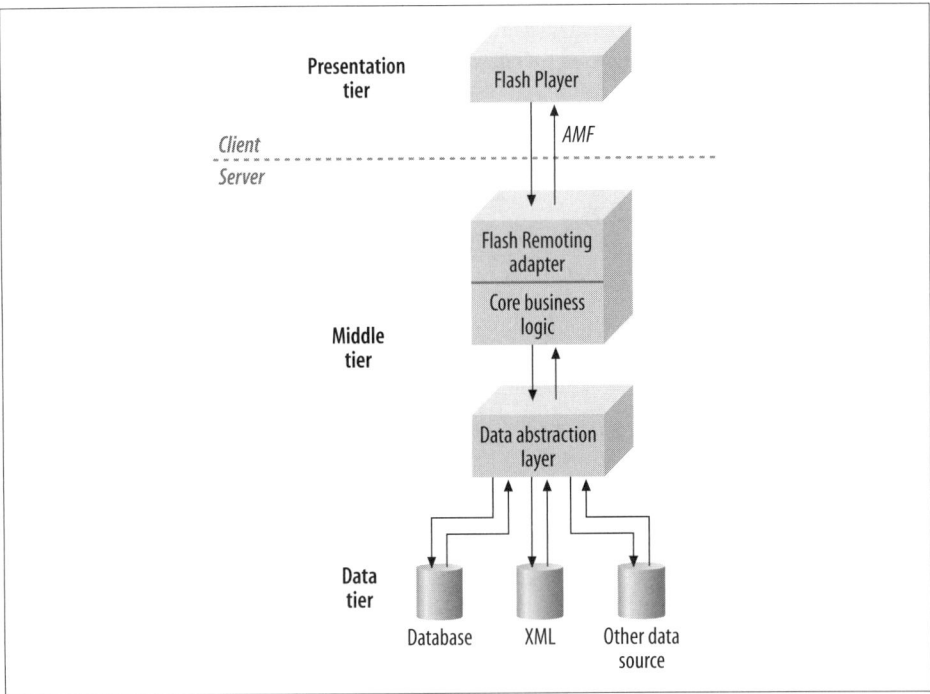

Figure 1-10. N-tiered architecture with data abstraction layer

By having multiple tiers, each tier can be optimized for its particular task and environment. This is particularly important when using Flash as the presentation layer, since Flash runs on the client side, which can be a much more variable and unknown environment than the server.

For example, you can filter large sets of data in the middle tier where you have a known environment and resources, versus doing it on the client side within Flash where, depending on the client's machine, it might not perform well. In this case, you may want to initially sort the data set on the server and then have any user-initiated sorts occur within the Flash Player. This is a good tradeoff between client-side processing concerns and the extra bandwidth required to transfer data sets to and from the server. Components such as the DataGrid from Macromedia further abstract the implementation of this logic and allow complex sorting and filtering directly within the Flash movie. I address these topics in subsequent chapters, using examples where appropriate.

It is much easier to update the application's core business logic when it is centralized in the middle tier, verses spreading it out across multiple tiers and technologies. Furthermore, keeping business logic out of the presentation tier allows you to test the business logic separate from the presentation tier, isolate any problems, deploy changes, and integrate it with the other tiers of the architecture.

Finally, this multitiered architectural structure mirrors the common divisions of labor during Flash application development. Often, a Flash developer creates the Flash movie and client-side ActionScript, while another developer creates the server-side code. They can program and test their code independently, making development much easier, faster and less error-prone. Provided that the interfaces between the levels are defined, the Flash developer can use temporary data hardcoded into the application to test the application. The server-side developer simply needs to ensure that his code implements the defined API to the presentation tier.

 Avoid the temptation to use ActionScript to implement the application's business logic within the Flash movie's presentation layer. Such an approach ties the Flash movie too closely to the lower levels of the architecture and exposes the business logic on the client side, making the application more difficult to maintain and update, as well as possibly affecting client-side performance adversely. When working with Flash Remoting, you are building a *client/server* application, not a standalone Flash movie. The application server is much better suited for the business logic. Chapter 12 goes into much greater detail about the best practices in building a Flash Remoting application.

Again, this is a very broad and general overview of client/server application architecture when using Macromedia Flash for the presentation layer. Later chapters discuss differences specific to additional technologies.

Wrapping Up

This chapter was only a brief introduction to the technology. You learned about the basic concepts of Flash Remoting, the benefits of Flash Remoting, and the advantages over traditional methods used in Flash 5. In addition, you saw a typical implementation of a Flash Remoting application and how it works in each server-side language.

Chapter 2 digs deeper into Flash Remoting. It covers installation of the server-side gateway (where necessary) and the authoring components. In addition, the Flash authoring environment is covered as it relates to Flash Remoting. Also, Flash UI components are covered, including additional components from Macromedia.

Installing, Configuring, and Using Flash Remoting

Being comfortable in a development environment is an important aspect of programming. Flash Remoting requires the utilization of several different technologies. Just getting all the pieces set up properly can be a challenge. This chapter gets you up and running with Flash Remoting. You'll install the components, set up the development environment, and build a simple Flash Remoting example.

Installing Flash Remoting

Flash Remoting is built into ColdFusion MX (and later) and JRun 4, making these two application servers attractive to begin working with Flash Remoting. ColdFusion Markup Language (CFML) has the added bonus of being relatively easy to learn. Flash Remoting is also available from Macromedia as an add-on for .NET and J2EE servers. Table 2-1 shows the languages that you can use to create server-side Flash Remoting services in each type of installation.

Table 2-1. Flash Remoting official language support

Flash Remoting installation	Languages
ColdFusion MX or later	CFML Server-Side ActionScript Java CFScript
JRun 4	Java Server-Side ActionScript
J2EE	Java
ASP.NET	VB C# JScript .Net C++ Any other ASP.NET language

Table 2-2 lists the open source projects underway that support Flash Remoting using various languages.

Table 2-2. Open source Flash Remoting language support

Project name	Language	URL
AMFPHP	PHP	*http://www.amfphp.org*
FLAP	Perl	*http://www.simonf.com/flap*
OpenAMF	Java	*http://www.openamf.org*

The following sections detail the installation and configuration of Flash Remoting in the server environments that are supported.

ColdFusion MX

ColdFusion MX and later run on a J2EE (Java 2 Enterprise Edition) platform. Therefore, you can write simple programs using CFML and the resulting application is compiled into a Java servlet.

Admittedly, the variants of ColdFusion can get confusing. There are three basic versions. Free 30-day trial versions of the two commercial versions are available. After 30 days, they revert to the Developer Edition, which restricts IP address access but is otherwise full-featured:

ColdFusion MX Server Developer Edition
> Included as part of Macromedia Studio MX or available as a free download from Macromedia's site. The Developer Edition is equivalent to the Enterprise Edition but can be accessed from only one remote IP address. It is intended for a single developer to use in testing.

ColdFusion MX Server Standard Edition
> A standalone version for Windows and Linux. This is the most basic and economical option for ColdFusion deployment on one server.

ColdFusion MX Server Enterprise Edition
> A standalone version for Windows, Linux, Solaris, and HP-UX for large-scale enterprise deployment, allowing server clustering and sandbox security. It also enhances J2EE integration by providing support for JavaServer Pages (JSP) servlets and JSP Tag Library imports. This version also runs atop an existing J2EE installation, including IBM WebSphere Application Server 4 or later, Macromedia JRun 4, Sun ONE Web Server 6 or later, and BEA WebLogic Server 6.1 or later.

Table 2-3 summarizes the platforms that ColdFusion MX Server will run on.

Table 2-3. ColdFusion MX Server supported platforms

Platform	Operating system	Web servers
Windows	98[a] ME[a] NT 4.0 Workstation SP6A NT 4.0 Server SP6A NT 4 Server, Enterprise Edition 2000 Professional SP2 2000 Server SP2 2000 Advanced Server 2000 Datacenter Server 2003 Server (a.k.a. .NET Server) XP Home XP Professional	Apache 1.3.12–1.3.27 Apache 2.x JRun HTTP Server iPlanet 6.x iPlanet 4.x Netscape 3.6x IIS 4.0 and higher (on OSes that support IIS)
Linux	Red Hat Linux 6.2 – 7.2 SuSE Linux 7.2, 7.3 TurboLinux 8 Server Red Hat Linux AS 2.1	Apache 1.3.12–1.3.27 Apache 2.x JRun HTTP Server iPlanet 6.x iPlanet 4.x Netscape 3.6x
Macintosh	Mac OS X[a]	JRun 4 Apache Tomcat
Solaris[b]	Solaris 7 Solaris 8 Solaris 9	Apache 1.3.12–1.3.27 Apache 2.x JRun HTTP Server iPlanet 6.x iPlanet 4.x Netscape 3.6x
HP-UX[b]	System 11.00	Apache 1.3.12–1.3.27 Apache 2.x JRun HTTP Server iPlanet 6.x iPlanet 4.x Netscape 3.6x

[a] Not recommended in a production environment
[b] Enterprise edition only

ColdFusion MX's J2EE underpinnings allow ColdFusion applications to be extended in Java. ColdFusion MX can also be deployed on top of an existing J2EE installation if you purchase the Enterprise edition. Using the Enterprise edition, you can run ColdFusion MX on a Macintosh as well, on top of a JRun 4 or Tomcat installation. Macromedia supports Macintosh installations for development only and not in a production environment. Installation on a Macintosh is covered at:

http://www.macromedia.com/support/coldfusion/j2ee/cfmx-mac-onjrunandtomcat. html

The system requirements for running ColdFusion MX on J2EE Servers are listed in Table 2-4. For web server requirements, consult your J2EE server documentation.

Table 2-4. J2EE Application Server supported platforms for ColdFusion MX

J2EE Application Server	Operating systems
IBM WebSphere Application Server Advanced Edition 4.0.3 and Application Server 5	Windows 2000, 2003 Windows NT4 Solaris 7, 8 Red Hat Linux 7.1, 7.2 SuSE Linux 7.2
Macromedia JRun 4	Windows 2000, 2003 Windows NT4 Solaris 7, 8 Red Hat Linux 6.2–7.2 SuSE Linux 7.2, 7.3
Sun ONE Web Server Version 6.02 and Version 7	Windows 2000, 2003 Windows NT4 Solaris 7, 8 Red Hat Linux 6.2–7.2
BEA WebLogic Version 6.1 and Version 7	Windows 2000, 2003 Windows NT4 Solaris 7, 8 Red Hat Linux 6.2–7.2

As per the Macromedia technote at *http://www.macromedia.com/support/coldfusion/ j2ee/#servers*, although you can deploy the Enterprise edition on any J2EE-compliant application server, not all are fully tested and supported for production use. For development and evaluation purposes, Macromedia has also tested Flash Remoting on Sun J2EE SDK 1.3 (the reference implementation) and Tomcat 4.1.12 (and later).

It is best to consult the Macromedia site for the current requirements. Macromedia's site explains the details of the different ColdFusion variants and pricing:

> *http://www.macromedia.com/software/coldfusion/productinfo*

Flash Remoting is also automatically installed as part of the ColdFusion MX Server package installation (Flash Remoting does not work with ColdFusion 5 or earlier versions). You can download and install the ColdFusion MX trial version, which will revert to a free developer's version after 30 days. The trial version is also included in the Studio MX package.

 As per Table 2-1, ColdFusion MX or JRun 4 is required for building the back end of the Flash Remoting application using Server-Side ActionScript.

ColdFusion MX can be installed in several different ways and on a multitude of platforms. ColdFusion MX Server can be installed atop your existing web server (IIS, Apache, or others) or using the built-in web server. The built-in web server is a limited functionality web server, recommended for testing only and not recommended for production environments. More information on the built-in web server can be found at:

http://www.macromedia.com/support/coldfusion/adv_development/config_builtin_ webserver

ColdFusion MX can also be installed side-by-side with an existing ColdFusion 5 installation, in which case it is installed with its own built-in web server on port 8500 rather than the standard web port 80. This port is crucial to making connections using Flash Remoting if you are running the standalone ColdFusion web server. You must specify the path to the server when you make your connection to a gateway URL, so if the server is running on port 8500 instead of port 80, the gateway connection code looks like this:

```
var myURL = "http://localhost:8500/flashservices/gateway";
var myServer = NetServices.createGatewayConnection(myURL);
```

Running side-by-side installations of ColdFusion 5 and ColdFusion MX lets you test existing ColdFusion 5 applications in the ColdFusion MX environment. Because ColdFusion MX was rebuilt from the ground up as a J2EE application, there may be compatibility problems with ColdFusion 5 applications, particularly with regard to the database connections, which have changed dramatically. There is a Compatibility Analyzer built into the ColdFusion MX Server that can help you determine the compatibility issues your older applications might have.

Installation of ColdFusion MX is straightforward and covered at length in the documentation that comes with the software and at *http://livedocs.macromedia.com*. Once installed, Flash Remoting is immediately available. You can test Flash Remoting on a standalone ColdFusion MX Server by browsing to the following URL:

http://yourservername:8500/flashservices/gateway

If you have a standard installation of ColdFusion MX Server that ties into your existing Apache, IIS, or other web server on port 80, you can test Flash Remoting by browsing to this URL:

http://yourservername/flashservices/gateway

If you see a blank page, you know that the gateway is working. If you see an error message or anything else on the page, something is wrong. Double-check your URL and port settings. There is no easy way to pinpoint and correct an installation error if you come across one. Usually, the only option is to recheck the steps you followed and reinstall the server. For more troubleshooting tips go to:

http://www.macromedia.com/support/coldfusion/installation.html

In a successful installation, you will not see a physical */flashservices/gateway* directory in your server root. This path is a virtual directory that is known to the ColdFusion MX Server. It does not correspond to any physical directory on your machine.

After a successful installation of ColdFusion MX, you will have the *flashgateway.ear* file in the *path_to_CFusionMX\runtime\servers\default* folder.

 If you have to reinstall the ColdFusion MX Server, you should delete the *CFusionMX* folder from your hard drive and restart the machine before attempting the reinstallation. Remnants of a past installation might cause errors, so when you run the installation program, select the option to uninstall a previous installation.

If you are upgrading a prior installation of ColdFusion Server, you can migrate your old ODBC and OLEDB data sources to ColdFusion MX Server, which uses JDBC. This can save you time when creating connections to existing databases. Existing ODBC data sources are migrated to JDBC format, which can exist side-by-side with the old ODBC data sources. Later modifying an ODBC data source will not affect the ColdFusion MX JDBC connections that bear the same data source name. JDBC data source configuration settings for ColdFusion MX Server are located in the *path_to_CFusionMX\runtime\servers\default\SERVER-INF\jrun-resources.xml* file.

Knowing how to create and connect to data sources is necessary for developing the server-side services of a Flash Remoting application. Data sources in ColdFusion MX are defined in the ColdFusion MX Administrator, the visual interface for administering ColdFusion applications. The ColdFusion MX documentation covers this topic thoroughly. Additionally, if you plan to develop your Flash Remoting services in Server-Side ActionScript rather than CFML, you will have full access to data sources defined in the ColdFusion MX Administrator.

As of this writing, there have been three major updaters to ColdFusion MX and a version upgrade to 6.1. Make sure you have the latest version of ColdFusion MX from the Macromedia site. Using Flash Remoting with ColdFusion MX is discussed at length in Chapter 5.

JRun 4

JRun 4 is Macromedia's enterprise-level J2EE application server, which supports JavaServer Pages (JSP). Although Flash Remoting is available as an add-on for other J2EE servers, the JRun 4 installation includes Flash Remoting out of the box, making it the easiest way to Flash-enable a J2EE site. When using JRun 4 for building Flash Remoting services, you will most likely be programming the server-side services in Java. In addition, JRun 4 allows Server-Side ActionScript to be used, which is unavailable in the Flash Remoting package for other J2EE servers.

JRun 4 also contains considerable enhancements that make it a worthy upgrade from previous versions of JRun, even without the Flash Remoting functionality. It is fully J2EE-compliant, having passed Sun's rigorous certification process for J2EE servers. In addition, it has full support for Enterprise JavaBeans (EJB) 2.0, hot-deployment technology (which avoids restarting the server when making changes), and enhanced support for web services.

Of the J2EE servers on the market, JRun is one of the easiest to get up and running, thanks to its visual installation wizard, and one of the easiest to administer because of the extensive administration interface. If you are just starting out and want to get your feet wet with the Java language in the J2EE arena, JRun 4 is a good choice.

 ColdFusion MX can also be purchased separately and installed on top of an existing JRun 4 installation, yielding an effective combination of the power of J2EE with the ease-of-use of ColdFusion.

JRun installs with its own built-in web server to port 8100 by default, rather than the standard web port 80, to avoid conflicts with any existing web servers. The administrative server interface is available at port 8000, using the URL *http://localhost:8000*. You can manually connect a JRun server to an existing web server as well, so that your pages can be accessed through the typical port 80. This can be done through the administrative interface of JRun. The built-in web server of JRun is recommended for developmental purposes only, not heavy use.

If you choose to develop your Flash Remoting applications using the default installation of the server on port 8100, you must specify the port in your connection to the Flash Remoting adapter:

```
var myURL = "http://localhost:8100/flashservices/gateway";
var myServer = NetServices.createGatewayConnection(myURL);
```

You can test the Flash Remoting functionality in a standard JRun 4 installation by pointing your browser to:

http://yourservername:8100/flashservices/gateway

where *yourservername* is the domain name or IP address of your web server. If you have set up a JRun server on the standard web port 80, you can point your browser to:

http://yourservername/flashservices/gateway

Again, just as in the ColdFusion installation, if you see a blank page, the Flash Remoting technology is working properly. If you don't see a blank page, check your JRun installation by testing the administrative interface or the samples included with JRun. If the server is working, you may have a problem with your gateway URL or port setting. If the server is not working, you may need to reinstall JRun. See the following URL for tips on JRun installation issues:

http://www.macromedia.com/support/jrun/installation.html

Chapter 7 shows how to install Flash Remoting in your web application rather than creating a server-wide testing installation.

Other J2EE Servers

Flash Remoting is available for purchase from Macromedia as a separate product, named Flash Remoting MX for J2EE, that will work in almost any J2EE-compatible server. There is a 30-day trial version available from *http://www.macromedia.com/software/trial_download*. The trial version reverts to a server-side development–only version after 30 days, with which you can continue to use the Flash Remoting servlet on your local machine for testing purposes.

Some of the servers that you can use with Flash Remoting include:

- IBM WebSphere
- Tomcat
- BEA WebLogic server
- HP Application Server
- Caucho Resin
- Oracle 9*i* AS
- JBoss
- ATG Dynamo

The following operating systems support the Flash Remoting gateway adapter:

Windows

- Windows NT Server 4.0 SP6a
- Windows 2000 Server SP2
- Windows 2003 (a.k.a. .NET server)

Linux

- Red Hat 7.3
- SuSE 7.3

Unix

- SPARC Solaris 2.7
- SPARC Solaris 8

These configurations are tested and supported by Macromedia, but other operating systems can be used at your discretion. I've successfully run Flash Remoting on Windows 2000 Professional with both JRun 4 and Tomcat in a testing environment. See *http://www.macromedia.com/software/flashremoting/productinfo/system_reqs* for the most recent system requirements for Flash Remoting.

To install Flash Remoting for J2EE in a server-wide test environment, follow these steps:

Windows

If you are loading from the CD-ROM, you can install from the CD-ROM's browser interface. If you are installing the trial version from the Macromedia web site, double-click the Flash Remoting for J2EE installer (named *flashremoting-java-win-en.exe* or something similar).

Linux

From a command line, type:

```
<prompt>./flashremoting-java-linux.bin -i console
```

This should begin the installation process.

Solaris

From a command line, type:

```
<prompt>./flashremoting-java-solaris.bin -i console
```

This should begin the installation process.

The installer gives you the choice of installing the *.war* or *.ear* archives with or without sample files and documentation. The installer creates a directory in which the archives are placed. After running the installer, follow these steps to deploy Flash Remoting on your server:

1. Find either the *flashgateway.war* or the *flashgateway.ear* file. These files are found in *C:\Program Files\Macromedia\Flash Remoting MX* in a default installation on Windows.

2. Deploy the *flashgateway.ear* or *flashgateway.war* file to the web application. The process varies from server to server. On Tomcat, for example, copy the *.war* file to the *webapps* directory and restart the Tomcat server. This deploys the *flashgateway.jar* file to the *site_root\flashgateway\WEB-INF\lib* directory. It also automatically deploys the *web.xml* file, which contains the servlet mappings for the *flashgateway* servlet, to the *WEB-INF* directory. The *flashgateway* directory is the default Flash Remoting location, but the *.jar* file can be deployed to other directories as well.

3. Find the *frconfig.txt* file and make sure it is in the classpath of your server. This is necessary for the license information to be available to Flash Remoting. In a trial or developer's edition, the serial number will be blank. In the commercial version of Flash Remoting, your serial number needs to be in this file.

4. Restart your server.

Test the functionality of the servlet by browsing to:

http://localhost/flashgateway/gateway

In a default Tomcat installation using port number 8080 instead of port 80, test the installation by browsing to:

http://localhost:8080/flashgateway/gateway

You should see a blank page. If the page is not blank, you must retrace your steps and make sure your web application mappings are correct. The Flash Remoting servlet is already mapped to /gateway in the *web.xml* file:

```
<servlet-mapping>
  <servlet-name>FlashGatewayServlet</servlet-name>
  <url-pattern>/gateway</url-pattern>
</servlet-mapping>
```

The *flashgateway.jar* file can be deployed in any of your web applications by specifying the servlet mapping in the *web.xml* file for each application. Each application on your server can use its own path to the gateway. Chapter 7 explains how to install Flash Remoting in your own application using Flash Remoting for J2EE Updater 1, which includes a *.jar* archive.

In your ActionScript code, the gateway URL is used to create the connection as follows (for the default installation):

```
var myURL = "http://localhost/flashgateway/gateway";
var myServer = NetServices.createGatewayConnection(myURL);
```

If you are having trouble making the connection, make sure your URL follows this general format:

> *http://domain_or_ip_address:port/context_or_folder/servlet_mapping_for_
> gateway_servlet*

A *flashgateway/samples* directory is also installed in the default gateway directory. These samples should work out of the box, assuming you are using a default web server at port 80. If not, you can open the *.fla* files in the subdirectories under the *samples* directory and change the paths in the ActionScript source.

ASP.NET

Flash Remoting is available for purchase from Macromedia as an add-on server component (DLL) for ASP.NET. There is also a 30-day trial version available from *http://www.macromedia.com/software/trial_download*. The trial version reverts to a server-side development–only version after 30 days, with which you can continue to use the DLL on your local machine for testing purposes.

Installation of Flash Remoting for ASP.NET is straightforward but requires that you have the Windows .NET SDK installed. The .NET SDK is available as a free download from the MSDN Download Center at:

> *http://www.microsoft.com/downloads/details.aspx?familyid=9B3A2CA6-3647-
> 4070-9F41-A333C6B9181D&displaylang=en*

You can also install the Flash Remoting samples to your web directory as part of the installation, which gives you a few sample C# and VB applications that utilize Flash Remoting. The samples can be run from the *webroot\flashremoting\samples\ default.htm* file.

The default installation of Flash Remoting places the files necessary for the Flash Remoting service to work in the *flashremoting* directory under your web root. This is also the directory where the samples are installed. They should work out of the box if the installation was successful. To test the installation of Flash Remoting for ASP. NET, point your browser to the following URL:

http://yourservername/flashremoting/gateway.aspx

Notice the differences between this connection and the ColdFusion and JRun connections:

- The directory under *yourservername* is called *flashremoting* instead of *flashservices*.
- The directory is a physical directory on your computer instead of a virtual directory.
- You are making a call to the *gateway.aspx* file, which actually exists in the directory as a dummy placeholder file with two lines in the file:

```
<%@Page %>
<!-- This file is intentionally blank. -->
```

Each .NET application on your server uses its own path to the gateway. The *Hello-World* sample application from Chapter 1 used the *flashremoting* directory, but if your application uses a different directory name, or none at all, you need to change the connection. A typical installation using the *gateway.aspx* file in a subfolder at the root of your web application might look like this:

http://www.yourservername.com/subfoldername/gateway.aspx

Or if you are developing locally, you can use the *localhost* URL:

http://localhost/subfoldername/gateway.aspx

The installation of the commercial Flash Remoting for ASP.NET product also places the *frconfig.txt* file in the *bin* directory of your web root. This file contains the serial number of Flash Remoting. Additional IP addresses can be placed in this file as well. Chapter 8 covers ASP.NET in detail, including other installation and configuration idiosyncrasies.

PHP with AMFPHP

AMFPHP adds the possibility of using Flash Remoting on PHP application servers, which are not supported by the commercial Macromedia tools. Because AMFPHP is open source, it may be used free of charge but it is subject to change and is being actively developed. The latest AMFPHP package can be obtained from its official web site:

http://www.amfphp.org

Installation of AMFPHP is quite simple. Once you've downloaded and extracted the AMFPHP package, copy its *flashservices* directory to your web server's document root. Using Apache, the default Windows directory may be *C:\Program Files\Apache Group\Apache\htdocs*. In Unix and Unix-flavored systems, it may be */usr/local/ apache/htdocs*. On Mac OS X systems, it may be */Library/WebServer/Documents*. Alternatively, you can put the *flashservices* directory in the `include_path` of your PHP environment. See the AMFPHP *readme* file for details.

The default *gateway.php* file should be sufficient to begin development of services, which should be placed under your *webroot/flashservices/services* directory and should follow the structure of your base classpath. After installing the gateway, browse to the gateway path:

> *http://localhost/flashservices/gateway.php*

If you see a blank page, the gateway is working. For more information on using Flash Remoting with PHP, see Chapter 9.

Typical Installations

The alphabet soup of technologies necessary to work with Flash Remoting can be confusing. Tables 2-5, 2-6, and 2-7 show several installations and typical components of each. These are not the only choices available by any means, but they represent the most typical configurations. Table 2-5 shows typical low-cost options for basic development.

Table 2-5. Typical low-cost Flash Remoting installation options for development

Operating system	Application server	Language	Web server	Database
Windows 98 or 2000 Professional	ColdFusion MX Developer's Edition	CFML or SSAS	Built-in HTTP server (port 8500)	MS Access
Red Hat Linux	Tomcat	Java	Apache (port 8080)	MySQL
Windows 2000 Professional	ASP.NET[a]	C#	IIS (port 80)	MS Access
Red Hat Linux	PHP[b]	PHP	Apache (port 80)	MySQL
Macintosh OS X	Tomcat/ColdFusion MX Developer's Edition	CFML or SSAS	Apache (port 80)	MySQL

[a] Requires add-on Flash Remoting server-side components
[b] Requires AMFPHP open source solution

Table 2-6 lists typical medium-cost installation options for medium- to high-traffic sites.

Table 2-6. Typical medium-cost Flash Remoting installation options

Operating system	Application server	Language	Web server (port 80)	Database
Windows 2000 Server	ColdFusion MX Professional	CFML or SSAS	IIS or Apache	SQL Server
Red Hat Linux	JRun 4	Java or SSAS	Apache	PostgreSQL

Table 2-6. Typical medium-cost Flash Remoting installation options (continued)

Operating system	Application server	Language	Web server (port 80)	Database
Windows 2000 Server	ASP.NET[a]	C#	IIS	SQL Server
FreeBSD Linux	PHP[b]	PHP	Apache	PostgreSQL

[a] Requires add-on Flash Remoting server-side components
[b] Requires AMFPHP open source solution

Table 2-7 lists typical high-end options for enterprise-level sites with high traffic.

Table 2-7. Typical high-end Flash Remoting installation options

Operating system	Application server	Language	Web server (port 80)	Database
Solaris 7 or 8	IBM WebSphere[a]	Java	IBM HTTP Server	DB2
Windows 2000 Advanced Server	ColdFusion MX for J2EE on top of JRun 4	CFML and Java	IIS	SQL Server
HP-UX or Solaris	Oracle 9i Application Server[a]	Java	Oracle HTTP Server	Oracle 9i
Red Hat Enterprise Linux AS	PHP[b]	PHP	Apache	IBM DB2

[a] Requires add-on Flash Remoting server-side components
[b] Requires AMFPHP open source solution

As you can see from Tables 2-5, 2-6, and 2-7, Flash Remoting can be deployed using a variety of different configurations. With the main ingredients of an application server (CFMX, J2EE, ASP.NET, or PHP), web server, database, and the Flash Remoting adapter in place, you can deploy the server-side services of Flash Remoting applications. Next, we'll talk about where these services go and how they are named.

Naming Your Services

I used to work with a guy named Jeff. One day, a new employee—also named Jeff—joined the company. Rather than try to deal with the potential name conflicts, we simply called the new guy "Jim." This worked so well that the boss began using the name Jim on his pay envelope. If someone named Jim were to join the company, however, the naming convention would have to have been reevaluated.

Just like real-life names, service names can have conflicts. It is important that you organize server-side services in such a way that your namespaces don't *collide* (i.e., conflict) with other namespaces. For example, if you name your service *HelloWorld*, users attempting to access it might unintentionally access another *HelloWorld* service of the same name. This is called a *namespace collision*.

To avoid collisions, service names should always include the directory structure, as used in the package-naming structure of Java, where the package name relates to the domain name and project information of the package. For example, a service from Macromedia for a "Remoting" project might be named *com.macromedia.Remoting*.

The next section describes in more detail how to create a namespace (and the directory structure it implies) that will work for examples in this book. Use this directory for all of your server-side services.

Creating the Sample Directories and Package Structure

After you've installed ColdFusion, JRun, or another application server and the Flash Remoting gateway adapter, follow these steps to create your directory structure for the samples and the package structure for your remote service files:

1. Set up a folder on your hard drive, such as *c:\frdg_samples*, in which to build the samples used in this book. You can download the finished code from the online Code Depot (cited in the Preface) and unzip them to this directory. This is the directory in which to place the *.fla* files for the Flash movies.

2. Determine the location of your root web directory (or site root directory) and make a subfolder named *frdg_web* within it. The example pages will run from this directory. On a typical Windows IIS server, this directory might be *c:\inetpub\ wwwroot\frdg_web*. You can access this URL from *http://localhost/frdg_web*.

3. The server-side service files (*.cfc*, *.dll*, *.class*, etc.) must be placed into an appropriate location, which varies depending on the type of server you are running:

   a. For CFCs, create the package structure as folders inside of your *web* root as shown in Step 4.

   b. For ASP.NET DLLs, create the package structure in the *bin* folder by creating a namespace to mimic the package structure detailed in Step 4.

   c. For Java classes, create the package structure at the root of your classpath folder as detailed in Step 4.

4. Set up the package structure in which to build the server-side services. For a ColdFusion Server or ASP.NET *.aspx* files, this package structure is simply folders under your web site root with the following subfolder structure: *webroot\com\ oreilly\frdg*. For the Java class files, simply create the identical structure under your classpath, which is usually in the *WEB-INF* (or *SERVER-INF*) directory in the web application.

 In order for the package structure to work properly, it needs to begin at the site root for ColdFusion, at the *bin* folder for ASP.NET, and at the root of the classpath for Java classes. If your web host has given you a folder under a site root but has not set up a virtual directory for you, the package will not work. Make sure a virtual directory has been created, or use an appropriate package path based on the physical location of the folders on the hard drive.

The examples in this book include further instructions about these package structures and the structure of the service within the package. The service structure is explained next under "The Services."

Using this structure, you can create server-side services that are named similarly to Java packages. The *com\oreilly* portion of the path is the domain name, *oreilly.com*, backwards. The third subdirectory, *frdg*, is the project or package name. When you create your own server-side packages, you can follow this structure using your own domain name.

Using a package name that includes your domain name ensures the path to the service is unique, so you can distribute a service without worrying about namespace collisions with other services. Conversely, it ensures that third-party services you install on your server won't cause namespace collisions with your own services.

The Services

References to server-side services have different meanings depending on the environment. Table 2-8 shows the services available for different Flash Remoting environments.

Table 2-8. Service types available to the Flash Remoting programmer

Environment	Service type	Service path	Methods
ColdFusion MX	ColdFusion pages	Directory path from site root	ColdFusion page (*.cfm*)
ColdFusion MX	CFC	Directory path from site root including ColdFusion Component (*.cfc*) name	Methods of the CFC
J2EE	EJB	JNDI name of the EJBHome binding	Method of the EJB
J2EE	Java class	Fully qualified Java class name	Methods of the class
J2EE	JavaBean	Fully qualified Java class name	Methods of the JavaBean
J2EE	Servlet	Directory path from site root	Servlet
JRun 4	JMX	MBean object name	Methods of MBean
ASP.NET	ASP.NET page	Directory path from site root	ASP.NET page (*.aspx*)
ASP.NET	DLL	Fully qualified class name	Methods of the DLL
Web Services	Web service	URL of the *.wsdl* file for the service	Methods of the remote service
Server-Side ActionScript	SSAS	Directory path from the site root including the SSAS	Methods of the SSAS (*.asr*) file
PHP	PHP page (class)	Directory path from the *services* folder in the site root	Methods of the PHP class

To put the concept of the server-side service and package structure into context, take a ColdFusion site using the *HelloWorld* service from Chapter 1 as an example. I'll show how the ActionScript service object might be created using two possible types of remote services: ColdFusion (*.cfm*) pages and ColdFusion Components (*.cfc* files).

To supply remote services to your Flash movie using a ColdFusion page:

- As shown in Figure 2-1, a ColdFusion *.cfm* file becomes the method name and the subfolder that the file is in becomes the service object path. A folder named *HelloWorld* will be placed in the *webroot\com\oreilly\frdg* directory. When creating the service object, the slashes (or backslashes) in the directory path become dots in the service's pathname, so *com\oreilly\frdg\helloworld* becomes *com.oreilly.frdg.helloworld*. This is the name via which you'll access the service object in ActionScript.

- The methods of this service object, which your Flash movie calls, are ColdFusion pages in that directory (without the *.cfm* file extension). A ColdFusion page named *sayHello.cfm* would supply a remote method named *sayHello( )* to your Flash movie.

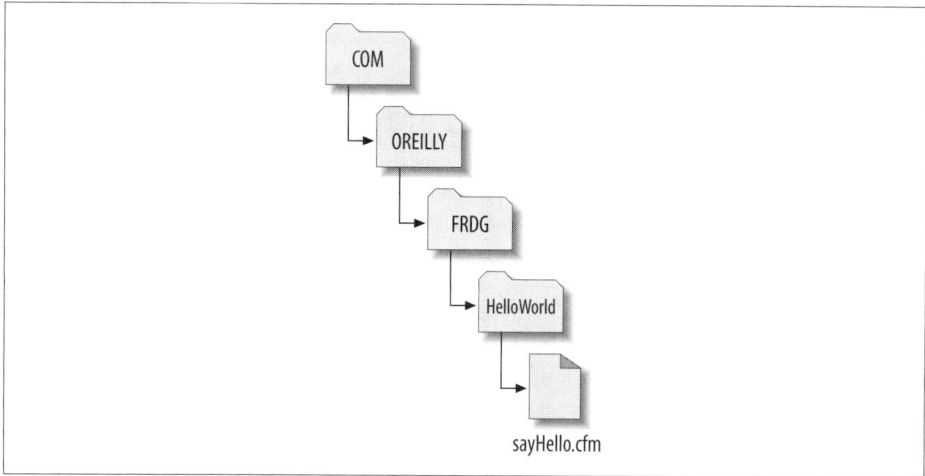

Figure 2-1. A subfolder becomes the remote service, and the ColdFusion page becomes the remote method

In contrast to using a *.cfm* page, to supply a remote service using a CFC:

- As shown in Figure 2-2, the CFC file path and filename (without the *.cfc* file extension) becomes the service object in Flash. The same example directory used earlier, *webroot\com\oreilly\frdg*, contains a CFC file named *HelloWorld.cfc*. The service object name is the same as in the *.cfm* example—*com.oreilly.frdg.helloworld*—but the service object here references a file and not a folder.

- The functions defined within the CFC become the methods that you can call from the Flash movie. The method named *sayHello( )* is a function inside the CFC file.

As you can see, certain types of remote services are more easily utilized with Flash Remoting. Whereas each ColdFusion page can contain only one method, requiring multiple *.cfm* pages in the directory, a CFC can implement many methods for a

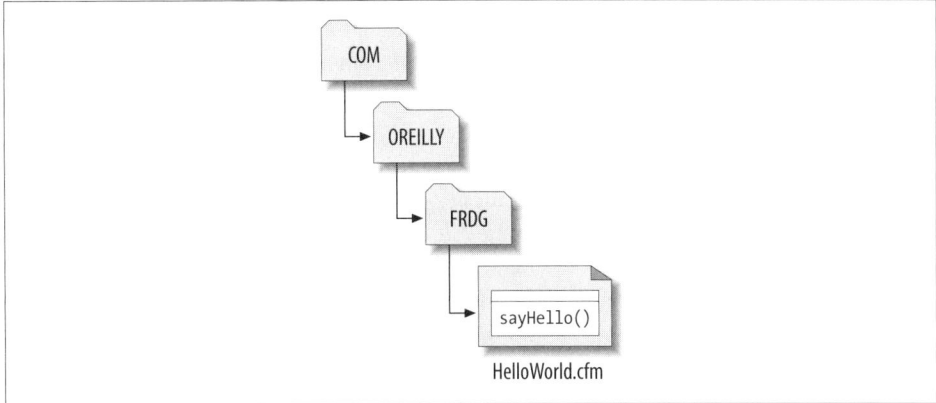

Figure 2-2. A ColdFusion Component becomes the remote service and the function inside becomes a method

service by simply defining multiple functions within the CFC. The same holds true of an ASP.NET (*.aspx*) page versus the ASP.NET DLL, and a Java servlet versus a Java class or JavaBean.

The Authoring Environment

The Flash authoring environment resembles standard software development interfaces familiar to Visual Basic and Delphi programmers. The features specifically advantageous for the Flash Remoting programmer are:

UI components
> The built-in Flash UI components allow for drag-and-drop construction of interfaces and easy connection to a data source through Flash Remoting using the *DataGlue* class. UI components are also extensible, allowing third-party developers to easily add to the core functionality of Flash.

ActionScript code hints and syntax highlighting
> The Actions panel (F9) provides lists of methods and properties as you type, as long as you use identifiers consistent with the code-hinting guidelines shown in Table 2-9 later in this chapter. For example, to enable code hinting, include the _ mc suffix in the names of movie clip instances.

Object-oriented programming (OOP)
> OOP standards and conventions drastically reduce the complexity of a Flash Remoting application when used properly. Flash is ideally suited for object-oriented methodologies, which reduce application development time and allow more complex applications to be built.

Property inspector
> The Property inspector is common to the Macromedia MX family of tools and is helpful for naming your objects.

Flash Remoting Components

The Flash Remoting components, which must be installed separately from Flash, are not visual components like the UI components; they include ActionScript classes for communicating with a server, two new UI panels, and code editor enhancements that make it easier to develop Flash Remoting applications in Flash. You can download the Flash Remoting components from *http://www.macromedia.com/go/flashremoting* or obtain them from the *\Flash MX\Extending Flash MX* folder on the Studio MX CD-ROM.

 The Flash Remoting components are required for working with Flash Remoting and must be installed in order to create Flash Remoting applications. Be sure you have the latest versions from the Macromedia web site. As of this writing, there has been one updater for Flash MX.

Installing the Flash Remoting components adds useful new classes to ActionScript. As shown in Figure 2-3, the new classes are located in the Flash MX program folder in the *Configuration\Include* directory. You can include one or more of these classes in your Flash movie using the #include directive at the top of your main move script (usually in the first frame following any preloader). When using #include, you can omit the folder name, because *Configuration\Include* is the default folder in which Flash MX looks for included files.

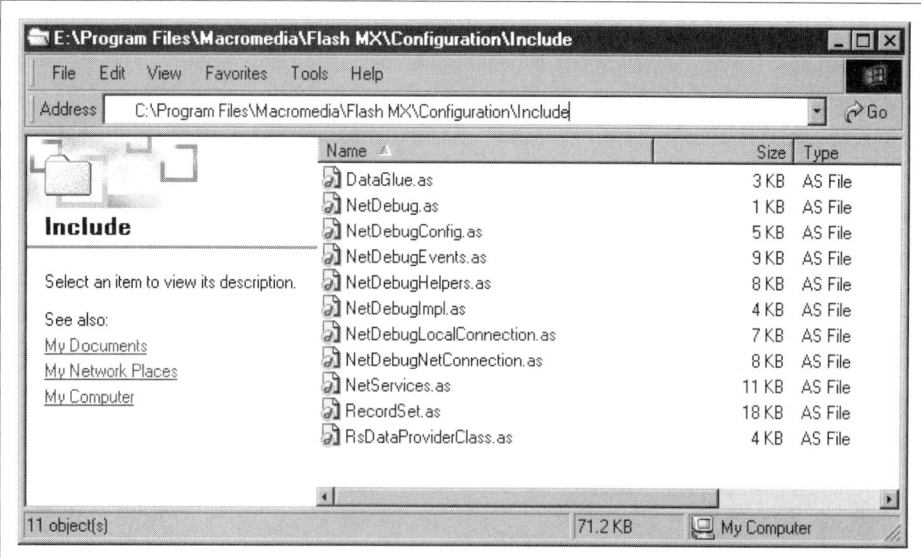

Figure 2-3. The ActionScript classes added by installation of the Flash Remoting components

These classes are discussed in depth in Chapter 4, but you should familiarize yourself with them briefly now.

NetServices class

The *NetServices* class provides a standard way to connect to remote services with a *NetConnection* object and provides standard methods that make it easy to call remote methods (services). The *NetServices.as* file should be included in every Flash Remoting application you build. You can include it in your Flash movie like this:

```
#include "NetServices.as"
```

RecordSet class

The *RecordSet* class adds support for a multirecord datatype, which can be delivered from the server or created on the client. The *RecordSet* class's methods make it easy to manipulate data within the Flash movie. A recordset delivered from a server-side service is serialized and sent to the Flash movie using the AMF protocol. The *RecordSet.as* class file is included automatically when you include the *NetServices* class, but you can include it by itself in applications that don't use Flash Remoting:

```
#include "RecordSet.as"
```

DataGlue class

The *DataGlue* class allows you to bind UI components to a *RecordSet* object or other data provider. You can use the *bindFormatStrings( )* method to attach data providers to interface controls that support *DataGlue*. Include *DataGlue.as* in your Flash movie as follows:

```
#include "DataGlue.as"
```

DataGlue.as, unlike *RecordSet.as*, is not included when you include the *NetServices.as* file. You must explicitly include *DataGlue.as* if you wish to utilize the *DataGlue* class.

NetDebug class

The *NetDebug* class ties your Flash movie to the server-side debugging capability of Flash Remoting and provides an interface from your movie to the NetConnection Debugger panel. The *NetDebug* class should never be included with your final movie, because it adds considerable code weight. Use it during development only by including it in your Flash movie:

```
#include "NetDebug.as"
```

 If you include the *NetDebug.as* file in your Flash Remoting application, anyone running the Flash authoring tool with the NetConnection debugger open will be able to see the debugging information in the panel.

Flash Remoting Windows and Menu Options

In addition to behind-the-scenes features, installing the Flash Remoting components adds two new panels to the Flash MX interface. It also adds some menu options.

NetConnection Debugger

The NetConnection Debugger panel (Window → NetConnection Debugger) helps to analyze and debug communication with the server. It lets you examine objects and variables to pinpoint problems. The NetConnection debugger is covered in Chapter 13.

Service Browser

The Service Browser panel (Window → Service Browser), shown in Figure 2-4, can list all your Flash Remoting connections and services. Services (and gateways) must be added manually to the Service Browser. Thereafter, the Service Browser can retrieve information about the service's methods and display them in a convenient tree view.

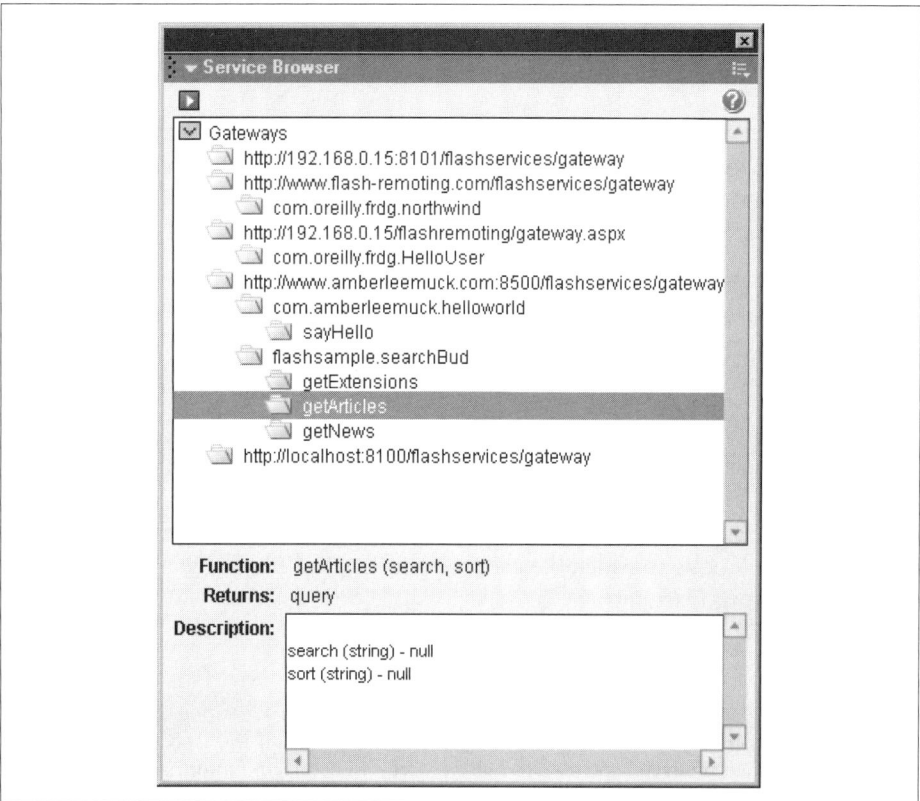

Figure 2-4. The Service Browser installs as part of the Flash Remoting components

To add a new service to the Service Browser, click the blue arrow in the upper-left corner of the panel and choose Add Service from the drop-down menu, which lists these largely self-explanatory options:

- Add Gateway
- Remove Gateway
- Add Service
- Remove Service
- Refresh Service Description
- Refresh All Service Descriptions
- Add Service to Actions Panel
- Remove Service from Actions Panel
- Expand All
- Collapse All

Adding a service to the panel is a two-step process. First, you must add the gateway. Choose Add Gateway to add the URL of a Flash Remoting gateway to the Service Browser. If you have already set up a local or remote server with a Flash Remoting gateway, you can add it to the Service Browser by typing in the actual gateway URL, such as:

http://localhost:8500/flashservice/gateway

With the gateway defined, you can now add a service—such as the *HelloWorld* service created in Chapter 1, or any other service—by choosing Add Service and typing in the service name, such as:

com.oreilly.frdg.helloworld

When you add a service using Add Service, the Service Browser displays the arguments and return datatypes of the remote methods comprising the service.

If you've defined a gateway and the URL is accessible over a live connection, the Service Browser should display the current *HelloWorld* service and its methods (only one, in this case). As your services become more numerous and complex, use the Service Browser to organize them and list their methods in one central location.

Help menu

When you install the Flash Remoting components, a new menu item—Welcome To Flash Remoting—is installed in Flash MX's Help menu. Its submenu contains three items:

Using Flash Remoting
    An overview of Flash Remoting technology

Flash Remoting Tutorial
    A tutorial intended as a brief introduction to Flash Remoting

The Actions Panel

The Actions panel is your most important friend as you develop Flash Remoting applications. It is where the action is, so to speak. All of the coding occurs here, unless you are using an external text editor. The Flash authoring environment can be a little claustrophobic at first, but keyboard shortcuts keep your tools close at hand. It is important to be comfortable in the coding environment if you are going to be programming in it for hours on end. If you find yourself writing ActionScript in the Actions panel's cramped default mode, follow the simple steps in the next section.

Setting up the Actions panel

When you first open Flash MX, the Actions panel appears as a little rectangle, as shown in Figure 2-5.

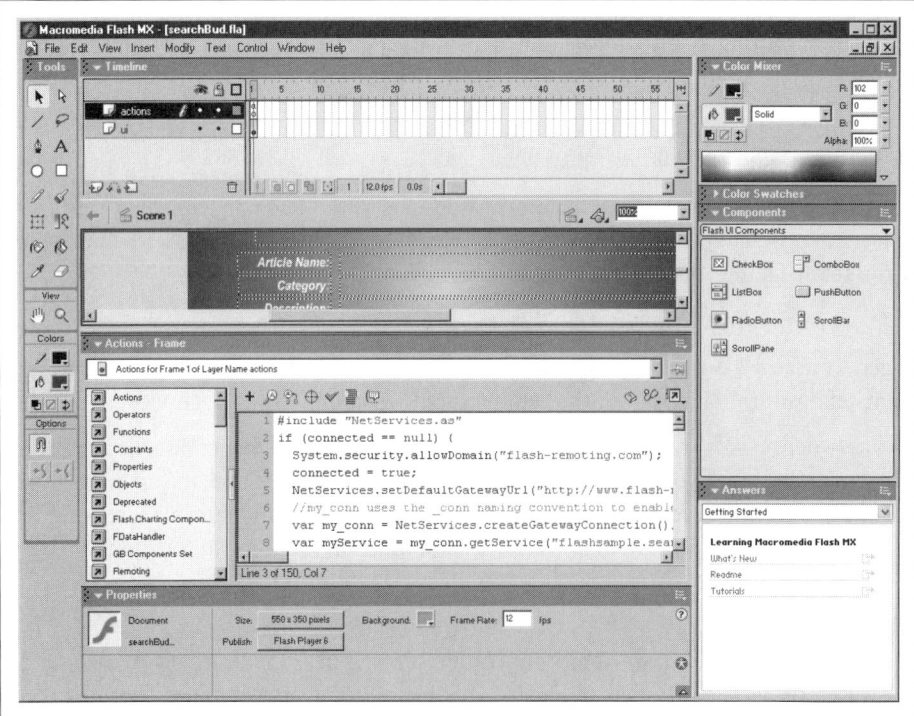

Figure 2-5. The default Flash MX interface

The first thing you'll need to do is to make the Actions panel's editable area bigger:

1. Close the Property inspector, which is for designing your interface, not programming it. The Property inspector is context-sensitive, so if you put all your code in frame 1, the Property inspector simply displays the main movie properties.

2. Open the Actions panel and drag the top of it up to the very top of the Flash interface with your mouse.

3. Select Expert Mode from the Actions panel pop-up Options menu.

4. Press F9—your magic key to toggle between the design and programming environments. Hitting it once will bring back the Stage and timeline. Hitting it again brings back the Actions panel.

5. With the Stage and timeline visible, open the Property inspector again. Now when F9 is pressed, the Property inspector also opens and closes when the Actions panel is toggled.

6. Eliminate the Answers panel, and open the Align panel and the Service Browser. The latter are both in the Window menu and can be dragged to the right side of the Stage with the rest of the panels. The Service Browser comes in handy as you develop your Flash Remoting applications. The Align panel is helpful when adding UI components to the interface visually.

7. Save the configuration of your panels by going to Window → Save Panel Sets and name it FR. You can retrieve this panel layout using Window → Panel Sets → FR, should the panels ever become disorganized.

Your environment should now look like Figure 2-6, ready for developing ActionScript.

Code hints and code completion

Installing the Flash Remoting components adds syntax highlighting and code completion to the ActionScript code editor (the Actions panel) for Flash Remoting objects.

You may have heard of Microsoft's Intellisense technology: you create an object in your code and you can access the properties, methods, and events of that object with code hints and code completion. Macromedia's implementation is "semi-intelligent"—it supplies the code hints and code completion, but it needs a little help in the form of naming conventions or comments. For example, if your variable name ends with _rs, such as `myresult_rs`, typing a period after the variable name displays the methods of the *RecordSet* class in a drop-down list.

Code hinting and code completion improve your coding speed and help avoid having to look up common properties, methods, and events as you type. Code completion also keeps spelling and capitalization consistent, which is not required in ActionScript but is required in many other languages and may be enforced in ActionScript someday. It is good coding practice to maintain capitalization consistency.

Flash's naming conventions for ActionScript objects are shown in Table 2-9. (See Table 3-1 for more code-hinting suffixes for user interface components.) Use these

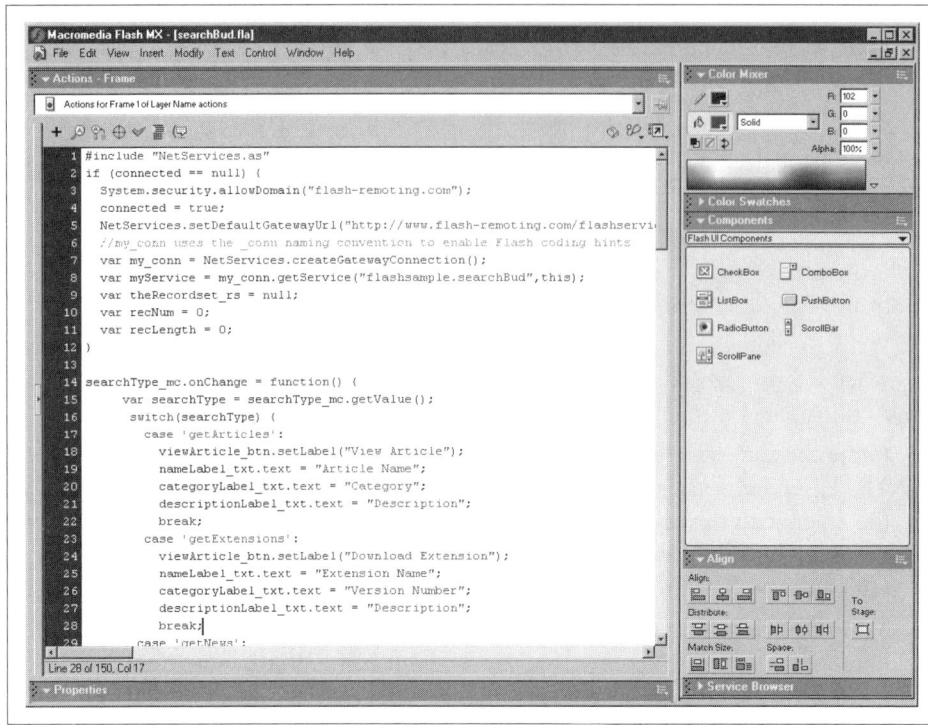

Figure 2-6. The Flash MX environment set up for Flash Remoting ActionScript coding

suffixes for variable names pertaining to the corresponding object type. For example, you might use a variable named deadline_date to hold a *Date* object. Note the suffixes for the *NetConnection* (_conn) and *RecordSet* (_rs) objects, which require installation of the Flash Remoting components.

Table 2-9. Suffixes used in ActionScript for code hinting

Object	Suffix
Array	_array
Button	_btn
Camera	_cam
Color	_color
Date	_date
Local Connection	_connection
Microphone	_mic
MovieClip	_mc
NetConnection	_conn
NetStream	_stream
RecordSet	_rs
SharedObject	_so

Table 2-9. Suffixes used in ActionScript for code hinting (continued)

Object	Suffix
Sound	_sound
String	_str
TextField	_txt
TextFormat	_fmt
Video	_video
XML	_xml
XMLSocket	_xmlsocket

The naming conventions used in Flash are somewhat controversial. They go against some OOP principles and naming strategies, which argue that the name of the object should not indicate an object's datatype because the datatype may change. For example, if you name an object employees_array and later change your code to implement the array as a *RecordSet* instance, the name would no longer relate to the object. You should rename the variable to employees_rs in such a case. That said, naming your objects with the standard naming conventions is an easy, intuitive way to speed up your coding. If a variable's datatype changes, correcting the variable's suffix is trivial compared to other changes that might need to be made.

Figure 2-7 shows code hints in use. If you are using the recommended naming conventions, as soon as you type a period, the list of possible methods pops up, along with their suggested arguments. You can choose one from the list or simply keep typing until your method is selected. Then you can hit Tab or Enter to insert the method name automatically. In addition, if there are arguments that need to be passed, the code completion feature inserts the opening parenthesis and gives you another code hint.

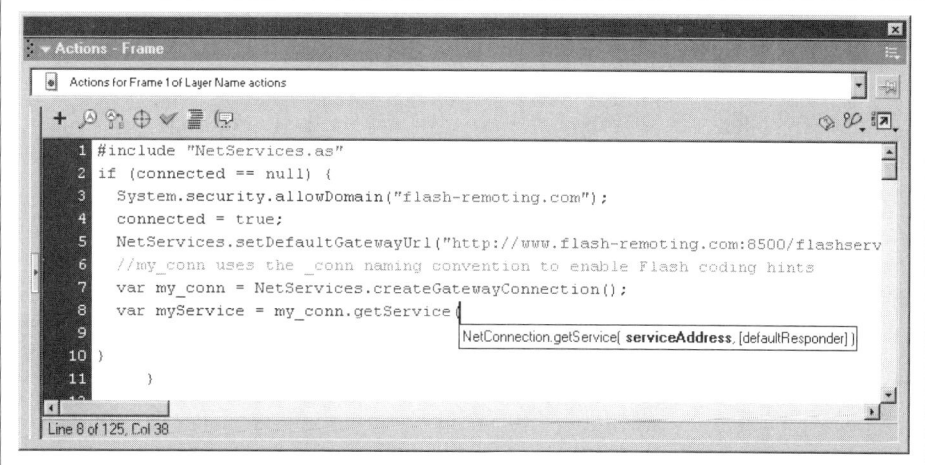

Figure 2-7. Code hints allow for quick coding

You can also enable code hints and code completion in the ActionScript editor by creating a comment for each object of interest. For example, to enable code hints for a *RecordSet* object named `rsGetEmployees`, add this comment to your script:

```
// RecordSet rsGetEmployees;
```

The ActionScript editor reads these comments and uses them to determine when to supply code hints and code completion.

> The semicolon at the end of the comment is necessary in this particular case. Even though the statement is a comment and not functioning code, it is treated as an ActionScript editor directive when used in this fashion.

Using explicit comments to enable code completion avoids being forced into using the Flash naming conventions. It also assists in documenting the program, as all your variables and objects can be set up in the beginning of your code.

Code hints and code completion are both fed by XML files whose location depends on your operating system. In a single-user environment, such as Windows 98 or Mac OS 9, they are stored in the main Flash program folder under the following directory:

> *Flash_program_directory\Configuration\ActionsPanel*

The Flash Remoting additions to these XML files are located in a subfolder named *CustomActions*. In a multiuser system, such as Windows 2000, Windows XP, or Mac OS X, the files are located in your multiuser applications directory.

Under Windows 2000, the files are located in:

> *C:\Documents and Settings\username\Application Data\Macromedia\Flash MX\ Configuration\ActionsPanel*

These directories and files are typically hidden in Windows, so you may need to show hidden items using the File Explorer's Tools → Folder Options → View → Show Hidden Files and Folders option.

On a Mac OS X machine, that directory is at:

> *mac_system_disk:Users:username:Library:Application Support:Macromedia:Flash MX:Configuration:*

As you create your own ActionScript classes, you can add code hints and code completion to them as well by building an XML file in the same format as the files in this directory. This technique is covered in conjunction with building custom UI controls in Chapter 11.

Additional Flash Remoting Developer's Tools

Man does not live by bread alone, and the Flash Remoting developer cannot develop an application solely with Flash MX. The following sections describe some of the applications you should keep in your arsenal as you develop Flash Remoting applications.

Database server and development environment

If you are developing a dynamic application, you should have a local copy of your database files and a database environment for testing purposes. In many cases, this might be an Access, MySQL, or Microsoft SQL Server database. These programs will give you easy access to your data as well as the query-building tools of these environments. In many cases, developmental versions of these programs are available free or for a small fee. In addition, using a local copy of a database before deploying your application lets you debug coding issues before adding server connectivity to the equation.

Local copy of application server

While not strictly necessary, it is easier to create applications on your local machine if you can test code locally rather than deploy to a production server. Under Windows, you can run a local copy of ASP.NET, ColdFusion, JRun 4, or a J2EE server to gain access to Flash Remoting on your local machine. To run ColdFusion with JRun or Tomcat locally on a Mac, see:

> *http://www.macromedia.com/support/coldfusion/j2ee/cfmx-mac-onjrunandtomcat. html*

If you're not able to develop on your local machine, it is wise to develop on a staging server before deploying to a production server. One serious mistake in your code, such as an endless loop, can bring down a server.

Code editor

Flash's Actions panel is well-suited to ActionScript coding, but many developers prefer to use an external text editor. Furthermore, you must use an external editor if you're creating external ActionScript (*.as*) files to be included at compile time (that is, the Actions panel in Flash MX and Flash 2004 can't edit external files, although Flash Pro supports editing external files). HomeSite+ and Dreamweaver MX, both included on the Macromedia Studio MX CD-ROM, make ideal ActionScript editors. Dreamweaver MX has code-coloring built into the program, and third-party code-coloring enhancements can be downloaded for HomeSite+. Figure 2-8 shows the Dreamweaver MX interface editing an ActionScript file.

Both HomeSite+ and Dreamweaver MX support Snippets (reusable code excerpts) to speed development. Dreamweaver MX—which also works well with ColdFusion (*.cfm*), JSP (*.jsp*), and ASP.NET (*.aspx*) files—is both customizable and extensible.

 For more information on Dreamweaver MX, see *Dreamweaver MX: The Complete Reference* (Osborne), which was co-authored by Ray West and myself, or see *Dreamweaver MX: The Missing Manual* by David Sawyer-McFarland (O'Reilly).

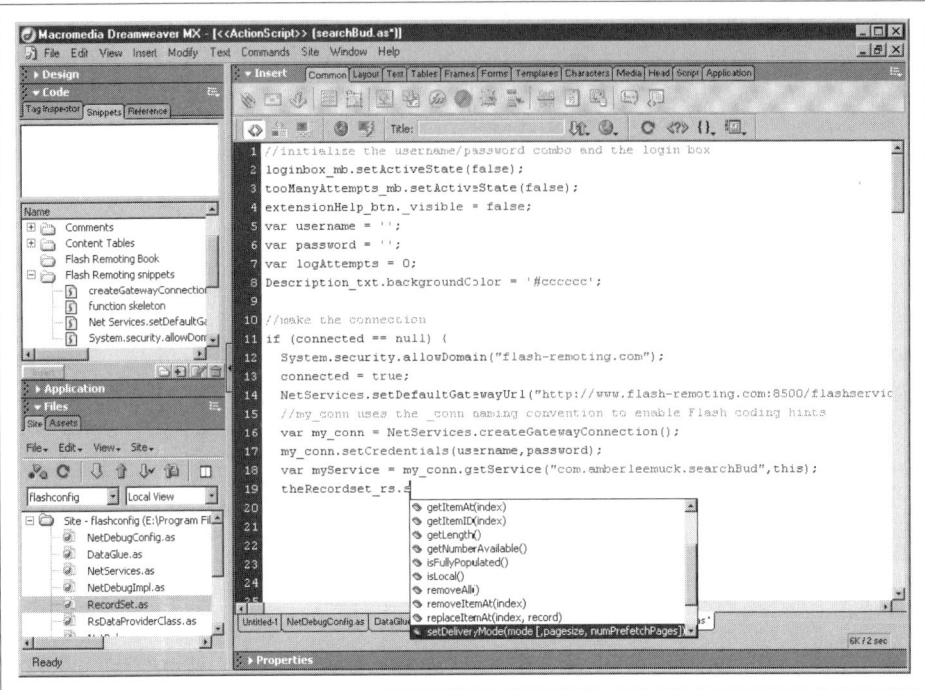

Figure 2-8. The Dreamweaver MX environment also has code hints and code completion

Other popular code editors include Ultraedit-32, Editplus, BBEdit, and Textpad. Many of these editors have built-in or third-party support for ActionScript code-coloring.

SWF decompiler

An SWF decompiler is a valuable debugging tool as you test your movie. It lets you explore your *.swf* files in greater depth than you can in the Flash authoring environment, examine reports, and print complete ActionScript files that include otherwise hidden code. ActionScript Viewer (*http://www.buraks.com/asv*), shown in Figure 2-9, is my favorite decompiler because it can save *.swf* files as plain text and create printouts.

Also, flasm (*http://flasm.sourceforge.net*) is an application that gives you the ability to modify a disassembly and optimize the bytecode.

Extensions

Flash is an extensible program, which means that you can create your own additions that will enhance your workflow or add features and components to the program. The Flash Remoting ActionScript classes, for example, can be expanded or enhanced. Components can be created from scratch or copied and enhanced from existing components. You can find extensions for Flash at the Macromedia Flash

---

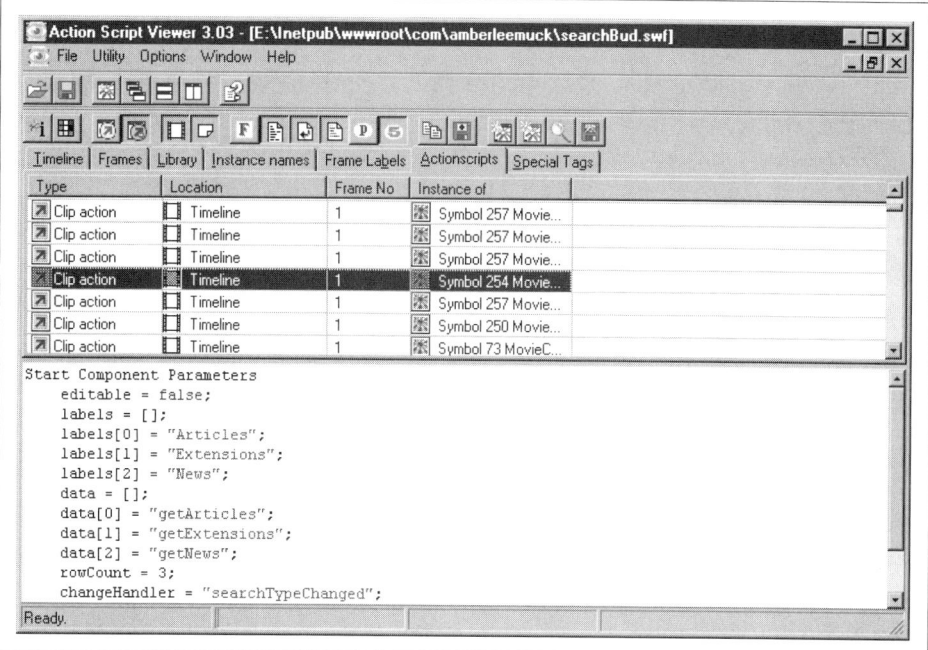

Figure 2-9. ActionScript Viewer .swf decompiler

Exchange (*http://www.macromedia.com/exchange/flash*) and elsewhere. The Macromedia Flash Exchange is a Flash Remoting application itself, showcasing some of the advantages of Flash Remoting.

The Flash Exchange features many Flash extensions. Of particular use to the Flash Remoting developer are the Macromedia-authored and third-party UI components. In addition, the Dreamweaver Exchange (*http://www.macromedia.com/exchange/dreamweaver*) has many Dreamweaver extensions, helpful if you are using Dreamweaver for ActionScript, HTML, or server-side page development.

Several Macromedia-authored extensions, such as the UI component additions and the DataGrid, are covered in this book, because they are important for the development of applications that utilize Flash Remoting.

Sequence of Events in Flash

To access a remote service from Flash, your movie must initiate a connection using the *NetServices.createGatewayConnection( )* method, which returns a *NetConnection* object through whose properties, methods, and events you'll manage the connection. You need to know the gateway URL for your Flash Remoting server in order to make a connection. The connection is defined one time for ColdFusion and J2EE servers, even if your movie accesses multiple services via the gateway. However, each ASP.NET service requires its own call to *createGatewayConnection( )*. In either case, each *NetConnection* object persists for the entire session. Note that when you create this connection object no call has been made to the server yet.

You'll call methods of the *NetConnection* object to manage the connection and access the remote service. The two *NetConnection* methods used most frequently in Flash Remoting applications are *setCredentials( )* and *getService( )*. The *setCredentials( )* method is used to authenticate a user.

 As of this writing, *setCredentials()* is available for ColdFusion MX and JRun 4 only. It is covered in Chapter 5.

The *getService( )* method sets up the call to a remote service by creating a *service object*, which contains the required information for Flash Remoting to make subsequent calls to methods of that remote service. The *getService( )* method's parameters are the same when using any of the service types shown previously in Table 2-8; the service is called by name and Flash makes no assumption about the type of service being called. The syntax for calling the *getService( )* method of the *NetConnection* object looks like this:

```
myService = myConnection_conn.getService(serviceName[, responderObject]);
```

where *myConnection_conn* is a *NetConnection* object returned by an earlier call to *createGatewayConnection( )*. The first parameter, *serviceName*, is a service name such as *com.oreilly.frdg.HelloWorld*. The optional second parameter, *responderObject*, is an object that will handle responses from future calls to methods of the remote service. We'll defer a detailed discussion of the many different ways to set up responder objects and service callbacks until Chapter 4. For now, simply note that our responder object defines *onResult( )* and *onStatus( )* methods that handle the results or errors returned when we invoke methods of the remote service.

When you call a method of your service, an AMF packet is sent to the remote service. The response of that remote service is automatically sent to *responderObject*.

 The *responderObject* argument does not receive the result of the *getService()* call itself, which we stored in myService. Instead, *responderObject* is used to obtain the results from subsequent calls to methods of the service. Therefore, *responderObject* isn't used until a remote method call is executed. The myService object is simply a proxy through which you can make calls to methods of the remote service.

After initializing the connection with *createGatewayConnection( )* and specifying a service with *getService( )*, you can call methods of the service using the object returned by *getService( )*. We stored that object in myService, so we can access methods of the remote service this way:

```
myService.myMethodName(optionalArguments);
```

Each call to a method of the remote service returns an AMF packet, as described in Chapter 1. That packet is automatically sent to the responder object specified in the earlier call to *getService( )*. Your ActionScript code should handle the response events using *onStatus( )* and *onResult( )* functions as methods of the responder object. Alternative ways to handle these events are covered in Chapter 4.

 An *onStatus* event is returned from the remote service if there were any errors. The *onStatus( )* function must handle the errors and act accordingly. An *onResult* event is returned from the remote service if there were no errors. The *onResult( )* function must handle the results of the service call and act accordingly.

Don't confuse the *onStatus* and *onResult* events with the *onStatus()* and *onResult()* methods that handle them. The events are returned in a serialized form from the server and deserialized by the *NetServices* class on the client. When that happens, the associated event handler is triggered. That is, the *onStatus( )* and *onResult( )* methods act as callback functions for the *onStatus* and *onResult* events.

Making a Remote Call

Now that we have some preliminaries out of the way, it's time to do some Remoting! The steps for a successful Flash Remoting call to a remote service are as follows:

1. Include the *NetServices.as* library.
2. Optionally, initialize variables to hold the URL of the gateway path and the name of the remote service.
3. Create a connection object that initializes a path to the Flash Remoting gateway.
4. Create a service object, which will be used to invoke remote services and dispatch results and error events.
5. Create *onResult( )* and/or *onStatus( )* callback methods to handle the *onResult* and *onStatus* events. These can be contained in a responder object or on the current timeline.
6. Call the remote service as a method of the service object. The Flash movie continues to execute while waiting for the response, so your code must not assume that the results are returned immediately.
7. When an *onResult* or *onStatus* event is returned, the appropriate callback function is triggered, and the movie reacts as programmed.

The following sections describe the preceding steps in greater detail by going through a slightly more advanced version of the *HelloWorld* service, called *HelloUser*. The *HelloUser* service collects a user-supplied parameter, checks the time on the server, concatenates a string, and passes the whole thing back as a result to the Flash movie. The responder object processes the results of the remote call and displays the string onscreen. This example demonstrates the following concepts not shown in the *HelloWorld* example:

- The *setDefaultGateway( )* method of the *NetConnection* object is utilized.
- A custom class is created to serve as a responder object.
- The remote call is triggered by the user.
- An argument is passed to the remote service method.
- The server does some processing before returning a string.

This example and others in the book can be downloaded from the online Code Depot at *http://www.flash-remoting.com*.

Example 2-1 shows the complete code for the client-side movie. The movie has three text fields—an unnamed label, userName_txt (the input element), and results_txt (to contain the result). In addition, a PushButton component named submit_pb triggers the call to the remote service. The interface is shown in Figure 2-10.

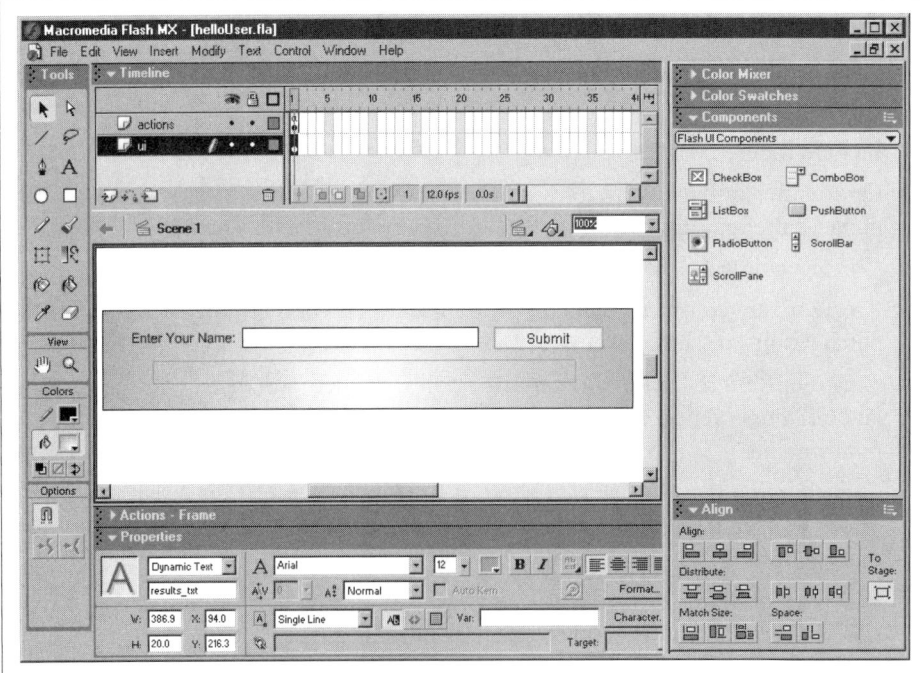

Figure 2-10. Simple interface for the HelloUser movie

The user fills in his name, clicks the Submit button, and is greeted with "Hello Tom. It is 11:02:32 PM" or something similar. Review the code briefly, and we'll discuss portions of it in subsequent sections.

Example 2-1. HelloUser.fla ActionScript code

```
#include "NetServices.as"

// Set up variables for the URL and service paths
var myURL = "http://localhost/flashservices/gateway";
var servicePath = "com.oreilly.frdg.HelloUser";

// Define the custom SimpleResult class
function SimpleResult () {
  // Set up onResult() and onStatus() handlers as methods of the SimpleResult class
  this.onResult = function (myResults) {
    results_txt.text = myResults;
  };

  this.onStatus = function (myError) {
    results_txt.text = myError.description;
  };

  // Set the system status to be handled by the
  // responder object's onStatus() handler as well
  System.onStatus = this.onStatus;
}

// If connection hasn't been initialized, create connection and service objects
if (initialized == null) {
  initialized = true;
  NetServices.setDefaultGatewayURL(myURL);
  var myConnection_conn = NetServices.createGatewayConnection();
  var service = myConnection_conn.getService(servicePath, new SimpleResult());
}

// Set up the callback function to handle mouseclicks
submit_pb.setClickHandler("callSayHello");

// Call the service when the user clicks the Submit button.
function callSayHello () {
  service.sayHello(userName_txt.text);
}
```

Initialize Objects as Needed

Before making a connection, you should initialize necessary variables. Don't forget to include the *NetServices.as* file:

```
#include "NetServices.as"

// Set up variables for the URL and service paths
var myURL = "http://localhost/flashservices/gateway";
var servicePath = "com.oreilly.frdg.HelloUser";
```

As should be familiar by now, the myURL variable holds the Flash Remoting gateway URL (you should specify the URL of your own Flash Remoting gateway). The servicePath variable, following the preferred namespace conventions, specifies the name of the remote service.

Next, Example 2-1 defines a new class, *SimpleResult*, an instance of which is used as a responder object to handle the results of the remote service call. This differs from the *HelloWorld* example, which used a generic object of the *Object* class. When movies are complex, it is easier to manage the code if your responder objects are instances of self-contained classes.

Each remote service call triggers either an *onResult* or *onStatus* event. The *SimpleResult* class handles these events with two class methods: *onResult( )* and *onStatus( )*. These methods simply set the text in the results_txt field:

```
function SimpleResult () {
  // Set up result and status handlers as methods of the SimpleResult class
  this.onResult = function (myResults) {
    results_txt.text = myResults;
  };

  this.onStatus = function (myError) {
    results_txt.text = myError.description;
  };

  // Set the system status to be handled by the result status handler as well
  System.onStatus = this.onStatus;
}
```

Subsequent chapters cover other ways to set up callback functions using *methodname_Result( )* and *methodname_Status( )* functions, as shown in some of the Macromedia documentation.

Create a Connection and Service Object

The path to the Flash Remoting gateway (the remote server) is set once on the main timeline. Generally, it is a good idea to keep all of your initialization scripting in the first frame (following any preloader) of your main *actions* layer. Our initialization script creates the connection and service objects.

Create a connection to the Flash Remoting services. Since this has to be done only once, we check for a variable flag that we create, named initialized. If it doesn't exist, we know that this is the first time our script has executed. The first time through, we set this variable so that we won't execute this section of code again on subsequent passes:

```
if (initialized == null) {
  initialized = true;
```

Next, set a default gateway URL using the *NetServices.setDefaultGatewayURL( )* method:

```
NetServices.setDefaultGatewayURL(myURL);
var myConnection_conn = NetServices.createGatewayConnection( );
```

This approach is slightly different from the one used in the previous example, *HelloWorld.fla*. Since we use the *setDefaultGateway( )* method here, we don't have to specify the gateway in the call to *createGatewayConnection( )*, as we did in *HelloWorld.fla*. Chapter 4 shows how to pass the URL to the movie dynamically to avoid hardcoding the URL within the movie. The *createGatewayConnection( )* method returns a *NetConnection* object, which is stored in `myConnection_conn`.

At this point, the connection object to the server is simply created; no connection to the server has been attempted yet. The `initialized` flag is set to `true` to say "we have set up the connection URL." Don't confuse this with checking whether a connection attempt was successful, which we'll do later.

Create a Service Object

Next, Example 2-1 creates the ActionScript service object, which is a reference to the server-side service that you are going to create. Creating a service object lets us call methods of the service later.

```
    var service = myConnection_conn.getService(servicePath, new SimpleResult( ));
  }
```

The second parameter, the responder object, is created as a new instance of the *SimpleResult* class. When a remote method is called and the service returns a result, the *onResult( )* method of the responder object is triggered. Again, at this point we still have not contacted the remote service.

Create Callback Methods or Functions

The initialization code defines callback methods—*onResult( )* and *onStatus( )*—for the *SimpleResult* class that we created.

The *PushButton* instance named `submit_pb` also needs a callback function, which we've named *callSayHello( )*, attached to it. The *callSayHello( )* function uses the service object that was set up previously (i.e., `service`) to call the remote *sayHello( )* method. It passes the text of the `username_txt` field as an argument:

```
    submit_pb.setClickHandler("callSayHello");
    // Call the service when the user clicks the Submit button.
    function callSayHello ( ) {
      service.sayHello(userName_txt.text);
    }
```

Call the Remote Service

Clicking the Submit button triggers the call to the remote service, as is typical of most Flash Remoting movies. You can extrapolate this concept to more complex interfaces, where each user interface element triggers a different remote method. For example, in a database results page, you could have Update, Insert, and Delete buttons that allow changes to your remote database. Each button could call a different remote method.

Wait for the Response

Because Flash Remoting is asynchronous, the Flash movie continues to execute while it awaits a response. In a simple movie such as this, the playhead is presumably paused in a frame and the movie simply displays the results when they are received. In a more complex movie, your ActionScript code must deal gracefully with extended delays that may be associated with calling a complex remote method.

When the response occurs, the *onResult( )* handler of the responder object is called. This is one of the key concepts of event-driven programming. The Flash movie is continuously executing, but when the remote method returns the result, an event occurs (*onStatus* or *onResult*) and the appropriate method within the responder object is called.

Act on the Response or Error

In this example, the response from the remote method is a string, and our responder object is an instance of the *SimpleResult* class. Regardless, the response is passed as a parameter to the responder object's *onResult( )* method, which sets the text of the field named results_txt to the incoming myResult variable:

```
this.onResult = function (myResult) {
  results_txt.text = myResult;
};
```

If an error occurs, the *onStatus( )* method is triggered instead of *onResult( )*. Our *onStatus( )* method sets the text of the results_txt field to the description property of the incoming status object (i.e., an object indicating the type of error), myError:

```
this.onStatus = function (myError) {
  results_txt.text = myError.description;
};
```

 The datatype of the parameter passed to the *onResult( )* handler is dictated by the return value of the remote service. The return value is specified using the <CFRETURN /> tag in CFML; the *return* statement in Server-Side ActionScript, C#, VB, CFScript, or Java; or the Flash.Result object in ASP.NET or ColdFusion pages. The parameter passed to the *onStatus( )* function is always an error object, with predefined properties including description, as described in Chapter 4.

The Server-Side Code

The following sections describe the server-side counterparts to the client-side Action-Script from Example 2-1. The different server-side examples are written in CFML, Server-Side ActionScript, Java, ASP.NET, and PHP.

ColdFusion MX

Example 2-2 shows a ColdFusion Component named *HelloUser.cfc*, containing the CFML that implements the remote service. It is stored in the *webroot\com\oreilly\ frdg* directory. This CFC is based on the *HelloWorld* code from Example 1-2. The changes are noted in bold.

Example 2-2. ColdFusion MX Component HelloUser.cfc

```
<cfcomponent>
    <cffunction name="sayHello" returntype="string" access="remote">
        <cfargument name="username" type="string" default="">
        <cfreturn "Hello #username#. It is #TimeFormat(now( ),"H:MM:SS TT")#" />
    </cffunction>
</cfcomponent>
```

The only differences from the *HelloWorld* CFC in Chapter 1 are the addition of an argument and the processing of the time on the server. Passing an argument to a CFC is simply a matter of including a <cfargument> tag inside of the <cffunction> tag.

Server-Side ActionScript

Example 2-3, which is an enhanced version of Example 1-3, shows the Server-Side ActionScript to implement the remote service. It is stored in a file named *HelloUser.asr* and saved in the *webroot\com\oreilly\frdg* directory. If you created the ColdFusion CFC named *HelloUser.cfc* earlier, you should rename it to *SomethingElse.cfc* to prevent it from being called instead of the SSAS file.

Example 2-3. Server-Side ActionScript file name HelloUser.asr

```
function getTime ( ) {
  var d = new Date( );
  // Format the time with leading zeroes for the seconds and minutes
  var seconds = d.getSeconds() < 10 ? "0" + d.getSeconds( ) : d.getSeconds( );
  var minutes = d.getMinutes() < 10 ? "0" + d.getMinutes( ) : d.getMinutes( );
  // Format the hours with a 12-hour clock and AM/PM
  var hours = d.getHours( );
  var am_pm = hours > 12 ? " PM" : " AM";
  hours = hours > 12 ? hours-12 : hours;
  // Return the time in hh:mm:ss AM/PM format
  return hours + ":" + minutes + ":" + seconds + am_pm;
}

function sayHello (username) {
    return "Hello " + username + ". It is " + getTime( );
}
```

The custom *getTime( )* function creates the current time string using a *Date* object in SSAS. The username argument from the Flash movie is concatenated with some literal text and the current server time to form the return string. As you can see, working with dates in SSAS is similar to working with dates in client-side ActionScript.

J2EE

The J2EE *HelloWorld* in Example 1-4 used a Java class. A Java class is stateless—each call to the class creates a new instance of the class. Example 2-4 shows how a JavaBean can be used instead, with the added advantage that a JavaBean can be stateful. The user's JSESSIONID is appended to the AMF packet by both the Flash Remoting server and the Flash movie. Flash Remoting automatically maintains the JavaBean state in the user session, provided the JavaBean implements the *java.io. Serializable* interface, as shown in Example 2-4. If not, the Flash Remoting adapter on the server will not store an instance of the class in the session and the service acts as a regular stateless Java class.

The steps to compile the JavaBean service vary from server to server. Typically you can run the javac compiler on the source file from a command prompt and place the resulting *.class* file in the classpath of your web application, using the folder structure outlined earlier (*com\oreilly\frdg*):

```
c:\>javac HelloUser.java
```

The source code for the JavaBean service is shown in Example 2-4.

Example 2-4. JavaBean HelloUser.java

```
package com.oreilly.frdg;

import java.util.*;
import java.text.SimpleDateFormat;
import java.io.Serializable;

public class HelloUser implements Serializable {
  public HelloUser () { // constructor
    message="";
  }
  private String message;

  public String getMessage () {
    this.setMessage();
    return this.message;
  }

  public void setUsername (String username) {
    this.username = username;
  }

  public void setMessage () {
    this.message = "Hello " + this.username + ". It is " + getTime();
  }

  public String getTime () {
    SimpleDateFormat formatter = new SimpleDateFormat("hh:mm:ss a");
    Date d = new Date();
```

Example 2-4. JavaBean HelloUser.java (continued)

```
    return formatter.format(d);
  }

  public String sayHello(String username) {
    this.setUsername(username);
    return this.getMessage();
  }
}
```

Example 2-4 has five methods: *getMessage( )*, *setUsername( )*, *setMessage( )*, *getTime( )*, and *sayHello( )*. The *sayHello( )* method is called by Flash Remoting, which returns the message. Again, the username argument is concatenated to the greeting, which consists of some literal text and the current time on the server, to form the return string.

ASP.NET

As mentioned earlier, ASP.NET remote methods can take different forms, including *.aspx* pages. Example 2-5 shows server-side ASP.NET implemented as an *.aspx* page named *sayHello.aspx*. The code, written in C#, that implements the remote service is stored in the *webroot/com/oreilly/frdg/HelloUser* directory.

Example 2-5. ASP.NET code implemented in C# as an .aspx page

```
<%@ Page Language="C#"%>
<%@ Register TagPrefix="MyTag" Namespace="FlashGateway" Assembly="flashgateway" %>
<MyTag:Flash ID="Flash" Runat="Server" />
<%
if (Flash.Params.Count > 0) {
  String username = Flash.Params[0].ToString();
  String currentTime = DateTime.Now.ToLongTimeString();
  Flash.Result = "Hello " + username + ". It is " + currentTime;
}
%>
```

In this ASP.NET example, the page name of the *.aspx* page becomes the method name in the Flash movie. When using *.aspx* pages in this way, you have to register the tag prefix "MyTag", as shown, and create the namespace *FlashGateway*, along with the assembly (*flashgateway.dll*) that creates the functionality of the *flashgateway* control. Using ASP.NET pages has a few other caveats as well:

- Arguments passed to the movie must be accessed as properties of the `Flash.Params` object.
- Results must be returned to the Flash movie with the `Flash.Result` object.

Given these Flash-specific requirements, it is easy to see why the preferred method is to create a .NET DLL, as shown in Example 1-5, rather than use an *.aspx* page. Using a DLL allows you a cleaner separation between client- and server-side code.

PHP

An AMFPHP implementation of this service utilizes a *HelloUser* class. The following PHP code implements the *HelloUser* service and should be placed in the file *webroot/ flashservices/services/com/oreilly/frdg/HelloUser.php*, assuming a standard installation of AMFPHP:

```php
<?php
class HelloUser {
  function HelloUser () { /* constructor */
    $this->methodTable = array(
      'sayHello' => array(
        'description' => 'Says a friendly hello to the user.',
        'access' => 'remote',
        'arguments' => array('username')
      )
    );
  }

  function sayHello ($username) {
    return "Hello $username. It is " . date('H:M:s', time());
  }
}
?>
```

In this example, we use PHP's built-in *date( )* and *time( )* functions to get the date and time, which we concatenate with the text greeting. Again, we must define the method table for AMFPHP to function properly and to allow our code to have web documentation.

Wrapping Up

In this chapter, we set up the Flash authoring environment for Flash Remoting. We enhanced our *HelloWorld* example from Chapter 1 to create a *HelloUser* application that demonstrates how to pass a parameter to the server and process some data on the server as well. The example also utilized a custom responder class, which is a preferred way to handle the response from the server. Chapter 3 introduces user interface components and shows how to connect them to remote recordsets.

CHAPTER 3

Client/Server Interaction, UI Components, and RecordSets

The most important aspect of building any application—and especially a web application—is to create a comfortable user experience. If the user is bored, frustrated, or uninterested, she will go elsewhere and probably never return. A good Flash movie can hold a user's attention, but the way in which the user interacts with the web application makes the difference between an application that is usable and one that just looks nice.

One of Flash Remoting's prime uses is to create a user interface that does one of several things:

- Allow the user to search a remote site or database
- Display information to a user
- Collect information from a user
- Allow interaction with remote databases or programs

Flash components make it easy to create user interfaces, and Flash Remoting adds features that allow easy connection to databases and other programs.

User Interface Components

Flash Remoting complements the client-side UI components of the Flash authoring environment. This rigorously pretested set of components, all based on the *FUIComponentClass* class, brings the familiar user interface elements of HTML to the Flash developer's arsenal. The UI components expose an API that is easy to use and consistent across components.

Prior to Flash MX, you could create movie clips that acted as reusable user-interface controls (a.k.a. Smart Clips), but they were harder to use than Flash's UI components. You can simply drag UI components from the Components panel onto your interface or create new instances programmatically in ActionScript by using the *MovieClip.attachMovie( )* method (assuming the Library contains the desired component symbol).

UI components add size to the final Flash movie, but the benefits of using the components far outweigh the downside. In addition, after adding an element of one type to the movie, each additional element of that type does not increase the movie size; your movie is roughly the same size whether you use one ListBox or ten ListBoxes.

 Flash 2004 and Flash Pro components share a larger common framework (which provides enhanced accessibility, focus management, and so on) than did Flash MX components. The Flash 2004/Pro framework is optimized for movies that include multiple components. If you're including only one or two components and download size is critical, you may prefer to manually implement custom components that are more streamlined.

Table 3-1 lists the UI components that come preinstalled with Flash MX, along with their object type and optional code-hinting suffix. The suffixes are not required, but they enable code hints and code completion when utilized. Data-aware components (components that can be populated by a data provider such as a *RecordSet* object) are noted. As of this writing, the components included with Flash 2004 and Flash Pro have not been finalized. It is anticipated that Flash 2004 will include a set of components similar to those included with Flash MX. Flash Pro is expected to include all the components available for Flash 2004, plus additional components that support features available in Flash Pro only. This chapter focuses on the components available in Flash MX.

Table 3-1. Basic UI components, object types, and code hint suffixes

Component	Object type	Code hints suffix
CheckBox	FCheckBox	_ch
ComboBox[a]	FComboBox	_cb
ListBox[a]	FListBox	_lb
PushButton	FPushButton	_pb
RadioButton	FRadioButton	_rb
ScrollBar	FScrollBar	_sb
ScrollPane	FScrollPane	_sp

[a] Data-aware component

The methods of these standard components are fully documented in the online Flash Help system (under Help → Using Flash) and the Reference panel (Window → Reference). Each component also has its own Property inspector (Window → Properties). The Property inspector (PI) for the ComboBox is shown in Figure 3-1.

You can use the Property inspector to set the Instance Name and other properties of the component.

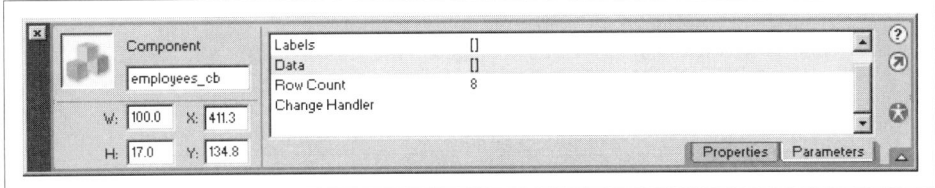

Figure 3-1. The Property inspector exposes properties of UI components and other objects

 Use the Property inspector to specify an instance name for your component or you won't be able to address the component by name via ActionScript.

Other component properties can be set from the PI as well, but you should set them via ActionScript instead so that your code is isolated from the UI and more understandable. For example, the ComboBox component has a Change Handler property. You could enter a function name, such as getMyUrl, in the PI to act as the callback function—the function to be called when the ComboBox changes. Then you could define the callback function, in this case *getMyUrl( )*, in your Flash movie. However, there is no easy way, by looking at the ActionScript, to identify or change what triggers the callback function; you have to select the component on stage and open the PI to see or change the callback function specified.

Callback functions are popular in other visual development environments such as Delphi, C++ Builder, and Visual Basic. In these environments, however, when you attach a function to a component event, the association is visible in the code. This is not the case in Flash. Therefore, if you're using the PI to set the callback function, you should always comment your code clearly to remind you of the function's purpose and what triggers it:

```
///////////////////////////////
// FUNCTION NAME: getMyUrl( )
// PURPOSE: callback function myComboBox_cb
// EVENT: onChange
///////////////////////////////

function getMyUrl () {
  // function body code
}
```

The preferred method, however, is to define your callback function inside the ActionScript code, like this:

```
employees_cb.setChangeHandler(getMyUrl);
function getMyUrl () {
  // function body code
}
```

or by using the method of an object, like this:

```
myObject = new Object( );
myObject.getMyUrl = function (component) {
  // function body code
};
employees_cb.setChangeHandler("getMyUrl", myObject);
```

By defining the callback function via ActionScript, the code is centralized rather than being attached to components in your timeline. The same can be said for defining the labels and data values of the ComboBox or any other component. As your interfaces get more complex, you'll appreciate all the code being in one place rather than attached to timeline elements directly.

```
myComboBox_cb.addItem("Choose Search Type", "0");
myComboBox_cb.addItem("Any word", "1");
myComboBox_cb.addItem("All words", "2");
myComboBox_cb.addItem("Exact Phrase", "3");
```

Components are "live" in the Flash environment. As you make changes to the component's properties in the PI, such as changing a label, the change is reflected in the design environment. This can, however, affect the overall performance of the authoring tool.

 If you find the program slowing down as you add more user interface components to the Stage, you can disable the Control → Enable Live Preview option. Changing properties via ActionScript has no effect on the Live Preview.

Some of the UI components work with the *DataGlue* class, a special ActionScript class that is installed with the Flash Remoting authoring components. The *DataGlue* class dynamically populates UI components with items from a *DataProvider*, such as a *RecordSet* object. The *DataGlue* class is described later in this chapter.

Here is a brief description of each of the standard UI components:

CheckBox

> The CheckBox component adds a typical checkbox with a label. The hit area of the CheckBox is the combined area of the label and the box. The *FCheckBox. getValue( )* method returns true (if checked) or false (if unchecked). You can specify a CheckBox's change handler using *FCheckBox.setChangeHandler( )*.

ComboBox

> The ComboBox component combines a plain text field and a select list—a combination that is unavailable in HTML but often used in desktop applications. A user can enter text into the ComboBox or choose an item from the list. Use *FComboBox.setEditable(false)* to disable user input. You can obtain the value of the selected element from the data and label properties of the object returned by *FComboBox.getSelectedItem( )*. You can specify a ComboBox's change handler using *FComboBox.setChangeHandler( )*.

ListBox

The ListBox component allows for single and multiple selections within a scrollable list. The ListBox also responds to mouse and keyboard input. You can retrieve the values of the selected elements from the data and label properties of the array of objects returned by *FComboBox.getSelectedItems( )*. You can specify a ListBox's change handler using *FListBox.setChangeHandler( )*.

PushButton

The PushButton component is a simple button with a label. You can specify a PushButton's click handler using *FPushButton.setClickHandler( )*.

RadioButton

The RadioButton component creates a standard radio button and allows grouping of multiple radio buttons by setting the group name using *FRadioButton. setGroupName(nameOfGroup)*. You can specify a RadioButton's change handler using *FRadioButton.setChangeHandler( )*.

ScrollBar

A ScrollBar component can be added to a dynamic or input TextField by dropping it from the Components panel onto the TextField in your movie. A ScrollBar added in this manner is automatically added as a listener of the TextField so that it can respond to text scroll events.

ScrollPane

The ScrollPane component adds the ability to display movie clips within a smaller area that become scrollable.

Flash UI Components Set 2 and Flash Charting Controls

Flash developers can create custom components and other Flash authoring elements, called *extensions*. The Extension Manager allows developers to package and share their own extensions or install packages developed by others. Many developers have already done this, and you can find extensions all over the Internet, particularly on the Macromedia Exchange, as noted earlier. Components are one type of extension. Flash 2004 and Flash Pro offer a new JavaScript extensibility layer that allows you to customize the Flash authoring tool interface, but here we are referring to ActionScript extensions, which offer enhanced runtime features.

Macromedia has released its own free extensions, including the UI Components Set 2 and the Flash Charting Controls, both outlined in Table 3-2. Each of these useful sets of components is available as a separate download from the Macromedia Exchange at *http://www.macromedia.com/exchange*, and also on the Studio MX CD-ROM in the *\Flash MX\Extending Flash MX* folder. Once installed, the UI Components Set 2 and Flash Charting Controls are fully documented under Window → Component Help - UI Set 2 and Window → Component Help - Charts, and within the Reference panel (Window → Reference) in Flash MX and under the Help panel in Flash 2004 and Flash Pro.

Table 3-2. Standard UI Components Set 2 and Charting Controls, showing code hint suffixes and object types

Component	Object type	Code hints suffix
BarChart[a]	FBarChart	_bc
Calendar	FCalendar	None
DraggablePane	FDraggablePane	_dp
IconButton	FIconButton	_ib
LineChart[a]	FLineChart	_lc
MessageBox	FMessageBox	_mb
PieChart[a]	FPieChart	_pc
ProgressBar	FProgressBar	_pr
SplitView	FSplitView	None
Ticker	FTicker	_tick
Tree[a]	FTree	_tr
TreeNode (individual nodes of a Tree)	FTreeNode	_tn

[a] Data-aware component

Here is a brief description of each of these additional UI components. Of particular interest to the Flash Remoting developer are the Calendar, MessageBox, Tree, and ProgressBar components:

Calendar

The Calendar component is extremely useful because it offers a visual way to input a date or range of dates. You can specify a Calendar's change handler using *FCalendar.setChangeHandler( )*.

DraggablePane

The DraggablePane component gives you an interface within an interface; you can attach other interface elements to the DraggablePane so that you can have a draggable interface that floats on top of your Flash movie.

IconButton

The IconButton component is similar to a standard PushButton, but you can attach a custom image to the face of the button. IconButton instances, unlike PushButtons, react to *onChange* events rather than *onClick* events. You can specify an IconButton's change handler with *FIconButton.setChangeHandler( )*.

MessageBox

A MessageBox component creates a convenience pop-up dialog box, much like a JavaScript alert box, with one of four configurations: Info, Question, Warning, or Error. The MessageBox has a close handler that can be specified with *FMessageBox.setCloseHandler( )*. The close handler callback function receives two arguments: the name of the MessageBox and the index of the button that was clicked.

ProgressBar

The ProgressBar component is typically used in preloaders, but it will graphically show the progress of anything that takes a long time to execute. It can be used within a Flash Remoting application to indicate the load time for a recordset from a remote method.

SplitView

The SplitView component allows you to split the user interface into distinct areas that can be scrolled or resized.

Ticker

The Ticker component gives you a way to scroll content perpetually in the Flash movie, such as in a stock ticker. In a Flash Remoting application, this content can be easily loaded dynamically from a remote source.

Tree

The Tree component, which displays a typical tree of content, is one of the more useful data-aware components. The content can be created manually or it can come from an XML feed or other data source, such as a recordset.

Charting Controls

The Charting Controls are a separate package from the UI Components Set 2, and they must be installed separately. The package includes BarChart, Line-Chart, and PieChart components. Charts are a huge part of dynamic application development. Using the Charting Controls, you can create a dynamic bar, line, or pie chart using the data returned by a remote service. The Charting Controls work in a fashion similar to the other UI components and are data-aware. Later in this chapter, under "Using the RecordSet Class," I present an example that uses the Flash Charting Controls in conjunction with a *RecordSet* object. Third-party charting components are also available. For example, B-Line Express (*http://www.blinex.com*) sells a package of charting components that provide a flexible and extensible library of charting and graphics functions for displaying data as pie charts, bar charts, and much more.

Macromedia's DRK

In October 2002, Macromedia released the first Developer Resource Kits (DRK), containing the UI Components Set 3 and one of the most important Flash extensions to date—the DataGrid component. The DataGrid component is especially important if you are going to be using Flash Remoting. Whereas the standard Flash UI components are included with Flash MX and the UI Components Set 2 are a free download, the DRK is a commercial product available from Macromedia for $99 at:

http://www.macromedia.com/go/drk

UI Components Set 3

The UI components that come with Flash MX provide some useful functionality and interaction with some standard user interface elements. The free UI Components Set 2 adds some more esoteric functionality to the Flash developer's toolbox, such as a calendar control and a ticker. The UI Components Set 3 is available only as part of the DRK and offers more advanced message boxes, tooltips, and loading boxes. None of the UI components in this third set, listed in Table 3-3, are data-aware.

Table 3-3. UI Components Set 3, code hint suffixes, and object types

Component	Object type	Code hints suffix
AdvancedMessageBox	FAdvancedMessageBox	None available
LoadingBox	FLoadingBox	None available
PromptBox	FPromptBox	None available
Tooltip	FTooltip	None available
TooltipLite	FTooltipLite	None available

Here is a brief description of the components in the UI Components Set 3:

PromptBox
> The PromptBox component is handy for getting an item of data from a user, such as prompting the user for a password. You could then use the *NetConnection.setCredentials( )* method to submit the password to a remote service. The PromptBox component allows you to specify a close handler programmatically with *FPromptBox.setCloseHandler( )*. The close handler callback function receives three arguments: the PromptBox name, the index of the button that was clicked, and any user input to the PromptBox.

AdvancedMessageBox
> The AdvancedMessageBox component creates message boxes with multiple buttons. The AdvancedMessageBox component has functionality similar to the MessageBox component of UI Components Set 2 but adds features such as scrollable message content.

LoadingBox
> The LoadingBox component can be used to display progress of any code that takes a long time to execute, such as when a remote method is executed or a recordset loads in.

Tooltip
> The Tooltip components (Tooltip and TooltipLite) can be attached to other UI components to give your visual interface an added professional look.

DataGrid Control

The DataGrid component is the high point of the DRK, and the DRK is the only place you can get it. The DataGrid component implements a complex, navigable grid that you can tie to a *RecordSet* object with one line:

```
myGrid_dg.setDataProvider(myRecordset_rs);
```

This gives you a default grid that displays the entire recordset that is returned to your Flash movie, including clickable column headers that sort the data. Later in this chapter, under "Gluing the DataGrid," I present a simple example using the Data-Grid and its additional features. First, see "The RecordSet Class" to familiarize yourself with the *RecordSet* class.

Other Content, DRKs, and Components

In addition to the DataGrid component and the UI Components Set 3, the DRK 1 contains much valuable information, including an email services ActionScript library and stock services ActionScript library that both utilize Flash Remoting and Cold-Fusion. Also included are several top Flash extensions from the Macromedia Exchange (including UI Components Set 2 and the Flash Charting Components), and many articles from Macromedia DevNet, several of which are focused on Flash Remoting.

Macromedia has committed to a quarterly DRK. Each DRK contains content for Flash and other Macromedia products. As of this writing, DRK Volumes 1, 2, and 3 have been issued. The Flash UI Components Sets 4 and 5 include additional advanced components and are available only as part of the DRK.

Macromedia has also released a set of components called the Data Connection Kit (DCK), or Firefly, as it is also known. The DCK contains sophisticated controls that can be utilized with Flash Remoting, or directly with XML or SQL Server. More information on the DCK can be found at:

http://www.macromedia.com/go/dck

Text Objects

Text fields are available in the Flash authoring tool from the Tools panel by clicking the Text Tool icon. This allows you to draw a text field on your movie interface. The text that you place in your movie using the Text Tool is an ActionScript object as well—the *TextField* object.

There are three distinct types of text fields: Static, Dynamic, and Input. A text field's type can be set using the drop-down list in the Property inspector, as shown in Figure 3-2.

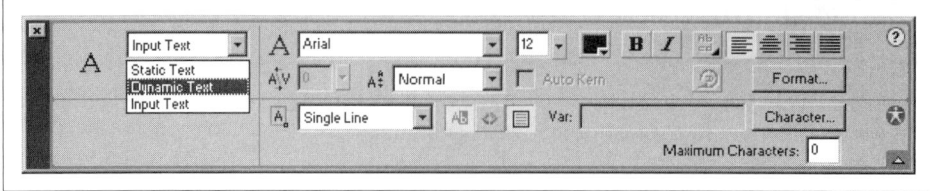

Figure 3-2. The Property inspector for a TextField object

Static Text Fields

To create a static text field, click the Text Tool in the Tools panel and draw an outline on the Stage. A static text field can be used as a label or to display text to the user. However, you can't set an instance name for a static text field, and the field's contents or other properties can't be manipulated via ActionScript. You can enter text in the field during authoring or change its properties through the Property inspector. If you put it in a movie clip, you can alter its appearance indirectly by changing the clip's properties.

Dynamic Text Fields

Unlike a static text field, you can modify a dynamic text field programmatically. You should use dynamic text fields in your Flash Remoting applications to give you the flexibility to change a field programmatically or alter the labels with localized text.

To control a dynamic text field programmatically, you must give it an instance name using the Property inspector and refer to it by this name from ActionScript. You can activate code hinting for a *TextField* object by giving it a name ending in _txt.

For example, this sets the text property of a field named myTextField_txt:

```
myTextField_txt.text = "Some dynamic text";
```

You can also set other properties of the text field programmatically:

```
myTextField_txt.multiline = true;
myTextField_txt.border = true;
myTextField_txt.text = "News for today, " + getMyDate( );
```

You can use a with construct to set multiple properties for a given object:

```
with (myTextField_txt) {
  multiline = true;
  border = true;
  text = "News for today, " + getMyDate( );
};
```

Dynamic text fields have three different formatting options available:

Single line
 Used for a single line of text.

Multiline

Used when the text might span multiple lines. If the text is too long, it automatically wraps to the next line.

Multiline no-wrap

Used for multiple lines in a text field, but it requires that you manually create line breaks with a \n or newline line break character.

Input Text Fields

An input text field is roughly equivalent to the HTML `<input type="text">` tag. An input text field can be used to gather user input. As with dynamic text fields, you must set the input text field's instance name in the Property inspector. An input text field has the same three formatting options that dynamic text fields have (single line, multiline, and multiline no-wrap) plus password formatting, in which input text is shown as asterisks.

To retrieve text that a user has typed into an input text field, access the field's text property:

```
var myUsername = username_txt.text;
var myPassword = password_txt.text;
myService.myLoginMethod(myUsername, myPassword);
```

Adding Text Fields from ActionScript

A new *TextField* object can be added directly from ActionScript using the *MovieClip. createTextField( )* method and passing in the new field's name, position, and properties:

```
movieclip.createTextField(name, depth, x, y, width, height);
```

For example, to programmatically create a user interface identical to the one built visually for the *HelloUser* example in Chapter 2, you might use the code in Example 3-1. The example also demonstrates creating a PushButton UI component dynamically. To dynamically create a UI component, the component's symbol must exist in the document's Library. You can drag a component instance from the Components panel to the Stage and then delete it to add the component to the Library.

Example 3-1. Creating TextFields and UI components in ActionScript

```
// Create the TextFields
this.createTextField("label_txt", 1, 25, 35, 125, 20);
this.createTextField("username_txt", 2, 150, 35, 125, 20);
this.createTextField("results_txt", 3, 25, 60, 300, 20);
// Create the PushButton
this.attachMovie("FPushButtonSymbol","submit_pb",4);
// Position and label the PushButton
with (submit_pb) {
  _x = 300;
```

```
  _y = 35;
  setLabel("Submit");
}
// Set the properties for the TextFields
label_txt.text = "Enter your name";
username_txt.border = true;
username_txt.type = "input";
```

Example 3-1 is combined with the *HelloUser* code from Chapter 2 in the online example *HelloUser_dynamic.fla* to form a completely ActionScript-generated Flash Remoting example. You can find it at the online Code Depot.

Building Forms in Flash MX

HTML forms are structured elements, consisting of a <FORM> tag surrounding form elements. In Flash, there is no encompassing form tag. The *form elements* can be text fields, UI components, or other Flash objects and can reside anywhere in the movie. Because Flash is an object-oriented interface, you need only reference the objects by name to access their properties and methods. You can utilize the text property of a *TextField* object in your Flash Remoting service calls like this:

```
    myService.myMethod(somefield_txt.text);
```

When you do that, you are essentially posting the contents of somefield_txt to the remote service. This is equivalent to sending a form and the contents of a form field to a server-side page. Because your remote services are expecting the argument, they don't need to process and parse a form field—they need only access the value.

For that reason, building forms in Flash is somewhat of a misnomer. You are not actually building a web form, per se; you are simply creating interface elements that act as collectors of user data and passing this data to your remote services. No form is ever created; no post is ever made to the server. This highlights a key difference between Flash Remoting and working with the *LoadVars* class (or working with *loadVariables( )* in Flash 5).

When working with the *LoadVars* class, your server-side page has to parse the incoming form data and determine what to do with it. Working with Flash Remoting is almost like working in one environment: you simply pass arguments to remote methods and process the return value. The fact that the methods can be halfway around the world makes Flash Remoting powerful. Flash 2004 handles forms the same way as Flash MX. Flash Pro introduces an alternative to the timeline metaphor—variously called *slides*, *screens*, or *forms*—which should not be confused with submitting data from forms, as discussed here.

The UI components and other ActionScript objects each have their own properties, and some of them have methods to address these properties. Table 3-4 shows several objects that might be used in a Flash Remoting application and how their values can be grabbed through dot notation by accessing a method of the object (or accessing the text property directly in the case of a text field).

Table 3-4. Accessing properties of various ActionScript objects

Object	Get the data
AdvancedMessageBox	FAdvancedMessageBox.getButtons( )[*buttonIndex*]
Calendar	FCalendar.getSelectedItem( ) or FCalendar.getSelectedItems( )
Checkbox	FCheckBox.getValue( )
ComboBox	FComboxBox.getSelectedItem( )
DataGrid	FDataGrid.getSelectedItem( ) or FDataGrid.getItemAt(*index*)
IconButton	FIconButton.getLabel( ) or FIconButton.getValue( )
ListBox	FListbox.getSelectedItem( ), FListbox.getSelectedItem( ), FListbox.getSelectedIndex( ), or FListbox.getSelectedIndices( )
MessageBox	FMessageBox.getButton( )[*buttonIndex*]
PromptBox	FPromptBox.getUserInput( )
PushButton	FPushButton.getLabel( )
RadioButton	FRadioButton.getData( ) or FRadioButton.getValue( )
TextField	TextField.text
Tree	FTree.getSelectedNode( )

The AdvancedMessageBox and MessageBox components have a roundabout way of retrieving the user input. You must retrieve the index number of the button that was clicked and use it to read the label of the button from the Buttons array.

To do so, define a close callback handler, using *setCloseHandler( )*, that accepts two arguments: the component instance and the index of the clicked button. A typical callback function for a MessageBox or AdvancedMessageBox is shown in Example 3-2.

Example 3-2. Message Box demo

```
// Set up the MessageBox component named delete_mb
delete_mb.setButtons(["OK","Cancel"]);
delete_mb.setMessage("Are you sure?");
delete_mb.setTitle("Delete Record");
delete_mb.setCloseHandler("myCloseHandler");

myCloseHandler = function (myMessageBox_mb, buttonIndex) {
  // Get the label of the button that was pressed
  var buttonLabel = myMessageBox_mb.getButtons( )[buttonIndex];
  // Do something based on which button was pressed
  switch (buttonLabel.toLowerCase( )) {
    case "cancel":
      trace("cancel");
      // In practice, do nothing when cancelled
      return;
    case "ok":
```

Example 3-2. Message Box demo (continued)

```
        trace("ok");
        // In practice, call the remote service when user clicks OK, such as:
        // myRemoteService.deleteRecord(myRecordNumber);
        return;
    }
};
```

The RecordSet Class

Now that we've seen the ease and power of UI components, let's see how interactivity is enhanced using one of the most impressive aspects of Flash Remoting technology: the *RecordSet* class. Remote method calls commonly return recordsets, which are converted to ActionScript *RecordSet* objects, to the Flash movie. The *RecordSet* class has methods that make it easy to work with data returned from a remote method and placed in a *RecordSet* object. For example, to find the number of records in a *RecordSet* object, use the *getLength( )* method:

```
    my_rs.getLength( );
```

To sort the items in a *RecordSet* object from within the Flash movie—without making another round trip to the server—you can use the *sortItemsBy( )* method:

```
    my_rs.sortItemsBy(columnName, order);
```

where *order* is asc (ascending) or desc (descending). In truth, specifying anything other than desc as the *order* parameter performs an ascending sort, but using asc explicitly is considered a best practice.

Other methods of the *RecordSet* class are just as easy to use. Here are several possibilities:

- List or otherwise display a set of results to the user.
- Populate a UI component, such as a ListBox or ComboBox, with the recordset data.
- Create dynamic charts.
- Create dynamic sortable grids.
- Create multidimensional arrays.

A *RecordSet* object works seamlessly with a ColdFusion MX *query* object: the *query* object in ColdFusion is also used when addressing directories, POP email servers, and FTP servers, in addition to standard database calls. For example, to return a directory listing from the remote server to the Flash movie, you could create a Cold-Fusion Component with one method and one tag:

```
    <cfcomponent displayName="searchDirectory">
      <cffunction name="getDirectory" access="remote" returnType="query">
        <cfdirectory directory="c:\documents"
          name="myDirectory"
```

```
        sort="name ASC, size DESC">
      <cfreturn myDirectory>
    </cffunction>
  </cfcomponent>
```

Inside the Flash movie, you can call this method using Flash Remoting and attach the query results to a Tree component to display a list of documents in this directory:

```
myTree_tree.setDataProvider(myResult_rs);
```

Because ColdFusion allows you to work with certain structures as if they were recordsets, Flash allows you to work with them as *RecordSet* objects as well. Cold-Fusion is covered at length in Chapter 5.

The *RecordSet* class performs client-side operations only—local modifications affect only the client and cannot be returned to the server. To perform batch updates or other client/server manipulation of data, you must use arrays, strings, or other data structures and process each record in the batch as you normally would within a server-side solution. See "Updating Data on the Server" in Chapter 5 and the sample application in Chapter 14 for examples.

Structure of a RecordSet Object

A recordset is essentially a multidimensional array, and managing such arrays can be somewhat tricky. A *RecordSet* object works just like a recordset at the application level: it contains rows and columns. Each row represents a record of data returned from the query. The columns represent the field names and values of data returned from the server. Consider a recordset that contains the field names ProductID, ProductName, Supplier, and Category, which could be represented by the following SQL statement:

```
SELECT ProductID, ProductName, Supplier, Category
FROM Products
```

A typical output from the database might look like that shown in Table 3-5 (available as *RecordSetDemo.fla* at the online Code Depot).

Table 3-5. The results of an imaginary database query

ID number	Index number	ProductID	ProductName	Supplier	Category
0	0	1001	Flash MX	Macromedia	Software
1	1	1002	Dreamweaver MX	Macromedia	Software
2	2	1003	Flash Remoting: The Definitive Guide	O'Reilly	Book
3	3	1004	Windows 2000 Professional	Microsoft	Software
4	4	1005	Programming ColdFusion	O'Reilly	Book
5	5	1006	Grandma's Extensions	Grandma	Extensions

The *RecordSet.getItemAt( )* method allows you to access the data by row number to get an entire row as an object:

```
var myRow = my_rs.getItemAt(0);            // Returns entire first row
```

You can access the data by row number and field name to get a specific item:

```
var temp = my_rs.getItemAt(3).ProductName;   // Returns "Windows 2000 Professional"
```

The index number that is used in record retrieval, which is maintained internally by the Flash movie, is a zero-based index. It reflects the physical positioning of the items in the *RecordSet* object. The records also have an internal ID number that remains attached to each record, accessible using the _ _ID_ _ property (note the two underscores on either side of the name, ID):

```
var myID = my_rs.getItemAt(0)._ _ID_ _;         // Returns 0
```

The _ _ID_ _ property reflects the index of the record within the *RecordSet* object as it was first created. If you perform a sort on the recordset, the index numbers change, but the internal ID numbers continue to be attached to the records to which they were originally bound. For example, if you sort the *RecordSet* object in Table 3-5 by ProductName, like this:

```
my_rs.sortItemsBy("ProductName");
```

you receive the results shown in Table 3-6. Note that the index numbers are sequential, but the ID numbers are not. The earlier statement would return a different result:

```
var myID = my_rs.getItemAt(0)._ _ID_ _;         // Returns 1
```

Table 3-6. RecordSet results

ID number	Index number	ProductID	ProductName	Supplier	Category
1	0	1002	Dreamweaver MX	Macromedia	Software
0	1	1001	Flash MX	Macromedia	Software
2	2	1003	Flash Remoting: The Definitive Guide	O'Reilly	Book
5	3	1006	Grandma's Extensions	Grandma	Extensions
4	4	1005	Programming ColdFusion	O'Reilly	Book
3	5	1004	Windows 2000 Professional	Microsoft	Software

Let's say you want to get the fourth item of the newly sorted recordset. If you attempt to get it using the *getItemAt( )* method, as follows:

```
trace(my_rs.getItemAt(3).ProductName);      // Returns "Grandma's Extensions"
```

you get "Grandma's Extensions" as the result, because index 3 is now associated with the original sixth record in the recordset. You can also access the fields and the items in the recordset as properties directly (although it isn't recommended) by accessing the items property using the following syntax:

```
my_rs.items[3].ProductName;                // Returns "Grandma's Extensions"
```

Using the items array will also access the record that is physically in that position at that time (by index number, not by ID number).

Using the *getItemID( )* method instead of *getItemAt( )*, you can retrieve an item's ID number (i.e., its original position in the recordset):

```
trace(my_rs.getItemID(3));                    // Returns 5
```

The preceding code returns the number 5, because "Grandma's Extensions" was originally the sixth item in the recordset (with a zero-based item number of 5). Using *getItemID( )* is preferable to accessing the _ _ID_ _ property directly.

There is no built-in method to retrieve an item by its original ID number (i.e., to retrieve its current record number based on its original position in the recordset). If you need to do so, you can write a custom function to resort the records by their _ _ID_ _ property, or you can write a loop to check the _ _ID_ _ property of each record and extract the desired match as shown under "RecordSet.getItemID( ) Method" in Chapter 15.

Using the RecordSet Class

The *RecordSet.as* file is included automatically when you include the *NetServices.as* file in your Flash movie. However, you can use the *RecordSet* class by itself, even in Flash movies that don't utilize Flash Remoting, by including the *RecordSet.as* class directly:

```
#include "RecordSet.as"
```

This approach can be used when you need to create a custom structure that can benefit from the many built-in methods of the *RecordSet* class. For example, the *RecordSet.sort( )* method, which allows you to sort on any column, is better suited to sorting multidimensional data than the basic *Array.sort( )* method.

There are many methods available for working with client-side *RecordSet* objects, which are examined in Chapter 4 and documented fully in Chapter 15.

Flash Remoting Using a RecordSet

Although client-side recordsets are handy, the real power lies in returning server-side recordsets to your Flash movie and putting them into an ActionScript *RecordSet* object. The following example demonstrates how to pull a recordset resulting from a remote method call into Flash.

The example is built using the sample *Northwind* database that is included with MS Access and MS SQL Server. The database is shipped with the ASP.NET version of Flash Remoting as well. If you don't have either of these database programs, you can download the database file from the following location:

http://office.microsoft.com/downloads/9798/nwind.aspx

The only thing you'll need to work with the sample database is a connection from your application server.

 A MySQL script to generate the *Northwind* database for a MySQL server is available for download from *http://www.flash-remoting.com* as well.

The Flash interface is very simple and can be downloaded from the online Code Depot (*SearchProducts.fla*). It consists of a search field, several text fields, and a Submit button. The interface allows a search of the *Northwind* Products table using the following SQL statement:

```
SELECT ProductName, UnitPrice, QuantityPerUnit
FROM Products
WHERE ProductName LIKE '%searchfield%'
```

This time, I'll show you the server-side code first, beginning with ColdFusion MX.

ColdFusion

Here, we use a CFC to build the remote service. The CFC in Example 3-3 should be named *SearchProducts.cfc* and placed in the *webroot\com\oreilly\frdg* directory. You'll need a data source named "Northwind" set up in the ColdFusion administrator.

Example 3-3. ColdFusion implementation of SearchProducts.cfc

```
<cfcomponent displayName="SearchProducts">
  <cffunction name="getSearchResult" access="remote" returnType="query">
    <cfargument name="search" type="string" default="%">
    <cfquery name="rsGetProducts" datasource="Northwind">
     SELECT ProductName, UnitPrice, QuantityPerUnit
     FROM Products
     WHERE ProductName LIKE '%#search#%'
    </cfquery>
    <cfreturn rsGetProducts>
  </cffunction>
</cfcomponent>
```

Again, this component isn't much different from the *HelloWorld* example, except for the addition of a <cfquery> within the function. Note the returnType of "query" in the <cffunction> tag. The <cfreturn> tag returns the entire query to the caller. This query object becomes an instance of the *RecordSet* class in Flash.

Server-Side ActionScript

This example of Server-Side ActionScript (SSAS) demonstrates a way to utilize the *CF* object of SSAS and its *query( )* method. The code is shown in Example 3-4.

Example 3-4. Server-Side ActionScript implementation of SearchProducts.asr

```
function getSearchResult (search) {
  var theSql = "SELECT ProductName, UnitPrice, QuantityPerUnit";
  theSql += " FROM Products";
  if (search) {
    theSql += " WHERE ProductName LIKE ";
    theSql += "'%" + search + "%'";
  }
  return CF.query({datasource:"Northwind", sql:theSql});
}
```

The remote method name, *getSearchResult( )*, must match the function name in the *.asr* file. This file should be named *SearchProducts.asr* and saved in the *webroot\com\ oreilly\frdg* directory. Once again, if you've already created the *SearchProducts.cfc* file, you'll have to rename it to *SomethingElse.cfc* so that it doesn't respond to the service call before this SSAS service is able to.

The search parameter is empty if there is no argument passed in, so I use a conditional WHERE clause in the SQL statement. The query returns all results if no search parameter is given.

The variable theSql is used to hold the SQL statement, because spanning multiple lines with SQL statements causes errors in SSAS. For that reason, you should create your SQL statement as a string, as shown in Example 3-4, before calling the *CF.query( )* method.

The *CF.query( )* method takes several parameters. This example uses only the datasource and sql parameters.

More information on the *CF.query( )* method and SSAS can be found in Chapter 6.

JRun and J2EE

The JRun version is implemented as a JavaBean named *SearchProducts.java*, also available at the online Code Depot. The JavaBean should be set up with a JDBC driver available for the sample *Northwind* database. The listing in Example 3-5 uses the Sun JDBC:ODBC bridge driver. The JavaBean should be compiled as before. You will also need *sun.jdbc.rowset.CachedRowSet* class for the resulting data, available from:

> *http://developer.java.sun.com/developer/earlyAccess/crs*

Chapter 7 explains the techniques for returning data from a server. The *java.sql. ResultSet* class is not recommended, as it is not a disconnected resultset like the *CachedRowSet*.

Example 3-5. Java implementation of SearchProducts.java

```
package com.oreilly.frdg;

import java.sql.*;
```

Example 3-5. Java implementation of SearchProducts.java (continued)

```java
import java.io.Serializable;
import sun.jdbc.rowset.*;

public class SearchProducts implements Serializable{
  public SearchProducts () {}

  private String myDriverString = "sun.jdbc.odbc.JdbcOdbcDriver";
  private String myConnectionString = "jdbc:odbc:northwind";
  private String myUsername = "myUsername";
  private String myPassword = "myPassword";
  private Connection conn = null;

  public ResultSet getSearchResult(String search) throws Exception {
    String errors = "";
    CachedRowSet rowset = new CachedRowSet();

    try {
      Class.forName(myDriverString);
      conn = DriverManager.getConnection(myConnectionString, myUsername, myPassword);
    } catch (ClassNotFoundException e) {
      errors = "Incorrect JDBC Driver\n";
    }
  if (errors == "") {
    try {
      Statement s = conn.createStatement();
      String sql = "SELECT ProductName,UnitPrice,QuantityPerUnit FROM Products";
      if (search != "") {
        sql += " WHERE ProductName LIKE '%" + search + "%'";
      }
      ResultSet rs = s.executeQuery(sql);
      rowset.populate(rs);
      rs.close();
      s.close();
      } catch (SQLException e) { //catch any SQL errors
        errors += e.toString() ;
      } finally {
        if (conn != null) {
          conn.close();
        }
      }
    }
    if (errors!="") {
      throw new Exception (errors) ;
    };
    return rowset;
  }
}
```

The Java implementation has some minor error handling, but it is intended mostly for demonstration purposes. Your own Java classes will be more robust. The Java errors are in fact passed to the Flash client even if they aren't handled in the class; the errors are returned in the *onStatus* event. You will have to handle them in Action-Script, as we've done here by throwing a new Exception with a custom error message.

All JavaBeans should implement the *java.io.Serializable* interface. This interface allows the object instance (an instance of the *SearchProducts* class, in this case) to be serialized and deserialized. Flash Remoting automatically maintains the state of the object if the JavaBean uses the *Serializable* interface. If not, Flash Remoting does not store an instance of the class in the session.

ASP.NET

The ASP.NET version is implemented as an *.aspx* page using C# as the language. The code in Example 3-6 calls a SQL Server database and delivers a DataSet to the Flash movie. Using a DataSet is just one way to deliver a dynamic SQL resultset to Flash Remoting.

Example 3-6. The ASP.NET implementation of getSearchResult.aspx

```
<%@ Page Language="C#"%>
<%@ Import Namespace="System.Data" %>
<%@ Import Namespace="System.Data.SqlClient"%>
<%@ Register TagPrefix="FRDG" Namespace="FlashGateway" Assembly="flashgateway" %>
<script runat="server" >
void Page_Load ( ) {
  SqlConnection myConnection;
  SqlCommand myCommand;
  SqlDataAdapter myDataAdapter;
  DataSet myDataSet;
  String sql = "SELECT ProductName,UnitPrice,QuantityPerUnit FROM dbo.Products";
  String conn = " Server=192.168.0.4;uid=myUsername;pwd=mypwd;database=Northwind";
  if (Flash.Params.Count > 0) {
    sql += " WHERE ProductName Like '%" + Flash.Params[0].ToString( ) + "%'";
  }
  myConnection = new SqlConnection(conn);
  myConnection.Open( );
  myCommand = new SqlCommand(sql, myConnection);
  myDataAdapter = new SqlDataAdapter(myCommand);
  myDataSet = new DataSet( );
  myDataAdapter.Fill(myDataSet,"Products");
  Flash.DataSource = myDataSet.Tables["Products"];
  Flash.DataBind( );
  myConnection.Close( );
}
</script>
<FRDG:Flash ID="Flash" Runat="Server" />
```

The page is saved as *getSearchResult.aspx* in the *com\oreilly\frdg\SearchProducts* directory. Just as with the *HelloUser* example page, the *FlashGateway* assembly is registered as a tag (FRDG) and utilized in the page.

PHP

PHP has a rich set of database extensions that allow you to use it with all sorts of databases (MySQL, Oracle, PostgreSQL, MS SQL, and mSQL, just to name a few). Example 3-7 uses MySQL, as it is fast, reliable, and the database most commonly used with PHP. With PHP, the functions to access the database change for each database, but for MySQL we use the *mysql_pconnect( )* function to connect to the database.

Example 3-7. PHP example for SearchProducts.php

```php
<?php
class SearchProducts {

  function SearchProducts () { /* constructor */
    $this->methodTable = array(
      'getSearchResult' => array(
        'description' => 'Searches the database and returns a result.',
        'access' => 'remote',
        'arguments' => array('search')
      )
    );
  }

  function getSearchResult ($search) {
    if (!$link = mysql_pconnect('localhost', 'myUsername', 'myPassword'))
      return mysql_error();
    if (!mysql_select_db('Northwind', $link)) return mysql_error();

    $query = 'SELECT ProductName, UnitPrice, QuantityPerUnit FROM Products';
    $query .= (!empty($search)) ? " WHERE ProductName LIKE '%$search%'" : '';

    if (!($result = mysql_query($query, $link))) return mysql_error();
    return $result;
  }
}
?>
```

The page is saved as *SearchProducts.php* in the *services\com\oreilly\frdg* directory. One handy thing about PHP services is that you can paste the URL of the service into a browser to test the service for errors. If you see a blank page, the service does not have syntax errors.

The client-side ActionScript code

With the server-side code in place, it's time to build the Flash movie. Add a layer named *actions* to the movie timeline, and add the script shown in Example 3-8 to the first frame of the timeline.

Example 3-8. Client-side ActionScript file SearchProducts.fla

```
#include "NetServices.as"

// Connect to the gateway and create a service object
if (connected == null) {
  connected = true;
  NetServices.setDefaultGatewayUrl("http://localhost/flashservices/gateway");
  var my_conn = NetServices.createGatewayConnection();
  var myService = my_conn.getService("com.oreilly.frdg.SearchProducts", this);
  var Products_rs = null;
}

// Set up event handlers for buttons
submit_pb.setClickHandler("onSubmit");

// Event handlers for buttons
function onSubmit () {
  myService.getSearchResult(search_txt.text);
}

// Responder function for onResult event
function getSearchResult_Result (result_rs) {
  Products_rs = result_rs;
  var temp = "";
  temp += "There were " + Products_rs.getLength();
  temp += " records returned.";
  results_txt.text = temp;
}

// Responder function for onStatus event
function getSearchResult_Status (error) {
  results_txt.text = "There was an error: " + error.description;
}
```

The code includes *NetServices.as*, which includes the reference to *RecordSet.as*, so you don't have to include the latter explicitly.

Next, it creates a connection to the Flash Remoting gateway and defines the service object. The remote service uses the same naming convention as the previous examples (*com.oreilly.frdg.serviceName*):

```
// Connect to the gateway and create a service object
if (connected == null) {
  connected = true;
  NetServices.setDefaultGatewayUrl("http://localhost/flashservices/gateway");
  var my_conn = NetServices.createGatewayConnection();
  var myService = my_conn.getService("com.oreilly.frdg.SearchProducts", this);
  var Products_rs = null;
}
```

Next, it assigns and defines the Submit button click handler function. The Submit button calls the *getSearchResult( )* method. The contents of the text field named search_txt are sent to the method:

```
// Set up event handlers for buttons
submit_pb.setClickHandler("onSubmit");

// Event handlers for buttons
function onSubmit ( ) {
  myService.getSearchResult(search_txt.text);
}
```

Next, the code handles the results from the database search. A remote method invocation always returns one of two events: *onResult* or *onStatus*. The *NetServices* class can handle these events in several different ways. To capture responses from the *HelloWorld* and *HelloUser* services (Examples 1-1 and 2-1), we used a responder object that had two methods: *onResult( )* and *onStatus( )*.

Alternatively, the events can be handled with functions that follow a specific naming convention.

 Results are returned to a function named using the name of the remote method with a suffix of *_Result*. Similarly, status (error) events are returned to a function named with a *_Status* suffix.

In this case, the remote method is *getSearchResult( )*, so the result and status functions are named *getSearchResult_Result( )* and *getSearchResult_Status( )*.

The remote service returns an entire recordset, which I've called result_rs, to *getSearchResult_Result( )*. Because the result is a recordset, using a variable name ending in _rs lets you take advantage of ActionScript's code hints and code completion features:

```
// Responder function for onResult event
function getSearchResult_Result (result_rs) {
  Products_rs = result_rs;
```

The *RecordSet.getLength( )* method returns the number of records in the recordset. The code displays the count in the results_txt text field along with some descriptive text. The text is first concatenated in a temporary variable, which is much quicker than setting the text property incrementally:

```
  var temp = "";
  temp += "There were " + Products_rs.getLength( );
  temp += " records returned.";
  results_txt.text = temp;
}
```

If the remote call is unsuccessful, the *_Status* function is called instead of the *_Result* function. The *_Status* function receives an error object with properties, including description, which identifies the error. The *getSearchResult_Status( )* function simply displays the descriptive text of any error message that is returned:

```
// Responder function for onStatus event
function getSearchResult_Status (error) {
  results_txt.text = "There was an error: " + error.description;
}
```

If you run the movie—either by publishing it and browsing to it, or by testing it in the authoring environment—you should be able to enter something into the search field and get a count of the results as a message in the interface.

If you get an error message, you'll probably wonder where the error occurred. This seemingly simple example uses several different technologies and demonstrates just how complex a Flash Remoting application can be. This example uses the following technologies:

- Flash and ActionScript
- A database (Access, SQL Server, MySQL, or other)
- Structured Query Language (SQL)
- The connection to the database (ODBC, JDBC, OLE DB)
- The application server (CF, ASP.NET, JSP)
- The Flash Remoting gateway
- The HTTP protocol

Obviously, when using this many different technologies, errors can happen at any step along the way. Chapter 13 covers debugging and troubleshooting in depth.

Once you have the code that counts the records returned to Flash working, you can add code to display the data and page through the recordset. The *RecordSet* class does not have client-side paging built in; it doesn't support the notion of a "current" record. Let's enhance the *RecordSet* class to include two custom methods: *move( )* and *getCurrentRecord( )*.

ActionScript allows you to augment a class by assigning custom methods and properties directly to its prototype property. This is not the only way to add functionality to a class, but in this case it fits the bill nicely. First, add a currentRecord property to the *RecordSet* prototype along with a "getter" method, *getCurrentRecordNum( )*:

```
RecordSet.prototype.currentRecord = 0;
RecordSet.prototype.getCurrentRecordNum = function () {
  return this.currentRecord;
};
```

Next, add the custom *move( )* method, which accepts a parameter specifying the direction ("first", "previous", "next", or "last"):

```
RecordSet.prototype.move = function (direction) {
  direction = direction.toLowerCase();
  switch (direction) {
```

```
      case "first":
        this.currentRecord = 1;
        break;
      case "previous":
        if (--this.currentRecord < 1) {
          this.currentRecord = 1;
        }
        break;
      case "next":
        if (++this.currentRecord > this.getLength()) {
          this.currentRecord = this.getLength();
        }
        break;
      case "last":
        this.currentRecord = this.getLength();
        break;
    }
  };
```

The custom *move( )* method sets the currentRecord property of the *RecordSet* object, depending on which of the four buttons—First, Previous, Next, or Last— the user clicked. You have seen this typical recordset navigation scheme a thousand times before.

Finally, create the *getCurrentRecord( )* method, which retrieves the current record. Keep in mind that by the time these methods are called, the entire recordset is in memory. There are no more round trips to the server.

```
  Recordset.prototype.getCurrentRecord = function () {
    return this.getItemAt(this.currentRecord-1);
  };
```

When you call *RecordSet.getCurrentRecord( )*, an entire record is returned, but you can retrieve individual fields from the record using the field name, like this:

```
  myRecordsetName.getCurrentRecord().myFieldName;
```

Now that the *RecordSet* class has been enhanced to support a current record and a navigation method, you can attach *onClick* event handlers to the First, Previous, Next, and Last buttons. The function is written as a callback function named *moveToRec( )* and assigned to the buttons (named moveFirst, movePrevious, moveNext, and moveLast):

```
  function moveToRec (button) {
    Products_rs.move(button.label);
    getRecord();
  }
  moveFirst.setClickHandler("moveToRec");
  movePrevious.setClickHandler("moveToRec");
  moveNext.setClickHandler("moveToRec");
  moveLast.setClickHandler("moveToRec");
```

Since the button label supplies the necessary argument to the *RecordSet.move( )* method, one generic function is sufficient for all four buttons.

Now we need to display fields extracted from the recordset data in some text fields. This task can be accomplished in several ways, but I'll use a function named *getRecord( )* that is called from the *moveToRec( )* click handler:

```
function getRecord () {
  if (Products_rs.getLength() == 0) {
    ProductName_txt.text = UnitPrice_txt.text = QuantityPerUnit_txt.text = "";
    navStatus_txt.text = "No Records";
  } else {
    var currentRecord = Products_rs.getCurrentRecord();
    ProductName_txt.text    = currentRecord.ProductName;
    UnitPrice_txt.text      = currentRecord.UnitPrice;
    QuantityPerUnit_txt.text = currentRecord.QuantityPerUnit;
    var temp =  "Rec. No. " + (Products_rs.getCurrentRecordNum());
    temp += " of " + Products_rs.getLength();
    navStatus_txt.text = temp;
  }
}
```

The preceding code simply sets the text elements in the Flash movie to the current record's field values, or sets them to blank if there are no records. It retrieves the current record with the *getCurrentRecord( )* method created earlier and then extracts each field individually.

You can test this movie from the Flash environment, or you can publish it to your site and browse to the resulting HTML page. When you browse to the page, the browser doesn't need to reload the page, even if you search the database repeatedly. The communication with the server is done by Flash behind the scenes. Figure 3-3 shows the interface in use. The completed example, *SearchProducts.fla*, is available at the online Code Depot. Chapters 4 through 9 show more examples that utilize the *RecordSet* class.

This section described a simple search interface in Flash that relied on ActionScript to manually set the text elements in the movie to the incoming recordset field values. The next section describes a much simpler approach that can be utilized with some types of UI components using another Flash Remoting class: *DataGlue*.

DataGlue

Typically, when working with recordsets in server-side applications and HTML pages, the most tedious part is formatting the recordset on a page or in a user-interface element, such as a list box. Fortunately, the *RecordSet* class, in combination with the *DataGlue* class, simplifies this immensely. The DataGrid and the Dynamic Chart components are perhaps the most impressive, but any data-aware component can be dynamically populated with a *RecordSet* object with one line of code:

```
myComponent.setDataProvider(myRecordset_rs);
```

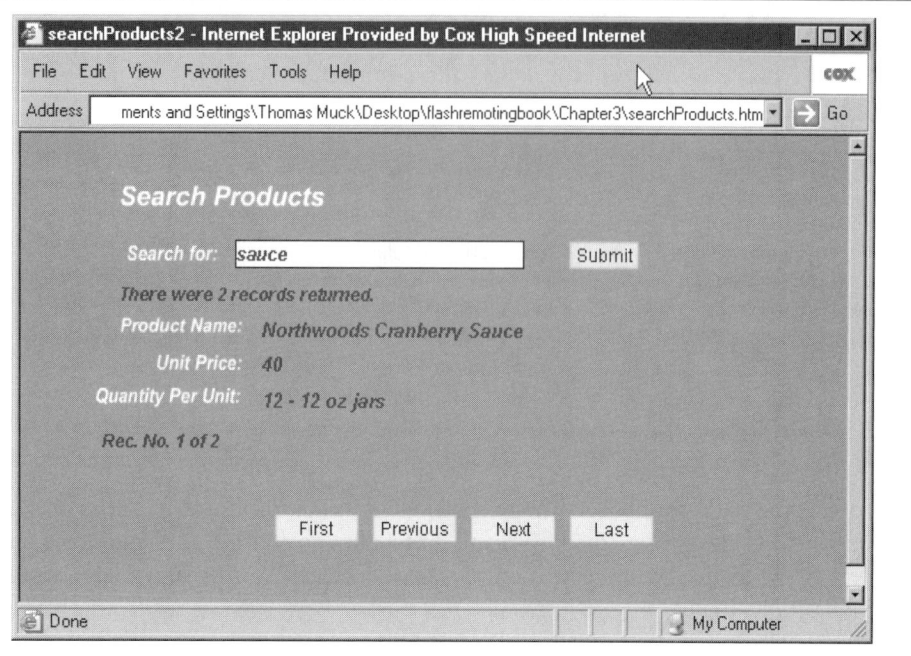

Figure 3-3. The Flash interface for SearchProducts.fla

This code effectively binds the recordset to the component and creates the visual output in the Flash movie.

Using the DataGlue Class

So-called data-aware components can interact with *DataProviderClass* objects to easily attach a data source to the component. Components that support *DataProvider-Class* objects include:

- ComboBox
- ListBox
- Tree
- BarChart
- LineChart
- PieChart
- DataGrid

These items support *DataProviderClass* methods, such as *addItem( )*, *addItemAt( )*, *getLength( )*, *removeAll( )*, *removeItemAt( )*, *replaceItemAt( )*, *setDataProvider( )*, and *sortItemsBy( )*. These methods are handy when you're working with static data, but when you're working with a *RecordSet* object there is one added bonus: changes to the *RecordSet* object are reflected automatically in the UI component's display. The

DataGlue.bindFormatStrings( ) class-level method effectively glues the recordset to the UI component; so, when you use one of the *RecordSet* methods, the component that is tied to the *RecordSet* object is also affected. For example, deleting an item from the client-side *RecordSet* object with the following code:

```
myRecordset_rs.removeItemAt(myRecordNumber);
```

automatically removes the item from any components that are tied to the *RecordSet*, such as a ListBox or ComboBox.

Take a ComboBox as an example. A ComboBox can be thought of as two arrays: one containing the `label` property for each item in the list, and one containing the data property. The label is displayed in a drop-down list, but the data can be almost anything, including a recordset row. Let's look at a simple example, which allows a server-side service to populate a ComboBox. The examples use the same server-side services as the last example: *com.oreilly.frdg.SearchProducts*.

The UI has a ComboBox to hold the resulting recordset, a ListBox to hold items chosen by the user, and two buttons to add and remove items from the ListBox. The code is listed in Example 3-9 and is also available at the online Code Depot as *DataGlueDemo.fla*.

Example 3-9. DataGlueDemo.fla

```
#include "NetServices.as"
#include "DataGlue.as"

if (connected == null) {
  connected = true;
  NetServices.setDefaultGatewayUrl("http://localhost/flashservices/gateway");
  var my_conn = NetServices.createGatewayConnection( );
  var myService = my_conn.getService("com.oreilly.frdg.SearchProducts", this);
}
// Call method inline when movie loads
myService.getSearchResult('');

// Set up event handlers for buttons
add_pb.setClickHandler("onAdd");
remove_pb.setClickHandler("onRemove");

// Event handlers for buttons
function onAdd ( ) {
  products_lb.addItem(allproducts_cb.getSelectedItem( ).label);
}

function onRemove ( ) {
  products_lb.removeItemAt(products_lb.getSelectedIndex( ));
}

function getSearchResult_Result (result_rs) {
  DataGlue.bindFormatStrings(allProducts_cb,result_rs,
                             "#productname#", "#unitprice#");
}
```

The first thing you should notice is the new include file, *DataGlue.as*:

```
#include "DataGlue.as"
```

The connection and service creation are the same as seen earlier. The *getSearchResult( )* remote method is called inline rather than triggered by an event; the recordset is loaded from the remote server when the movie loads. Two buttons add items to the ListBox from the ComboBox and remove items from the ListBox. They are set up with click handler functions:

```
// Set up event handlers for buttons
add_pb.setClickHandler("onAdd");
remove_pb.setClickHandler("onRemove");

// Event handlers for buttons
function onAdd () {
  products_lb.addItem(allproducts_cb.getSelectedItem( ).label);
}

function onRemove () {
  products_lb.removeItemAt(products_lb.getSelectedIndex( ));
}
```

The only other code in this example is the *_Result* function, which handles the result from the remote method. This is where *DataGlue.bindFormatStrings( )* is used to tie the recordset to the UI component:

```
function getSearchResult_Result (result_rs) {
  DataGlue.bindFormatStrings (allProducts_cb,result_rs,"#productname#");
}
```

The *bindFormatStrings( )* method takes four parameters:

Data consumer
> The ComboBox in this case

Data provider
> The *RecordSet* object in this case

Label data
> Using the current ProductName field from the recordset

Value data
> Not used here

The *DataGlue.bindFormatStrings( )* method essentially glues your recordset to the ComboBox. When the recordset is loaded from the remote server, it is automatically placed in the ComboBox.

The next section describes the *DataGlue* class (or simply DataGlue) as it applies to the DataGrid component.

Gluing the DataGrid

The previous example showed a simple recordset feeding a ComboBox using the *DataGlue* class. However, DataGlue works just as easily with more sophisticated components. The DataGrid component comes with its own method for handling the *DataProviderClass*, called *setDataProvider( )*:

```
myGrid.setDataProvider(myRecordset_rs);
```

Calling *DataGrid.setDataProvider( )* causes a DataGrid component to display an entire recordset in a sortable grid, as shown in Figure 3-4. Because the DataGrid contains its own DataGlue functionality, you don't have to specifically include *DataGlue.as* in your Flash file.

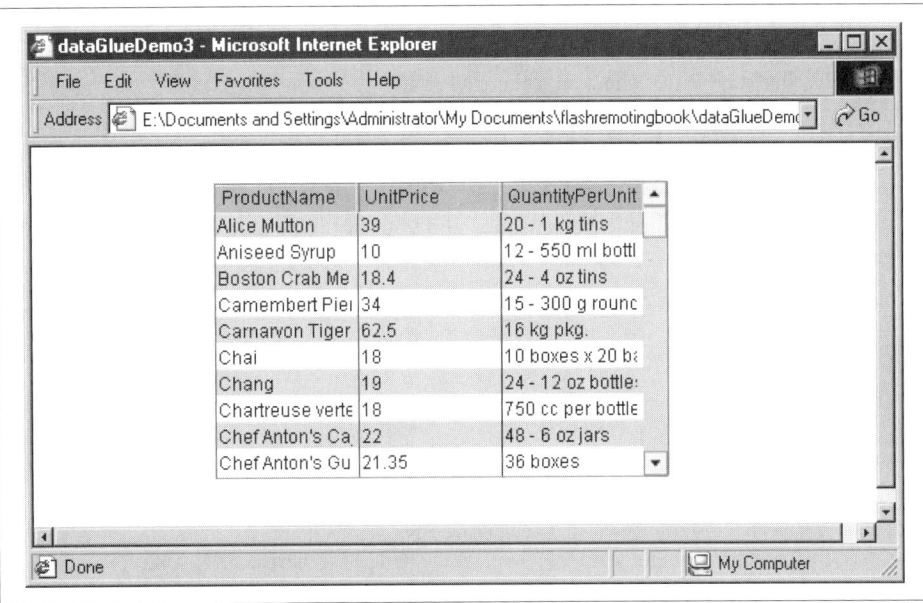

Figure 3-4. The DataGrid component in use

You'll notice that the row colors are alternating in Figure 3-4. This was done by adding one line of code:

```
myGrid_dg.alternateRowColors(0xCCCCCC,0xFFFFFF);
```

The entire code listing for the DataGrid demo (*DataGridDemo.fla*), which you'll find at the online Code Depot, is shown in Example 3-10.

Squashing a DataGrid Bug

There is a bug in the DataGrid implementation that is documented in the DataGrid help files. It has to do with the way that conflicting classes are dealt with in Flash MX. If you add a DataGrid to your page and you find that it displays nothing but blank results, you are seeing the bug.

To work around the DataGrid bug, follow these steps:

1. Open the Library of your *.fla*.
2. Navigate to Flash UI Components → Component Skins → Global Skins in the Library.
3. Select the skin called FLabel and delete it from the Library.
4. A dialog box appears, asking if you're sure.
5. There will be a checkbox prompting you to delete symbol instances. Make sure this checkbox is not checked, then click OK.
6. Drag another DataGrid instance from the Components panel to the Stage.
7. A dialog box appears, asking you to replace existing components. Say yes, and then delete the grid from the Stage.

At this point, the bug should be squashed and you should be able to see the results in your DataGrid.

Example 3-10. DataGridDemo.fla

```
#include "NetServices.as"

if (initialized == null) {
  initialized = true;
  NetServices.setDefaultGatewayUrl("http://localhost/flashservices/gateway");
  var my_conn = NetServices.createGatewayConnection();
  var myService = my_conn.getService("com.oreilly.frdg.SearchProducts", this);
}

myService.getSearchResult('');

function getSearchResult_Result(result_rs) {
  myGrid_dg.alternateRowColors(0xCCCCCC,0xFFFFFF);
  myGrid_dg.setDataProvider(result_rs);
}
```

 The online example files utilizing the DataGrid do not contain the grid component, due to licensing issues, as it is a commercial component. You need to add a DataGrid component to the *.fla* and give it an instance name of myGrid_dg in order to make the examples work.

Gluing the Dynamic Chart Components

Flash's Dynamic Chart Components are perhaps the most sophisticated components available from Macromedia. Attaching a *RecordSet* object to one of these charts is just as simple as it was using a ComboBox or DataGrid component. Just like Data-Grid components, the Chart Components have their own *DataProviderClass* built in and don't need *DataGlue.as*.

To demonstrate, I'll go back to the *Northwind* database and create a service that queries the Category Sales for 1997 view. The SQL statement used for this service is simply:

```
SELECT * FROM [Category Sales for 1997]
```

The MySQL version of the database does not have built-in views or queries like MS SQL Server or MS Access. If you are using the MySQL database, you can substitute the following SQL statement for the previous query:

```
SELECT Categories.CategoryName,
Sum((order_details.UnitPrice * Quantity * (1-Discount)/100)*100)
AS CategorySales
FROM Categories
INNER JOIN Products ON Categories.CategoryID = Products.CategoryID
INNER JOIN Orders ON Orders.OrderID = order_details.OrderID
INNER JOIN order_details
ON Products.ProductID = order_details.ProductID
WHERE Orders.ShippedDate Between '19970101' And '19971231'
GROUP BY Categories.CategoryName
```

The server-side code is identical to the *SearchProducts* service that was created earlier, with the exception of the previous SQL statement and the method name: *getCategorySales( )*. The code for the server-side service is not shown here but is available as a CFC for ColdFusion, a Java class for J2EE, an *.aspx* page for ASP.NET, and a *.php* page for PHP at the online Code Depot.

The Flash source file, *ChartDemo.fla*, can also be downloaded from the online Code Depot. It contains one item: a PieChart object named *myChart*. Example 3-11 shows the commented ActionScript code.

Example 3-11. ChartDemo.fla

```
#include "NetServices.as"

if (connected == null) {
  connected = true;
  NetServices.setDefaultGatewayUrl("http://localhost/flashservices/gateway");
  var my_conn = NetServices.createGatewayConnection( );
  var myService = my_conn.getService("com.oreilly.frdg.getStats", this);
}
// Set up the chart title, the label field, and the value field
myChart.setChartTitle("Category Sales for 1997");
myChart.setLabelSource("CategoryName");
```

Example 3-11. ChartDemo.fla (continued)

```
myChart.setValueSource("CategorySales");

// Get the remote service
myService.getCategorySales();

// Handle the result by setting the DataProvider of the chart
function getCategorySales_Result(result_rs) {
  myChart.setDataProvider(result_rs);
}
```

This code provides a simple pie chart based on the data returned from the server. If you roll your mouse over the pie elements, you can see the data from the recordset (shown in Figure 3-5).

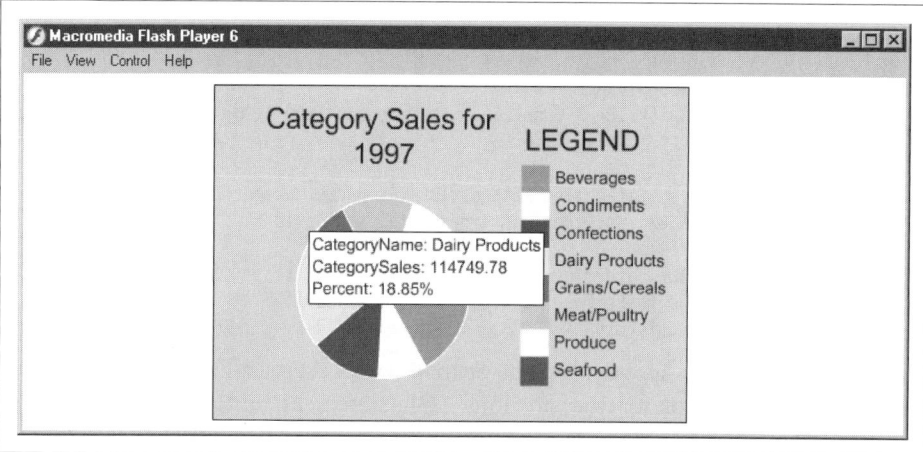

Figure 3-5. The dynamic PieChart component in use

To change this PieChart to a BarChart, simply remove the PieChart object from the Flash movie and replace it with a BarChart object. Name the BarChart myChart, using the PI. If you test the movie at this point, you should see the data displayed in bar chart format.

Wrapping Up

This chapter has covered many of the user interface basics that you need to create your own Flash Remoting interfaces and allow them to interact with remote services. You learned about many of the UI components that are available and how they interact with Flash Remoting through DataGlue and other techniques. Chapter 4 covers details about the Flash Remoting components and what makes them tick.

CHAPTER 4

Flash Remoting Internals

I learned how to program by pulling apart existing programs and trying to figure out how they worked. This was back in 1982, when the hottest computer around was the Commodore 64. My approach was to load an existing program, run it, and then look at the code line by line. I would comment each line of the code with my observations of what the program was doing. After some practice, I got pretty good at discovering what other people's code did. I also got pretty good at writing my own code.

The code was assembly language. Although the properties, methods, and events of modern-day languages make it easy to accomplish complex tasks with one or two lines of code, a simple statement like `myService.getSearchResults(string)` might require hundreds of lines of assembly language. Little wonder that I went through 7,000 sheets of tractor-feed printer paper. Despite its drawbacks, the flip side of assembly language is that it gives you access to the core underpinnings of the software and hardware. If you understand the assembly language, you really understand everything the program does.

The goal of Flash Remoting is to take complex tasks and abstract them so that you, the programmer, can accomplish more with each line of code than was previously possible. But saying "it just works" isn't very satisfying to programmers who want to understand Flash Remoting at a deeper level. Especially because sometimes it doesn't "just work," a deeper technical understanding can help you solve otherwise vexing problems.

The preceding chapters have shown you a few examples of the technology and how to use it. Now that Flash Remoting's concepts are familiar to you, it is a good time to dive more deeply into the different classes, objects, and components of Flash Remoting. What exactly are *NetServices* and *createGatewayConnection( )* and why do they work as they do?

Following the discussion of some of Flash Remoting's internals, this chapter explores other topics in depth. This chapter includes many practical details on responder objects and callback functions, recordset objects, error trapping, and registering objects for transmission between the client and server. This chapter gives a new understanding of Flash Remoting, so you can decide when to sit back and enjoy the cruise control and when to tinker under the hood. It should be read carefully by all developers, so buckle up.

The NetConnection Class

The *NetConnection* class is available to the Flash Player when you install the Flash Remoting authoring components. A *NetConnection* object provides you with a proxy through which you connect to the Flash Remoting gateway on the remote server. It also gives you a way to call remote methods. All you need to know is the URL of the Flash Remoting gateway and the methods that you want to access. The *NetConnection* class takes care of the minutiae involved in making the connection, calling the services, and handling the results.

The *NetConnection* class contains several methods that can be accessed directly, but they are most often called indirectly through the *NetServices* class, as shown in the previous chapters. The methods of *NetConnection* are:

- *connect(url)*
- *call(remoteMethod, responderObject[, arg1, arg2,...])*
- *close( )*

These three core methods are used internally by the *NetServices* class to connect to and use the Flash Remoting gateway on the server. But what exactly is the relation between the *NetConnection* and *NetServices* classes?

Using NetServices

In the examples in the preceding chapters, the *NetServices.as* file was included to allow you to use two methods of the *NetServices* class: *createGatewayConnection( )* and *setDefaultGateway( )*.

There is also a *NetServices.getVersion( )* method, which returns the current version of the *NetServices* class. You can check the version number to maintain backward compatibility if future versions of the *NetServices* class contain new functionality. Several other methods are used internally as well.

The *NetServices* class also gives you an interface to the *NetConnection* class and enhances the *NetConnection* class to include several new methods:

- *getService(remoteMethod, responderObject[, arg1, arg2,...])*
- *setCredentials(username, password)*
- *RequestPersistentHeader( )*
- *ReplaceGatewayUrl(url)*

The first two methods should be accessed through the connection that you set up with the *createGatewayConnection( )* method. The last two methods are reserved for future use by the Flash Remoting gateway.

Establishing the Gateway Connection

Calling the *NetServices.createGatewayConnection( )* method initializes a *NetConnection* object and returns that object to the Flash movie. The new *NetConnection* object can be used to connect to the Flash Remoting gateway on the server.

Here, a hardcoded URL for the gateway is passed as an argument to *createGateway-Connection( )*:

```
var myURL = "http://localhost/flashservices/gateway";
var myConnection_conn = NetServices.createGatewayConnection(myURL);
```

Alternatively, the URL can be defined with another method, *NetServices.setDefault-Gateway( )*. The *NetServices.setDefaultGateway( )* method provides a way to hard-code a default gateway URL within your Flash movie while retaining the flexibility to pass a gateway URL to the movie from the HTML page. When you use *setDefault-Gateway( )* to specify the URL, the URL is stored as a property of the *NetConnection* object. When the *createGatewayConnection( )* method is called, the *NetConnection* object determines the gateway URL as follows:

1. If the Flash developer included a URL in the call to *createGatewayConnection( )*, as in Example 1-1, that URL is used.

2. Otherwise, the *NetConnection* object checks whether the HTML page request is an HTTP or HTTPS request. If so, it uses the URL specified by the `gatewayURL` variable within the `FlashVars` attribute of the `<OBJECT>` or `<EMBED>` tag.

3. If the URL is still not found, the *NetConnection* object uses the gateway URL specified in the earlier call to *setDefaultGateway( )* method, if any.

4. If no URL is found, an error message is sent back to the Flash movie and displayed in the Output window (in authoring mode only). In a production environment, the attempt to create the gateway connection fails silently.

For the purposes of demonstration, I have hardcoded the Flash Remoting gateway's URL path in previous examples. Passing the URL into the movie as a variable from HTML makes it easier to move your Flash Remoting application to a different server without having to recompile the *.swf* file.

To change the URL at runtime, add a `FlashVars` attribute to the `<OBJECT>` and `<EMBED>` tags of the HTML page containing the Flash movie. `FlashVars`, first supported in Flash Player 6, allows you to pass name/value pairs from the HTML page to the Flash movie. The HTML for a typical Flash movie might look like this, with the `FlashVars` attributes in bold:

```
<OBJECT classid="clsid:D27CDB6E-AE6D-11cf-96B8-444553540000"
  codebase="http://download.macromedia.com/pub/shockwave/cabs/flash/
```

```
swflash.cab#version=6,0,0,0" WIDTH="550" HEIGHT="400"
id="mymovie" ALIGN="">
<PARAM NAME=movie VALUE="mymovie.swf">
<PARAM NAME=FlashVars
 VALUE="gatewayURL=http://www.flash-remoting.com/flashservices/gateway">
<PARAM NAME=quality VALUE=high>
<PARAM NAME=bgcolor VALUE=#FFFFFF>
<EMBED src="mymovie.swf" quality=high bgcolor=#FFFFFF  WIDTH="550"
 HEIGHT="400" NAME="Untitled-2" ALIGN=""
 TYPE="application/x-shockwave-flash"
 FlashVars="gatewayURL=http://www.flash-remoting.com/flashservices/gateway"
 PLUGINSPAGE="http://www.macromedia.com/go/getflashplayer">
</EMBED>
</OBJECT>
```

The FlashVars attribute should specify the variable name gatewayURL and give it a value that is the path to the Flash Remoting gateway on your server, because gatewayURL is the variable that the *NetConnection* object is expecting:

```
gatewayURL=http://www.flash-remoting.com/flashservices/gateway
```

The best scenario is to use a *setDefaultGateway( )* method to create a default URL in the ActionScript code, but then override that within your final web page using a gatewayURL variable within the FlashVars attribute. This gives you the flexibility to test your movie in authoring mode and change the URL when publishing the movie to the Web:

```
// Create the connection and service objects
NetServices.setDefaultGatewayURL("http://localhost/flashservices/gateway");
var myConnection_conn = NetServices.createGatewayConnection( );
```

After executing the preceding code, the variable myConnection_conn contains an instance of the *NetConnection* class. Notice that there is no need to parse the gatewayURL variable from the HTML page; this is done automatically behind the scenes by the *NetConnection* object.

If you examine the *NetServices.as* file, you can see the last few lines of code in the definition for the *createGatewayConnection( )* method:

```
NetServices.createGatewayConnection = function (url) {
  //... snipped code ...
  var nc = new NetConnection( );
  nc.connect(url);
  return nc;
};
```

You can see that it creates a new *NetConnection* object and uses the *connect( )* method to create a connection before returning the object to the caller. The method is named *connect( )*, but the actual connection to the remote server isn't made until making a call to the remote service.

Creating the Service Object

When you set up a connection using *createGatewayConnection( )*, the resulting *Net-Connection* object can be used to gain access to a service by calling its *getService( )* method as shown here:

```
var myService = myConnection_conn.getService("com.oreilly.frdg.HelloUser", this);
```

The last parameter passed to *getService( )*—in this case, the current object this—is sometimes called a *default responder object*. This object will handler future results returned in response to remote calls on the service. See "Creating Responder Functions" later in this chapter for many more details on responder objects.

The service object returned by *getService( )* is used to invoke methods or functions of the remote service. Although the way in which you access methods of a service is similar for most server models, details for each server-side platform are covered in Chapters 5 through 9.

Calling *getService( )* also automatically sets up a *NetServiceProxy* object and the *Net-ServiceProxyResponder* object. You shouldn't have to deal with these directly, as they are used behind the scenes, but they are explained next.

NetServiceProxy

For each service established via *getService( )*, Flash automatically generates an object of the *NetServiceProxy* class to pass the remote call to the server and handle the results from the remote call as well. It makes sure that the AMF packets to and from the remote service are deserialized and registered properly as ActionScript objects. See "Registering Objects" later in this chapter for more information.

When you connect to a remote service with a *getService( )* call like this:

```
var myService = myConnection_conn.getService("com.oreilly.frdg.HelloUser", this);
```

getService( ) returns an instance of the *NetServiceProxy* class. The *NetServiceProxy* object acts as a proxy or middleman to the remote service and initiates the call to methods of the remote service.

NetServiceProxyResponder

For each service established via *getService( )*, Flash also automatically generates an object of the *NetServiceProxyResponder* class. The *NetServiceProxyResponder* object dispatches *onResult* events containing the response from a remote method call, as described under "Creating Responder Functions." Similarly, the *NetServiceProxyResponder* object also dispatches *onStatus* events if an error occurs when invoking a method of a remote service. Again, see "Creating Responder Functions" for many important details on the order in which *NetServiceProxyResponder* searches for the callback functions to handle *onResult* and *onStatus* events.

User Authentication

Authenticating a user is a tedious but necessary task eventually faced by every application programmer. Although different application servers have different methods of authenticating users, the *NetConnection.setCredentials( )* method provides a standard way to send authentication information to your server-side application. At the time of this writing, *setCredentials( )* is supported by ColdFusion MX and JRun 4 only.

The *setCredentials( )* method sends a credentials header with userid and password name/value pairs to the remote server. The server, in turn, must be equipped to handle the header. The *setCredentials( )* method is covered at length in Chapters 5 and 7.

Using the NetConnection Object Directly

Flash Remoting includes a *NetConnection* class as part of its core classes. The *NetServices* class simply provides a higher-level interface to the *NetConnection* class. The *NetServices.as* file contains the classes used by Flash Remoting to communicate with the server. You don't have to include the *NetServices.as* file if you use the *NetConnection* class directly. That is, the classes contained in the *NetServices.as* file are not required, but they are easier to use than native *NetConnection* methods. However, let's look at the *NetConnection* methods for comparison.

To utilize the *NetConnection* class directly you can first create a connection object:

```
var myConn = new NetConnection( );
```

Then connect to the Flash Remoting gateway using the *NetConnection.connect( )* method:

```
myConn.connect("http://127.0.0.1/flashservices/gateway");
```

To call a method of a remote service, you can use the *NetConnection.call( )* method, specifying the service and method names together in one argument, the responder object as the next argument, followed by any arguments to send to the remote method. In this case, there are no arguments supplied to the remote method:

```
myResult = new Object( );
myConn.call("com.oreilly.frdg.HelloWorld.sayHello", myResult);
```

Notice that you must specify the complete namespace of the service (com.oreilly. frdg.HelloWorld), along with the method name without parenthesis (sayHello) in the call to the server. The Flash Remoting gateway treats this call the same as invoking a method on the service object returned by *getService( )*, as shown in Example 1-1, portions of which are reproduced here:

```
#include "NetServices.as"
// Set the URL for the gateway connection
var myURL = "http://localhost/flashservices/gateway";
// Specify the path to the service
var myServicePath = "com.oreilly.frdg.HelloWorld";
```

```
// Create a responder object (event handlers are not shown)
myResult = new Object();
// Establish the gateway connection
var myServer = NetServices.createGatewayConnection(myURL);
// Access the remote service
var myService = myServer.getService(myServicePath, myResult);
// Invoke a remote method on the service
myService.sayHello();
```

One or more arguments can be specified following the service and method names and the responder object. For example, you can call the *HelloUser* service from Chapter 2 and pass it a username as follows:

```
myConn.call("com.oreilly.frdg.HelloUser.sayHello", myResult, username_txt.text);
```

Again, the Flash Remoting gateway treats this call the same as using the *NetServices* class, as shown in Example 2-1.

Although our brief examples of using *NetConnection* directly don't include callback handlers to handle the results or status errors, you can set up event handlers in the manner shown in Examples 1-1 and 2-1. You can't, however, use named callback functions, such as *methodName_Result* (as shown in Example 3-8) without the *NetServices* class.

Although the *NetConnection* object can be used directly, the *NetServices* class provides several advantages:

- The service object can be created once (using *getService( )*) and methods can be invoked on that service by name, which is more intuitive.
- You can specify result-handling functions using the *methodname_Result* naming convention.
- The *NetServiceProxy* object created automatically by *getService( )* acts as a proxy to handle any necessary deserialization of the results into ActionScript objects.
- Connection URLs can be set up using a *setDefaultGatewayUrl( )* method and then overridden by the parameters coming from HTML sent to the movie.

If you choose to call the *NetConnection* methods directly, the *NetConnection.close( )* method can be used to close a connection to the Flash Remoting gateway:

```
myConnection_conn.close();
```

Furthermore, the *NetConnection.addHeader( )* method allows you to attach a header to the AMF packet sent to the server, as follows:

```
myConnection_conn.addHeader(name, mustUnderstand, object)
```

The *name* argument is a header name that you specify (such as credentials). The second argument, *mustUnderstand*, is a Boolean value; if it is true, the server must process the header before any further processing can take place. It is up to your server-side code to process the header. The third argument can be any ActionScript object. A typical call to *addHeader( )* is included in the *NetServices.as* file, which you can examine by looking at the source file in the Flash *Include* folder. The *NetConnection. setCredentials( )* method, covered in Chapter 5, uses *addHeader( )* to process the login information in a Flash movie.

NetConnection debugging methods

The *NetConnection* class also has several methods that you can use to debug your Flash Remoting application:

- *NetConnection.getDebugConfig( )*
- *NetConnection.getDebugID( )*
- *NetConnection.setDebugID( )*
- *NetConnection.trace( )*

These methods are covered in Chapter 13, where we talk about debugging. They are also documented in Chapter 15.

Creating Responder Functions

You've seen different ways of creating a responder function for a remote service call. There are two broad categories of responder functions:

- The responder functions can be methods named *onResult( )* and *onStatus( )* (or, more accurately, they are functions assigned to the onResult and onStatus properties of a responder object).
- Responder functions can also be named functions, in which case the function name must match the name of the remote method followed by *_Result* or *_Status*, such as *methodname_Result( )* and *methodname_Status( )*. This approach is used in some of the Macromedia documentation and in Example 3-8.

Now that you understand the basics, here is the twist. A responder object can be passed to *getService( )*, in which case the same responder object is used for all future method invocations on that service. Alternatively, a responder object can be passed separately each time a method is invoked on the service, in which case a responder object should not be passed in the initial call to *getService( )*.

Using onResult( ) and onStatus( ) Responder Functions

Let's first look at passing a responder object to *getService( )*. Recall the syntax for calling the *getService( )* method, where *myConnection_conn* is a *NetConnection* object returned by an earlier call to *createGatewayConnection( )*:

```
myService = myConnection_conn.getService(serviceName[, responderObject]);
```

The first parameter, *serviceName*, is a service name such as com.oreilly.frdg. HelloWorld. The optional second parameter, *responderObject*, is any object that defines *onResult( )* and *onStatus( )* methods, which will handle responses from future calls to methods of the remote service. The Macromedia documentation sometimes refers to *responderObject* as a *result-handler callback object*, we use the term *responder object*.

The *responderObject* argument does not receive the result of the *getService( )* call itself, which we stored in myService. Instead, *responderObject* is used to obtain the results from subsequent calls to methods of the service. The myService object is simply a proxy through which you can make calls to methods of the remote service.

Many examples from Macromedia and elsewhere use the keyword this as the responder object, which causes Flash to look for callback functions defined on the object from which the *getService( )* method is invoked. The only requirements for a responder object is that it defines an *onResult( )* and *onStatus( )* method, or uses named callback functions as described later in this section.

The responder object can take different forms. In this excerpt from Example 1-1, a generic instance of the *Object* class was created to handle the response from remote method calls:

```
myResult = new Object( );

myResult.onResult = function (data) {
  trace("Data received from Server : " + data);
};

myResult.onStatus = function (info) {
  trace("An error occurred : " + info.description);
};

// ...other code omitted
var myService = myServer.getService(myServicePath, myResult);
```

Note how the myResult object is passed as the *responderObject* parameter of the *getService( )* method. After a remote method call on the service completes, the *onResult( )* method of the myResult object will receive the results (unless an error occurs, in which case the *onStatus( )* method will be invoked instead).

The following example defines the *onResult( )* and *onStatus( )* handlers on the current Flash object, as specified by the keyword this, and passes this as the responder object. This technique is also commonly seen throughout this book and in Macromedia's documentation:

```
this.onResult = function (myResult) {
    results_txt.text = myResult;
};

this.onStatus = function (myError) {
    results_txt.text = myError.description;
};
```

```
// Setting up of myConnection_conn and servicePath variables are not shown
var myService = myConnection_conn.getService(servicePath, this);
```

Recall that you can invoke any service function as a method of the service object returned by *getService( )*:

```
// Call a service function named functionA() on myService with no parameters.
myService.functionA();
```

If the service function expects parameters, you can pass the parameters to it just as with any other method invocation:

```
// Call a service function named functionB() on myService with two parameters.
myService.functionB("sample1", "sample2");
```

If you passed a *responderObject* parameter when calling *getService( )* earlier, the response from each remote method call is passed to the responder object's *onResult( )* handler.

However, if you didn't specify a responder object when calling the *getService( )* method, you can specify named callback functions for each remote method called (as discussed later).

First, let's discuss another option: passing a responder object as the first argument when invoking a remote function on the service. If the first argument is an object defining an *onResult( )* method, the *NetServiceProxyResponder* object strips it from the argument list passed to the remote service function and uses it as a responder object instead (the responder object parameter is not sent to the service function).

For example:

```
// Create the service object without specifying a responder object.
myService = myConnection.getService("serviceName");

// Call functionA(), specifying that myResponseObjectA should handle the
// results, but without passing any additional parameters.
// The definition of myResponseObjectA is not shown.
// myResponseObjectA is not sent to the service function.
myService.functionA(myResponseObjectA);

// Call functionB(), specifying that myResponseObjectB should handle
// the results, and pass two additional parameters. myResponseObjectB is not
// sent to the service function, but the two string parameters are sent.
// The definition of myResponseObjectB is not shown.
myService.functionB(myResponseObjectB, "sample1", "sample2");
```

Specifying the responder object when invoking a remote method on the service lets you specify different responder objects for each remote method call, as shown in the preceding example. You don't have this flexibility if the responder object is set when calling *getService( )*. If you set a responder object via *getService( )* and attempt to specify another responder object when invoking a remote function, it won't work. The responder object will be passed as a parameter to the remote function instead of being stripped out of the argument list.

Using Named Responder Functions

An alternative to using *onResult( )* and *onStatus( )* responder functions is to use named responder functions that match the name of the method. For example, here we define two named responder functions for the *sayHello( )* method:

```
function sayHello_Result (myResult) {
    results_txt.text = myResult;
}

function sayHello_Status (myError) {
    results_txt.text = myError.description;
}
```

When a remote service call returns a result, the *NetServiceProxyResponder* object, which handles the result from the remote call, looks for a function that follows the *methodName_Result( )* naming convention. Thus, *onResult* events generated by the *say-Hello( )* function cause Flash Remoting to invoke the *sayHello_Result( )* function. Similarly, error events generated by the *sayHello( )* function cause Flash Remoting to invoke the *sayHello_Status( )* function

Using named functions in this way keeps the result and status callback functions separate for each remote method call. Contrast this with the approach in which the *onResult( )* and *onStatus( )* handlers of a responder object passed to *getService( )* handle the results of all remote method calls on that service.

Response Dispatch Hierarchy

Now that we know about the various ways that responder objects and functions can be specified, how does Flash Remoting decide which responder function to invoke when results are returned from a remote method call?

We saw earlier that when a service is established via *getService( )*, Flash generates a *NetServiceProxyResponder* object. When a remote method call returns a result, a corresponding *onResult* (or *onStatus*) event is serialized by the Flash Remoting gateway as part of the AMF packet that is sent back to your Flash movie.

The *NetServiceProxyResponder* object dispatches the *onResult* event from a remote call in this order:

1. First, it looks for a function that is named using the *methodname_Result( )* convention. If it finds one, results are sent to that function. This function can be defined on the responder object or the current timeline.

2. If the *methodname_Result( )* function isn't found and a responder object with an *onResult( )* method was specified in the call to *getService( )*, results are sent to that responder object's *onResult( )* method.

3. If a responder object wasn't specified in the call to *getService( )* and the first argument passed to the remote method invocation is an object that defines an

onResult( ) method, the first argument is assumed to be a responder object and results are sent to its *onResult( )* method.

4. If no responder object is specified (or if the specified responder object lacks an *onResult( )* method), the *NetServiceProxyResponder* object sends the results to the Output window if the movie is playing in the authoring environment. Otherwise, the results are lost.

The *NetServiceProxyResponder* object also handles the *onStatus* event of the remote service in this order:

1. First, it looks for a function that is named using the *methodname_Status( )* convention. If it finds one, status errors are sent to that function.

2. If the *methodname_Status( )* function isn't found and a responder object with an *onStatus( )* method was specified, results are sent to the responder object's *onStatus( )* method.

3. If no responder object is specified (or if the specified responder object lacks an *onStatus( )* method), the _root level is checked for an *onStatus( )* method. If it is found, it is used.

4. If that is not found, the *_global.System.onStatus( )* method, if any, is used.

5. Finally, if none of the preceding handlers are found, the *NetServiceProxyResponder* object sends the status to the Output window in the authoring environment. Otherwise, the status is lost.

In the authoring environment, if you don't specify responders, the results are displayed in the Output window. This can be handy when testing applications.

Choosing the Appropriate Type of Responder Function

Now that you understand your options, which type of responder function should you use? The answer depends on your application's structure and requirements.

Named result functions are typically used when you have specified a default responder object for a service object (that is, when you've passed a responder object to the *getService( )* method). This technique allows a single responder object to define separate responder functions for each remote service function (because of the naming convention used).

You should use *onResult( )* and *onStatus( )* responder functions when you are passing a responder object as the first parameter to each service function invocation. This technique is quite flexible: you can define different responder objects for each service function invocation, or you can share a single responder object among multiple service function invocations.

Provided you understand the mechanisms, you can mix and match the techniques to suit your situation. Now we will we explore various possible situations and solutions.

By passing a responder object to *getService( )*, you can use one event handler to handle all the results or errors for multiple remote method calls, if appropriate. For example, if you have a service that accessed a company employees database, you might have various methods like this:

```
myService.addEmployee(name);
myService.deleteEmployee(ID);
myService.updateEmployee(ID, record);
```

Each method can return true if it is a successful database transaction. If you use named functions to handle the results, each of these remote method calls needs its own set of responder functions, as in this code snippet:

```
updateEmployee_Result (result) {
  if (result != true) results_txt.text = "There was an error.";
}
deleteEmployee_Result (result) {
  if (result != true) results_txt.text = "There was an error.";
}
addEmployee_Result (result) {
  if (result != true) results_txt.text = "There was an error.";
}
updateEmployee_Status (status) {
  results_txt.text = status.description;
}
deleteEmployee_Status (status) {
  results_txt.text = status.description;
}
addEmployee_Status (status) {
  results_txt.text = status.description;
}
```

Using the responder object approach, this example could be written using one *onResult( )* handler and one *onStatus( )* handler attached to a generic object:

```
Responder = new Object();
Responder.onResult = function (result) {
  if (result != true) results_txt.text = "There was an error.";
};

Responder.onStatus = function (status) (
  results_txt.text = status.description;
};
```

Or, if you pass this (i.e., the current object) as the responder object, you can simply write:

```
onResult = function (result) {
  if (result != true) results_txt.text = "There was an error.";
};
onStatus = function (status) (
  results_txt.text = status.description;
};
```

Using a responder object is more concise in this particular case. In addition, it is in keeping with object-oriented design. The named handler functions are easy to comprehend and use, but they are more typical of procedural programming.

However, you may need to process the results of each remote method call differently. For example, suppose the *addEmployee()*, *deleteEmployee()*, and *updateEmployee()* methods each require special handling. In such cases, you can pass a responder object as the first argument in the remote method call, as described earlier under "Using onResult( ) and onStatus( ) Responder Functions."

Applying this technique to the hypothetical *addEmployee()*, *deleteEmployee()*, *updateEmployee( )* methods, the resulting ActionScript might look like Example 4-1.

Example 4-1. SampleDatabaseMethods.fla

```
#include "NetServices.as"
// Set up variables for the URL and service paths.
var myURL = "http://localhost/flashservices/gateway";
var servicePath = "com.oreilly.frdg.SampleDatabaseMethods";

// Define the custom responder class for the remote updateEmployee() method.
function UpdateResult () { }

// Define a custom onResult() handler for the UpdateResult class.
UpdateResult.prototype.onResult = function (myResults) {
  results_txt.text = "Update employee successful";
  // Do some housekeeping after updating an employee
};

UpdateResult.prototype.onStatus = errorHandler;

// Define the custom responder class for the remote addEmployee() method.
function AddResult () { }

// Define a custom onResult() handler for the AddResult class.
AddResult.prototype.onResult = function (myResults) {
  results_txt.text = "Add employee successful";
  // Do some housekeeping after adding an employee
};

// AddResult and subsequent classes all share a single error handler.
AddResult.prototype.onStatus = errorHandler;

// Define the custom responder class for the remote deleteEmployee() method.
function DeleteResult () { }

// Define a custom onResult() handler for the DeleteResult class.
DeleteResult.prototype.onResult = function (myResults) {
  results_txt.text = "Delete employee successful";
  // Do some housekeeping after deleting an employee
};
```

Example 4-1. SampleDatabaseMethods.fla (continued)

```
DeleteResult.prototype.onStatus = errorHandler;

System.onStatus = errorHandler;

function errorHandler (myError) {
  results_txt.text = myError.description;
}

// Connection hasn't been initialized; create connection and service objects.
if (initialized == null) {
  initialized = true;
  NetServices.setDefaultGatewayURL(myURL);
  var myConnection_conn = NetServices.createGatewayConnection();
  var myService = myConnection_conn.getService(servicePath);
}

// Set up the callback functions to handle mouseclicks.
add_pb.setClickHandler("callAdd");
update_pb.setClickHandler("callUpdate");
delete_pb.setClickHandler("callDelete");

// Call the remote service when the user clicks the buttons.
function callAdd () {
  myService.addEmployee(new AddResult(), "Jack O'Lantern");
}
function callUpdate () {
  myService.updateEmployee(new UpdateResult(), myRecordNum, myRecord);
}
function callDelete () {
  myService.deleteEmployee(new DeleteResult(), myRecordNum);
}
```

Each remote method call has a corresponding responder object that defines a custom *onResult( )* handler. Notice, however, that all responder objects share a common error handler function. This allows you to process the results of each remote method differently while economizing with a single error handler.

We've seen how to invoke different responder functions for different remote methods, but you may want to distinguish between multiple calls to the same remote method. Remember that remote method invocations are asynchronous, and you cannot rely on results being returned to Flash in the same order in which the functions are invoked. Therefore, if you are using the same responder function for multiple calls to the same remote service function, you can't tell which service function invocation returned a particular result. To distinguish between the results from multiple calls to the same remote method, you can use a separate instance of a custom class for each responder object. Attach a custom property to each responder object instance and check its value when the result is returned to the responder function.

This solution adds an id parameter to the *AddResult* class constructor. You can create multiple instances of the *AddResult* class—one for each function invocation—and assign each one a unique id. Then, you can distinguish between results using the id property of the responder object. Replace the following functions in Example 4-1 with these new versions:

```
// Define the custom responder class for the remote addEmployee() method.
// Assign an id property to each instance.
function AddResult (id) {
  this.id = id;
}

// Define a custom onResult() handler for the AddResult class.
AddResult.prototype.onResult = function (myResults) {
  // Process the result differently, depending on the value of the id property.
  results_txt.text = "Employee " + this.id + " added successfully";
};
```

Now you can invoke the same service function multiple times. In each case, use an instance of the *AddResult* class as the responder object, but assign each instance an id corresponding to the employee name so that you can distinguish between them when the results are returned.

```
myService.addEmployee(new AddResult("Jack Sprat"),     "Jack Sprat");
myService.addEmployee(new AddResult("Jack Beanstalk"), "Jack Beanstalk");
myService.addEmployee(new AddResult("Jack O'Lantern"), "Jack O'Lantern");
```

Let's look at one more scenario for creating and managing responder objects. You can create a common responder class (named *BaseResult* in the following code snippet) and then create new responder objects that inherit from the base class for each remote method:

```
// Define a BaseResult class. This class is never called directly,
// but it acts as a base class for responder objects.
function BaseResult () { }

BaseResult.prototype.onResult = function (myResults) {
  trace("success");
};

BaseResult.prototype.onStatus = function (myError) {
  results_txt.text = myError.description;
};

system.onStatus = BaseResult.prototype.onStatus;

UpdateResult.prototype = new BaseResult();

function UpdateResult() { // Empty constructor
}

UpdateResult.prototype.onResult = function (myResults) {
  results_txt.text = "Update employee successful";
```

```
    // Do some housekeeping after updating an employee.
};
// etc.
```

In this scenario, the *onStatus( )* handler is defined in the parent class (*BaseResult*) and is available to all of the classes that inherit from it. Each class that is created implements its own *onResult( )* method. The full code listing for this example is available at the online Code Depot as *SampleDatabaseMethods2.fla*.

You can also establish a hierarchy of result handlers in your Flash movie. You can do this if you have several methods that can share a result handler but some methods that need special handling. For example, the following script defines two dedicated result handlers and one generic handler that will handle all other remote method calls:

```
function myMethod1_Result (result) {
  // Do some stuff for myMethod1( )
}
function myMethod2_Result result) {
  // Do some stuff for myMethod2( )
}
function onResult (result) {
  // Do some generic stuff for all other methods
}
```

The first two functions correspond to method names, and the third function simply acts as a generic method that all other remote method calls will use as a result handler.

Of course, the bottom line is that these techniques are all available and you should use what you feel comfortable with or what the situation demands. "Responder objects in OOP" in Chapter 12 shows other techniques for responder objects that rely on callback functions or broadcasters to handle results more elegantly.

RecordSet Object

The one class that truly separates Flash Remoting from other techniques for dealing with remote data in Flash is the *RecordSet* class. The *RecordSet.as* file is installed as part of the Flash Remoting authoring components, which makes available the *RecordSet* class. We introduced the *RecordSet* class in the Chapter 3, but let's examine it further and describe some of its available methods. For more information, refer to Chapter 15, which documents the *RecordSet* class, among others. For brevity in the following sections, I use the term "recordset" interchangeably with "client-side *RecordSet* object" where the equivalence is clear from context.

Anyone who works with databases every day, like I do, will tell you that the recordset is king. Everything you can do with data—from displaying lists of products to summarizing account information, analyzing web traffic, totaling a shopping cart, or viewing threads in a forum—ultimately depends on recordsets. A recordset is simply a way of organizing data, usually into rows and columns. The Flash *RecordSet* class offers a way to pass this organized data from the server to the client and manipulate it on the client with simple, intuitive methods. The following sections explain the methods of the *RecordSet* class. The lines of code can be typed in consecutively to follow along with the results that are obtained.

When working with *RecordSet* objects, it is handy to be able to examine the contents of the object. For that reason, I've created a custom *RecordSet.showData( )* method that displays the contents of a *RecordSet* object in the Output window. Put the code from Example 4-2 into a file named *RecordSetDebug.as* and save it in your Flash *Configuration\Include* folder.

Example 4-2. The RecordSet.showData( ) method

```
/////////////////////////////////////////////
// RecordSet.showData
// Purpose: trace the contents of a RecordSet object in the Output window
/////////////////////////////////////////////

RecordSet.prototype.showData = function () {
  var fields = this.getColumnNames();
  var i, j, tempfield="", temprow="", temprec="";
  trace("--Recordset Properties--");
  trace("Recordset length: " + this.getLength());
  trace("Fields: " + fields);
  trace("Begin records...");
  var tempLength = this.getLength();
  for (var i = 0; i < tempLength; i++) {
    temprec = this.getItemAt(i);
    for (var j=0; j < fields.length; j++) {
      tempfield = fields[j];
      temprow += tempfield + ': "' + temprec[tempfield] + '"; ';
    }
    trace(temprow);
    temprow="";
  }
  trace("End records...");
  trace("--End Recordset Properties--");
};
```

Now you can include this extension to the *RecordSet* class by adding this line to a Flash movie during debugging:

```
#include "RecordSetDebug.as"
```

You can invoke the *showData( )* method on a *RecordSet* object that you want to display:

```
myRecordset_rs.showData();
```

This dumps the contents of the *RecordSet* object to your Output window. Use this method when typing in the examples in subsequent sections. Later in the chapter, we'll add to the *RecordSetDebug.as* file to make it more versatile.

The RecordSet Constructor

RecordSet objects must be instantiated from the *RecordSet* class, as is common for ActionScript objects. You need to include the *RecordSet.as* file or the *NetServices.as* file, which includes *RecordSet.as*, in your Flash movie in order to use the *RecordSet* class. To create a new, empty *RecordSet* object, use the new keyword and pass an array of field names to the constructor:

```
var myRecordset_rs = new RecordSet(["First", "Last", "Email"]);
```

This creates a client-side recordset with three fields. Recordsets created in this way don't interact with the server, but they can be useful for client-side storage and manipulation of data. The *recordsetname*_rs naming convention activates code hinting in the Flash and Dreamweaver authoring environments.

When a remote method call returns a recordset, a *RecordSet* object is automatically created on the client side (there is no need to create one manually). The fields from the database query become the field names of the client-side *RecordSet* object. Of course, once a recordset is returned, you can use any of the client-side *RecordSet* class methods on it.

 The client-side recordset is not tied to the remote database. If you return a recordset from the remote server, any changes you make to the *RecordSet* object on the client from Flash have no effect on the remote database. See "Updating Data on the Server" in Chapter 5.

The addItem( ) Method

A recordset is essentially a two-dimensional array. Each record in the recordset can be represented as an associative array of field names and values:

```
var tempRecord = {First:"Tom", Last:"Muck", Email:"tom@tom-muck.com"};
```

A record can be added to a recordset with the *RecordSet.addItem( )* method:

```
myRecordset_rs.addItem(tempRecord);
```

This adds the new record to the end of the recordset and increases the length of the recordset by 1.

The addItemAt( ) Method

The *addItemAt( )* method is similar to the *addItem( )* method, except you specify the position at which to insert the item by passing an index number as the first argument:

```
recordsetname.addItemAt(index, record)
```

For example:

```
tempRecord = {First:"John", Last:"Jehosephat", Email:"john@jehosephatlodge.com"};
myRecordset_rs.addItemAt(0,tempRecord);
```

This adds the record into the first position (index 0) of the recordset and pushes all other records down. If you use an index number less than 0, the record is not inserted. If you use an index number greater than the total number of records in the recordset, the record is added to the end of the recordset at the position specified, and blank records are added before the newly inserted record, as in this example:

```
tempRecord = {First:"Adam", Last:"Susquhanna", Email:"adam@susquehannahats.com"};
myRecordset_rs.addItemAt(10,tempRecord);
```

The newly added record appears at index 10. Given that only indexes 0 and 1 contain records from the previous examples, records 2 through 9 are empty (undefined). You can verify this with the custom *showData( )* method from Example 4-2:

```
myRecordset_rs.showData( );
```

When using *addItemAt( )*, be careful about possible error conditions. For example, an error occurs if you try to call *addItemAt( )* when a server-side recordset is not fully loaded into the client-side *RecordSet* object. Therefore, you should wait until the recordset is loaded before reading or writing to the *RecordSet* object. For example, if you invoke a remote function that returns a recordset, you should wait until the responder function, such as *onResult( )*, is called, at which point you know that the recordset is fully loaded. However, refer to the *RecordSet.isFullyPopulated( )* method in Chapter 15 for more information about loading pageable recordsets in Cold-Fusion (see also Chapter 5).

The getLength( ) Method

You can count the number of records in a recordset with the *RecordSet.getLength( )* method:

```
var myRecordsetLength = myRecordset_rs.getLength( );
trace(myRecordsetLength);
```

The length is always 1 greater than the index of the last record, because the index is zero-based. The length of this particular recordset is 11 because there is a record at index 10.

The getItemAt( ) Method

It is often convenient to retrieve a record by its index number using the *RecordSet.getItemAt( )* method:

```
var myRecord = myRecordset_rs.getItemAt(0);
```

Records within a recordset are copied by reference, not by value. Therefore, any changes to the fields of myRecord are reflected in record 0 of myRecordset_rs and vice versa.

Once your variable contains a copy of a record (a row of the recordset), you can access individual fields by name:

```
var tempFirst = myRecord.First;
var tempLast = myRecord.Last;
trace(tempFirst + ' ' + tempLast);
```

The preceding example should output "John Jehosephat" if you've been typing in the code examples as we go along.

Fields can also be addressed using associative array notation:

```
var tempFirst = myRecord["First"];
var tempLast = myRecord["Last"];
```

The index of the last element of a recordset is 1 less than the recordset's length:

```
var tempLength = myRecordset_rs.getLength();
var myRecord = myRecordset_rs.getItemAt(tempLength - 1);
```

The removeItemAt( ) Method

The *removeItemAt( )* method removes the record at the specified index number:

```
recordsetname.removeItemAt(index)
```

Removing a record moves up the subsequent elements of the recordset to fill in the vacated index. The fact that removing a record decreases a recordset's length by 1 can cause confusion within a loop. To demonstrate, we'll loop through the *Record-Set* object created earlier and attempt to remove empty elements:

```
var tempLength = myRecordset_rs.getLength();
for (var i=0; i < tempLength; i++) {
  trace("i=" + i + ": current record=" + myRecordset_rs.getItemAt(i));
  if (myRecordset_rs.getItemAt(i) == undefined) {
    myRecordset_rs.removeItemAt(i);
  }
}
trace(myRecordset_rs.getLength());
```

Figure 4-1 shows the results in the Output window.

You might expect the recordset's length to be 3 after removing the eight empty elements, but the recordset is getting shorter after each iteration of the loop. The code doesn't properly account for the fact that when a record is removed, the index number of each subsequent record is decremented by 1. As the example is written, when a record is removed (and replaced by the next record) the next record is never tested. Therefore, by the time the loop reaches record 6 (the seventh element) there are no more records to test. To remove empty elements properly, you can iterate through the records in reverse:

```
trace(myRecordset_rs.getLength())
var tempLength = myRecordset_rs.getLength()-1;
for (var i=tempLength; i >= 0; i--) {
```

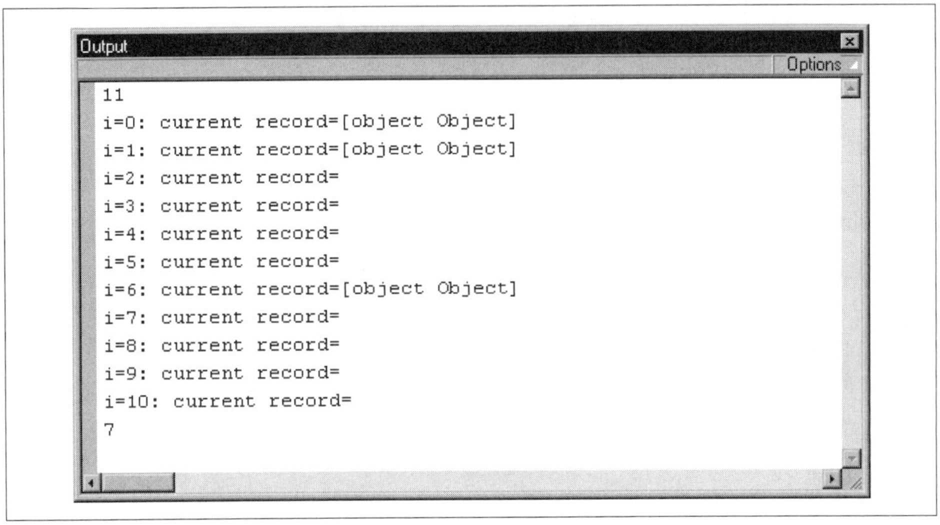

```
Output                                                                    ×
                                                              Options ◢
11
i=0: current record=[object Object]
i=1: current record=[object Object]
i=2: current record=
i=3: current record=
i=4: current record=
i=5: current record=
i=6: current record=[object Object]
i=7: current record=
i=8: current record=
i=9: current record=
i=10: current record=
7
```

Figure 4-1. The Output window after running the script

```
trace("i=" + i + ": current record=" + myRecordset_rs.getItemAt(i));
if (myRecordset_rs.getItemAt(i) == undefined) {
  myRecordset_rs.removeItemAt(i);
}
}
trace(myRecordset_rs.getLength( ));
```

This gives you the expected length of 3 when finished, because the individual empty records are removed from the end of the recordset.

The replaceItemAt( ) Method

Use the *replaceItemAt( )* method to replace the contents of a given record:

```
recordsetname.replaceItemAt(index, record)
```

For example:

```
var newRecord = {First:"Jim", Last:"Zatoichi", Email:"jim@theblindswordsman.com"};
myRecordset_rs.replaceItemAt(1, newRecord);
```

After running this code, the record with name "Tom Muck" in element 1 of the recordset is replaced with "Jim Zatoichi." You can verify this change with the custom *showData( )* method.

The getItemID( ) Method

The *getItemID( )* method returns the internal ID that Flash uses to keep track of the recordset records. This is different from the index number, as explained in "Structure of a RecordSet Object" in Chapter 3. The ID number is assigned by Flash when the record is created, and it doesn't change.

The setField( ) Method

The *setField( )* method is useful for changing the value of a given field in a record. Invoke it with the index number of the record, the field to set, and the new value of the field:

```
recordsetname.setField(index, field, newValue)
```

For example, if Jim Zatoichi from the previous example changed his email address, you could update the recordset as follows:

```
myRecordset_rs.setField(1, "Email", "jz@somenewemailaddress.com");
```

Again, I must reiterate that changing a client-side *RecordSet* object has no effect on the database that resides on your remote server. You have to specifically create code to update the remote database, as shown in "Updating Data on the Server" in Chapter 5.

The getColumnNames( ) Method

The extremely useful *RecordSet.getColumnNames( )* method returns a comma-separated list of the field names in a *RecordSet* object. This can be handy for creating generic classes, methods, or functions that work with different remote recordsets. After the recordset is loaded into the Flash movie, the *getColumnNames( )* method can be used to determine exactly what is in the recordset so that you can work with individual fields. You can call it like this:

```
var myFieldNames = myRecordset_rs.getColumnNames();
trace(myFieldNames);
```

The Output window displays "First, Last, Email", the three fields in the recordset.

The filter( ) Method

The *filter( )* method filters the recordset by predefined criteria and returns a new *RecordSet* object. This method works a little differently than you might expect if you're coming from a server-side programming background.

The filter method requires that you define a function to determine how the recordset is filtered. You pass a function name to the method and a value to filter by:

```
recordsetname.filter(function, value)
```

For example, to filter a recordset by its last name field, create a function called *filterByLastName( )* that accepts two arguments: the record and the last name to filter by:

```
function filterByLastName (theRecord, theLastName) {
  return (theRecord.Last != theLastName);
}
```

The *filter( )* method cycles through each record of the recordset and calls the filtering function. If the callback function returns true, the record is included in the filtered output. If it returns false, the record is removed.

If you don't store the return value of the *filter( )* method as follows, the return value is discarded:

```
myRecordset_rs.filter(filterByLastName,"Zatoichi");
```

Regardless, the *filter( )* method does not affect the original recordset; instead, it returns an entirely new *RecordSet* object. Therefore, you can maintain the original recordset while creating a filtered version as well by simply specifying a new variable to contain the filtered recordset:

```
var theNewRecordset_rs = myRecordset_rs.filter(filterByLastName,"Zatoichi");
```

After executing this code, theNewRecordset_rs contains the filtered recordset and myRecordset_rs contains the original recordset.

Records within a recordset are copied by reference, not by value. Therefore, although *filter( )* creates a new *RecordSet* object, the records within the filtered recordset are still linked to the records in the original recordset. To create a separate copy of a record, you must manually construct a new record object and manually copy the fields from the original record to it.

To change the original recordset permanently, you can store the return value of the *filter( )* method in the variable holding the original *RecordSet* object:

```
myRecordset_rs = myRecordset_rs.filter(filterByLastName,"Zatoichi");
```

Refer to "The sortItemsBy( ) and sort( ) Methods" later in this chapter for sorting recordsets without filtering them.

The getNumberAvailable( ) Method

The *getNumberAvailable( )* method is used only with *RecordSet* objects that are retrieved from a remote server via Flash Remoting. It indicates how many records have been downloaded up until that point. You can use this method to determine whether it is safe to call other methods of the *RecordSet* class that depend on the entire *RecordSet* object being loaded into memory. If the number returned by *getLength( )* matches the number returned by *getNumberAvailable( )*, the entire recordset has been downloaded:

```
if (myRecordset_rs.getLength( ) == myRecordset_rs.getNumberAvailable( )) {
  // Do something
}
```

This method pertains to pageable recordsets in ColdFusion (see Chapter 5).

The setDeliveryMode( ) Method

The *setDeliveryMode( )* method allows you to create pageable server-side recordsets that relate to a *RecordSet* object in a Flash movie. You pass the method a mode, page size, and number of records:

```
recordsetname.setDeliveryMode(mode, pagesize, number)
```

The first argument specifies one of three possible modes of operation—"ondemand" (the default), "fetchall", or "page".

If the delivery mode is not specified via *setDeliveryMode( )*, the default mode is "ondemand", which returns all records from the remote server. The "fetchall" and "page" modes tell the server to hold records in memory and deliver only the needed pages of records. For example, if your remote recordset includes 1,000 records, you can group them into pages of 20 records each:

```
myRecordset_rs.setDeliveryMode("page", 20, 5);
```

That allows your Flash movie to download 5 pages at a time, with 20 records on each page. Using "fetchall" mode, records are delivered when available (like "ondemand" mode), but they are delivered as pages so that you can use the results as they come in. Pageable recordsets are available only in ColdFusion MX. See "Implementing Pageable Recordsets on the Server" in Chapter 5 for more details.

The sortItemsBy( ) and sort( ) Methods

There are two ways to sort a *RecordSet* object in Flash: by field or by defining a custom sort function. When you sort by field using the *sortItemsBy( )* method, you are in effect sorting a multidimensional array. The individual records (rows) of the *RecordSet* object are reordered by the values within the field name passed to the *sortItemsBy( )* method. You can pass a second argument to specify ascending or descending order:

```
recordsetname.sortItemsBy(field, direction)
```

If the second argument is "desc", the sort will be in descending order; otherwise, the sort is ascending.

For example, to sort the recordset created earlier in this chapter by last name, you can use:

```
myRecordset_rs.sortItemsBy("Last");
myRecordset_rs.showData( );
```

The first element in the sorted recordset will be John Jehosephat.

The *sort( )* method allows you to specify a user-defined sort function:

```
recordsetname.sort(function)
```

This method is much slower than the *sortItemsby( )* method, so it should be used sparingly, such as when you need to sort the recordset by two fields. In the following example, *sortByFirstAndLast( )* is a custom sorting function:

```
function sortByFirstAndLast (rec1, rec2) {
  if (rec1.Last  < rec2.Last)  return -1;
  if (rec1.Last  > rec2.Last)  return 1;
  if (rec1.First < rec2.First) return -1;
  if (rec1.First > rec2.First) return 1;
  return 0;
}

// Perform the sort
myRecordset_rs.sort(sortByFirstAndLast);

// Display the results
for (var i=0; i<myRecordset_rs.getLength(); i++) {
  trace(myRecordset_rs.getItemAt(i).Last + ", " +
      myRecordset_rs.getItemAt(i).First);
}
```

The *sort( )* method uses a custom function, *sortByFirstAndLast( )* in this example, to compare rows of your *RecordSet* object. The function is called repeatedly to compare two records and must return a value indicating how the two records should be ordered. The function returns 1 if the first record is greater than the second record, -1 if the second record is greater, and 0 otherwise. Likewise, your sort function should return a positive number if the first record should precede the second, a negative number if the second record should precede the first (i.e., swap the records), and 0 if the order doesn't matter.

Refer to "The filter( ) Method" earlier in this chapter for filtering recordsets based on a particular criterion.

The addView( ) Method

The *addView( )* method allows you to specify the callback function to be executed when something changes in the *RecordSet* object, such as when a user edits an item in a DataGrid, sorts the results, or deletes a record. Changes made via the following methods can be tracked:

sort( )
updateAll( )
addRows( )
updateRows( )
allRows( )
fetchrows( )
deleteRows( )

The object passed to the *addView( )* method must define a *modelChanged( )* method:

```
var myObject = new Object();
myObject.prototype.modelChanged = function (myInformationObject) {
  trace(myInformationObject.event);
};
```

When *modelChanged( )* is called, it receives as an argument an information object whose event property indicates the triggering event. For example, this code detects when the recordset is sorted:

```
// Create a generic object
var myObject = new Object();
// Define a modelChanged( ) handler for the object
myObject.prototype.modelChanged = function (myInformationObject) {
  if (myInformationObject.event == "sort") {
    trace("The recordset was sorted");
  }
};
// Call addView( ) to set myObject.modelChanged( ) as the callback function,
myRecordset_rs.addView(myObject);
```

To demonstrate the functionality, add the code in Example 4-3 to the *RecordSetDebug.as* file that was created earlier. The *showData( )* method from Example 4-2 remains unchanged and should be included in the same *RecordSetDebug.as* file. Example 4-3 traces any change made to the recordset in the Output window (works in the authoring tool only).

Example 4-3. RecordSetDebug.as

```
/////////////////////////////////////////////
// RecordSet.debug
// Purpose: Trace all changes to the recordset or its properties
/////////////////////////////////////////////

// Main public method to debug the recordset. Activate it like this:
//   myRecordset_rs.debug(true);
// Turn it off like this:
//   myRecordset_rs.debug(false);

RecordSet.prototype.debug = function (enabled) {
  if (enabled) {
    if (!this.debugObject)
      this.debugObject = new RecordSetDebugObject(this);
  } else {
    this.debugObject.modelChanged = null;
    this.debugObject = null;
  }
};

// Create a new object that debugs a recordset passed to it
function RecordSetDebugObject (rs) {
  this.init(rs);
}
```

Example 4-3. RecordSetDebug.as (continued)

```
// Class initialization, including the addView( ) method
RecordSetDebugObject.prototype.init = function (rs) {
  this.rs = rs;
  this.rs.addView(this);
};

// This method is called whenever a change is made in a recordset.
// It displays the event and start/end rows affected, as
// well as the RecordSet.showData( ) information
RecordSetDebugObject.prototype.modelChanged = function (info) {
  trace("");
  trace("--Recordset event occurred--");
  trace("Event: " + info.event);
  switch info.event) {
    case("sort"):
      trace("The RecordSet has been sorted.");
      break;
    case("updateAll"):
      trace("The RecordSet has changed in some way")
      break;
    case("addRows"):
      trace("firstRow:" + info.firstRow);
      trace("lastRow:" + info.lastRow);
      trace("Row numbers " + info.firstRow +
        " through " + info.lastRow + " have been added.");
      break;
    case("updateRows"):
      trace("firstRow:" + info.firstRow);
      trace("lastRow:" + info.lastRow);
      trace("Row numbers " + info.firstRow + " through " +
        info.lastRow + " have been changed.");
      break;
    case("deleteRows"):
      trace("firstRow:" + info.firstRow);
      trace("lastRow:" + info.lastRow);
      trace("Row numbers " + info.firstRow + " through " +
        info.lastRow + " have been deleted.");
      break;
    case("allRows"):
      trace("All records have arrived from the server.");
      break;
    case("fetchrows"):
      trace("firstRow:" + info.firstRow);
      trace("lastRow:" + info.lastRow);
      trace("Row numbers " + info.firstRow + " through " +
        info.lastRow + " have been requested from the server.");
      break;
  }
  this.rs.showData(); // Call showData( ) to display the contents
  trace("--End recordset event--");
};
```

You can see that each *RecordSet* event is traced in the *modelChanged( )* method after it occurs. The argument passed to *modelChanged( )* is an object that contains three possible properties:

event
> Name of the event that triggered the handler

firstRow
> First row of the recordset that has changed

lastRow
> Last row of the recordset that has changed

To use the custom *debug( )* and *showData( )* methods, include *RecordSetDebug.as* in your Flash movie:

```
#include "RecordSetDebug.as"
```

Then you can activate debug mode for a *RecordSet* object like this:

```
myRecordset_rs.debug(true);
```

Try it out on some of the earlier examples and you'll see that it traces the changes made to the recordset as well as its contents. For example, upon adding a row to a new empty recordset, like this:

```
var tempRecord = {First:"Tom", Last:"Muck", Email:"tom@tom-muck.com"};
myRecordset_rs.addItem(tempRecord);
```

the Output window displays:

```
--Recordset event occurred--
Event: addRows
firstRow:0
lastRow:0
Row numbers 0 through 0 have been added.
  --Recordset Properties--
Recordset length: 1
Fields: First,Last,Email
Begin records...
First: "Tom"; Last: "Muck"; Email: "tom@tom-muck.com";
End records...
  --End Recordset Properties--
--End recordset event--
```

The removeAll( ) Method

The *removeAll( )* method clears out a *RecordSet* object, leaving a length of 0. The *RecordSet* object still exists with the field name structure in place but with no items in the array. If you use the custom *debug( )* method on the recordset, you can see the length is zero but the field names still exist. To destroy a *RecordSet* object completely, set it equal to null:

```
myRecordset_rs = null;
```

The Timeline

Flash's timeline controls both animation and the order in which events occur in the movie. Flash MX and Flash 2004 use the timeline metaphor, although the latter offers *timeline effects* to simplify common interactions with the timeline for repetitive tasks. Furthermore, Flash Pro offers a screen-based metaphor that helps disguise the underlying timeline for programmers coming from Visual Basic and similar environments. If you are a programmer unfamiliar with the timeline, you can imagine it as a piece of audio tape. When a musician records a song, the various instruments are recorded on different tracks. The guitar might be on one track, the drums on another, the lead vocals on another, and backing vocals on yet another. There might be many separate tracks of music, but as the tape head glides across the final tape, all tracks are played together, making one cohesive collage of sound.

This is similar to how the Flash timeline works, only the tracks are called *layers*, and each layer can contain audio, video, animation, or ActionScript code. Also, playback is not continuous like an audio tape, but more like a motion picture, with individual frames that the playback head displays at a typical rate of 10 to 30 frames per second.

That said, a Flash application that acts as an interface to a dynamic web application might not follow these general principles. The movie might have a static interface with several screens that can be displayed. In these cases, the timeline can be used to break up individual screens of the user interface. Each screen can occupy a frame or several frames in the movie and can be displayed in response to a triggering event.

To give you an example, let's say you have an interface with six main screens: user login, display data, drill down to a detail of the data, update the data, insert new data, and delete the data. Each of these six screens of user interface can each occupy several frames on the timeline with specific starting and ending points. As a particular screen is needed, the playback head can be sent to the starting point on the timeline that begins that particular element, and it will stop at the end of that section. In effect, you have six individual scenes that are meant to be played individually rather than sequentially.

How does the timeline fit into Flash Remoting? Well, the short answer is that it doesn't. All of your Flash Remoting code can be placed into frame 1 of the main timeline (or the first frame following any preloader) so that it executes and initializes when the movie loads. Your remote methods will be available to all other parts of your movie if you do this.

You can place a *stop( )* function in the code to make sure that the movie doesn't begin playing until all of the Flash Remoting initialization code has executed. Your methods and event handlers can all be contained in one central location on one layer in one frame of the timeline. This isn't always necessary or even possible, but it is a goal to shoot for when developing your Flash Remoting application.

 If all of your code is self-contained, you can put it into an external *.as* file and use an #include directive to incorporate it in your Flash movie.

Catching Errors

Error handling is one of the most often overlooked parts of application development. How often have you been to a web page and seen a database error, JavaScript error, connection error, or page not found error? These are examples of errors that are not handled properly. It is up to you to decide how you want to recover from a particular error, but I will show you where the errors can occur in a Flash Remoting application and give you some basic strategies for developing your own error handling.

Error Types

Errors can occur in any aspect of your Flash movie or in the server-side code of a Flash Remoting application. Errors can be broken down into these basic types:

Syntax errors
>   Syntax errors are caused by malformed code (you typed something incorrectly, such as a misplaced comma or quote). If the syntax error is in the client-side code, Flash's Output window generally displays the error when you attempt to compile your *.swf* file. Consult the online help, Chapter 15, or *ActionScript for Flash MX: The Definitive Guide* for the correct syntax for a given command. Although author-time syntax errors are usually easy to find and fix, those that occur because of user input are more difficult to detect. For example, a user entering a single quote into a form field might cause a syntax error in a SQL statement. Server-side syntax errors should be identified by the server-side development environment, although the exact process varies depending on the server technology in use.

Application errors
>   Application errors are general errors in logic. Although the syntax is correct, the code doesn't perform the desired actions accurately. These errors are generally more difficult to detect because they might occur under only specific conditions. These include errors like trying to access an element past the end of an array (such as when using an incorrect index variable). Another common error is using data of the wrong datatype (or trying to perform an invalid operation on a given datatype). For example, if you are trying to add values obtained from user input or XML, which are always strings, you must first convert them to numbers. Flash Remoting can handle native ActionScript datatypes, which reduces this type of error.

Database errors

Errors at the database level can be caused by bad data, bad datatypes, bad user input, or any combination of things that affect your database. For example, a record may be locked because another user is sorting the database. Or a database field may contain invalid data that confuses your application. You can and should validate the data in your ActionScript code whenever possible. For example, you should check whether the entry in a field is empty or out of range before submitting it to the server (although the server-side database may also validate the data). You can minimize potential problems by writing test routines that examine every record in a database for potential errors before deploying your application.

Filesystem errors

Errors can occur when reading to or writing from the hard disk if the permission of a file or folder is not set correctly, or if a file is in use. Another common error is running out of disk space (or, for example, exceeding the allotted space for a local shared object).

Connection errors

Errors in connecting to the Flash movie can occur for many reasons, such as name lookup problems with a DNS server, too many connections on the server, or a misspelled page name inside a web page, database, or Flash movie.

Although the errors themselves can't be eliminated, by adding validation code inside your Flash movie you can recover from the inevitable errors gracefully. Many errors are caused by users using your application in ways that you hadn't anticipated. Perform extensive beta testing and add code to prevent or gracefully handle the errors you discover. An ounce of prevention is worth a pound of cure when it comes to user input. For example, restricting the length and allowed characters in a user input field can eliminate most errors and make it simpler to handle those that occur.

External data, whether coming from user input or a remote server, is a common source of error. That said, server errors are handled quite nicely by Flash Remoting and most of them can be trapped easily inside of your Flash movie.

Trapping Server-Side Errors

An error that is detected is said to be *trapped*. Once an error is trapped, you usually need to handle it in some useful way. For example, if the server is inaccessible, you might automatically try again in several seconds, or you might display a message explaining the problem to the user. Server errors are passed to the Flash movie in the serialized *onStatus* event of a remote call, which triggers an *onStatus* event in the Flash movie, which in turn is handled by the *onStatus( )* method of the responder object or the *methodName_Status( )* function, as described earlier. A *status object*, which you can use to understand and handle the error, is passed to the error handler (either *onStatus( )* or *methodName_Status( )*). In previous examples, I displayed the `description` property of the status object, which contains a human-readable error message, in the Output window or a text field. The complete properties of the status object are shown in Table 4-1.

Table 4-1. Properties of the status object

Property	Contents
code	Text indicating where the error occurred (usually the literal string "SERVER.PROCESSING")
level	The literal string "error"
description	Human-readable description of the error message
details	A stack trace of the error from the server
type	The class name of the error
rootcause	Another error object that has additional information about the cause of the error (available only if a Java servletException is thrown)

Most errors in services should be captured at the server level. That is, you can write your CFML, C#, Java, or other server-side code to detect certain types of errors. After capturing the error on the server, you must decide how to handle the particular error:

- Return an object to the Flash movie to be dealt with in the *onResult( )* method. While this might seem appealing, the Flash movie might not have sufficient knowledge of or control over the server to handle the error effectively.

- Throw a controlled error on the server to pass a code back to the *onStatus( )* method. For example, errors can be indicated by numeric codes, human-readable text, or both. In general, numeric error codes are easiest to deal with programmatically, but human-readable text is most useful for providing information to the user. A *controlled error* is one in which the server returns a more limited or informative error message than is generated by the original error. We explore this option in more detail later in this chapter and in "Handling Errors with try/catch" in Chapter 6.

- Handle the error completely on the server. While this might seem tempting, a one-size-fits-all approach unnecessarily restricts the flexibility of clients that connect to the server. For example, if the server code waits indefinitely for a locked database record to become available, the client-side code won't know what's happening and has no choice but to wait indefinitely for a response. It is often preferable for the server to trap the error, notify the client, and let the client decide how best to proceed. See "Retrying the Query" in Chapter 6 for an example.

Of course, you can leave the error unhandled or even untrapped on the server, which would leave the error trapping and handling up to the Flash movie entirely. Abdicating control over errors that can and should be trapped or handled at the server level is a poor approach because it leads to errors that can't be prevented or detected on the client side.

Of the various options, the most appealing is to trap the error on the server and send a controlled response to the client where specific and appropriate action can be taken. This approach keeps your error-trapping code on the server separate from your responder code on the client. Typically, you would have a try/catch block on the server to capture the error and then use a throw statement to create your own error message to pass back to Flash. This way, you can control how the error appears to the Flash movie. The ColdFusion code in Example 4-4 demonstrates.

Example 4-4. Capturing errors on the server with testError.cfc

```
<cfcomponent>
  <cffunction name="myFunction" access="remote" returntype="string">
    <cfargument name="myArgument" type="string" required="true">
    <cftry>
      <cfquery name="myQuery" datasource="northwind">
       SELECT * FROM Customers WHERE CustomerID = '#myArgument#'
      </cfquery>
      <cfcatch type="database">
        <cfthrow message="Database error">
      </cfcatch>
      <cfcatch type="any">
        <cfthrow message="Other error">
      </cfcatch>
    </cftry>
    <cfif myQuery.recordcount EQ 0>
      <cfthrow message="User not defined">
    </cfif>
    <cfreturn myQuery>
  </cffunction>
</cfcomponent>
```

The corresponding ActionScript code is shown in Example 4-5.

Example 4-5. Responding to server errors in Flash with testError.fla

```
#include "NetServices.as"

var my_conn;        // Connection object
var my_service;     // Service object
// Responder for general service methods
var Responder = new Object();
var myURL = "http://localhost/flashservices/gateway"

// Capture connection errors and attempt connection up to 5 times
Responder.onResult = function (myResults) {
  trace("No errors");
  // put responder code here
};

// General error-handling routing
Responder.onStatus = function (theError) {
```

```
  switch (theError.description) {
    case("HTTP: Failed"):
      trace("Connection error.");
      // In actual practice, send the user to a general error page
      break;
    case("Service threw an exception during method invocation: Database error"):
      trace("There was a database error");
      break;
    case("Service threw an exception during method invocation: Other error"):
      trace("There was an undefined error");
      break;
    case("Service threw an exception during method invocation: User not defined"):
      trace("The user was not found in the database");
      break;
    default:
      trace("There was a general error");
  }
  trace(theError.description);
};

// General connection errors or other errors use the Responder object as well
System.onStatus = Responder.onStatus;

function init( ) {
  NetServices.setDefaultGatewayUrl(myURL);
  my_conn = NetServices.createGatewayConnection( );
  myService = my_conn.getService("com.oreilly.frdg.testError");
}

// Start
init( );

myService.myFunction(Responder,"test");
```

As you can see from the *onStatus( )* function, the error messages returned by the *.cfc* method are trapped in the switch statement. You should handle the errors as you see fit, such as by redirecting the user to a general error page where you display information about the error.

Registering Objects

Flash makes it easy to create code that follows OOP principles. OOP is not the only methodology for writing code, but it fits well with the framework of Flash Remoting. We've been using OOP techniques for many of the ActionScript examples in the book, but up to now we've used ActionScript objects only. What if we could instantiate an object on the client, pass it to the server, manipulate it in some way on the server, and pass it back to the client? This is possible with Flash Remoting.

Using Object.registerClass( )

If you've written Flash applications that use shared objects or extend the *MovieClip* class, you've probably used the *Object.registerClass( )* method. The method allows you to register a specific class by name with ActionScript so that you can utilize the class in your movie simply by using its name:

```
Object.registerClass("MyObjectClass", MyObject);
```

The first argument is the name that you want to associate with the class, and the second argument is the actual class constructor. For the previous example to work, you must first define a class constructor:

```
function MyObject () {
  // Some class initialization code
}
```

This technique is typically used when creating UI components or other objects that inherit from the *MovieClip* class. However, when used with Flash Remoting, *Object. registerClass( )* associates a Flash object in a movie with an object that is returned from the server. This ensures that the return object is deserialized into your Flash movie as an instance of the custom class that we set up.

When you instantiate a class, the various properties and methods of the class are known to the Flash movie and can be used in your ActionScript code. When you pass this object to a remote service, the properties remain intact but the methods of the original class are stripped off. Likewise, a return object is not associated with a custom class by default. Even if the return object contains the same properties as the original object, Flash treats it as a generic object of the *Object* class. The custom methods of the original class are no longer available to the object.

Using *Object.registerClass( )* allows Flash to assign a class identifier (the arbitrary name that we pass to the *Object.registerClass( )* method) to the instance of the class. This identifier is passed along with the object to Flash Remoting and is returned along with any results to the responder's *onResult( )* method. The return object is associated with the class once again when it is deserialized in the Flash movie, thus reinstating the object's methods before being passed to the *onResult( )* method.

This is extremely simple to do using Server-Side ActionScript for your remote methods. You can merely pass the ActionScript object to the remote method, and the return object is automatically recreated as the ActionScript object that originated from your movie. For example, suppose you have a remote method named *computeTimeDifference( )* and a client-side ActionScript class named *TimeDifference*. The remote method can compute the difference between the client time and the server time. The *TimeDifference* object on the client holds the properties date, days, hours, minutes, seconds, and milliseconds and a method named *getTimeDifference( )*. You might have a client-side ActionScript class constructor like the code in Example 4-6.

Example 4-6. Class constructor for the TimeDifference class

```
// Class constructor
function TimeDifference( ) {
  // Initialize the class only if it isn't already initialized
  if (!this.inited)
    this.init( );
}

TimeDifference.prototype.init = function ( ) {
  this.date = new Date( );
  this.days = 0;
  this.hours = 0;
  this.minutes = 0;
  this.seconds = 0;
  this.milliseconds = 0;
  this.inited = true; // Instance is initialized
};

TimeDifference.prototype.getTimeDifference = function ( ) {
  var d = this.days;
  var h = this.hours < 10 ? "0" + this.hours: this.hours;
  var m = this.minutes < 10 ? "0" + this.minutes : this.minutes;
  var s = this.seconds < 10 ? "0" + this.seconds: this.seconds;
  var ms = this.milliseconds < 100 ? "0" + this.milliseconds : this.milliseconds;
  return d + " D " + h + ":" + m + ":" + s + "." + ms;
};

Object.registerClass("TimeDifferenceClass", TimeDifference);
```

The last line of Example 4-6 registers the class. This line is key to the serialization and deserialization of objects in Flash Remoting. If the class is registered, the return object will be deserialized into an object of the same type. Take a look at the rest of the client-side ActionScript code for the Flash Remoting application:

```
var Responder = new Object( ); // Create the responder object

Responder.onResult = function (myResults) {
  trace(myResults.getTimeDifference( ));
};

Responder.onStatus = function (theError) {
  trace(theError.description);
};

if (initialized == null) {
  initialized = true;
  NetServices.setDefaultGatewayUrl("http://localhost/flashservices/gateway");
  my_conn = NetServices.createGatewayConnection( );
  myService = my_conn.getService("com.oreilly.frdg.DebugFunctions", Responder);
}

myService.computeTimeDifference(new TimeDifference( ));
```

The *onResult( )* method here is doing something a little peculiar: it invokes a method on the result from the remote service, as received in the myResults parameter! This is made possible through the registering of the *TimeDifference* class—the remote service attaches properties to the returned object, and the registered class's methods are reattached by reinstantiating the object on the client side. We can reinstantiate the object without losing any of its properties by using an *init( )* method, which is called only if the inited property does not exist, in the constructor:

```
function TimeDifference( ) {
  // Initialize the class only if it isn't already initialized
  if (!this.inited)
    this.init( );
}
```

Now look at the Server-Side ActionScript in Example 4-7.

Example 4-7. Server-Side ActionScript for the computeTimeDifference() method

```
function computeTimeDifference(t) {
  var d = new Date( );
  var e = new Date(t.get("date"));
  var difference = e.getTime( ) - d.getTime( );
  var days = Math.floor(difference/1000/60/60/24);
  difference -= days*1000*60*60*24
  var hours = Math.floor(difference/1000/60/60);
  difference -= hours*1000*60*60
  var minutes = Math.floor(difference/1000/60);
  difference -= minutes*1000*60
  var seconds = Math.floor(difference/1000);
  difference -= seconds*1000
  var milliseconds = difference;
  t.put("days", days);
  t.put("hours", hours);
  t.put("minutes", minutes);
  t.put("seconds", seconds);
  t.put("milliseconds", milliseconds);
  return t;
}
```

The Server-Side ActionScript method takes one argument: a custom object of type *TimeDifference*, named t, that we pass to the method from the Flash movie. The date property of the object (which holds the current time of the client) is extracted with a *get( )* method:

```
var e = new Date(t.get("date"));
```

Then the date is reconstructed as an ActionScript *Date* object and compared to the server date. The days, hours, minutes, seconds, and milliseconds are computed and packed into the *TimeDifference* object using the *put( )* method. The object is then sent back to the Flash movie.

When you run the movie, you should see a result that shows the difference between your server time and the client time in the Output window. If you are using your local machine as the testing server, this difference may be only milliseconds. The results are traced to the Output window using the *TimeDifference.getTimeDifference( )* method:

```
trace(myResults.getTimeDifference( ));
```

This tells us that the Flash movie is taking the results from the remote call and placing them back into an instance of our custom *TimeDifference* class.

To verify that this is happening, try commenting out the last line of the client-side ActionScript by prepending two slashes:

```
// Object.registerClass("TimeDifferenceClass", TimeDifference);
```

If you comment out the line, you can still access all of the properties of the `myResults` parameter, as you can verify by tracing the object's properties in the Output window, but the *getTimeDifference( )* method does not work. That is because without the *registerClass( )* call, the object is treated as a generic object with simple properties but no methods.

Registering Objects for ColdFusion MX, Java, ASP.NET, and PHP

When you're using Server-Side ActionScript, the passing of an object back and forth from client to server is straightforward. In CFML, Java, and ASP.NET, on the other hand, the object needs to be massaged on the server by creating the object and setting the type manually. This is done using the techniques described in the following sections.

ColdFusion MX

Create a serializable object of type *flashgateway.io.ASObject* (i.e., an ActionScript object) in ColdFusion using a <cfobject> tag in CFML or a *CreateObject( )* function within CFScript. The object type should be set to "java" and the class set to "flashgateway.io.ASObject":

```
<cffunction access="remote" name="myMethod" returntype="any">
  <cfobject type="java"
   class="flashgateway.io.ASObject"
   name="myObject"
   action="create" />
  <cfset myInstance = myObject.init( )>
  <cfset myInstance.setType("MyFlashObject") />
  <cfset myInstance.put("inited", 1) />
  <cfreturn myInstance />
</cffunction>
```

A few things about the ColdFusion MX code need explanation. First, the *flashgateway.io.ASObject* datatype needs to be created inside of the function with the <cfobject> tag. This allows the creation of a serializable representation of an ActionScript object. Next, an instance of the object is instantiated with:

```
<cfset myInstance = myObject.init( )>
```

The *init( )* method is not an internal method of the *ASObject* class; it is a built-in ColdFusion construct that initiates a call to the constructor of the class. This is a requirement to create an instance of the object. Next is a call to the *setType( )* method.

```
<cfset myInstance.setType("MyFlashObject") />
```

This procedure associates the custom client-side ActionScript class specified in the call to *Object.registerClass( )* with the server-side *ASObject* datatype. Next, the inited property is set to 1, ColdFusion's equivalent of the Boolean true. The inited property was the custom property that we set in the client-side ActionScript to trick the class constructor into creating the object without clearing out the properties. We could have also used the inited property of the arguments structure, which will be shown in the next example.

Finally, we return the object to Flash. Let's put the concept to use using the Flash movie that was created in Example 4-6. The ColdFusion MX code is shown in Example 4-8 and is commented inline.

Example 4-8. ColdFusion MX remote service DebugFunctions.cfc

```
<cfcomponent>
  <cffunction name="computeTimeDifference" access="remote">
<!--- Create the ActionScript object --->
    <cfobject type="java"
     class="flashgateway.io.ASObject"
     name="myObject"
     action="create">
<!--- Create an instance of the object --->
    <cfset t = myObject.init()>
<!--- Set the type to our custom TimeDifferenceClass for deserialization --->
    <cfset t.setType("TimeDifferenceClass")>
<!--- Do the math for the time difference --->
    <cfset d = now()>
    <cfset e = createodbcdatetime(arguments.date)>
    <cfset difference = DateDiff("s", d, e)>
    <cfif difference LT 0>
      <cfset difference = difference = difference * -1>
    </cfif>
    <cfset days = int(difference/60/60/24)>
    <cfset difference = difference - days*60*60*24>
    <cfset hours = int(difference/60/60)>
    <cfset difference = difference - hours*60*60>
    <cfset minutes = int(difference/60)>
    <cfset seconds = difference - minutes*60>
<!--- Put the properties into the custom object --->
    <cfset t.put("days", #days#)>
    <cfset t.put("hours", #hours#)>
    <cfset t.put("minutes", #minutes#)>
    <cfset t.put("seconds", #seconds#)>
<!--- Set the inited property to the inited property of the object
      passed to this method --->
    <cfset t.put("inited", arguments.inited)>
```

Example 4-8. ColdFusion MX remote service DebugFunctions.cfc (continued)

```
<!--- Finally, return the object --->
    <cfreturn t />
  </cffunction>
</cfcomponent>
```

You can name this file *DebugFunctions.cfc* and put it into the *webroot\com\oreilly\frdg* directory. The Flash movie created earlier in Example 4-6 will work with this service with no change. Notice this line:

```
<cfset t.setType("TimeDifferenceClass")>
```

This line sets up the class type so that when it is returned to the Flash movie it will be deserialized into our custom *TimeDifference* class.

The same service can be written using CFScript, as shown in Example 4-9. The CFScript version uses a *CreateObject( )* function rather than a <cfobject> tag.

Example 4-9. The DebugFunctions.cfc file using CFScript instead of CFML

```
<cfcomponent>
  <cffunction name="computeTimeDifference" access="remote">
    <cfscript>
    myObject = CreateObject("java", "flashgateway.io.ASObject");
    t = myObject.init();
    t.setType("TimeDifferenceClass");
    d = now();
    e = createodbcdatetime(arguments.date);
    difference = DateDiff("s", d, e);
    if (difference LT 0) {difference = difference * -1;}
    days = int(difference/60/60/24);
    difference = difference - days*60*60*24;
    hours = int(difference/60/60);
    difference = difference - hours*60*60;
    minutes = int(difference/60);
    seconds = difference - minutes*60;
    t.put("days", #days#);
    t.put("hours", #hours#);
    t.put("minutes", #minutes#);
    t.put("seconds", #seconds#);
    t.put("inited", arguments.inited);
    return t;
    </cfscript>
  </cffunction>
</cfcomponent>
```

Java

You saw in the ColdFusion version of the remote service that we were creating an instance of a Java class that allowed the serialization of the data into a copy of our ActionScript object. The Java class is also used in the Java version of the code, shown in Example 4-10.

Example 4-10. Java version of the service named DebugFunctions.java

```java
// Java Document
package com.oreilly.frdg;
import flashgateway.io.*;
import flashgateway.util.*;
import java.util.*;
import java.lang.*;
import java.io.Serializable;

public class DebugFunctions {
  public DebugFunctions( ) {
  }
  public ASObject computeTimeDifference (ASObject t) {
    Date d = new Date( );
    Date e = (Date)t.get("date");
    double difference = (double)e.getTime( ) - (double)d.getTime( );
    difference = Math.abs(difference);
    int days = (int)(Math.floor(difference/1000/60/60/24));
    difference -= days*1000*60*60*24;
    int hours = (int)(Math.floor(difference/1000/60/60));
    difference -= hours*1000*60*60;
    int minutes = (int)Math.floor(difference/1000/60);
    difference -= minutes*1000*60;
    int seconds = (int)Math.floor(difference/1000);
    difference -= seconds*1000;
    int milliseconds = (int)difference;
    String daysStr = String.valueOf(days);
    String hoursStr = String.valueOf(hours);
    String minutesStr = String.valueOf(minutes);
    String secondsStr = String.valueOf(seconds);
    String millisecondsStr = String.valueOf(milliseconds);
    t.put("days",  daysStr);
    t.put("hours", hoursStr);
    t.put("minutes", minutesStr);
    t.put("seconds", secondsStr);
    t.put("milliseconds", millisecondsStr);
    return t;
  }
}
```

The Java code uses the *ASObject* class, just as the ColdFusion version did. In the *computeTimeDifference( )* method, an *ASObject* (ActionScript object) was passed to the method, and the method returns the same *ASObject*:

```java
public ASObject computeTimeDifference (ASObject t) {
```

Again, the methods of the client-side ActionScript object passed to the remote method are not accessible through Java, but the properties can be read with the *get( )* method of the *ASObject* and they can be written using the *put( )* method.

The Java class should be compiled and placed in the classpath of your application server. It will be used by the Flash movie created in Example 4-6.

When using the *flashgateway.io.ASObject* class, you need to put the *flashgateway.jar* file in your application's classpath; otherwise, you might get an error such as "Service threw an exception during method invocation: flashgateway/io/ASObject".

 Even if Flash Remoting is working on your server, your application may not have access to the *flashgateway* classes unless you explicitly add the path of the *flashgateway.jar* file to your application. If you are going to be using the *ASObject*, you need access to these classes.

ASP.NET

The ASP.NET version of Flash Remoting also allows the use of the *ASObject* class from the *FlashGateway.IO* assembly. Just as in the ColdFusion and Java versions, the *TimeDifference* object is passed into the method, the time difference is computed, and the properties are packed back into an ActionScript object, which is passed back to the Flash movie. The C# code is listed in Example 4-11.

Example 4-11. C# class for computeTimeDifference( )

```csharp
// C# Document
using System;
using FlashGateway.IO;

namespace com.oreilly.frdg {
  public class DebugFunctions {
    //protected FlashGateway.Flash Flash;
    public DebugFunctions( ) {
    }
    public ASObject computeTimeDifference (ASObject t) {
      // Set the type of the ActionScript object
      t.ASType = "TimeDifferenceClass";
      DateTime d = DateTime.UtcNow;
      DateTime e = (DateTime)t["date"];
      TimeSpan tsDuration;
      // Use an absolute value for the time difference
      tsDuration = DateTime.Compare(d, e) < 0 ? e - d : d - e;
      t["days"] = tsDuration.Days;
      t["hours"] = tsDuration.Hours;
      t["minutes"] = tsDuration.Minutes;
      t["seconds"] = tsDuration.Seconds;
      t["milliseconds"] = tsDuration.Milliseconds;
      t["serverDate"] = d;
      return t;
    }
  }
}
```

PHP

The PHP implementation of Flash Remoting (AMFPHP) also contains the functionality required to pass an ActionScript object from the client to the server and back again. Using PHP, you simply set up the name of the custom class in the returns element in the methodTable for the method used, as shown in Example 4-12. The AMFPHP gateway handles the serialization and deserialization of the custom object.

Example 4-12. Utilizing the custom computeTimeDifference() method in PHP

```php
<?php
class DebugFunctions {
  function DebugFunctions () {
    $this->methodTable = array(
      "computeTimeDifference" => array(
      "description" => "Returns an instance of TimeDifferenceClass (Custom Class)",
      "access" => "remote", // available values are private, public, remote
      "roles" => "role, list", // currently inactive
      "arguments" => array ("t"),
      "returns" => "TimeDifferenceClass" // name of Custom Class
      )
    );
  }
  function computeTimeDifference ($t) {
    $d = time();
    $e = $t["date"] / 1000 // PHP date is in seconds;
    $difference = ($d <= $e) ? ($e - $d) : ($d - $e);
    $days = floor($difference/60/60/24);
    $difference -= $days*60*60*24;
    $hours = floor($difference/60/60);
    $difference -= $hours*60*60;
    $minutes = floor($difference/60);
    $difference -= $minutes*60;
    $seconds = floor($difference);
    $t["days"] = $days;
    $t["hours"] = $hours;
    $t["minutes"] = $minutes;
    $t["seconds"] = $seconds;
    return $t;
  }
}
?>
```

The Real Power of Object.registerClass( )

You've seen ActionScript objects on the client be passed to the server and back again. This should give you a feel for what is possible with Flash Remoting. When you consider that an ActionScript object can be as simple or as complex as you make it, you will start to appreciate the power of this technique. Imagine an initialization script that loads recordset data into 10 drop-down lists in your Flash movie. This can be done with 10 calls to remote methods, or it can be accomplished with one complex ActionScript object where each recordset is a property of the object. That way, you can make just one remote call, as shown in the following imaginary object:

```
function MyInitObject () {
  if (!this.inited) this.init();
}
MyInitObject.prototype.init = function () {
  this.clients = new RecordSet(["ClientName", "ClientID"]);
  this.states = new RecordSet(["State", "StateAbrev"]);
  this.products = new RecordSet(["ProductID", "ProductName", "ProductDesc"]);
  this.categories = new RecordSet(["CatID", "CatDesc"]);
  this.colors = new RecordSet(["ColorID", "Color"]);
  this.shoppingCart = new RecordSet(["ProductID", "Quantity", "UnitPrice"]);
};
var currentCart = new MyInitObject();
```

Application performance can be improved dramatically by caching server-side recordsets and reducing the remote calls using *Object.registerClass( )*.

The technique is now in your hands. How you use it is up to you.

Wrapping Up

In this chapter, we've covered a lot of ground. You learned about the *NetServices* class in depth and how the *NetConnection* object and *NetServices* are related. You also learned how to create responder functions in several different ways. The *Record-Set* object was explored in greater depth, and client-side recordsets were introduced as well. Basic error-handling techniques were covered as they relate to responder objects.

One of the best features of Flash Remoting is the ability to transfer ActionScript objects between the client and server, keeping the properties and methods of that object. This functionality was explored using each of the server technologies that Flash Remoting supports.

The next five chapters cover the server-side languages individually. This will allow us to go into greater detail about the implementation of services in each of the languages and also allow us to explore the strengths of each of the technologies as they relate to Flash Remoting. We'll begin with the server-side technology that is best supported by Flash Remoting—ColdFusion—in Chapter 5.

The Server-Side Languages

Part II covers the server-side languages that Flash can communicate with via Flash Remoting. Individual chapters cover Remoting in conjunction with ColdFusion, Server-Side ActionScript, Java, ASP.NET, and PHP. You should at least skim all the chapters, even for languages you don't intend to use, because they contain useful information that pertains to multiple environments.

- Chapter 5, *Flash Remoting and ColdFusion MX*
- Chapter 6, *Server-Side ActionScript*
- Chapter 7, *Flash Remoting and Java*
- Chapter 8, *Flash Remoting and .NET*
- Chapter 9, *Flash Remoting and PHP*

Flash Remoting and ColdFusion MX

Flash Remoting is supported on a number of different platforms, but perhaps the best supported, simplest, and most popular platform for Flash Remoting is ColdFusion MX. The ColdFusion MX server provides you with three primary means for implementing the server-side portion of your Flash applications:

1. ColdFusion Markup Language (CFML) pages
2. ColdFusion Components (CFCs)
3. Server-Side ActionScript

This chapter covers CFML and CFCs in detail, while Chapter 6 covers Server-Side ActionScript. Additionally, this chapter examines the fundamental differences between using ColdFusion pages and ColdFusion Components, and how their advantages and disadvantages should influence your application architecture.

Introduction to ColdFusion MX

ColdFusion is a tag-based language, built as an extension to HTML. It is designed for simplicity of use and rapid application development. The ColdFusion programmer can create complex business logic using a few simple tags.

ColdFusion tags and their attributes implement commonly needed functionality. These attributes can be likened to the properties of an object. For example, a <cfmail> tag has to, from, and subject attributes. When the ColdFusion application server sees a <cfmail> tag, it sends an email according to the specified attributes. It's that simple.

ColdFusion MX is written in Java and runs as a Java servlet. The ColdFusion application server is a page preprocessor. User requests are passed from the web server to the ColdFusion Server. Tags in the page are executed sequentially. The first time the page is accessed on the Web, the page is compiled into a Java servlet. Each access after that benefits from the speed of compiled code.

ColdFusion Components are the closest thing in ColdFusion to the concept of object-oriented programming. With a CFC, you have a self-contained object containing methods that can be called by other ColdFusion pages, CFCs, or Flash applications. They can also act as web services to allow virtually any consumer of web services to access their methods. CFCs as they relate to Flash don't follow the concept of instantiation; when you call a CFC, you are calling a *static object*. CFCs support the notion of an instance of a CFC, but this involves the use of the session or application scope, which is not accessible from Flash.

 While CFC instances are not accessible to Flash, you can create other CFCs that act as *wrapper objects*, allowing the use of session or application instances of other CFCs.

How ColdFusion Fits into Flash Applications

I like to think of *remote services* (services provided by a computer other than the computer the client is running on) as extensions of the client. In fact, once you get used to incorporating a server-side aspect to your Flash applications—and especially once you have a library of reusable services in place—it is difficult to think of application development without integrating server-side functionality.

Writing services in ColdFusion provides some nice options to Flash application developers. ColdFusion is simple enough to allow the Flash developer to also write the remote services that his application needs. Alternatively, projects can be organized to create more of a division between remote services and the client code that uses them. One team of developers can provide various remote services, such as database interaction or email capability, while another team builds the front end of the application that makes use of those services.

Regardless of who on the team does the work, you should divide your application or set of services into presentation logic and business logic. *Business logic* is the rules and workflow that model your enterprise. Code that handles account creation or credit card transactions is an example of business logic. *Presentation logic* is the portion of your application that presents data to the user and allows for interactivity. Code that allows users to drag items into a shopping cart or display error messages is an example of presentation logic. Flash is an excellent choice for developing and deploying sophisticated presentation logic that allows for a high degree of interaction and contains rich, compelling content. ColdFusion MX is a fitting choice for business logic implementation because of its ease-of-use, versatility, and seamless integration with Flash.

To successfully implement an application or service using two different technologies, we need an efficient way for the two technologies to communicate, which in the programming world usually means passing objects and other forms of data back and forth. The basis for communication between Flash and ColdFusion is, of course, Flash Remoting. Figure 5-1 demonstrates the relationship between Flash and Cold-Fusion in the context of an integrated application.

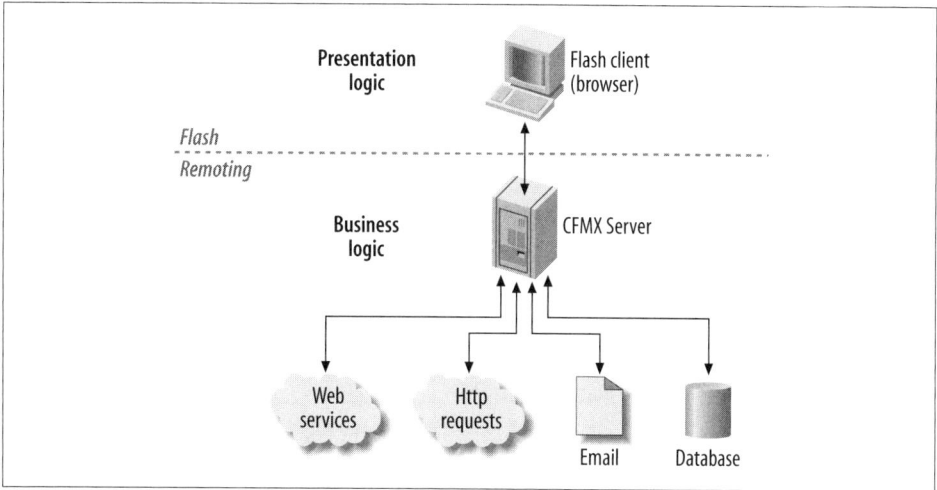

Figure 5-1. The relationship between Flash, ColdFusion, and Flash Remoting

Datatype Conversions

Before we get into examples of how data can be passed back and forth between Flash and ColdFusion, let's take some time to examine how datatypes are handled between client-side ActionScript code and server-side ColdFusion. In other words, as objects and primitive datatypes are passed from client to server and vice versa, how do those datatypes change?

Datatypes in Flash

Flash supports both primitive datatypes and reference datatypes (also called *composite* or *complex* datatypes). *Primitive datatypes*, such as *string*, *number*, and *boolean* have distinctive characteristics:

- They contain a single data value.
- Primitive datatypes are *passed by value*, meaning that when they are passed as parameters to a function, a copy of the value of the data is passed, not a reference to the data. The value of a primitive datatype in a calling routine cannot be changed from within the called routine.
- Making a copy of a primitive datatype and then changing its value does not change the value of the original variable.

Reference datatypes, such as *Object*, *Array*, *RecordSet*, and *MovieClip*, have the following characteristics:

- They do not contain data themselves; rather, they contain references to objects that usually contain data and functions. They point to a place in memory where the data of interest resides.

- Attributes or elements of a reference datatype can change without changing the fact that a variable can refer to the object's or array's container. For example, you might have a reference to an object with a certain set of properties, and those properties are free to change while you maintain a reference to that object. Likewise, adding or deleting elements from an array doesn't change the fact that a variable might refer to the array.

- Making a copy of a reference datatype generally creates another reference to the datatype in memory (similar to the way that creating a Windows shortcut or Macintosh alias doesn't create a new filename but rather points to an existing file).

- Reference datatypes are generally *passed by reference*, meaning that when they are passed as parameters to a function, changes made to the data within the called routine may affect the data in the calling routine as well.

The *null* and *undefined* datatypes are used to indicate the absence of a value or reference.

Datatypes in ColdFusion

Although ColdFusion uses different terminology, ColdFusion datatypes are very similar to ActionScript datatypes. ColdFusion uses the term *simple* (as opposed to *primitive*) to describe datatypes that can contain a single value, such as *numbers*, *strings*, and *booleans*.

Since ColdFusion does not support objects to the extent that ActionScript does, it does not support an exact equivalent of Flash's reference datatypes. However, ColdFusion does have a collection of complex datatypes (a.k.a. *data containers* or *data structures*), such as *arrays*, *queries*, and *structures*, that contain data that can change.

ColdFusion also supports a *binary* datatype, which handles the contents of things like image files or MP3s, and an *external object* datatype that is used for things like Java objects. These two datatypes cannot be returned to a Flash application.

Passing data between Flash and ColdFusion

Even though datatypes are similar between Flash and ColdFusion, some differences must be accounted for when passing data back and forth. Table 5-1 shows datatype conversions between Flash and ColdFusion.

Table 5-1. Datatype conversions between ActionScript and ColdFusion

Flash (ActionScript)	ColdFusion
ActionScript object	Struct (or ASObject)
Array	Array
Associative array	Struct
Boolean	Boolean

Table 5-1. Datatype conversions between ActionScript and ColdFusion (continued)

Flash (ActionScript)	ColdFusion
Date	Date
Number	Number
RecordSet	Query object
String	String
Undefined	Null
XML	XML document
Null	Null

As you can see, there is a close correlation between ActionScript and ColdFusion datatypes. This helps to make integration of the two technologies virtually seamless. The Flash Remoting gateway does the work of converting the objects from ColdFusion into ActionScript and back again.

Flash Variable Scope

ColdFusion supports the Flash variable scope, which is used primarily when ColdFusion pages are accessed as remote services. The Flash scope is used like other variable scopes in ColdFusion, such as URL, Session, and Request. For example, Flash.Result is the Result variable of the Flash scope.

> For ColdFusion pages, the Flash scope is the only way to pass data to and from the service. Although the Flash scope can also be used with services built as CFCs, the recommended approach is to receive arguments using the <cfargument> tag and return data using the <cfreturn> tag.

There are three built-in variables in the Flash scope to pass data to and from the Flash movie:

Flash.Params
: An array of parameters passed from the Flash movie

Flash.Result
: A return object that is passed back to the Flash movie from the ColdFusion page

Flash.Pagesize
: The number of records to return from a <cfquery> to the Flash movie

The Params variable is an array of arguments passed to your remote service call. They have to be accessed in your ColdFusion page by number, starting with 1 as ColdFusion arrays do. For example, if you call a method from your client-side ActionScript:

```
var first="Tom";
var last="Muck";
```

```
var email="tom@tom-muck.com";
myService.saveEmployeeRecord(first, last, email);
```

you can access the arguments on the ColdFusion page like this:

```
<cfset first = Flash.Params[1]>
<cfset last = Flash.Params[2]>
<cfset email = Flash.Params[3]>
```

You can also use the `Flash` variable scope to access named elements of an Action-Script object. The shorthand way of creating an object in Flash is to use an object literal, where each name/value pair has the syntax *label:value*:

```
var first="Tom";
var last="Muck";
var email="tom@tom-muck.com";
myService.saveEmployeeRecord({first:first, last:last, email:email});
```

Again, you could access the variables in ColdFusion using the `Flash` scope:

```
<cfset first = Flash.first>
<cfset last = Flash.last>
<cfset email = Flash.email>
```

The `Flash.Result` variable is used to return results from the service to the Flash movie. In a ColdFusion page, unlike the CFC services that we built in earlier examples, `Flash.Result` is the only way to return a parameter to the Flash movie. This variable can contain any type of result, such as a struct, recordset, string, or Boolean. Simply setting the `Flash.Result` variable triggers the return of the parameter to the Flash movie.

Service Name Mappings

The different types of services that ColdFusion supports are referenced in different ways from the client when calling *NetConnection.getService( )*. For example, you must reference a service implemented as a ColdFusion page differently than a ColdFusion Component. Table 5-2 shows how different types of services should be referenced using *getService( )*.

Table 5-2. How to reference remote services in ColdFusion

Service type	Name of service	Name of remote function
ColdFusion page	The directory that the ColdFusion page (*.cfm* file) resides in, expressed in dot notation	The name of the ColdFusion page that you want to invoke in the specified directory
ColdFusion Component	The entire path to the ColdFusion Component (*.cfc* component file) from the web root, expressed in dot notation	The name of the function in the specified *.cfc* file
Server-Side ActionScript	The full path to the SSAS file (*.asr* file) from the web root, expressed in dot notation	The name of the function in the specified *.asr* file

Order of Service Lookup

In order to adapt to a variety of software architectures and personal preferences, ColdFusion supports Flash Remoting services implemented in a few different ways. You can write your remote services as ColdFusion pages, ColdFusion Components, or Server-Side ActionScript. When the Flash client references a remote service on the ColdFusion Server, ColdFusion looks up the service on the server and invokes it, returning the result to the Flash client. Flash Remoting looks for services in this order:

1. ColdFusion page (*.cfm* or *.cfml*)
2. ColdFusion Component (*.cfc*)
3. Server-Side ActionScript (*.asr*)

 ColdFusion Components can also be used to create web services that can be accessed with Flash Remoting, as covered in Chapter 10.

Now that we have covered some of the fundamentals of Flash Remoting with Cold-Fusion, let's look at some more specific elements of Flash and ColdFusion integration.

Invoking a ColdFusion Page Service from Flash

To invoke a ColdFusion page from a Flash application, follow these steps:

1. Set the gateway URL.
2. Create a connection object using *NetServices.createGatewayConnection( )*.
3. Create a service object by invoking *getService( )* on the connection object obtained in Step 2. The service path includes the directory name, but not the *.cfm* page name.
4. Invoke the page as a method of the service object obtained in Step 3. (That is, use the page name, without the *.cfm* extension, as the method name.)

The first two steps should be very familiar by now:

```
NetServices.setDefaultGatewayUrl("http://localhost/flashservices/gateway");
var myConnection_conn = NetServices.createGatewayConnection();
```

To create the service object in Step 3, specify the service name in the call to *getService( )*. The service name is the name of the directory containing the *.cfm* file (relative to the web root), substituting dots for slashes, but it does not include the *.cfm* file's name. For example, to invoke a *.cfm* page called *sendEmail.cfm* located in the directory *wwwroot/com/oreilly/frdg/Email*, create a reference to the service, as follows:

```
var emailService = myConnection_conn.getService("com.oreilly.frdg.Email", this);
```

Use the *.cfm* page name (without the extension) as the remote function name. The following code invokes the *sendEmail.cfm* ColdFusion page:

```
emailService.sendEmail( );
```

 The name of the ColdFusion page is not case-sensitive on a Windows server, so *emailService.sendEmail( )* works as well as *emailService.Send-Email( )*. However, it is good practice to use the correct case in your code for compatibility with Unix servers.

You can send as many arguments to the *sendEmail.cfm* page as you want:

```
emailService.sendEmail(toAddress, fromAddress, subject, body);
```

Using the Flash variable scope to pass data between Flash and a ColdFusion page

To access the arguments passed from Flash, use the `Flash.Params` variable within your ColdFusion page. `Flash.Params` is an array containing sequentially numbered elements, one for each argument passed in from the Flash application.

 Unlike ActionScript arrays, which start from 0, ColdFusion arrays start from 1.

For example, the following ColdFusion code accesses the four variables passed into the *sendEmail.cfm* page from Flash:

```
<cfmail to="#Flash.Params[1]#" from="#Flash.Params[2]#"
 subject="#Flash.Params[3]#">
 #Flash.Params[4]#
</cfmail>
```

 In ColdFusion, you can use variables as tag attributes without using pound signs (#). If the variables are not being used as attributes, or if you use quotes around the variables, you have to use pound signs.

Therefore, the preceding example could be written as:

```
<cfmail to=Flash.Params[1] from=Flash.Params[2]
subject=Flash.Params[3]>
 #Flash.Params[4]#
</cfmail>
```

Using named parameters to pass data from a Flash application to a ColdFusion page

Instead of passing ordered arguments to a ColdFusion page, you can also attach properties to an object and pass that object to your remote function. Any properties attached to the object become *named arguments* to the function. This example passes the `to`, `from`, `subject`, and `body` arguments as named arguments:

```
var args = new Object();
args.to = toAddress;
args.from = fromAddress;
args.subject = subject;
args.body = body;
emailService.sendEmail(args);
```

You can express the same thing in a more succinct manner using an object literal:

```
emailService.sendEmail(
    {to:toAddress, from:fromAddress, subject:subject, body:body});
```

To access named arguments on the server, treat the Flash variable as though it were a structure:

```
<cfmail to=Flash.to
 from=Flash.from
 subject=Flash.subject>
#Flash.body#
</cfmail>
```

You can also use the attribute name inside of single quotes within brackets. Don't forget to use pound signs and double quotes to surround each element, as follows:

```
<cfmail to="#Flash['to']#"
 from="#Flash['from']#"
 subject="#Flash['subject']#">
#Flash['body']#
</cfmail>
```

Because named arguments are accessed by property name and not by order, the preceding ColdFusion examples work even if the arguments are attached to the object in a different order, such as:

```
emailService.sendEmail(
    {subject:subject, from:fromAddress, to:toAddress, body:body});
```

Returning data to Flash from a ColdFusion page

Returning data from a ColdFusion page to Flash is as simple as assigning the return value to the Flash.Result variable. For example, to return the string "Email sent!" to the Flash client making the remote call, use the following code:

```
<cfset Flash.Result="Email sent!" />
```

As soon as the variable is defined, the data is returned to the client.

> Remember, you can also return complex objects like *Arrays*, *Structs*, *Dates*, *Queries* and *XML* objects to the Flash client.

Example 5-1 shows the complete CF code, including some basic error handling and sending a return value. You can save the file in the remote services directory *webroot\ com\oreilly\frdg\cfpages* under the name *sendEmail.cfm*.

Example 5-1. ColdFusion code for the remote service sendEmail.cfm

```
<cftry>
  <cfmail to = Flash.to
    from = Flash.from
    subject = Flash.subject>
#flash.body#
  </cfmail>
  <cfcatch type="Any">
    <cfthrow message = "There was an error">
  </cfcatch>
</cftry>
<cfset Flash.Result = "Email sent">
```

The corresponding client-side ActionScript code is shown in Example 5-2. It assumes that a MessageBox component (from the Macromedia UI Components Set 2) named status_mb is available to display messages upon a successful send or an error. It assumes that the movie has text fields named to_txt, from_txt, subject_txt, and body_txt and containing appropriate text. The final *sendEmail.fla* file can be downloaded from the online Code Depot.

Example 5-2. ActionScript code for sendEmail.fla

```
#include "NetServices.as"

var my_conn;         // Connection object
var emailService;    // Service object
var myURL = "http://localhost/flashservices/gateway";
// Responder for general service methods
function Responder () {
  this.onResult = function (myResults) {
    if (myResults == null)
      myResults = "Email sent!";
    status_mb._visible = true;
    status_mb.setMessage(myResults);
  };

  this.onStatus = function (theError) {
    status_mb._visible = true;
    status_mb.setMessage(theError.description);
    System.onStatus = this.onStatus;
  };
}

// Close the message box when OK is clicked
status_mb.setCloseHandler("closeBox");
function closeBox () {
  status_mb.visible = false;
}

// Initialize Flash Remoting
function init () {
  initialized = true;
```

Example 5-2. ActionScript code for sendEmail.fla (continued)

```
  NetServices.setDefaultGatewayUrl(myURL);
  my_conn = NetServices.createGatewayConnection( );
  emailService = my_conn.getService("com.oreilly.frdg.cfpages");
}

init( );

// Send the email when the send_pb button is clicked
send_pb.setClickHandler("send");

function send ( ) {
  var args     = new Object( );
  args.to      = to_txt.text;
  args.from    = from_txt.text;
  args.subject = subject_txt.text;
  args.body    = body_txt.text;
  // Call the service, passing the responder and then the arguments
  emailService.sendEmail(new Responder( ), args);
}
```

Flash Remoting Services as ColdFusion Components

Writing Flash Remoting services as ColdFusion pages is relatively quick and easy. However, ColdFusion pages primarily are designed to return dynamic HTML to web browsers, as opposed to providing generic services to a variety of clients. ColdFusion Components (CFCs), on the other hand, are specifically designed to provide services to various clients.

The theory behind ColdFusion Components

CFCs are loosely modeled after Java objects and should be designed and written with many of the same principles in mind. The objective of a CFC should be to provide well-encapsulated functionality to a variety of clients. *Encapsulation* refers to a service's ability to provide functionality to a client without exposing anything about the implementation behind the functionality.

For example, consider a CFC called *UserServices.cfc*, containing a function called *createUser( )*, which takes several arguments pertaining to typical user data and returns a numeric key that is associated with the new user. To clients invoking *createUser( )*, it is not apparent whether the user information is written to a database or saved in a text file. In theory, the client shouldn't care even if the implementation behind *createUser( )* changes completely, as long is it continues to take the same arguments and return a numeric key.

Now, consider an implementation of *createUser( )* that requires database connection parameters to be passed to the method in addition to user information. If the implementation of *createUser( )* changes to use text files, clients must change their code to pass in a file path rather than database connection parameters. It's easy to see how small changes can require changes elsewhere in an application, requiring rewriting and retesting the code.

CFCs can be invoked from Flash, ColdFusion pages, and even other CFCs. Since CFCs are typically *client-agnostic* (they don't care what type of client invokes them), it is important that their implementations be kept free of client-specific code. For example, if you were to access arguments passed into the CFC through the Flash variable scope, your CFC couldn't be called successfully from a ColdFusion page or another CFC. Conversely, if your CFC used the <cfoutput> tag to return HTML, it would no longer be usable from Flash. For that reason, it is also advisable not to use constructs such as session or application variables in your CFCs, as that breaks the encapsulation of the component functionality.

The other primary goal of a CFC should be code re-use. Whenever you find yourself implementing the same logic in more than one place in your code, you should consider abstracting the logic into a CFC. Once your CFC properly encapsulates your logic, you can reuse it from anywhere, including different applications and different types of clients.

Additionally, CFCs support *inheritance*, which means you can "layer" your CFC to get the most functionality out of the fewest lines of code. Multiple layers of abstraction allow you to maintain code in a single location, and they also allow you to change the implementation behind certain services without having to rewrite every client that depends on that CFC.

For example, let's say you create a component method called *getUsStates( )* that returns a *Query* object with the names and abbreviations of all the U.S. states. The logic is generic enough that it could be used by multiple clients or applications without concern for whether the list of states is hardcoded or stored in a text file or database. As long as the CFC's interface never changes, none of the applications or clients calling *getUsStates( )* need to change. Let's explore how ColdFusion provides everything you need to keep your CFC generic and well-encapsulated.

The structure of ColdFusion Components

As you can see from the following general structure of a CFC, the component is wrapped in a single <cfcomponent> tag containing any number of nested <cffunction> tags or inline ColdFusion code:

```
<cfcomponent extends="superComponent" displayName="displayName">
  <cffunction name="functionName"
   returnType="dataTypeToReturn"
   roles="securityRole"
   access="clientAccess"
   output="trueOrFalse"
   hint="functionHint "
   description="functionDescription">
    <cfargument name="variableName"
```

```
          type="argumentDataType"
          required="trueOrFalse"
          default="defaultValue"
          description="argumentDescription"/>
      <!--- Component implementation here --->
      <cfreturn dataToReturn />
    </cffunction>
    <cffunction name="anotherFunction">
      <!---body of function --->
    </cffunction>
  </cfcomponent>
```

Any code that is not contained in a function is executed whenever the component is called. Your CFC needs to be stored in a file with a *.cfc* extension, which must reside in or below your web root.

The <cfcomponent> tag

Table 5-3 describes the possible attributes of a <cfcomponent> tag.

Table 5-3. Attributes of the ColdFusion <cfcomponent> tag

Attribute name	Type	Required	Description	Possible values
extends	string	No	Indicates another CFC that the current component inherits functionality from	Any local CFC name
displayName	string	No	Descriptive name used for self-documentation	An arbitrary description
hint	string	No	Display hint for Dreamweaver MX, CFC Explorer, or other introspection mechanism	Any descriptive hint
output	string	No	Specifies whether to suppress output from the component	"yes" or "no"

When a component *extends* another component, it inherits the properties and functions from the component it is extending. When structuring your CFC, remember that any functions or properties a component inherits from its parent must be just as valid for the inheriting component as it is for the parent. Any component that extends another component should be a *subclass*, or a more specific version, of the component it is extending.

For example, let's say you've written an ecosystem simulation using a component called *PrayingMantis.cfc* with the functions *getLegCount( )* and *getPrimaryDiet( )*. You decide that your simulation needs a grasshopper, so you create *Grasshopper.cfc* and add *getLegCount( )* and *getPrimaryDiet( )* functions to it. Although praying mantises and grasshoppers have different diets, they both have six legs. Rather than duplicating *getLegCount( )* in two places, you create a third component called *Insect.cfc* that contains the function *getLegCount( )*. Any function or property that is common to all insects goes in *Insect.cfc*, while functionality specific to one type of insects should go in a subclass of *Insect.cfc*. Even if you have 20 different types of insects inheriting from *Insect.cfc*, you need to write the code only once. And if entomologists discover they have been miscounting all these years and insects actually have seven legs, you only have to change the *getLegCount( )* function in a single location to automatically change your entire insect collection.

The <cffunction> tag

Table 5-4 describes the possible attributes of a <cffunction> tag.

Table 5-4. Attributes of the <cffunction> tag

Attribute name	Type	Required	Description	Possible values
name	string	Yes	The name of function, which is the name by which it will be invoked	Any valid string
returnType[a]	string	No	The datatype of the value returned by the component	"any", "array", "binary", "boolean", "component name", "date", "guid", "numeric", "query", "string", "struct", "uuid", "variable name", "void", "xml"
access	string	No	Indicates what type of clients have access to the function	"public", "private", "package", or "remote"
roles	string	No	Indicates security roles for this function	Any valid user role
output	string	No	Indicates whether output from the component is written back to the client	"yes" or "no"
hint	string	No	Usage hint for self-documentation	Any string hint
description	string	No	Displayed when introspecting components, such as while browsing remote services from the Flash authoring environment	Any string description

[a] Use "void" when there is no return value and use "any" when returning an object of type *ASObject*.

The access attribute of the <cffunction> tag determines what type of clients can access your component functions. It has four possible values:

"public"
  Function is available to all local pages or other CFCs

"private"
  Function is available only to other functions in the same CFC

"package"
  Function is available only to CFCs in the same directory, including the CFC in which the function is declared

"remote"
  Function can be invoked remotely (access must be "remote" to work with Flash Remoting)

Roles are discussed in detail later in this chapter in the section "Using Role-Based Security with ColdFusion Components."

The <cfargument> tag

Table 5-5 describes the possible attributes of a <cfargument> tag.

Table 5-5. Attributes of the <cfargument> tag

Attribute name	Type	Required	Description	Possible values
name	string	Yes	The argument's variable name	Any valid variable name
type[a]	string	No	The argument's datatype	"any", "array", "binary", "boolean", "component name", "date", "guid", "numeric", "query", "string", "struct", "uuid", "variable name", "xml"
required	Boolean	No	Whether the argument is required	"yes" or "no" (defaults to "no")
default	string	No	A default value if argument it is not defined	Any value valid for the argument's datatype
description	string	No	Displayed when browsing remote services from the Flash authoring environment	Any string description

[a] Use "any" when passing an object of type *ASObject* to the function.

An argument whose required attribute is "yes" must be passed in at the time the function is invoked (unless the default attribute is also specified); otherwise, the function invocation fails. In the case of Flash Remoting, the responder object's *onStatus( )* method is called with an error object indicating which arguments were missing.

Organizing ColdFusion Components using packages

The directory structure you use to organize your CFCs is called a *package structure*. Packages are useful for grouping files in logical ways. For example, I might put the *PrayingMantis.cfc* and *Grasshopper.cfc* files discussed earlier in the directory *webroot\com\oreilly\frdg\bugs*. All ColdFusion Components in the *bugs* directory in the *frdg* project should relate to little critters with several legs, whether they are insects or arachnids. The actual package name is relative to the document root and uses dots rather than slashes; so, in the previous example, the package name would be "com.oreilly.frdg.bugs". As discussed in Chapter 2, using domain names as directory structures prevents namespace collisions and keeps your code better organized.

Invoking ColdFusion Components From Flash

Invoking a CFC from Flash is very similar to invoking a ColdFusion page. To create an instance of a service in your Flash movie, you call *getService( )* on your *NetConnection* instance, passing in the fully qualified component name (the entire name of the CFC, including the package name). Remember that package names are relative to the document root and use dots in place of slashes.

To invoke a CFC from a Flash application, follow these steps:

1. Set the gateway URL.
2. Create a connection object using *NetServices.createGatewayConnection( )*.
3. Create a service object by invoking *getService( )* on the connection object obtained in Step 2. The service path includes the directory name and the name of the *.cfc* file, excluding the *.cfc* extension.
4. Invoke a function within the component as a method of the service object obtained in Step 3. Any functions defined within the component can be accessed as methods of the service object.

The following code creates an instance of the service, which points to our *Grasshopper* component and invokes the *getLegCount( )* method:

```
var myURL = "http://localhost/flashservices/gateway";
var myService = "com.oreilly.frdg.bugs.Grasshopper";
NetServices.setDefaultGatewayUrl(myURL);
var my_conn = NetServices.createGatewayConnection( );
var grasshopperSevice = my_conn.getService(myService, responderObject);
grasshopperService.getLegCount( );
```

As with the earlier ColdFusion page example, we pass the service name to *get-Service( )*. However, note that when using a CFC the service path includes the name of the *.cfc* file (in this case *Grasshopper.cfc*) without the *.cfc* extension. Contrast this with the case of a ColdFusion page, in which the *.cfm* file is not part of the service path passed to *getService( )* but is instead invoked as the method on the service object returned by *getService( )*.

Remember that a component can define multiple functions (one for each `<cffunction>` tag), and each one can be accessed as a method of the service object returned by *getService( )*. That is, as long as the responder object passed to *get-Service( )* is capable of handling different types of results, you can reuse the same service instance to call other functions on the same component:

```
grasshopperService.getPrimaryDiet( );
```

You can pass arguments into a remote CFC function the same way you pass arguments to the ColdFusion page. For example, if the component defines a *setSpecies( )* function, you can pass arguments to it as follows:

```
grasshopperService.setSpecies("Melanoplus Differentialis");
```

Examples of Flash Remoting Using ColdFusion Components

ColdFusion Components are extremely versatile, because the code inside of the `<cffunction>` tags can be written in CFML or CFScript and can be included from external files. Including code in your functions using the `<cfinclude>` tag is a good way to reuse code, and it allows you to add layers of abstraction to your application. CFC functions can also invoke each other (as long as the access attributes allow for it). They can even create instances of Java objects and use them.

The next three subsections demonstrate various techniques. The first section is a working example of a CFC that performs a service (sends an email) and doesn't return anything to the client. The next section demonstrates performing a database query and returning data to the client. It also shows the benefit of component functions calling other component functions. The last subsection shows how to wrap a Java class in a CFC so it is more easily accessible to Flash through Flash Remoting.

Using a ColdFusion Component to send email

Sending email is a common task that nearly all web-based applications support. There is no way to send email directly from a Flash movie unless you use a *mailto* URL in conjunction with the *getURL( )* function, which is far from ideal since it assumes the user is on his own computer and has a mail client and server properly configured. These are not necessarily things you can count on, since Flash runs on many different types of devices and in many different places. The solution is to use Flash Remoting to delegate the task to a server. Using ColdFusion, the entire procedure can be done in just a few lines of code.

Example 5-3 shows code for a CFC capable of sending email on behalf of a client. It is analogous to the ColdFusion page of Example 5-1 but is written as a component. Name the component *Email.cfc* and put it in the package *com.oreilly.frdg*.

Example 5-3. Sending an email with a CFC using Email.cfc

```
<cfcomponent>
  <cffunction name="sendEmail" access="remote">
    <cfargument name="to" required="true" />
    <cfargument name="from" required="true" />
    <cfargument name="subject" required="true" />
    <cfargument name="body" required="true" />
    <cftry>
      <cfmail to = to
       from = from
       subject = subject>
#body#
      </cfmail>
      <cfcatch type="Any">
        <cfthrow message = "There was an error">
      </cfcatch>
    </cftry>
  </cffunction>
</cfcomponent>
```

In order for *Email.cfc* to work, you must have an email server configured through the ColdFusion administrator.

The component in Example 5-3 is a simple, generic service that can be invoked remotely from a Flash application (since the access attribute is "remote") or locally from a ColdFusion page or even another CFC. The ActionScript code from Example 5-2, used with the ColdFusion page, must be modified slightly to invoke the *sendEmail( )* method from the component. On the last line of the *init( )* function in Example 5-2, change the *getService( )* invocation to use the path to the new component (omit the *.cfc* extension):

```
emailService = my_conn.getService("com.oreilly.frdg.Email");
```

Note that we've named our function *sendEmail( )* in imitation of the ColdFusion page named *sendEmail.cfm* from Example 5-1. This allows us to invoke *sendEmail( )* using the same client-side code from the original Example 5-2; however, in the earlier case *sendMail* was the name a *.cfm* page, and here it is the name of a function within a CFC:

```
emailService.sendEmail(new Responder(), args);
```

Even though the *sendEmail( )* method doesn't return anything to the client, the responder object's *onResult( )* method is called when the function completes. No argument is passed back to the *onResult( )* function. Notice that the ActionScript code in Example 5-2 created a default message to be displayed if there was no result from the server.

Returning a Query object

Let's see how to return a value from a CFC. The CFC listed in Example 5-4 defines two functions, which become methods of the component. The *getAllStates( )* method performs a database query to retrieve information on all the U.S. states and returns the result. Notice how the *getStatesByRegion( )* method first calls *getAllStates( )* to avoid unnecessarily repeating code. The code in Example 5-4 can go in a file called *StatesEnum.cfc* in the package *com.oreilly.frdg*.

Example 5-4. Returning a query with StatesEnum.cfc

```
<cfcomponent>
  <cffunction name="getAllStates" access="remote" returnType="query">
    <cfquery datasource="Northwind" name="allStates">
      SELECT StateID, StateName, StateAbbr, StateRegion
      FROM USStates
    </cfquery>
    <cfreturn #allStates# />
  </cffunction>
  <cffunction name="getStatesByRegion" access="remote" returnType="query">
    <cfargument name="region" type="string" required="true" />
    <cfset allStates=this.getAllStates() />
    <cfquery dbtype="query" name="regionalStates">
      SELECT *
      FROM allStates
      WHERE StateRegion = '#region#'
    </cfquery>
    <cfreturn #regionalStates# />
  </cffunction>
</cfcomponent>
```

In order for Example 5-4 to work, you must have an appropriate data source configured through the ColdFusion administrator. A *.csv* file named *USStates.csv* filled with a listing of U.S. states and regions is available from the online Code Depot and can be imported to your database of choice for use in this example. Import the file to a new table called USStates.

The *StatesEnum.cfc* component takes advantage of a nice feature of ColdFusion called *queries of queries*. The *getAllStates( )* method returns a *Query* object that was returned from the <cfquery> tag used to query the database. Rather than have the *getStatesByRegion( )* method use its own <cfquery> tag to run the same query, we can extract the subset of interest by performing a more specific query on the allStates *Query* object returned by *getAllStates( )*. Using ColdFusion's query of query capability is efficient in terms of both performance and coding practice.

Example 5-5 shows the client-side ActionScript code for invoking the *getAllStates( )* and *getStatesByRegion( )* functions remotely.

Example 5-5. ActionScript code for StatesEnum.fla

```
NetServices.setDefaultGatewayUrl("http://localhost:8500/flashservices/gateway");
var con = NetServices.createGatewayConnection( );
var statesSevice = con.getService("com.oreilly.frdg.StatesEnum", this);
statesService.getAllStates( );
statesService.getStatesByRegion("south");

function onResult (states) {
  // states_cb is the instance name of a ComboBox UI component.
  states_cb.setDataProvider(states);
}
```

The states parameter passed to the *onResult( )* function is cast (or transformed) into an ActionScript *RecordSet* object by the Flash Remoting gateway. Notice how the function is not concerned with whether it is being passed a recordset of all the U.S. states or a subset based on region. Its only job is to populate a ComboBox with the data it receives. Because we can use the same responder object for calls to both *getAllStates( )* and *getStatesByRegion( )*, we again are able to reuse code.

ColdFusion supports *cached queries*, which allow data to be held in memory on the server. The allStates query in Example 5-4 is an ideal candidate for caching. To cache a query, define a cachedwithin attribute such as cachedwithin="#CreateTimeSpan(7,0,0,0)#", which caches the query in memory for 7 days. Therefore, the query executes no more than once per week, unless the server restarts (depending on your CF administrative settings, which can limit the number of cached queries).

Although you can access arguments to a component function using the Flash.Params array or as named parameters, you should use <cfargument> tags instead.

There is also an additional variable scope you can use with components, called the arguments scope. The arguments scope can be used with dot notation (arguments. *argumentName*) or the Structure model (arguments["*argumentName*"]). If you are going to use a variable scope, you should use the arguments scope instead of the Flash scope for two reasons:

- It keeps your components generic so that they can be invoked by clients other than remote Flash applications.

- It is easier to keep track of the variables that are prepended with their scopes. For example, if the *getStatesByRegion( )* function is very long, referring to the region argument as arguments.region makes your code clearer. Even if your function contains <cfargument> tags, it's a good idea to use the arguments scope for the sake of readability.

Wrapping a Java class in a ColdFusion Component

Although ColdFusion does not support creating or calling methods on Java objects directly, you can easily create CFCs or ColdFusion pages that can delegate to Java objects. That is, you can use a CFC as a thin layer between your Flash Remoting application and the Java object layer. Chapter 7 covers Java and Flash Remoting integration in detail, but here is a short, simple example in the context of a CFC. This example demonstrates the following process:

1. The Flash client invokes a remote CFC function.

2. The CFC function instantiates a Java object, passing it the argument that was sent from the Flash client.

3. The CFC calls a method on an instance of the Java class, which returns a string.

4. The string returned from the Java method is returned by the CFC to the Flash client.

Figure 5-2 illustrates the process of calling a Java object wrapped in a ColdFusion Component.

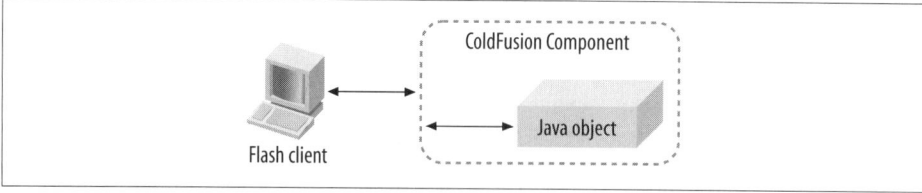

Figure 5-2. Wrapping a Java object in a ColdFusion Component

There are three parts to this example:

- The client-side ActionScript code
- The ColdFusion Component
- The Java object

Let's work backward and start with the Java object.

The Java object, called *StringReverser* and shown in Example 5-6, has a constructor that accepts a *String* object. There is only one method on *StringReverser*, called *getReversedString( )*, which reverses the order of the characters in the string and returns it as a new string.

Example 5-6. Java class StringReverser.java

```
package com.oreilly.frdg;

public class StringReverser {
  private String target;

  public StringReverser (String target) {
    this.target = target;
  }

  public String getReversedString ( ) {
    StringBuffer reversedString = new StringBuffer( );
    char[] chars = target.toCharArray( );
    for (int i = chars.length; i > 0; --i) {
      reversedString.append(chars[i-1]);
    }
    return reversedString.toString( );
  }
}
```

You can compile the *StringReverser.java* file with any Java IDE or with the command-line compiler *javac.exe*. Once the Java file is compiled, place the resulting *.class* file in any directory included in ColdFusion's classpath. In a typical installation of ColdFusion MX on a Windows machine, this would be at *C:\CFusionMX\ runtime\servers\lib*.

If you choose to put your classes in a package, remember to add the package declaration to the top of the *.java* file, as we have done here, and to create the appropriate directory structure. The *StringReverser.class* should go into a directory structure of *classpath\com\oreilly\frdg*. You can also put your class files into a Java archive (*.jar*) file, as long as the *.jar* files are included in ColdFusion's classpath.

Let's look at the CFC that serves as a proxy between the Flash client and the *StringReverser* Java object. The code in Example 5-7 is contained in a file called *JavaExamples.cfc*, located in the package *com.oreilly.frdg*.

Example 5-7. JavaExamples.cfc

```
<cfcomponent>
  <cffunction name="reverseString" access="remote" returnType="string">
    <cfargument name="target" type="string" required="true">
    <cfobject type="Java" action="create" class="StringReverser"
     name="reverserClass" />
    <cfset reverser = reverserClass.init(#target#) />
    <cfset reversedString = reverser.getReversedString( ) />
    <cfreturn #reversedString# />
  </cffunction>
</cfcomponent>
```

We use the <cfobject> tag to get a reference to the *StringReverser* class, not an instance of *StringReverser*. At this point, you have access to only static members of the class. The instance of *StringReverser* is actually created and returned from the *init( )* method call on the line following the <cfobject> tag.

The *StringReverser* class does not have an explicit *init( )* method. *init( )* is a ColdFusion function that is required to be called whenever instantiating a Java object. Calling *init( )* from ColdFusion invokes the corresponding class constructor. If you attempt to reference a nonstatic member of a Java object before calling an *init( )* method, the object's default no-argument constructor is called if one exists. If the object does not have any constructors at all, allowing the default no-argument constructor to be called in this manner is fine. However, if your object has one or more constructors and does not explicitly define a no-argument constructor, attempting to access nonstatic members before initializing the Java object results in an exception being thrown and propagated up to the Flash client.

By passing the target variable into the *init( )* method, *StringReverser*'s constructor is called, returning an instance of *StringReverser*, which has the value of target set as a member variable. The instance is assigned to the ColdFusion variable reverser, which is the instance that you call methods on. Calling *getReversedString( )* on reverser returns the value of target, except with its characters in reverse order, which is assigned to the ColdFusion variable reversedString. We then return reversedString, which, in this case, is returned to the Flash client. The instance of *StringReverser* goes out of scope and is ready for garbage collection at the moment the CFC function returns. In the case of ColdFusion pages and CFCs, instances of Java objects go out of scope when the entire page has finished executing.

Now let's take a look at the client-side ActionScript for this exercise, shown in Example 5-8.

Example 5-8. ActionScript code for JavaExample1.fla

```
NetServices.setDefaultGatewayURL("http://localhost:8500/flashservices/gateway");
var my_conn = NetServices.createGatewayConnection( );
var javaExService = my_conn.getService("com.oreilly.frdg.JavaExamples", this);
javaExService.reverseString("this is a top secret code");
```

Example 5-8. ActionScript code for JavaExample1.fla (continued)

```
function onResult (response) {
  trace(response);
}

function onStatus (error) {
  trace("error: " + error.description);
}
```

The ActionScript code for this example is straightforward. Calling the remote *reverseString( )* function on *JavaExamples.cfc* returns the reversed string to the *onResult( )* callback function. The result should be the string "edoc terces pot a si siht" printed in your Output window.

ColdFusion Component Introspection

Like Java class definitions, CFCs are self-documenting, which means that the components themselves—or, more precisely, the *cfexplorer.cfc* located in *wwwroot/CFIDE/componentutils*—can describe how each component is used. A component's ability to reflect upon itself is referred to as *introspection* or *component metadata*. There are two primary advantages to component metadata:

- It exposes components' application programming interface (API) without exposing the implementation of the component.
- It is always up-to-date.

Clients using your components should not care or rely upon how a function is implemented; they should be concerned only with how a function is used and what data it returns. Hiding the internal implementation of a component is a key requirement of abstraction and encapsulation. Component metadata is a great way for developers to access the information they need without looking through the component's code, which not only defeats the goal of encapsulation but also takes a great deal of time.

Component metadata also allows CFC developers to concentrate on their code, rather than manually keeping the documentation current. Component metadata is generated as HTML, so it can be viewed by simply referencing the *.cfc* file's URL directly from a web browser, like this:

> *http://localhost/com/oreilly/frdg/MyCFC.cfc*

When the ColdFusion Server receives a request for a CFC file rather than a request to invoke a particular function within it, the request is redirected to *webroot\CFIDE\componentutils\cfexplorer.cfc*. For security reasons, you are prompted to enter the ColdFusion Remote Development Security (RDS) password, after which you should see a document similar to Figure 5-3, which shows the documentation for *StatesEnum.cfc* from Example 5-4.

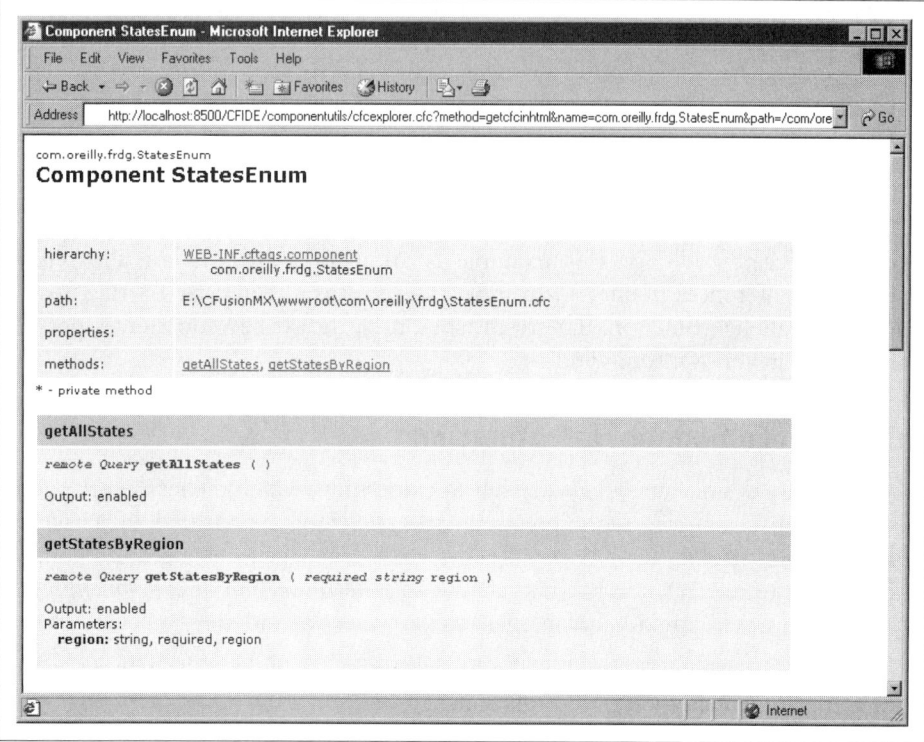

Figure 5-3. Introspecting StatesEnum.cfc

ColdFusion metadata includes the following information:

- The inheritance tree of the component
- The directory the component is in
- The package the component is in
- The display name of the component, if the displayName attribute is present
- Each property that the component contains
- All the functions the component contains
- What arguments each function accepts, the arguments' datatypes, and whether they are required
- The ColdFusion variable name used to reference each argument
- Arguments' default values, if present
- What type of access each function allows
- The value of the function's hint attribute, if present
- Whether output is enabled for each function
- The datatype of the return value of each function

If you are not sure which component you are looking for, you can use the Component Browser to browse all the components on the ColdFusion Server. To access the Component Browser, enter a URL of the following form in your web browser:

wwwroot/CFIDE/componentutils/componentdoc.cfm

For example:

http://localhost:8500/CFIDE/componentutils/componentdoc.cfm

Dreamweaver MX also allows you to introspect CFCs from its Components panel. In Dreamweaver MX, after you've defined a site and set your server model to ColdFusion, the Components panel displays all components that are available on the server, in a tree, as shown in Figure 5-4. Right-clicking (in Windows) or Ctrl-clicking (on the Macintosh) on a component, method, or argument within the panel gives details about that particular item.

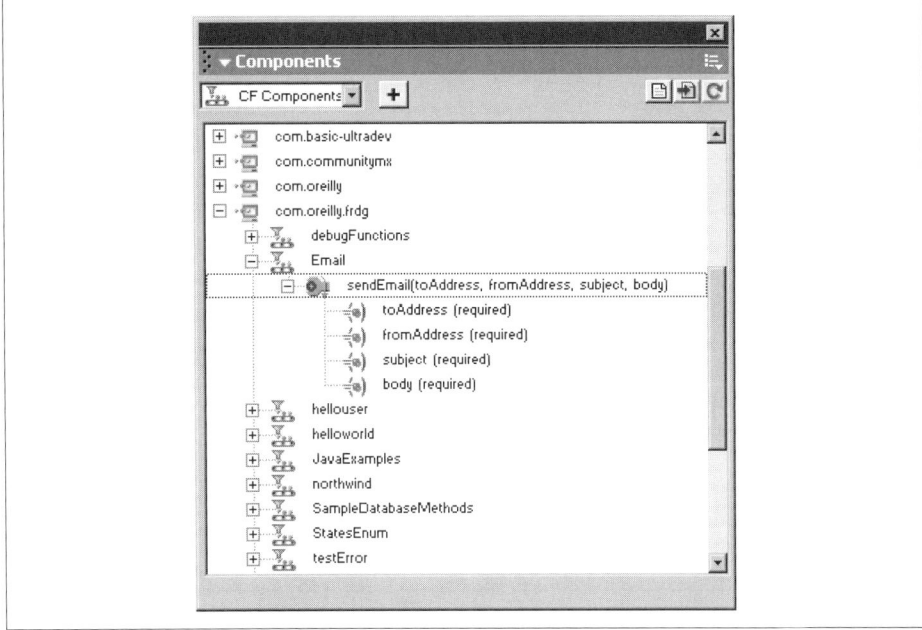

Figure 5-4. Introspecting the Email.cfc component from within Dreamweaver MX

You can also create your own interface for introspecting CFCs.

Discovering ColdFusion Components from Flash

In addition to being able to browse CFC services from your browser and from Dreamweaver MX, you can also browse them directly from the Flash authoring environment through the Service Browser (Window → Service Browser). You cannot discover unknown services, because you must enter the address of the service in order to find it; however, it is a convenient way to keep important component APIs available while you write ActionScript code against them. Chapter 2 describes the Service Browser, which is shown in Figures 2-4 and 5-5.

The Description field in the Service Browser contains, at a minimum, a list of arguments the function accepts and their datatypes. If you have added the description attribute to your <cffunction> tag, its value is displayed in the Description field. Additionally, you can define a description attribute for each argument a function accepts to provide the Service Browser with additional information. Be sure to refresh the service descriptions often if other developers could be working on the component files, to make sure you are always viewing the most recent versions.

Figure 5-5 shows the Service Browser exposing the *Email.cfc* ColdFusion Component.

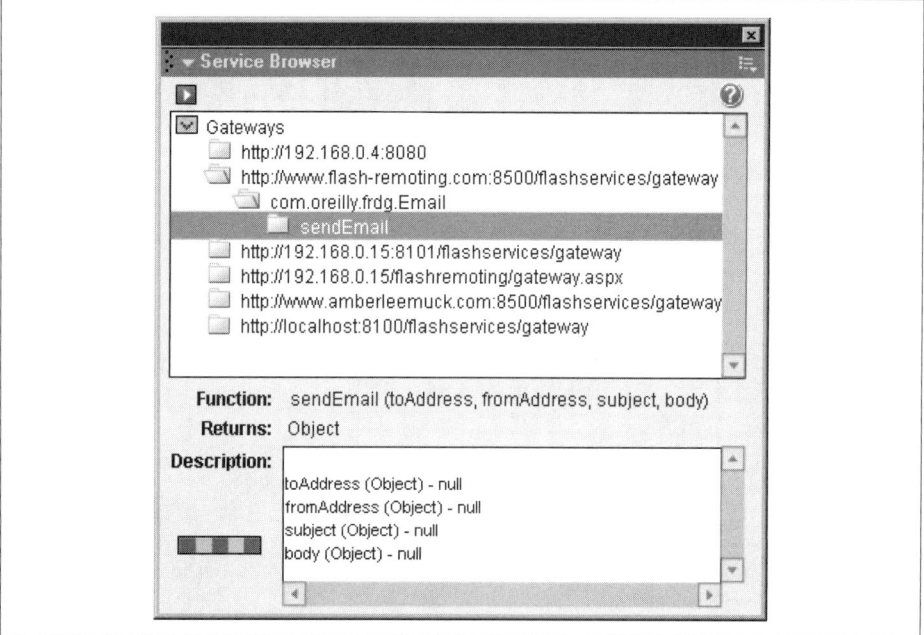

Figure 5-5. The Flash Service Browser exposing the Email CFC

ColdFusion Pages Versus ColdFusion Components

Typically, my preference for a particular type of technology or architecture is driven by the nature of the task I need to accomplish. I favor that which gets the job done most efficiently and allows the project to be maintained most easily. I can't think of any situation in which I would recommend using ColdFusion pages rather than ColdFusion Components to provide Flash Remoting services. Using ColdFusion pages and the `Flash` variable scope might be faster initially for developers not familiar with CFCs. However, I strongly recommend learning to write CFCs and appreciate the theory behind them.

There are three things CFCs offer that ColdFusion pages do not:

Documentation

CFCs provide an excellent and completely automatic form of documentation, and you can browse them from the Flash and Dreamweaver authoring environments.

Automatic validation

Since CFCs allow you to define the arguments that a function accepts, the Cold-Fusion Server can automatically validate the parameters passed to a function. You must hand-code such validation for ColdFusion pages.

Re-use

Writing Flash Remoting services as ColdFusion pages requires the `Flash` variable scope for retrieving arguments and returning data, making the pages incompatible with clients other than Flash. ColdFusion Component code can and should be kept generic enough that you can invoke the same functions from various clients, such as Flash Remoting, ColdFusion pages, other CFCs, and through URLs.

Some advantages of CFCs can be simulated with ColdFusion pages, although it often requires additional work. For example, the clever use of includes can achieve the same result as inheritance and allow a high degree of code re-use and modularity. A set of well-planned ColdFusion pages can be maintained easily and can provide the same level of encapsulation as CFCs. Although each developer must make his own choice, CFCs were designed with advanced, object-oriented development in mind, whereas the same concepts are afterthoughts in the context of ColdFusion pages.

Loading Query Data Incrementally

You should never make your user wait longer than necessary. And if the wait is unavoidable, at least make it seem shorter. For example, since browsers are usually accessing remote resources over which they have very little control, they are designed to display partial content as it becomes available. Modern browsers improve performance where it is under their control and give the illusion of performance when issues are beyond their control (such as connection speed, site design, server traffic, and so on).

Browsers use sophisticated caching and rendering algorithms to decrease the amount of work that has to be done between a request and a fully rendered response. Where performance is out of their hands, they employ user feedback to ease the pain of waiting as much as possible. For example, browsers use loader bars to indicate the page's load progress and render available content before the remainder is fully loaded. Most browsers use an animated icon in the upper-right corner to imply that the browser is making steady progress even though the animation has nothing to do with what the browser is loading.

One of the most appealing aspects of using Flash to develop web-based applications is that a well-designed UI can perform very well. Not only does Flash content stream, but once the page is fully loaded a well-designed Flash application requires fewer round trips to the server than traditional HTML-based applications. And when it is necessary to retrieve data from the server through Flash Remoting, incremental or pageable recordsets can be used to get data in front of users as quickly as possible.

Implementing Pageable Recordsets on the Server

A *pageable recordset* is returned to the client over the course of more than one request, allowing the application to start rendering results sooner than if all the results were returned at once. By default, when a recordset is returned to Flash, the entire recordset is returned in a single response. If you are not returning very many records, or if everyone using the application has a high-speed connection, the default behavior is probably fine; however, when returning large numbers of records over slower connections, it is more practical to return them incrementally.

A *page* is a subset of a recordset, and *page size* refers to the number of records in a given page. The default page size is the size of the entire recordset, which means that if the page size isn't explicitly set on the server, all records are returned in a single page. To change the page size, simply assign a value to the Flash.Pagesize variable before returning your *Query* object, as shown in Example 5-9. Although setting the Flash.Pagesize variable might appear to make our CFC function Flash-specific, it is ignored by non-Flash clients. See the full discussion under "Passing the Page Size from Flash Dynamically" later in this chapter.

Example 5-9. Customers.cfc

```
<cfcomponent>
  <cffunction name="getCustomers"
   access="remote"
   returnType="query">
   <cfquery name="rsCustomers" datasource="Northwind">
    SELECT ContactName FROM Customers
   </cfquery>
   <cfset Flash.Pagesize = 10 />
   <cfreturn #rsCustomers# />
  </cffunction>
</cfcomponent>
```

Example 5-9 can be saved as *Customers.cfc* in the *webroot\com\oreilly\frdg* directory. Notice how we set the Flash.Pagesize to 10 before returning the *Query* object. The server returns 10 records for each client request, but the server cannot push data to the client without the client asking for it. Setting the Flash.Pagesize variable to 10 means that the first 10 records are returned initially and the rest of the records are pageable. The server returns the remaining records when requested; however, the server does not limit responses to 10 records at a time. After the initial 10 records are returned, it is up to the client to decide how and when the rest of the data is loaded.

The Flash paging implementation is different than the type of recordset paging that uses the `maxrows` attribute of the `<cfquery>` tag, which might be more familiar to ColdFusion programmers. Once the CFML code sets the `Flash.Pagesize` variable, the server takes care of the details of paging when the client requests another page.

Implementing Pageable Recordsets on the Client

Since the server doesn't limit the number of records returned to the client after the initial records have been returned, it is up to the client to establish a delivery mode for incrementally loading the remaining data. A *delivery mode* is essentially a policy for how and when pageable data is retrieved from the server. To set a delivery mode, you use the *setDeliveryMode( )* method on the *RecordSet* instance returned from the server, passing in the appropriate arguments. Table 5-6 describes each of the three delivery modes and how to use them.

Table 5-6. Delivery modes for pageable recordsets

Delivery mode	Description	Usage
"ondemand"	Loads each record individually each time a record is requested through the *RecordSet.getItemAt( )* function on the object. This is the default behavior for pageable recordsets.	`rs.setDeliveryMode("ondemand");`
"fetchall"	Loads all the records in the recordset unconditionally, but tells the server to return them in pages, or sets, as opposed to one at a time.	`rs.setDeliveryMode("fetchall", 10);` The second argument (10) indicates the number of records per page, meaning the number of records to be returned from the server with each response. It makes sense for this number to be the same as the Flash.Pagesize variable you set on the server, but it does not have to be.
"page"	When an individual record is retrieved from a particular page, not only are all the other records from that page returned, but also some specified number of subsequent pages are returned to the client if they have not already been retrieved.	`rs.setDeliveryMode("page", 10, 2);` The second argument (10) indicates the page size while the third argument (2) indicates the number of subsequent pages to be retrieved and cached. If the third argument is 0, only the current page is returned.

Here is a description of when to use each delivery mode:

"ondemand"

Use "ondemand" mode when each record is needed individually and at different times. Do not use this mode if you are iterating through the entire *RecordSet* at once, because it forces the client to make a separate request for each record, which is very inefficient. This mode is efficient only if you won't eventually load all the records and you want to limit network traffic to only those records that must be loaded.

"fetchall"

Use "fetchall" mode when you know that you are going to load all the data but would like to start displaying the data incrementally rather than having to wait for it all to load. For example, if you know you have 300 records to load, it makes sense to load them over the course of 10 requests, 30 records at a time, so that you can start displaying data as soon as possible.

"page"

The "page" mode lies somewhere between "ondemand" and "fetchall". Use "page" mode when you don't expect to need all the data in the recordset, but you don't want the overhead of loading each record individually. For example, you don't want to make the user wait for 10 pages of search results to load, because she will most likely find what she needs in the first two or three pages. Therefore, load the first two or three pages initially, and then load the other pages as they are needed.

If you are handing off your recordset to a Flash UI component through the component's *setDataProvider( )* method, set the delivery mode on the recordset before passing it into the component. The component will automatically load the data as specified in the call to *setDeliveryMode( )*. Since the best reason to load data incrementally is to display it to users, you may never need to load data incrementally outside of the context of a Flash UI component. If you need to handle or process incrementally loaded data yourself, however, the next section explains how Action-Script implements recordset paging.

Managing Incrementally Loaded Data by Hand

Remember that if the Flash.Pagesize variable is set on the server, the server returns only the specified number of records in the initial query. Unless the client requests the remainder of the data, it is never sent.

The *RecordSet.addView( )* method is the key to handling pageable records. Any object that is passed into the *addView( )* function should contain a function called *modelChanged( )*. The *RecordSet* object calls the *modelChanged( )* function whenever its state changes in any way, passing into the function an object with the following properties:

event

Describes the type of event that occurred. Possible values for the event property are as follows:

"addRows"

Indicates that rows have been added to the recordset. Use the firstRow and lastRow properties to determine which rows were affected.

"allRows"

> The recordset is completely populated, meaning all rows have been returned from the server. The firstRow and lastRow properties will not have values.

"fetchRows"

> Rows have been requested from the server, but a response containing the data has not been received. Use the firstRow and lastRow properties to determine which rows were affected.

"sort"

> Indicates that the records in the recordset have been sorted. The firstRow and lastRow properties will not have values.

"updateAll"

> Indicates that the recordset has changed. This event occurs when a new view is added to the recordset.

"updateRows"

> Indicates that rows have been changed. Use the firstRow and lastRow properties to determine which rows were affected.

firstRow

> The index of the first row that was affected by the event.

lastRow

> The index of the last row that was affected by the event.

Example 5-10 shows code for a simple ActionScript example that handles a pageable recordset manually (as opposed to allowing a Flash UI component to handle retrieving and displaying the data). The example simply retrieves the pageable data associated with a remote CFC function call and displays it in the Flash Output window. Assume that the remote service—*com.oreilly.frdg.Customers*—sets the Flash. Pagesize variable to 10 just before returning a *RecordSet* object of unknown length, containing a column called ContactName.

Example 5-10. Customers1.fla

```
#include "NetServices.as"

// Establish the connection to the service.
NetServices.setDefaultGatewayURL("http://localhost/flashservices/gateway");
var my_conn = NetServices.createGatewayConnection();
var customerService = my_conn.getService("com.oreilly.frdg.Customers", this);
// Invoke the getCustomers() function within the .cfc file.
customerService.getCustomers();

// Declare the IncomingDataHandler class's constructor.
function IncomingDataHandler (rs) {
  this.rs = rs;
}

// Get the rows that the server sent back immediately. This should be
// equal to the Flash.Pagesize variable set on the server (10 in this case).
```

Example 5-10. Customers1.fla (continued)

```
IncomingDataHandler.prototype.getData = function () {
  for (var i = 0; i < this.rs.getNumberAvailable(); ++i) {
    trace(this.rs.getItemAt(i)["ContactName"]);
  }
};

// This function is called automatically as data is returned from the server.
IncomingDataHandler.prototype.modelChanged = function (info) {
  if (info.event == "updateRows") {
    for (var i = info.firstRow; i <= info.lastRow; ++i) {
      trace(this.rs.getItemAt(i)["ContactName"]);
    }
  }
};

function onResult (result_rs) {
  // Fetch all records, but only 10 at a time.
  result_rs.setDeliveryMode("fetchall", 10);
  var dataHandler = new IncomingDataHandler(result_rs);
  result_rs.addView(dataHandler);
  dataHandler.getData();
}

function onStatus (error) {
  trace("error: " + error.description);
}
```

Let's start analyzing Example 5-10 at the beginning of the *onResult( )* function, which is automatically called when the remote *getCustomers( )* function returns a result. The first thing we do is set the delivery mode to "fetchall" for the *RecordSet* object that has been passed into *onResult( )*. This mode indicates we want all the results to be returned as soon as they are available. However, we also specify a page size of 10, so that the data is returned 10 records at a time over the course of as many requests and responses between the client and the server as are necessary to deliver all the data.

Although we are not responsible for writing the code that requests the data, we must implement an object that knows what to do with the data once it is returned from the server, so let us digress momentarily to discuss the *IncomingDataHandler* class. As you can see in Example 5-10, the *IncomingDataHandler* class defines a *modelChanged( )* function, which is used to listen for records arriving on the client from the server, as follows.

The *onResult( )* handler instantiates an *IncomingDataHandler* object, passing in the result_rs *RecordSet* object as an argument. It then passes the *IncomingDataHandler* instance named dataHandler to the *addView( )* function of the result_rs recordset. Therefore, dataHandler's *modelChanged( )* function is called whenever the state of the result_rs recordset changes. The final line of code in the *onResult( )* function calls the *getData( )* method on `dataHandler`, which manages the flow of data between the client and the server.

The *getData( )* method merely iterates through the records that were already returned, which is determined by the value of the `Flash.Pagesize` variable set on the server and accessible through the recordset's *getNumberAvailable( )* method. The rest of the paging is up to the *modelChanged( )* function, which the recordset calls automatically as the data arrives from the server (10 records at a time). When the *model-Changed( )* function receives an "updateRows" event, it extracts the data from the rows that were most recently loaded.

If, in the *onResult( )* function, we had set the delivery mode to "ondemand" rather than "fetchall", we would have seen very different results. Recall that setting the delivery mode to "fetchall" causes all the data from the server to be returned to the client as quickly as possible, but the data is divided into pages over several requests and responses. When the delivery mode is set to "ondemand", however, no additional records beyond the initial page are returned until they are requested by the client through the *RecordSet.getItemAt( )* method. Therefore, in "ondemand" mode, we would have seen the initial data sent from the server written to the Flash Output window in the *IncomingDataHandler.getData( )* function, but until we tried to access records that hadn't been loaded yet, the *IncomingDataHandler.modelChanged( )* method would never be called. It is important to note that once a record has been loaded, whether it was loaded on demand or fetched automatically, it gets cached on the client, so there is no need to make additional trips to the server when accessing data that has been loaded previously.

Passing the Page Size from Flash Dynamically

You may recall that one advantage of CFCs is that they tend to be more generic and reusable, since there is generally no need for a CFC function to contain Flash-specific code. They generally do not use the `Flash` variable scope to access arguments, and they use the `<cfreturn>` tag instead of the `Flash.Result` variable to return data. This concept seems to break down the moment you define the `Flash.Pagesize` variable in your ColdFusion Component; however, setting the `Flash.Pagesize` variable does not prevent other types of clients from invoking your ColdFusion Component functions. If the `Flash` variable scope is irrelevant in the context of the current request, setting the `Flash.Pagesize` variable has no effect whatsoever.

However, for the purists who simply cannot stand the sight of client-specific code in their components, there is actually a way to be rid of the tag entirely and set the page size from the client. Consider the following client-side ActionScript excerpt:

```
NetServices.setDefaultGatewayURL("http://localhost/flashservices/gateway");
var my_conn = NetServices.createGatewayConnection( );
var customerService = my_conn.getService("com.oreilly.frdg.Customers", this);
customerService.getCustomers2({pagesize:10});
```

When the preceding ActionScript code invokes the remote *getCustomers2()* ColdFusion function, it passes in an object containing a pagesize property. The Cold-Fusion Server understands the argument to mean that the query returned by the function should be pageable, sparing your ColdFusion Component function from unsightly client-specific code. The *getCustomers2()* function is listed in Example 5-11.

Example 5-11. The getCustomers2( ) function in the Customers.cfc file

```
<cffunction name="getCustomers2"
 access="remote"
 returnType="query">
  <cfquery name="rsCustomers" datasource="Northwind">
   SELECT ContactName FROM Customers
  </cfquery>
  <cfreturn #rsCustomers# />
</cffunction>
```

The only difference from the previous *getCustomers( )* function in Example 5-9 is that the Flash-specific line, `<cfset Flash.Pagesize = 10 />`, has been removed from *getCustomers2( )*. The full code can be found at the online Code Depot as *Customers2.fla* and *Customers.cfc*.

ColdFusion Security: Authenticating Users

It is possible to associate a particular *NetConnection* instance with a username and password combination that allows you to secure both ColdFusion page services and ColdFusion Components. You can secure services by user, role, or application.

Client-Side Security Implementation

The required client-side ActionScript code is straightforward. Simply call the *setCredentials( )* method on the *NetConnection* instance from which you will get your secured services:

```
NetServices.setDefaultGatewayURL("http://localhost/flashservices/gateway");
var my_conn = NetServices.createGatewayConnection();
my_conn.setCredentials("someUsername", "somePassword");
var someService = my_conn.getService("com.oreilly.util.someService", this);
someService.execute();
```

To properly implement an authentication scheme, the services being called have to be properly protected (a process we will review shortly). The username and password are sent to the server in the same request that actually invokes the remote function. If authentication is successful, the service will process normally; upon failure to authenticate, execution halts and an error is returned to the client through the *onStatus( )* function of your responder object. It is perfectly acceptable to call *setCredentials( )* on a *NetConnection* instance more than once if different credentials are being used for different functions.

The username and password arguments passed into *setCredentials( )* can be the username and password of a particular user (for example, the user who is currently using your application), or it can be more general, such as a username and password combination pertaining to your application rather than who is using it. For example, if only one or two people have access to certain services on your ColdFusion Server, you should authenticate at the level of the particular user.

If all or most users of a particular application are allowed to access essentially the same set of services, you may want to authenticate at the level of the application itself. You could even come up with a single username and password combination that all your users and applications could use, which would simply protect against any party not associated with any of your applications from invoking services. The differences between the levels of authentication granularity are not at all reflected in the code itself. In other words, there is actually no difference between the way in which you authenticate a particular user and how you would authenticate an entire application or even a set of applications. The difference is purely in the significance that you decide to attach to the usernames and passwords that are chosen and how you architect your application.

As mentioned previously, you may also choose to protect services by user role. A *role* is just a group of users who have the same security restrictions. The Flash client does not explicitly specify a user's role when setting credentials on the *NetConnection* instance, since roles are typically not exposed to the client. For example, when you log into an account on either a Unix or a Windows computer, your role (or the sets of permissions that are granted to you) is unconditionally associated with your authentication information, meaning you don't say your name is "frank", your password is "frank123", and you would like your role to be "root" or "administrator". The computer you are logging into determines your role based on who you say you are. In this case, the computer you are logging into or authenticating against is the ColdFusion Server.

Security on the Server

ColdFusion MX supports three tags and two functions associated with authentication:

`<cflogin>`
> This tag is typically to implement your authentication code. It is usually placed in your *Application.cfm* page and can be customized to authenticate in any manner you choose, such as checking a username and password against a database, text file, or LDAP server. The tag is executed only if the request is coming from a user who ColdFusion determines is not already logged in.

`<cfloginuser>`
> This tag tells the ColdFusion Server that the user has successfully authenticated. The `<cfloginuser>` tag has three attributes: `name`, `password`, and `roles`. Executing

this tag associates those three attributes with the current request and all future requests from the user's client for the remainder of the user's session.

`<cflogout>`

Tells the ColdFusion Server that the current user is no longer logged in. Any future requests from the client automatically invoke the `<cflogin>` tag and require authentication again.

IsUserInRole("role")

Determines whether the user making the present request is assigned to the specified role. If so, this function returns `true`; otherwise, `false` is returned.

GetAuthUser( )

Returns the name of the user making the present request, if he is logged in.

In addition to the preceding tags, the `<cffunction>` tag used in this chapter also takes a `roles` attribute that allows you to manage security and define user roles for individual functions.

Example 5-12 uses basic web authentication to prompt or challenge users who have not yet successfully logged in. Basic web authentication is a simple protocol supported by most web servers and browsers. When a web server that has been configured to use basic authentication receives a request that does not have an Authorization header containing a base 64–encoded username and password, or if the username and password are incorrect, it returns a 401 code to the client, which indicates that the client is responsible for gathering a username and password and returning it in all subsequent requests.

Most browsers ask users for their authentication information by opening up a small dialog box in which the user can enter a username and password. The username and password are then base 64–encoded (so they are not visible as plain text to anyone spying on HTTP traffic) and returned to the server as the value of the Authorization header. If the username and password are correct, the resource that was originally requested is returned. If the username and password are not correct, an authorization failure policy is executed, which usually means that an error page is returned to the browser. The code in Example 5-12, when placed in an *Application.cfm* file (preferably at the top so that it is executed first), uses a combination of basic authentication and ColdFusion security to authenticate users.

Example 5-12. Application.cfm file for authenticating a user

```
<cfapplication name="myApplication">
<cflogin>
  <cfif IsDefined("cflogin")
   AND cflogin.name EQ "someUsername"
   AND cflogin.password EQ "somePassword">
    <cfset roles = "administrator" />
    <cfloginuser
     name = "#cflogin.name#"
     password = "#cflogin.password#"
```

Example 5-12. Application.cfm file for authenticating a user (continued)

```
     roles = "#roles#" />
  <cfelse>
   <cfheader statuscode = "401">
   <cfheader name = "WWW-Authenticate"
    value="Basic realm=""SomeRealm""">
   <cfoutput><html><body><b>Not authorized</b></body></html></cfoutput>
   <cfabort />
  </cfif>
</cflogin>
```

The `cflogin` variable scope is available within the `<cflogin>` tag, if the Authorization header was defined in the request. If the user has not yet been prompted to enter a username and password, the `cflogin` variable scope is not available, which is why you must ensure it is defined before trying to access its properties.

If the `cflogin` variable scope is not available or the username and password contained in the Authorization header are not `"someUsername"` and `"somePassword"` respectively, Example 5-12 uses the `<cfheader>` tag to return a 401 status code. In addition, the `<cfheader>` tag passes the `"WWW-Authenticate"` header, which indicates to the client that it is responsible for prompting the user for authentication information and returning it in the next request. It is then necessary to use the `<cfabort>` tag to ensure that the rest of the page is not processed and no more content is returned.

There is a problem with the default IIS settings when you try to use the `<cflogin>` tag with ColdFusion MX and an IIS web server. To get the `<cflogin>` tag to work properly with the *setCredentials( )* method, you need to open the IIS admin interface, right-click on your web application, and choose Properties → Directory Security → Anonymous Access and Authentication Control → Edit. Uncheck the Integrated Windows Authentication, which only allows users that are set up under Windows to access pages in a directory protected by a system. The `<cflogin>` system works perfectly with the built-in CFMX web server using its default settings.

If the `cflogin` variable scope exists and it contains username and password properties that equal `"someUsername"` and `"somePassword"`, the user is logged into the ColdFusion Server using the `<cfloginuser>` tag. At this point, you can associate roles with a specific user using the `roles` attribute. To associate more than one role with a user, specify a comma-delimited list of roles. When using the *IsUserInRole( )* function, ColdFusion checks the roles against the value specified by the `roles` attribute of the `<cfloginuser>` tag.

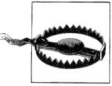

Roles are case-sensitive and must follow the rules of ColdFusion lists. Spaces should not be used, because they become part of the items in the list. For example, if you specify `"user, admin"`, the second role would be `" admin"` with a leading space.

Although the preceding code has the username and password hardcoded as "someUsername" and "somePassword", you should implement your own form of authentication, such as comparing the information against a database table or an LDAP server.

If you make a request from your browser for any page inside the same directory as the *Application.cfm* file containing the preceding authentication code, you are prompted to enter a username and password, as shown in Figure 5-6.

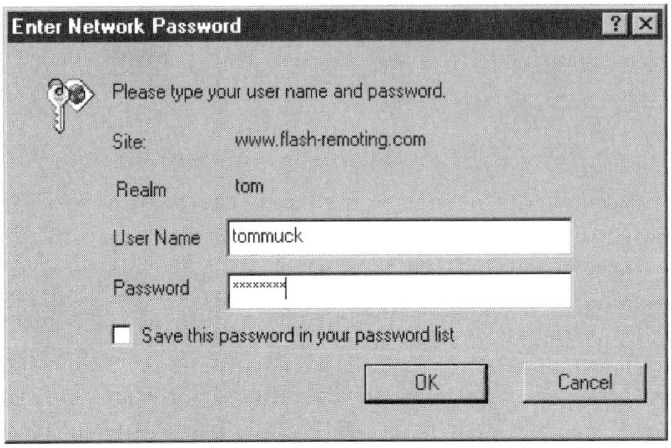

Figure 5-6. The standard browser login window

When accessing a secure resource through Flash Remoting, the process of authentication works slightly differently. As previously mentioned, the username and password are sent along in the same request that either calls the ColdFusion page or invokes the CFC function. If authentication is successful, processing of the service continues; if it fails, the *onStatus( )* method of your responder object is called.

Using Role-Based Security with ColdFusion Components

You can control access to your CFC functions by specifying the roles attribute in the <cffunction> tag. Notice that you are associating either a role or a comma-delimited list of roles with the protected function rather than an actual username and password. It is obviously much more practical to associate a group of users with a function than it is to associate a single username and password combination per function. If you need that type of fine-grained access control, however, you can simply assign one user per role, which essentially accomplishes the same thing.

Here is an example of a CFC that allows access only for users who have the role of either "manager" or "admin":

```
<cfcomponent>
  <cffunction name="getEmployees"
  access="remote"
```

```
    roles="manager,admin"
    returnType="query">
     <cfquery name="rsEmployees" datasource="someDatasource">
      SELECT lastName FROM Employees
     </cfquery>
     <cfreturn #rsEmployees# />
   </cffunction>
  </cfcomponent>
```

A user who is not logged in or who does not have the role of either "manager" or "admin" is not permitted to invoke the *getEmployees( )* method. When the ColdFusion Server encounters such a request, it looks for authentication code to run, such as the login code we reviewed earlier in the *Application.cfm* file. The username and password that your authentication code uses should be set using *NetConnection. setCredentials( )*:

```
NetServices.setDefaultGatewayURL("http://localhost/flashservices/gateway");
var my_conn = NetServices.createGatewayConnection( );
my_conn.setCredentials("someUsername", "somePassword");
var myService = my_conn.getService("com.oreilly.frdg.admin.adminServices", this);
myService.getEmployees( );
```

If the user successfully authenticates according to your authentication implementation inside of the <cflogin> tag and the <cfloginuser> tag is used to log the user into the ColdFusion Server, the ColdFusion Server compares the role of the user who made the request with the value of the roles attribute in the <cffunction> tag. If a match is found, the function is allowed to execute normally; otherwise, the responder object's *onStatus( )* method is invoked with an error object indicating an authorization failure.

Implementing security at such a low level (the component level as opposed to putting all the logic on the client) has the following advantages:

- Since one of the goals of Flash Remoting services is code re-use, it is nice to be able to reuse your security logic across clients in addition to reusing the code it is securing. When you associate roles with services in the services themselves, you can assume they are secure regardless of what types of clients are accessing them.

- The closer your security is to your data, the more sure you can be that your data is safe. In other words, there is less room or opportunity for the wrong user to either get a hold of or update data he is not authorized to access. If a function is a security risk when executed by the wrong party, take the extra time to make sure the code is secure. A function that assumes its invoker has been properly authenticated is potentially vulnerable; therefore, use verification at the function level to ensure security.

Updating Data on the Server

One frequent question about Flash Remoting is, "How do I get the recordset back to the server?" The short answer is that you have to program your Flash movie to manually parse the data and send it to the server. For example, when using the DataGrid component, changes made to the data are not uploaded to the server automatically. In the next few sections, however, I'll show you a few techniques that can be used to ease the passing of data back to the server.

Passing a Record to the Service Manually

In Chapter 3, you saw a Products display using text fields in Examples 3-3 through 3-8. The examples added several new properties and methods to the *RecordSet* class. We'll expand on that example to show the updating, inserting, and deleting of data. I'll go through the server-side code first. The component is called *ProductsAdmin.cfc* and should be saved in the *webroot\com\oreilly\frdg\admin* folder. As you recall from the previous ColdFusion security discussion, this directory is protected by an *Application.cfm* file. Therefore, to access the remote methods in this directory, your Flash code must log into the application. For the purposes of the example, the authentication code is hardcoded into the Flash file.

The server-side code

We need these main services:

getSearchResult(search)
> Gets a subset of the products, or all products

addProduct(record)
> Adds a new product to the Products table

updateProduct(record)
> Updates an existing product

deleteProducts(ids)
> Deletes one or more records from the Products table

In addition to the main services, we need some utility services to feed two Combo-Boxes in the Flash user interface:

getSuppliers( )
> Gets a list of suppliers so that the SupplierID can be used as a foreign key in the Products table

getCategories( )
> Gets a list of categories so that the CategoryID can be used as a foreign key in the Products table

The complete CFC for the required services is shown in Example 5-13. The SQL statements in the example are built up using the preceding-comma method, such as:

```
INSERT INTO Products
 (ProductName
 ,UnitPrice
 ,QuantityPerUnit
 ,CategoryID
 ,SupplierID)
```

The preceding commas might look funny, but when you are debugging complex SQL statements, this style of coding makes it easy to comment out individual lines of SQL code without having to reformat the rest of the SQL statement.

Example 5-13. The ProductsAdmin.cfc file

```
<cfcomponent displayname="Administer Products"
 hint="Add, update, delete, and search Northwind product list">

<!--- Search the Products table in the Northwind database --->
  <cffunction name="getSearchResult" access="remote"
   returnType="query" hint="Pass a search string to get a list of products,
   or nothing to get all products">
    <cfargument name="search" type="string" default="">
    <cftry>
      <cfquery name="rsGetProducts" datasource="Northwind">
        SELECT ProductID, ProductName, UnitPrice,
        QuantityPerUnit, CategoryID, SupplierID FROM Products
<!--- If no argument is passed, return all records --->
        <cfif search NEQ "">
         WHERE ProductName LIKE '%#search#%'
        </cfif>
      </cfquery>
      <cfcatch type="Any">
        <cfthrow message="There was a database error">
      </cfcatch>
    </cftry>
    <cfreturn rsGetProducts />
  </cffunction>

<!--- Add a product to the Northwind Products table --->
  <cffunction name="addProduct" returntype="string"
   access="remote" hint="Pass a record to add a product">
    <cfargument name="ProductName" type="string" required="true" />
    <cfargument name="UnitPrice" type="numeric" default=0 />
    <cfargument name="QuantityPerUnit" type="string" default="0" />
    <cfargument name="CategoryID" type="numeric" default=0 />
    <cfargument name="SupplierID" type="numeric" default=0 />
    <cftry>
      <cfquery name="rsSuppliers" datasource="Northwind">
       INSERT INTO Products
       (ProductName
        ,UnitPrice
        ,QuantityPerUnit
```

Example 5-13. The ProductsAdmin.cfc file (continued)

```
        ,CategoryID
        ,SupplierID)
      VALUES
      ('#ProductName#'
      ,#UnitPrice#
      ,'#QuantityPerUnit#'
      ,#CategoryID#
      ,#SupplierID#)
    </cfquery>
    <cfcatch type="Any">
      <cfthrow message="There was a database error">
    </cfcatch>
  </cftry>
  <cfreturn "Record inserted" />
</cffunction>

<!--- Update a product using a product record --->
  <cffunction name="updateProduct"
   returntype="string"
   access="remote"
   hint="Pass a record including the ProductID to update a product">
    <cfargument name="ProductName"     type="string"  required="true" />
    <cfargument name="UnitPrice"       type="numeric" default=0 />
    <cfargument name="QuantityPerUnit" type="string"  default="0" />
    <cfargument name="CategoryID"      type="numeric" default=0 />
    <cfargument name="SupplierID"      type="numeric" default=0 />
    <cfargument name="ProductID"       type="numeric" required="true" />
    <cftry>
      <cfquery name="rsSuppliers" datasource="Northwind">
       UPDATE Products
       SET ProductName='#ProductName#'
          ,UnitPrice=#UnitPrice#
          ,QuantityPerUnit='#QuantityPerUnit#'
          ,CategoryID=#CategoryID#
          ,SupplierID=#SupplierID#
       WHERE ProductID = #ProductID#
      </cfquery>
      <cfcatch type="Any">
        <cfthrow message="There was a database error">
      </cfcatch>
    </cftry>
    <cfreturn "Record updated" />
  </cffunction>

<!--- Delete products from a list of ProductIDs --->
  <cffunction name="deleteProducts" returntype="string" access="remote"
   hint="Pass a ProductID or comma-separated list
   of ProductIDs to delete records">
    <cfargument name="productids" type="string" default="0" />
    <cftry>
      <cfquery name="rsSuppliers" datasource="Northwind">
<!--- The following query will delete products.
```

Example 5-13. The ProductsAdmin.cfc file (continued)

```
      The alternate query will merely set the Discontinued field to 1
       DELETE FROM Products WHERE ProductID IN (#productids#)--->
       UPDATE Products SET Discontinued = 1 WHERE ProductID in (#productids#)
      </cfquery>
      <cfcatch type="Any">
        <cfthrow message="There was a database error">
      </cfcatch>
    </cftry>
    <cfreturn "Record deleted" />
  </cffunction>

<!--- Get a list of suppliers to feed a dropdown list --->
  <cffunction name="getSuppliers" returntype="query"
   access="remote" hint="Get a list of all suppliers">
    <cftry>
      <cfquery name="rsSuppliers" datasource="Northwind"
       cachedwithin=#CreateTimespan(7,0,0,0)#>
       SELECT SupplierID, CompanyName FROM Suppliers
      </cfquery>
      <cfcatch type="Any">
        <cfthrow message="There was a database error">
      </cfcatch>
    </cftry>
    <cfreturn rsSuppliers />
  </cffunction>

<!--- Get a list of categories to feed a dropdown list --->
  <cffunction name="getCategories" returntype="query"
   access="remote" hint="Get a list of product categories">
    <cftry>
      <cfquery name="rsCategories" datasource="Northwind"
       cachedwithin=#CreateTimespan(7,0,0,0)#>
       SELECT CategoryID, CategoryName FROM Categories
      </cfquery>
      <cfcatch type="Any">
        <cfthrow message="There was a database error">
      </cfcatch>
    </cftry>
    <cfreturn rsCategories />
  </cffunction>

</cfcomponent>
```

The methods of the *ProductsAdmin* service are self-documenting using the hints of
the <cffunction> tag and the inline comments. The methods each contain a basic
error handler of a <cftry> and <cfcatch> block that simply throws an error message
to the Flash movie upon any type of error. The *getCategories( )* and *getSuppliers( )*
methods demonstrate the cachedwithin attribute of the <cfquery> tag— each query is
executed only once every seven days, or upon a restart of the server. This improves
the speed of the queries dramatically because they exist in the server's memory.

The client-side code

The ActionScript code for the *ProductsAdmin.fla* file is shown in Example 5-14.

Example 5-14. ProductsAdmin.fla

```
#include "NetServices.as"
#include "DataGlue.as"

// Set up the combo boxes to be able to pick a value
FComboBoxClass.prototype.pickValue = function (value) {
  for (var i=0; i<this.getLength(); i++) {
    if (this.getItemAt(i).data == value) {
      this.setSelectedIndex(i);
      break;
    }
  }
};

// General error handler for authoring environment
function errorHandler (error) {
  trace(error.description);
}

// Responder objects
var SearchResult = new Object();

SearchResult.onResult = function (result_rs) {
  Products_rs = result_rs;
  results_txt.text = "There were " + Products_rs.getLength() +
    " records returned.";
  Products_rs.move("First");
  getRecord();
};

SearchResult.onStatus = errorHandler;

// Set up a responder object to handle recordsets for ComboBoxes
function ComboBoxResponder (cbName) {
  this.cbName = cbName;
}
// The responder assumes that data is coming in with
// ID column in [0] position and description column
// in the [1] position
ComboBoxResponder.prototype.onResult = function (result_rs) {
  var fields = result_rs.getColumnNames();
  var idField = '#' + fields[0] + '#';
  var descField = '#' + fields[1] + '#';
  DataGlue.bindFormatStrings(this.cbName, result_rs, descField,idField);
};
ComboBoxResponder.prototype.onStatus = errorHandler;

// Main responder for the Update, Insert, and Delete functions.
// Display is to the Output window only.
```

Example 5-14. ProductsAdmin.fla (continued)

```
function MainServiceResponder () {
}
MainServiceResponder.prototype.onResult = function (result) {
  trace(result);
};
MainServiceResponder.prototype.onStatus = errorHandler;

// Init code
if (connected == null) {
  connected = true;
  NetServices.setDefaultGatewayUrl("http://localhost/flashservices/gateway");
  var my_conn = NetServices.createGatewayConnection( );
  my_conn.onStatus = errorHandler;
  my_conn.setCredentials("admin", "1234");    // hardcoded username and password
  var myService = my_conn.getService("com.oreilly.frdg.admin.ProductsAdmin");
  var Products_rs = null; // Main RecordSet object for product list
}

// Set up the two ComboBoxes
myService.getCategories(new ComboBoxResponder(categories_cb));
myService.getSuppliers(new ComboBoxResponder(suppliers_cb));

// Create new functionality for the RecordSet class
RecordSet.prototype.currentRecord = 0;
RecordSet.prototype.getCurrentRecordNum = function () {
  return this.currentRecord
};

RecordSet.prototype.move = function (direction) {
  direction = direction.toLowerCase( );
  switch (direction) {
    case "first":
      this.currentRecord = 1;
      break;
    case "previous":
      if (--this.currentRecord < 1) this.currentRecord = 1;
      break;
    case "next":
      if (++this.currentRecord > this.getLength( ))
        this.currentRecord = this.getLength( );
      break;
    case "last":
      this.currentRecord = this.getLength( );
      break;
    default:
      // Not a direction: must be a number
      this.currentRecord = direction;
  }
};

Recordset.prototype.getCurrentRecord = function () {
  return this.getItemAt(this.currentRecord-1);
```

Example 5-14. ProductsAdmin.fla (continued)

```
};

// Set up event handlers for buttons
submit_pb.setClickHandler("getRecordset");

moveFirst.setClickHandler("moveTo");
movePrevious.setClickHandler("moveTo");
moveNext.setClickHandler("moveTo");
moveLast.setClickHandler("moveTo");

insert_pb.setClickHandler("insertRecord");
update_pb.setClickHandler("updateRecord");
delete_pb.setClickHandler("deleteRecord");
// Event handlers for buttons
function getRecordset ( ) {
  myService.getSearchResult(SearchResult, search);
}

function moveTo (button) {
  Products_rs.move(button.label);
  getRecord( );
}

function updateRecord ( ) {
  myService.updateProduct(new MainServiceResponder( ), getUpdatedRecord( ));
  getRecordset( );
}

function insertRecord ( ) {
  if (insert_pb.getLabel( ) == "Add New Product") {
    Products_rs.addItem(getNewRecord( ));
    Products_rs.move("last");
    getRecord( );
    insert_pb.setLabel("Insert To Database");
    insert_txt.text = "Click again to insert to database";
  } else {
    insert_pb.setLabel("Add New Product");
    myService.addProduct(new MainServiceResponder( ), getUpdatedRecord( ));
    getRecordset( );
    insert_txt.text = "";
  }
}

function deleteRecord ( ) {
  var productID = Products_rs.getCurrentRecord( ).ProductID;
  myService.deleteProducts(new MainServiceResponder( ), ProductID);
  getRecordset( );
}

// Display the current record
function getRecord ( ) {
  if (Products_rs.getLength( ) == 0) {
```

Example 5-14. ProductsAdmin.fla (continued)

```
      ProductName_txt.text = "";
      UnitPrice_txt.text = "";
      QuantityPerUnit_txt.text = "";
      navStatus_txt.text = "No Records";
    } else {
      ProductName_txt.text = Products_rs.getCurrentRecord( ).ProductName;
      UnitPrice_txt.text = Products_rs.getCurrentRecord( ).UnitPrice;
      QuantityPerUnit_txt.text = Products_rs.getCurrentRecord( ).QuantityPerUnit;
      categories_cb.pickValue(Products_rs.getCurrentRecord( ).CategoryID);
      suppliers_cb.pickValue(Products_rs.getCurrentRecord( ).SupplierID);
      navStatus_txt.text =
        "Rec. No. " + (Products_rs.getCurrentRecordNum( )) + " of " +
        Products_rs.getLength( );
    }
}

// Pack the updated record from the display into the RecordSet object
// and return the record to the caller
function getUpdatedRecord ( ) {
  var ProductName = ProductName_txt.text;
  var UnitPrice = UnitPrice_txt.text;
  var QuantityPerUnit = QuantityPerUnit_txt.text;
  var CategoryID = categories_cb.getSelectedItem( ).data;
  var SupplierID = suppliers_cb.getSelectedItem( ).data;
  var ProductID = Products_rs.getCurrentRecord( ).ProductID;
  var theRecord = { ProductName:ProductName
                   ,UnitPrice:UnitPrice
                   ,QuantityPerUnit:QuantityPerUnit
                   ,CategoryID:CategoryID
                   ,SupplierID:SupplierID
                   ,ProductID:ProductID
                  };
  Products_rs.replaceItemAt(Products_rs.getCurrentRecord, theRecord);
  return theRecord;
}

// Get a blank record
function getNewRecord ( ) {
  var theRecord = { ProductName:''
                   ,UnitPrice:''
                   ,QuantityPerUnit:''
                   ,CategoryID:''
                   ,SupplierID:''
                   ,ProductID:''
                  };
  return theRecord;
}
```

I'm not going to explain this code line by line, because much of it was explained in Chapter 3; however, several parts of the code warrant further explanation.

Enhancing the ComboBox component

When using ComboBoxes, there is no built-in method to pick a particular field in the box. Again, the flexibility of the UI components comes to our rescue—we can simply add new functionality to the ComboBox class. After including the required files, I add a custom method, *pickValue( )*, to the *FComboBoxClass* class:

```
// Set up the combo boxes to be able to pick a value
FComboBoxClass.prototype.pickValue = function (value) {
  for (var i=0; i<this.getLength(); i++) {
    if (this.getItemAt(i).data == value) {
      this.setSelectedIndex(i);
      break;
    }
  }
};
```

This method allows you to pass a value to a ComboBox to display that particular record. Since there are two ComboBoxes in the file, I decided to build onto the *FComboBoxClass* class rather than call a generic function. This is useful in the display of the current record:

```
ProductName_txt.text = Products_rs.getCurrentRecord( ).ProductName;
UnitPrice_txt.text = Products_rs.getCurrentRecord( ).UnitPrice;
QuantityPerUnit_txt.text = Products_rs.getCurrentRecord( ).QuantityPerUnit;
categories_cb.pickValue(Products_rs.getCurrentRecord( ).CategoryID);
suppliers_cb.pickValue(Products_rs.getCurrentRecord( ).SupplierID);
```

Response handlers

Example 5-14 defines a generic error handler that is used for all of the responder objects for the remote methods being called:

```
// General error handler for authoring environment
function errorHandler (error) {
  trace(error.description);
}
```

We simply set the *onStatus( )* methods of the responders equal to this function to be able to use one generic error handler for all of the remote calls. The *NetConnection* object my_conn uses this error handler as well.

Another aspect of the file that deserves a bit of explanation is the use of the responder objects. I've used three different responder objects for the six different services called in the example.

The *getSearchResult( )* method uses a generic instance of the *Object* class with *onResult( )* and *onStatus( )* methods as a responder:

```
var SearchResult = new Object( );
SearchResult.onResult = function (result_rs) {
  Products_rs = result_rs;
  results_txt.text = "There were " + Products_rs.getLength( )+
    " records returned.";
```

```
    Products_rs.move("First");
    getRecord();
};

SearchResult.onStatus = errorHandler;
```

The two utility methods, *getCategories( )* and *getSuppliers( )*, both feed Combo-Boxes, so I set up a responder class, *ComboBoxResponder*, that works with ComboBoxes:

```
function ComboBoxResponder (cbName) {
  this.cbName = cbName;
}
// The responder assumes that data is coming in with
// ID column in [0] position and description column
// in the [1] position
ComboBoxResponder.prototype.onResult = function (result_rs) {
  var fields = result_rs.getColumnNames();
  var idField = '#' + fields[0] + '#';
  var descField = '#' + fields[1] + '#';
  DataGlue.bindFormatStrings(this.cbName, result_rs, descField,idField);
};
ComboBoxResponder.prototype.onStatus = errorHandler;
```

The *ComboBoxResponder* class accepts the ComboBox name in its constructor, which is packed with the recordset from the remote method. The services are called later in the code with inline statements:

```
// Set up the two ComboBoxes
myService.getCategories(new ComboBoxResponder(categories_cb));
myService.getSuppliers(new ComboBoxResponder(suppliers_cb));
```

The main service responder (for the update, insert, and delete functionality) simply displays the message from the server in the Output window:

```
// Main responder for the Update, Insert, and Delete functions.
// Display is to the Output window only.
function MainServiceResponder () {
}
MainServiceResponder.prototype.onResult = function (result) {
  trace(result);
};
MainServiceResponder.prototype.onStatus = errorHandler;
```

Calling the services

The three main service functions are called when the user clicks the corresponding button. The *updateProduct( )* remote method in Example 5-13 takes the current record as an argument. It is called from the client-side *updateRecord( )* function of Example 5-14, which is triggered by a click of the update_pb button:

```
function updateRecord () {
  myService.updateProduct(new MainServiceResponder(), getUpdatedRecord());
  getRecordset();
}
```

The two arguments passed to the remote service are the responder object (stripped off by Flash before making the remote call) and the result of the *getUpdatedRecord( )* function. The *getUpdatedRecord( )* function updates the current client-side *Record-Set* object to match the currently displayed record, and it returns the current record to the caller:

```
// Pack the updated record from the display into the RecordSet object
// and return the record to the caller
function getUpdatedRecord ( ) {
    var ProductName = ProductName_txt.text;
    var UnitPrice = UnitPrice_txt.text;
    var QuantityPerUnit = QuantityPerUnit_txt.text;
    var CategoryID = categories_cb.getSelectedItem( ).data;
    var SupplierID = suppliers_cb.getSelectedItem( ).data;
    var ProductID = Products_rs.getCurrentRecord( ).ProductID;
    var theRecord = { ProductName:ProductName
                    ,UnitPrice:UnitPrice
                    ,QuantityPerUnit:QuantityPerUnit
                    ,CategoryID:CategoryID
                    ,SupplierID:SupplierID
                    ,ProductID:ProductID
                    };
    Products_rs.replaceItemAt(Products_rs.getCurrentRecord, theRecord);
    return theRecord;
}
```

For the sake of the example, we assume that the currently displayed record has been modified if (and only if) the user clicks the Update Product button. In a production situation, you can set "dirty" flags to indicate that a record needs to be updated (as shown in Example 5-16). One option is to check the current display against the client-side *RecordSet* object; if the displayed recordset differs in any way from the *RecordSet* object in memory, then you know it has been changed. You can also disable the Update button until the record has been changed by the user. Similarly, you should generally allow the user to confirm that she wants to submit changes by explicitly clicking an Update button; updating the server data automatically whenever the data changes on the client side may lead to unintentional database updates.

The record is sent to the server, which treats the fields of the record as named arguments. If you recall from our *.cfc* file in Example 5-13, all the fields for the database update were named as arguments in the function:

```
<cfargument name="ProductName" type="string" required="true" />
<cfargument name="UnitPrice" type="numeric" default=0 />
<cfargument name="QuantityPerUnit" type="string" default="0" />
<cfargument name="CategoryID" type="numeric" default=0 />
<cfargument name="SupplierID" type="numeric" default=0 />
<cfargument name="ProductID" type="numeric" required="true" />
```

We can simply pass an ActionScript object (the current record) to the remote service.

The insert functionality is similar, although the ProductID is generated by the database. It deserves a bit of explanation, though, because it has to be done in two parts:

```
function insertRecord () {
  if (insert_pb.getLabel() == "Add New Product") {
    Products_rs.addItem(getNewRecord());
    Products_rs.move("last");
    getRecord();
    insert_pb.setLabel("Insert To Database");
    insert_txt.text = "Click again to insert to database";
  } else {
    insert_pb.setLabel("Add New Product");
    myService.addProduct(new MainServiceResponder(), getUpdatedRecord());
    getRecordset();
    insert_txt.text = "";
  }
}
```

When the user clicks the Add New Product button, the display has to be cleared out and a new record needs to be inserted into the client-side *RecordSet* object. At this point, nothing has happened on the server. The display on the button changes to "Click again to insert into database." The user can type into the blank display to fill in the fields of the new record. When the user clicks the button again, the code adds the newly created record to the remote database.

The delete functionality is straightforward as well. The currently displayed record's ProductID field is sent to the server. The remote method deletes the record:

```
function deleteRecord () {
  var productID = Products_rs.getCurrentRecord().ProductID;
  myService.deleteProducts(new MainServiceResponder(), ProductID);
  getRecordset();
}
```

The completed code can be found at the online Code Depot. Keep in mind that any updates, inserts, and deletes will permanently change your database. Always make backups and keep clean copies of the *Northwind* database on hand for other examples.

Passing a Record to the Service Automatically

The DataGrid component is one of the commercial add-ons available from Macromedia in the first Developer Resource Kit (DRK), available from *http://www.macromedia.com/go/drk*. This section describes one way to update remote data from within a client-side DataGrid. The example uses the same remote services as the previous example—*ProductsAdmin.cfc*—with one additional method.

 Because the DataGrid is a commercial product, licensing restrictions prevent distributing it from the online Code Depot. You must add your own DataGrid component to the movie for the example to work.

The updateProducts( ) method

The *ProductsAdmin.cfc* file from Example 5-13 contains an *updateProduct( )* method for updating a single database record. Example 5-15 adds a new method, *updateProducts( )*, that allows batch updates of data.

Example 5-15. The updateProduct( ) method added to ProductsAdmin.cfc

```
<cffunction name="updateProducts"  returntype="string"
   access="remote" hint="Batch update a group of products">
   <cfargument name="Products" type="array" required="true" />
   <cfloop index=i from="1" to=#ArrayLen(Products)#>
     <cfset temp =
     updateProduct(Products[i].ProductName,
                   Products[i].UnitPrice,
                   Products[i].QuantityPerUnit,
                   Products[i].CategoryID,
                   Products[i].SupplierID,
                   Products[i].ProductID)>
   </cfloop>
   <cfreturn "Products updated" />
</cffunction>
```

The *updateProducts( )* method updates multiple records by calling the *update-Product( )* method within the same *.cfc* file (see Example 5-13) for each record passed in. This is typically how a batch update process is done. The client-side code is shown in Example 5-16.

The client-side ActionScript

Most of the client-side code remains the same as Example 5-14. The new code in Example 5-16 that is related to the DataGrid component is commented inline.

Example 5-16. ActionScript for ProductsAdminGrid.fla

```
#include "NetServices.as"
#include "DataGlue.as"

// Set up the combo boxes to be able to pick a value
FComboBoxClass.prototype.pickValue = function (value) {
  for (var i=0; i<this.getLength( ); i++) {
    if (this.getItemAt(i).data == value) {
      this.setSelectedIndex(i);
      break;
    }
  }
};

// General error handler for authoring environment
function errorHandler (error) {
  trace(error.description);
}
```

Example 5-16. ActionScript for ProductsAdminGrid.fla (continued)

```
// Responder objects
var SearchResult = new Object( );
SearchResult.onResult = function (result_rs) {
  // Put the contents of the recordset into the DataGrid
  allProducts_dg.setDataProvider(result_rs);
  // Don't allow editing of the ProductID primary key
  allProducts_dg.getColumnAt(0).setEditable(false);
};

SearchResult.onStatus = errorHandler;

// Set up a responder object to handle recordsets for ComboBoxes
function ComboBoxResponder (cbName) {
  this.cbName = cbName;
}
// The responder assumes that data is coming in with
// ID column in [0] position and description column
// in the [1] position
ComboBoxResponder.prototype.onResult = function (result_rs) {
  var fields = result_rs.getColumnNames( );
  var idField = '#' + fields[0] + '#';
  var descField = '#' + fields[1] + '#';
  DataGlue.bindFormatStrings(this.cbName, result_rs, descField,idField);
}
ComboBoxResponder.prototype.onStatus = errorHandler;

// Main responder for the Update, Insert, and Delete functions.
// Display is to the Output window only.
function MainServiceResponder ( ) {
}
MainServiceResponder.prototype.onResult = function (result) {
  trace(result);
};
MainServiceResponder.prototype.onStatus = errorHandler;

// Initialization code
if (connected == null) {
  connected = true;
  NetServices.setDefaultGatewayUrl("http://localhost/flashservices/gateway");
  var my_conn = NetServices.createGatewayConnection( );
  my_conn.onStatus = errorHandler;
  my_conn.setCredentials("admin", "1234"); // hardcoded username and password
  var myService = my_conn.getService("com.oreilly.frdg.admin.ProductsAdmin");
}

// Set up the two combo boxes
myService.getCategories(new ComboBoxResponder(categories_cb));
myService.getSuppliers(new ComboBoxResponder(suppliers_cb));
// Set up change handlers for combo boxes
categories_cb.setChangeHandler("setCategory");
suppliers_cb.setChangeHandler("setSupplier");
```

Example 5-16. ActionScript for ProductsAdminGrid.fla (continued)

```
// Set up the DataGrid
allProducts_dg.setEditable(true);
allProducts_dg.setSelectMultiple(true);

// Each time a row is edited, flag it for update
allProducts_dg.setEditHandler("flagForUpdate");
// Create an array to hold flagged product records
allProducts_toUpdate = new Array();    // Records marked for update

// When the user selects a row, set the combo boxes to match the data
allProducts_dg.setChangeHandler("setCombos");

// Get the Product list
function getRecordset () {
  myService.getSearchResult(SearchResult, '');
}
getRecordset();

// Set up event handlers for buttons
insert_pb.setClickHandler("insertRecord");
update_pb.setClickHandler("updateRecords");
delete_pb.setClickHandler("deleteRecords");

// Event handlers for buttons

// Update a batch of records stored in the allProducts_toUpdate array
function updateRecords () {
  myService.updateProducts(new MainServiceResponder(), allProducts_toUpdate);
  getProductList();
}

function insertRecord () {
  if (insert_pb.getLabel() == "Add New Product") {
    allProducts_dg.addItem(getNewRecord());
    allProducts_dg.setSelectedCell(allProducts_dg.getLength()-1,"ProductName");
    insert_pb.setLabel("Insert To Database");
    insert_txt.text = "Click again to insert to database";
  } else {
    insert_pb.setLabel("Add New Product");
    myService.addProduct(new MainServiceResponder(),
      allProducts_dg.getSelectedItem());
    getRecordset();
    insert_txt.text = "";
  }
}

// Delete all selected records -- pass the ProductID numbers as a list
function deleteRecords () {
  var deletedIndices = allProducts_dg.getSelectedIndices();
  var deletedItems = new Array();
  for (var i=0; i < deletedIndices.length; i++) {
    deletedItems.push(allProducts_dg.getItemAt(deletedIndices[i]).ProductID);
```

Example 5-16. ActionScript for ProductsAdminGrid.fla (continued)

```
    allProducts_dg.removeItemAt(deletedIndices[i]);
  }
  myService.deleteProducts(new MainServiceResponder(), deletedItems.join());
}

// Get a blank record
function getNewRecord () {
  var theRecord = { ProductID:''
                   ,ProductName:''
                   ,UnitPrice:''
                   ,QuantityPerUnit:''
                   ,CategoryID:''
                   ,SupplierID:''
                  };
  return theRecord;
}

function flagForUpdate (grid_dg) {
  // This row has been modified; save it for update
  allProducts_toUpdate.push(grid_dg.getSelectedItem());
}

function setCombos () {
  categories_cb.pickValue(allProducts_dg.getSelectedItem().ProductID);
  suppliers_cb.pickValue(allProducts_dg.getSelectedItem().SupplierID);
}

// Utility function to set the current CategoryID to the value in the combo
function setCategory (combo) {
  allProducts_dg.setCellData(allProducts_dg.getSelectedIndex(),
                            "CategoryID", combo.getValue());
}

// Utility function to set the current SupplierID to the value in combo
function setSupplier (combo) {
  allProducts_dg.setCellData(allProducts_dg.getSelectedIndex(),
                            "SupplierID", combo.getValue());
}
```

The main functional differences between Example 5-16 and Example 5-14 are:

- Results can be seen for many records at once in a grid display.

- Rows can be deleted in bulk by multiselecting the rows and pressing the Delete
  Selected Products button.

- Updates are made in bulk as well; "dirty" (edited) records are stored in an array
  and passed to the server at once when the user clicks Update Products.

The DataGrid's changeHandler function, *setCombos( )*, is called whenever the user
selects another row. This updates the combo boxes in the display. The DataGrid's

editHandler function, *flagForUpdate( )*, adds the edited row to an array, which can then be passed to the server upon clicking the Update Products button.

The DataGrid is a highly versatile component that can be used by itself or in conjunction with other components, as shown here. You can also enhance the DataGrid so that the cells contain other components such as CheckBoxes, ComboBoxes, and other items, as described in Chapter 11.

Wrapping Up

This chapter covered Flash Remoting specifically for ColdFusion applications. ColdFusion is perhaps the most popular platform for building Flash Remoting applications because of its tag-based syntax and ease of use. Several features of ColdFusion MX—ColdFusion Components, the authentication system, tag-based functions, and the <cfobject> tags—are ideally suited for Flash Remoting.

In this chapter, you learned about ColdFusion Components (CFCs) in depth and explored the authentication system using ActionScript's *setCredentials( )* method. You also saw two extended examples that demonstrated inserting, updating, and deleting data.

The ColdFusion MX Server can also be host to Flash Remoting applications written in Server-Side ActionScript, which is covered in Chapter 6. Much of the discussion in Chapter 7, which focuses on Flash Remoting and Java, also pertains to the ColdFusion implementation.

CHAPTER 6

Server-Side ActionScript

ActionScript has evolved over the years into a highly sophisticated object-based language. ActionScript 1.0 is based on the ECMA-262 standard, which was designed to standardize the features of JavaScript across platforms and implementations. JavaScript Versions 1.3 and higher conform to this standard, and Flash MX ActionScript conforms closely—but not entirely—to the standard. Server-Side ActionScript (SSAS) is Macromedia's way of allowing ActionScript developers to leverage their experience in coding ActionScript to be able to develop server-side services without having to learn a new language like ColdFusion or Java. Now you can query databases directly with ActionScript, albeit executed on the server-side and not on the client-side in the Flash Player.

What Is Server-Side ActionScript?

Server-Side ActionScript is more accurately JavaScript—it is built entirely using the Rhino JavaScript parser (*http://www.mozilla.org/rhino*). The Rhino implementation of JavaScript was a project begun by Netscape for a never-used all-Java browser. The Rhino project took on a life of its own, however, and is now an open source project housed at the Mozilla web site. Rhino is essentially a JavaScript parser built in Java. For that reason, it is a perfect fit for ColdFusion MX and JRun 4. Macromedia used the Rhino engine for the Server-Side ActionScript implementation in both ColdFusion MX and JRun 4. Currently, these are the only two platforms that support SSAS (the .NET, Java, PHP, and Perl versions of Flash Remoting don't support SSAS).

 Flash Communication Server has its own implementation of JavaScript as Server-Side ActionScript, but it is based on the Mozilla Spidermonkey JavaScript engine (written in C). It offers no interoperability with Flash Remoting SSAS. You can find more information about Spidermonkey at *http://www.mozilla.org/js/spidermonkey*.

SSAS files have an *.asr* file extension and reside within a ColdFusion or JRun 4 web directory. The *.asr* files can be viewed in any web browser as plain text files unless you take precautions, such as adding the *.asr* file extension to the list of excluded file types in your web server.

An SSAS file consists entirely of functions, which become the methods of the remote service that you call with Flash Remoting. You cannot call or execute an SSAS file on its own or through any mechanism other than Flash Remoting. For that reason, SSAS files have these limitations:

- SSAS files cannot execute inline code, such as variable declarations or other inline statements, except when calling methods. When you call a remote method, all inline code on the page is executed as well.

- SSAS files cannot include other files, which precludes you from using SSAS to develop server-side classes that reside in separate files.

SSAS consists of the core ECMAScript language, without any of the client-side features you have come to know from writing ActionScript in Flash MX. SSAS uses the same basic expressions, operators, and objects as ActionScript (or JavaScript), but does not include support for movie clips, components, the *LoadVars* class, XML, or other Flash-specific features. SSAS is intended only for access by Flash through Flash Remoting. It can't be accessed from outside of the Flash environment.

SSAS is stripped to the bare essentials of the ActionScript 1.0 language (the version supported in Flash MX), but it has some added features that may surprise a few ActionScript developers:

- Full use of regular expressions (the RegExp object)
- The *try/catch/finally* construct for error trapping, as in JavaScript
- The full use of *eval( )*, which is only partially supported in client-side Action-Script
- Ability to access Java classes from within SSAS

Using SSAS, you can build server-side objects and methods much like you would build client-side objects and methods. For ActionScript developers that have access to a ColdFusion MX Server, however, the real strength of SSAS is in the new CF object that is specifically designed for Flash Remoting. The CF object has two methods:

CF.query( )
    Adds the ability to access ColdFusion data sources with SSAS

CF.http( )
    Adds the functionality of the ColdFusion <cfhttp> tag to the SSAS developer's arsenal

These two methods will be the focus of much of this chapter.

 The CF object is not available in the SSAS implementation of JRun 4; however, you can use Java classes within SSAS to simulate the CF object, as shown later in this chapter.

The CF Object

The CF object allows SSAS to perform queries and HTTP calls through the Cold-Fusion server.

Using CF.http( )

ColdFusion supports the <cfhttp> tag, which allows ColdFusion applications to post to and retrieve content from remote web servers—or from your own web server. The *CF.http( )* method mimics the functionality of this tag, as well as its child tag <cfhttpparam>.

 *CF.http( )* doesn't include all of the functionality of the <cfhttp> tag. The ability to dynamically create queries using a *.csv* file is conspicuously absent from the *CF.http( )* arsenal.

CF.http( ) has many possible uses:

- Post searches and retrieve search results from different search engines
- Access web services, such as stock services
- Load XML files from remote locations
- Create downloadable links that don't reveal the file location to the end user
- Dynamically create and save to the server HTML documents that can later be browsed as static pages

There are many more uses as well. *CF.http( )* can be called like this:

```
var myVar = CF.http(method, url, username, password,
                    resolveurl, params, path, file);
```

The *CF.http( )* method accepts up to eight arguments, as listed in Table 6-1.

Table 6-1. Arguments of the CF.http( ) method

Property	Description
method[a]	"get" or "post". The "get" option retrieves a file, and the "post" option posts data to a server.
url[a]	The URL of the server where you are getting the file or posting the data. This needs to be a fully qualified URL (including the http:// or other protocol).
username	Username (if required) for authentication.
password	Password (if required) for authentication.

Table 6-1. Arguments of the CF.http( ) method (continued)

Property	Description
resolveurl	"yes" or "no" (defaults to "no"). If the file content you are retrieving has links or URLs inside of certain tags, they will be resolved. See Table 6-2.
params	Array of parameter objects that can be passed to the http operation. Each object can contain name, type, and value properties.
path	If storing a file, use both the path and file properties.
file	Filename of file. In "get" operations this defaults to the filename in the url argument.

ᵃ Required

The params array deserves a little further explanation. This array should contain one or more objects with the following properties:

name
> The name of the field that you are posting

type
> One of the following five types:

> "url"
>> URL-encoded data

> "formfield"
>> Indicates a value to be passed as a field in a form

> "cookie"
>> Cookie data

> "cgi"
>> CGI script to execute

> "file"
>> File to be uploaded

value
> Any value that conforms to the limitations of the type of field you are passing (you shouldn't pass a 10 KB cookie field, for example)

You should build the array of parameter objects before sending it to the *CF.http( )* method, as shown in the following examples.

Table 6-2 shows HTML tags resolved by passing "yes" in the *resolveurl* argument to *CF.http( )*

Table 6-2. HTML tags resolved by using "yes" in the resolveurl argument of CF.http()

Tag	Attribute	Tag	Attribute
img	src	frame	src
a	href	bgsound	src
form	action	object	data

Tag	Attribute	Tag	Attribute
applet	code	object	classid
script	src	object	codebase
embed	src	object	usemap
body	background		

You can call *CF.http( )* using the standard technique in which the arguments must be specified in the expected order. Here, only the required arguments are passed:

```
var myObj = CF.http("get","http://www.flash-remoting.com/feeds/rss.cfm");
```

Named arguments can be passed to *CF.http( )*, shown here using an object literal, in which case the position of the arguments is irrelevant:

```
var myObj = CF.http(
  {
    method:"get",
    url:"http://www.someremoteservice.com/news.xml",
    resolveurl:"yes"
  }
);
```

Here is an example using the "post" method and passing an array of parameters:

```
// Define the parameters to pass
var myParams = new Array();
myParams.push({name:"username",type:"formfield",value:"tom"});
myParams.push({name:"password",type:"formfield",value:"mypassword"});
// Pass the myParams array along with the other parameters
var myObj = CF.http(
  {
    method:"post",
    url:"http://www.someremoteservice.com",
    params:myParams,
    path:"c:\downloads",
    file:"myfile.xml"
  }
);
```

The *CF.http( )* method returns an object that contains seven built-in properties. You can access the properties of this object on the client side as you would any other ActionScript object:

charset
> The character set used in the document that is returned

filecontent
> The contents of the requested file

header
> The response header

mimetype

The MIME type of the file that is returned, such as `"text/xml"`

responseheader

Response header from the server, in the form of a single header or array of headers

statuscode

HTTP error code and error string from the remote call

text

The value `"true"` if the file content is textual; otherwise, `"false"`

The `filecontent` property is the most useful, allowing you to access the contents of the file you requested with the *CF.http( )* method.

The next section shows an example of a possible use of the *CF.http( )* functionality.

Creating a proxy for a remote service

One of the limitations of Flash is that it can't access content outside of the Flash movie's domain. For example, a Flash movie hosted on *www.communitymx.com* can't load content from *www.flash-remoting.com*. One way around this is to use a *proxy*, a middleman that allows communication between two different servers. The proxy can be written with a few simple lines of Server-Side ActionScript code in a remote function. The code in Example 6-1 can be saved as *Proxy.asr* in the *webroot\ com\oreilly\frdg* directory.

Example 6-1. Remote service proxy code in Proxy.asr

```
function proxy (location) {
  // Request the data
  var theFile = CF.http (location);
  // Return the filecontent property of the object returned by CF.http( )
  return theFile.get("filecontent");
}
```

In this code, the *CF.http( )* method grabs the file content from the specified URL (`location`). The *proxy( )* method simply passes back the contents of the requested file to the Flash movie, which can do whatever it wants with the data.

Example 6-2 shows the client-side ActionScript necessary to display a remote XML file through the *Proxy* service set up in Example 6-1. In this case, the XML document is an RSS feed for my weblog located at *http://www.flash-remoting.com*. It will load through the proxy to a movie served from any domain. The text field is created dynamically, so no interface is needed. To get the dynamic scrollbar to work with the movie, you'll have to drag an instance of the ScrollBar component from the Components panel to the Stage and then delete it. This populates the Library with the symbols needed for the component.

Example 6-2. Retrieving a URL via a SSAS proxy

```
#include "NetServices.as"

// You must set the myURL and servicePath variables to
// your own Flash Remoting path and service path
var myURL = "http://localhost/flashservices/gateway";
var servicePath = "com.oreilly.frdg.Proxy";

// Create a text field to show the results
createTextField("myTextfield",1,10,10,400,200);
myTextfield.multiline = true;
myTextfield.wordWrap = true;
myTextfield.html = true;
myTextfield.border = 1;

// Add the ScrollBar component to the dynamic text field.
// This assumes you've added the FScrollBarSymbol symbol
// to the library by dragging a ScrollBar instance to the
// Stage and deleting it.
init = {_targetInstanceName:"myTextfield", horizontal:false};
_root.attachMovie("FScrollBarSymbol", "myScrollbar", 2, init);
myScrollbar._x = myTextfield._width + 10; // put it next to textfield
myScrollbar._y = myTextfield._y ;          // put it next to textfield

myScrollbar.setSize(myTextfield._height);
myScrollBar.setEnabled(true);

myTextfield.htmlText = "Reading blog...";

// Perform initialization only once
if (!initialized) {
  initialized = true;
  NetServices.setDefaultGatewayUrl(myURL);
  var my_conn = NetServices.createGatewayConnection();
  var myService = my_conn.getService(servicePath);
}

function textfieldNews (xml) {
  // Extract news items in item nodes of channel node
  var channelTag = xml.childNodes[1].nextSibling.childNodes[1];
  var temp = "";
  var newsitem, currentTag, link, newsdate;
  myTextfield.htmlText = "";
  for (var i=0; i < channelTag.childNodes.length; i++) {
    newsitem = channelTag.childNodes[i];
    newsitem.ignoreWhite = true;
    for (var j=0; j<newsitem.childNodes.length; j++) {
      currentTag = newsitem.childNodes[j];
      currentText = currentTag.firstChild.nodeValue;
      switch (currentTag.nodeName) {
        case "title":
          title = currentText;
```

Example 6-2. Retrieving a URL via a SSAS proxy (continued)

```
            break;
        case "link":
          link = "<font color='#9966CC'>";
          link += "<a href='" + currentText + "'>" + title + "</a></font>";
          break;
        case "pubDate":
          newsdate = currentText;
          temp += newsdate + "<br>";
          temp += link + "<br><br>";
          break;
      }
    } // end for j
  } // end for i
  myTextfield.htmlText = temp;
}

// Responder object to displays the result or an error
function MyResponder () {}
MyResponder.prototype.onResult = function (myResult) {
  var fr_news = new XML(myResult);
  textfieldNews(fr_news);
};

MyResponder.prototype.onStatus = function (myStatus) {
  trace("Error: "+ myStatus.description);
};
myService.proxy(new MyResponder(), "http://www.flash-remoting.com/rss.xml");
```

Using CF.query( )

ColdFusion developers have always had access to a simple tag that creates database connections, executes SQL statements, and returns resultsets to the caller. The <cfquery> tag is simple to use and simple to understand. The ColdFusion implementation of SSAS contains a method, *CF.query( )*, that works in a fashion similar to the <cfquery> tag.

CF.query( ) properties

The *CF.query( )* method accepts up to six arguments, as listed in Table 6-3. Only the datasource and sql arguments are required. A ColdFusion Server's database connections are defined in the CF Administrator. These connections are known as *datasource names* and are the basis of all data operations in ColdFusion. Once you have a datasource name set up, you can access the database to select, update, insert, or delete the data; invoke stored procedures calls; create tables; or perform any other database operation. All of this is accessible through SSAS.

Table 6-3. Arguments of the CF.query( ) method

Argument	Description
datasource[a]	ColdFusion datasource set up in the CF Administrator
sql[a]	SQL statement that you are sending to the database
username	Login name for the database connection, which overrides the datasource username from the CF Administrator
password	Password for the database connection
maxrows	Number of rows to deliver to the Flash movie
timeout	Number of seconds to wait for the query to finish before returning an error

[a] Required

The sql argument is the SQL statement that you want to send to the database. If this is a simple SELECT statement, the *CF.query( )* method returns a resultset, or *Query* object as it is known to ColdFusion programmers.

Just like the *CF.http( )* method, you can pass your arguments to the *CF.query( )* method in several different ways. This is how the method is called using the basic function call:

```
var myVar = CF.query(datasource, sql, username, password, maxrows);
```

You cannot use the timeout argument when calling *CF.query( )* with sequential arguments. To use timeout, you must use the named argument style:

```
var myVar = CF.query(
  {
    datasource:datasource,
    sql:sql,
    username:username,
    password:password,
    maxrows:maxrows,
    timeout:timeout
  }
);
```

The SQL argument

Common questions about Flash Remoting and SSAS involve the sql argument in the *CF.query( )* method. The important thing to remember is that the sql argument is just a SQL statement in the form of a string; there is nothing magical about it. You can build a SQL statement manually, create a loop to add fields, or concatenate several parts together. The resulting string must be a valid SQL statement that can be sent to the database for processing. For example, you might pass an object to your Server-Side ActionScript containing the parameters for the query:

```
myService.searchProducts({productname:"s%",unitprice:15});
```

Then, your SSAS code can build the SQL statement string using the object properties:

```
function searchProducts (searchobj) {
    var sql = "SELECT * FROM Products WHERE ";
    sql += "ProductName LIKE '" + searchobj.get("productname") + "'";
    sql += " AND UnitPrice > " + searchobj.get("unitprice");
    return CF.query("northwind", sql);
}
```

The variable sql in the previous example would contain the following SQL statement:

```
SELECT * FROM Products WHERE ProductName LIKE 's%' AND UnitPrice > 15
```

When you are creating your SQL statements, make sure to use single quotes for string or character delimiters and no quotes for numeric data. If you're using a Microsoft Access database, you should use # for date and time data.

Retrieving results

The most basic form of database interaction involves the SELECT statement to retrieve results from the server. This is easily implemented in SSAS using *CF.query( )*, as in the following code:

```
function getProducts () {
    var sql = "SELECT ProductID, ProductName FROM Products";
    var myResults = CF.query("northwind", sql);
    return myResults;
}
```

This code returns an entire resultset back to the Flash movie in the form of an ActionScript *RecordSet* object. This is the same as calling a <cfquery> tag in a ColdFusion Component or ColdFusion page, as shown in Chapter 3.

Inserting, updating, and deleting results

When you perform a database SELECT, you retrieve a resultset. When you do other database operations such as inserting, updating, or deleting from a database, nothing is returned. These types of statements can also be executed from SSAS, as can other types of SQL statements that create and drop database objects, set permissions, or perform any other valid form of database transaction.

To demonstrate, I'll use the client-side code that was set up in Example 5-14. The functions in the SSAS file all work in a fashion similar to the ColdFusion example. If you set up the *ProductsAdmin.cfc* file in Example 5-13, you'll have to rename it to *SomethingElse.cfc* in order to allow the SSAS *.asr* file to take precedence.

The code in Example 6-3 is the full source listing for *ProductsAdmin.asr*. It should be saved in the *webroot\com\oreilly\frdg\admin* directory in order to allow it to work with the *ProductsAdmin.fla* file.

Example 6-3. Updating, inserting, and deleting data using SSAS in ProductsAdmin.asr

```
function getSearchResult (search) {
  // Retrieves records that match the search criteria
  var sql = "SELECT ProductID, ProductName, UnitPrice,";
  sql += " QuantityPerUnit, CategoryID, SupplierID";
  sql += " FROM Products"
  // If no argument is passed, all records are returned
  if (search)
    sql += " WHERE ProductName LIKE '%" + search + "%'";
  try { // Execute the query and capture errors
    var rsGetProducts = CF.query("northwind", sql);
  } catch (e) {
    throw "There was a database error";
  }
  return rsGetProducts;
}
function addProduct (Product) {
  var sql = "INSERT INTO Products (";
  sql += " ProductName";
  sql += " , UnitPrice";
  sql += " , QuantityPerUnit";
  sql += " , CategoryID";
  sql += " , SupplierID ";
  sql += ") VALUES (";
  sql += " '" + Product.get("ProductName") + "'";
  sql += " , " + Product.get("UnitPrice");
  sql += " , '" + Product.get("QuantityPerUnit") + "'";
  sql += " , " + Product.get("CategoryID");
  sql += " , " + Product.get("SupplierID");
  sql += ")";
  try { // Execute the query and capture errors
    CF.query("northwind", sql);
  } catch (e) {
    throw "There was a database error";
  }
}

function updateProduct (Product) {
  var sql = "UPDATE Products";
  sql += " SET ProductName='" + Product.get("ProductName") + "'";
  sql += " , UnitPrice=" + Product.get("UnitPrice");
  sql += " , QuantityPerUnit='" + Product.get("QuantityPerUnit") + "'";
  sql += " , CategoryID=" + Product.get("CategoryID");
  sql += " , SupplierID=" + Product.get("SupplierID");
  sql += " WHERE ProductID = " + Product.get("ProductID");
  try { // Execute the query and capture errors
    CF.query("northwind", sql);
  } catch (e) {
    throw "There was a database error";
  }
}
```

```
function deleteProducts (ProductIDs) {
  // Delete one or more products. ProductIDs can be one ProductID or
  // a comma-separated list of ProductIDs.
  // The next statement is the delete statement. It is commented out
  // so that you can use the Discontinued column to delete products.
  // var sql = "DELETE FROM Products WHERE ProductID IN (" + ProductIDs + ")";
  var sql= "UPDATE Products SET Discontinued = 1
  sql += "WHERE ProductID IN (" + ProductIDs + ")";
  try { // Execute the query and capture errors
    CF.query("northwind", sql);
  } catch (e) {
    throw "There was a database error";
  }
}

function getSuppliers () {
  // Retrieve a list of suppliers for a ComboBox.
  var sql = "SELECT SupplierID, CompanyName FROM Suppliers";
  try {  // Execute the query and capture errors
    var rsSuppliers = CF.query("northwind", sql);
  } catch (e) {
    throw "There was a database error";
  }
  return rsSuppliers;
}

function getCategories () {
  // Retrieve a list of categories for a ComboBox.
  var sql = "SELECT CategoryID, CategoryName FROM Categories";
  try {  // Execute the query and capture errors
    var rsCategories = CF.query("northwind", sql);
  } catch(e) {
    throw "There was a database error";
  }
  return rsCategories;
}
```

The remote methods operate exactly as the methods from the CFML in Example 5-13. Following are a few comments about the code.

To access properties of objects passed to remote methods, you have to use *objectName*.get("*propertyName*"), as in this line from Example 6-3:

```
sql += " SET ProductName='" + Product.get("ProductName") + "'";
```

This is because the ActionScript objects coming from the client are actually Java objects of type *ASObject* when they are parsed by your SSAS file.

The SQL statements in Example 6-3 are built up using the preceding-comma approach of building SQL strings, as in this code:

```
var sql = "UPDATE Products";
sql += " SET ProductName='" + Product.get("ProductName") + "'";
```

```
sql += " , UnitPrice=" + Product.get("UnitPrice");
sql += " , QuantityPerUnit='" + Product.get("QuantityPerUnit") + "'";
sql += " , CategoryID=" + Product.get("CategoryID");
sql += " , SupplierID=" + Product.get("SupplierID");
sql += " WHERE ProductID = " + Product.get("ProductID");
```

The code might look funny, but when you are debugging complex SQL statements, this style of coding makes it easy to comment out individual lines of SQL code without having to reformat the rest of the SQL statement.

SQL statements in Server-Side ActionScript must be contained on one line with no line breaks. For that reason, it is wise to build your SQL statement as a string before sending it to the database.

When to Use Server-Side ActionScript

Server-Side ActionScript is a powerful addition to the developer's arsenal, but it is not always the best way to create Flash Remoting services. It is merely a convenience for Flash ActionScript developers to create server-side services without having to learn another language.

That said, however, there are also some pluses to creating SSAS services. For example, if you are running JRun 4 and need a simple service and don't want to get your Java programmers to create a Java source file, compile it, and deploy it, you can write your service in SSAS and simply upload it to the proper folder.

In addition, you might find that a particular service requires an ActionScript object to be sent to the server, manipulated on the server, and sent back to the client. This can be done using a language such as CFML, but using SSAS makes this much simpler. Chapter 4 showed the process of transferring ActionScript objects back and forth from client to server.

Datatype Conversions

Most datatypes in SSAS are interchangeable with client-side ActionScript datatypes. The notable exception is the client-side *Object* type, which is actually an object of type *ASObject* on the server (an extension of the Java class *java.util.HashMap*). For that reason, when you access properties of an ActionScript object that you have passed to the server, you have to use the *get( )* and *put( )* methods of the object, as you saw earlier in Example 6-3.

A resultset created with a *CF.query( )* method on the server is automatically transformed into a *RecordSet* object in Flash. This is taken care of behind the scenes by the Flash Remoting adapter on the server and the *RecordSet* class on the client.

Handling Errors with try/catch

Server-Side ActionScript contains the *try/catch/finally* construct of ECMAScript. If you have used JavaScript, Java, or ColdFusion before, you may be familiar with this construct, which is missing from client-side ActionScript. You use it like this:

```
try {
  // Code here
} catch(exception) {
  // Error handling code here
} finally {
  // Do this in either case
}
```

 A *try/catch/finally* construct says, "Try to execute the code inside the *try* block. If there is an error (*exception*), execute the code in the *catch* block. In either case, execute the code in the *finally* block."

To demonstrate, look at this SSAS code:

```
function getProducts () {
  var sql = "SELECT ProductID, ProductName FROM Products";
  try {
    var myResults = CF.query("northwind", sql);
  } catch (e) {
    sendEmailAdmin(e);
    throw("There was an error connecting to the database");
  }
  return myResults;
}
```

In this case, the query to the database is wrapped in a *try/catch* block. This allows us to capture any error when connecting to the database and perform some additional steps. In this case, we've called an imaginary function called *sendEmailAdmin( )* that resides in the same file, allowing us to send a notification email to the administrator that an error occurred. After sending the email, we create our own error using the throw keyword. When we throw an error, we are in control of what is sent to the Flash movie. We can use this to send a code or an error message of our own rather than a system error message. When you use throw, the *onStatus* event is sent to the Flash movie, so the myResults resultset would not be returned in this case.

Retrying the Query

Many times, there are things that you can do on the server to circumvent an error or gracefully handle an error. We could have tried to execute another query to a backup data source on another server within the *catch* block:

```
function getProducts () {
  var sql = "SELECT ProductID, ProductName FROM Products";
```

```
  var myResults;
  try {
    myResults = CF.query("northwind", sql);
  } catch (e) {
    try {
      myResults = CF.query("backupServer", sql);
      } catch (e) {
        sendEmailAdmin(e);
        throw("There was an error connecting to the database");
      }
  }
  return myResults;
}
```

We could have also read the information from a static text file on the server, retrieved it from an XML document, or inserted some static code to return to the Flash movie in order to allow the person viewing the Flash movie to keep on working. The point is that we are in control of what happens to the error on the server side. Errors that can be handled gracefully on the server are errors that don't have to be handled by Flash.

Debugging

Using *try/catch* can also benefit you while you are debugging an application. Look at the following code:

```
function updateProducts (Product) {
  var sql = "UPDATE Products SET ProductDesc=" + Product.get("ProductDesc");
  sql += ", ProductName=" + Product.get("ProductName");
  sql += " WHERE ProductID = " + Product.get("ProductID");
  try {
    CF.query("northwind", sql);
  } catch (e) {
    throw "Error in updateProducts: sql=" + sql; // debugging info
  }
  return true;
}
```

If you run this example, it causes an error because there are no quotes around the ProductDesc and ProductName fields. Suppose you send a Product record to this function that looks like this:

```
myService.updateProduct({
  ProductID:33,
  ProductDesc:"Test product description",
  ProductName:MyProduct"});
```

The error thrown back to the Flash movie would look like this: "Error in updateProducts: sql=UPDATE Products SET ProductDesc=Test product description, ProductName=MyProduct WHERE ProductID=33".

You can now pinpoint the problem. You can fix your code by adding single quotes around the values for the `ProductDesc` and `ProductName` fields:

```
function updateProducts (Product) {
  var sql = "UPDATE Products SET ProductDesc='"+Product.get("ProductDesc") + "'";
  sql += ", ProductName='" + Product.get("ProductName") + "'";
  ...
}
```

Finally

The *finally* construct allows you to execute a code block regardless of whether there was an error. This can be useful for freeing resources that are used in the script, as in this example:

```
function writeLinesToFile (myArray) {
  var success = true;
  try {
    writeMyFile(myArray);
  } catch (e) {
    success = false;
  } finally {
    closeMyFile();
  }
  return success;
}
```

The *finally* construct is optional and therefore not always used in *try/catch* constructs.

Custom Exception Objects

You can also create your own *exception objects*, which can act as error types for your remote services. For example, a validation service might contain exception objects that you set up for each type of validation. An object that accepts a valid email address is shown in Example 6-4.

Example 6-4. The EmailAddress.asr service with custom exceptions

```
// The exception object
function EmailAddressException (address) {
  this.value = address;
  this.message = " is not a valid email address";
  this.toString = function () {
    return this.value + this.message;
  };
}

// The email address object
function EmailAddress (email, name) {
  var theExpression = /^[A-Za-z0-9\_\-]+\@[A-Za-z0-9\_\-]+.*\.\w{2,6}$/;
  if (theExpression.test(email)) {
```

```
    this.address = email;
    this.name = name;
  } else {
    throw new EmailAddressException(email);
  }
}

function validateEmail (email, name) {
  var myEmailObject;
  try {
    myEmailObject = new EmailAddress(email, name);
  } catch (e) {
    if (e instanceof EmailAddressException) {
      return e.toString();
    } else {
      return "Undefined error";
    }
  }
  return myEmailObject;
}
```

This example checks for an exception of type *EmailAddressException* (our own error type). If the error is of that type, we return the error message that is part of the *EmailAddressException* object. If another type of error occurs, we send back an "Undefined error" message. Note that in this example all errors are trapped. If it were a complex service with many different validation types, you might have different exception types.

The Flash Remoting adapter effectively implements a *try/catch* construct: successful calls to a remote method return the *onResult* event, and errors return the *onStatus* event. Using *try/catch* explicitly within SSAS just gives you a little finer control over how your errors are handled.

The *try/catch* construct is important when executing Java code within Server-Side ActionScript, as discussed in the next section.

Extending Server-Side ActionScript with Java

Server-Side ActionScript is written entirely in Java, and one of the tremendous advantages of SSAS is that you can extend it in Java as well. If your workplace consists of ActionScript programmers who will be assembling server-side methods using SSAS, a few custom Java functions can provide any functionality that SSAS is missing. For example, the JRun 4 implementation of SSAS is missing the CF object, which is required for database queries. The functionality of the CF object can be mimicked in Java and used from within SSAS. Similarly, the file and directory manipulation techniques of ColdFusion, Java, and ASP.NET are missing from SSAS; these too can be added using

Java. I'll show a few simple examples of possible extensions to SSAS and then show a simple CF object with a *query( )* method that can be used from within JRun 4.

The Principles of Extending SSAS

Server-Side ActionScript uses the Rhino JavaScript parser, which allows you to call Java methods as follows. To invoke a method of a Java class contained within the *java* package, first use the *new* operator to create an instance of the Java class:

```
var myVar = new java.packagename.classname;
```

Then call methods on the instance of the class as usual:

```
myVar.methodname(params);
```

You can also reference classes that are not in the java package by using the Packages prefix:

```
var myVar = new Packages.myPackagename.myClassname;
```

As an example of using a class that is not in the *java* package, consider the *String-Reverser* class from Example 5-6. Simply create a new *.asr* file named *StringReverser. asr* with the method *reverseString( )* in it, as shown in Example 6-5.

Example 6-5. The StringReverser in SSAS

```
function reverseString (target) {
  var temp = new Packages.com.oreilly.frdg.StringReverser(target);
  return temp.getReversedString( );
}
```

If you use the Flash movie created in Example 5-8, *JavaExample1.fla*, it should give you the same results as the CFC using the same Java class.

 When referencing Java classes that aren't in the *java* package, you have to make sure the classes are in the classpath of the ColdFusion MX or JRun 4 server—not the web directory path where the SSAS file resides.

More information on the Rhino parser and the techniques for accessing Java from SSAS can be found at *http://www.mozilla.org/rhino/scriptjava.html*.

One of the key benefits to invoking Java inside of SSAS is to take advantage of the numerous classes that are already part of the *java* and *javax* packages. The following examples show some of the simple Java classes that can be used.

Adding a Sleep( ) function

When creating client/server communication, you often want to add a delay to the processing. This can be done in SSAS using some fancy scripting and the *Date* object, but you can do it more easily with a simple Java class, shown in Example 6-6.

Example 6-6. The Sleep( ) method of Sleep.asr pauses a script

```
function Sleep (howManySeconds) {
  var mySleeper = new java.lang.Thread;
  mySleeper.sleep(howManySeconds * 1000);
}
```

This function allows you to pass a count, in seconds, of how long you want the script to delay. The following code will cause a three-second sleep:

```
Sleep(3);
```

Getting a directory list from the server

Unlike ColdFusion, SSAS does not support any built-in directory access methods. Again, this can be accomplished rather easily with Java. The remote method *getDirectory( )*, shown in Example 6-7, returns a directory in an array, with recursive entries for subdirectories. The function can be saved in a file named *Directory.asr* in the *webroot\com\oreilly\frdg* directory.

Example 6-7. Retrieving a directory with SSAS

```
function getDirectory (theDirectory) {
  // Create a file object for the root directory
  var myFile = new java.io.File (theDirectory) ;
  // Get all the files and directories under the directory
  var myFileList = myFile.listFiles();
  var theList = new Array();
  for (var i = 0 ; i < myFileList.length ; i ++ ) {
    if (myFileList[i].isDirectory()) {
      // If it is a directory, create an object containing
      // the directory name and file list.
      theList.push({directory:myFileList[i].toString(),
                    files:getDirectory(myFileList[i])});
    } else if (myFileList[i].isFile()) {
      theList.push(myFileList[i].toString())
    }
  }
  return theList;
}
```

The *getDirectory( )* function accepts a directory path as an argument. The path should be in a string format, such as "e:/cfusionmx/wwwroot/com/oreilly". The path can use slashes (/) to maintain compatibility with Unix servers or backslashes (\) for Windows servers. If you use backslashes, you'll also have to escape them with another backslash, such as "e:\\cfusionmx\\wwwroot\\com\\oreilly". The function uses the *File* class in the *java.io* package. The *listFiles( )* method grabs an array of files in the directory. The list elements can be files or directories. If the current item is a directory, as indicated by *isDirectory( )*, we create an ActionScript object with a directory property (the directory path) and a files property. The files property is an array created by calling the *getDirectory( )* function recursively. This will play an important part in the process on the client once we return the result. If the current item is not a directory, we add it to the current directory's file list. Finally, we return the list to the caller.

Example 6-8 shows the client-side ActionScript for the *Directory* service. The method uses a *Tree* object from the Flash UI Components Set 2. We assume the *Tree* object is named directory_tree and we populate it with the contents of the remote directory.

Example 6-8. Retrieving the contents of a directory on the server with DirectoryList.fla

```
#include "NetServices.as"

// The directory to list the contents of
var theDirectory = "e:\\cfusionmx\\wwwroot\\com\\oreilly";

var myURL = "http://localhost/flashservices/gateway";
if (initialized == null) {
  initialized = true;
  NetServices.setDefaultGatewayUrl(myURL);
  var my_conn = NetServices.createGatewayConnection( );
  var myService = my_conn.getService("com.oreilly.frdg.Directory");
}

// Call the remote service to retrieve a directory, given the path
myService.getDirectory(new MyResponder( ), theDirectory);

// Set up the Tree control named directory_tree, assumed to exist already
var myRootNode = new FTreeNode(theDirectory).setIsOpen(true);
directory_tree.setRootNode(myRootNode);

// Responder object for the directory list, with private methods
function MyResponder ( ) {
  this.onResult = function (myResult) {
    listDirectory(myResult, myRootNode);
    directory_tree.refresh( );
  };
  this.onStatus = function (myStatus) {
    trace("Error: "+ myStatus.description);
  };
  function listDirectory (myArray, node) {
    // Populate the Tree object using the directory list from the server
    for (var i=0; i< myArray.length; i++) {
      if (myArray[i] instanceof Object) {
        var new_tree_node = new FTreeNode(myArray[i].directory);
        node.addNode(new_tree_node);
        listDirectory(myArray[i].files, new_tree_node);
      } else {
        node.addNode(new FTreeNode(getFile(myArray[i]), getFile(myArray[i])));
      }
    }
  };
  function getFile (filePath) {
    var lastSlash = filePath.lastIndexOf("\\");
```

```
    if (lastSlash != -1) filePath = filePath.substring(lastSlash+1);
    return filePath;
  }
}
```

Example 6-8 uses recursion again—this time on the client. The array of directories and files is returned from the server, so we cycle through the array and test each item. If it is an object, it is a directory, so we create a root node for the tree using the directory property (the path of the directory) and call the *listDirectory( )* method recursively. If it is not an object, then it must be a file path, so we get the filename from the path (using another private method—*getFile( )*) and add a child node to the current root node of the tree. Figure 6-1 shows the *Directory* service in use.

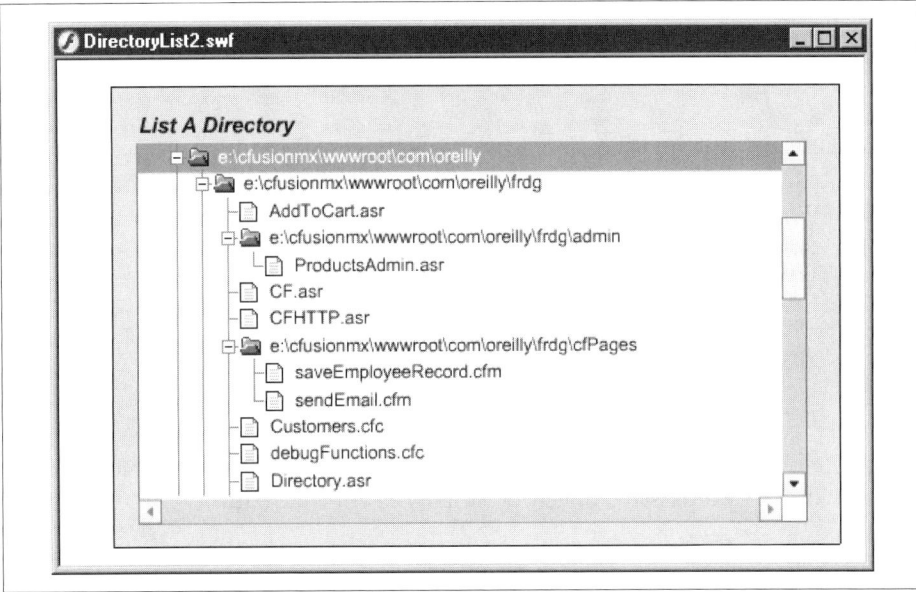

Figure 6-1. Recursively listing the contents of a directory on the server

This example demonstrates one of the striking things about using SSAS for remote services—the separation between client and server is almost seamless. You could, for example, add a filtering mechanism to the *Directory* service to filter filenames based on their file extensions. The functionality could be placed on the client or on the server. In fact, the same code would work in either place, because it is simply Action-Script code.

File methods on the server

The preceding section showed how to use Java from within SSAS to access the filesystem. Following are some general utility functions that can be used in SSAS inside of your remote methods.

 Object-oriented techniques don't work as well in SSAS as in client-side ActionScript because of the nature of the language. There are no includes, and the remote methods are accessed when needed, so instantiating objects doesn't make as much sense from a programming perspective. For that reason, the file methods shown in this section are shown as individual functions rather than methods of a class.

The *moveFile( )* method shown in Example 6-9 moves a file on the server given a source file path and destination file path.

Example 6-9. Moving a file on the server

```
function moveFile (source, destination) {
  var myFile = new java.io.File(source);
  if (!myFile.exists( ))
    return false;
  return myFile.renameTo(new java.io.File(destination));
}
```

The *renameFile( )* method shown in Example 6-10 renames a file on the server.

Example 6-10. Renaming a file on the server

```
function renameFile (sourcepath, newFilename) {
  var myFile = new java.io.File(sourcepath);
  if (!myFile.exists( ) || myFile.isDirectory( ))
    return false;
  newFilename = myFile.getParent( ) + java.io.File.separator + newFilename;
  return myFile.renameTo(new java.io.File(newFilename));
}
```

The *deleteFile( )* method shown in Example 6-11 deletes a file on the server. It deletes an entire directory if passed a directory path instead of a file path.

Example 6-11. Deleting a file or a directory on the server

```
function deleteFile (filepath) {
  var success = false;
  var theFile = new java.io.File(filepath);
  var f;
  if (!theFile.exists( ))
    return success;
  if (theFile.isDirectory( )) {
    var allFiles = theFile.list( );
    for (var i=0; i < allFiles.length; i++) {
      f = theFile.getAbsolutePath( ) + java.io.File.separator + allFiles[i];
      deleteFile(f);
    }
  } else {
    try {
      success = theFile.delete( );
    } catch(e) { // noop }
  }
```

Example 6-11. Deleting a file or a directory on the server (continued)

```
  return success;
}
```

The *createDirectory( )* method shown in Example 6-12 creates a directory on the server.

Example 6-12. Creating a directory on the server

```
function createDirectory (directoryPath) {
  var theDirectory = new java.io.File(directoryPath);
  if (theDirectory.exists())
    return true;
  return theDirectory.mkdir();
}
```

Sending an email with Server-Side ActionScript

SSAS does not contain any methods for working with SMTP servers, so there is no way to send an email from SSAS…or is there? Using the *javax.mail.** package, you can script a method that sends emails through a SMTP server. The method shown in Example 6-13 can be saved in *webroot\com\oreilly\frdg* as *Email.asr*. It will send an email, given the recipient, sender, subject line, and message body.

Example 6-13. Sending an email from Server-Side ActionScript

```
function send (to, from, subject, message) {
  try {
    var mailobj = Packages.javax.mail;
    var props = new java.util.Properties();
    // Substitute your SMTP server address here
    props.put("mail.smtp.host","mail.YourServerNameHere.com");
    var mySession = new mailobj.Session.getInstance(props);
    var myMessage = new mailobj.internet.MimeMessage(mySession);
    var myToField = new mailobj.internet.InternetAddress(to);
    var myFromField = new mailobj.internet.InternetAddress(from);
    var recipientType = mailobj.Message.RecipientType.TO;
    myMessage.setFrom(myFromField);
    myMessage.addRecipients(recipientType, myToField);
    myMessage.setSubject(subject);
    myMessage.setText(message);
    mailobj.Transport.send(myMessage);
  } catch (e) {
    throw ("Error in sending email:" + e);
  }
  return true;
}
```

The first line of the function inside the *try* block sets an ActionScript variable to the *javax.mail* package. This technique is not immediately intuitive to the Java programmer, but it is allowed in SSAS. The Java package can be referenced with the `mailobj` variable thereafter.

The only change you need to make to this script is to supply a SMTP server address in place of "*mail.YourServerNameHere.com*". This remote method can be used with the simple email interface created in Chapter 5. Example 6-14 shows the client-side ActionScript code for generating the email application's interface. The interface elements required by Example 6-14 are shown in Table 6-4.

Table 6-4. Interface elements used in Example 6-14

Interface Element	Name
Input text field	to_txt
Input text field	from_txt
Input text field	subject_txt
Input text field	body_txt
PushButton	send_pb
MessageBox	status_mb

Example 6-14. The client-side ActionScript code for sendEmailASR.fla

```
#include "NetServices.as"

var my_conn;          // Connection object
var emailService;     // Service object
var myURL = "http://localhost/flashservices/gateway";
// Message box that displays status messages
status_mb.visible = false;

// Responder for general service methods
function Responder () {}
Responder.prototype.onResult = function (myResults) {
  if (myResults == true) myResults = "Email sent!";
  status_mb._visible = true;
  status_mb.setMessage(myResults);
};

Responder.prototype.onStatus = function (theError) {
  status_mb._visible = true;
  status_mb.setMessage(theError.description);
  System.onStatus = this.onStatus;
};

// Close the message box when OK is clicked
status_mb.setCloseHandler("closeBox");
function closeBox () {
    status_mb.visible = false;
}

// Initialize Flash Remoting
function init () {
  initialized = true;
  NetServices.setDefaultGatewayUrl(myURL);
```

Example 6-14. The client-side ActionScript code for sendEmailASR.fla (continued)

```
  my_conn = NetServices.createGatewayConnection();
  emailService = my_conn.getService("com.oreilly.frdg.Email");
}

init();

// Send the email when the send_pb button is clicked
send_pb.setClickHandler("send");
function send () {
  var toAddress = to_txt.text;
  var fromAddress = from_txt.text;
  var subject = subject_txt.text;
  var body = body_txt.text;
  // Call the service, using the responder in the first argument
  emailService.send(new Responder(), toAddress, fromAddress, subject, body);
}
```

Retrieving emails using Server-Side ActionScript

You can enable SSAS to retrieve email from a POP3 server using the methods of the
javax.mail package. The code shown in Example 6-15 demonstrates the steps
required to access a POP3 server:

1. Pass your authentication information to a POP3 server.

2. Retrieve a folder.

3. Parse the messages in the folder, retrieving message ID numbers, subjects, from
   lines, and any other information you might need.

4. Get the content of each email as part of the multipart email.

To do this, I've created an *Inbox* class that acts as a simple wrapper on the server for
the POP3 access. For the sake of simplicity, the Flash interface is done in three parts:

1. Get the user's login information.

2. Grab the contents of the inbox and display the headers.

3. If the user clicks on an individual email, show the body.

First, the Server-Side ActionScript is shown in Example 6-15. The code is explained
with inline comments.

Example 6-15. Retrieving email from a POP3 account in SSAS

```
function Inbox (myHost, myUsername, myPassword) {
  // The Inbox object opens the connection to the POP3 server
  // and provides methods to receive messages and close connections
  var mailobj = Packages.javax.mail;
  var props = new java.util.Properties();
  var mySession = new mailobj.Session.getInstance(props);
  this.popAccount = mySession.getStore("pop3");
  this.popAccount.connect(myHost, myUsername, myPassword);
```

Example 6-15. Retrieving email from a POP3 account in SSAS (continued)

```
    this.folder = this.popAccount.getFolder("INBOX");
    this.folder.open(mailobj.Folder.READ_ONLY);

    // The getMessages() method retrieves all messages
    this.getMessages = function () {
      return this.folder.getMessages()
    };

    // The getMessage() method retrieves one message given a message number
    this.getMessage = function(messageNumber) {
      return this.folder.getMessage(messageNumber);
    };
    // The close() method simply closes connections to the POP3 server
    this.close = function () {
      this.folder.close(false);
      this.popAccount.close();
    };
}

// retrieveMessages() retrieves a list of headers given three arguments:
// myHost (POP3 account), myUsername (login name), myPassword (password)
function retrieveMessages (myHost, myUsername, myPassword) {
  var myInbox = new Inbox(myHost, myUsername, myPassword);
  var myMessages = myInbox.getMessages();
  // The raw headers can't be sent via Flash Remoting,
  // so we serialize them manually
  var serializedHeaders = serializeHeaders(myMessages);
  // Close the connection to the inbox
  myInbox.close();
  return serializedHeaders;
}

// retrieveMessage() retrieves one message given four arguments:
// myHost (POP3 account), myUsername (login name), myPassword (password),
// and the message number.
function retrieveMessage (myHost, myUsername, myPassword, messageNumber) {
  var myInbox = new Inbox(myHost, myUsername, myPassword);
  var myMessage = myInbox.getMessage(messageNumber);
  // The raw message can't be sent via Flash Remoting,
  // so we serialize it manually
  var serializedMessage = serializeMessage(myMessage);
  // Close the connection to the inbox
  myInbox.close();
  return serializedMessage;
}

// serializeHeaders() takes a messages array and extracts/serializes
// the header information (from, subject, messagenumber)
function serializeHeaders (messages) {
  var serializedHeaders = new Array();
  var header;
  for (var i=0; i < messages.length; i++) {
```

Example 6-15. Retrieving email from a POP3 account in SSAS (continued)

```
    // Call our own general-purpose header serialization routine
    header = serializeHeader(messages[i]);
    serializedHeaders.push(header);
  }
  return serializedHeaders;
}

// serializeHeader( ) takes one message argument and extracts header information
function serializeHeader (message) {
  var header = new Object( );
  header.messageNumber = message.getMessageNumber( );
  header.from = message.getFrom( );
  header.subject = message.getSubject( );
  return header;
}

// serializeMessage( ) takes a message as an argument and extracts only
// the text portion of the message. The rest of the parts are simply
// counted as attachments. You can enhance this function to return other
// parts of messages as well.
function serializeMessage (message) {
  var serializedMessage = serializeHeader(message);
  serializedMessage.attachments = 0;
  var tempPart;
  if (message.isMimeType("multipart/*")) {
    var content = message.getContent( );
    for (var i=0; i<content.getCount( ); i++) {
      tempPart = content.getBodyPart(i);
      if (tempPart.isMimeType("text/plain")) {
        serializedMessage.text = tempPart.getContent( );
      } else {
        serializedMessage.attachments++;
      }
    }
  } else if (message.isMimeType("text/plain")) {
      serializedMessage.text = message.getContent( );
  } else {
      serializedMessage.attachments++;
  }
  return serializedMessage;
}
```

Next, we must write the client-side ActionScript. This interface will have three "pages"—login, headers, and message. Because this is a simple demonstration, the message is retrieved from the server when the user wants to read it. In practice, you would probably set up a class to handle the messages on the client side and save the messages into a local *SharedObject*. The commented client-side code is shown in Example 6-16.

Example 6-16. Client-side ActionScript code for email retrieval

```
#include "NetServices.as"

// Set up the components
status_mb._visible = false;
grid_lb._visible = false;
message_pb.setClickHandler("messageClicked");
login_pb.setClickHandler("loginClicked");
message_pb._visible = false;

// Set up global vars
var login;
var password;
var popServer;

// Set up the gateway URL and initialization function
var myURL = "http://localhost/flashservices/gateway";
function init () {
  NetServices.setDefaultGatewayUrl(myURL);
  var my_conn = NetServices.createGatewayConnection();
  // Set up the Email service
  var myService = my_conn.getService("flashremoting.com.oreilly.frdg.Email");
}
init();

// Click handler for Login button:
// Get the message headers
function loginClicked () {
  status_mb._visible = true;
  status_mb.setButtons();
  login = login_txt.text;
  password = password_txt.text;
  popserver = popserver_txt.text;
  myService.retrieveMessages(new HeaderResponder(), popserver, login, password);
  gotoAndPlay("login");
}

// Display the headers
function headersClicked () {
  grid_lb._visible = true;
  gotoAndPlay("headers");
}

// Get the current message
function messageClicked()  {
  var message = grid_lb.getSelectedItem().data;
  if (message)
    myService.retrieveMessage(new MessageResponder(),
                              popserver, login, password, message);
}

// Responder to grab all headers and display in list box
function HeaderResponder () {}
```

```
HeaderResponder.prototype.onResult = function(myResults) {
  status_mb._visible = false;
  grid_lb._visible = true;
  for (var i in myResults)
    grid_lb.addItem(myResults[i].subject,myResults[i].messageNumber);
  message_pb._visible = true;
  gotoAndPlay("headers");
};

HeaderResponder.prototype.onStatus = function (theError) {
  trace(theError.description);
};

// Responder to grab messages and display in message page
function MessageResponder () {}

MessageResponder.prototype.onResult = function (myResults) {
  status_mb._visible = false;
  grid_dg._visible = false;
  gotoAndPlay("message");
  subject_txt.text = myResults.subject;
  from_txt.text = myResults.from + " <" + myResults.address + ">";
  date_txt.text = myResults.date;
  body_txt.text = myResults.body;
};

MessageResponder.prototype.onStatus = function (theError) {
  trace(theError.description);
};

stop();
```

The client-side code uses a ListBox component rather than a DataGrid, since the ListBox component is preinstalled with Flash and freely available. You could just as easily use a DataGrid for your own implementation.

The two service calls—*retrieveMessages( )* and *retrieveMessage( )*—each use their own responder object. When retrieving multiple messages, only the headers are retrieved, which are placed in the ListBox. When retrieving one message, the body of the message is also retrieved.

Creating a CF.query( ) Method for JRun 4

ColdFusion MX users have access to databases from SSAS using the *CF.query( )* method. JRun 4 users have no way to access databases from within SSAS unless they know Java and know how to extend SSAS in Java. At the time of this writing, there is no way to return a resultset from a Java application to a Flash movie, as you would do with ColdFusion or ASP.NET. Resultsets have to be manually parsed on the server and placed into arrays or *CachedResultSets*. (See Chapter 7 for more details on the Java implementation of Flash Remoting.)

The code shown in Example 6-17 partially emulates the *CF.query( )* method from within your JRun 4 SSAS files, but it returns the result as an array of objects that you can parse manually in the Flash movie. The *CF.query( )* method for JRun uses data sources that are defined in the JRun administrative interface and takes two arguments: datasource and sql.

Example 6-17. The CF object created for a JRun SSAS implementation

```
CF = new Object( );
CF.query = function (datasource, sql) {
  // InitialContext for JRun data source names
  var ctx = new Packages.javax.naming.InitialContext( );
  // Find the data source
  var ds = ctx.lookup(datasource);
  var dbConnection = ds.getConnection( );
  var stmt = dbConnection.prepareStatement(sql);
  if (sql.match(/^select\s*/i)) {
    var rs = stmt.executeQuery( );
    var rsmd = rs.getMetaData( );
    var myRecordSet = new Object( );
    myRecordSet.columnNames = getColumnNames(rsmd);
    rs_hasData = rs.next( );
    if (rs_hasData) {
      myRecordSet.items = serializeData(rs, myRecordSet.columnNames);
    }
    myRecordSet.totalCount = (rs_hasData) ? myRecordSet.items.length : 0;
    rs.close( );
  } else {
    return stmt.executeUpdate( );
  }
  stmt.close( );
  dbConnection.close( );
  return myRecordSet;
};

// Get the column names of the resultset
function getColumnNames (metadata) {
  var columns = new Array( );
  for (var i=1; i<= metadata.getColumnCount( ); i++)
    columns.push(metadata.getColumnLabel(i));
  return columns;
}

// Serialize the data for returning to Flash
function serializeData (rs, columns) {
  var rs_hasData = true;
  // rows holds the rows
  var rows = new Array( );
  // currentRow will hold individual row
  var currentRow = new Object( );
```

```
// z is a mapping -- integer indexes that match column names
var z = new Array( );
var columnCount = columns.length;
// Get index mapping of column names
for (var i = 0; i < columnCount; i++)
  z.push(rs.findColumn(columns[i]));
while (rs_hasData) {
  for (i = 0; i < columnCount; i++) {
    currentRow[columns[i]] = (rs.getObject(z[i]));
  }
  // Add to our permanent recordset
  rows.push(currentRow);
  // Clear the row out again
  currentRow = new Object( );
  rs_hasData = rs.next( );
}
return rows;
}
```

Simply add the code shown in Example 6-17 to an SSAS file, and you will be able to access *CF.query( )* functionality from a JRun 4 SSAS file. The data is returned as an array of row objects, but a little bit of client-side ActionScript code added to your Flash movie converts it into a *RecordSet* object:

```
JRunRecordset.prototype = new Recordset( );
function JRunRecordset (rs) {
  super (rs.columnNames);      // Call the RecordSet constructor
  for (i in rs.items)
    this.addItem(rs.items[i]);  // Add records to RecordSet
}
```

Now you can convert the returned array of objects into an ActionScript *RecordSet* object by instantiating a new *JRunRecordset* object. Here is the updated responder object for the *ProductsAdmin.fla* file from Example 5-14 (changes are shown in bold):

```
SearchResult.onResult = function (result_rs) {
  Products_rs = new JRunRecordset(result_rs);
  results_txt.text = "There were " + Products_rs.getLength( )+
   " records returned.";
  Products_rs.move("First");
  getRecord( );
};
```

Example 5-14 also contains two *RecordSet* objects that feed data to the drop-down ComboBoxes. These ComboBoxes are created in the *ComboBoxResponder* object. Change the *ComboBoxResponder.onResult( )* method from Example 5-14 to add the *JRunRecordset* (changes are shown in bold):

```
function ComboBoxResponder (cbName) {
  this.cbName = cbname;
}
ComboBoxResponder.prototype.onResult = function (result_rs) {
```

```
result_rs = new JRunRecordset(result_rs);
var fields = result_rs.getColumnNames();
var idField = '#' + fields[0] + '#';
var descField = '#' + fields[1] + '#';
DataGlue.bindFormatStrings(this.cbName, result_rs, descField,idField);
};
```

The custom *CF.query( )* method for JRun 4 will work with most of the online examples that you'll find for Server-Side ActionScript at the Macromedia web site and other places.

Wrapping Up

In this chapter, you learned about ActionScript's cousin—Server-Side ActionScript. You learned that SSAS is in reality an implementation of JavaScript that is also scriptable with Java, making it a highly customizable language. Also in this chapter, several missing features were added using Java, including the ability to read directories and files on the server and the ability to send and retrieve emails. In addition, the limitations of the SSAS implementation for JRun were shown.

Chapter 7 focuses on the Java language and the J2EE implementation of Flash Remoting.

Flash Remoting and Java

Flash Remoting for J2EE (Java 2 Enterprise Edition) allows Flash clients to communicate efficiently with Enterprise Java applications running on the server. J2EE is a collection of core Java features plus standard application programming interfaces (APIs) for enterprise-level services such as messaging, naming, and remote components. This chapter discusses the details of using Flash Remoting with Java applications. It assumes that you are familiar with writing Flash Remoting clients as covered in earlier chapters and with web application development in Java application servers that support the Servlet 2.2 or 2.3 specifications. If you are not schooled in Java and have trouble following the examples in this chapter, consult the resources cited in Appendix B.

Flash Remoting for J2EE must be purchased separately from Macromedia, although a trial version is available. For an open source implementation, refer to "OpenAMF" at the end of this chapter.

The Flash Remoting Gateway

Flash Remoting for J2EE is essentially a servlet that uses Java *introspection*, also called *reflection*, to invoke methods on objects running in a Java application server. This servlet and its supporting classes are collectively named the *Flash Remoting gateway*. Combined with the client-side Flash Remoting components, Flash Remoting for J2EE gives Flash clients a simple object-oriented interface to locate Java objects as services, call methods on them, and handle the results.

It is worth noting that the implementation of Flash Remoting for J2EE is the same implementation that supports Flash Remoting for ColdFusion. Flash Remoting for ColdFusion includes the additional service types of ColdFusion pages, ColdFusion Components, and web services, but the core gateway implementation is the same. Much of the discussion in this chapter concerning the internal behavior of the gateway also applies to Flash Remoting for ColdFusion.

Supported Platforms

Any application running on a Java application server that supports the Servlet 2.2 or 2.3 specifications can use Flash Remoting to provide services to Flash clients.

Macromedia explicitly supports JRun 4.0, IBM WebSphere Application Server 4, BEA WebLogic, and Sun ONE Web Server. The Remoting gateway determines the application server platform by looking for known classes in its *classpath*, a list of locations in which to look for Java classes and other resources. For Sun ONE Web Server, Flash Remoting does not support Enterprise JavaBean (EJB) services. For IBM WebSphere and BEA WebLogic, Remoting supports the standard service types described later in this chapter.

Flash Remoting supports several additional features on JRun. The user credentials specified using *NetConnection.setCredentials( )* are used to define the user and user role in *Container-Managed Security*, the J2EE standard way of authenticating and authorizing users, and for access to EJBs. Flash Remoting can be used to give Flash clients access to JRun's JMX MBeans. Finally, Flash Remoting writes its log messages using JRun's logging infrastructure.

Flash Remoting also runs correctly on numerous other J2EE application servers, including Caucho Resin, Tomcat, JBoss, ATG Dynamo, Oracle 9i AS, and HP Application Server. However, do not take this list as complete. The next section describes how to set up Flash Remoting for these and other application servers so you can try additional platforms yourself.

Setting Up Flash Remoting for J2EE

Chapter 2 describes using the Flash Remoting for J2EE installer to install Flash Remoting. Be sure to use the latest update from Macromedia, which at the time of this writing is the Flash Remoting MX for J2EE Updater 1. The updater is available in ZIP archive format from *http://www.macromedia.com/support/flash_remoting/updaters.html*.

The updater provides several different distributions of Flash Remoting:

- WAR archive with no examples
- WAR archive with examples
- EAR archive with no examples
- EAR archive with examples
- JAR archive

If you want to run the examples in a servlet container, install the WAR archive with examples. If you want to run the examples in a servlet and EJB container, install the EAR archive with examples. The installation procedure is described under "Other J2EE Servers" in Chapter 2.

To install Flash Remoting for use in your own application, place the JAR archive, *flashgateway.jar*, in your web application's *WEB-INF/lib* directory and add the following servlet definition and mapping to your web application's *WEB-INF/web.xml* file:

```
<servlet>
  <servlet-name>FlashGatewayServlet</servlet-name>
  <servlet-class>flashgateway.controller.GatewayServlet</servlet-class>
</servlet>

<servlet-mapping>
  <servlet-name>FlashGatewayServlet</servlet-name>
  <url-pattern>/gateway</url-pattern>
</servlet-mapping>
```

The servlet definition maps the Flash Remoting gateway servlet to the */gateway* URL within your web application. If your web application context root is */mywebapp* and viewable at *http://localhost/mywebapp/*, the Flash Remoting gateway URL that Flash clients will connect to is *http://localhost/mywebapp/gateway*.

It is important to install Flash Remoting as a servlet in your web application so that it can find your classes. If you install Flash Remoting using the WAR or EAR archives provided by Macromedia, the classes in your web application will not be visible to the gateway servlet configured in those archives.

Once you have installed the Remoting gateway, you need to put the Flash Remoting license file, *frconfig.txt*, in your web application's classpath, such as in *WEB-INF/ classes*, so that the Remoting gateway can find it. If you are using Flash Remoting for multiple web applications, you can put a single copy of *frconfig.txt* in your application server's classpath so that it will found by the Remoting gateway in each of your web applications.

For application servers with an enabled Java security manager, you may need to edit the Java security policy to allow Flash Remoting to access your services. Refer to "Restricting Service Access" later in this chapter for a discussion of Java security and Flash Remoting.

Logging

When you configure the Remoting gateway in your *web.xml* file, you can configure the log level of the gateway:

```
<servlet>
  <servlet-name>FlashGatewayServlet</servlet-name>
  <servlet-class>flashgateway.controller.GatewayServlet</servlet-class>
  <init-param>
   <param-name>LOG_LEVEL</param-name>
   <param-value>ERROR</param-value>
  </init-param>
</servlet>
```

The options for the LOG_LEVEL parameter are ERROR, WARNING, INFO, DEBUG, and NONE.

The gateway logs messages to *System.err* and *System.out,* which will appear in your application server's logs. In development, set the log level to DEBUG to see the services being invoked by the Remoting gateway and the results of each invocation.

Service Types

Flash clients can communicate with several different service types running on a Java server. This section provides an overview of the different service types and how they are used with Flash Remoting.

JavaBean Services

Macromedia uses the term *JavaBean service* to refer to a Java class accessed through Flash Remoting that implements the *java.io.Serializable* interface (a.k.a. "implements *Serializable*"). While *JavaBean* means many things to many people, we will use Macromedia's term to identify this service type. In the case of JavaBean services, the fact that a class implements *Serializable* tells Flash Remoting that the service class can be stored in the user's session.

JavaBean services must have a *no-argument constructor* (a constructor that does not take any arguments) to be used with Remoting. If you have no other constructors, the default no-argument constructor implicit in the class is sufficient. If you have other constructors, you must explicitly implement a no-argument constructor. Otherwise, the Remoting gateway returns an error of type *java.lang.InstantiationException* because the gateway cannot create an instance of the service even though it can find the service class.

Error conditions are indicated by passing back an error object whose properties can be examined for additional details about the error. For the remainder of the chapter, we say "throws a *SuchAndSuchException*" as a shorthand way of saying that the gateway returns an error object whose type property is set to "SuchAndSuchException".

JavaBean service methods are implemented as instance methods of a JavaBean object. When the Remoting gateway invokes a JavaBean service method, it creates a new instance of the JavaBean object and invokes the service method with the arguments provided by the Flash client.

After the Remoting gateway invokes a JavaBean service, it stores the JavaBean instance in the user session and reuses it for subsequent service method calls by that same user. If the state of the JavaBean changes with one method call, the Remoting gateway uses it in its changed state for subsequent method calls. Use JavaBean services only if you want to maintain state in the Remoting service between service method calls, such as is necessary to create pageable resultsets, as discussed under "Create a Business Delegate" later in this chapter.

The following example shows a JavaBean service implementation with an *echo( )* method that simply takes an argument and returns it back to the client. Note that this example implements *java.io.Serializable* and does not need to explicitly define a no-argument constructor, since it has no other constructors. When a Flash client calls *echo( )*, the Remoting gateway stores an instance of *JavaBeanService* in the session and reuses it for subsequent calls to the same service by the same client.

```
public class JavaBeanService
  implements java.io.Serializable {
  public Object echo (Object obj) {
    return obj;
  }
}
```

Java Class Services

Java class services are simply Java classes with no restrictions other than that they do not implement *java.io.Serializable*. Java class services must have a no-argument constructor as described for JavaBean services.

Like JavaBean services, Java class service methods are implemented as instance methods of the Java object. For each service method invocation, the Remoting gateway creates a new instance of the Java class service. The following example of a Java class service provides the same functionality as the previous JavaBean service example. The difference is that it does not implement *java.io.Serializable*, so the Remoting gateway creates a new instance of the Java class service each time *echo( )* is called by a Flash client (recall that, in contrast, JavaBean instances are stored in the user session for subsequent service method calls by that same user):

```
public class JavaClassService {
  public Object echo (Object obj) {
    return obj;
  }
}
```

Enterprise JavaBean (EJB) Services

Enterprise JavaBeans (EJBs) are the J2EE model for distributed component development. For more information on EJB design and development, refer to *Enterprise Java-Beans* by Richard Monson-Haefel (O'Reilly). Any EJB available to the web application within which Flash Remoting is running can be used as an *EJB service*. That is, you may use both remote and local entity and session EJBs as Flash Remoting services.

To use an EJB service, a Flash client identifies the service using the EJB's *JNDI name* (see "Locating Services" later in this chapter for more on JNDI names). The Flash client can then invoke any home interface method using this service. The most common use is to call *create( )*, but the Flash client can also call finders on entity bean home interfaces. If the result of the call on the home interface is an EJB, Flash Remoting stores that instance in the user session and sends the Flash client back a *NetServices* object, which can be used to call methods on that EJB.

 If you are not familiar with remote and local entity sessions, home interfaces, and finders, refer to the EJB resources cited in Appendix B.

Example 7-1 shows the client-side ActionScript code for using an EJB with the JNDI name *java:comp/env/ejb/EjbService*. The service variable is essentially a reference to the EJB home interface, and the Flash client invokes the *create( )* method on it. Invoking the *create( )* method creates a new instance of the EJB and passes it as the result to the *create_Result( )* method on the Flash client. The *create_Result( )* method then calls the *echo( )* method on the EJB. Thus, we have demonstrated how to create an EJB, pass a reference to it back to Flash, and allow Flash to invoke methods on the EJB as a Remoting service itself.

Example 7-1. Invoking a method on an EJB from Flash

```
// Identify the EJB with JNDI name "java:comp/env/ejb/EjbService"
var service = gatewayConnection.getService("java:comp/env/ejb/EjbService", this);

// Create an instance of the EJB
service.create();

// The result handler for create() receives a reference to the EJB
function create_Result(ejb) {
  // Call echo on the created EJB
  ejb.echo("Flash says 'say hi.'");
}

// Handle the result of calling echo().
function echo_Result(result) {
  trace("The EJB said " + result);
}
```

Servlet Services

Servlet services are simply servlets running in the web application container. A Flash client uses a servlet service by using the web application context name as the service name and the servlet name, as it is identified in the *web.xml* file, as the service method name. For example, consider a web application named *remotingbook* and a servlet named *ServiceServlet* mapped in its *web.xml* file:

```
<servlet>
 <servlet-name>ServiceServlet</servlet-name>
 <servlet-class>
```

```
        com.oreilly.frdg.java.service.ServiceServlet
    </servlet-class>
    </servlet>
```

Example 7-2 shows the client-side ActionScript code, which creates a service object by specifying the web application name in quotes ("remotingbook") as the service name. It then invokes the servlet service as a method of the service object returned by *getService( )*.

Example 7-2. Invoking a servlet service from Flash

```
// The web application name is used as the service name
var service = gatewayConnection.getService("remotingbook", this);

// Call the servlet service as a method of the service object
service.ServiceServlet("Hello.");

// Handle the service servlet result
function ServiceServlet_Result(result) {
  trace("ServiceServlet_Result:" + result);
}
```

Example 7-3 shows a servlet service that accepts an argument list from a Flash client and, for demonstration purposes, simply returns the same arguments back to Flash. The servlet service receives the Flash arguments via the FLASH.PARAMS attribute of the request object. It returns a result by setting the FLASH.RESULT attribute of the request object:

Example 7-3. Servlet service implementation

```
public class ServiceServlet
  extends HttpServlet
{
  public void service(HttpServletRequest request,
                      HttpServletResponse response)
    throws ServletException
  {
    // Retrieve the parameter list from the Flash invocation of ServiceServlet()
    List params = (List) request.getAttribute("FLASH.PARAMS");

    // Just echo the parameters back to Flash
    request.setAttribute("FLASH.RESULT", params);
  }
}
```

There is always a *java.util.List* in *request.getAttribute("FLASH.PARAMS")*. If the Flash client provides no arguments in the service method call, the *List* is empty.

Macromedia provides a servlet implementation, *flashgateway.adapter.java. FlashServlet*, that handles fetching the parameters from and setting the results in the request object's attributes. The following example shows a *ServiceFlashServlet* class, which extends *FlashServlet* to replicate the functionality of Example 7-3. The

FlashServlet.service( ) method accepts a list of parameters from Flash and returns an object as the result. The *ServiceFlashServlet.service( )* method does not throw any exceptions, so if you need to throw a *checked exception* (an exception that must be caught somewhere in the call chain) from your servlet service, you must implement your servlet service manually, as shown in the Example 7-3. Adding a checked exception when extending a method will cause a compiler error.

```
import flashgateway.adapter.java.FlashServlet;

public class ServiceFlashServlet
  extends FlashServlet
{
  public Object service (ServletRequest request,
                         ServletResponse response,
                         List params) {
    // Just echo the parameters back to Flash
    return params;
  }
}
```

In application servers that support the Servlet 2.3 specification, you can configure JSPs as servlets in your *web.xml* file as follows:

```
<servlet>
 <servlet-name>JspService</servlet-name>
 <jsp-file>/WEB-INF/jsp/service/jspService.jsp</jsp-file>
</servlet>
```

With this configuration, you can use the JSP file as a Remoting service in the same way you used a servlet as a service. Here is what the client-side ActionScript code looks like:

```
// The web application name is used as the service name
var service = gatewayConnection.getService("remotingbook", this);

// Call the JSP service
service.JspService ("Hello.");

// Handle the JSP servlet result
function JspService_Result(result) {
  trace("JspService_Result:" + result);
}
```

Here is the server-side code in *jspService.jsp*:

```
<%@ page language="java"%>

<%
// Retrieve the parameters sent from Flash
java.util.List params = (java.util.List) request.getAttribute("FLASH.PARAMS");

// Just echo the parameters back to Flash
request.setAttribute("FLASH.RESULT", params);
%>
```

Servlet services are awkward to use because the service method arguments and result must be accessed through attributes of the request object. Additionally, developers must implement a new servlet for each service method they provide to the Flash client. However, servlet services are the only service type that has direct access to the user request and, therefore, the user session. This access can be very helpful for developers who need to access, from Remoting services, information that has been stored in the user session by other objects running in the application.

JMX MBean Services

The Java Management Extensions (JMX) is an optional extension to the core Java technologies that standardizes management interfaces to remote services. Typically, it is used to manage services running in a J2EE application server. A *managed bean (MBean)* is a Java object that represents a JMX manageable resource. For more information on JMX and MBeans, see *http://java.sun.com/products/JavaManagement*.

When used with JRun, Flash Remoting gives Flash clients direct access to MBeans running in JRun as MBean services. With access to these MBeans, a Flash client can inspect the state of services deployed in JRun.

Server-Side ActionScript (SSAS) Services

SSAS is not a standard J2EE technology. It is a feature of JRun and ColdFusion. When used with JRun and ColdFusion, Flash Remoting gives Flash clients the ability to invoke methods on SSAS objects.

Server-Side ActionScript is covered in detail in Chapter 6 and is not addressed in this chapter.

Datatype Conversions

The Flash Remoting gateway translates ActionScript objects to Java objects when passing ActionScript objects as method parameters for Remoting service method calls. When it gets the results of the service call, the gateway translates the Java object results to ActionScript objects for Flash. It does these translations regardless of the service type and according to the mappings listed in Tables A-3 and A-4 in Appendix A.

There are specialized behaviors in these translations that are worth describing here.

ActionScript-to-Java Data Conversion

The Remoting gateway converts objects from ActionScript to Java arbitrarily deep. This means that a graph of nested objects in ActionScript will become a graph of nested objects in Java, converted according to the mappings listed in Table A-3.

Because the gateway traverses nested ActionScript objects to do the conversion, it is possible to cause a *java.lang.StackOverflowException* in the gateway by passing objects with recursive references. This example shows one way to get into trouble:

```
var service = gatewayConnection.getService(
                "com.oreilly.frdg.java.service.JavaClassService", this);

// Create two objects that reference each other.
var top = new Object();
var bottom = new Object();
top.bottom = bottom;
bottom.top = top;

// Creates a stack overflow because of infinite recursion
// when the gateway tries to convert the objects to Java
service.echo(top);
```

While the preceding example is oversimplified, it is not hard to create recursive references in your own applications (intentionally or otherwise). Be sure not to use objects with recursive references as arguments to Remoting service methods.

The gateway preserves references even when converting nested data structures. So, an ActionScript array of two references to the same ActionScript object will become a Java *List* of two references to the same object. For example:

```
var service = gatewayConnection.getService(
                "com.oreilly.frdg.java.service.JavaClassService", this);

// Create an array of two references to the same object
var obj = new Object();
var refs = new Array(obj, obj);

// Ask the service if the objects on the server are equivalent
service.checkReferences(refs);

// The server returns true
function checkReferences_Result (result) {
  trace("checkReferences_Result:");
  trace("  Should be true: " + result);
}
```

The following service implementation compares the two objects in the *List* for referential equality and returns the result:

```
public class JavaClassService {
  public boolean checkReferences (List objs) {
    return objs.get(0) == objs.get(1);
  }
}
```

In Table A-3, note that ActionScript objects that are not one of the known types are converted to a Java object of type *flashgateway.io.ASObject*. An *ASObject* is derived from *java.util.Map* with case-insensitive keys and with an additional field named type. Its interface is shown here:

```
package flashgateway.io;

public class ASObject
  extends flashgateway.util.CaseInsensitiveMap
{
  public ASObject();
  public ASObject(String type);
  public String getType();
  public void setType(String type);
}
```

The Remoting gateway sets the type property of an *ASObject* to the key used when registering an ActionScript object in Flash using *Object.registerClass(key, class)*, as discussed in "Registering Objects for ColdFusion MX, Java, ASP.NET, and PHP" in Chapter 4.

Since the Remoting gateway converts ActionScript objects to only the Java objects listed in Table A-3, it cannot call service methods that take parameters that are not in the list. A Flash client calling a service method *updateUser(User user)* written as:

```
public class UserService {
  public void updateUser (User user) {
    Directory.updateUser(user);
  }
}
```

with client-side ActionScript code written as:

```
var service = gatewayConnection.getService(
                "com.oreilly.frdg.java.service.UserService", this);

// Create an object with a username property
var user = new Object();
user.username = "Flash User";

// Send the object to the service's updateUser() method
service.updateUser(user);
```

will cause a Flash Remoting error similar to: "Service com.oreilly.frdg.java.service. JavaClassService does not have a method 'updateUser' that matches the name and parameters provided."

This problem is that *UserService.updateUser( )* expects a *User* object, but Flash passes an *ASObject*. The type mismatch results in an error.

In order for it be invoked by the Remoting gateway, we must write the service as follows (changes are shown in bold):

```
import flashgateway.io.ASObject;

public class UserService {
```

```
public void updateUser (ASObject asUser) {
  // Create a User object from the ASObject
  String username = (String) asUser.get("username");
  User user = new User(username);

  Directory.updateUser(user);
  }
}
```

This example changes the *UserService.updateUser( )* method to accept an *ASObject* instead of a *User* object. It creates a *User* object from the properties of the *ASObject* so that it can use the application's *Directory.updateUser( )* implementation.

Java-to-ActionScript Data Conversion

After the Remoting gateway receives the results of calling a service method, it converts the result object for sending back to Flash, according to the conversions listed in Table A-4.

As with ActionScript-to-Java conversion, the conversion is deep in that it accesses nested elements; however, references are not preserved. The following example shows a method, *getTwoOfTheSame( )*, that returns a *List* of two references to the object passed in. We'll invoke this service from Flash to see if the references point to the same object when they are passed back to the responder function, *getTwoOfTheSame_Result( )*.

```
public class JavaClassService {
  public List getTwoOfTheSame (Object obj) {
    // Create a List with two references to the same object
    List list = new ArrayList();
    list.add(obj);
    list.add(obj);
    return list;
  }
}
```

The following ActionScript shows a Flash client calling *getTwoOfTheSame( )* and checking whether the two objects returned are references to the same object:

```
var service = gatewayConnection.getService(
              "com.oreilly.frdg.java.service.JavaClassService", this);

service.getTwoOfTheSame(new Date());

function getTwoOfTheSame_Result (result) {
  trace("Are they equal? " + (result[0] == result[1]));
}
```

This ActionScript code traces:

```
Are they equal? false
```

ResultSet

Table A-4 indicates that the Remoting gateway converts a *java.sql.ResultSet* returned from a service method call to an ActionScript *RecordSet* object. However, you should not return a *ResultSet* that you have received as the result of a direct JDBC call. Such *ResultSets* are connected, meaning that they are backed by an open database connection. If you close the *Connection* object and close the live *ResultSet* before returning it, the gateway cannot convert it. If you do not close the *ResultSet* so that the gateway can do the conversion, you will quickly run into issues in the server-side application, caused by a lack of available database connections or unpredictable behavior in the *ResultSet* object itself.

The Flash Remoting Updater release notes mention this issue at *http://www.macromedia.com/support/flash_remoting/releasenotes/mx/releasenotes.html*:

> Do not serialize a Java ResultSet from JDBC code directly back to Flash. ResultSets are live, connected objects associated with pooled resources and I/O socket resources such as Statements and Connections. When a Statement or Connection is closed in JDBC code, all ResultSets associated with them are also automatically closed. Even if a user decides not to close a Statement or Connection, they could be closed and reclaimed by the application server at any time because they are pooled resources. If the ResultSet was closed for any reason, it will not be available to Flash Remoting for serialization. (#N-36858)

To return the data in a live *ResultSet* from a service method call, you must first create a disconnected *ResultSet*. The JDBC 2.0 API includes an interface, *javax.sql.RowSet*, that implements *java.sql.ResultSet* and is designed to be used in disconnected environments. Sun provides an implementation of *RowSet* called *sun.jdbc.rowset.CachedRowSet* that is suitable for this purpose and available from *http://developer.java.sun.com/developer/earlyAccess/crs*.

To convert a connected *ResultSet* to a disconnected *ResultSet*, create a *RowSet* from the connected *ResultSet*, as shown Example 7-4.

Example 7-4. Returning a disconnected ResultSet

```java
import java.sql.*;
import javax.sql.*;
import sun.jdbc.rowset.*;

public class JavaClassService {
  public ResultSet getResultSet () {
    Connection conn = null;
    try {
      DataSource ds = (DataSource) new InitialContext().lookup(
                              "java:comp/env/jdbc/remotingbook");
      conn = ds.getConnection();

      // Create and execute a SQL statement
      Statement stmt = conn.createStatement();
      ResultSet resultset = stmt.executeQuery("SELECT * FROM test");
```

Example 7-4. Returning a disconnected ResultSet (continued)

```
    // Create and populate a disconnected ResultSet (CachedRowSet)
    // from the connected ResultSet
    CachedRowSet rowset = new CachedRowSet();
    rowset.populate(resultset);

    // Close resources
    resultset.close();
    stmt.close();
    conn.close();

    // Return the disconnected ResultSet
    return rowset;
    // Exception handling omitted
  } catch (Exception e) {
    // handle exception
  } finally {
    // Close the connection if it exists and is not yet closed
    try {
      if (conn != null && !conn.isClosed()) conn.close();
    } catch (SQLException e) {}
  }
  return null;
}
```

Using this technique, the Remoting gateway converts the disconnected *ResultSet* to an ActionScript *RecordSet*. For details on using *RecordSets* in your Flash client, see "RecordSet Object" in Chapter 4.

PageableResultSet

To enable paging of the results of a service method call using the paging features of ActionScript's *RecordSet* object, the result of your service method must implement *flashgateway.sql.PageableResultSet*.

For paging of *ResultSets*, Macromedia provides *flashgateway.sql.PagedResultSet*, which implements *flashgateway.sql.PageableResultSet* and wraps a *ResultSet*. The constructor of *PagedResultSet* accepts the *ResultSet* to be wrapped and the page size. Using the *getResultSet( )* method from Example 7-4 to obtain a disconnected *ResultSet*, we create and return a *PageableResultSet* as follows:

```
import java.sql.*;
import javax.sql.*;
import sun.jdbc.rowset.*;
import flashgateway.sql.*;

public class JavaClassService {
  public PageableResultSet getPagedResultSet()
    throws SQLException
  {
    // Create and return a PagedResultSet with 20 records per page
    return new PagedResultSet(getResultSet(), 20);
  }
```

```
  public ResultSet getResultSet () {
    // See Example 7-4 for implementation
  }
}
```

Java object

When the Remoting gateway converts a Java object that is not one of the known types listed in Table A-4, it converts it to an ActionScript object using a strategy similar to standard Java serialization. For each Java object, it creates a new ActionScript object with properties that have the same name as the internal member variables, regardless of visibility, of the source Java object.

For example, given the following class:

```
public class User
  implements java.io.Serializable
{
  private String _username;

  public User() {}

  public User(String username) {
    setUsername(username);
  }

  public String getUsername() {
    return _username;
  }

  public void setUsername(String username) {
    _username = username;
  }
}
```

and the following service method:

```
public class UserService {
  public User getUser(String username) {
    return Directory.getUser(username);
  }
}
```

a Flash client calling *getUser( )* through Flash Remoting receives an ActionScript object with a single property: _username (not username, as a Java programmer might expect). The Remoting gateway uses a *pass by value* strategy for converting Java objects. It converts Java objects to ActionScript objects by creating a new Action-Script object for each Java object and converting the instance variables of the object to the type defined in the standard conversions. If the member instance is another regular Java object, it is converted according to the same rules.

There are a couple of issues with this approach. In Java development, a convention has emerged from the JavaBean specifications in which Java developers create public property accessors for private object state. They define an object's interface using methods called *property accessors*, named *getPropertyName( )*, *setPropertyName( )*, and *isPropertyName( )*. The *java.beans* Java APIs provide developers with an easy-to-use implementation for inspecting objects that describe themselves in this manner. Many APIs and frameworks including the Java Standard Tag Libraries (JSTL), and Jakarta Struts make extensive use of JavaBean property introspection.

Flash Remoting does not use an object's property accessors when converting a Java object to ActionScript. It uses the object's internal state, which ends up giving the Flash client a view of the object's internal state but not the interface defined by the developer of the Java object. Not only does this conversion technique expose information to Flash clients that is not available even to Java code running on the server, but it does not send the information to Flash that the developer of the Java object intended all clients of the object to see.

While Macromedia's pass by value approach for converting Java objects is one valid way to convert an object's state for use in Flash, it is not very useful for Java or Flash developers who end up with Java and ActionScript versions of the same objects that may look nothing alike. A more intuitive and useful approach is to convert Java objects to ActionScript using the Java object interfaces rather than their internal state. The following section discusses techniques for applying this approach.

Converting Using JavaBean Introspection

Automatic conversion between Java objects and ActionScript objects using JavaBean introspection is provided by an open source project called ASTranslator (Action-Script Translator). ASTranslator is available and documented at *http://carbonfive. sourceforge.net/astranslator* and is sponsored by Carbon Five, Inc.

Converting datatypes from ActionScript to Java

We have seen that service methods called through Flash Remoting can only take the Java objects listed in Table A-3 as their parameter types. This leaves the job of converting *ASObjects* to application-specific Java objects up to the Java developer. For simple objects, this is not a difficult task. However, for complex objects that are composed of other objects, this task quickly becomes tedious and the implementation becomes brittle.

ASTranslator gives Java developers a mechanism to convert *ASObjects* to native Java objects using JavaBean introspection. The following example uses ASTranslator to convert the asUser *ASObject* object to a *User* object:

```
import flashgateway.io.ASObject;
import com.carbonfive.flash.ASTranslator;

public class UserService {
  public void updateUser (ASObject asUser) {
    ASTranslator translator = new ASTranslator();
```

```
    User user = (User) translator.fromActionScript(asUser);

    Directory.updateUser(user);
  }
}
```

ASTranslator requires that the type field of the *ASObject* parameter equal the class name of the Java object it should be converted to. With this information, ASTranslator converts a complex *ASObject* to a complex Java object arbitrarily deep. To set the type field, the ActionScript object must be registered in Flash with an identifier that equals the destination Java object class name.

The following example shows how to define an ActionScript *User* class and register it with a key equal to the class name of the *User* Java object on the server. This key becomes the value of the type field of the destination *ASObject* when the *User* object is sent by Flash to the Remoting gateway. This example creates a new ActionScript *User* object, sets its username property, and calls the *updateUser( )* service method shown in the preceding code excerpt:

```
var service = gatewayConnection.getService(
                "com.oreilly.frdg.java.service.UserService", this);

User = function () {};
Object.registerClass("com.oreilly.frdg.java.user.User", User);

var user = new User();
user.username = "Flash User";

service.updateUser(user);
```

ASTranslator creates a new instance of the destination Java object type and sets its properties using JavaBean introspection according to the keys and their values in the source *ASObject*. The destination Java object must have a no-argument constructor and implement *java.io.Serializable* in order to be created by ASTranslator. ASTranslator preserves references as it does this conversion.

Converting datatypes from Java to ActionScript

Table A-4 lists the datatype conversions that the Remoting gateway performs when going from Java to ActionScript. ASTranslator converts Java objects to *ASObjects* using JavaBean introspection so that the *ASObject* can be returned as the result of a service method call. ASTranslator respects the conversions explicitly handled by the Remoting gateway and preserves object references when converting Java objects to ActionScript objects. Any object that is not converted by ASTranslator is left as-is, to be converted by the Remoting gateway. The Remoting gateway converts Java *ASObjects* to ActionScript objects by creating a new ActionScript object for each *ASObject* and setting an ActionScript object property for each key in the *ASObject*. The Flash client receives ActionScript objects that have property names and values that match the original Java object properties on the server.

The following example converts a Java *User* object to an *ASObject* using ASTranslator and returns the *ASObject*. The Remoting gateway converts the *ASObject* return value to an ActionScript object that has the same properties as the properties of the original *User* Java object:

```
import flashgateway.io.ASObject;
import com.carbonfive.flash.ASTranslator;

public class UserService {
  public ASObject getUser (String username) {
    User user = Directory.getUser(name);

    return (ASObject) new ASTranslator().toActionScript(user);
  }
}
```

Since they are being converted for sending over the network, Java objects must implement *java.io.Serializable* to be converted by ASTranslator.

ASTranslator also sets the type property of each *ASObject* it creates to the class name of the source Java object. Combined with the behavior of *Object.registerClass( )*, discussed in Chapter 4, and the ASTranslator convention of registering classes in ActionScript using the Java class name they should be converted to, ASTranslator facilitates a seamless mapping between ActionScript objects in Flash and Java objects in the server-side application.

Service Lookup

This section describes the process for identifying, locating, and invoking services through the Remoting gateway.

When multiple services methods are invoked in a single frame of a Flash movie, Remoting on the Flash client aggregates multiple service method calls in a single HTTP request. On the server, The Remoting gateway handles each service method call individually. The following discussion applies to both individual and aggregated service method calls.

Identifying Services

When a Flash client connects to a service using *NetConnection.getService( )*, the gateway tries to locate the named service that is passed as the first argument. For Java-Bean and Java class services, the service name (or, more formally, the *service identifier*) is the full class name, including the package, of the service implementation class. This ActionScript example creates a service reference to a Java class service with class name "com.oreilly.frdg.java.JavaClassService":

```
var service = gatewayConnection.getService(
              "com.oreilly.frdg.java.JavaClassService", this);
```

For EJBs, the service name is the JNDI name of the EJB as it is accessed from within the servlet container. The following ActionScript example creates a service reference to an EJB service with JNDI name `"java:comp/env/ejb/EjbService"`.

```
var service = gatewayConnection.getService(
                "java:comp/env/ejb/EjbService", this);
```

For servlets, the service name is the web application context name (i.e., the URL prefix that identifies your web application). The following ActionScript example creates a service reference to the web application named *mywebapp*. The service name does not include any servlet services that may invoked on the service object reference at a later time.

```
var service = gatewayConnection.getService("mywebapp", this);
```

For MBeans, the service name is the name of the JMX object under which the MBean is registered. This ActionScript example creates a service reference to an MBean named *DeployerService* in the *DefaultDomain* MBean server. The format of this identifier is defined by the JMX standards.

```
var service = gatewayConnection.getService(
                "DefaultDomain:service = DeployerService", this);
```

Locating Services

Calling *gatewayConnection.getService( )* does not result in the Flash client communicating with the server. The Flash client doesn't contact the server until the client-side ActionScript makes the first method call on the service. When the Remoting gateway receives the first service method call, it tries to locate the service. If it is found, the gateway tries to invoke the specified service method on it on behalf of the Flash client. Because they are two separate steps, the gateway may succeed in finding the service but fail to invoke the service method.

The gateway uses the service identifier to locate services in the following order:

1. JavaBean
2. Java class
3. EJB
4. Servlet
5. JMX MBean
6. Server-Side ActionScript

For platforms in which a particular service type is not supported, the gateway does not try to locate a service of that type. For example, Flash Remoting does not support EJBs when running on Sun ONE Web Server, so the gateway would not look for EJB services in that case.

The gateway identifies JavaBean services by looking for the identified class in the classpath of the gateway's *classloader*. If it finds the class and the class implements *java.io.Serializable*, the gateway uses the JavaBean as the service.

Classloaders in J2EE web applications can get interesting. A classloader is responsible for locating Java classes in its classpath. In an application server, classloaders have a hierarchy. Each web application has a classloader with a classpath specific to that web application. If the web application classloader can not find a class, the next classloader above it tries to locate the class within its classpath, and so on until either the class is found or all classloaders in the hierarchy have failed to find the class.

Our installation instructions for Flash Remoting recommend installing the *flashgateway.jar* file in the *WEB-INF/lib* directory of your web application. In this location, the Remoting gateway uses the classloader for your web application when trying to locate Java classes. It will be able to locate all classes in your web application and in the classpath of all classloaders above your web application. If you install *flashgateway.jar* in another location—say, the classpath of your application server—it will not be able to see classes in classloaders lower in the hierarchy and will therefore fail to find services implemented by those classes.

If the gateway does not find a JavaBean service, it simply looks for the identified class in the classpath of the gateway's classloader. It uses the class as a Java class service if it finds it.

The gateway next looks for an EJB in JNDI using the service identifier. JNDI (Java Naming and Directory Interface) is the standard J2EE interface for organizing and locating objects regardless of their actual location. The entry point to JNDI is an *InitialContext* object. The Remoting gateway uses the default *InitialContext* returned by *new InitialContext( )* to look up the EJB. Configuration of your default *InitialContext* depends on your application server platform. Basically, the JNDI name you use to look up the EJB from within a servlet in your web application is the JNDI name to use as the service identifier in Flash. If the gateway finds the named EJB in JNDI, it uses the named EJB as the service.

The gateway next looks for servlet services by first locating a web application *ServletContext* object with same name as the service identifier. If it finds the *ServletContext*, the gateway then looks for a servlet with the same name as the service method in that *ServletContext*. If it finds both the named *ServletContext* and the servlet, the gateway uses the servlet as the service. As described in "Servlet Services" earlier in this chapter, the name of the service method in ActionScript must match the name of a servlet defined in your application's *web.xml* file.

This example shows a servlet named *ServiceServlet*:

```
<servlet>
 <servlet-name>ServiceServlet</servlet-name>
 <servlet-class>
   com.oreilly.frdg.java.service.ServiceServlet
```

```
      </servlet-class>
    </servlet>
```

If the gateway is running in JRun and the service has not been found yet, the Remoting gateway continues trying to locate the service by next looking for a JMX MBean. It looks for an MBean with the name provided as the service identifier in Flash. If it finds the MBean, the gateway uses it as the service.

Finally, if it has found none of the other service types and it is running in JRun, the gateway looks for a Server-Side ActionScript service. The gateway locates the SSAS service by mapping the dot-separated service identifier to a file path that the gateway looks for, relative to the web application root. Using Example 6-7, the SSAS service *com.oreilly.frdg.Directory* maps to the file *com/oreilly/frdg/Directory.asr* in the web application root. If it finds the file, the gateway uses it as the service. Note that the gateway ignores SSAS services in the protected *WEB-INF* and *META-INF* directories.

If the gateway is unable to find a service with the name identified by the Flash client, it throws a *flashgateway.adapter.NoSuchServiceException*, which is returned to Flash's *onStatus( )* handler as an error object. The `description` property of the error object includes the name of the service it was trying to find.

Invoking Service Methods

Once the gateway has successfully located the service identified by the Flash client, it tries to invoke the service method called by the client. The gateway must first get a reference to an instance of the service. It uses introspection to locate the service method and then call it.

For each service type, the gateway uses a different technique to get a reference to an instance of the service. Regardless of the service type, once the gateway has a reference to the service it invokes the service method in the same manner. It looks for a method that has the same case-insensitive name and parameters that match the converted parameters from ActionScript. If it can not find a matching service method, the gateway throws a *java.lang.Exception* with the message "Service [service name] does not have a method [method name] that matches the name and parameters provided." Refer to "ActionScript-to-Java Data Conversion" earlier in this chapter for an example of how to remedy this error.

If the gateway finds the service method, it invokes the method using introspection and returns the result to the Flash client after converting the Java objects in the result to ActionScript objects. If the result implements *flashgateway.sql.PageableResultSet*, the gateway saves a reference to the result in the user session so that the Flash client can use the paging features of the *RecordSet* component.

Invoking Service Methods on JavaBeans

For JavaBean services, the gateway first looks to see if an instance of the service is already in the user session. It looks for the JavaBean instance using the service class name as the attribute name in the user session. If the service is not already there, the gateway creates a new instance using *Class.forName("JavaBeanService").newInstance( )* and the service identifier, *"JavaBeanService"* in this example, as the name of the class to instantiate and puts the new instance in the user session.

Invoking Service Methods on Java Classes

To get a reference to a Java class service method, the Remoting gateway simply creates a new instance of the Java class using *Class.forName("JavaClassService").newInstance( )* and the service identifier, *"JavaClassService"* in this example, as the name of the class to instantiate.

Invoking Service Methods on EJBs

The Remoting gateway gets a reference to an EJB service by looking it up in JNDI using the service identifier as the EJB name to look up.

In addition to the standard handling of method invocation, if the result of a method call on an EJB service implements *javax.ejb.EJBObject* or *javax.ejb.EJBLocalObject*, the gateway stores a reference to it in the user session and returns the EJB to the Flash client, wrapped as a *NetServices* object that may then be used to call methods directly on the EJB. This process is shown in Example 7-1.

Invoking Service Methods on Servlets

As described earlier under "Locating Services," the gateway obtains a reference to a servlet service by first locating a *ServletContext* with the same name as the service identifier provided by Flash and then looking for a servlet in that context with a name that matches the method name called by Flash. As with other service types, the gateway throws a *flashgateway.adapter.NoSuchServiceException* if it cannot find the servlet; however, the error message identifies the web application name and the service identifier it cannot find, not the servlet name.

The gateway puts the method parameters in the FLASH.PARAMS attribute of the request property and forwards the request and response to the servlet. The servlet's *service( )* method is invoked as a result of this forwarding action, not as a result of using introspection.

When the servlet's *service( )* method completes, the gateway returns to Flash the object that the servlet has set in the FLASH.RESULT attribute of the request property. Refer to the discussion following Example 7-3 under "Servlet Services."

Invoking Service Methods on MBeans

When running in JRun, the Remoting gateway invokes a service method on a JMX MBean using the standard JMX APIs. It creates a standard JMX server invocation from the service identifier and method parameters provided by the Flash client.

Exceptions

Regardless of the service type, if a service method call throws an exception, the Remoting gateway returns the exception of type *java.lang.reflect. InvocationTargetException* to the Flash client. This example shows a service method, *throwException( )*, that always throws an exception of type *java.lang.Exception*:

```
public class JavaClassService {
  public void throwException()
    throws Exception
  {
    throw new Exception("This is a service exception.");
  }
}
```

The exception is returned to the *onStatus( )* method of the ActionScript responder object as an error object. See Chapter 4 for information on handling errors returned from Flash Remoting. Tracing the contents of the error returned to the Flash client when it calls the *throwException( )* service method, we get:

```
code:        SERVER.PROCESSING
level:       error
type:        java.lang.reflect.InvocationTargetException
rootcause:
description: Service threw an exception during method invocation: null
details:     java.lang.reflect.InvocationTargetException
  at sun.reflect.NativeMethodAccessorImpl.invoke0(Native Method)
  ...
  at flashgateway.Gateway.invoke(Gateway.java:194)
  at flashgateway.controller.GatewayServlet.service(GatewayServlet.java:56)
  ...
  at java.lang.Thread.run(Thread.java:536)
Caused by: java.lang.Exception: This is a service exception.
  at com.oreilly.frdg.java.service.JavaClassService.throwException
  (JavaClassService.java:124)
  ...          ...
```

Note that the preceding listing shows the exception type property as the string "java.lang.reflect.InvocationTargetException" and not "java.lang.Exception". This discrepancy is an oversight in the design of the Remoting gateway. The *InvocationTargetException* is created when a method called using introspection throws an exception. The *InvocationTargetException* wraps the source exception (in this case, *java.lang.Exception*) and makes it available in Java via *InvocationTargetException.getTargetException( )*. We can see the nested target exception under `Caused by:` in the details of the error. However the type, description, and `details` fields of the error object are populated by the properties of the *InvocationTargetException*, not the exception thrown by the service method. The Remoting gateway should return an error object to Flash populated by the target exception, not by the *InvocationTargetException*.

This behavior is unfortunate. Throwing exceptions is a well-established way of handling exceptional cases in Java applications. Code that is using an object that can throw exceptions can inspect the exception to determine what went wrong and what to do about it.

A Flash client could make a decision based on the type of exception if it were passed the real exception thrown by the service method as an error object. If the type field were the class name of the exception thrown by the service (in this case, *java.lang. Exception*), not an *InvocationTargetException*, the Flash client could perform its own error handling based on the type of exception.

The Remoting gateway's behavior of throwing an *InvocationTargetException* when a service method throws an exception doesn't pertain when using servlet services. Since servlet services are invoked using standard servlet dispatching and not introspection, exceptions thrown by servlet services are returned directly to the Flash client.

Architecture and Design

Flash Remoting provides the means for Flash clients to communicate efficiently with server-side applications. When using Flash Remoting for J2EE, you are either building a new application with a Flash interface or adding Flash Remoting to an existing application to support a new Flash interface. In either case, you may be supporting both Flash and traditional HTML interfaces.

This section presents strategies for including Flash Remoting in your Java application architecture.

Use a Service-Oriented Architecture

Although you can directly access and invoke methods on servlets, JSPs, MBeans, and entity and session EJBs with Flash Remoting for J2EE, you shouldn't necessarily do so. If possible, you should avoid exposing Flash developers to the details of how you have implemented the application functionality. Instead, you should create Java-Bean and Java class services that provide a simple, clean interface for Flash clients. Have the JavaBean and Java class services invoke methods of your application to provide those services to Flash clients.

A *service-oriented architecture* (SOA) describes an application designed to expose a set of loosely coupled business services that can be accessed by a range of clients to assemble application functionality. Clients may be J2EE or .NET applications or Flash clients. A service-oriented architecture makes for applications that are flexible, scalable, and able to collaborate with other applications running on the network.

Enterprise application developers are rapidly adopting service-oriented architectures. In the J2EE world, session EJBs are enterprise service implementations. Across technology platforms, SOAP-based web services are rapidly becoming a popular technology for supporting service-oriented architectures. The EJB 2.1 specification requires that all J2EE application servers provide the ability to expose Stateless Session Beans as web services. Microsoft's .NET architecture already relies heavily on web services. In addition, the major packaged application vendors, such as SAP, PeopleSoft, and Siebel, have announced support to varying degrees for web services and are providing SOAP interfaces to their core products.

Flash Remoting is designed to facilitate creating applications that use a service-oriented architecture to expose services to Flash clients. While Flash Remoting uses Macromedia's own AMF message format, the philosophy is very similar to SOAP-based web services. Expect Macromedia to leverage standards such as SOAP-based web services moving forward. For example, Flash Pro and Flash Player 7 have native support for SOAP-based web services in addition to AMF-based Flash Remoting.

Developers should use Flash Remoting to support a service-oriented architecture in their own applications. These applications will be flexible enough to be used by rich Flash clients to support traditional HTML-based presentation layers and to expose their functionality through web services.

Create a Business Delegate

To use a service-oriented architecture with Flash Remoting, simply create an object within your web application that is designed to explicitly expose services to Flash. Using another object to get the real work done is called *delegation*. In the terminology of the Sun J2EE Blueprints, such objects are *Business Delegates*. They can be used to present an encapsulated, Flash-friendly interface, exposed through the Flash Remoting gateway, that invokes methods on EJBs or any other object in the application server on behalf of the client. For more information on the Business Delegate pattern, see *http://java.sun.com/blueprints/patterns/BusinessDelegate.html*.

Using a Business Delegate addresses the need to create Remoting service methods that accept *ASObjects* as method parameters instead of business objects appropriate to your application. The Business Delegate has service methods that accept and return the known Flash Remoting object types. All that a service method needs to do is convert the Remoting objects, usually *ASObjects*, to application-specific objects, invoke methods on other application objects to get the work done, and convert the results back to Remoting objects for returning back to Flash.

In most cases, the Business Delegate can be a simple Java class service. Consider an application that has a *Directory* class that manages user information stored in *User* objects. Clients to a *Directory* object can retrieve users by name, update a user's data, and retrieve a list of all users. Here is a simplistic implementation:

```
public class Directory {
  static Map users = new HashMap();

  public static void updateUser (User user) {
    users.put(user.getUsername(), user);
  }

  public static User getUser (String username) {
    if (!users.containsKey(username)) {
      users.put(username, new User(username));
    }
    return (User) users.get(username);
  }

  public static Collection getAllUsers () {
    return users.values();
  }
}
```

The *Directory* class provides simple methods for creating, updating, and retrieving *User* objects. In this example, the *Directory* class stores *User* objects in a *HashMap* object in memory. In the real world, the *Directory* class would probably use a database for storage.

The *Directory* class cannot be used directly through Flash Remoting, because its methods accept and return native Java *User* objects, not *ASObjects*. The Remoting gateway will not convert method parameters sent from Flash into *User* objects, so the *Directory* class will not be able to find a service method with a matching name and parameters. The solution is to create a Business Delegate for Flash clients to access through Remoting.

The following example shows a Business Delegate for the *Directory* class, implemented as a Java class service called *UserService*. The *UserService* class has a method for each method in the *Directory* class but it accepts and returns *ASObjects* instead of *User* objects. The *UserService* class uses ASTranslator to convert *ASObjects* to *User* objects and then invokes a method of the *Directory* class with the same name. When a method of the *UserService* class obtains the results from a corresponding method of the *Directory* class, *UserService* converts the *User* objects back to *ASObjects* using ASTranslator again:

```
public class UserService {
  public void updateUser (ASObject asUser) {
    User user = (User) new ASTranslator().fromActionScript(asUser);
    Directory.updateUser(user);
  }
```

```
    public ASObject getUser (String name) {
      User user = Directory.getUser(name);
      return (ASObject) new ASTranslator().toActionScript(user);
    }

    public List getAllUsers () {
      Collection users = Directory.getAllUsers();
      return (List) new ASTranslator().toActionScript(users);
    }
  }
```

Usually, a Business Delegate strategy is sufficient to expose your application's features to Flash clients through Remoting while keeping your original application architecture intact.

However, in some cases, it is useful to have the Remoting service be *stateful*, meaning that an instance of a service persists between service method calls. JavaBean services are stateful. Consider the *getAllUsers( )* implementation in the preceding example. In a real-world application, it is likely that the list of users is too large to efficiently return in one chunk to the Flash client. Using a JavaBean service implementation of the Business Delegate, we can provide simple paging features to the Flash client.

The following example shows a Business Delegate for the *Directory* class, implemented as a JavaBean service called *UserService*. The *getUsers( )* method gives a Flash client an interface to page through the entire list of users, count users at a time:

```
    public class UserService
      implements Serializable
    {
      List users = null;
      int index  = 0;

      public List getUsers (int count) {
        // Get the list of users if we don't have it yet
        if (users == null) users = new ArrayList(Directory.getAllUsers());

        // Based on count, determine the range of indexes for the list of users
        int from = index;
        int to   = index + count;
        index += count;

        // Get the sublist of users limited to the range
        List result = users.subList(from, to);

        // Convert the User objects to ASObjects and return the result
        return (List) new ASTranslator().toActionScript(result);
      }
    }
```

The preceding example omits the obvious need for boundary checking and additional information for the Flash client, such as the number of users available, but it illustrates the utility of stateful JavaBean services. The Remoting gateway will persist a single instance of the *UserService* bean in the user session for a series of calls to *getUsers()*, so that the Flash client can request a small chunk of users at a time.

With Java class and JavaBean services, Java developers should be able to handle all service implementations for Flash clients. If you wish to expose a service available from a session EJB, create a Java class service that delegates to the session EJB. In the preceding example, the *Directory* class could be implemented as a session EJB that the *UserService* bean looks up in JNDI to handle the work of each service method call.

When integrating Flash Remoting with an existing application, the trick is to identify the services needed by the Flash client. It is possible that business logic that would support these services is combined with code that renders HTML views. In this case, refactoring is required to extract the business logic code to classes independent of presentation code.

 *Refactoring* is the process of changing a software system in such a way that it does not alter the external behavior of the code yet improves its internal structure. See *Refactoring* by Martin Fowler (Addison-Wesley). Refactor code to improve reusability and readability and to make it easier to make changes and add functionality.

The newly refactored classes will become the application services used by both the Remoting Business Delegate services and the presentation code to carry out their respective tasks.

Referencing the Request and Session

Flash Remoting services do not have access to the *HttpServletRequest* request object created by the Flash client Remoting service call. Nor do they have access to the *HttpSession* user session object associated with that request. Many developers using Flash Remoting find that they need access to both. The request object has useful information about the user making the request. Developers frequently use the user session object to store information specific to that user while the user is using the application.

The most common reason for accessing the request and user session objects is to integrate with a user-authentication system, either standard Container-Managed Security supported by Servlet 2.3 J2EE application servers or a homegrown system that stores information in the user session object.

If we can gain access to the *HttpServletRequest* object, we can also access the user session via *HttpServletRequest.getSession()*, so let's focus on the first goal. One solution is to write a servlet filter, available in Servlet 2.3 application servers, that associates the request with the current thread before the request is handled by the Remoting gateway. Servlet filters can act on the request and response objects before and after they are handled by a servlet.

By associating the request with the current thread before the request is handled by the Remoting gateway, any code running in the same thread can retrieve a reference to the request. Two classes provide this implementation: *RequestContextFilter* and *RequestContext*. Let's look at *RequestContextFilter* first:

```
public class RequestContextFilter
  implements javax.servlet.Filter
{
  public void init(FilterConfig config) throws ServletException { }
  public void destroy() { }

  public void doFilter(ServletRequest request,
                       ServletResponse response,
                       FilterChain chain)
    throws IOException, ServletException
  {
    RequestContext.setRequest(request);
    chain.doFilter(request, response);
  }
}
```

RequestContextFilter sets the request in the *RequestContext* and calls the next filter in the filter chain. A filter is defined and mapped to a URL in the application's *web.xml* file similarly to a servlet. You should map *RequestContextFilter* to the Flash Remoting gateway URL, as shown here, to set the request in *RequestContext* for every Remoting service call:

```
<filter>
  <filter-name>RequestContextFilter</filter-name>
  <filter-class>com.oreilly.frdg.java.RequestContextFilter</filter-class>
</filter>

<filter-mapping>
  <filter-name>RequestContextFilter</filter-name>
  <url-pattern>/gateway</url-pattern>
</filter-mapping>
```

RequestContext, shown here, provides methods for setting and retrieving the current request and for getting the *HttpSession* directly from the current request:

```
public class RequestContext {
  // ThreadLocal() is associated with the current thread.
  private static ThreadLocal localRequest = new ThreadLocal();

  // Get the request from the current thread.
  public static ServletRequest getRequest () {
    return (ServletRequest) localRequest.get();
  }
```

```
// Set the request in the current thread.
public static void setRequest (ServletRequest request) {
  localRequest.set(request);
}

// If it is an HttpServletRequest, get the request from the current thread.
public static HttpServletRequest getHttpRequest () {
  if (getRequest() instanceof HttpServletRequest) {
    return (HttpServletRequest) getRequest();
  }
  return null;
}

// Get the session from the HttpRequest in the current thread.
public static HttpSession getSession () {
  if (getHttpRequest() == null) return null;
  return getHttpRequest().getSession(true);
}
}
```

RequestContext relies on the magical behavior of the *java.lang.ThreadLocal* class, which gives developers the ability to associate different instances of an object with each thread in an application. For more details on using *ThreadLocal*, see one of the Java books cited in Appendix B.

Use *RequestContext.getHttpRequest( )* to get a reference to the current request from a Remoting service method when using the *RequestContextFilter* and *RequestContext* implementation we just discussed. The following example is a Remoting service, *ContainerLoginService*, with a method, *isUserLoggedIn( )*, that returns true if the current user has logged in using Container-Managed Security. *HttpServletRequest. getUserPrincipal( )* returns a *java.security.Principal* object if the user has logged in through Container-Managed Security:

```
public class ContainerLoginService {
  public boolean isUserLoggedIn () {
    HttpServletRequest request = RequestContext.getHttpRequest();
    return request.getUserPrincipal() != null;
  }
}
```

We add another method, *getLoggedInUser( )*, to *ContainerLoginService* in the following example. The *getLoggedInUser( )* service method uses the *Directory* service to return the logged-in user to a Flash client. *Principal.getName( )* returns the username of the logged-in user, which we use to look up the user in the *Directory*:

```
public class ContainerLoginService {
  public ASObject getLoggedInUser () {
    if (!isUserLoggedIn()) return null;

    Principal p    = RequestContext.getHttpRequest().getUserPrincipal();
    User      user = Directory.getUser(p.getName());

    return (ASObject) new ASTranslator().toActionScript(user);  }
}
```

Saving and Sharing State

Applications that use Flash for the entire application interface can rely on the Flash client maintaining state while making multiple calls to the server. *State* in this context refers to data being held in memory in either the Flash client or on the server. Unlike traditional HTML interfaces, where the browser redraws the page for each server request, Flash clients that use Remoting remain as a single stateful instance while handling multiple server requests. As soon as the Flash client is unloaded or reloaded, however, the state that the Flash client held is lost. Flash and Java developers have to work together to preserve the state of the Flash client and restore it when the Flash interface is loaded again.

Additionally, applications that have both HTML and Flash interfaces will often find that they want to share state between the two. One example that we have already discussed is a homegrown security system that uses a *User* object saved in the user session both to determine if a user is logged in and to retrieve information about that user. A Flash client, the Remoting services it uses, and the code that handles the HTML interface all need to access this user information.

For applications that have Flash-only interfaces, one option for saving state is to use an ActionScript local shared object (an instance of the *SharedObject* class) to save data to and retrieve data from the user's computer. Local shared objects are effective as long as the size of the data does not exceed the maximum configured by the user in his Flash Player settings. That said, you can make additional requests for local storage by passing the optional `minimumDiskSpace` parameter to the *SharedObject. flush( )* method. Furthermore, you can open the user's Flash Player Settings dialog box, where he can increase the allowed space for local storage, using *System. showSettings(1)*.

However, for situations when the amount of data is too large to save locally, when having the user approve using additional disk space is undesirable, or when the data needs to be accessed by more than the Flash client, applications must store and share the state of the data on the server.

Using JavaBean Services to Store Session State

The preceding "Referencing the Request and Session" section offers a generic solution for accessing the user session, which can be used as a place on the server side to store object state. Another solution for storing and sharing state takes advantage of the fact that JavaBean services are already stored in the user session by the Remoting gateway. Objects that have access to the user session can access a stored JavaBean service to change its stored state.

Consider a homegrown authentication system that uses the following custom *Authenticator* class to log users in. The *Authenticator.login( )* method looks for a user in the *Directory* object with the supplied username. If it finds the user, it stores the

User object in the user session under the session attribute key USER_KEY. Once the *User* object is stored in the user session, other code can retrieve the logged-in user by calling *Authenticator.getLoggedInUser( )* and passing in the current request:

```
public class Authenticator {
  private static final String USER_KEY = "user";

  public static User login(String username,
                                    HttpServletRequest request)
    throws Exception
  {
    // Look for a user in the Directory with this username
    User user = Directory.getUser(username);

    // If we don't find it, return null
    if (user == null) return null;

    // Store the logged-in user in the session
    request.getSession().setAttribute(USER_KEY, user);

    // Return the logged-in user
    return user;
  }

  public static User getLoggedInUser(HttpServletRequest request)
    throws Exception
  {
    // Return the user stored in the session
    return (User) request.getSession().getAttribute(USER_KEY);
  }
}
```

As is, Remoting services cannot use the *Authenticator* class, because they do not have access to the current request. We have looked at a solution for getting access to the current request from a Remoting service by associating the request with the running thread using a servlet filter.

Another solution to this problem is to give the Remoting service a reference to the logged-in user when the user logs in. So, instead of the Remoting service needing access to the request or user session, we now need a way to get access to the Remoting service from our application code in the *Authenticator*.

The following example is a JavaBean Remoting service called *LoginService* that gives Flash clients access to user login information through the service methods *isUserLoggedIn( )* and *getLoggedInUser( )*. It uses an instance variable, currentUser, to support these service methods.

```
public class LoginService
  implements java.io.Serializable
{
  private User currentUser = null;
```

```
  public User getCurrentUser () {
    return currentUser;
  }

  public void setCurrentUser (User user) {
    this.currentUser = user;
  }

  public boolean isUserLoggedIn () {
    log.info("Checking if user is logged in");
    return currentUser != null;
  }

  public ASObject getLoggedInUser () {
    log.info("Getting logged in user");
    return (ASObject) new ASTranslator().toActionScript(currentUser);
  }
}
```

Since it is a JavaBean service, the Remoting gateway stores *LoginService* in the user session under a session attribute key equal to *LoginService*'s full class name. The following implementation of the custom *ServiceProvider* class has a single, static method, *getJavaBeanService( )*, that looks for a JavaBean service in the user session (given the class of the JavaBean service) and returns a reference to the JavaBean service. If it does not find an existing JavaBean service, it creates the service and stores it in the user session so that it will be there when a Flash client accesses it through Remoting.

```
public class ServiceProvider {
  public static Object getJavaBeanService(HttpServletRequest request,
                                          Class serviceClass)
    throws InstantiationException, IllegalAccessException
  {
    // Look for an existing instance of the service.
    String sessionKey = serviceClass.getName();
    Object service    = request.getSession(true).getAttribute(sessionKey);

    // If it's not there, create it.
    if (service == null) {
      service = serviceClass.newInstance();
      if (service instanceof Serializable) {
        request.getSession(true).setAttribute(sessionKey, service);
      }
    }

    return service;
  }
}
```

The following example shows a modified *Authenticator.login( )* method that uses *ServiceProvider.getJavaBeanService( )* to get a reference to the *LoginService* Remoting service when the user logs in. The *Authenticator.login( )* method then gives the

LoginService a reference to the logged-in user using *LoginService.setCurrentUser( )* so that the *LoginService* can support its service methods for Flash clients.

```
public class Authenticator {
  private static final String USER_KEY = "user";

  public static User login(String username,
                            HttpServletRequest request)
    throws Exception
  {
    // Look for a user in the Directory with this username.
    User user = Directory.getUser(username);

    // If we don't find it, return null.
    if (user == null) return null;

    // Store logged-in user in the session.
    request.getSession().setAttribute(USER_KEY, user);

    // Get the login service.
    LoginService service = (LoginService)
        ServiceProvider.getJavaBeanService(request, LoginService.class);

    // Set logged-in user in the login service.
    service.setCurrentUser(user);

    // Return the logged-in user.
    return user;
  }
}
```

This technique of accessing JavaBean services stored in the user session is an easy way to share information between Remoting services and other application classes.

Using Servlet Services to Store Session State

Servlet services are the only service type that has direct access to the request and user session. Servlet services do not need additional support to access application functionality that requires a request or user session to store shared user information.

The following example shows a servlet service called *LoginServletService* that uses the *Authenticator* class from the preceding example to provide a login service to a Flash client. The *LoginServletService.service( )* method retrieves the username from the first item in the FLASH.PARAMS attribute of the request object, logs the user in using *Authenticator.login( )*, and returns the logged-in *User* object to the Flash client by setting it in the FLASH.RESULT attribute of the request object.

```
public class LoginServiceServlet
  extends HttpServlet
{
  public void service(HttpServletRequest request,
                       HttpServletResponse response)
```

```
      throws ServletException
  {
    // Get the method parameters.
    List params = (List) request.getAttribute("FLASH.PARAMS");

    // If no parameters just return;
    if (params.isEmpty()) return;

    // The username should be the first parameter.
    String username = (String) params.get(0);

    try {
      // Log in using the Authenticator class.
      User user = Authenticator.login(username, request);

      // Set the logged-in user as the result of this service call.
      request.setAttribute("FLASH.RESULT",
                           new ASTranslator().toActionScript(user));
    } catch (Exception e) {
      throw new ServletException("Error logging in.", e);
    }
  }
}
```

A Flash client would log into the application using the *LoginServiceServlet* (presented in the preceding code listing) as follows:

```
// Get service references.
var servletServices = gatewayConnection.getService("remotingbook", this);

// Log in as "flashuser".
servletServices.LoginServiceServlet("flashuser");

// Handle the result of calling LoginServiceServlet.
function LoginServiceServlet_Result (user) {
  trace("LoginServiceServlet_Result:");
  trace("  Logged in: " + user);
}

// Define and register the User class
User = function (name) {
  if (this.username == null) this.username = username;
  this.toString = function () { return "User[" + this.username + "]"; };
};
Object.registerClass("com.oreilly.frdg.java.user.User", User);
```

Databinding

Chapter 3 discusses databinding Remoting *RecordSet* results to UI components using ActionScript *DataGlue* and *DataProviderClass* objects. Databinding is a powerful technique for streamlining Flash and server application integration.

Most enterprise Java applications encapsulate data access in a layer that hides JDBC code from business application classes. The data access layer accepts and returns business objects instead of JDBC *ResultSets*, which means that Remoting services in Java usually send collections of objects back to Flash instead of sending *ResultSets*. Collections of objects in Java become arrays of objects in Flash.

It would be great to be able to databind arrays of objects using *DataGlue*, just as we do *RecordSets*. Fortunately, this is quite easy with a class that extends the *DataProviderClass* implementation, *RsDataProviderClass*, that comes with the Flash Remoting components. The custom *ArrayDataProvider*, shown here, extends *RsDataProviderClass* by defining a constructor that takes an array as an argument and by defining a method, *addAll( )*, that calls the *RsDataProviderClass* implementation of *addItem( )* to add each object in the array to the data provider:

```
#include "RsDataProviderClass.as"

_global.ArrayDataProvider = function (list) {
  this.init();
  this.addAll(list);
};

// ArrayDataProvider subclasses (i.e., extends) RsDataProviderClass.
ArrayDataProvider.prototype = new RsDataProviderClass();

ArrayDataProvider.prototype.addAll = function (list) {
  if (list != null && list.length != 0) {
    for (var i = 0; i < list.length; i++) {
      this.addItem(list[i]);
    }
  }
};

ArrayDataProvider.prototype.checkLocal = function () {
  return true;
};
```

In your client-side ActionScript, you can use *ArrayDataProvider* with *DataGlue* to bind an array of objects to a UI component with *DataGlue.BindFormatStrings( )*. Use the object property names as the values in the format strings. The following example uses *ArrayDataProvider* to bind an array of users to a ListBox component named lb_users:

```
#include "DataGlue.as"
#include "ArrayDataProvider.as"

// Define User class.
User = function (username, realname) {
  this.username = username;
  this.realname = realname
};
```

```
// Create an array of Users.
var users = new Array();
users.push(new User("mike", "Mike Wynholds"));
users.push(new User("sam",  "Sam Borgeson"));
users.push(new User("don",  "Don Thompson"));
users.push(new User("alon", "Alon Salant"));

// Create a data provider with the array.
var dataprovider = new ArrayDataProvider(users);

// Associate (glue) the array of Users to the ListBox component (lb_users).
DataGlue.BindFormatStrings(lb_users, dataprovider,
                    "#realname# (#username#"), "#username#");
```

To use the *ArrayDataProvider* class to glue Remoting service results to UI components, create the data provider and bind the array in the service call result handler. The following example demonstrates calling a Remoting service method, *service. getAllUsers( )*, and databinding the results of the service call to the lb_users ListBox component using *ArrayDataProvider*:

```
service.getAllUsers();

function getAllUsers_Result (users) {
  trace("getAllUsers_Result:" + users);

  var dataprovider = new ArrayDataProvider(users);

  DataGlue.BindFormatStrings(lb_users, dataprovider,
                    "#realname# (#username#"), "#username#");
}
```

Security

In this section, we address the various security aspects of using Flash Remoting with Java. Application security is a broad topic in Java and encompasses many aspects of Java application development. There are user authentication and authorization systems for managing individual user access to protected application features. There are the Container-Managed Security features of a J2EE application server that manage method-level access to EJBs and user authentication security constraints in the servlet container. There are also the core Java security features that manage system resource, class, and method access within the JVM (Java Virtual Machine). There are the security features provided by specific technologies, such as web services. Finally, there is the fuzzy task of trying to guess how malicious users might try to attack the system and plugging the holes before they are exploited.

User Authentication and Authorization

Authentication is the process of identifying a user or entity accessing a system. This is usually implemented with a login process that requires a user to provide a username and password. *Authorization* is the process of determining the privileges of an authenticated user. Authorization may be implemented with custom application logic or using configuration in a J2EE application server to restrict access to resources based on the user's role.

Container-Managed Security

When used with JRun, Flash Remoting clients can provide user credentials using *NetConnection.setCredentials( )*, as shown here (note that the call to *NetServices.createGatewayConnection( )* returns a *NetConnection* object):

```
var gatewayConnection = NetServices.createGatewayConnection();
gatewayConnection.setCredentials("username", "password");
```

The user is authenticated by JRun when the Remoting gateway handles service method calls. JRun uses the user role to authorize access to EJBs and other container-managed resources.

When not running in JRun, applications using Container-Managed Security may have users log in through an HTML interface or have Flash communicate directly with the security service of the application server exposed through the standard j_security_check form action.

The following example shows a function, *cmLogin( )*, that submits an HTTP POST request to the application server's authentication service. The j_security_check portion of the URL, "http://localhost:8400/remotingbook/j_security_check", and the request parameters, j_username and j_password, are dictated by the Container-Managed Security portions of the Servlet 2.3 specification. We are essentially using Flash to mimic submitting an HTML form tied into the form-based login of the container as specified and standardized by the Servlet 2.3 specification:

```
// Function to handle container-managed login
function cmLogin (username, password) {
  // Create the object to load the url
  var loader = new LoadVars();
  loader.j_username = username;
  loader.j_password = password;

  // Create the target to handle the result
  var target = new LoadVars();
  target.onLoad = function (result) {
    trace("cmLogin.onLoad: " + result);
  };

  // Log in against the container's j_security_check.
  loader.sendAndLoad("http://localhost:8400/remotingbook/j_security_check",
                    target);
}
```

For more information on using standard form-based login with Container-Managed Security, see *http://www.onjava.com/pub/a/onjava/2001/08/06/webform.html* or the books *Java Servlet Programming* and *JavaServer Pages* (both from O'Reilly).

Once a user is logged in, the container makes a *java.security.Principal* object and role available for performing authorization checks. This information is available through the two methods *HttpServletRequest.getUserPrincipal( )* and *HttpServletRequest.isUserInRole( )*. The "Referencing the Request and Session" section earlier in this chapter explains techniques for gaining access to the user request so that Remoting services can access the container-managed authentication and authorization information.

With an authenticated user, the servlet container will use the user's information when authorizing use of other container-managed resources, such as EJBs and security constraints configured in the application's *web.xml* file. To restrict access to the Remoting gateway to only logged-in users, add a security constraint to your application's *web.xml* file as shown in the following example. Replace *rolename* with the name of a role that you have defined in your application and wish to have access to Remoting services.

```
<security-constraint>
  <web-resource-collection>
    <url-pattern>/gateway</url-pattern>
    <auth-constraint>
      <role-name>rolename</role-name>
    </auth-constraint>
  </web-resource-collection>
</security-constraint>
```

Home-grown systems

Home-grown authentication and authorization systems range widely in implementation and complexity. Most rely on storing information in the user session. The sections "Referencing the Request and Session" and "Saving and Sharing State" earlier in this chapter explain techniques for accessing the user session from Remoting services that can be used to support custom authentication and authorization.

For tasks such as limiting access to the Remoting gateway based on user information, a servlet filter that can deny access based on your own custom criteria and is mapped to the gateway URL is an appropriate solution.

Service authentication

Authentication in service-oriented architectures is a topic of much discussion, especially as it relates to SOAP-based web services. Many developers believe that services should handle authentication and authorization for every service method call. Applied to Flash Remoting, this approach requires that the Flash client provide the user credentials for every service method call. The service method authenticates the user according to the provided credentials every time a Flash client invokes it.

While authenticating the user every time may seem like overkill, it makes it easier to write standalone services that are not dependent on the application server or other application code to authenticate users. If a service needs to know about the user in order to run, it looks up the user using her credentials and continues.

Restricting Service Access

Flash Remoting is essentially a servlet that uses introspection to invoke methods on a class in the application server. The class and method are both named by the Flash client. A Flash client can invoke any method through the Flash Remoting gateway on any class in the application server that has a no-argument constructor.

This arrangement gives the client a great deal of power over what classes are instantiated on the server side. A malicious user could write a Flash client to manipulate the server state, access internal information about the server and application, or use up all the server memory by using classes in the application server or application. While all classes with no-argument constructors are vulnerable to this exploit, the ones of greatest concern are classes with easily accessible documentation. The application server classes and standard Java classes fit this profile. A malicious user can easily find out what classes are available in any application server or Java distribution by reading the documentation available online.

A simple exploit of this vulnerability is shown in the following example. In this example, the Flash client connects to *java.util.ArrayList* as a Remoting service from a Flash client through Flash Remoting and invokes *ArrayList.addAll( )* in an infinite loop. This is basically a *denial of service attack*, which will fill up the available memory of the application server. Before long, it will crash the JVM running the application server:

```
// Use java.util.ArrayList as a JavaBean service.
var service = gatewayConnection.getService("java.util.ArrayList", this);

// Build a nice big list of strings.
var list = new Array();
for (var i = 0; i < 100; i++) {
  list.push("Let's eat memory");
}

// Add the list forever.
this.onEnterFrame = function () {
  for (var i = 0; i < 100; i++) {
    service.addAll(list);
  }
};
```

Other, more sophisticated exploits may use application server classes as services to change the state of the running server or access protected information. The following sections outline defensive measures you can take against certain types of attacks.

Use Java security

Flash Remoting does not provide a mechanism to restrict Flash client access to specific services. Macromedia recommends restricting access to services by enabling the Java security manager for your application server and editing the Java security policy to allow only the Remoting gateway to access your service classes.

 The Java security manager is responsible for enforcing the security policy for an application. A *security policy* is a collection of permissions that are defined in a *security policy file* or in code. See Sun's security documentation at *http://java.sun.com/j2se/1.4/docs/guide/security/index.html* or *Java Security* by Scott Oaks (O'Reilly) for complete coverage of configuring security in Java.

Refer to your application server's documentation for information on enabling the Java security manager for your application and for the location of the security policy file it uses. Some application servers install with the Java security manager already enabled, in which case you probably need to give the Flash gateway access to your service classes to use Flash Remoting at all. For example, in an installation of IBM Web-Sphere with the security manager enabled, grant clients permission to access the package that contains the service class by adding a line to the default permissions granted to all domains in the *websphere_root/AppServer/java/jre/lib/security/java.policy* file. For example, the following line lets users access the Flash Remoting sample classes in the *my.services* package:

```
permission java.lang.RuntimePermission "accessClassInPackage.my.services"
```

A properly configured security policy will prevent the Remoting gateway from accessing the classes that it does not need to access in the application server, core Java libraries, and your application.

Unfortunately, using the Java security manager to limit service access has its limitations. Most application servers do not install with the security manager enabled, because it degrades performance and introduces configuration hassles for developers. The security manager degrades performance because it has to check permissions for almost everything that happens in the JVM. The extent of the performance degradation depends on the application server. It is usually from 1 to 10%.

Configuring a security policy can be a tricky task. Simply enabling the security manager and finding the right location for the security policy file may require digging into the depths of your application server documentation. Editing a policy file requires a good understanding of the behavior of the Java security manager and the range of security threats to your application and application server. Testing the security policy configuration and ensuring that it does not prevent other aspects of your application from running correctly also add complexity to your development process.

The final limitation to using the Java security manager to limit service access is that you cannot write a security policy that prevents the gateway from using the core Java libraries as services, because the gateway needs them to operate correctly. A security policy file cannot distinguish between classes used in the gateway Java code and classes invoked by the gateway as services. So, the *ArrayList* exploit discussed earlier is still available.

FlashGatekeeper

In the process of writing the security section of this chapter, I became increasing frustrated with the available options for restricting service access through the Remoting gateway. The security manager solution recommended by Macromedia is inadequate. It is hard to implement and does not address all of the issues.

 Java developers using Flash Remoting need a simple solution for limiting service access to the services they have created. The solution should forbid all service access except those explicitly indicated by the developer. Flash Remoting for J2EE should provide such a solution but it does not. So, I created one and I describe it here.

The solution is a Servlet 2.3 filter implementation called *FlashGatekeeper*. FlashGatekeeper is documented and available as an open source project at *http://carbonfive. sourceforge.net/flashgatekeeper*. FlashGatekeeper uses classes that come with the Flash Remoting *flashgateway.jar* file to inspect the AMF message sent by the Flash client. It extracts information about the services that the Flash client is trying to invoke and determines if the services are allowed based on the FlashGatekeeper configuration.

If a Flash client tries to invoke a service that is not allowed by FlashGatekeeper, FlashGatekeeper writes details about the Flash Remoting request to the application server's log files and returns a standard 403 Forbidden HTTP header. If the service is allowed, FlashGatekeeper allows the request to continue on to the Flash Remoting gateway.

FlashGatekeeper installs as a JAR file in your application's *WEB-INF/lib* directory. Configure FlashGatekeeper in your application's *WEB-INF/web.xml* file as a servlet filter mapped to the URL of the Flash Remoting gateway servlet. If the Remoting gateway is mapped to */gateway,* configure the FlashGatekeeper filter as follows:

```
<filter>
  <filter-name>GatekeeperFilter</filter-name>
  <filter-class>com.carbonfive.flashgateway.security.GatekeeperFilter
    </filter-class>
  <init-param>
```

```
      <param-name>config-file</param-name>
      <param-value>flashgatekeeper.xml</param-value>
    </init-param>
  </filter>

  <filter-mapping>
    <filter-name>GatekeeperFilter</filter-name>
      <url-pattern>/gateway</url-pattern>
  </filter-mapping>
```

FlashGatekeeper looks for its configuration file in the classpath of your web application. In this example, you should put *flashgatekeeper.xml* in *WEB-INF/classes* or in another directory in your web application's classpath. The FlashGatekeeper configuration file is an XML description of permitted services and service methods. The configuration allows for identifying several services by using a package name instead of a class or using a JNDI context instead of an object in JNDI.

A sample *flashgatekeeper.xml* configuration file follows:

```
<config>
  <service>
    <name>com.oreilly.frdg.java.service</name>
    <method>
      <name>*</name>
    </method>
  </service>
  <service>
    <name>com.oreilly.frdg.java.FlashService</name>
    <method>
      <name>serviceMethod</name>
    </method>
  </service>
  <service>
    <name>remotingbook</name>
    <method>
      <name>*</name>
    </method>
  </service>
  <service>
    <name>java:comp/env/ejb</name>
    <method>
      <name>*</name>
    </method>
  </service>
</config>
```

This configuration file allows access to only services in or below the package *com. oreilly.frdg.java.service*, the service method implementation *com.oreilly.frdg.java. service.FlashService.serviceMethod( )*, servlet services in the *remotingbook* web application, and any EJB services in JNDI under *java:comp/env/ejb*.

In addition to restricting access to services by service name and service method, FlashGatekeeper supports restricting service access by user role, as determined by

Container-Managed Security. For detailed information on FlashGatekeeper configuration and features, refer to the FlashGatekeeper web site.

OpenAMF

OpenAMF is an emerging open source alternative to Macromedia's Flash Remoting for J2EE. OpenAMF is based on the AMFPHP implementation of Flash Remoting for PHP covered in Chapter 9 and is available from *http://www.openamf.org*. The goals of the project are to provide an open source alternative to Flash Remoting for J2EE and to extend its features to include web services support, flexible configuration, and more. OpenAMF is maturing quickly, supports the features of Remoting for J2EE functionality, and provides several additional features.

Much of the discussion in this chapter also applies to the behavior of the OpenAMF gateway. The architecture and design strategies are certainly applicable. OpenAMF also includes the ASTranslator project to provide developers with the option of using JavaBean introspection to convert between Java and ActionScript objects without explicitly referencing ASTranslator in their service implementations.

Wrapping Up

In this chapter, we've looked under the hood of the Flash Remoting for J2EE gateway to understand how it locates and invokes service methods on the different types of Remoting services available in Java. We've also looked at techniques for managing application security, sharing information between Remoting services and other application classes, and binding the results of Remoting service method calls to Flash UI components.

Today, Flash Remoting for J2EE is the smoothest technology for creating rich Flash interfaces to enterprise Java applications. Flash clients communicating with service-oriented enterprise Java applications through Flash Remoting present a model architecture for the next generation of enterprise applications in which smart, stateful clients assemble remote services to create dynamic feature-rich user experiences.

CHAPTER 8

Flash Remoting and .NET

The goal of this chapter is to provide an overview of connecting Flash to a Microsoft .NET application. We assume basic familiarity with .NET concepts in order to focus on Flash Remoting as it related to ASP.NET development. If you need more background information on .NET, consult the resources cited in Appendix B. This chapter covers:

- The best way to implement a Flash Remoting connection to a .NET application
- Converting .NET datatypes into ActionScript datatypes and vice versa
- Using the ADO.NET database connectivity library to connect with SQL, Access, and XML data sources
- Dealing with state management between .NET and Flash Remoting
- Error handling and throwing exceptions from a .NET application to a Flash application

Flash Remoting for .NET must be purchased separately from Macromedia, although a trial version is available. Refer to Chapters 1 and 2 for more on .NET support and configuration.

Overview of .NET

ASP.NET is the web development element of Microsoft's .NET platform. N-tier programming methodology is at the core of ASP.NET and the .NET platform. This methodology uses an object-oriented approach for dividing business logic, data access, and presentation logic. This separation, almost nonexistent in ASP 3.0, allows designers to easily retool business logic for use on platforms other than web browsers. It also allows developers to easily provide hooks into an application's logic by sharing business logic as XML web services.

The .NET Framework, sometimes referred to as the Base Class Library (BCL), is an extensive library of classes that provide basic functionality. By using these classes, developers can decrease development time with comprehensive implementations for data access, sending email, XML document manipulation, and much more.

The .NET Framework also allows developers a choice of programming languages, including JScript.NET, C# (pronounced "C sharp"), and Visual Basic.NET (VB.NET). Accessing the Framework varies only slightly across these three languages. A single ASP.NET application can mix modules written in different languages. Following are three analogous code snippets in the three languages. Each example displays "Hello World!" on the screen when the web page loads.

Visual Basic.NET example:

```
Sub Page_Load (Sender As Object, E As EventArgs)
   HelloWorld.Text = "Hello World!"
End Sub
```

C# example:

```
public void Page_Load (Object Sender, EventArgs E) {
   HelloWorld.Text = "Hello World!";
}
```

JScript.NET example:

```
Public void Page_Load (Object Sender, EventArgs E) {
   HelloWorld.Text = "Hello World!";
}
```

The .NET platform also uses the common type system (CTS) to map common datatypes among all supported .NET languages. This means a .NET object built in C# can pass parameters to a VB.NET object without a problem.

Connecting to .NET

Flash Remoting supports integration with ASP.NET pages (*.aspx* files), .NET class libraries (*.dll* files), and XML web services. This support allows developers to construct hooks for Flash interfaces using whatever back-end implementation they prefer; however, each implementation provides certain advantages and disadvantages when it comes to Flash Remoting, as shown in Table 8-1.

Table 8-1. Comparison of ASP.NET implementations for Flash Remoting

Connection method	Advantages	Disadvantages
ASP.NET page	Fast development time Built-in session and application state management Good performance	Limited to one result per page Breaks with object-oriented design practices if used without code behind Not remotely accessible to other applications
.NET class library	Object-oriented design Exposes multiple methods and properties Good performance	Longer development time and more planning Not remotely accessible to other applications Session and application state management is not built-in
.NET XML web service	Accessible to remote applications. .NET allows quick development time Built-in session and application state management	Slow runtime performance

ASP.NET pages (pages with an *.aspx* extension) must be service-oriented (SO) in Flash Remoting because they can return only one value to the calling Flash movie. Developing ASP.NET pages is extremely quick and allows developers to separate presentation and business logic within a page. However, ASP.NET pages lack the structure of properly programmed and developed assemblies if done without the benefit of *code behind* (which we cover later in this chapter under "Using code behind with ASP.NET pages"). This lack of an object-oriented structure can make it hard to reuse code across multiple ASP.NET pages without duplicating that code.

ASP.NET pages also have built-in support for session and application state management. State management allows developers to store values unique to each user session and share variables across all pages within an ASP.NET application. ASP.NET pages and XML web services are the only .NET implementations with state management built in. Developers creating assemblies (*.dll* files) must build a custom system for handling state management. State management with *.aspx* pages and web services is covered later in this chapter.

Typically, developers build ASP.NET applications as collections of object-oriented assemblies, each encompassing a different focus and containing exposed properties and methods. When an assembly is called by Flash Remoting, all of the assembly's public methods and properties are exposed to the Flash application. Unlike ASP.NET pages, which are compiled at runtime, assemblies must be compiled using a tool like Visual Studio .NET (VS.NET) or #Develop (See the ".NET Editors" sidebar). You can also create .NET applications in a text editor like Notepad and use the command-line compiler that comes with the free .NET SDK.

.NET Editors

Though you can develop all of your .NET applications using Dreamweaver MX, you may want to use a third-party editor for other tasks such as compiling assemblies:

Visual Studio .NET (http://msdn.microsoft.net/vstudio)
> The de facto .NET development environment. Features such as IntelliSense make it a very attractive solution.

#Develop (http://www.icsharpcode.net)
> Totally free and totally open source. Coded completely in C#, and including many Visual Studio .NET features such as IntelliSense, #Develop can hold its own against any other .NET editor.

PrimalCode (http://www.sapien.com)
> Comes with all the standard features you might expect, such as PrimalSense (Sapien's version of IntelliSense) and syntax coloring. Sapien claims that their editor is very fast due to its small file size footprint.

Of course, you could always just use Notepad. ;-)

A class library can, and should, require more planning at the beginning of your application's development. Because you need to decide on the methods and properties to expose via its public interface, it's up to the developers to create the framework for the application. ASP.NET pages inherit from existing classes in the *System.Web* namespace with the intent of making implementation as quick as possible. It is also important to remember that most class libraries don't do anything by themselves. They usually require an ASP.NET page (or other client, such as a Windows form) to display output. Properly structured, object-oriented applications connect to and reuse business logic through these exposed methods and properties. Class libraries, therefore, prevent replication of commonly used code and allow developers to easily build an application upon a pre-existing foundation.

Developers use classes as a key component to object-oriented programming (OOP) by grouping methods and properties based on a specific business method or object. However, when connecting Flash applications to a .NET back end, issues with datatype conversion can make connecting directly to business logic a bad idea. The best way to avoid this problem is by developing your classes using service-oriented (SO) programming. SO programming means creating a wrapper that provides a specific service by manipulating several business logic components or handling the implementation itself. This way, a service can be built that is optimized for Flash Remoting and manipulates an existing .NET back end while exposing multiple methods to your Flash movie.

.NET XML web services are the best development choice when you wish to share data or functionality over the Internet or other distributed networks. .NET provides a strong API for quickly developing XML web services based on WSDL 1.0 and other W3C standards. Chapter 10 covers connecting with XML web services.

Connecting to an ASP.NET Page

ASP.NET pages use a custom server control to send and receive data through Flash Remoting. *Server controls* are compiled blocks of code that can be reused. (The server control is sometimes known as the *Flash Remoting gateway* or *Flash Remoting adapter*.) A server control also allows developers to add functionality or create visual elements with very little code. The Flash Remoting custom server control can grab parameters passed from the Flash Player, return results to the Flash Player, and bind database data directly to our Flash application.

Let's create a Hello World ASP.NET page that returns a simple string to our Flash application. To get started, create a new plain text file in any text editor and name it *helloWorldpage.aspx*.

In our new ASP.NET page, we need to register the Flash Remoting server control, which allows us to place the server control tag onto the page. To register the Flash Remoting server control, add this tag to your ASP.NET page:

```
<%@ Page Language="C#" debug="true" %>
<%@ Register TagPrefix="MM" Namespace="FlashGateway" Assembly="flashgateway" %>
```

The `TagPrefix` parameter should always be set to the same thing, for consistency's sake. We'll use "MM" for Macromedia. The `Namespace` and `Assembly` parameters provide the location of our Flash Remoting server control.

Once our Flash Remoting server control has been registered with the ASP.NET page, we can begin to communicate with our Flash application. The following code example implements our Flash Remoting server control using ASP.NET's custom tag structure:

```
<MM:Flash id="Flash" runat="server" />
```

Notice the tag's name, `MM:Flash`, which corresponds to the `TagPrefix` we set when registering the server control and the name embedded in the server control. Our Flash assembly will always use the name "Flash". The `id` parameter creates a unique identifier for us to reference this server control programmatically; we'll call our control "Flash". The `runat` parameter tells our web server to process this line of code on the server; the server control will not work without this parameter set to "server".

With the instance of our server control created, we can send and receive data to and from our Flash application. To do this, we access our Flash Remoting server control instance and use its methods and properties to communicate with Flash. The main properties for communicating with Flash are:

Params
:   The `Params` property is an array of parameters passed by the Flash Player to the ASP.NET page (used to determine the number of parameters passed and access the parameter values).

Result
:   Setting the `Result` property passes the results of our ASP.NET page to the Flash application, as would a typical `return` command in most languages.

DataSource
:   The `DataSource` property allows us to bind Flash with an ADO.NET–compatible data source (SQL, XML, Access, etc.). See "Connecting to a .NET Assembly" later in this chapter for details on binding data sources.

We'll access our server control's properties from the ASP.NET *Page_Load( )* event, which is called automatically after our ASP.NET page loads but before any data is shown to the user. The following example shows how to set the `Result` property to "Hello World!", the text string that will be returned to Flash. In this example, we use `Flash.Result`, where the portion before the period, `Flash`, matches the `id` attribute that labeled the control with the identifier `Flash`. Here is the C# code:

```
<%@ Page Language="C#" debug="true" %>
<%@ Register TagPrefix="MM" Namespace="FlashGateway" Assembly="flashgateway" %>
<MM:Flash id="Flash" runat="server" />
<script runat="server">
public void Page_Load (Object Sender, EventArgs E) {
  Flash.Result="Hello World!";
}
</script>
```

As written, our ASP.NET Hello World page is already available as a Flash Remoting service (assuming you've uploaded it to your web server).

To build our Flash application that accesses this ASP.NET page, we'll create a standard Flash Remoting connection. However, instead of specifying a gateway in the same fashion as we do for ColdFusion, we create a blank ASP.NET file and name it *gateway.aspx*. A physical *gateway.aspx* file is always required when using Flash Remoting through .NET to establish a connection to the service. Flash can also use the filename without the *.aspx* extension to establish a connection to the ASP.NET page. Here is an example:

```
NetServices.setDefaultGatewayUrl("http://localhost/myASPApp/gateway.aspx");
gatewayConnection = NetServices.createGatewayConnection();
ASPXservice = gatewayConnnection.getService("helloWorldPage", this);
```

Make sure that your *web.config* file has the following entry within its main `<configuration>` tag:

```
<system.web>
  <httpModules>
    <add name="GatewayController"
         type="FlashGateway.Controller.GatewayController,flashgateway" />
  </httpModules>
</system.web>
```

Once Flash has established a connection to the service, we can call our method. Naturally, we should create the *_Result* and *_Status* callback methods to handle the results returned before invoking the remote method. Since our ASP.NET page does not have a method for Flash to call, Flash treats the entire ASP.NET page as a method. To call this implicit method, use the identifier *helloWorldPage*, the same name as our ASP.NET page (without the *.aspx* extension):

```
ASPXservice.helloWorldPage();

function helloWorldPage_Result (Results) {
  trace(Results);
}

function helloWorldPage_Status (Status) {
  trace(Status);
}
```

When our Flash application runs, it accesses our ASP.NET page, establishes a Flash Remoting service, and displays "Hello World!" in the Output window.

Using code behind with ASP.NET pages

Microsoft learned from the shortcomings of ASP 3.0 and has allowed .NET developers to provide better separation of presentation and business logic within an ASP.NET page. This implementation, called *code behind*, allows us to create and register server controls within the presentation layer of the code and implement that code programmatically in .NET assemblies.

With code behind, a separate page is created to hold the business logic. To keep things consistent, the name for the code-behind page should be the complete name of the ASP.NET page (including the *.aspx* extension), followed by the proper extension for the given programming language. For example, if the ASP.NET filename is *helloWorldPage.aspx*, the code-behind file should be named *helloWorldPage.aspx.cs* if programmed in *C#*, or *helloWorldPage.aspx.vb* if programmed in VB.NET. If you're using Visual Studio .NET as your programming environment, this is done for you automatically.

In our *helloWorldPage.aspx* file, we need to change the Page tag to properly reference the code-behind page. The Page tag references the namespace and class name for our code-behind page, using the Inherits tag. If you're using Visual Studio .NET, you'll notice that an extra property is set; the CodeBehind property is purely a Visual Studio .NET construct and not necessary for those using other editors or IDEs:

```
<%@ Page language="c#" debug="true" CodeBehind="helloWorldPage.aspx.cs"
Inherits="FRDG.helloWorldPage" %>
```

We can also remove the script tag from our ASP.NET page, since we will reimplement the script in our code-behind page.

In a new file named *helloWorldPage.aspx.cs*, we create a class named *helloWorldPage* within the *FRDG* namespace. This class is used by our ASP.NET page to implement our Flash server control.

In our code-behind page, we need to reference the necessary .NET namespaces so that we can access their classes from within our application. You'll notice we also reference the Flash Remoting assembly as FlashGateway so that we can have access to its classes in the code-behind page:

```
Using System;
Using System.Web.UI;
Using System.Web.UI.WebControls;
Using FlashGateway;
```

Finally, let's build a class to implement our ASP.NET page. This class inherits from the ASP.NET Page object, which every ASP.NET page automatically inherits. (Technically, the ASP.NET page inherits from the code-behind page, and the code-behind page manually specifies that it inherits from Page.) Among other things, the Page object invokes the *Page_Load( )* callback function when the page loads.

Within our class, we must create an instance of the Flash server control to access its properties and methods. This object must have the same identifier as we used in our server control's id parameter. Notice that the type, FlashGateway.Flash, is referenced using the namespace, despite the namespace being imported at the top of the file. The reason for this is that since our server control instance is called "Flash", it would cause a name clash if we didn't use the full namespace path. We also define the *Page_Load( )* event handler to provide result data to Flash:

```
namespace FRDG {
  public class helloWorldPage : System.Web.UI.Page {
    protected FlashGateway.Flash Flash;

    public void Page_Load () {
      Flash.Result="Hello World!";
    }
  }
}
```

We can reference the code-behind ASP.NET pages from Flash using the same ActionScript code as the previous section. When the Flash movie is run, the Action-Script *trace( )* method prints "Hello World!" to the Output window.

Connecting to a .NET Assembly

Class libraries allow Flash to connect directly to business logic. This allows Flash to access multiple methods and properties from one service.

To explain how an assembly is called from Flash, we'll develop a Hello World assembly and access it as a Flash Remoting service. To get started, create a new text file named *HelloWorldAssembly.cs*, because we're writing it in C#; name it *HelloWorldAssembly.vb* if you're programming in VB.NET.

Before writing the skeleton for our assembly, we must reference the required namespaces. For our example file, we'll need the base namespace—*System*—as well as Flash's namespace *FlashGateway.IO*:

```
using System;
using FlashGateway.IO;
```

 Assemblies and code-behind pages require a different namespace than ASP.NET pages to implement the Flash component. Assemblies use *FlashGateway.IO*, while ASP.NET pages use *FlashGateway*.

Within our file, let's create the skeleton of an assembly by defining its namespace and class name. Every assembly requires a class name, but the namespace is an optional item used to help developers categorize assemblies based on their responsibilities. You'll notice our Flash Remoting namespace differs from our ASP.NET pages. This is because the ASP.NET page includes a server control object with additional functionality for use in ASP.NET pages.

```
using System;
using FlashGateway.IO;

namespace FRDG {
  public class HelloWorldAssembly {
```

```
      // statements go here...
  }
}
```

Next, we'll add a constructor to initialize any variables for the object and our *Say-HelloWorld( )* method, which returns a string to our Flash application:

```
public HelloWorldAssembly () {
}

public string SayHelloWorld () {
  return "Hello World!";
}
```

Compile the assembly into a DLL and place it in your web server's */bin* directory.

 Unlike their COM predecessors, .NET assemblies need not be registered with the server. To make an assembly active and available, just place it in the */bin* directory.

Once the DLL file is placed in your web application's */bin* folder, Flash Remoting can access the assembly's methods and properties. Establishing the service in Flash is similar to accessing our ASP.NET page. The difference is that we use the class's full name (including namespace) as the service name. Also, unlike our ASP.NET page, we can call the assembly's service methods directly and create wrappers to catch their results. (Although an *.aspx* page is compiled into an assembly by the .NET application server, it is not available in assembly form to Flash Remoting, hence the difference in the way Flash Remoting deals with assemblies and ASP.NET pages.)

```
NetServices.setDefaultGatewayUrl("http://localhost/myASPApp/gateway.aspx");
gatewayConnection = NetServices.createGatewayConnection();
AssemblyService = gatewayConnnection.getService("FRDG.HelloWorldAssembly", this);
```

With a reference to our assembly available as a service, we can access any of its methods directly. Invoke our assembly's *SayHelloWorld( )* method and trace the Results returned from our *SayHelloWorld_Result( )* callback function as follows:

```
AssemblyService.SayHelloWorld();

function SayHelloWorld_Result (Results) {
  trace(Results);
}

function SayHelloWorld_Status (Error) {
  trace(Error);
}
```

When run, our Flash application displays "Hello World!" in the Output window.

Datatype Conversions

As with Java, ColdFusion, and PHP, Flash Remoting allows several ASP.NET native types to be passed and converted to ActionScript datatypes. Table 8-2 shows a list of ASP.NET datatypes and how they are converted to ActionScript datatypes and vice versa. Datatype conversion is bidirectional, unless more than one ActionScript type is converted to a given ASP.NET type (see the *Null* and *Hashtable* ASP.NET types).

Table 8-2. ASP.NET-to-ActionScript datatype conversions

ASP.NET datatype	ActionScript datatype
Double	Number
Bool	Boolean
String	String
Hashtable	ActionScript object
Null	Null
Null	Undefined
Array	Ordered (integer-indexed) array
Hashtable	Associative (named) array
DateTime	Date object
Hashtable	XML object
DataView/DataTable	RecordSet

Flash Remoting transforms most native ASP.NET datatypes into a comparable ActionScript datatype. However, complex ASP.NET types, such as classes and structures, are converted into Flash objects with only the properties intact by means of the *ASObject*, which I cover later in this chapter. This means that ASP.NET objects that depend on methods to access properties will not work once converted to ActionScript datatypes in your Flash application.

Flash also provides supports for arrays, but native arrays only. Complex ASP.NET array objects such as the *ListArray*, *Enumerable*, and *StringDictionary* cannot be converted into Flash objects. Considering the size and scope of the .NET Base Class Library, it would be impossible to list all unsupported datatypes. As a rule of thumb, if it's not in the list provided in Table 8-2, it's not supported. However, see Tables A-5, A-6, A-7, and A-8 in Appendix A, which show datatype conversions between ActionScript and C# or Visual Basic.NET in more detail.

Receiving Complex Datatypes from .NET

The Flash Remoting gateway allows .NET to build an ActionScript object and return it to Flash. Provided the necessary steps are taken, Flash Remoting can return ActionScript objects with custom types (rather than creating generic *ASObjects* only).

For example, if we've defined and registered a custom ActionScript class, *Book*, we can create an *ASObject* of the *Book* type and access the returned data intact from our Flash application. Let's see how this is done.

Example 8-1 shows the client-side ActionScript to define our *Book* class with three properties (`title`, `author`, and `price`) and a single method, *bookCost( )*, in Flash.

Example 8-1. Declaring a custom class and registering it for remote usage

```
function Book () {
  this.title = "";
  this.author = "";
  this.price = 0;
}

Book.prototype.bookCost = function (qty) {
  return (this.price * qty);
};

Object.registerClass("BookClass", Book);
```

Notice that the ActionScript code registers the object with Flash as a *Book* type. This is used to recreate objects of the *Book* class when they are returned from the .NET service. Now that we've seen the client-side implementation, let's look at the server side.

In the Flash Remoting for .NET implementation, the *ASObject* object inherits from a .NET *Hashtable* object and consists of the following important property and method:

ASType

> The `ASType` property takes a string that identifies the name of the *ASObject*'s Flash counterpart. This is explained in the following example.

Add( )

> The *Add( )* method adds name/value pairs to an *ASObject*. The method accepts two parameters: a name and its corresponding value, such as *Add("Name", "Value")*. Note that both the name and value must be strings. To retrieve a value, use syntax similar to an array. In C#, specify the name of the value to retrieve surrounded by brackets, such as *myASObject["Name"]*. In VB.NET, use parentheses, such as *myASObject("Name")*.

To return an object through Flash Remoting, we need to define an instance of *ASObject* in the *FlashGateway.IO* namespace. With the object created, we can define the `ASType` our object will use. Here we define a remote method called *GetBook( )* that creates and returns a *Book* object to Flash:

```
using System;
using FlashGateway.IO;
```

```
namespace FRDG {
  public class BookAssembly {
    public ASObject GetBook () {
      ASObject aso = new ASObject();
      aso.ASType = "Book";
      aso.Add("title", "FRDG");
      aso.Add("author", "Tom Muck");
      aso.Add("price", "39.99");
      return aso;
    }
  }
}
```

The Flash Remoting adapter converts our *ASObject* into the corresponding Action-Script object—in this case, an object of type *Book*—on the Flash client.

 Flash Remoting does not return an object to Flash if the ASType property is not set. If nothing else, set ASType to "Object", which generates a generic instance of the *Object* class for return to the Flash client.

The final piece of the puzzle is to create the client-side ActionScript that acts as a callback function to receive the *Book* object from the .NET service:

```
function GetBook_Result (Results) {
  // Display the book's title and the cost of one dozen copies
  trace(Results.title);
  trace(Results.bookCost(12));
}
```

Now invoke the .NET remote method as follows:

```
#include "NetServices.as"

var myURL = "http://localhost/frdg/flashservices/gateway.aspx";
var servicename = "FRDG.BookAssembly";

NetServices.setDefaultGatewayURL(myURL);
var connection = NetServices.createGatewayConnection()
var bookService = connection.getService(servicename, this);

bookService.GetBook();
```

Once our *GetBook_Result( )* callback handler receives the object, it calls the *book-Cost( )* method and traces the book's cost in the Output window (in this case, it displays the cost of a dozen books).

Sending Complex Datatypes to .NET

Flash Remoting also has strong support for sending complex datatypes from Flash to .NET applications. This feature is typically used to pass classes or structures as parameters to a .NET method.

First, we declare the object on the client side. The ActionScript code is the same as shown in Example 8-1 in the previous section.

When you pass a complex ActionScript object to a .NET remote method, it arrives as an object of type *ASObject*. The following C# class defines an *InsertBook( )* method that accepts an *ASObject* but accesses the object's properties as if it were a *Book* object. We access the object's properties by specifying the name of the property to retrieve in quotes. In C#, surround the property name in brackets; in VB.NET, use parentheses.

```
using System;
using FlashGateway.IO;

namespace FRDG
{
  public class BookService
  {
    public bool InsertBook (ASObject asbook)
    {
      string title = asbook["title"].ToString( );
      string author = asbook["author"].ToString( );
      decimal price = (decimal)asbook["price"];

      // Code to insert book into database, or similar, is omitted

      // Return a successful status.
      return true;
    }
  }
}
```

Notice that the properties' names are always specified as strings and the values are stored as objects of the generic *Object* type. We must convert the title and author properties to strings using the *ToString( )* method supported by all .NET objects. To convert the price property to a number, we explicitly *cast* it by using (decimal) before the object.

Invoke the service as you would any other Flash Remoting service. Simply create a *Book* object and pass it into the *InsertBook( )* method, as shown in the following client-side ActionScript code:

```
#include "NetServices.as"

var myURL = "http://localhost/frdg/flashservices/gateway.aspx";
var servicename = "FRDG.BookService";

NetServices.setDefaultGatewayURL(myURL);
var connection = NetServices.createGatewayConnection( )
var bookService = connection.getService(servicename, this);

book = new Book( );
book.title = "ASP.NET Development with Dreamweaver MX";
```

```
book.author = "Joel Martinez";
book.price = 30.00;

bookService.InsertBook(book);
```

The ability to send and retrieve objects of custom datatypes is valuable when you're creating an object-oriented architecture for your application.

Convert Custom Classes to an ASObject

The .NET framework has a robust Reflection API. *Reflection* allows you to peer into the inner workings of any .NET class. Because of this, we can create a generic function that can accept any .NET class and convert its public properties into an *ASObject*. Here is a small utility function, written in C#, for converting a .NET class or struct into an *ASObject* for easy transmission to Flash:

```
using System;
using System.Reflection;
using FlashGateway.IO;

public class Util
{
  public static ASObject ConvertToASO (Object obj, string astype)
  {
    Type type = obj.GetType();

    // Initialize the ASObject
    ASObject aso = new ASObject();
    aso.ASType = astype;

    // Iterate through the member fields
    foreach(FieldInfo field in type.GetFields())
    {
      aso.Add(field.Name, field.GetValue(obj));
    }

    return aso;
  }
}
```

Note that the preceding code extracts only public fields, those intended to be exposed by the developer.

The *ConvertToASO()* function accepts two parameters. The first is of type *Object*, so you can pass any type of object into it. The second is a string used to represent the ActionScript type.

To demonstrate its usage, we create a struct of type *Book* in C# (notice it has the same properties as the ActionScript object we constructed in earlier examples):

```
public struct Book
{
  public string title;
  public string author;
```

```
    public decimal price;
  }
```

Call the *ConvertToASO( )* function whenever you need to return an object to Flash. The following method, written in C#, instantiates a new *Book* object and sets its properties. It then uses *ConvertToASO( )* to convert the struct to an *ASObject*:

```
public ASObject GetABook( )
{
  Book book = new Book( );
  book.title = "FRDG";
  book.author = "Tom Muck";
  book.price = 39.99

  ASObject aso = Util.ConvertToASO(book,"Book");

  return aso;
}
```

Receiving Arrays from .NET

Flash Remoting also supports native .NET arrays but does not support complex array types such as Lists and Collections.

.NET can create a native array from any set of variables with the same type. The disadvantage of an array is that it requires a developer to provide a list of the objects within the array. This prevents the array from dynamically expanding past a preset size.

To create an array in .NET, use the [ ] operator. Initialize (a.k.a. *dimension*) the array with the desired number of elements. For example, here is some C# code to initialize an array:

```
String[] nameArray = new String[5];
```

You can initialize the array with literals by immediately providing a list of the items you'd like store in it:

```
String[] nameArray = new String[]{"Joel Martinez", "Tom Muck"};
```

By default, specifying an array literal sets the maximum number of elements to the number of items specified, but we can set a maximum while initializing only a few array elements:

```
String[] nameArray = new String[5]{"Joel Martinez", "Tom Muck"};
```

Access the .NET objects from the array using a zero-relative numeric index. Here we change the value of the first two elements of the array:

```
nameArray[0] = "Angelina Jolie";
nameArray[1] = "Lara Croft";
```

Like in ActionScript, all .NET array indexes start from 0, not 1. This means the first element in our array will always be 0, so the previous array has 2 full slots.

.NET arrays provide support for all native .NET datatypes, including structures and classes. We can create an array of *ASObject* objects and return the array to Flash, which is a convenient way to return more than one object, such as an array of search results, to Flash. The following C# code creates an *ASObject* array with two indexes and stores two *Books* as elements of the array (technically, it converts the *Book* objects to *ASObjects* and stores the *ASObjects* in the array):

```csharp
using System;
using FlashGateway.IO;

namespace FRDG {
  public class BookService {
    public ASObject[] GetBookList () {
      ASObject[] asoArray = new ASObject[2];

      Book bookItem0 = new Book();
      bookItem0.title = "Flash Remoting: The Definitive Guide";
      bookItem0.author = "Tom Muck";
      asoArray[0] = Util.ConvertToASO(bookItem0);

      Book bookItem1 = new Book();
      bookItem1.title = "ActionScript Cookbook";
      bookItem1.author = "Joey Lott";
      asoArray[1] = Util.ConvertToASO(bookItem1);

      return asoArray;
    }
  }
}
```

As with our complex objects, Flash automatically converts our .NET array to Action-Script's *array* datatype. The developer can immediately access the array's values from the Results object returned by our Flash Remoting service. In the following client-side ActionScript code snippet, our Flash application displays the title of the first book in the array returned by our Flash Remoting services' *GetBookList( )* method:

```actionscript
#include "NetServices.as"

var myURL = "http://localhost/frdg/flashservices/gateway.aspx";
var servicename = "FRDG.BookService";

NetServices.setDefaultGatewayURL(myURL);
var connection = NetServices.createGatewayConnection()
var bookService = connection.getService(servicename, this);

bookService.GetBookList();

function GetBookList_Result (Results) {
  trace(Results[0].title);
}
```

You can view the array and *Book* objects by opening Flash's interactive debugger. For more information on debugging, see Chapter 13.

Sending Arrays to .NET

Sending arrays as a parameter from Flash to a .NET application is straightforward. We can build an array of any of our supported datatypes and pass those values to .NET. For example, to pass an array of strings containing book titles to our .NET application, we could use the following client-side ActionScript code:

```
#include "NetServices.as"

var myURL = "http://localhost/frdg/flashservices/gateway.aspx";
var servicename = "FRDG.BookService";

NetServices.setDefaultGatewayURL(myURL);
var connection = NetServices.createGatewayConnection()
var bookASPnetService = connection.getService(servicename, this);

bookTitleArray = new Array();
bookTitleArray[0] = "FRDG";
bookTitleArray[1] = "ASDG2";

bookASPnetService.AddTitles(bookTitleArray);
```

Our .NET application can receive this array and access it as a native array object:

```
public void AddTitles (string[] books) {
  foreach (string book in books) {
    // statements...
  }
}
```

Flash Remoting also allows Flash to create arrays of complex objects to pass to a .NET application. For example, we can use the ActionScript *Book* class, which we defined earlier, to create several instances of a Flash object and pass them all as parameters to our .NET service. Here is the client-side ActionScript code the invokes the remote *AddBooks()* method, shown next:

```
bookArray = new Array();

bookItem = new Book();
bookItem.title = "FRDG";
bookItem.author = "Tom Muck";
bookArray[0] = bookItem;

bookItem = new Book();
bookItem.title = "ASDG2";
bookItem.author = "Colin Moock";
bookArray[1] = bookItem;

// The code to initialize bookASPnetService is shown in the preceding example
bookASPnetService.AddBooks(bookArray);
```

Once our designated .NET method receives the parameter, it can access the array of objects natively. The following .NET code snippet shows the remote *AddBooks( )* method iterating through the array of objects:

```
public void AddBooks (ASObject[] books)
{
  foreach (ASObject book in books)
  {
    // Do something with each individual "book"
  }
}
```

Naturally, you can use the methods and properties of the .NET *Array* class to perform operations on the array or its elements. For example, the *Array.GetLength( )* method returns the length of the array (the number of elements in the array). Refer to the .NET resources cited in Appendix B for more information on .NET's *Array* class.

Database Access with ADO.NET

ADO.NET is the .NET Framework's class library for reading and manipulating data sources. This section identifies the major classes used when selecting and inserting data into an Access database, as well as reading XML with ASP.NET.

> These examples connect with an Access database using the OLEDB ADO.NET library. Implementation for SQL databases and other data sources differs slightly.

In many ways, ADO.NET has surpassed its predecessor ADO. The new version of the database connectivity library provides tighter integration with Microsoft databases, increasing the speed of calls to a Microsoft SQL database. The library also allows binding to Microsoft's server controls, making it easy to build HTML tables and grids of database information. One of the most notable features is a new *DataSet* object that provides disconnected access to data sources. This allows developers to reduce the load on the SQL back end while maintaining access to data.

ADO.NET with Flash Remoting also allows binding to Flash objects. This feature works similar to binding data to a *DataGrid* or other ASP.NET server control and provides Flash with a *RecordSet* object containing ADO.NET's results. We'll describe this feature in more detail later in this section.

> The following sample uses the *Northwind.mdb* file, a sample database bundled with Microsoft Access. The database can usually be found in the directory *C:\Program Files\Microsoft Office\Office\Samples*.
>
> Once you've found the file, make a copy of it and place the copy in a directory named *database* in the root of your web site.

Selecting from a Database

Establishing a connection to an Access data source and selecting data with ADO.NET is similar to using the older ADO methods. However, ADO.NET has made a few notable name changes to key ADO objects.

The following code snippet shows an example of an *OleDb* database connection to our *Northwind* Access database with ADO.NET. When run, this ASP.NET page passes a recordset of all products in the *Northwind* database to our Flash application:

```
<%@ Page Language="C#" debug="true" %>
<%@ Register TagPrefix="MM" Namespace="FlashGateway" Assembly="flashgateway" %>
<%@ import namespace="System.Data" %>
<%@ import namespace="System.Data.OleDb" %>

<html>
<head>
<title>ADO.NET to Flash Remoting connection</title>
</head>

<body bgcolor="#ffffff" text="#000000">
<MM:Flash id="Flash" runat="server" />
</body>

<script langauge="C#" runat="server">
void Page_Load (Object sender, EventArgs e) {
  // Create an OLE database connection and adapter
  OleDbConnection connection = new OleDbConnection
        ("Provider=Microsoft.Jet.OLEDB.4.0; Data Source=Northwind.mdb");
  OleDbDataAdapter adapter = new OleDbDataAdapter
        ("SELECT * FROM Products", connection);

  // Fill your DataSet and close your connection
  DataSet dataset = new DataSet();
  adapter.Fill(dataset,"table");
  connection.Close();

  // Bind your data to Flash
  Flash.DataSource = dataset;
  Flash.DataBind();
}
</script>
</html>
```

The first four lines of our code alert ASP.NET to the language used on our page, register our Flash server control, and set the namespaces required for our application. You'll notice two new namespaces—*System.Data* and *System.Data.OleDb*—which give us access to the required ADO.NET classes for database access. If our application used a Microsoft SQL server, we could use the *System.Data.SqlClient* namespace.

With the page initialized, we can create an instance of the Flash server control. As before, it uses the tag prefix we defined earlier:

```
<MM:Flash id="Flash" runat="server" />
```

Next, the code creates an ADO.NET database connection, executes our SQL command on the database, and allows us to capture the results of the operation.

The call to *new OleDbConnection( )* establishes a connection to the *Northwind* database. The constructor accepts a semicolon-delimited string containing the database driver, location of the database, and optional security information (username and password). Our example creates a DSN-less connection using the *Northwind* database's filename and the valid Access driver:

```
OleDbConnection connection = new OleDbConnection
    ("Provider=Microsoft.Jet.OLEDB.4.0; Data Source=Northwind.mdb");
```

After the connection to the database is established, we pass our SQL statement to the database and begin our operation. The *OleDbDataAdapter* object allows us to execute this SQL statement and pass our returned results to a *DataSet* object:

```
OleDbDataAdapter adapter = new OleDbDataAdapter
    ("SELECT * FROM Products", connection);

// Fill your DataSet and close your connection
DataSet dataset = new DataSet( );
adapter.Fill(dataset,"table");
connection.Close( );
```

From the *DataSet*, we can bind the results to our Flash server control:

```
Flash.DataSource = dataset;
Flash.DataBind( );
```

Flash Remoting also allows us to implement our database connection as a .NET assembly. The following is an example assembly implementation written in C#:

```
Using System.Data;
Using System.Data.OleDb;
Using FlashGateway.IO;

Public namespace FRDG {
  public class SelectFromDatabase {

    public DataTable Select ( ) {
      OleDbConnection connection = new OleDbConnection
        ("Provider=Microsoft.Jet.OLEDB.4.0; Data Source=Northwind.mdb");
      OleDbDataAdapter adapter = new OleDbDataAdapter
        ("SELECT * FROM Products", connection);

      // Fill your DataSet and close your connection
      DataSet dataset = new DataSet( );
      adapter.Fill(dataset, "table");
      connection.Close( );
```

```
      return dataset.Tables[0];
   }
 }
}
```

When we bind our database operation's results (a .NET *ResultSet*) to our Flash application, Flash Remoting passes this data to the Flash client as an ActionScript *RecordSet* object. From this object, we can bind our database data to Macromedia's UI components, such as the DataGrid or DropDownList component. More information on using the *RecordSet* object is available in Chapters 3 and 4.

For our Flash application to use the passed data, we can bind it to one of our components using the *DataGlue* class or access the results directly with a *RecordSet* object. The following example demonstrates each component.

The *DataGlue* class allows us to bind our database results to a Flash UI component. This comes in handy when a developer needs to create a drop-down list or other UI component based on the contents of your Flash Remoting data results. Our application glues the results of our database query to a DropDownList UI component.

First, create a call to our ASP.NET page as a Flash Remoting web service. This allows us to populate our *RecordSet* object and bind the data to our drop-down list:

```
#include "NetServices.as"
#include "DataGlue.as"

var myURL = "http://localhost/frdg/flashservices/gateway.aspx";
var servicename = "FRDG.SelectFromDatabase";

NetServices.setDefaultGatewayURL(myURL);
var connection = NetServices.createGatewayConnection()
var dataservice = connection.getService(servicename, this);

dataservice.Select();
```

Next, drag an instance of the DropDownList component from the Components panel onto the Stage, where it becomes a movie clip instance. Name your movie clip instance cmptDropDpwnList using the Property inspector. This allows us to manipulate the drop-down list dynamically from ActionScript.

Finally, we can bind our *RecordSet* object to the DropDownList using the *DataGlue.bindFormatStrings( )* method in the responder function that receives the results:

```
function Select_Result (result_rs) {
  DataGlue.bindFormatStrings(comboBox,result_rs,"#productName#","#productName#");
}
```

This Flash application displays a list of products pulled from the *Northwind* database as a drop-down list. We could add functionality to the drop-down list to show more information when a specific product is selected.

Our application can also access the *RecordSet* object directly. This allows us to loop through database results or validate content for specific criteria. The following example loops through the entire contents of our database results and displays them in the Output window:

```
function Select_Result (result_rs) {
  for (i=0; i < result_rs.getLength(); i++) {
    var row = result_rs.getItemAt(i);
    trace(row["productName"]);
  }
}
```

Manipulating a Database

ADO.NET also allows applications to manipulate databases by inserting, updating, or deleting data. These operations are similar to our SQL SELECT statement, but these commands don't return blocks of data like a SELECT statement.

The following assembly shows the implementation of an ADO.NET application, written in C#, that inserts a new product into our *Northwind* database:

```
Using System.Data;
Using System.Data.OleDb;

Public namespace FRDG {
  public class InsertIntoDatabase {

    public bool Insert () {
      OleDbConnection connection = new OleDbConnection
        ("Provider=Microsoft.Jet.OLEDB.4.0; Data Source=Northwind.mdb");
      OleDbCommand command = new OleDbCommand
        ("INSERT INTO product(productName, UnitPrice, UnitsInStock)
            VALUES('FRDG',39.99,5000)", connection);
      command.ExecuteNonQuery();
      connection.Close();

      return true;
    }
  }
}
```

This database connection is similar to our ASP.NET database select code, with a few differences:

- Our *OleDb* code does not create a *DataSet* when it executes the SQL.
- Our function returns a *boolean* type to our Flash caller.

Because the assembly does not return a *RecordSet* object to our Flash application, we don't need to include the *FlashGateway.IO* library used in our earlier example.

Once the method is called by our Flash application, the specified product is inserted into the *Northwind* database. The code also returns a Boolean value that informs our Flash application that the product was inserted successfully. Of course, our example is a degenerate one insofar as it always inserts the same record. If the number of fields in the record is relatively low, you can pass them as parameters to the method, as in the following C# snippet:

```
Using System.Data;
Using System.Data.OleDb;

Public namespace FRDG {
  public class InsertIntoDatabase {

    public bool Insert (string name, decimal price, int stock) {
      string sql = "INSERT INTO product(productName, UnitPrice, UnitsInStock)
        VALUES('"+ name +"',"+ price.ToString() +","+ stock.ToString() +")";

    OleDbConnection connection = new OleDbConnection
      ("Provider=Microsoft.Jet.OLEDB.4.0; Data Source=Northwind.mdb");
    OleDbCommand command = new OleDbCommand
      (sql, connection);
    command.ExecuteNonQuery();
    connection.Close();

    return true;
    }
  }
}
```

Now, we have a generalized remote service that is useful. You can use it to insert new records straight from Flash.

 You shouldn't store sensitive data, such as passwords or connection strings, in your Flash movie. It is possible for others to decompile your *.swf* file. Consider anything in your ActionScript code public information. Refer to the Windows .NET Server (a.k.a. Windows Server 2003) documentation for details on authenticating users and securing the server.

Using an XML Data Source

In addition to typical databases, ADO.NET provides access to other data sources, such as Excel documents, comma-delimited text files, and XML documents. This allows developers to apply the same SQL operations typically used with SQL data sources to XML applications.

In our example, we'll develop an XML file named *products.xml* that stores a list of hair products:

```
<products>
  <product>
    <id>12345</id>
    <name>FRDG Hair Remover</name>
    <description>New spray-on hair remover gives you that balding look
you've always wanted!!</description>
```

```
      <price>$19.95</price>
    </product>
  </products>
```

Next, we need to use ADO.NET to connect to our XML file. This allows us to manipulate this XML data as a *RecordSet* object in Flash.

```
<%@ Page Language="C#" debug="true" %>
<%@ Register TagPrefix="MM" Namespace="FlashGateway" Assembly="flashgateway" %>
<%@ import namespace="System.Data" %>
<%@ import namespace="System.Data.OleDb" %>

<script langauge="C#" runat="server">
void Page_Load (Object sender, EventArgs e) {
  DataSet oDataset = new DataSet( );
  oDataset.ReadXml(Server.MapPath("products.xml"));

  Flash.DataSource = oDataset.Tables[0];
  Flash.DataBind( );
}
</script>

<MM:Flash id="Flash" runat="server" />
```

You may notice that our ASP.NET page uses a structure very similar to our ADO.NET select code. In this code block, the XML file is loaded and stored into a *DataSet* object. You can use that *DataSet* object just as if it had been loaded straight from a database. That is one of the things that the *DataSet* class was developed for. With it, you can have any number of data backends, and still interface with the same ADO.NET component.

Writing to an XML File

Not only does the *DataSet* class have the ability to natively read from an XML data source, it also gives you the ability to write to an XML data source. This can be a very useful technique for caching queries from a database.

The following code example checks to see whether there is a *products.xml* file in the same directory as the *.aspx* page that is executing. If the *.xml* file is not present, the code queries the database and writes the file:

```
<%@ Page Language="C#" ContentType="text/html" ResponseEncoding="iso-8859-1" %>
<%@ Import Namespace="System.Data" %>
<%@ Import Namespace="System.Data.OleDb" %>
<%@ Register TagPrefix="MM" Namespace="FlashGateway" Assembly="flashgateway" %>
<script runat="server">
protected void Page_Load (Object Src, EventArgs E) {
  // Declare main variables
  string xmlpath = Server.MapPath("products.xml");
  DataSet datasetToBind;
```

```
  // Check to see if the file exists
  if (!System.IO.File.Exists(xmlpath)) {
    // The file is missing, let's create it
    datasetToBind = GenerateXmlFile(xmlpath);
  } else {
    // The file exists, so let's retrieve it
    datasetToBind = new DataSet();
    datasetToBind.ReadXml(xmlpath);
  }

  flash.DataSource = datasetToBind.Tables["product"];
  flash.DataBind();
}
```

Let's examine the code in more detail. First, the code declares a few variables for use later in the script. Next, it uses the *System.IO.File* class to check whether the XML file exists. If the XML file exists, the code reads the data from the file into the dataset. Otherwise, the code creates a new XML file using the *GenerateXmlFile( )* function, which looks like this:

```
DataSet GenerateXmlFile (string path)
{
  // Declare database variables
  string connectionString = "Provider=Microsoft.Jet.OLEDB.4.0;Data Source=" +
                            Server.MapPath("/frdg/Northwind.mdb") + ";";
  string sql = "SELECT * FROM Products";
  OleDbConnection connection;
  OleDbDataAdapter adapter;

  // Connect to the database
  connection = new OleDbConnection(connectionString);
  connection.Open();

  // Fill the dataset and close connection
  adapter = new OleDbDataAdapter(sql, connectionString);
  DataSet oDataset = new DataSet("products");
  adapter.Fill(oDataset,"product");
  connection.Close();

  // Write the file for later use
  dataset.WriteXml(path);

  return dataset;
}
</script>
<asp:DataGrid id="flash" runat="server" />
```

The *GenerateXmlFile( )* function retrieves all the products in the Products database. Once it fills the dataset, the function calls the *DataSet.WriteXml( )* method to store the data in an XML file. And there you have it, a very simple caching mechanism. Although ASP.NET has its own caching mechanism, caching isn't supported within an assembly. With just a little work, this example could be enhanced to be more robust for use in an assembly. For example, you could generalize it to store the results of any query in an XML file. And you could use .NET's file I/O capabilities to check the file creation date to decide whether to requery the database and update the XML file.

State Management

Flash Remoting provides support for ASP.NET state management by maintaining the session ID on all requests to the server. This allows ASP.NET to identify an existing session and application state.

In essence, a session is the server-side corollary of a client-side cookie. It is an object in the server's memory that retains key information on a user throughout his visit to a web site. An example of state management across multiple pages is a login and validation system. A web form can pass login criteria, such as username and password, to an application. If the username and password are acceptable, a session variable containing the username is created. All subsequent requests to ASP.NET pages within the application can check if the user is logged in and, if so, display the user's name.

ASP.NET also allows developers to customize their state management settings to loosen or tighten security. Typically, if a web user is inactive for 20 minutes, the session object for the user is destroyed. This time limit can be changed by tweaking the *web.config* file for your ASP.NET application.

 Session and application state management is supported by ASP.NET pages and .NET XML web services, but not assemblies. Class libraries requiring state management must implement a custom solution or establish state through an ASP.NET page.

In addition to the benefits for ASP.NET applications, state management can be used by Flash Remoting. This can allow Flash applications to provide personalized data or allow multiple Flash applications using Remoting to share data specific to a user.

In our example of state management with Flash Remoting, we develop a web form (shown in Figure 8-1) that collects a user's name and age and stores it in the session. We then create a Flash application that uses this session information to display the user's name and age.

Please supply your name and age

Name:

Age:

Submit

Figure 8-1. An ASP.NET web form used to collect session data

The web form uses two ASP.NET text objects and a Submit button to collect the age and name information:

```
<!DOCTYPE html PUBLIC "-//W3C//DTD XHTML 1.0 Transitional//EN" "http://www.w3.org/TR/
xhtml1/DTD/xhtml1-transitional.dtd">
<%@ Page Language="C#" ContentType="text/html" ResponseEncoding="iso-8859-1" %>
<script runat="server">
protected void submit_click (Object Src, EventArgs E) {
  Session["name"] = name.Text;
  Session["age"] = age.Text;
}
</script>
<html xmlns="http://www.w3.org/1999/xhtml">
<head>
<title>FRDG</title>
<meta http-equiv="Content-Type" content="text/html; charset=iso-8859-1" />
</head>
<body>
<h1>Flash Remoting MX: The Definitive Guide </h1>
<p>Please supply your name and age</p>
<form runat="server">
Name: <asp:textbox id="name" runat="server" />
<br />
Age: <asp:textbox ID="age" runat="server" />
<br />
<asp:button ID="submit" Text="Submit" OnClick="submit_click" runat="server" />
</form>
<object classid="clsid:D27CDB6E-AE6D-11cf-96B8-444553540000" codebase="http://
download.macromedia.com/pub/shockwave/cabs/flash/
swflash.cab#version=6,0,29,0" width="300" height="150">
  <param name="movie" value="../../../../userInfo.swf" />
  <param name=quality value=high />
  <embed src="../../../../userInfo.swf" quality=high pluginspage="http://www.
macromedia.com/shockwave/download/
index.cgi?P1_Prod_Version=ShockwaveFlash" type="application/
x-shockwave-flash" width="300" height="150"></embed>
</object>
</body>
</html>
```

As you see in the preceding code snippet, the name and age variables are stored in the Session object as Session["name"] and Session["age"]. This allows us to access the variables in our Flash file through Flash Remoting.

 State management works only when viewing your Flash application through a browser. The Test Player in the Flash development environment does not work with cookies, thus handicapping ASP.NET's state management features. This is why the .swf file is tested from an .aspx page, rather than in the Flash Test Player.

The ASP.NET page that acts as our Flash Remoting service merely creates an *ASObject* with two properties for the name and age. If the Session variable is undefined, the page returns a null value to Flash:

```
<%@ Page Language="C#" ContentType="text/html" ResponseEncoding="iso-8859-1" %>
<%@ Import Namespace="FlashGateway.IO" %>
<%@ Register TagPrefix="MM" Namespace="FlashGateway" Assembly="flashgateway" %>
<script runat="server">
protected void Page_Load (Object Src, EventArgs E)
{
  ASObject userinfo = new ASObject();
  userinfo.ASType = "UserInfo";

  userinfo.Add("name", Session["name"]);
  userinfo.Add("age", Session["age"]);

  flash.Result = userinfo;
}
</script>
<MM:Flash id="flash" runat="server" />
```

To set up our Flash application, define two dynamic text fields, lblName_txt and lblAge_txt, to display our two session properties, name and age. Remember that our remote service is returning an ActionScript object with two properties, so we must define and register the *UserInfo* class:

```
#include "NetServices.as"

var myURL = "http://localhost/frdg/flashservices/gateway.aspx";
var servicename = "frdg.com.oreilly.frdg.stateservice";

NetServices.setDefaultGatewayURL(myURL);
var connection = NetServices.createGatewayConnection()
var stateservice = connection.getService(servicename, this);

function UserInfo () {
  this.name="";
  this.age=0;
}

Object.registerClass("UserInfoClass", UserInfo);
stateservice.getUserInfo();

function getUserInfo_Result (result) {
  lblName.text = result.name;
  lblAge.text = result.age;
}
function getUserInfo_Status(err) {
  trace("Error: " + err.description);
}
```

Using this approach, you can create a Flash application that checks for a session variable indicating whether the user is logged in, and display information accordingly.

Error Handling in Flash Remoting with .NET

One of the true marks of a good programmer is how she handles errors in the code. Programmers coming from a Classic ASP background likely have very brief experience with good error handling. Flash taps directly into .NET's robust error-handling mechanisms. This section discusses how to trap errors and expose them to your Flash application. We also discuss different error-handling techniques and how to use them with Flash. For related information, see "Handling Errors with try/catch" in Chapter 6.

Catch Me If You Can

The .NET languages support the *try/catch* construct for error handling. When an error occurs, code execution stops and the .NET Framework raises an exception. The following C# snippet includes code that may raise an exception, depending on the value of divisor:

```
int divideIt (int numerator, int divisor) {
    return = numerator / divisor;
}
```

This code will raise a *DivideByZeroException* if divisor is 0, because dividing by zero is a mathematical impossibility. Though you can avoid the exception by checking the divisor for a zero value before performing the division, there are situations where anticipating an exception is difficult if not impossible. For example, if you write code that connects to a remote SQL Server and the remote server reboots while your code is running, you're going to find yourself with a big fat exception.

Luckily, handling exceptions is easy. You can handle the *DivideByZeroException* by adding a *try/catch* block, as follows. If the exception is raised (which occurs when divisor is 0), the function simply returns 0:

```
int divideIt (int numerator, int divisor) {
    try {
        return = numerator / divisor;
    } catch (Exception ex) {
        return = 0;
    }
}
```

Any code the invokes the preceding function will never see an exception, because the function's error handling is self-contained. However, there are times when server-side code should transfer the responsibility for exception handling to the client side. As discussed in "Catching Errors" in Chapter 4, you have several choices about how to handle errors, including throwing a custom exception.

Simply throw the exception when you detect the error condition of interest:

```
int divideIt (int numerator, int divisor) {
    if (divisor == 0) {
```

```
      throw new Exception("Divisor cannot be zero");
    } else {
      return numerator / divisor;
    }
  }
```

Therefore, when the divisor parameter is 0, the *divideIt( )* function throws an exception with a custom message detailing the problem. Utility functions are prime candidates for this type of error handling. It allows developers using that code to see any problems early in the development phase, and the remaining code in the utility function can assume that it won't have to deal with any invalid values.

Exceptional Flash

What does all this mean to Flash applications? Flash Remoting for .NET allows you to call a remote method, and if an unhandled exception is encountered, you can react accordingly.

In the earlier ActionScript examples in this chapter, we used a *methodName_Result( )* callback handler to handle the response of a remote method invocation. No doubt, you noticed the *methodName_Status( )* function defined in most of the examples, which is called instead of *methodName_Result( )* when an error occurs. In that case, the *methodName_Status( )* function receives an error object containing information about the exception that was thrown by the server.

The error object has several properties, as shown in this output from the NetConnection debugger:

```
Status (object #2)
.....code: "SERVER.PROCESSING"
.....description: "this is a custom exception"
.....details: "   at FlashGateway.Delegates.ASPAdapter.InvokeService(ActionContext
action)
   at FlashGateway.Delegates.ServiceCommander.InvokeAdapter(ActionContext
      flashContext)
   at FlashGateway.Delegates.ServiceFilter.preInvoke(ActionContext flashContext)"
.....level: "error"
.....type: "System.Exception"
```

The properties of interest include the description and the type. You can use the description property to display an error for debugging purposes or send yourself an email with that error (through Flash Remoting, of course). The type property is useful when the possibility exists of several different types of exceptions being thrown. See Chapter 4 for more information on the error object and exception handling.

Here is an example of how to handle a simple exception in your ActionScript code:

```
serviceObject.divideIt (365, 0);

divideIt_Result (result) {
  lblMessage.text = "The result is " + result;
```

```
  }

divideIt_Status (error) {
  lblMessage.text = "Error: " + error.description;
}
```

You can also easily check for several different types of exceptions:

```
divideIt_Status (error) {
  var tmpMsg = "";
  switch (error.type) {
    case "System.DivideByZeroException":
      tmpMsg = "Error: your input must not be a zero";
      break;
    case "System.Exception":
      tmpMsg = "Error: " + error.description;
      break;
  }

  lblMessage.text = tmpMsg;
}
```

As you can see, you can easily build a robust error-handling system into your Flash application. This is especially true if you spend a bit of extra time at the beginning of your project planning out where you can apply error handling. With a bit of practice, you'll be a pro.

Wrapping Up

We've explored several different ways to use Flash Remoting with .NET pages and assemblies in this chapter. We also addressed database conversion, database access, and other issues. Refer to Chapter 10 for more information about using .NET to create XML web services.

CHAPTER 9

Flash Remoting and PHP

When Flash Remoting was first introduced, you had no choice but to use either ColdFusion MX (which comes with Flash Remoting) or purchase Flash Remoting MX for J2EE (Java) or .NET from Macromedia. The reason for this was that the protocol used by Flash Remoting, Action Message Format (AMF), is proprietary to Macromedia and they chose not to release any specifications about it.

Since then, a resourceful programmer named Wolfgang Hamann managed to reverse engineer AMF. Soon after AMF was decoded, an open source project with the goal of creating a fully compatible PHP-based Flash Remoting gateway was born. This project, AMFPHP (*http://www.amfphp.org*), is well on its way to meeting its goal. At the time of this writing, AMFPHP supports connecting Flash to specially defined PHP classes or SOAP-based web services.

There are a few other open source projects that have applied Wolfgang's work to other languages. These include OpenAMF (*http://www.openamf.org*), a Java implementation, and FLAP (*http://www.simonf.com/flap*), a Perl implementation.

This chapter covers how to install AMFPHP on a server and write PHP classes that AMFPHP can utilize. In addition, this chapter examines a few of the more common uses of PHP with Flash.

It's important to note that AMFPHP is a fluid project, so for the final word on its current features be sure to check the documentation on its web site.

Introduction to PHP

PHP, which stands for PHP: Hypertext Preprocessor (yes, it is a recursive acronym), is an open source scripting language that borrows its syntax from C, Java, and Perl, just to name a few. The result is a language that feels familiar to many programmers. This makes a lot of sense, since the stated goal of PHP is to help web developers create dynamic content quickly, and nothing speeds up coding like knowing the language!

PHP's capabilities are similar to other server-side languages, such as ColdFusion, ASP, and JSP. In addition, because it's an open source language, PHP is constantly gaining new capabilities via extensions. There are even a few extensions that allow PHP to create Flash content dynamically. Furthermore, the PHP Extension and Application Repository (PEAR) offers a huge online repository of PHP components, available at *http://pear.php.net* or via the special *pear* command-line tool, which is installed with PHP.

PHP installs onto nearly every server platform available, and it integrates with all of the major web servers, including both Apache and IIS. As its name suggests, PHP is a preprocessor that executes code in PHP pages when they are requested. The result is then sent to the web server and finally delivered to the client. You never have to compile PHP pages explicitly; PHP handles all of the processing of PHP pages for you.

PHP code can be written in either a procedural or object-oriented manner. That said, AMFPHP requires that you write your code as PHP classes. Be aware, though, that if you've used other object-oriented languages in the past, you'll find the OOP capabilities of PHP to be relatively limited. These limitations will be addressed with the upcoming PHP 5.0, so be sure to check out the excellent documentation at *http://www.php.net* to get the most up-to-date information.

There are two fundamental pieces to PHP's syntax that tend to trip up newcomers. The first is that all variables must begin with a $ symbol. The second is that a period (.), rather than the usual + or &, is used to concatenate strings.

How PHP Fits into Flash Applications

The fact that PHP is available on so many platforms for free means that many hosting providers include it in their service packages. AMFPHP offers a number of installation options; you can even set it up without requiring administrative access to your server. So, while ColdFusion may be the easiest language to use Flash Remoting with from a technical standpoint, PHP is the easiest from an economic standpoint.

The fact that AMFPHP also allows you to connect to SOAP-based web services allows you to use it as a simple connector to pre-existing web services you've written in other languages. Thus, you can add a Flash front end to an existing application without any cost on the server side.

Besides these monetary advantages, using Flash Remoting with PHP provides the same advantages that all of the other Flash Remoting–enabled languages provide. These include the ability to separate architecture and development tasks in a clean manner. Plus, if you design your code well, it's much easier to reuse PHP code you've written for use with Flash Remoting than it is if you were using Flash's *Load-Vars* or *XML* classes.

Installing AMFPHP

First, you need to download AMFPHP from *http://www.amfphp.org*. As with many open source projects, you can download either the most recent stable build or the absolutely latest version of the code from the project's source code repository. Unless you plan on helping out with the development of AMFPHP, it's generally best to use the stable build. The following directions assume that you are using Version 0.5.1 of AMFPHP, so be sure to check the documentation that comes with AMFPHP if you are using a more recent version.

There are a number of ways to install AMFPHP, depending on your exact requirements, but the following two approaches are the most common.

The first approach assumes you can modify the `include_path` variable for your PHP environment or that you know the current `include_path` and can copy files to that location. For more information on how to modify `include_path`, be sure to check out the PHP documentation and your web server's docs. (For example, for Apache, you can modify `include_path` with either your *httpd.conf* file or an *.htaccess* file). Once you have `include_path` set up to your liking, simply copy the *flashservices* directory included in AMFPHP to a directory specified in `include_path`.

The second approach doesn't require any kind of special access to your server, but you may want to have access to your domain's web root if you would like to do a single installation for your whole domain (which is recommended). To install AMF-PHP this way, just upload the *flashservices* directory to some location under your web root and note the path to that directory.

So far, the steps have involved getting the core AMFPHP code up on your server. The next step is to set up the *gateway.php* file, which acts as the gateway for your projects. With AMFPHP, you can have multiple gateways set up on your server, which is handy if you want to keep the services (the actual PHP classes you write) of each project separate.

The code inside the *gateway.php* file is quite short; it merely includes the rest of the code for the project and specifies where your services are located. You can find a sample *gateway.php* file in the *examples/basic/* directory. You simply modify this file to fit your setup. It can be uploaded to any directory under your server's web root.

The lines you'll need to modify in *gateway.php* are:

```
include "flashservices/app/Gateway.php";
```

and:

```
$gateway->setBaseClassPath("services/");
```

If you've installed the *flashservices* directory using the `include_path` approach, you won't need to modify the first line at all. Otherwise, you'll have to modify the path so that it properly reaches your *flashservices* directory. For example, on my server, that line looks like this:

```
include "/usr/local/apache/htdocs/flashservices/app/Gateway.php";
```

Simply change the second line to point to the path where you keep your services. The default path, *services/*, points to the *services* directory underneath where you installed the *flashservices* directory. Again, as an example, here's what I have on my server:

```
$gateway->setBaseClassPath("/usr/local/apache/htdocs/amfServices");
```

To summarize how to install AMFPHP:

1. Download the AMFPHP source files from *http://www.amfphp.org*.
2. Copy the *flashservices* directory from AMFPHP somewhere on your server. You can place it in one of the path's specified in your `include_path` PHP variable or somewhere under your web root.
3. Dig down into the *examples/basic* directory of AMFPHP and modify the *gateway.php* file to reflect your setup.
4. Upload the *gateway.php* file somewhere under the web root of your server.

Note that AMFPHP is completely server-based. There is no client-side installation, and there are no client-side *.as* library files to include when using AMFPHP, except for the *NetServices.as* file, which you should include whenever using Flash Remoting, regardless of the server-side technology.

Because AMFPHP returns binary data to the Flash client, rather than returning HTML, debugging your setup can be a bit difficult. If you're having trouble, you may want to temporarily add the following lines to the beginning of your *gateway.php* file:

```
ini_set( 'display_errors', false );
ini_set( 'log_errors', true );
```

These two lines suppress sending errors back to Flash and instead log errors to your web server's error log.

Configuring AMFPHP for Web Services

To use AMFPHP with web services, you need to complete a few more steps. AMFPHP works with two different PHP SOAP implementations: PEAR::SOAP (*http://pear.php.net*) and nuSOAP (*http://dietrich.ganx4.com/nusoap*). At the time of this writing, PEAR::SOAP is compatible with a larger number of web services than nuSOAP.

The PEAR::SOAP package is part of the PHP Extension and Application Repository, which provides a library of PHP code. There are a number of ways to install PEAR packages, but the easiest by far is to use the *pear* command line tool that ships with PHP 4.3.0 and later.

To install the PEAR::SOAP package using the *pear* tool, go to a command line on your server and type:

```
pear install SOAP
```

If the command displays an error and lists dependent modules, simply install the missing modules one by one. For example, if the error message says that the *HTTP_Request* module is missing, install it using:

```
pear install HTTP_Request
```

Once all of the dependent modules are installed, try to install SOAP again. Once SOAP installs successfully, you're done.

If you prefer to use nuSOAP instead:

1. Download it from *http://dietrich.ganx4.com/nusoap*.
2. Create a new directory underneath the *flashservices* directory on your server, and name it *lib*.
3. Copy all of the decompressed nuSOAP files into *lib*.

Datatype Conversions

The conversion of datatypes between PHP and ActionScript is straightforward, as shown in Table 9-1. These conversions work in both directions, from PHP to Action-Script and vice versa, with the exception of PHP arrays.

Table 9-1. PHP-to-ActionScript datatype conversion

PHP	Flash (ActionScript)
Null	Null
Integer	Integer
Double	Float
String	String
Array (normal)	Array
Array (associative)	Object
Object	Object
Resource[a]	Recordset

[a] The only supported databases are MySQL, ODBC, and PostgreSQL.

The conversion of PHP arrays to Flash ActionScript can be a bit confusing. In PHP, all arrays are *associative arrays*. Associative arrays can use any type of symbol, rather than just integers, for the index. This means that the following PHP code is perfectly legal:

```
$myList = new Array();
$myList[0] = "apple";
$myList["foo"] = 12;
```

This fact means that, when coming from Flash, ActionScript objects of type *Array* and *Object* (a.k.a. *structures*) are converted to the PHP *Array* datatype. When converting an ActionScript *Array* to PHP, a PHP *Array* using entirely integer indexes is created.

The problem comes when translating PHP arrays to ActionScript. AMFPHP has to guess what is the best kind of ActionScript datatype to create from the PHP array. It does this by a simple process of elimination; if the PHP array contains any noninteger indexes, it is converted to the ActionScript *Object* datatype; otherwise, it is converted to the ActionScript *Array* datatype.

As of this writing, AMFPHP doesn't support the sending of PHP objects to Flash. Nor does it fully support the sending of objects created from custom ActionScript classes to PHP (they are seen as simple objects with no associated methods). The AMFPHP team is actively working on implementing these features, and they will probably be in place by the time you read this. Check the AMFPHP site for more information.

Using AMFPHP with Web Services

If you'd like to use AMFPHP to connect to pre-existing SOAP-based web services, you don't have to write a single line of PHP. As long as your installation of AMFPHP is set up properly, connecting to web services with it is a breeze and is nearly identical to the process you would with ColdFusion (ColdFusion is the only other Remoting gateway that automatically supports connecting to external web services). See Chapter 10 for more information about web services with ColdFusion and .NET.

Not all web services work with AMFPHP. This is a limitation of the SOAP libraries that AMFPHP uses rather than a limitation of the AMFPHP library itself. If you want to test to make sure a particular web service is accessible before you start doing heavy development against it, download the CMX Remoting Testing Tool from *http://www.communitymx.com/abstract.cfm?cid=E79F1303C1E096ED*. The tool is a free extension that adds a new CMX Remoting Testing Tool panel to the Flash MX authoring environment and allows you to quickly execute remote methods and see the results.

To use a web service with AMFPHP, you first need to know the URL of that web service's WSDL file. A *WSDL file* is an XML file that describes a web service, including its URL, the methods it supports, and the arguments and return types of those methods. You can, in fact, open a WSDL file in a text editor and read this information from it. Of course, you also need to know the URL of the *gateway.php* file up on your server.

The only slightly odd process in using a web service with AMFPHP is that you must pass all of the arguments to the web service via properties of an object. For example, XMethods (*http://www.xmethods.com*) provides a free web service that returns the current temperature for any U.S. Zip Code. The WSDL file for this web service dictates that there's a single method named *getTemp( )*, which expects a single argument specifying the Zip Code. Example 9-1 shows the client-side ActionScript code that connects to this web service and prints the result to the Output window.

Example 9-1. Accessing the getTemp( ) web service via Flash Remoting

```
#include "NetServices.as"

onResult = function (temp) {
  trace("Got temp: " + temp);
};

gatewayURL = "http://localhost/frdg/gateway.php";
serviceURL = "http://www.xmethods.net/sd/2001/TemperatureService.wsdl";
gateway = NetServices.createGatewayConnection(gatewayURL);
service = gateway.getService(serviceURL);
service.getTemp(this, {zipcode:20781});
```

Example 9-1 creates an anonymous object to transmit the arguments to the *getTemp( )* remote service. You could also pass the arguments by attaching properties to a generic instance of the *Object* class:

```
data = new Object( );
data.zipcode = 20781l
service.getTemp(this, data);
```

When the web service is written in ColdFusion, you can often get away without creating such an object and just calling the service like this:

```
service.getTemp(this, 207811);
```

Using AMFPHP with PHP Classes

If you want to connect Flash to PHP code via AMFPHP, you need to write your PHP code as a PHP class. The remote methods that your ActionScript code calls are the methods of your custom classes. A PHP class uses the following syntax:

```
class MyClass {
  var local1 = 1;
  var local2 = 2;

  function MyClass ( ) {
    // do something
  }

  function someMethod ($val) {
    // do something else
  }

  function someOtherMethod ($val0, $val1) {
    // and something else
  }
}
```

In this case, local1 and local2 are *instance variables* (unique variables associated with each instance of this class). The function *MyClass( )* is this class's constructor, which runs when an instance of this class is first created. This method performs necessary setup for an instance of this class. Finally, *someMethod( )* and *someOther-Method( )* are two sample methods to which all instances of this class have access.

For AMFPHP to work properly, each class must be defined in its own file and the file must have the same name (including capitalization) as the class. In addition, the class's constructor must include a *method table*, specific code to define the signatures and permissions of all methods of the class. This information is used primarily by the Service Browser in Flash MX to help you write the correct ActionScript, but the permission information is used by AMFPHP to limit which methods of your class are accessible via Flash Remoting. This approach lets you define private methods that can be called internally only.

An example method table is shown in Example 9-2, along with methods for the class. This code should be placed in *MyClass.php*.

Example 9-2. Defining a method table for a PHP class

```
class MyClass {
  function MyClass ( ) {
    // Create the method table for AMFPHP
    $this->methodTable = array(
      "someMethod" => array(
        "description" => "Retrieve the list of countries",
        "roles" => "list",
        "access" => "remote",
        "arguments" => array("state")
      ),
      "someOtherMethod" => array(
        "description" => "Retrieve a list of companies in a given country",
        "roles" => "list",
        "access" => "remote",
        "arguments" => array("country", "postalCode")
      )
    );
  }

  function someMethod ($val) {
    // Just echo back the value
    return $val
  }
  function someOtherMethod ($val0, $val1) {
    // and something else
  }
}
```

As you can see, this code defines a variable named methodTable that is an array of all the methods this services supports, along with information about each method. The access property can be set to "remote", "public", or "private". AMFPHP closely mirrors ColdFusion in the way that method permissions are set. If you want your method accessible only to this class, define its access property as "private". If you want the method accessible to other classes, declare access as "public". Finally, if you want the method to be callable via Flash Remoting, set access to "remote". Refer to "The <cffunction> tag" in Chapter 5 for more information about the access property.

Although Version 0.5.1 of AMFPHP doesn't use the roles property, by the time you read this AMFPHP will most likely use the roles property to implement a security system similar to how ColdFusion works (see "Using Role-Based Security with Cold-Fusion Components" in Chapter 5 for related information). In general, if you don't plan on using the roles information, simply leave the roles property out of your code.

The two remaining properties, description and arguments, provide a description of the method and the arguments that the method accepts. At this time, the arguments property is used only for documentation purposes and won't cause an error if it doesn't match the actual arguments specified in the method declaration.

 Make sure that you keep the method table current. If a method in your class doesn't have a corresponding entry in the method table, Flash Remoting displays an error saying that no such method exists in your class.

If there are any syntax errors in your class constructor, Flash Remoting displays an error, usually one that doesn't provide a lot of information about the problem. However, you can check for syntax errors easily by opening a web browser to the URL of your service (i.e., the URL of the .php file). Any syntax errors are displayed along with their line numbers.

If no syntax errors exist but you are still receiving an error in Flash (often the Bad Version error), make sure that AMFPHP is properly installed and that your class isn't accidentally outputting any extra characters, such a spaces, tabs, or other whitespace directly around your <?php> tag.

Once you have created a PHP class, you need to write the client-side ActionScript to connect to it. The URL you give for the gateway is just the normal URL to your *gateway.php* file. However, the URL you specify for your service is a bit different. Instead of being a URL delimited by slashes, it is a dotted path to your PHP class's file, starting from the directory that you specified to be the base path of your classes in your *gateway.php* file. For example, if you specified your classpath as:

```
/usr/local/apache/htdocos/frdg/services/
```

and your actual PHP class is located at:

```
/usr/local/apache/htdocos/frdg/services/stuff/MyClass
```

then the URL of the class would be:

```
stuff.MyClass
```

Example 9-3 shows the client-side ActionScript code to access *MyClass*.

Example 9-3. Accessing a PHP class via Flash Remoting

```
#include "NetServices.as"

onResult = function (result) {
  trace("Received result: " + result);
};

gatewayURL = "http://localhost/frdg/gateway.php";
serviceURL = "stuff.MyClass";
gateway = NetServices.createGatewayConnection(gatewayURL);
service = gateway.getService(serviceURL);
service.someMethod(this, {testString:"Testing..."});
```

Working with a Database

PHP works with many different databases, but the one most often associated with it is MySQL. The following example assumes you have both PHP and MySQL set up and running and that you have the *Northwind* database set up with a user named "northwind" and a password of "northwind". The *Northwind* database is provided by Microsoft as a sample for SQL Server (*http://office.microsoft.com/downloads/2000/ Nwind2K.aspx*) and can be translated into a MySQL database via the *mssql2mysql* VBScript (*http://www.kofler.cc/mysql/mssql2mysql.html*). A MySQL version of the *Northwind* database is also available at the online Code Depot cited in the Preface.

This example defines a custom PHP class, *CustomersAdmin*, which is assumed to live inside of a file named *CustomersAdmin.php* in your *services* directory. The information about the database (database name, hostname, username, and password) are all stored as properties of the class. In addition, the connection to the database is set up as a persistent connection in the class's constructor; consequently, the class methods don't have to worry about setting up that connection. Example 9-4 shows the server-side PHP code to access a database. Example 9-5 implements the client-side Action-Script code that goes along with it.

Example 9-4. Server-side code for accessing a database

```
<?PHP
  class CustomersAdmin {

    // Login information for the database
    var $dbhost = "localhost";
    var $dbname = "northwind";
    var $dbuser = "northwind";
    var $dbpass = "northwind";

    // Constructor
    function CustomersAdmin () {
```

Example 9-4. Server-side code for accessing a database (continued)

```
     // Create the method table for AMFPHP
     $this->methodTable = array(
       "getCountries" => array(
         "description" => "Retrieve the list of countries",
         "access" => "remote",
         "arguments" => array( )
       ),
       "getCustomersByCountry" => array(
         "description" => "Retrieve a list of companies in a given country",
         "access" => "remote",
         "arguments" => array("country")
       ),
       "getContact" => array(
         "description" => "Retrieve all of the information about a customer",
         "access" => "remote",
         "arguments" => array("customerID")
       ),
       "updateContact" => array(
         "description" => "Update the contact information for a customer",
         "access" => "remote",
         "arguments" => array("customerID", "contactName", "contactTitle",
                              "phone", "fax")
       )
     );

     // Create the connection to the database server and select the database
     $this->conn = mysql_pconnect($this->dbhost, $this->dbuser, $this->dbpass);
     mysql_select_db($this->dbname);
   }

   // Get a list of the countries
   function getCountries ( ) {
     $result = mysql_query("SELECT Distinct(Country) FROM Customers
                            ORDER BY Country");
     return $result;
   }

   // Get the customers in a given country
   function getCustomersByCountry ($country) {
     $query = "SELECT CustomerID, CompanyName FROM Customers ";
     if ($country != "All") {
       $query .= "WHERE Country = '".$country."' ";
     }
     $query .= "ORDER BY CompanyName";

     $result = mysql_query($query);
     return $result;
   }

   // Get all of the information for a contact at a given customer
   function getContact ($customerID) {
     $customer = array( );
```

Example 9-4. Server-side code for accessing a database (continued)

```
    $result = mysql_query("SELECT * FROM Customers
                          WHERE CustomerID = '".$customerID."'");
    $customer = mysql_fetch_array($result);
    return $customer;
  }

  // Update the contact at a given customer
  function updateContact ($customerID, $contactName, $contactTitle, $phone, $fax) {
    $query = "UPDATE Customers SET ";
    $query .= "ContactName = '".$contactName ."', ";
    $query .= "ContactTitle = '".$contactTitle ."', ";
    $query .= "Phone = '".$phone."', ";
    $query .= "Fax = '".$fax."' ";
    $query .= "WHERE CustomerID = '".$customerID."'";
    $result = mysql_query($query);
    return $result;
  }
 }
?>
```

Notice that the *getCountries( )* method returns the exact resource that is returned from the database, but the *getContact( )* method pulls out a single row of a resource and sends it back as an array. It's up to you to determine the most appropriate kind of data to send back to Flash. Just keep in mind that you probably don't want to return more data than the client will actually use.

Now that the server-side code is set up, you must set up the client-side interface for the example (or download the *.fla* file from the online Code Depot), as shown in Figure 9-1. The instance names of each interface element, as indicated in Figure 9-1, should be set using the Property inspector.

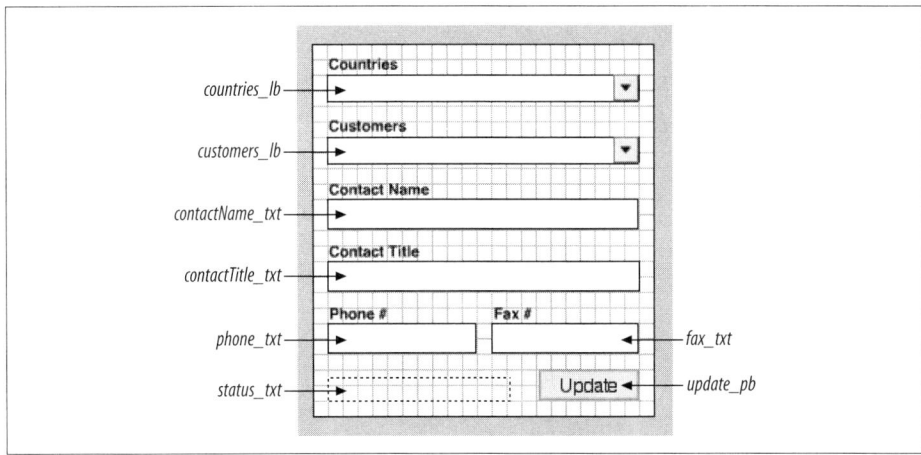

Figure 9-1. Client-side interface for a database access application

The interface operates as follows. The countries are listed in the countries_lb list-box; once a country is selected, the customers in that country are displayed in the customers_lb listbox. Once a user selects a customer, the customer's contact name, contact title, phone number, and fax number are displayed. If the user wants to update the information about the customer, he simply changes the listbox selections or text field text and clicks the Update button. The status_txt text field tells the user what is going on at any given time.

Example 9-4 showed the server-side PHP code to access the database on the server. The client-side ActionScript code to implement the user interface, as listed in Example 9-5, lives entirely on the main timeline.

Example 9-5. Client-side code for user interface

```
#include "NetServices.as"

//-------------------------------------------------------------------
// Define the URLs
//-------------------------------------------------------------------
gatewayURL = "http://localhost/frdg/gateway.php";
serviceURL = "CustomersAdmin";

//-------------------------------------------------------------------
// General purpose functions
//-------------------------------------------------------------------

// Turn the entire interface on or off
enableInterface = function (state) {
  var textType = state ? "input" : "dynamic";
  var textColor = state ? 0xFFFFFF : 0xBEBEBE;

  countries_cb.setEnabled(state);
  customers_cb.setEnabled(state);
  update_pb.setEnabled(state);

  contactName_txt.type = textType;
  contactTitle_txt.type = textType;
  phone_txt.type = textType;
  fax_txt.type = textType;

  contactName_txt.backgroundColor = textColor;
  contactTitle_txt.backgroundColor = textColor;
  phone_txt.backgroundColor = textColor;
  fax_txt.backgroundColor = textColor;
};

//-------------------------------------------------------------------
// Event handlers for the components
//-------------------------------------------------------------------

onSelectCountry = function () {
  var country = countries_cb.getSelectedItem().label;
```

Example 9-5. Client-side code for user interface (continued)

```
    service.getCustomersByCountry(customerResponder, country);

    customers_cb.removeAll();
    customers_cb.addItem("Loading...");
    enableInterface(false);
    status_txt.text = "Getting customers...";
};

onSelectCustomer = function () {
    customerID = customers_cb.getSelectedItem().data;
    service.getContact(contactResponder, customerID);

    contactName_txt.text = "";
    contactTitle_txt.text = "";
    phone_txt.text = "";
    fax_txt.text = "";

    enableInterface(false);
    status_txt.text = "Loading contact...";
};

onUpdate = function () {
    var customerID = customers_cb.getSelectedItem().data;
    var contactName = contactName_txt.text;
    var contactTitle = contactTitle_txt.text;
    var phone = phone_txt.text;
    var fax = fax_txt.text;
    service.updateContact(updateResponder, customerID, contactName,
                contactTitle, phone, fax);

    enableInterface(false);
    status_txt.text = "Updating contact...";
};


//-------------------------------------------------------------------
// Create the responder objects
//-------------------------------------------------------------------

// Responder for loading countries
countryResponder = new Object();
countryResponder.onResult = function (countries_rs) {
    var max = countries_rs.getLength();

    countries_cb.setEnabled(true);
    countries_cb.addItem("All", 0);

    for (var i=0; i<max; ++i) {
        countries_cb.addItem(countries_rs.getItemAt(i).Country, i+1);
    }
    countries_cb.setSelectedIndex(0);
};
```

Example 9-5. Client-side code for user interface (continued)

```
// Responder for loading customers
customerResponder = new Object( );

customerResponder.onResult = function (customers_rs) {
  var customer;
  var max = customers_rs.getLength( );
  customers_cb.setEnabled(true);
  customers_cb.removeAll( );

  for (var i=0; i<max; ++i) {
    customer = customers_rs.getItemAt(i);
    customers_cb.addItem(customer.CompanyName, customer.CustomerID);
  }

  customers_cb.setSelectedIndex(0);
};

// Responder for loading a contact
contactResponder = new Object( );

contactResponder.onResult = function (contact) {
  enableInterface(true);
  contactName_txt.text = contact.ContactName;
  contactTitle_txt.text = contact.ContactTitle;
  phone_txt.text = contact.Phone;
  fax_txt.text = contact.fax;

  status_txt.text = "Ready.";
};

// Responder for updating a contact
updateResponder = new Object( );

updateResponder.onResult = function ( ) {
  enableInterface(true);
  status_txt.text = "Ready.";
};

//--------------------------------------------------------------------
// Create the gateway and service objects
//--------------------------------------------------------------------
gateway = NetServices.createGatewayConnection(gatewayURL);
service = gateway.getService(serviceURL);

//--------------------------------------------------------------------
// Set up the components' event handlers
//--------------------------------------------------------------------
countries_cb.setChangeHandler("onSelectCountry", this);
customers_cb.setChangeHandler("onSelectCustomer", this);
update_pb.setClickHandler("onUpdate", this);

//--------------------------------------------------------------------
```

Example 9-5. Client-side code for user interface (continued)

```
// Set up the interface and load the countries
//-----------------------------------------------------------------
contactName_txt.borderColor = 0x666666;
contactTitle_txt.borderColor = 0x666666;
phone_txt.borderColor = 0x666666;
fax_txt.borderColor = 0x666666;
enableInterface(false);
status_txt.text = "Loading countries..."
service.getCountries(countryResponder);
```

Wrapping Up

The open source AMFPHP project allows you, for free, to implement Flash Remoting with both PHP classes and SOAP-based web services. While not yet complete, AMFPHP is already very useful. This is an exciting new option for Flash developers who don't have access to a gateway server and for developers who program exclusively in PHP. The way that you utilize AMFPHP from Flash is no different than the other gateway implementations, with the exception of arguments when dealing with web services.

Please remember that AMFPHP is a rapidly evolving project and the information presented here is highly subject to change. For the most recent information about AMFPHP be sure to visit the project's site at *http://www.amfphp.org*.

Advanced Flash Remoting

Part III covers advanced Flash Remoting techniques and applied topics. It includes details on accessing SOAP-based web services, enhancing objects and UI controls, implementing best practices, and debugging strategies. Also included are a detailed real-world application (an online script repository) and Flash Remoting API documentation.

- Chapter 10, *Calling Web Services from Flash Remoting*
- Chapter 11, *Extending Objects and UI Controls*
- Chapter 12, *Flash Remoting Best Practices*
- Chapter 13, *Testing and Debugging*
- Chapter 14, *Real-World Application*
- Chapter 15, *Flash Remoting API*

Calling Web Services from Flash Remoting

Cooking is a topic that everyone is familiar with. When you cook dinner, you are creating a meal from scratch. You take the ingredients, mix them together, cook them, and serve them. In many cases, this can be the preferred method of getting food on the table. Sometimes, however, it's simpler to pick up the phone and call for food, such as when you are staying in a hotel. Utilizing a prebuilt web service is like ordering room service: someone else has done the work for you, and all you have to do is consume the results.

Creating remote services for your Flash Remoting applications and connecting to them has been the focus of the previous chapters. We were, in effect, cooking our meals from scratch. Flash Remoting also works with prebuilt web services that you might find on the Internet. Web services are based on the Standard Object Access Protocol (SOAP). This protocol is spoken fluently by Flash Remoting and your application server.

What Is a Web Service?

Strictly speaking, web services have been around for many years. By definition, a *web service* is any form of service that can be accessed by an application over the Internet. In the past few years, however, the term *web services* has come to mean any service that utilizes one of the standardized XML web service technologies, such as SOAP or XML-RPC.

The advantages of XML are widely known. Any technology can communicate with any other technology if they share a common language. XML is a standardized way of transferring information that almost every technology can understand. XML does, however, have some disadvantages. It is cumbersome, because the data has to be described using plain text tags. So, while it is human-readable, it doesn't provide the best format for transmitting binary data across wires. Flash Remoting circumvents this problem by passing data between the Flash Remoting adapter (the proxy for the web service) and the Flash client (the movie in the user's browser) using the AMF format discussed in Chapter 1.

 A thorough discussion of web services is beyond the scope of this book. For more information on SOAP and web services, see *Programming Web Services with SOAP* by Pavel Kulchenko, James Snell, and Doug Tidwell (O'Reilly), which is a great introduction to SOAP-based web services. You can also find information at the W3C at *http://www.w3.org/TR/SOAP*.

A web service consists of three parts:

The service description
> This is usually stored in a Universal Description, Discovery, and Integration (UDDI) service repository, such as XMethods at *http://www.xmethods.com*.

The service provider
> The application server where the web service exists. The service provider generally provides a public description of the service, in the form of a Web Services Description Language (WSDL) document (an XML file with a *.wsdl* extension).

The service consumer
> The application that consumes the web service, usually by sending an XML request to the service provider. In our case, the Flash Remoting adapter on our server is the service consumer and our Flash movie on the user's browser will access the content provided by the service.

A typical web service might look like this ASP.NET web service, written in Visual Basic.NET:

```
<%@ WebService language="VB" class="HelloUser" %>

Imports System
Imports System.Web.Services
Imports System.Xml.Serialization
<WebService(Namespace:="http://oreilly.com/frdg/")>Public Class HelloUser

    <WebMethod> Public Function sayHello(username as String) As String
       Dim currentTime as String
       currentTime = DateTime.Now.ToLongTimeString( )
       return "Hello " & username & ". It is " + currentTime
    End Function

End Class
```

The process of consuming a web service begins with a request to the server for a *.wsdl* document.

WSDL

The *.wsdl* file is where the publicly accessible service description lives. The language is XML, but it is strictly formatted to specifications so that a consumer of a web service can know exactly what is in the web service and how to utilize it. The *.wsdl* file is akin to a contract between the service provider and the consumer of the service. It contains information about what is needed by the service and what will be returned.

The *.wsdl* file consists of the following:

- Information on all publicly available methods and how to interface to them
- Datatype information for all method responses and requests
- Address where the service can be found
- Information about the protocol to be used

In many cases, the *.wsdl* file is an automatically generated document (as you saw earlier in the ColdFusion example in Chapter 1). The *.wsdl* file for a *HelloUser* web service, shown as a *.cfc* in Chapter 2, might look like this:

```
<?xml version="1.0" encoding="utf-8"?>
<definitions xmlns:http="http://schemas.xmlsoap.org/wsdl/http/"
xmlns:soap="http://schemas.xmlsoap.org/wsdl/soap/"
xmlns:s="http://www.w3.org/2001/XMLSchema" xmlns:s0="http://oreilly.com/frdg/"
xmlns:soapenc="http://schemas.xmlsoap.org/soap/encoding/"
xmlns:tm="http://microsoft.com/wsdl/mime/textMatching/"
xmlns:mime="http://schemas.xmlsoap.org/wsdl/mime/"
targetNamespace="http://oreilly.com/frdg/xmlns=
"http://schemas.xmlsoap.org/wsdl/">
  <types>
    <s:schema elementFormDefault="qualified" targetNamespace="http://oreilly.com/
frdg/">
      <s:element name="sayHello">
        <s:complexType>
          <s:sequence>
            <s:element minOccurs="0" maxOccurs="1" name="username"
             type="s:string" />
          </s:sequence>
        </s:complexType>
      </s:element>
      <s:element name="sayHelloResponse">
        <s:complexType>
          <s:sequence>
            <s:element minOccurs="0" maxOccurs="1" name="sayHelloResult"
             type="s:string" />
          </s:sequence>
        </s:complexType>
      </s:element>
      <s:element name="string" nillable="true" type="s:string" />
    </s:schema>
  </types>
  <message name="sayHelloSoapIn">
    <part name="parameters" element="s0:sayHello" />
  </message>
  <message name="sayHelloSoapOut">
    <part name="parameters" element="s0:sayHelloResponse" />
  </message>
  <portType name="HelloUserSoap">
```

```
  <operation name="sayHello">
    <input message="s0:sayHelloSoapIn" />
    <output message="s0:sayHelloSoapOut" />
  </operation>
</portType>
<binding name="HelloUserSoap" type="s0:HelloUserSoap">
  <soap:binding transport="http://schemas.xmlsoap.org/soap/http"
    style="document" />
  <operation name="sayHello">
    <soap:operation soapAction="http://oreilly.com/frdg/sayHello"
  style="document" />
    <input>
      <soap:body use="literal" />
    </input>
    <output>
      <soap:body use="literal" />
    </output>
  </operation>
</binding>
<service name="HelloUser">
  <port name="HelloUserSoap" binding="s0:HelloUserSoap">
    <soap:address location="http://localhost/HelloUser.asmx" />
  </port>
</service>
</definitions>
```

The *.wsdl* file tells consumers how to use the service. Specifically, it tells us the name of the service:

```
<service name="HelloUser">
```

the methods available:

```
<s:element name="sayHello">
```

the arguments of the method:

```
<s:element minOccurs="0" maxOccurs="1" name="username" type="s:string" />
```

and the response:

```
<s:element minOccurs="0" maxOccurs="1" name="sayHelloResult" type="s:string" />
```

More information on the WSDL specification can be found at *http://www.w3.org/TR/wsdl*.

The next point to consider is where to find the *.wsdl* files. In many cases, this is handled by UDDI.

UDDI

UDDI is the specification that allows web services to be listed in central service registries. Typically, the WSDL description of a web service is embedded into a UDDI registry. You can think of a UDDI registry as a table of contents to publicly available web services. A UDDI registry contains listings of WSDL documents and other web services. Three large UDDI registries can be found at *http://www.xmethods.com, http://uddi.microsoft.com, and http://www-3.ibm.com/services/uddi.*

Currently, the most popular technology for web services is SOAP.

SOAP

SOAP is nothing more than a standardized XML format that acts as an envelope for the service request and result. You pass your request to the web service using a SOAP envelope, and the service responds with a SOAP envelope. Because SOAP is based in XML, it is free of environmental dependencies, so you can use SOAP freely among different environments. SOAP envelopes are typically sent over HTTP, as the HTTP port 80 is readily available and accessible by most systems, and open to most firewalls.

Flash Remoting allows you to call your web service using familiar ActionScript syntax. The details of SOAP translation are hidden in the Flash Remoting adapter on the server. You call the service from Flash using a simple method name, and the Flash movie sends an AMF packet with the request to the Flash Remoting adapter on the server. The Flash Remoting adapter issues the request for the *.wsdl* file on the application server (a GET request). The server (ColdFusion MX, ASP.NET, PHP, or Java) proxies the request and creates a SOAP request to the web service. The SOAP response is sent back to Flash Remoting, which translates the response back to an AMF packet that the Flash Player can understand. (If using Flash Player 7, SOAP support is built into the Player and does not require a server-side Remoting adapter.)

The SOAP packet consists of two parts: the header and the body. The header is an optional element that contains information about the content. The body is contained in a <soap:Envelope> tag and contains the information about the request or the response.

A typical request envelope might look like this:

```
POST /com/oreilly/frdg/HelloUser.asmx HTTP/1.0
Content-Length: 355
Host: 192.168.0.15
Content-Type: text/xml; charset=utf-8
SOAPAction: "http://oreilly.com/frdg/sayHello"

<?xml version="1.0" encoding="UTF-8"?>
<SOAP-ENV:Envelope xmlns:SOAP-ENV="http://schemas.xmlsoap.org/soap/envelope/"
xmlns:xsd="http://www.w3.org/2001/XMLSchema"
xmlns:xsi="http://www.w3.org/2001/XMLSchema-instance">
<SOAP-ENV:Body>
<sayHello xmlns="http://oreilly.com/frdg/">
<username>Tom</username>
</sayHello>
</SOAP-ENV:Body>
</SOAP-ENV:Envelope>
```

This request was created by an ASP.NET application server upon receiving the GET request from the Flash Remoting adapter on the server. The *sayHello( )* method of the web service can be plainly seen within the envelope body, along with the username parameter that was supplied in the Flash movie, "Tom". A response to that request might look like this:

```
HTTP/1.1 200 OK
Server: Microsoft-IIS/5.0
Date: Wed, 01 Jan 2003 01:20:19 GMT
Cache-Control: private, max-age=0
Content-Type: text/xml; charset=utf-8
Content-Length: 371

<?xml version="1.0" encoding="utf-8"?>
<soap:Envelope xmlns:xsi="http://www.w3.org/2001/XMLSchema-instance"
xmlns:xsd="http://www.w3.org/2001/XMLSchema"
xmlns:soap="http://schemas.xmlsoap.org/soap/envelope/">
<soap:Body>
<sayHelloResponse xmlns="http://oreilly.com/frdg/">
<sayHelloResult>Hello Tom. It is 8:20:19 PM</sayHelloResult>
</sayHelloResponse>
</soap:Body>
</soap:Envelope>
```

Again, the *sayHello( )* method response can be identified as a <sayHelloResponse> tag in this envelope. The response from the server is contained within the <sayHelloResult> tag. In the case of Flash Remoting, the SOAP packets are processed entirely on the server. An AMF packet is returned to the Flash movie.

Handy utilities exist to examine SOAP packets. Check *http://msdn.microsoft.com/webservices/downloads/microsoft/default.aspx* for Microsoft's SOAP Toolkit, which contains the Trace Utility for ASP.NET web services. For Java, the TCPTunnelGUI tool, which is part of the Apache SOAP package at *http://xml.apache.org/soap*, works well. More information on SOAP can be found at *http://www.w3.org/TR/SOAP*.

As you saw in Chapter 1, you can create your own web services easily using Cold-Fusion. This chapter, however, focuses on consuming web services from Flash, not creating your own. One of the nice things about Flash Remoting is that you don't have to know about UDDI, WSDL, SOAP, or XML. All you need is the location of the *.wsdl* file, and the requirements of the service. You can usually find human-readable descriptions of web services from the service provider, or you can examine the *.wsdl* file to determine the services requirements.

Why Use Flash Remoting?

One of the common questions about Flash is whether you can access web services using the Flash client only. Although Flash Player 6 requires Flash Remoting to access web services, Flash Player 7 has built-in SOAP support. However, the basic Flash 2004 authoring tool does not include the SOAP-based components that are standard in Flash Pro. Therefore, you must use Flash Pro (instead of Flash 2004) if you intend to use the built-in SOAP features of the Flash Player 7. As of this writing, it isn't clear how Macromedia will prevent developers from extending Flash 2004 to support the SOAP enhancements available in Flash Pro. Licensing restrictions and encrypted libraries have been raised as possibilities.

Table 10-1 summarizes the compatibility issues.

Table 10-1. Flash Remoting and SOAP-based web services support

Server platform	Flash Player	Flash Remoting via AMF support	SOAP-based web service support
ColdFusion MX 6.0 or later	Version 6.0.65 or later	Built into ColdFusion Server	Built into ColdFusion Server
JRun 4 or later	Version 6.0.65 or later	Built into JRun	Built into JRun
J2EE	Version 6.0.65 or later	Requires Flash Remoting for J2EE, or OpenAMF	Requires Flash Remoting for J2EE, or OpenAMF
J2EE	Version 7	Requires Flash Remoting for J2EE, or OpenAMF	Built into Flash Player 7 but requires Flash Pro for authoring
.NET	Version 6.0.65 or later	Requires Flash Remoting for .NET	Requires Flash Remoting for .NET
.NET	Version 7	Requires Flash Remoting for .NET	Built into Flash Player 7 but requires Flash Pro for authoring
PHP	Version 6.0.65 or later	Requires AMFPHP	Requires AMFPHP and nuSOAP or PEAR::SOAP
PHP	Version 7	Requires AMFPHP	Built into Flash Player 7 but requires nuSOAP or PEAR::SOAP
Perl	Version 6.0.65 or later	Requires FLAP	Not supported

So, should you switch to SOAP-based web services or stick with AMF? The answer is "it depends." If you need to support Flash Player 6 or access any web service outside your domain, you'll need Flash Remoting (or an open source equivalent) installed on the server side. If you want to use a SOAP-based solution without Flash Remoting, you must wait for Flash Player 7 to infiltrate the installed base. Within 18 months of its release (September 2003), Flash Player 7 should have sufficient penetration (greater than 80%) to justify shipping a SOAP-based solution, even if you're using a J2EE or .NET server without Flash Remoting. If you want to develop Flash applications that access SOAP-based web services from Flash Player 7, you must upgrade to Flash Pro because the basic Flash 2004 authoring environment doesn't include the libraries or prewritten behaviors for SOAP-based web services.

The major advantage of using SOAP is that J2EE and .NET servers understand SOAP messages without requiring Flash Remoting to be installed on the server side. This is very attractive if you don't have the privileges to install Flash Remoting on the server. So, when using J2EE and .NET, should you always use SOAP-based web services? Not necessarily. For one thing, you'll want to wait until Flash Player 7 is widely installed in the user base. Furthermore, the AMF format is more compact and efficient for transferring binary data, so Flash Remoting may yield better performance than SOAP-based web services. If you decide that Flash Player 7 is sufficiently ubiquitous to drop support for Flash Player 6, should you use SOAP-based web services when communicating with ColdFusion, JRun, or PHP? Not necessarily. ColdFusion and JRun come with Flash Remoting preinstalled, and it is a free installation for PHP. There is no reason not to use AMF format if you can guarantee that the Flash Remoting gateway is available on the server, as it is in these cases. (Likewise, the free OpenAMF Java implementation makes sense for developer's who have shied away from Flash Remoting for J2EE due to cost.)

Until you switch to Flash Player 7 and SOAP-based web services, you must use the Flash Remoting adapter on the server in order to translate your web service into an AMF packet that Flash Player 6 can understand. So, let's return to using SOAP-based web services in Flash MX. In many cases, this is as simple as adding the Flash Remoting adapter URL into your Flash movie. No hand-written server-side code is necessary. The Flash Remoting adapter on the server takes care of the necessary translation, so your Flash movie can simply use the service. Figure 10-1 shows a diagram of how Flash Remoting fits into the picture.

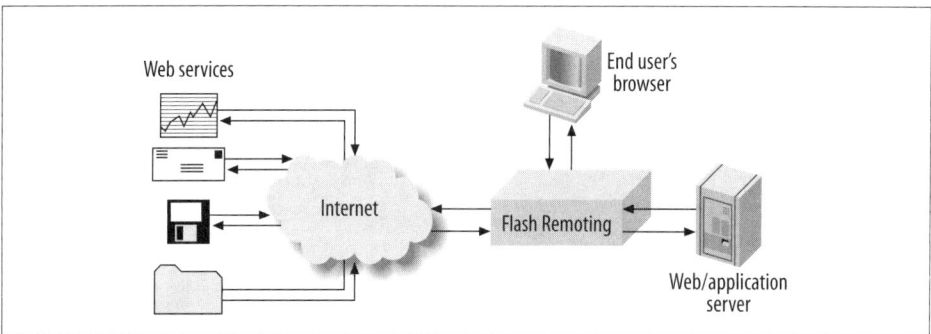

Figure 10-1. Flash Remoting and web services

This is the order of operations:

1. The Flash client (browser) makes the request via client-side ActionScript. The ActionScript code refers to the Flash Remoting gateway and the web service *.wsdl* file by name (except in the case of J2EE, which will be discussed shortly).

2. The Flash Remoting gateway uses a proxy on the application server to translate the request into SOAP. In ColdFusion MX and ASP.NET, the application server creates the proxy automatically.

3. The proxy then sends the request to the remote web service.

4. The remote web service responds to the application server with a SOAP envelope.

5. The Flash Remoting gateway gets the results back from the application server and translates the results into ActionScript objects.

6. The gateway passes the result back to the Flash client.

Why wasn't Flash Player 6 built to utilize SOAP directly? There are several reasons for this:

- SOAP is a large protocol. It is based in XML and requires major parsing inside of the Flash plugin. Flash Player 6 excluded SOAP support in order to keep the plugin footprint small and accelerate deployment. Adding SOAP deserialization to Flash Player 7 increases the footprint over Flash Player 6 somewhat.

- The Flash Player has security restrictions that prevent it from loading content from other domains. This is a good thing, as it keeps the level of acceptance of the Flash player very high; having Flash on your computer is regarded as safe.

- The AMF format of Flash Remoting is a terse binary format, which results in fast transfer speeds between the Flash Remoting gateway and the Flash movie. Furthermore, there is faster processing because of less serialization and deserialization.

As a contrast in size, look at the AMF response passed to the Flash movie for the simple *HelloUser* SOAP example shown earlier:

```
HTTP/1.1 200 OK
Server: Microsoft-IIS/5.0
Date: Wed, 01 Jan 2003 01:40:30 GMT
Cache-Control: private
Content-Type: application/x-amf
Content-Length: 59

.......1/onResult..null.......Hello Tom. It is 8:40:30 PM..
```

The Content-Length header tells the story: the SOAP version was 371 characters, whereas the AMF version was 59 characters. You can imagine that, with more complex web services, the savings in bandwidth can be enormous. Macromedia's reluctance to release the AMF specification hasn't dampened developer enthusiasm for the format in the guise of projects such as AMFPHP (*http://www.amfphp.org*) and OpenAMF (*http://www.openamf.org*).

There are other techniques to access a web service from Flash, such as parsing the SOAP on the server using server-side code, but Flash Remoting is by far the easiest method to use. This chapter discusses the different implementations of Flash Remoting and how to use web services in each.

Limitations

Using Flash Remoting for consuming web services is a viable option in many cases; however, there are a few limitations:

- Flash Remoting is able to connect only to SOAP web services that have a WSDL descriptor file. At this time, XML web services are not supported.

- You have to supply all of the parameters to a web service, even if they are optional parameters.

- Datatypes that aren't supported in your platform (ColdFusion MX, Java, ASP.NET, or PHP) aren't supported by Flash Remoting. For example, ColdFusion supports a *Query* datatype, but it is not accessible from ASP.NET because ASP.NET does not support a multidimensional array type.

Some of these limitations may be addressed in future versions of Flash Remoting.

Web Services from a ColdFusion Server

When the server environment for web services is ColdFusion MX, you don't have to do anything on the server side to consume a web service. The Flash movie merely has to reference the Flash Remoting adapter on the server. The ColdFusion MX Server contains the necessary SOAP translation requirements and creates a proxy for the web service. The Flash Remoting gateway translates the SOAP reply from the proxy into the ActionScript objects that Flash will understand.

As of ColdFusion Updater 3, web services are not enabled by default in ColdFusion MX. This is for security reason; a malicious user can hijack a Flash Remoting gateway to call web services. To enable the web services, the *web.xml* file in the ColdFusion MX installation needs to be changed. Read the Updater 3 release notes at *http://www.macromedia. com/support/coldfusion/releasenotes/mx/releasenotes_mx_updater01.html* for more information.

ColdFusion MX creates Java stub classes as a proxy for the web service behind the scenes. These proxy classes are located in *ColdFusion_MX_root\stubs*. Upon first calling the web service, the proxy is created. It remains in place for subsequent calls. For that reason, the first call to the service will take more time. The same is true for a web service called through Flash Remoting using ASP.NET.

To demonstrate a simple example, we'll call the *Whois* web service at *http://www. soapclient.com/xml/SQLDataSoap.wsdl*. Services such as these can be found at *http:// www.xmethods.com* and other UDDI registries.

The availability of a particular web service comes and goes, but the code shown in Example 10-1 should work for any similar *Whois* service, including the one at *http://www.flash-remoting.com/whois.wsdl*, which takes one simple argument: domain.

Example 10-1 shows the client-side ActionScript code necessary to call a remote web service. The Flash movie also contains a text field named domain_txt to get the user input, a text field named results_txt to hold the results, and a button named submit_pb to call the service. Notice that the service name is a fully qualified URL of the *.wsdl* file for the web service. The ColdFusion MX Server creates a proxy for the service. Again, the myURL variable in the sample code contains the reference to a local

ColdFusion Server at port 8500, but you should change this URL to your own Flash Remoting location.

Example 10-1. Client-side ActionScript code for accessing a Whois service

```
#include "NetServices.as"

// Set up variables for the URL and service paths
var myURL = "http://localhost:8500/flashservices/gateway";
var servicePath = "http://www.soapclient.com/xml/SQLDataSoap.wsdl";

// Define the custom class SimpleResult
function SimpleResult() {
}
// Set up onResult and onStatus handlers as methods of the SimpleResult class
SimpleResult.prototype.onResult = function (myResults) {
  results_txt.text = myResults;
};
SimpleResult.prototype.onStatus = function (myError) {
  results_txt.text = myError.description;
};
// Set the system status to be handled by the result status handler as well
System.onStatus = SimpleResult.prototype.onStatus;

// Connection hasn't been initialized; create connection and service objects
if (initialized == null) {
  initialized = true;
  NetServices.setDefaultGatewayURL(myURL);
  var myConnection_conn = NetServices.createGatewayConnection();
  var myService = myConnection_conn.getService(servicePath, new SimpleResult());
}

submit_pb.setClickHandler("getWhois");
// Call the service when the user clicks the Submit button
function getWhois () {
  myService.ProcessSRL("WHOIS.SRI","whois",domain_txt.text);
}
```

Upon running the movie, you are prompted for a domain name. You can enter a domain name and click Submit. The web service responds with the *Whois* data for that particular domain.

Web Services from an ASP.NET Server

Accessing a web service from Flash using Flash Remoting on an ASP.NET server is almost as easy as it is from a ColdFusion MX Server. Like ColdFusion MX, you do not have to supply any extra code on the server to use a remote web service. The only difference is that you need to set up the proper permissions on the ASP.NET server. ASP.NET contains a utility called *wsdl.exe*, which Flash Remoting uses to automatically generate proxies for web services. The ASP.NET server creates a *.dll* file in your local assembly cache that acts as a proxy for the web service when you first call the service. This proxy remains in place for future calls to the service. For that reason, the first call to the service takes a little longer than subsequent calls. It's a good idea to delete these files manually during development, to prevent the use of a cached web service.

The Windows user *ASPNET* (found in Administrative Tools → Computer Management → Users and Groups) needs to be set up with permissions to write to the *bin* directory in your Flash Remoting application. This allows the ASP.NET server to create the *.dll* files necessary to consume the web service. ASP.NET also creates a C# source file for the DLL that can be modified and recompiled. The *ASPNET* user also needs Script execute permission from the IIS management console.

 If you can't access a web service, even after applying the proper permissions, check the permission level on the *wsdl.exe* file, which resides in *C:\Program Files\Microsoft.NET\FrameworkSDK\Bin* in a default installation of the .NET Framework SDK. This file also needs to allow the *ASPNET* user to access it.

You can use Example 10-1 to call the web service using an ASP.NET server, by changing only one line, the reference to the gateway:

```
var myURL = "http://localhost/flashremoting/gateway.aspx";
```

You should substitute your own Flash Remoting URL here.

Upon running the example, the *webroot\flashremoting\bin* directory contains two new files: *SQLDataSoap.cs* and *SQLDataSoap.dll*. If you recall, the web service *.wsdl* file was named *SQLDataSoap.wsdl*, and the *.dll* proxy is always named after the web service. If you create *.dll* files manually, you should follow this naming convention as well. The *.cs* file is the C# source code for the proxy to the web service. The code is listed in Example 10-2. Nothing else has to be done to the code, but it is listed here for your perusal or if you need to modify the file in any way.

Example 10-2. C# code for the web service proxy

```
//------------------------------------------------------------------------------
// <autogenerated>
//     This code was generated by a tool.
//     Runtime Version: 1.0.3705.0
//
//     Changes to this file may cause incorrect behavior and will be lost if
//     the code is regenerated.
// </autogenerated>
//------------------------------------------------------------------------------

//
// This source code was auto-generated by wsdl, Version=1.0.3705.0.
//
using System.Diagnostics;
using System.Xml.Serialization;
using System;
```

Example 10-2. C# code for the web service proxy (continued)

```csharp
using System.Web.Services.Protocols;
using System.ComponentModel;
using System.Web.Services;


/// <remarks/>
[System.Diagnostics.DebuggerStepThroughAttribute()]
[System.ComponentModel.DesignerCategoryAttribute("code")]
[System.Web.Services.WebServiceBindingAttribute(Name="SQLDataSoapBinding",
 Namespace="http://www.SoapClient.com/xml/SQLDataSoap.wsdl")]
public class SQLDataSoap : System.Web.Services.Protocols.SoapHttpClientProtocol {

    /// <remarks/>
    public SQLDataSoap() {
        this.Url = "http://soapclient.com/xml/SQLDataSoap.wsdl";
    }

    /// <remarks/>
    [System.Web.Services.Protocols.SoapRpcMethodAttribute(
"http://soapclient.com/SQLDataSRL",
RequestNamespace="http://www.SoapClient.com/xml/SQLDataSoap.xsd",
ResponseNamespace="http://www.SoapClient.com/xml/SQLDataSoap.xsd")]
    [return: System.Xml.Serialization.SoapElementAttribute("return")]
    public string ProcessSRL(string SRLFile, string RequestName, string key) {
        object[] results = this.Invoke("ProcessSRL", new object[] {
                    SRLFile,
                    RequestName,
                    key});
        return ((string)(results[0]));
    }

    /// <remarks/>
    public System.IAsyncResult BeginProcessSRL(string SRLFile, string
RequestName, string key, System.AsyncCallback callback, object asyncState) {
        return this.BeginInvoke("ProcessSRL", new object[] {
                    SRLFile,
                    RequestName,
                    key}, callback, asyncState);
    }

    /// <remarks/>
    public string EndProcessSRL(System.IAsyncResult asyncResult) {
        object[] results = this.EndInvoke(asyncResult);
        return ((string)(results[0]));
    }

    /// <remarks/>
    [System.Web.Services.Protocols.SoapRpcMethodAttribute(
"http://soapclient.com/SQLDataSRL",
RequestNamespace="http://www.SoapClient.com/xml/SQLDataSoap.xsd",
ResponseNamespace="http://www.SoapClient.com/xml/SQLDataSoap.xsd")]
    [return: System.Xml.Serialization.SoapElementAttribute("return")]
    public string ProcessSRL2(string SRLFile, string RequestName, string key1,
```

Example 10-2. C# code for the web service proxy (continued)

```
string key2) {
        object[] results = this.Invoke("ProcessSRL2", new object[] {
                    SRLFile,
                    RequestName,
                    key1,
                    key2});
        return ((string)(results[0]));
    }

    /// <remarks/>
    public System.IAsyncResult BeginProcessSRL2(string SRLFile, string
RequestName, string key1, string key2, System.AsyncCallback callback, object
asyncState) {
        return this.BeginInvoke("ProcessSRL2", new object[] {
                    SRLFile,
                    RequestName,
                    key1,
                    key2}, callback, asyncState);
    }

    /// <remarks/>
    public string EndProcessSRL2(System.IAsyncResult asyncResult) {
        object[] results = this.EndInvoke(asyncResult);
        return ((string)(results[0]));
    }

    /// <remarks/>
    [System.Web.Services.Protocols.SoapRpcMethodAttribute(
"http://www.SoapClient.com/SQLDataSQL",
RequestNamespace="http://www.SoapClient.com/xml/SQLDataSoap.xsd",
ResponseNamespace="http://www.SoapClient.com/xml/SQLDataSoap.xsd")]
    [return: System.Xml.Serialization.SoapElementAttribute("return")]
    public string ProcessSQL(string DataSource, string SQLStatement, string
UserName, string Password) {
        object[] results = this.Invoke("ProcessSQL", new object[] {
                    DataSource,
                    SQLStatement,
                    UserName,
                    Password});
        return ((string)(results[0]));
    }

    /// <remarks/>
    public System.IAsyncResult BeginProcessSQL(string DataSource, string
SQLStatement, string UserName, string Password, System.AsyncCallback callback,
object asyncState) {
        return this.BeginInvoke("ProcessSQL", new object[] {
                    DataSource,
                    SQLStatement,
                    UserName,
                    Password}, callback, asyncState);
    }
```

Example 10-2. C# code for the web service proxy (continued)

```
    /// <remarks/>
    public string EndProcessSQL(System.IAsyncResult asyncResult) {
        object[] results = this.EndInvoke(asyncResult);
        return ((string)(results[0]));
    }
}
```

Wrapping J2EE and JRun Web Services

Accessing a remote web service from a Java application server or JRun 4 is a little more complicated than utilizing a web service from ColdFusion MX or ASP.NET. You need to manually create the proxy for the web service, using some tools that are readily available and preinstalled as part of the JRun 4 installation.

JRun 4 comes with a command-line tool called *wsdl2java.exe* (located in the *Jrun4\bin* directory), which is part of the Apache Axis implementation of SOAP. If you are using an alternate J2EE server, you can download the necessary components from *http://xml.apache.org/axis*. The *wsdl2java* tool from the Apache web site is a Java *.jar* file rather than a command-line program. More information on the classes can be found at *http://xml.apache.org/axis*.

The *wsdl2java* tool automatically creates most of the Java code necessary to consume the web service from Flash. It transforms a *.wsdl* file into a Java interface. You can use *wsdl2java* manually from a command line. To convert the *Whois* service shown earlier, navigate to the directory containing the *wsdl2java.exe* file and run it as follows:

```
wsdl2java -o yourSourceDir http://www.soapclient.com/xml/SQLDataSoap.wsdl
```

Using the *.jar* version of *wsdl2java*, you call it like this:

```
java org.apache.axis.wsdl.WSDL2Java
http://www.soapclient.com/xml/SQLDataSoap.wsdl -o yourSourceDir
```

If you are using the *wsdl2java.jar* file from the Apache site, make sure you include the following classes in your classpath when running the tool:

*   *axis_directory/lib/axis.jar*
*   *axis_directory/lib/jaxrpc.jar*
*   *axis_directory/lib/saaj.jar*
*   *axis_directory/lib/commons-logging.jar*
*   *axis_directory/lib/commons-dicovery.jar*
*   *axis_directory/lib/wsdl4j.jar*
*   An XML parser, such as Xerces

The *wsdl2java* conversion tool creates at least four *.java* stub and skeleton files in the *classes\com\SoapClient\www* directory, using the *o* switch to specify the output directory. Each web service has its own directory structure, based on the domain name of the service. These four files for this particular web service are:

SQLDataSoap.java
SQLDataSoapBindingStub.java
SQLDataSoapLocator.java
SQLDataSoapPortType.java

These Java source files need to be compiled. The packages needed by these stub and skeleton files are all included in *jrun_directory/lib/webservices.jar* for JRun 4. To utilize the classes from Flash Remoting, you have to create a wrapper JavaBean. The Java code shown in Example 10-3 acts as a wrapper bean for this particular web service. It can be easily modified to work with any web service.

Example 10-3. JavaBean wrapper code for the Whois web service

```
// Use the same package as the wsdl2java-generated classes
package com.SoapClient.www;

// Handle to the generated stub
public class SQLDataSoapBean {
  private com.SoapClient.www.SQLDataSoapBindingStub soap;

  // Empty constuctor
  public SQLDataSoapBean( ) throws java.net.MalformedURLException,
   org.apache.axis.AxisFault {
     final java.net.URL endPoint =
      new java.net.URL("http://www.SoapClient.com/xml/SQLDataSoap.wsdl");
     soap = new com.SoapClient.www.SQLDataSoapBindingStub(endPoint,
           new org.apache.axis.client.Service( ));
  }

  // Public method to call the web services method processSRL
  public String processSRL(String SRLFile, String requestName,
   String key) throws java.rmi.RemoteException {
    return soap.processSRL(SRLFile, requestName, key);
  }
}
```

After compiling the stub, skeleton, and JavaBean files, you should be able to use the Flash code shown in Example 10-1, changing the service path to the path of your JavaBean. When accessing a web service through a J2EE server, you don't access the service directly, as you would with a ColdFusion or ASP.NET server, but instead access the wrapper that you just created:

```
var servicePath = "com.SoapClient.www.SQLDataSoapBean";
```

As you can see, using web services from J2EE servers is slightly more complex than it is from ColdFusion or ASP.NET, but once you've consumed one service, you can easily adapt the code to consume other services.

Web Services from PHP

Setting up AMFPHP for web services is covered in Chapter 9. There are two web service options for AMFPHP: nuSOAP and PEAR::SOAP. The examples should work with either. The AMFPHP gateway requires that web services be called with the arguments attached to an ActionScript object. The *Whois* web service described earlier requires these three named arguments:

SRLFile
> The name of the Service Request Language File ("WHOIS.SRI" for domain checking).

RequestName
> This should always be "whois".

Key
> The domain name.

Other than that, the code can be used as-is from the ColdFusion MX example, substituting your own Flash Remoting gateway URL. The *getWhois( )* function looks like this in the PHP example:

```
function getWhois () {
  myService.ProcessSRL({
    SRLFile:"WHOIS.SRI",
    RequestName:"whois",
    Key:domain_txt.text});
}
```

In the function, we are simply creating a generic object in the function call.

BabelFish Web Service

The BabelFish translation service at XMethods (*http://www.xmethods.net*) is a sample that can be implemented easily with a couple of text fields, a combo box, and a button. With a few lines of ActionScript code, you can put language translation functionality into a Flash movie and into your site. The BabelFish method at *http://www.xmethods.net/sd/2001/BabelFishService.wsdl* takes two arguments: translationmode and sourcedata.

The translationmode argument is a special code for the two languages used in the translation, as shown in Table 10-2. This data is displayed in a combo box named language_cb.

Table 10-2. Translation modes for the BabelFish remote method

From	To	translationmode
English	French	en_fr
English	German	en_de

Table 10-2. Translation modes for the BabelFish remote method (continued)

From	To	translationmode
English	Italian	en_it
English	Portuguese	en_pt
English	Spanish	en_es
French	English	fr_en
German	English	de_en
Italian	English	it_en
Portuguese	English	pt_en
Russian	English	ru_en
Spanish	English	es_en

The sourcedata argument is the text that you want translated (limited to a string of 150 characters or less). The Flash UI, shown in Figure 10-2, allows the user to type into the from_txt text field, choose a language translation from the combo box, click a button, and get the result in a text field named to_txt.

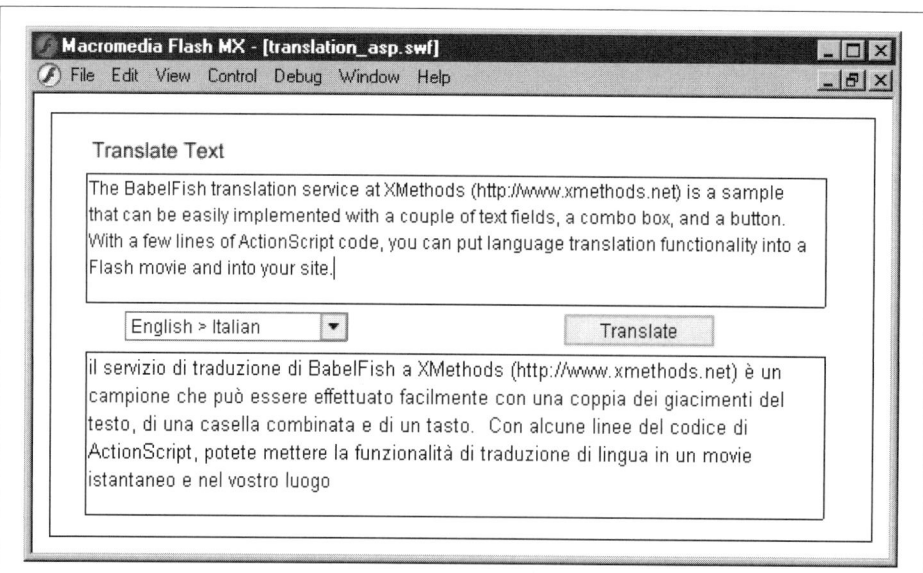

Figure 10-2. Translation interface

The client-side ActionScript code is shown in Example 10-4, using the ColdFusion gateway.

Example 10-4. ActionScript code for consuming the BabelFish web service

```
#include "NetServices.as"

// Set up variables for the URL and service paths
// Use your own Flash Remoting gateway URL
var myURL = "http://localhost:8500/flashservices/gateway";
var servicePath = "http://www.xmethods.net/sd/2001/BabelFishService.wsdl";

// Define the custom class SimpleResult
function SimpleResult () {
}
// Set up onResult() and onStatus() handlers as methods of SimpleResult class
SimpleResult.prototype.onResult = function (myResults) {
  to_txt.text = myResults;
};
SimpleResult.prototype.onStatus = function (myError) {
  to_txt.text = myError.description;
};
// Set the system status to be handled by the result status handler as well
System.onStatus = SimpleResult.protype.onStatus;

// Connection hasn't been initialized; create connection and service objects
if (initialized == null) {
  initialized = true;
  NetServices.setDefaultGatewayURL(myURL);
  var myConnection_conn = NetServices.createGatewayConnection();
  var myService = myConnection_conn.getService(servicePath, new SimpleResult());
}

// Call the service on click of the push button
translate_pb.setClickHandler("translate");
function translate () {
  myService.BabelFish(language_cb.getSelectedItem().data, from_txt.text);
}
```

The ActionScript code when using an ASP.NET server would differ only in the Flash Remoting gateway URL, as set in the myURL variable. Everything else remains the same.

The ActionScript code when using a PHP example is also similar. Once the gateway URL is set correctly, the only other difference is that the *translate( )* function must pass the parameters to the *BabelFish* service using an object with named properties:

```
function translate () {
  myService.BabelFish(
    {translationmode:language_cb.getSelectedItem().data,
     sourcedata:from_txt.text});
}
```

The Java version requires the wrapper JavaBean, similar to Example 10-3. The wrapper JavaBean needed for Example 10-4 is shown in Example 10-5. You will also have to use the *wsdl2java* tool as described earlier under "Wrapping J2EE and JRun Web Services."

Example 10-5. JavaBean wrapper for the BabelFish method

```
// Use the same package as the wsdl2java-generated classes
package net.xmethods.www;

public class BabelFishServiceBean implements java.io.Serializable {

// Handle to the generated stub
private net.xmethods.www.BabelFishBindingStub soap;

  // Empty constuctor
  public BabelFishServiceBean( ) throws java.net.MalformedURLException,
    org.apache.axis.AxisFault {
    final java.net.URL endPoint = new java.net.URL
    ("http://www.xmethods.net/sd/2001/BabelFishService.wsdl");
     soap = new net.xmethods.www.BabelFishBindingStub(endPoint,
       new org.apache.axis.client.Service( ));
  }

  // Public method to call the web services method babelFish
  public java.lang.String babelFish(java.lang.String translationmode,
   java.lang.String sourcedata) throws java.rmi.RemoteException {
     return soap.babelFish(translationmode, sourcedata);
  }
}
```

The ActionScript code for the Java example needs to have the URL to the service changed from the *.wsdl* file to the JavaBean on your server:

```
var servicePath = "net.xmethods.www.BabelFishServiceBean";
```

Datatype Conversions

Web services have specific simple types that are native to SOAP and other complex types that you can define. The SOAP datatypes and their ActionScript equivalencies are listed in Table 10-3.

Table 10-3. Datatype conversion between ActionScript and SOAP

ActionScript	SOAP
Null	Null
Undefined	Null
Boolean	Boolean
Number	Decimal, Float, Double, Integer, Int
String	String
Date	DateTime
Array (numeric index)	Array
Associative array	Complex type
RecordSet	N/A
Object	Complex type

ColdFusion also supports a *QueryBean* datatype, which allows you to transfer query objects as results from a web service. It is advisable, however, to create web services that will be more universally readable, such as an array. Not all consumers of web services will be able to access a *QueryBean*.

Passing Complex Datatypes to and from Web Services

Sending a complex datatype to a web service is sometimes as simple as defining it in the client-side ActionScript and passing it as an argument. An example of a web service that accepts a complex object as an argument and returns a complex object as a result is the Amazon.com web service. Unfortunately, this is not a service that is usable in different server environments. Example 10-6 works in ASP.NET and PHP environments only. The Flash Remoting gateway for Java and ColdFusion (essentially the same gateway) seems to have problems with this web service.

To make use of the Amazon.com web service, you must go to *http://www.amazon.com/webservices* and sign up for a free developer's kit. You are issued a developer's token that can be used as a key to use the service. Once you've done that, you are free to use their service in accordance with the licensing agreement.

One obvious use is to search Amazon.com's catalog of books. The Flash UI for Amazon.com web service example is shown in Figure 10-3. The source file, *amazon.fla*, can be downloaded from the online Code Depot.

We'll use the *KeywordSearchRequest( )* method of the Amazon.com web service for this example. The method accepts an object with the following properties as an argument (see the comments in Example 10-6 or the Amazon.com documentation for more information about each argument):

```
keyword
page
mode
tag
type
sort (optional)
devtag
```

The response from the service is also in the form of an object. The returned object has the following properties:

ListName
> Not used for the *KeywordSearchRequest( )* method.

TotalResults
> Contains the total number of search results (only 10 results are returned from the service, however).

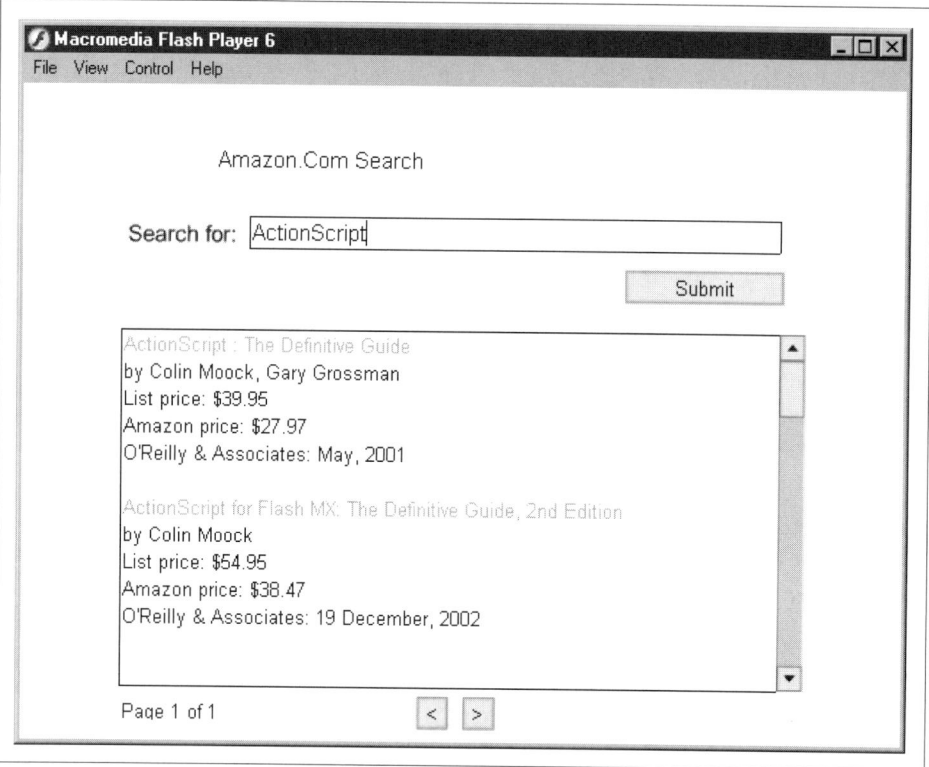

Figure 10-3. The Amazon.com service using Flash Remoting

Details

An array of objects containing the details of the books returned by the search. Each element of the array is an object that contains the following properties:

URL	Manufacturer
ASIN	ImageUrlSmall
ProductName	ImageUrlMedium
Catalog	ImageUrlLarge
Artists	ListPrice
Authors	OurPrice
ReleaseDate	UsedPrice

The Artists and Authors properties are arrays as well. The code shown in Example 10-6 creates the Flash MX interface to the Amazon.com web service, which takes a complex datatype as a parameter and returns a complex datatype to the caller. Because Amazon.com implements its own pageable results, we have to implement paging in our Flash movie to be able to display all of the results. The code is commented inline.

Example 10-6. Amazon.com web service implementing a keyword search (amazon.fla)

```
#include "NetServices.as"

if (!connected) {
  var connected = true;
  var gatewayURL = "http://localhost/flashremoting/gateway.aspx");
  NetServices.setDefaultGatewayURL(gatewayURL);
  var gatewayConnection = NetServices.createGatewayConnection();
  var myService = gatewayConnection.getService(
    "http://soap.amazon.com/schemas2/AmazonWebServices.wsdl", this);
}

var keywordSearchPages = 0;
var KeywordRequestArgument = new Object();

// Initialize the object with properties and methods
KeywordRequestArgument.init = function () {
  this.keyword = "";              // Search word or words
  this.page = "1";                // Page number of results
  this.mode = "books";            // Type of product we are searching
  this.tag = "myassociateID";     // Amazon.com associate ID if you have one
  this.type = "lite";             // Type is either "lite" or "heavy"
  this.devtag = "yourtaghere";    // The Amazon developer tag that is issued to you
  this.version = "2.0";           // Version number of the Amazon web service
// This ends the properties for the object

  // Methods will be stripped off before being sent to the service
  this.setPageNumber = function (page) {this.page = page.toString();};
  this.getPageNumber = function (page) {return this.page;};
  this.setKeyword = function (keyword) {this.keyword = keyword;};

  // Call the remote service
  this.callService = function (page) {
    this.setPageNumber(page);
    pagedisplay_txt.text = "...working";
    myService.KeywordSearchRequest(this);
  };
};

KeywordRequestArgument.init();  // Initialize the object

previous_pb.setClickHandler("previousPage");
function previousPage () {
  var page = KeywordRequestArgument.getPageNumber();
  // Decrement the page counter, but no less than 1
  page = (page-- < 1) ? 1 : page--;
  KeywordRequestArgument.callService(page);
}

next_pb.setClickHandler("nextPage");
function nextPage () {
  var page = KeywordRequestArgument.getPageNumber();
```

Example 10-6. Amazon.com web service implementing a keyword search (amazon.fla) (continued)

```
  // Increment the page counter, but no greater than total pages
  page = (page++ >= keywordSearchPages) ? keywordSearchPages : page++;
  KeywordRequestArgument.callService(page);
}

submit_pb.setClickHandler("getResults");
function getResults () {
  keywordSearchPages = 0;
  KeywordRequestArgument.setKeyword(search_txt.text);
  KeywordRequestArgument.callService("1");
}

// Turn a URL into a clickable link
function makeLink(theText,theLink) {
  return '<font color="#00cc00"><a href="' + unescape(theLink)+ '" target="_blank">' +
theText + '</a></font>';
}

function KeywordSearchRequest_Status (error) {
  trace(error.description);
}

// Display the results
function KeywordSearchRequest_Result (result) {
  results_txt.text = "";
  if (result.TotalResults == 0) {
    pagedisplay_txt.text = "No results";
  } else {
    keywordSearchPages = Math.ceil(result.TotalResults/10);
    var temp = "";
    var totalResults = (result.TotalResults < 10) ? result.TotalResults : 10;
    for (var i=0; i < totalResults; i++) {
    temp += makeLink(result.Details[i].ProductName, result.Details[i].Url)+
          "<br>";
    temp += "by " + result.Details[i].Authors.join(", ") + "<br>";
    temp += "List price: " + result.Details[i].ListPrice + "<br>";
    temp += "Amazon price: " + result.Details[i].OurPrice + "<br>";
    temp += result.Details[i].Manufacturer + ": " +
          result.Details[i].ReleaseDate + "<br>";
    temp += "<br>";
    }
    results_txt.htmlText = temp;
    pagedisplay_txt.text = "Page " + KeywordRequestArgument.getPageNumber() +
       " of " + keywordSearchPages;
  }
}
```

In this case, we attach the parameters required for the web service as properties of a generic *Object*, KeywordRequestArgument. The parameters are handled by the Flash Remoting adapter on the server and translated into the proper SOAP datatypes by the application server. An object is returned to the Flash movie and is parsed and displayed in the *KeywordSearchRequest_Result( )* function.

Example 10-6 uses the ASP.NET gateway. No server-side code is necessary. For PHP, the code should work as written (because it passes the parameters to the service as properties of an object), provided you update the gateway URL to point to the PHP gateway.

I hope that Macromedia makes the future versions of Flash Remoting more consistent across server implementations so that services such as Amazon.com can be used by ColdFusion MX and J2EE servers as well.

Passing Simple Arrays to Web Services

Web services can supply many different types of results to consumers of those services. Many web services pass simple strings or simple values. In Example 10-6, we saw the Amazon.com web service, which passes a complex object, making it incompatible with ColdFusion MX and J2EE servers when using Flash Remoting.

An array is a basic datatype in most languages, and SOAP is no exception. The web service at *http://www.communitymx.com/services/cmxfeed.wsdl* passes an array of simple objects to the consumer. The web service lists articles and other content available at Community MX, a support site for Studio MX and other web technologies. The array contains objects with the following properties:

```
Title
Author
Category
Description
Keywords
Type_description
Url
```

The ActionScript code for the simple interface is shown in Example 10-7. Notice that the service method *getContent( )* takes one argument: type. If you pass the argument "all", the service simply passes the latest content feed from Community MX. The interface consists of two text fields: results_txt and content_txt, with a scrollbar attached to content_txt. The source file, *communitymx.fla*, can be downloaded from the online Code Depot.

Example 10-7. Flash code for web service from Community MX (communitymx.fla)

```
#include "NetServices.as"

// Set up variables for the URL and service paths
var myURL = "http://localhost:8500/flashservices/gateway";
var servicePath = "http://www.communitymx.com/services/cmxfeed.wsdl";

// Define the custom SimpleResult class to display the results
function SimpleResult() {}
// Set up onResult() and onStatus() handlers as methods of SimpleResult class
SimpleResult.prototype.onResult = function (myResults) {
```

```
    results_txt.text = myResults.length + " records returned";
    var temp = "";
    for (var i=0; i < myResults.length; i++) {
      temp += makeLink(myResults[i].title,myResults[i].url) + "<br>";
      temp += "Author: " + myResults[i].author + "<br>";
      temp += "Category: " + myResults[i].category + "<br>";
      temp += "Description: " + myResults[i].description + "<br>";
      temp += "<br><br>";
      }
    content_txt.htmlText = temp;
};
SimpleResult.prototype.onStatus = function (myError) {
    results_txt.text = myError.description;
};
// Set the system status to be handled by the result status handler as well
System.onStatus = SimpleResult.prototype.onStatus;

// Make a clickable link out of the Title
function makeLink(theText,theLink) {
    var temp = '<font color="#00cc00"><a href="';
    temp += unescape(theLink);
    temp += '" target="_blank">' + theText + '</a></font>';
    return temp;
}

// Connection hasn't been initialized; create connection and service objects
if (initialized == null) {
    initialized = true;
    NetServices.setDefaultGatewayURL(myURL);
    var myConnection_conn = NetServices.createGatewayConnection();
    var myService = myConnection_conn.getService(servicePath, new SimpleResult());
}

// Call the service on load
results_txt.text = "...working";
myService.getContent("all");
```

The content is displayed when the movie loads.

Example 10-7 uses the ColdFusion gateway. The ASP.NET version is identical, except for the path to the Flash Remoting adapter on the server. The PHP version needs to have the arguments to the service packed into an object, so replace the last line of Example 10-7 with these two lines:

```
    var tempObj = {type:"all"};
    myService.getContent(tempObj);
```

The J2EE and JRun versions need a JavaBean wrapper, as described earlier under "Wrapping J2EE and JRun Web Services." The JavaBean shown in Example 10-8 will work for this service after following the instructions outlined for Example 10-3 under "Wrapping J2EE and JRun Web Services."

Example 10-8. JavaBean wrapper code for the Community MX web service

```
// Use the same package as the wsdl2java-generated classes
package services;

public class CmxfeedBean implements java.io.Serializable {

  // Handle to the generated stub
  private services.CmxfeedCfcSoapBindingStub soap;

  // Empty constuctor
  public CmxfeedBean() throws java.net.MalformedURLException,
   org.apache.axis.AxisFault {
    final java.net.URL endPoint = new java.net.URL
     ("http://www.communitymx.com/services/cmxfeed.wsdl");
      soap = new services.CmxfeedCfcSoapBindingStub(endPoint,
      new org.apache.axis.client.Service());
    }

  // Public method to call the web services method getContent()
  public Object[] getContent(String myArg) throws java.rmi.RemoteException {
    return soap.getContent(myArg);
  }
}
```

Creating a Flash MX Web Service Extension

Flash MX and the other MX programs allow you to install Flash panels that become part of the authoring environment. The Community MX and Amazon.com examples from this chapter can be placed in the *WindowSWF* folder in the multiuser *Configuration* folder of Flash MX, located in the following location in a typical Windows 2000 installation:

> *C:\Documents and Settings\username\Application Data\Macromedia\Flash MX\ Configuration\WindowSWF*

Note that the folder is a hidden folder by default in Windows. Hidden folders can be shown with Tools → Folder Options → View → Hidden files and folders → Show Hidden files and folders. For Macintosh OS X, the folder is located at:

> *Hard Drive/Users/Library/Application Support/Macromedia/FlashMX/ Configuration/WindowSWF*

If you have a single-user operating system, such as Windows 98 or Macintosh OS 9, the folder can be found in your main Flash MX installation folder.

Simply dropping a *.swf* file in this folder allows you to use the Flash interface as a dockable panel in Flash MX. You can easily add other types of panels that utilize other public web services or ones of your own design, and even package these as extensions for consumption by other users of Studio MX products. To package a Flash *.swf* file as an extension, you have to create an extension package. This is done by first creating a special XML file with a *.mxi* file extension.

 More information on the Macromedia Extension Installation file format (MXI) can be found at the Macromedia site at *http://download. macromedia.com/pub/exchange/mxi_file_format.pdf.*

The *.mxi* file for the Community MX Content extension might look like this:

```
<macromedia-extension
    name="Community MX Content"
    version="1.0.0"
    type="Flash Panel">

    <author name="Thomas Muck" />

    <products>
      <product name="Flash" version="6" primary="true" />
    </products>

    <description>
    <![CDATA[
    The Community MX Content panel shows the latest content from Community MX  ]]>
    </description>

    <ui-access>
    <![CDATA[
    After installing the extension, you can find the Community MX Content panel in
    the Window menu of Flash MX.
    ]]>
    </ui-access>

    <files>
      <file source="Community MX.swf" destination="$flash/WindowSWF" />
    </files>

</macromedia-extension>
```

Using the $flash variable in the *.mxi* file, you don't have to know the path to Flash on the user's machine; the Extension Manager takes care of the details of installing the panel to the user's *Flash\WindowSWF* folder.

If you place this *.mxi* file in the same folder as your *.swf* file and double-click it, the Macromedia Extension Manager launches in its packaging mode. It prompts you to create a new package and save it on your hard drive. The package is created with an *.mxp* file extension (the *.mxi* file is bundled inside). The Flash extension package (the *.mxp* file) can be installed by anyone with Flash MX or later. The Extension Manager is shown in Figure 10-4.

This technique for packaging extensions can be used with many types of Flash movies, allowing you to create your own interface elements of the Flash MX environment. The NetConnection debugger and the Service Panel are examples of Flash MX extensions built as *.swf* files in this way. The Community MX panel is shown in Figure 10-5.

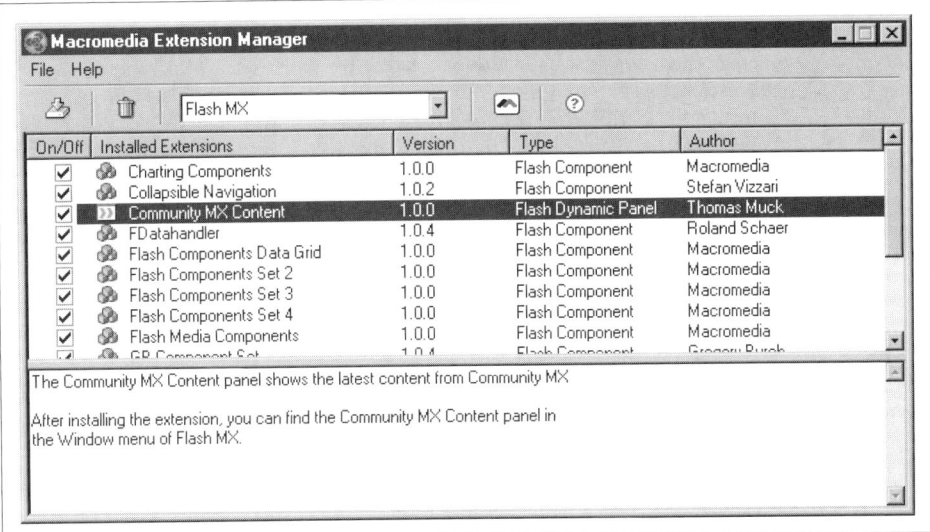

Figure 10-4. The Macromedia Extension Manager

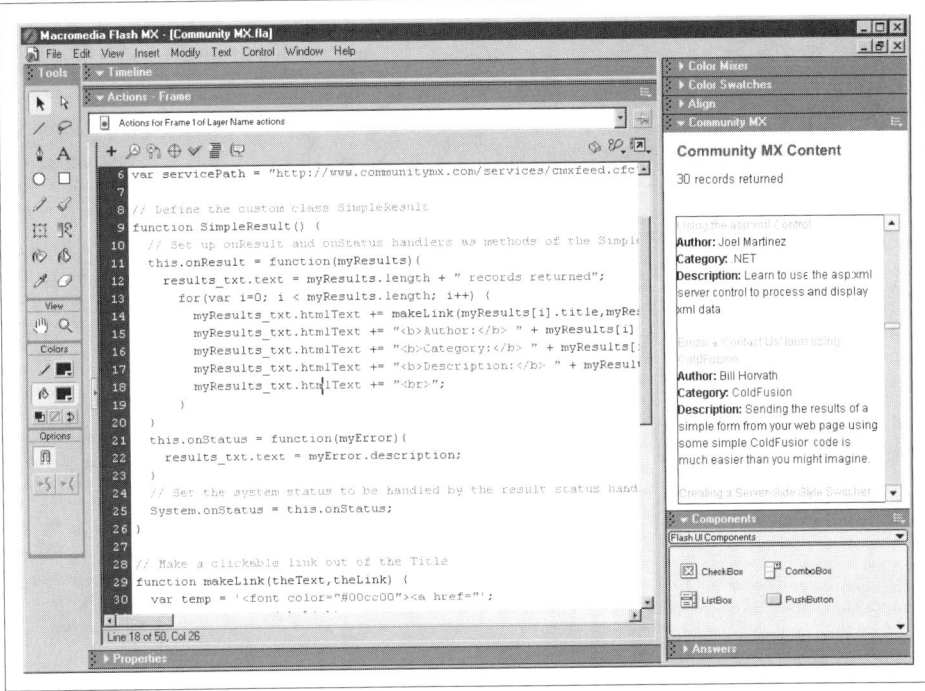

Figure 10-5. The Community MX web service example as a Flash panel

 MXI creator programs are available to help create MXI files for Macromedia extensions, such as one created by Muzak at *http://www. muzakdeezign.com/mxi_creator/about.asp*. Flash 2004 and Flash Pro feature a JavaScript extensibility layer, such as that available in Dreamweaver MX, so expect to see more Flash extensions in the future. Consult the resources cited in Appendix A.

Wrapping Up

In this chapter, we've looked at how you might use Flash Remoting to consume web services from service providers, rather than create your own remote services. You've seen examples that work in each implementation of Flash Remoting, and you've seen some limitations of dealing with web service datatypes that might prevent you from using a given server solution for a particular web service. You've also seen how a Flash Remoting example of a web service can be used inside of the Flash environment as a Flash panel.

At the time of this writing, support for SOAP-based web services in Flash MX Professional 2004 is still in flux. That said, the existing Flash Remoting feature set remains supported in Flash Player 7 and Flash MX 2004. Even if enhanced support for SOAP-based web services in Flash MX Professional 2004 obviates the need for Flash Remoting to be installed on the server, these examples should work in Flash Player 7. If necessary, see the online Code Depot for updated *.fla* files for Flash Player 7, which may differ slightly from the Flash 6 versions presented here if you're not using Flash Remoting on the server.

Chapter 11 delves into one of the coolest areas of Flash MX and ActionScript programming—building user interface components and enabling them to be data-driven by a remote service.

Extending Objects and UI Controls

ActionScript facilitates easy extension of objects. By extending an existing component or object, you are in effect extending the functionality of ActionScript and Flash. The Flash UI components and other custom objects are, in fact, merely custom ActionScript code. Components can be customized, copied, or linked together through ActionScript. In fact, Flash MX components are simply ActionScript objects and, as such, are flexible with regard to the properties, methods, and events that you can attach to them.

Principles Behind UI Components

UI components are essentially movie clips that have three added features:

- A Property inspector, in which you can set properties at authoring time.
- A live preview that shows a display of what the component might look like.
- The ability to be loaded in once, at the time the movie loads. If you have one instance of a component or a hundred instances, the overhead is the same.

A properly built component is created as a class, with all methods declared on the prototype. This insures that the component code exists in only one place—in the prototype—and not in each individual instance of a component. This is unlike Flash 5 SmartClips, in which each instance had its own copies of methods.

UI components also offer the ability to create rich interfaces and give Flash developers the ability to put together these interfaces with the same ease that Visual Basic (VB) developers can create interfaces.

 Flash Pro includes a new screens-based metaphor intended to appeal to VB developers, but here were cover using UI components with Flash's traditional timeline-based metaphor supported in Flash MX and Flash 2004.

UI components, however, are easily modified using simple ActionScript. The next section shows several enhancements you can make to components to make your Flash Remoting application development easier.

DataProviderClass and DataGlue

The *DataProviderClass* class binds data to a user interface control or other object. Flash Remoting would not be as easy to use if it were not for the hidden functionality of *DataProviderClass*.

 Jesse Warden has made documentation on *DataProviderClass* available in standard Flash MX Reference format at *http://www. jessewarden.com/downloads/DataProvider.mxp*.

DataProviderClass operates behind the scenes on the components listed in Table 11-1.

Table 11-1. UI components that use the DataProviderClass class

Component	Found here
FComboBox	Flash UI Components
FListBox	Flash UI Components
FTicker	Flash UI Components Set 2
FTree	Flash UI Components Set 2
FTreeNode	Flash UI Components Set 2
FAdvancedCalendar	Flash UI Components Set 4
FSimpleMenu	Flash UI Components Set 4
FSmartComboBox	Flash UI Components Set 4
FDataGrid	Flash UI DataGrid
FBarChart	Flash Charting Components
FLineChart	Flash Charting Components
FPieChart	Flash Charting Components
FAccordianPane	Flash UI Components Set 5
FTabView	Flash UI Components Set 5
FWeekView	Flash UI Components Set 5

The *RecordSet* class inherits from *RSDataProviderClass*, a class with the same methods as *DataProviderClass*. *RecordSet* objects use a format of rows and columns, as do many of the Flash UI components tied to *DataProviderClass*, so this parallel makes sense.

You can picture a data consumer (the element that consumes the data from the data provider) as shown in Figure 11-1.

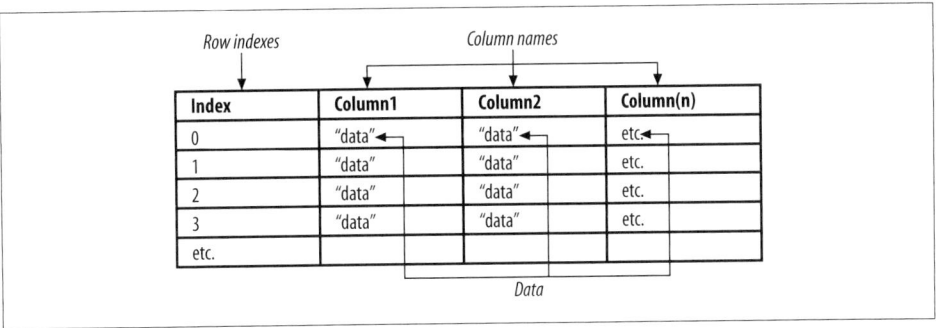

Figure 11-1. A conceptual view of the DataProvider class

Some components support data and label properties, such as the ComboBox and the ListBox. Typically, you store an ID number of some sort in the data property and store the textual representation of the data in the label property. This is roughly the equivalent of a <select> tag in HTML, where your option values are hidden and usually contain numbers. When using the *Northwind* database as a data provider, it is convenient to use the CategoryID column to populate the data properties and the CategoryDescription column to populate the label properties of the elements within a ListBox or ComboBox, as shown in Table 11-2.

Table 11-2. Categories table in Northwind, as it relates to a ComboBox or ListBox

CategoryID (data)	CategoryDescription (label)
1	"Beverages"
2	"Condiments"
3	"Confections"
4	"Dairy Products"
5	"Grains/Cereals"
6	"Meat/Poultry"
7	"Produce"
8	"Seafood"

Most components that use the *DataProviderClass* support these methods:

addItem( )
> Adds an item to the end of the data set

addItemAt( )
> Adds an item at the specified position in the data set

getLength( )
> Returns the length of the data (number of rows)

removeAll( )
> Removes all rows of data

replaceItemAt( )
> Replaces an item (row) in the data

removeItemAt( )
> Removes a specific item (row)

setDataProvider( )
> Sets the data provider for this data consumer

sortItemsBy( )
> Sorts the items by a specific column in the data

Using *setDataProvider( )* on a ComboBox or ListBox, however, displays the entire contents of a recordset row in each line of the ComboBox or ListBox. Therefore, use the *DataGlue.bindFormatStrings( )* method to bind a descriptive label and a data item to the rows of ComboBox and ListBox components:

```
DataGlue.bindFormatStrings(dataConsumer, dataProvider, label, data);
```

However, you can pass the *DataGlue.bindFormatFunction( )* method a custom function to handle the binding of the data. This allows you to load data that does not conform to the label/data structure into a ComboBox or ListBox component. You can create complex structures within the data property of the component rows. *DataGlue* passes each row of data in the recordset to your format function, which should return an object that looks like this:

```
{label:yourLabel, data:yourData}
```

DataGlue hides the details of the binding of the data to the component. Your format function should simply create an object with a label property and a data property. What you put into those properties is up to you.

For example, suppose you want to pass six fields to a Flash movie and display them within a ListBox. You could display one item in the label property and pass the other fields into the data property as an ActionScript object. Figure 11-2 shows the user interface for this demo, which simply displays all of the database fields in text fields as the row is selected in the ListBox.

The code is shown in Example 11-1.

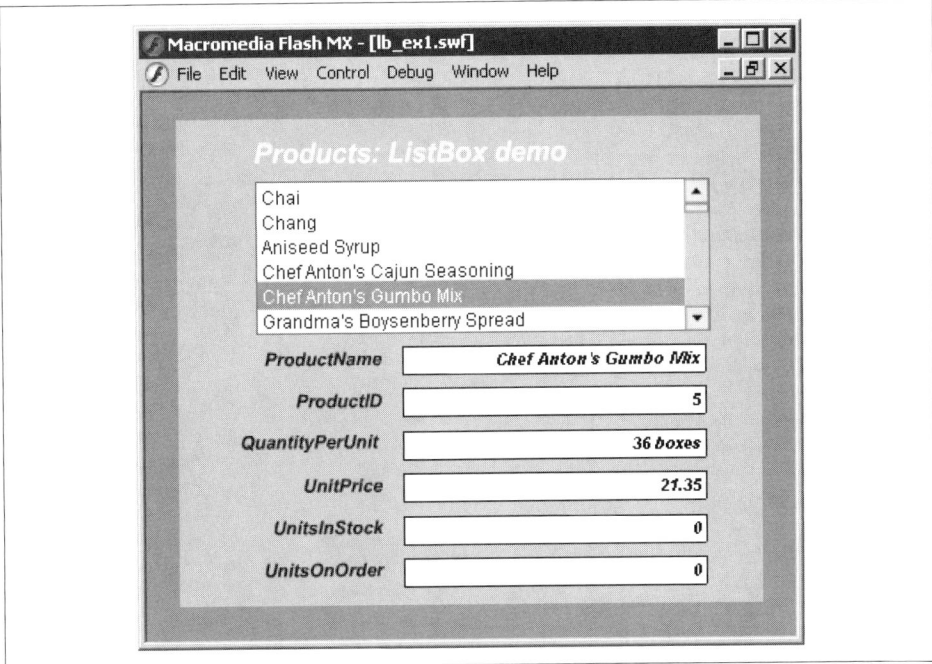

Figure 11-2. DataGlue can populate a ListBox or ComboBox with a complete record

Example 11-1. The ListBox demo

```
#include "NetServices.as"
#include "DataGlue.as"

// Set up a responder object to handle recordsets for ListBoxes
function ListBoxResponder (lbName) {
  this.lbName = lbName;
}
ListBoxResponder.prototype.onResult = function (result_rs) {
  // Use a format function to bind the data to the individual rows
  DataGlue.bindFormatFunction(this.lbName, result_rs, formatTheData);
};
ListBoxResponder.prototype.onStatus = function (error) {
  trace(error.description);
};

// Create an object to pass to the data property of the ListBox
function formatTheData (record) {
  label = record.ProductName;
  temp = {};
  temp.ProductID = record.ProductID;
  temp.ProductName = record.ProductName;
  temp.QuantityPerUnit = record.QuantityPerUnit;
  temp.UnitPrice = record.UnitPrice;
  temp.UnitsInStock = record.UnitsInStock;
```

Example 11-1. The ListBox demo (continued)

```
    temp.UnitsOnOrder = record.UnitsOnOrder;
    return {label:label, data:temp}
}

// Initialization code
if (connected == null) {
    connected = true;
    NetServices.setDefaultGatewayUrl("http://localhost/flashservices/gateway");
    var my_conn = NetServices.createGatewayConnection( );
    my_conn.onStatus = errorHandler;
    var myService = my_conn.getService("com.oreilly.frdg.SearchProducts");
    var Products_rs = null; // Main RecordSet object for product list
}

// Call the service and populate the ListBox
myService.getSearchResult(new ListBoxResponder(products_lb));

products_lb.setChangeHandler("updateDisplay");

// Display properties of object contained in data property of the ListBox
function updateDisplay (lb) {
    var record = lb.getSelectedItem( ).data;
    ProductID_txt.text = record.ProductID;
    ProductName_txt.text = record.ProductName;
    QuantityPerUnit_txt.text = record.QuantityPerUnit;
    UnitPrice_txt.text = record.UnitPrice;
    UnitsInStock_txt.text = record.UnitsInStock;
    UnitsOnOrder_txt.text = record.UnitsOnOrder;
}
```

The key to this functionality is the *formatTheData( )* function, in which an object named temp is created to hold the data from the record. As you recall, each record is passed to this function by *DataGlue*. The temp object is populated with data from each individual record of the recordset and packed into the data property of the return value:

```
    return {label:label, data:temp}
```

The label property simply contains a product name from the recordset.

Enhancing a Standard Control

In the formal, object-oriented sense of the word, to *extend* an object means create a subclass that adds to the features of a given superclass. Here we use to term interchangeably with the more informal word *enhance*, by which we mean customizing an object's feature set either by adding methods to an existing class or by modifying a class to create a new one with the desired features.

It is often handy to enhance existing components that may lack the basic features for interacting with remote services. You can simply add the functionality to the prototype of the component, or overwrite the existing functionality. The basic syntax is:

```
FComponentNameClass.prototype.myMethod = function (args) {
    // Method code goes here
};
```

The advantage of defining the method on the prototype is that it will be available for all instances of the component.

The class names of most components follow the convention of using a capital *F* (Flash), the component name, and then the word *Class*. If you are in doubt about the name of the component class, you can check the component definition in the Library. For example, a CheckBox class definition is named *FCheckBoxClass*. Other components have similar names, as shown in Table 11-3.

Table 11-3. The class names for common Flash UI components

Component	Class definition name	Linkage symbol name
CheckBox	FCheckBoxClass	FCheckBoxSymbol
ComboBox	FComboBoxClass	FComboBoxSymbol
ListBox	FListBoxClass	FListBoxSymbol
PushButton	FPushButtonClass	FPushButtonSymbol
RadioButton	FRadioButtonClass	FRadioButtonSymbol
ScrollBar	FScrollBarClass	FScrollBarSymbol
ScrollPane	FScrollPaneClass	FScrollPaneSymbol
Tree	FTreeClass	FTreeSymbol
Ticker	FTickerClass	FTickerSymbol

Most Flash MX UI components are subclassed from the *FUIComponentClass* class. The *FUIComponentClass* class contains most of the everyday functionality that a component needs, such as initialization, setting colors and styles, setting callback methods, and setting focus. For more information on *FUIComponentClass*, see the third-party extension by Jesse Warden at *http://www.jessewarden.com/downloads/FUIComponent.mxp*.

Subsequent sections show examples of extending basic components.

Creating a ListBox with a Data-Driven Icon

An ActionScript programmer can visually and functionally extend the Flash MX components. There are numerous examples on the Web that demonstrate this, but I will show a way to add a custom icon to a ListBox, based on data from a remote service call, and, in doing so, create an enhanced version of the ListBox component.

You'll need two icons—a blank checkbox and a filled checkbox—to simulate a checkbox component for the data display. The files used in the procedure, *blankbox.gif* and *check.gif*, are also available at the online Code Depot, as are the completed *.fla* files.

As an exercise, you might want to experiment by adding a true CheckBox component rather than an icon to the ListBox. The icon is used for performance reasons, since we are simply displaying data and no user interaction is needed.

 Flash 2004 and Flash Pro components are larger than their Flash MX predecessors. The updated component architecture uses a larger common base class to support accessibility, tabbing, and other popular features. The shared code affords some economies of scale in applications that use five or six components; however, using only one or two components in Flash 2004 and Flash Pro results in larger file sizes than might be justified. If using only one or two components, a custom component will likely be more efficient.

The ListBox, and other components like it, have three main parts: the data provider, the item (row), and the component itself. Components and their assets can be found in the Library after you drag an instance of the component from the Components panel to the Stage. The assets are organized in folders under the *Flash UI Components* folder in the Library, as shown in Figure 11-3.

We'll add a checkbox icon to the *FListBoxItem* to create a new element named *FListCheckItem*. Use the *.fla* created in Example 11-1 as a starting point. The final version is available as *FListCheckItem.fla* from the online Code Depot.

1. Drag an instance of the ListBox component from the Components panel to the Stage. It appears as *FListBoxItem* in the Library panel under Core Assets - Developer Only → FUIComponent Class Tree → FUIComponent SubClasses → FSelectableItem SubClasses, as shown in Figure 11-3.

2. In the Library, right-click (Ctrl-click on Macintosh) *FListBoxItem* and choose Duplicate from the pop-up menu. If you've successfully duplicated the Library symbol and not an instance of it on the Stage, the Duplicate Symbol dialog box appears.

3. In the Duplicate Symbol dialog box, name the new symbol *FListCheckItem*. Select the Export for ActionScript checkbox, and set the Linkage Identifier to *FListCheckItemSymbol* (click the Advanced button to expand the dialog box if you don't see the Linkage properties).

4. Next, import the *blankbox.gif* and *check.gif* files to the Library using File → Import to Library.

5. Create a new symbol in the Library, name it *Checkbox_icons*, and open it for editing.

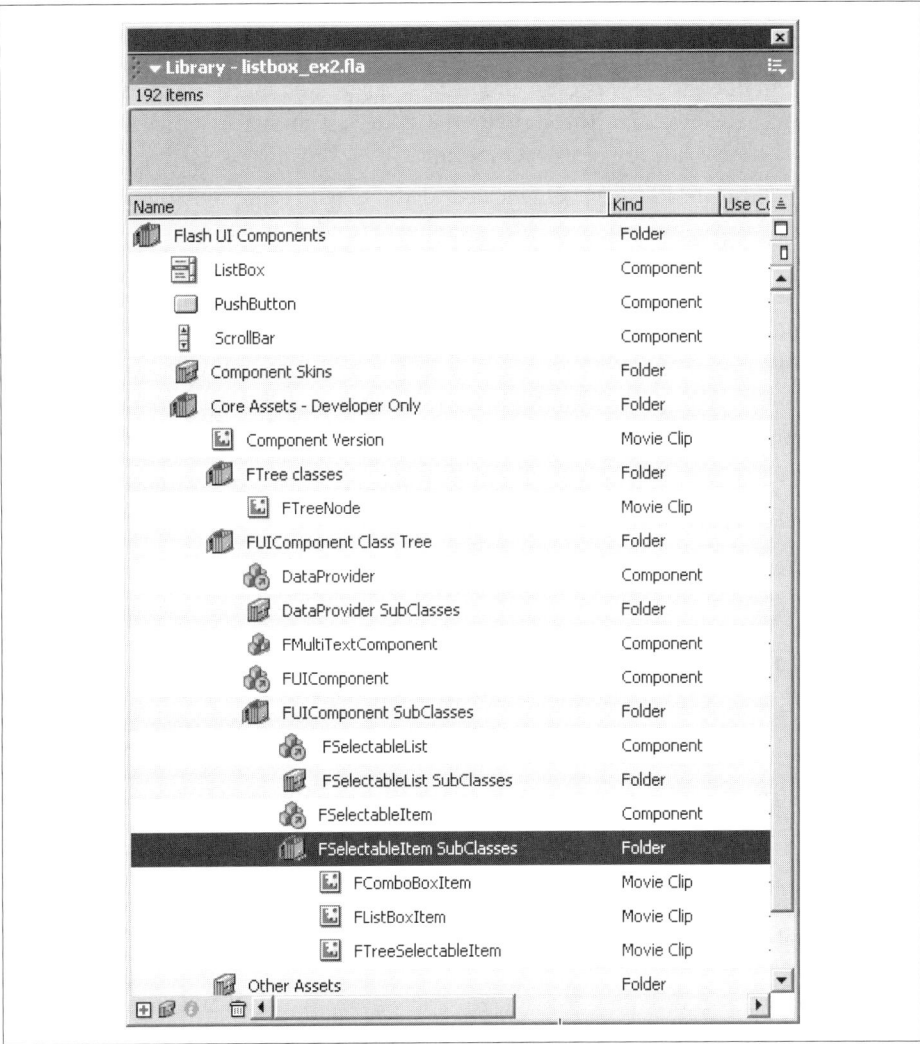

Figure 11-3. The hierarchy of components in the Library panel

6. Add *blankbox.gif* to the first frame of the *Checkbox_ icons* symbol, and add *check.gif* to a new second frame. You can position the images with their upper-left corners at the registration point of the movie clip.

7. Open the *FListCheckItem* symbol for editing, and add a new layer. On that layer, drag an instance of the *Checkbox_icons* symbol from the Library to the symbol's canvas, and give it the instance name check_mc in the Property inspector.

8. Next, select the first frame of the *Actions* layer of the *FListCheckItem* symbol, and open the Actions panel to show the existing code (which was duplicated

from the original *FListBoxItem* symbol). Modify the code, as shown in Example 11-2 (changes are shown in bold):

a. To define the *FListCheckItemClass* class, change `FListItemClass` to `FListCheckItemClass` throughout the code, as shown in bold. Also change `FListItemSymbol` to `FListCheckItemSymbol`.

b. Our custom *FListCheckItemClass* class extends the *FSelectableItemClass* class, but we must add the *layoutContent( )* and *displayContent( )* methods to handle the attaching of the icons. The *layoutContent( )* method overrides the *FSelectableItemClass* method of the same name. Copy the code for the *layoutContent( )* method from the first frame of the *Methods* layer of the *FSelectableItem* symbol in the Library, and make the changes shown in bold.

c. The *displayContent( )* method overrides the superclass method of the same name, which it calls via super. Again, enter the text shown in bold.

9. Finally, we'll add a few lines to the main *.fla*, as shown in Example 11-3, with the changes from Example 11-1 shown in bold.

Example 11-2. The FListCheckItem code

```
#initclip 3
/*
        FListCheckItemClass
        EXTENDS FSelectableItemClass
        This is mostly a code stub for extension purposes.
*/

function FListCheckItemClass()
{
  this.init();
}

FListCheckItemClass.prototype = new FSelectableItemClass();

// EXTEND this method to change the content of an item and its layout
FListCheckItemClass.prototype.layoutContent = function (width) {
  this.attachMovie("FLabelSymbol", "fLabel_mc", 2,
      {hostComponent:this.controller});
  this.fLabel_mc._x = 2;
  this.fLabel_mc._y = 0;
  this.icon_mc._x = width - this.icon_mc._width - 10;
  this.fLabel_mc.setSize(width - 10 - this.icon_mc._width);
  this.fLabel_mc.labelField.selectable = false;
};

FListCheckItemClass.prototype.displayContent = function(itmObj, selected) {
  // Execute the superclass method first
  super.displayContent(itmObj, selected);
  // Show an icon dependent on the data.checked property
  this.check_mc.gotoAndStop(itmObj.data.checked ? 1 : 2);
}
```

Example 11-2. The FListCheckItem code (continued)

```
Object.registerClass("FListCheckItemSymbol", FListCheckItemClass);

#endinitclip
```

Example 11-3. The main movie .fla code

```
#include "NetServices.as"
#include "DataGlue.as"

// Set up a responder object to handle recordsets for ListBoxes
function ListBoxResponder (lbName) {
  this.lbName = lbName;
}
ListBoxResponder.prototype.onResult = function (result_rs) {
  // Use a format function to bind the data to the individual rows
  DataGlue.bindFormatFunction(this.lbName, result_rs, formatTheData);
};
ListBoxResponder.prototype.onStatus = function (error) {
  trace(error.description);
};

// Create an object to pass to the data property of the ListBox
function formatTheData(record) {
  label = record.ProductName;
  temp = {};
  temp.ProductID = record.ProductID;
  temp.ProductName = record.ProductName;
  temp.QuantityPerUnit = record.QuantityPerUnit;
  temp.UnitPrice = record.UnitPrice;
  temp.UnitsInStock = record.UnitsInStock;
  temp.UnitsOnOrder = record.UnitsOnOrder;
  temp.checked = record.Discontinued;
  return {label:label, data:temp}
}

// Initialization code
if (connected == null) {
  connected = true;
  NetServices.setDefaultGatewayUrl("http://localhost/flashservices/gateway");
  var my_conn = NetServices.createGatewayConnection();
  my_conn.onStatus = errorHandler;
  var myService = my_conn.getService("com.oreilly.frdg.SearchProducts");
  var Products_rs = null; // Main RecordSet object for product list
}

// Set up the FListCheckItemSymbol to be the item for the ListBox
products_lb.setItemSymbol("FListCheckItemSymbol");

// Call the service and populate the ListBox
myService.getSearchResult(new ListBoxResponder(products_lb));

products_lb.setChangeHandler("updateDisplay");
```

Example 11-3. The main movie .fla code (continued)

```
// Display properties of object contained in data property of the ListBox
function updateDisplay (lb) {
  var record = lb.getSelectedItem( ).data;
  ProductID_txt.text = record.ProductID;
  ProductName_txt.text = record.ProductName;
  QuantityPerUnit_txt.text = record.QuantityPerUnit;
  UnitPrice_txt.text = record.UnitPrice;
  UnitsInStock_txt.text = record.UnitsInStock;
  UnitsOnOrder_txt.text = record.UnitsOnOrder;
}
```

Save and test the movie. It should show the checkbox icons in our custom ListBox, depending on the `Discontinued` field in the `Products` table. (The `Products` table does not have a `Discontinued` field by default, but you can add it to your test database easily, as we did in Chapter 5.)

The following line sets up *FListCheckItemSymbol* as the list item for the ListBox instance on the Stage:

```
    products_lb.setItemSymbol("FListCheckItemSymbol");
```

That's all there is to it. In this case, the original ListBox component was not touched, but a copy of it was enhanced to include an icon. That is, our custom *FListCheck-ItemClass* class extends the *FSelectableItemClass* class directly instead of extending *FListItemClass*, as could have been done. Regardless, a component like this can also be packaged and installed into the Components panel with very little effort.

Enhancing a ComboBox with Methods

In Chapter 4, we enhanced the ComboBox component to include a *pickValue( )* method. This method allows you to pass a result from a Flash Remoting call to the ComboBox and choose that value in the UI. I'll take that a step further now by adding *pickLabel( )*, *setDefault( )*, and *setDescriptor( )* methods. These new methods, and others like it, can make working with the ComboBox much easier, especially when working with Flash Remoting.

 The following examples add methods to the prototype of the ComboBox component. This adds functionality to an existing component without creating a new one. You could instead create a new component that inherits from (i.e., subclasses or extends) the ComboBox, and add your new methods to the custom component. Full details on the intricacies of component building are beyond the scope of the book.

When enhancing ActionScript objects in this way, make sure that your method names do not conflict with method names from other programmers. For example, if another programmer on your team creates a *pickValue( )* method for a ComboBox, the two namespaces will collide.

Using pickValue( ) and pickLabel( )

The custom *pickValue( )* and *pickLabel( )* methods can be used to set a value in a ComboBox. The methods are shown in Example 11-4.

Example 11-4. The pickValue() and pickLabel() methods for the ComboBox

```
// Set up the combo boxes to be able to pick a value
FComboBoxClass.prototype.pickValue = function (value) {
  var tempLength = this.getLength();
  for (var i=0; i < tempLength; i++) {
    if (this.getItemAt(i).data == value) {
      this.setSelectedIndex(i);
      break;
    }
  }
};

// Set up the combo boxes to be able to pick a label
FComboBoxClass.prototype.pickLabel = function (text) {
  var tempLength = this.getLength();
  for (var i=0; i < tempLength; i++) {
    if (this.getItemAt(i).label == value) {
      this.setSelectedIndex(i);
      break;
    }
  }
};
```

Typically, a ComboBox is populated from a remote database containing labels and values of a Categories table or some other related table. In a typical update of a database, you populate the user interface with a record from the database. In this situation, *pickValue( )* or *pickLabel( )* can be used to choose the correct value for the current record. You might use it like this, with a *RecordSet* object named myResults_rs:

```
myCombobox.pickValue(myResults_rs.getItemAt(0)["categoryid"]);
```

Using setDefault( )

Frequently, you may need to set a default value for a ComboBox or other UI component. The *setDefault( )* method, shown in Example 11-5, handles these situations.

Example 11-5. Default value functionality for the ComboBox

```
// Set up a "default" property, which will be the value picked if
// the setDefault() method is called.
FComboBoxClass.prototype._default = null;
```

Example 11-5. Default value functionality for the ComboBox (continued)

```
// setDefaultValue() sets up the default value when setDefault() is called
FComboBoxClass.prototype.setDefaultValue = function (value) {
  this._default = value;
};

// Getter method for the default value
FComboBoxClass.prototype.getDefaultValue = function () {
  return this._default;
};

// Set up the combo boxes to keep a default value
FComboBoxClass.prototype.setDefault = function () {
  this.pickValue(this.getDefaultValue());
};
```

The *setDefault( )* method comes in handy for situations where you are inserting data into a database. The ComboBox can display the default item. If the user doesn't pick an item for the ComboBox, the default value to enter in the database can be pulled from the ComboBox. For example, when requesting the user's shipping address, you might specify an appropriate default country and shipping method, like this:

```
myCombobox.setDefaultValue(1);    // Initialize the default value
```

Now, whenever you want to display the default item in the ComboBox, simply call:

```
myCombobox.setDefault();          // Displays the default item in the ComboBox
```

This technique is more flexible than simply choosing the value when you need to, because you can set the default value in one place in your movie and have the ability to set the ComboBox back to the default item at any time. If the default value changes at some point, your ComboBox code throughout your movie will still work. For example, if the user specifies his country as the United States, you might set the default shipping method to "UPS Ground." For other countries, you could set it to "Federal Express International".

Using setDescriptor( )

The last custom method in this section is *setDescriptor( )*. ComboBoxes frequently have a default label that states "—All options—" or "—Choose Shipping Method—". These types of items can be added easily to all of your ComboBoxes using the *setDescriptor( )* method, shown in Example 11-6.

Example 11-6. Adding the setDescriptor() method to the ComboBox

```
// Add a descriptive row to the ComboBox
FComboBoxClass.prototype.setDescriptor = function (text, value) {
  // Create a blank record
  var temp = {};
  // Get the RecordSet object
  var rs = this.dataProvider.dataProvider;
```

Example 11-6. Adding the setDescriptor() method to the ComboBox (continued)

```
  // Create a blank record
  rs.addItemAt(0, temp);
  // Get the recordset's field names in mTitles, and set the text and value
  rs.setField(0, rs.mTitles[1], text);
  rs.setField(0, rs.mTitles[0], value);
  this.pickValue(0);
};
```

The *setDescriptor( )* method works with ComboBoxes that have been set up with *DataGlue*. In those cases, if you try to set the label directly, you'll find that it can't be done easily. You can create a new record in the data provider, however, which will propagate down to the ComboBox:

```
    shipping_cb.setDescriptor("--Choose Shipping method-- ", 0);
    country_cb.setDescriptor("--Country--", 0)
```

The ComboBox enhancements can be saved to the *Flash MX\Configuration\Include\ com\oreilly\frdg* folder as *DataFriendlyCombo.as*. If you want to include the functionality in your Flash Remoting application, add the following #include directive to your code in the first frame:

```
    #include "com/oreilly/frdg/DataFriendlyCombo.as"
```

Enhancing the RecordSet Class for Interactivity

Chapter 3 showed an enhancement to the *RecordSet* class that facilitated a user interface showing only one record at a time—a common way of displaying resultset data to the end user. The enhancement added the concept of a current record and provided methods to move to specific records (first, previous, next, last, and record number). To augment this functionality, let's implement a feature to associate a field in a recordset with user interface controls and other elements (*DataGlue* style).

The Current Record Functionality

The current record functionality was described in Chapter 3, but we'll add a few new methods to implement the gluing of components to individual *RecordSet* fields. The basic functionality that we will begin with is shown in Example 11-7.

Example 11-7. Adding current record functionality to a RecordSet

```
// Initialize the current record number
RecordSet.prototype.currentRecord = 0;

// Return the current record
RecordSet.prototype.getCurrentRecord = function () {
```

Example 11-7. Adding current record functionality to a RecordSet (continued)

```
    return this.getItemAt(this.currentRecord-1);
};

// Return the current record number
RecordSet.prototype.getCurrentRecordNum = function () {
  return this.currentRecord
};

RecordSet.prototype.move = function (direction) {
  switch (direction.toLowerCase()) {
    case "first":
      this.currentRecord = 1;
      break;
    case "previous":
      if (--this.currentRecord < 1) this.currentRecord = 1;
      break;
    case "next":
      if (++this.currentRecord > this.getLength())
        this.currentRecord = this.getLength();
      break;
    case "last":
      this.currentRecord = this.getLength();
      break;
    default:
      // Not a direction: must be a number
      this.currentRecord = direction;
  }
  this.recordChanged();
};
```

The code is identical to what was shown in Chapter 3 under "Flash Remoting Using a RecordSet," with one exception: we added a call to *this.recordChanged( )* in the *move( )* method. The *recordChanged( )* method will be described in the next few sections.

Remember, the currentRecord property contains numbers from 1 to the length of the recordset. However, recordsets use a zero-relative index, so we'll add or replace records based on the currentRecord - 1.

Adding the glue( ) and recordChanged( ) Functionality

DataGlue effectively binds a *RecordSet* object to a ComboBox or a ListBox. In those cases, you are populating the component with the entire recordset (or specific fields of a recordset). This is possible because ComboBoxes and ListBoxes display items in rows. But what about components or objects that don't support multiple individual items, such as a CheckBox or a text field? These types of objects come in handy when you're displaying only one record from a resultset. The *recordChanged( )* method that we will create will change the components that are bound to the

RecordSet object, but first we have to bind the fields. We'll add another custom method to the *RecordSet* class, called *glue( )*. This is the method that effectively binds a recordset field to a component or text field. The *glue( )* method is shown in Example 11-8, along with the uiFields property that holds the fields to be glued from the *RecordSet*.

Example 11-8. The glue( ) method binds the component to the field

```
// Set up an array of UI components to bind to fields
RecordSet.prototype.uiFields = new Array( );

// The glue( ) method binds a control of controlType to a field
// controlTypes supported:
  //   "text"
  //   "combobox"
  //   "checkbox"
  //   "radiobutton"

RecordSet.prototype.glue = function (control, field, controlType) {
  // Create the uiField member as an object
  var controlObj = {};
  controlObj.control = control;
  controlObj.field = field;
  controlObj.controlType = controlType;
  // Replace the field if it is already defined.
  for (var i=0; i<this.uiFields.length; i++) {
    if (this.uiFields[i].control == controlObj.control) {
      uiFields[i] = controlObj;
      return;
    }
  }
  // If the field is not bound yet, add it to the array
  this.uiFields.push(controlObj);
};
```

You call the *glue( )* method like this, passing the component (or text field), the name of the database field you want to glue to the component, and the component type ("text", "combobox", or "checkbox"):

```
RecordSetname.glue(component, databaseField, componentType);
```

Typical calls to *glue( )* look like this:

```
// Glue the CategoryID field to the categories_cb ComboBox.
Products_rs.glue(categories_cb, "CategoryID", "combobox");
// Glue the ProductName field to the ProductName_txt TextField.
Products_rs.glue(ProductName_txt, "ProductName", "text");
```

The *glue( )* method is one piece of the puzzle. After the field is glued to the component, you have to be able to update the component in the UI. This is handled by a *recordChanged( )* method, shown in Example 11-9.

Example 11-9. The recordChanged( ) method

```
RecordSet.prototype.recordChanged = function ( ) {
  // Define variables to hold current field, component, and type of component
  var theField, theControl, theControlType;
  // The current record to be changed
  var record = this.getCurrentRecord( );
  // The uiFields property is an array of controlObj objects set up in glue( )
  var tempLength = this.uiFields.length;
  for (var i=0;i < tempLength; i++) {
    theField = this.uiFields[i].field;
    theControl = this.uiFields[i].control;
    theControlType = this.uiFields[i].controlType;
    switch (theControlType) {     // What kind of control is it?
      case "text":                // Text fields have the text property set
        theControl.text = record[theField];
        break;
      case "combobox":            // ComboBoxes use the custom pickValue( ) method
        theControl.pickValue(record[theField]);
        break;
      case "checkbox":            // CheckBoxes have the value set true or false
        theControl.setValue(record[theField]);
        break;
      default:                    // Other components not supported at this time
        trace(theControlType + " not supported")
    }
  }
};
```

The *recordChanged( )* method cycles through the `uiFields` array, updating each UI component to display the data that is in the glued field of the current record. The methods have been implemented for TextFields, ComboBoxes, and CheckBoxes, but you can add functionality for any type of UI component.

Now, components and text fields can be glued to a field in a recordset, and the field will change when the current record changes. Next, the *setCurrentRecord( )* method will update the current record in the recordset, based on what is in the fields that are glued to it.

The setCurrentRecord( ) Method

The UI is now capable of being updated as the user pages through the recordset. But TextFields, ComboBoxes, and other UI components might be changed by the user as well. We need a method to update the current displayed record directly from the fields that are glued in the recordset. The *setCurrentRecord( )* method, shown in Example 11-10, accomplishes this.

Example 11-10. The setCurrentRecord( ) method updates the recordset

```
// Update the current record based on values in the glued components
RecordSet.prototype.setCurrentRecord = function () {
  // Define variables to hold the current field, component, and type of component
  var theField, theControl, theControlType;
  // The current record to be changed
  var record = this.getCurrentRecord();
  // The uiFields property is an array of controlObj objects set up in glue()
  var tempLength = this.uiFields.length;
  for (var i=0;i < tempLength; i++) {
    theField = this.uiFields[i].field;
    theControl = this.uiFields[i].control;
    theControlType = this.uiFields[i].controlType;
    switch (theControlType) { // What kind of control is it?
      case "text":            // The TextField uses the text property
        record[theField] = theControl.text;
        break;
      case "combobox": /      // ComboBoxes use the data value of the selected item
        record[theField] = theControl.getSelectedItem().data;
        break;
      case "checkbox":        // CheckBoxes use the value true or false
        record[theField] = theControl.getValue();
        break;
      default:                // Other components not supported at this time
        trace(theControlType + " not supported")
    }
  }
};
```

The *setCurrentRecord( )* method operates in place on each component or TextField that is glued to the recordset. Whatever is currently displayed in the UI is written to the client-side recordset that the UI component or text field is glued to.

Putting It Together

With the *glue( )* functionality in place, you can now simplify the process of building a rich interface. The *ProductsAdmin.fla* code from Example 5-14 can be simplified, including using a checkbox to display the Discontinued status of the product. The interface fields that are glued include TextFields, ComboBoxes, and a CheckBox.

The administrative interface that is bound to a recordset is shown in Figure 11-4.

The code is shown in Example 11-11. The completed *.fla* file showing the interface can be downloaded from the online Code Depot.

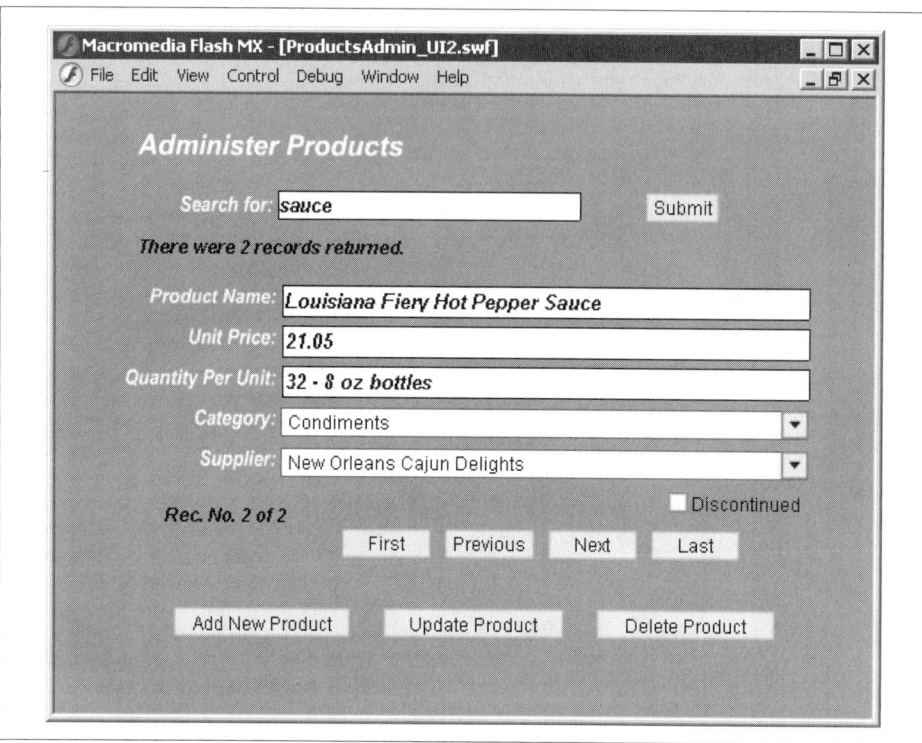

Figure 11-4. The administrative interface for the Products table of Northwind

Example 11-11. Using the glue( ) functionality simplifies the ActionScript code

```
#include "NetServices.as"
#include "DataGlue.as"
#include "NetDebug.as"
#include "com/oreilly/frdg/DataFriendlyCombo.as"
#include "com/oreilly/frdg/RecordSetPlus.as"

// General error handler for authoring environment
function errorHandler(error) {
  trace(error.description);
}

// Responder objects

// SearchResult( ) takes one optional argument: recNum
// When inserting or updating a record, the recNum can be specified
// to move the user interface to that record; otherwise, use "first"
function SearchResult(recNum) {
  if (recNum) {
    this.recNum = recNum;
  } else {
    this.recNum = "first";
```

Example 11-11. Using the glue( ) functionality simplifies the ActionScript code (continued)

```
  }
}

// The SearchResult responder object handles the gluing of the UI
SearchResult.prototype.onResult = function (result_rs) {
  Products_rs = result_rs;
  // Use the glue( ) method to bind the UI to the recordset
  Products_rs.glue(ProductName_txt, "ProductName", "text");
  Products_rs.glue(categories_cb, "CategoryID", "combobox");
  Products_rs.glue(UnitPrice_txt, "UnitPrice", "text");
  Products_rs.glue(QuantityPerUnit_txt, "QuantityPerUnit", "text");
  Products_rs.glue(suppliers_cb, "SupplierID", "combobox");
  Products_rs.glue(test_ch, "Discontinued", "checkbox");

  results_txt.text = "There were " + Products_rs.getLength( )+ " records returned.";
  Products_rs.move(this.recNum);
};

SearchResult.prototype.onStatus = errorHandler;

// Set up a responder object to handle recordsets for ComboBoxes
// This responder assumes that data is coming in with
// ID column in [0] position and description column
// in the [1] position
function ComboBoxResponder (cbName) {
  this.onResult = function (result_rs) {
    var fields = result_rs.getColumnNames( );
    var idField = '#' + fields[0] + '#';
    var descField = '#' + fields[1] + '#';
    DataGlue.bindFormatStrings(cbName, result_rs, descField,idField);
    cbName.setDescriptor("--Choose One--", 0);
    cbName.setDefaultValue(0);
  };
  this.onStatus = errorHandler;
}

// Main responder for the Update, Insert, and Delete functions
// Display is to the Output window only
function MainServiceResponder( ) {}
MainServiceResponder.prototype.onResult = function (result) {
  trace(result);
};
MainServiceResponder.prototype.onStatus = errorHandler;

// Initialization code
if (connected == null) {
  connected = true;
  NetServices.setDefaultGatewayUrl("http://localhost/flashservices/gateway");
  var my_conn = NetServices.createGatewayConnection( );
  my_conn.onStatus = errorHandler;
  var myService = my_conn.getService("com.oreilly.frdg.admin.ProductsAdmin");
```

Example 11-11. Using the glue( ) functionality simplifies the ActionScript code (continued)

```
  var Products_rs = null;      // Main RecordSet object for product list
  // Set up the two ComboBoxes
  myService.getCategories(new ComboBoxResponder(categories_cb));
  myService.getSuppliers(new ComboBoxResponder(suppliers_cb));
}

// Set up event handlers for buttons
submit_pb.setClickHandler("searchProducts");

// Move buttons
moveFirst.setClickHandler("moveTo");
movePrevious.setClickHandler("moveTo");
moveNext.setClickHandler("moveTo");
moveLast.setClickHandler("moveTo");

// Insert, Update, and Delete buttons
insert_pb.setClickHandler("insertRecord");
update_pb.setClickHandler("updateRecord");
delete_pb.setClickHandler("deleteRecord");

// Event handlers for buttons

// submit_pb click handler
function searchProducts ( ) {
  getRecordset( );
}

// moveFirst( ), movePrevious( ), moveNext( ), and moveLast( ) click handler
function moveTo (button) {
  // The label of the button indicates the direction to move the recordset:
  // "first", "previous", "next", "last"
  Products_rs.move(button.label);
  navStatus_txt.text =
      "Rec. No. " + (Products_rs.getCurrentRecordNum( )) + " of " +
      Products_rs.getLength( );
}

// update_pb click handler
function updateRecord ( ) {
  myService.updateProduct(new MainServiceResponder( ), getUpdatedRecord( ));
  var tempRec = Products_rs.getCurrentRecordNum( );
  getRecordset(tempRec);
}

// insert_pb click handler
function insertRecord ( ) {
  if (insert_pb.getLabel( ) == "Add New Product") {
    Products_rs.addItem(getNewRecord( ));
  Products_rs.move("last");
    insert_pb.setLabel("Insert To Database");
    insert_txt.text = "Click again to insert to database";
```

Example 11-11. Using the glue( ) functionality simplifies the ActionScript code (continued)

```
  } else {
    insert_pb.setLabel("Add New Product");
    myService.addProduct(new MainServiceResponder( ), getUpdatedRecord( ));
    getRecordset("last");
    insert_txt.text = "";
  }
}

// delete_pb click handler
function deleteRecord ( ) {
  var productID = Products_rs.getCurrentRecord( ).ProductID;
  myService.deleteProducts(new MainServiceResponder( ), ProductID);
  getRecordset( );
}

// Utility functions
function getRecordset (recNum) {
  // Call the remote method using a responder object with optional record number
  //   to move the recordset to
  myService.getSearchResult(new SearchResult(recNum), search);
}

// Pack the updated record from the display into the RecordSet object
// and return the record to the caller
function getUpdatedRecord ( ) {
  Products_rs.setCurrentRecord( );
  return Products_rs.getCurrentRecord( );
}

// Get a blank record
function getNewRecord ( ) {
  var theRecord = { ProductName:''
                  ,UnitPrice:''
                  ,QuantityPerUnit:''
                  ,CategoryID:0
                  ,SupplierID:0
                  ,ProductID:''
                  };
  return theRecord;
}
```

In Example 11-11, the *onResult( )* method updates the UI as the record changes and updates the client-side recordset if the user changes the UI:

```
// Use the glue( ) method to bind the UI to the recordset
Products_rs.glue(ProductName_txt, "ProductName", "text");
Products_rs.glue(categories_cb, "CategoryID", "combobox");
Products_rs.glue(UnitPrice_txt, "UnitPrice", "text");
Products_rs.glue(QuantityPerUnit_txt, "QuantityPerUnit", "text");
Products_rs.glue(suppliers_cb, "SupplierID", "combobox");
Products_rs.glue(test_ch, "Discontinued", "checkbox");
```

Adding Validation to a TextField

Text fields are used often in Flash Remoting applications, because you frequently need to accept user input for your remote calls. Any time a user can interact with an application, the possibility exists for major problems. One way to minimize the types of problems you might encounter is to validate the user-input data before it is sent to the remote server.

 Client-side validation is important for a smooth user experience, but you should also validate user-input data on the server, to avoid malicious attacks on your server-side services. Remember, when you set up a remote service, it is open to the world, whether a user uses your Flash interface or not.

The next example shows how you might implement a validation routine directly on the *TextField* class. (The TextField component on the DRK 3 CD-ROM also features validation functionality.) Simply calling *TextField.validate( )* causes all text fields that have a defined validator to be validated. The method returns an error message if there is a problem, or nothing if everything validates properly. First, enhance the *TextField* class to keep track of the validators for each *TextField* instance. The validators are stored in an array:

```
TextField.validators = new Array( );
```

Next, insert a routine to allow the programmer to set a specific validator type on a given text field:

```
TextField.prototype.setValidationType = function (theType, errMsg) {
  var validator = new Object( );
  validator.textfield = this;
  validator.theType = theType;
  validator.errMsg = errMsg;
  // If validator needs more arguments, set them up here
  if (arguments.length > 2) {
    for (var i=2; i< arguments.length; i++) {
      validator[i] = arguments[i];
    }
  }

  TextField.validators.push(validator);
};
```

The *setValidationType( )* method allows two or more arguments. The first argument, theType, specifies the type of validation. The errMsg argument allows you to set the error message. If you supply more than two arguments, the remaining arguments will be passed to the *validate( )* method for use by the given validation routine.

Finally, create the validation routines in the *validate( )* method. Because this is a simple example, I've implemented only a required field, an email field, a password field

---

between *n* and *n2* characters (arguments 3 and 4 are passed to the *setValidation-Type()* method), and a password confirmation validator (using argument 3 passed to *setValidationType()*). More *case* statements could be added for more validation types:

```
TextField.validate = function () {
  var errMsg = "";
  var temp;
  for (var i=0; i < this.validators.length; i++) {
    temp = this.validators[i];
    switch(temp.theType) {
      case 0:
        break;
      case 1:        // required field
        if (temp.textfield.text == "")
          errMsg += temp.errMsg + "\n";
        break;
      case 2:        // email address
        if (!isValidEmail(temp.textfield.text))
          errMsg += temp.errMsg + "\n";
        break;
      case 3:        // password between n and n2 characters
        if (temp.textfield.text.length < temp["2"] ||
            temp.textfield.text.length > temp["3"])
          errMsg += temp.errMsg + "\n";
        break;
      case 4:        // password must equal confirm fields
        if (temp.textfield.text != temp["2"].text)
          errMsg += temp.errMsg + "\n";
        break;
    }
  }
  function isValidEmail (theString) {
    var isValid = (
    (theString.lastIndexOf('.') < theString.length - 2) && // must have dot
    (theString.indexOf('@') != -1) &&                      // must have one @
    (theString.indexOf('@') == theString.lastIndexOf('@')) // must not have two @@
    )
    return isValid;
  }
  return errMsg;
};
```

To demonstrate the new method of the *TextField* class, set up a new movie with four input text fields named name_txt, email_txt, password_txt, and confirm_txt, along with a Submit button and a MessageBox component named validation_mb (from UI Components Set 2). Here is the code to set up the validators on the boxes:

```
name_txt.setValidationType(1, "Name must not be blank");
email_txt.setValidationType(2, "Email must be valid");
password_txt.setValidationType(3, "Password must be between 8 and 12 characters",
                        8, 12);
password_txt.setValidationType(4, "Passwords don't match", confirm_txt);
```

Each *TextField* that is to be validated is initialized with the *setValidationType( )* method, with two arguments. Simply pass the number of the validation type (1: required field; 2: email validation; 3: password of a given length, 4: password match). The password_txt field actually has two validations on it: a length validation and a confirmation validation. The code to submit the form and check the validity of the data is shown here:

```
submit_pb.setClickHandler("submitForm");
submitForm = function () {
  // Validate all TextFields
  var errorMessage = TextField.validate();
  // If there is an error message, there was a problem
  if (errorMessage != "") {
    validation_mb._visible = true;
    validation_mb.setMessage("Error in the data you provided\n" + errorMessage)
  } else { // No problem, pass the form to the remote method, when implemented
    trace("valid data!!!")
  }
};
```

There are other ways to perform validations, but this technique shows how you might implement a validator that performs all required validations at one time, by simply enhancing the *TextField* class.

Wrapping Up

In this chapter you saw how UI components and other ActionScript objects, such as the *RecordSets* class, can be enhanced to allow for better interaction with Flash Remoting. ActionScript is a flexible language that allows for extensibility of custom components or even its core objects.

CHAPTER 12

Flash Remoting Best Practices

The issue of *best practices* is a subjective topic. One person's idea of a best practice may be someone else's idea of a worst nightmare. As in all forms of programming, there is no single *right* way to perform a given task. For that reason, this chapter presents some of the common tactics employed by Flash Remoting developers. It is up to the developer to measure the options carefully and decide on the best course of action for a particular application.

We've touched on numerous best practices throughout the earlier chapters (see "best practices" in the index). Here we look at the big picture and cover additional best practices you should seriously consider. Refer also to the Macromedia white papers and articles on best practices cited in Appendix B.

Separation of Tasks

A Flash Remoting application can be constructed by one person or a team of designers and programmers. If working in a team environment, Flash Remoting utilizes several different technologies that can be easily broken down into tasks for different types of developers. In your team, individuals might wear different hats at different times, so there will be some overlap, but the division of tasks is fairly clear.

Designer

The designer concentrates on the visual and audio design of the application and deals with the look and feel of the application. He creates all the interfaces; he chooses the fonts, colors, graphics, and other elements of the application. He may know ActionScript and be able to program some functionality, or he may not. He should be able to create an application interface from specifications and be flexible enough to change visual elements easily.

Client-Side ActionScript Programmer

The client-side ActionScript programmer is responsible for all of the interaction in the application, and she works with the designer to implement this functionality. She might create the code that calls the various interface elements to display in the movie, and she would also create any code that is related to user input. The Action-Script programmer should know the Flash programming environment inside and out and be able to bring the project specifications to life.

If the designer has not completed a particular section, the interface should work as it stands, using dummy methods where user interactions or remote service calls might be (for example, if a user clicks "Login," an alert message might say "User logging in").

Flash Remoting ActionScript Programmer

The Flash Remoting programmer is also an ActionScript programmer, but he is responsible for connecting to the remote services and providing hooks for the client-side ActionScript programmer in the form of an API. He should work closely with the server-side developers to build the client-side code that calls remote services accurately. He should be able to test his service calls at all points, using dummy methods on the server that the server-side programmer has set up.

Database Programmer

The database programmer is responsible for setting up the database, including table definitions, relationships, and all stored procedure code necessary. She should also work closely with the server-side programmer. Typically, in an application that uses a database, the database needs to be in place before the server-side services are developed. The database is frequently the first part of the application to be built. All parts of the application revolve around the database.

The database programmer is also responsible for exposing items to the server-side programmer. From an ActionScript perspective, this is the equivalent of exposing methods or functions to the team. The database programmer exposes views, stored procedures, and possibly tables (in a MySQL environment) to the server-side programmer.

Server-Side Programmer

The server-side programmer might be versed in CFML, SSAS, Java, C#, VB.NET, or PHP. He should be able to create the remote services that can be accessed from the Flash movie. He should also be able to create HTML interfaces (test harnesses) for testing the remote services so that the server-side services can be completed before bringing Flash into the equation.

The server-side programmer exposes methods for the Flash Remoting ActionScript programmer to utilize.

HTML Developers

The HTML developer ties the whole application together on the HTML page and provides necessary code for alternate pages (if needed) and Flash detection. She also must create the HTML pages in such a way that they blend seamlessly with the Flash application. The HTML developer should work closely with the designer.

Separation of Functionality

A Flash Remoting application is a client/server application. You should have a clean separation of client and server duties, however. The server-side services should be operable in any situation, whether being accessed by a Flash interface, HTML interface, desktop application, or other web service. For that reason, it is not advisable to use the Flash object on the server. In Example 2-5, you saw the *HelloUser* service written using C# in an ASP.NET environment:

```
<%@ Page Language="C#"%>
<%@ Register TagPrefix="MyTag" Namespace="FlashGateway" Assembly="flashgateway" %>
<MyTag:Flash ID="Flash" Runat="Server" />
<%
  if (Flash.Params.Count > 0) {
  String username = Flash.Params[0].ToString( );
  String currentTime = DateTime.Now.ToLongTimeString( );
  Flash.Result = "Hello " + username + ". It is " + currentTime;
}
%>
```

I presented it because it is a part of Flash Remoting that you should know about—and it is frequently an easy way to accomplish a task—but it is not always a good way to code your remote service. The Flash object is available and easy to use, but you should carefully consider the consequences of using the Flash object, as it ties the remote service to the Flash application (preventing you from building a non-Flash interface to the service).

There are several other considerations to separating the client and server. Flash Remoting raises a dilemma—where does the functionality belong? Some functionality is plainly client-side functionality, and some is plainly server-side. Some of it might be in-between and could go either way. For example, you can filter large sets of data in the middle tier, where you have a known environment and resources, versus doing it on the client side within Flash, which, depending on the client's machine, might not perform well. In this case, you may want to initially sort the data set on the server, and then have any user-initiated sorts occur within the Flash Player. This is a good trade-off between client-side processing concerns and the extra bandwidth required to transfer data sets to and from the server.

The database should handle as much data processing as possible, because that is its function and it is good at it. Such things as sorting and filtering recordsets, especially large recordsets, should be left to the database whenever possible.

An example of how you might enhance a server-side method to be more versatile and separate from the client is to manually manipulate your resultset before sending it to Flash. To demonstrate what I mean, think of a resultset that feeds a ComboBox. Frequently, you want to add a display item or an option for "All" in a ComboBox. One of the ways to do this is to add the text manually on the client after the resultset is returned. Sometimes, it makes sense to add the logic to the server so that the client merely has to display what is returned, without doing any manipulation. Performing the processing on the server side makes for a faster client experience and, as an added benefit, if you have to create an HTML interface for the same type of Combo-Box, you don't have to do any client-side manipulation of code in your HTML page either. Example 12-1 shows the ColdFusion code to manipulate a *Query* object on the server, which populates a client-side ComboBox.

Example 12-1. Enhancing a recordset to include static items directly in the remote service

```
<cffunction name="getTypes" access="remote" returntype="query">
<!--- First, get the data from the database
      The cachedwithin attribute keeps the query in memory for
        quicker access--->
  <cfquery name="rsGetContentTypes"
   datasource="myDSN"
   cachedwithin="#CreateTimeSpan(7, 0, 0, 0)#">
   SELECT type_ID, type_Desc from mytypes
  </cfquery>
<!--- Next, add a row to the query result and
      set new fields for the static option --->
  <cfset temp = QueryAddRow(rsGetContentTypes)>
  <cfset Temp = QuerySetCell(rsGetContentTypes, "type_id", 0)>
  <cfset Temp = QuerySetCell(rsGetContentTypes, "type_desc", "ALL")>
<!--- Lastly, do a query of a query and return the query to the
      caller ordering on the type_id field --->
  <cfquery name="rsTypesDropdown" dbtype="query">
   SELECT * FROM rsGetContentTypes ORDER BY type_id
  </cfquery>
  <cfreturn rsTypesDropdown />
</cffunction>
```

In this case, we could have added the row on the Flash client using ActionScript code, but manipulating UI components can slow down an application—especially if you have more than a few in an interface. Example 12-1 shows another aspect of ColdFusion— the ability to cache a resultset. The attribute cachedwithin="#CreateTimeSpan(7, 0, 0, 0)#" creates a seven-day cache; the database is hit only once per week for this query.

This type of functionality can even be included in your database in a stored procedure:

```
CREATE PROCEDURE spGetCategoriesDropdown
AS
```

```
SELECT CategoryID, CategoryName
FROM categories
UNION
SELECT 0 as CategoryID, 'All' as CategoryName
ORDER BY CategoryID
```

The stored procedure returns the resultset with the values already in place for populating the drop-down list.

Server-Proofing the Application

The Flash Remoting application has many possible failure points. One of the more frequent failure points is the communication between client and server. *Server-proofing* involves testing the application in serverless environments to guarantee that the application will fail gracefully if the server is unavailable.

There are many possible reasons for communication failure:

The Internet is too busy
> This can happen during peak hours and may be a limitation of the end user's Internet Service Provider (ISP), or it may be tied to a global Internet virus, which seems to occur more and more each year.

The end user has saved the page for offline browsing
> If the end user has disconnected from the Internet, how will your application respond?

The server might be down temporarily
> This can happen when your ISP is rebooting a server, the server is down for maintenance, etc.

Whatever the reason, your application needs a reliable way to recover from the lack of a connection. In an HTML page, this is not a problem; the browser will force a timeout after a specified number of seconds waiting for a response. In a Flash movie, it is your responsibility to provide a fallback mechanism to handle the lack of a connection. You can do this in two ways:

Provide an offline option in your application
> In some applications this is not possible, but you may have an application that works well offline, such as an email program that allows a user to read the contents of previously downloaded email or compose an email offline.

Display a user-friendly error message
> The user should not see system error messages and other cryptic messages. Instead, handle the error gracefully in the ActionScript code and display a comprehensible message to the end user.

The System.onStatus event should be assigned to a function in your application so that any failed remote calls will be handled gracefully:

```
System.onStatus = function () {
    getURL("http://www.flash-remoting.com/try_again.html","_blank");
};
```

This code displays an HTML error page to the user when a connection to Flash Remoting cannot be made.

Component Use

Components are one of the cornerstones of Rich Internet Application (RIA) development using Flash and Flash Remoting. Components make it easy to create rich interfaces, but they can also be responsible for an application getting bogged down with poor performance. Many of the Macromedia user interface components are very code-intensive when it comes to doing things like populating the component, sorting, and adding data. You should be conservative in your use of client-side code when dealing with components. The DataGrid component, for example, can utilize 90–100% of the end user's system resources while being populated—from a remote service or local data.

The Flash 2004 component architecture is optimized for applications that use five or six components; the shared library that Flash 2004 components require adds more file size than is justified by using only one or two components.

Component Speed

The speed of a component is often dependent on the type of code you are utilizing. What looks more efficient to the ActionScript programmer is often slower in execution. If you're in doubt about the speed of a particular section of code, you can time it using the *Date( )* object. The code in Example 12-2 is a *CodeTimer* object, which can be used to time the execution of sections of code.

Example 12-2. The CodeTimer class facilitates easy timing of code

```
// Constructor accepts an optional message argument and starts the timer
function CodeTimer (message) {
  this.message = message; //optional message
  this.startTime = new Date( ).getTime( );
}

// CodeTimer.trace( ) calculates the elapsed time and traces it to the Output window
CodeTimer.prototype.trace = function ( ) {
  this.endTime = new Date( ).getTime( );
  this.elapsedTime = this.endTime - this.startTime;
  if (this.message != undefined) trace(this.message);
```

Example 12-2. The CodeTimer class facilitates easy timing of code (continued)

```
  trace("Elapsed Time: " + this.elapsedTime + " milliseconds");
  return this.elapsedTime;
};
```

To use the timer, simply start it by creating a new *CodeTimer* object at the start of the code you want to time, and call the *CodeTimer.trace()* method at the end of the code:

```
    // Initialize the timer
    var t = new CodeTimer("Testing DataGlue");

    // Some code to time
    var fields = result_rs.getColumnNames();
    var idField = '#' + fields[0] + '#';
    var descField = '#' + fields[1] + '#';
    DataGlue.bindFormatStrings(cbName, result_rs, descField, idField);

    // Display the elapsed time in milliseconds in the Output window
    t.trace();
```

The preceding example tests the speed of the *DataGlue.bindFormatStrings()* method. The example recordset that I tested yielded an average result of 10 milliseconds. The following code shows the time taken to manually populate the same ComboBox with the same recordset using an index loop:

```
    var t = new CodeTimer("Testing index loop");

    var fields = result_rs.getColumnNames();
    for (var i; i < result_rs.getLength(); i++) {
      cbName.addItemAt(i,
        result_rs.getItemAt(i)[fields[1]],
        result_rs.getItemAt(i)[fields[0]]);
    }
    t.trace();
```

The second example yielded an average result of 30 milliseconds. The last example uses a *for...in* loop and a much more concise coding style:

```
    var t = new CodeTimer("Testing for/in loop");

    for (var i in result_rs) cbName.addItem(i[0],i[1],root);

    t.trace();
```

The third example is less verbose and looks like it is more efficient, but it results in an elapsed time of 90 milliseconds—9 times slower than the first example—showing the efficiency of the *DataGlue* class. Looks are deceiving sometimes when coding, as this example demonstrates. It's best to not simply take the code at face value; measure your code's execution time and try different things to get the best possible results.

Shaving 80 milliseconds off the data-loading operation for one ComboBox can have a dramatic impact in the end user's experience if you have many user interface elements and can optimize some of them in similar ways. 80 milliseconds might not seem like a lot, but when you're dealing with a Flash interface it is wise to conserve where you can, to balance the initial load time of the movie, which might run into several seconds. 10 or 20 interface elements can increase this delay by 1 or 2 seconds for the user. Every little bit of optimization helps to improve the user experience.

Here is a simple technique for testing performance. When you're testing a brief operation, it may be so fast that you can't get an accurate measure of the time it takes. Furthermore, if an operation is performed hundreds or thousands of times during your program execution, the execution time may vary, and it isn't practical to add up the times of each execution manually. You can add a *for...in* loop to execute an operation, say, 100 times to give you a more accurate picture of the time required for execution. Here is the new code (additions shown in bold):

```
var t = new CodeTimer("Testing index loop 100 times");

for (var j; j < 100; j++) {
  var fields = result_rs.getColumnNames();
  for (var i; i < result_rs.getLength(); i++) {
    cbName.addItemAt(i,
      result_rs.getItemAt(i)[fields[1]],
      result_rs.getItemAt(i)[fields[0]]);
  }
}
// Displays total and average execution time
elapsedTime = t.trace();
trace("Average Elapsed Time: " + elapsedTime/100 + " milliseconds");
```

Don't forget to take the average time, and don't forget to remove the *for...in* loop when you're done testing (you can comment out the testing code so that it is easy to reinstate if you want to test it again later). Be sure to test the operations that you are trying to optimize. How would the timing differ if the call to *getColumnNames( )* were moved outside the second loop? Refer to "Looping" later in this chapter for hints on optimizing loop performance.

You can get much more elaborate with timing, but this simple example gives you the basic technique. Timing your code is very important when dealing with Flash Remoting or Flash interfaces in general. Sometimes, a call to the remote database will be quicker than trying to manipulate results on the client. Also, sometimes there are sections of code that execute too slowly in ActionScript and can be moved to the server.

Data Loading

Frequently, when building data-driven Flash interfaces, you test with a small amount of data with the knowledge that your application will grow in the future with more back-end data. The Flash UI components can generally handle a small amount of data, but when you start feeding thousands of records into them they start slowing down dramatically. How do you test with large amounts of sample data if the data doesn't exist yet?

One way is to use a temporary SQL statement in your server-side service that returns a lot more rows than your test data actually contains, by forcing a cross join on another table. A *cross join* gives you a result that contains every combination of rows of data from the joined tables. In other words, each row in the first table is joined to every row in the second table, giving you a huge resultset. A cross join has limited use in everyday data retrieval but is especially handy when you're testing application interfaces. Consider the following query on the *Northwind* database:

```
SELECT c.CategoryID, c.CategoryName
FROM Categories c
```

The query returns about eight rows of data. If you were to time this data being rendered into a ComboBox or DataGrid, you would not be able to discern any noticeable speed problem. Change the query to cross join the Products table:

```
SELECT c.CategoryID, c.CategoryName
FROM Categories c, products
```

Now the query returns over 600 rows by joining the Products table and returning a complete set of data from the Categories table for each row of data in the Products table. The fields that you are retrieving are the same as the fields in the first example, but they are duplicated many times. This gives you a better idea of what your final application will be able to handle and gives you a more accurate picture of where your bottlenecks are. (It also gives you a chance to test your screen layouts to see if they accommodate large recordsets and test your logic for pageable recordsets, if applicable.)

UI components can greatly speed up the development process, but they can also be a performance bottleneck if the code that uses the component is not optimized.

Clean API

Application programming interface (API) is a general term for how one block of code communicates with another. For example, each ActionScript class defines an API by making methods and properties available (or keeping them hidden). Keeping the API for your application clean, with well-defined properties, methods, and events, makes for fast programming by the rest of your team. A formal API helps to insulate one code module from changes in another module. Furthermore, updates to an application can be made more quickly if your properties, methods, and events are predesigned, documented, and consistent with the API that you set up.

Reusable Code

Making your code reusable is one of the ways that you can improve the speed of coding in future applications. You should maintain stock objects and snippets of code that have been programmed, tested, and optimized in the past. For example, most applications have users, so if you maintain a standard *User* object that interacts with a *User* remote service, the two parts can be utilized over and over. There is no sense in reinventing the wheel each time. Even if an object or piece of code can't be used in its entirety, it can be used as a starting point. Developing a useful library of ActionScript or server-side code (or benefiting from libraries made available by others) can increase your productivity by orders of magnitude.

Modularity

Keeping the program modular is not something that is confined to one style of programming; it is a concept that works in all cases. If you code is self-contained in modules, you have several advantages over code that is nonmodular:

- Code in a module can be tested without relying on other parts of the application, by simply knowing what the code requires and what it returns.
- Modules can be improved and replaced without affecting other elements of the application, assuming your new module does the same thing with the same properties, methods, and events associated with the old module (i.e., as long as the API to the module doesn't change).
- A test module can be plugged into the application in place of the real module, to facilitate easy testing.
- Other programmers who might need to work on the application can understand the code more easily.

Having modularized code does not simply mean separating the code into sections. I worked on an application once, built by a fellow programmer, that was broken down into several include files. At first glance, it seemed logical that the program was broken down as it was. However, after diving into the code, I could see that each file had elements that relied on other files (variables, functions, etc.), which made it very hard to update the application. In the end, I wasted more time trying to figure out what went where than the time it would have taken to rewrite the code using a more logical approach. Therefore, trying to maintain modularity can help alert you to poor application design. If you can't modularize your code, you probably need to redesign it, even if it means starting over.

Loops and Repeated Operations

Most of your performance problems are going to be the result of a repeated operation that is not optimized. A nonoptimized piece of code that executes one time is not likely to have an impact on an application; however a nonoptimized piece of code that executes 1,000 times in a loop is going to kill the performance. For that reason, any code that is executed repeatedly, such as an *onEnterFrame( )* handler or a *for* loop is a potential bottleneck.

Macromedia improved the performance of the Flash Remoting classes in the first updater, available at *http://www.macromedia.com*. One technique that was originally used throughout the Flash Remoting classes involves initializing a *for* loop in a nonoptimized way. In standard ECMA scripting, the middle section of the *for* loop (the *condition* in the *for(variable; condition; update)* construct) is evaluated each time the loop executes. For that reason, a static value should be used whenever possible.

Bad:

```
for (var i = 0; i < this.getLength( ); i++) {
  // Do something
}
```

Good:

```
var tempLength = this.getLength( );
for (var i = 0; i < tempLength; i++) {
  // Do something
}
```

However, counting down is even faster:

```
var tempLength = this.getLength( )-1;
for (var i = tempLength; i >= 0; i--) {
  // Do something
}
```

Optimizing a loop's *condition* expression is only the first step. Code within the loop should be optimized whenever possible, for this is where your application performance is going to suffer the worst. This is especially true if you are populating a UI component, such as a Tree. If a piece of code that takes 1 millisecond to execute can be removed from a loop that is repeated 1,000 times, you'll save 1 second (which can make an application feel much more responsive). The most basic technique is moving outside the loop any operation that doesn't need to be performed repeatedly. Consider the following two cases. In this case, the string is initialized to "Hello Tom!" within the loop:

```
for (var i = 0; i <= 10; i++) {
  myString = "Hello Tom!";
  trace(myString.substring(0, i));
}
```

In this case, the string is initialized outside the loop:

```
myString = "Hello Tom!";
for (var i = 0; i <= 10; i++) {
  trace(myString.substring(0, i));
}
```

In the first case, the string is initialized repeatedly, even though its value never changes. The second loop will execute faster (about 1.8 milliseconds versus 2 milliseconds). You might look for other ways to optimize the code. For example, the *trace( )* statement, because it displays text in the Output window, might slow things down. Here, we accumulate all the text in a variable, outputString, and display it once, rather than executing the *trace( )* statement repeatedly:

```
myString = "Hello Tom!";
outputString = "";
for (var i = 0; i < 10; i++) {
  outputString += myString.substring(0, i) + newline;
}
trace(outputString);
```

Surprise! This version takes an average of 2.4 milliseconds and is therefore slower than the *trace( )* version. It turns out that string concatenation is a more expensive operation than tracing the text in the Output window.

Loops should also be terminated (broken out of) as soon as possible. Take the following piece of code as an example:

```
var temp = myArray.length;
for (var i=0; i < temp; i++) {
  if (findItem(myArray, myItem))
    found = true;
}
trace("found it!");
```

The preceding example sets a flag when a specific item has been found in the array. The problem is that the loop continues even after the item has been found. This is wasteful, especially in a recursive loop that might be populating a UI component. A better solution is to break out of the loop as soon as the item is found:

```
var temp = a.length;
for (var i=0; i < temp; i++) {
  if (findItem(a[i], "50")) {
    found = true;
    break;
  }
}
trace("found it!");
```

A loop like this will run an average of 50% faster, because an item might be found at the beginning of the loop or the end of the loop but the average will be somewhere in the middle. The loop is ended as soon as the item is found.

The preceding techniques apply equally well to any code that is executed repeatedly. For example, don't initialize data within an event handler that is called repeatedly. Initialize it once outside the event handler and refer to it as needed. Likewise, once an event handler is no longer needed, you should cease executing it. For example, if you've added a listener with *addListener( )*, you can remove it with *removeListener( )* when it is no longer needed.

OOP or Not OOP

There are at least two different approaches to programming in ActionScript 1.0: object-oriented programming and procedural programming. Both have their strengths and weaknesses. You could add a third group of programmers as well: those who program procedurally and use OOP concepts in their applications. This section will show some ways of doing things with Flash Remoting using these approaches.

Procedural Programming

Procedural programming, also known as *top-down programming*, uses techniques that have been around since the beginning of computer programming. With procedural programming, you write code from beginning to end and call functions when they're needed. Assembly language is an example of procedural programming. There is nothing inherently wrong with procedural programming, yet it has fallen out of favor with the advent of OOP.

Task-oriented

Procedural programming focuses on the tasks. Using an example of the Products database from the earlier chapters, a procedural program asks the question "what has to be done?" and then proceeds to do it. For example, the code might follow like this (in pseudocode):

```
1. Initialize movie
2. Call remote methods to populate UI
3. Display results
4. Wait for user input
5. If "add" is clicked, show the addProduct screen
6. If "search" is clicked, call the remote method searchProducts()
```

Each section of the program (*addProduct*, *searchProducts( )*, etc.) would contain more code that executes sequentially, with conditional logic to branch off into other areas of the program.

ActionScript 1.0 promotes the use of procedural programming by the very nature of the ECMA-262 specification. ECMA-262 is not a true object-oriented specification, but it does allow for OOP. It's a very loose language in that it does not require entry points, strict datatyping, class definitions, or even variable declaration. That does not make procedural programming bad; it just means you have to structure your code to make it modular and maintain organization as you do so. One programming flaw in a program can have consequences further down the line. Because the code is executed sequentially, each line of code depends on what comes before it.

ActionScript 2.0, based on ECMAScript 4 and supported in Flash 2004 and Flash Pro, is geared more toward object-oriented programming, requiring strict typing, formal class declarations, and other constructs familiar to Java programmers. However, ActionScript 1.0 (the version supported by Flash MX) is still supported in Flash 2004 and Flash Pro. ActionScript 1.0 is not strictly case-sensitive in Flash Player 6. However, when exporting for Flash Player 7, ActionScript 1.0 is strictly case-sensitive, as is ActionScript 2.0.

Event-driven

Flash also operates as an event-driven application, and event-driven applications are procedurally oriented. When the movie loads, all of the code in the movie is executed (depending on the timeline, of course). Flash then waits for user input. The user input triggers events that can be trapped with event handlers. These event handlers become named functions when you're using procedural programming:

```
myButton_pb.setClickHandler("getProducts");
function getProducts( ) {
  myService.getProducts( );
}
```

When you're using procedural programming in a Flash Remoting application, it becomes even more important to keep the code structured and clean. A procedural program can quickly turn into spaghetti code if the program lacks structure and organization. That said, a procedural program can also be well-constructed and function perfectly.

Result handlers in procedural programming

When dealing with remote services, you have several choices in how you handle the results. The simplest and most documented way of retrieving results is to name a function using the remote method name with an appended _Result or _Status. Generally, a procedural approach would utilize this method:

```
myService.loginUser(user_txt.text, pwd_txt.text);
loginUser_Result = function (result) {
  if (result == true) {
    trace("User logged");
  } else {
    trace("User not logged");
  }
};
```

This method is simple, direct, and effective. It is self-documenting, because the remote method name is used in the naming of the callback function. However, it does become cumbersome when dealing with many remote calls. I would not discourage someone from using it, but I would not consider it a best practice. That said, there is nothing wrong with using this technique if you feel comfortable using it.

Procedural example

Example 12-3 is an example of a procedural program with structure.

Example 12-3. A procedural approach to the HelloUser program

```
#include "NetServices.as"
// Set up variables for the URL and service paths
var myURL = "http://localhost/flashservices/gateway";
var servicePath = "com.oreilly.frdg.HelloUser";

// Connection hasn't been initialized; create connection and service objects
if (initialized == null) {
  initialized = true;
  NetServices.setDefaultGatewayURL(myURL);
  var myConnection_conn = NetServices.createGatewayConnection();
  var service = myConnection_conn.getService(servicePath, this);
}
// Set up the callback function to handle mouseclicks
submit_pb.setClickHandler("callSayHello");

// Call the service when the user clicks the Submit button
function callSayHello () {
  var user_name = userName_txt.text;
  if (user_name == "") {
    user_name = "User";
  }
  service.sayHello(user_name);
}

// Set up onResult and onStatus event handlers
function sayHello_Result (myResults) {
  results_txt.text = myResults;
}

function sayHello_Status (myError) {
  results_txt.text = myError.description;
}
// Set the system status to be handled by the method status handler as well
System.onStatus = sayHello_Status;
```

The procedural style mixes the user interface logic (inside the *sayHello_Result( )* function) and is executed from the top down. Events that are triggered (such as when the submit_pb button is clicked) are handled by named functions. Events returned by a remote service are handled by functions, *sayHello_Result( )* and *sayHello_Status( )*, that are named after the calling method.

A procedural program such as this can easily grow into spaghetti code if you are not careful. Even in this simple example, the results_txt field is referenced in several places. If something were to change in the interface, you would have to find all of your user interface references and change them manually.

A better option is to use a custom responder object, as discussed in Chapter 4. Some of the more flexible options are shown in the next section, "Object-Oriented Programming."

Object-Oriented Programming

Object-oriented programming (OOP) is at the opposite end of the programming spectrum from procedural programming. In true OOP, everything is an object. Code in the program does not exist if it is not part of an object. For that reason, Flash MX is not a true OOP environment; you don't have to create objects in order for the program to operate, although inline code is technically part of the current object where the code resides. Also, some of the key principles of OOP, such as data hiding (private, protected, and public members), are not implemented in ActionScript. Even though strict OOP is not entirely possible with Flash MX, you can get pretty darn close by simply using OOP principles in your coding style.

 Flash 2004 and Flash Pro support ActionScript 2.0, which is much closer to a true OOP language than ActionScript 1.0. The following discussion applies whether you're using ActionScript 2.0 or trying to stretch ActionScript 1.0 to act as if it were truly object-oriented, although ActionScript 2.0 enforces stricter coding requirements.

Everything is an object

With OOP, you will want to create objects for everything. The application itself is an object; the user of the application is an object; every button on the screen is an object; the connection to the remote server is an object; the user's email address can be an object. An object is an instance of a class. A class is the coded blueprint for an object. Imagine the classes as rubber stamps, and the objects as the imprints you make when you use each rubber stamp. How you organize your classes and tie them together is one of the keys to understanding how OOP works.

OOP works in the exact opposite way that procedural programming works. In procedural programming, you ask yourself "What has to be done?" and then you do it. In OOP, you create abstract representations of each item in your application and ask yourself "How do they communicate?" Each class is created as a black box; you know what it does, you know what it needs, and you know what it returns. You don't have to know how it works, and you can remove it and substitute another black box with the same properties, methods, and events and the program will still work. Your class encapsulates the functionality and allows other classes to interact with it.

OOP in Flash Remoting

In Flash Remoting, there are several different ways you can encapsulate the functionality in objects:

Enclose your remote server calls in an object
Every remote method is mirrored in a method of an object in your Flash movie. For example, you might have a Products database, as was shown in Chapter 3. You would have a *Product* class and a *ProductList* class, which would be a collection of *Product* objects. The *ProductList* class might have a method called *getList( )* that would retrieve the entire product list from the remote server. The *Product* class might have a method called *addProduct( )* that would call an insert routine on the remote server to insert the product into the database.

Use broadcasters
A *broadcaster* is another object that you can use to simplify how remote method calls are handled on the client. When you use a broadcaster, you also have a *listener*. When the broadcaster broadcasts an event, the listener is automatically informed and performs some function. This is ideal for Flash Remoting, where a remote method does not provide an immediate response, but rather sends an *onResult* event back to the movie.

Use a Model/View/Controller (or Model/View/Presenter) architecture
The Model/View/Controller (MVC) design pattern allows you to separate functionality into distinct units. These patterns have been utilized by many Flash Remoting applications. The *Model* is the business object, handling the logic of the application; the *View* is the unit that handles the UI, such as the text fields, buttons, and UI components; and the *Controller* is the catalyst between the Model and the View, handling communication between them. In a Flash Remoting application, the Model is usually split between ActionScript on the client and the server-side services.

How to create your objects

There are several ways to implement OOP in Flash. Generally, the more abstract you make your classes, the easier the classes will be to understand for other programmers. I mean *abstract* in the sense of "evoking something's distilled essence," not "esoteric and obtuse." You should create classes that represent something meaningful. For example, your class should not be called *RemoteService* with methods that merely mirror your remote methods. This is obtuse and redundant, not abstract; it merely serves as a convenient way of accessing your services. An abstract class would be called *Product*, *User*, *EmailAddress*, or *Search*. These are human-readable objects that represent something meaningful to the application.

Objects are typically modeled before a line of code is written. *Modeling* involves identifying the objects in your application and documenting how they communicate via the properties, methods, and events of each object. Modeling can be done in many ways: using a Universal Modeling Language (UML) diagram, 3×5 cards (one for each object), or plotted on paper. In an OOP application, the more modeling you do in advance of coding, the easier it will be to create the objects and complete the coding successfully. In Flash Remoting, you must identify how an object will receive the remote result and how it will handle the result using an OOP mentality.

Responder objects in OOP

Throughout the book, I've shown a technique that makes sense in many situations—utilizing a custom responder object, like this:

```
function LoginResponder( ) {
  this.onResult = function (result) {
    if (result == true) {
      message_mc.message_txt.text = "User logged";
    } else {
      message_mc.message_txt.text = "User not logged";
    }
  };
  this.onStatus = function (error) {
    trace(error.description);
  };
}
myService.loginUser(new LoginResponder( ), user_txt.text, pwd_txt.text);
```

or this:

```
function LoginResponder ( ) {
}
LoginResponder.prototype.onResult = function (result) {
  if (result == true) {
    message_mc.message_txt.text = "User logged";
  } else {
    message_mc.message_txt.text = "User not logged";
  }
};
LoginResponder.prototype.onStatus = function (error) {
    trace(error.description);
};
myService.loginUser(new LoginResponder( ), user_txt.text, pwd_txt.text);
```

A better technique, however, is to use a *callback function* or a *broadcaster* within the responder object. The previous code is tied to the user interface, which is not an object-oriented approach; the user interface elements are not separate from the *LoginResponder* object. If you pass a callback function to the object, the *Login-Responder* is separate from the UI. You might start with a *Responder* class:

```
function Responder ( ) {}
Responder.prototype.onResult = function (results) {trace(results);};
Responder.prototype.onStatus = function (error) {trace(error.description);};
```

Then, create a *LoginResponder* class for specific functionality:

```
// LoginResponder extends Responder
#include "Responder.as"
function LoginResponder (myCallback) {
  this.prototype = new Responder();
  this.callback = myCallback;
}

LoginResponder.prototype.onResult = function (result) {
  if (result == true) {
    this.callback("User logged", result);
  } else {
    this.callback("User not logged", result);
  }
};
doMessage = function (message) {
  message_mc.message_txt.text = message
};
```

The preceding *LoginResponder* class defines a responder object that uses the callback function passed to it. You can use it from another class designed to gather information from the UI:

```
myUserObject = new UserObject();
myUserObject.loginUser("doMessage", user_txt.text, pwd_txt.text);
```

Inside the *UserObject* class you would have a *loginUser( )* method, which would call the remote service:

```
#include "LoginResponder.as"
UserObject.prototype.loginUser = function (callback, username, password) {
  this.service.loginUser(new LoginResponder(callback), username, password);
};
```

Problems with OOP

There are a few inconsistencies with Flash Remoting when working with objects. The asynchronous nature of Flash Remoting makes it difficult to create objects that separate UI and content from your remote results. Because the results are accessed within an *onResult( )* method, you might be tempted to access interface elements from within the same method. This would break the principle of *encapsulation*, which basically says that objects should behave as black boxes. In a properly encapsulated object, the internal workings of the object don't rely on external items such as UI elements. You can overcome the obstacle by using a broadcaster inside the *onResult( )* and *onStatus( )* methods, or by passing a callback method to the object, which would be called inside of *onResult( )* or *onStatus( )*, as we'll see shortly.

Another problem involves having a service object as part of a custom object that is sent to the server in a remote method. It is a natural tendency to want to encapsulate the object to be self-sufficient and exist as a unit. One way to do that is to have your remote service as a property of the object. Unfortunately, this causes the remote call to fail due to an internal fault with Flash Remoting. The Macromedia Pet Market blueprint application (*http://www.macromedia.com/devnet/mx/blueprint*) suffers from this problem, but the programmers worked around the issue by copying the object properties to another object before calling the remote service. Workarounds such as these are commonplace, as Flash Remoting is still in its infancy and has a few kinks to work out.

Callback example

This section demonstrates an example that uses callback functions and shows how the procedural code from Example 12-3 might be implemented as an OOP application. There are a few extra steps involved in turning a simple example into a full-fledged OOP application. You'll have to start with a new movie named *HelloUserOOP.fla* and follow these steps (the completed file is available at the online Code Depot):

1. Add 2 layers to the timeline: *actions* and *ui*.

2. In the *ui* layer, create the user interface that was shown in Chapter 2, with an input TextField named userName_txt, a dynamic TextField named results_txt, and a PushButton component named submit_pb. There is also one static Text-Field that contains the text "Enter your name".

3. Create a new MovieClip using Insert → New Symbol.

4. The dialog box that appears prompts you for a name. Name the symbol *HelloUser-Class*, select the Export for ActionScript checkbox, as shown in Figure 12-1, and click OK.

5. Inside the symbol, rename layer *Layer1* to *actions*.

6. Define a *HelloUserClass* class in the first frame of the *actions* layer, as follows. This class initializes the gateway and is the basis of our application:

```
#initclip
#include "NetServices.as"

function HelloUserClass (url) {
  this.init(url);
}

Object.registerClass("HelloUserSymbol", HelloUserClass);

HelloUserClass.prototype.init = function (url) {
  this.testingUrl = url;
  NetServices.setDefaultGatewayURL(this.testingUrl);
  this._conn= NetServices.createGatewayConnection( );
};

#endinitclip
```

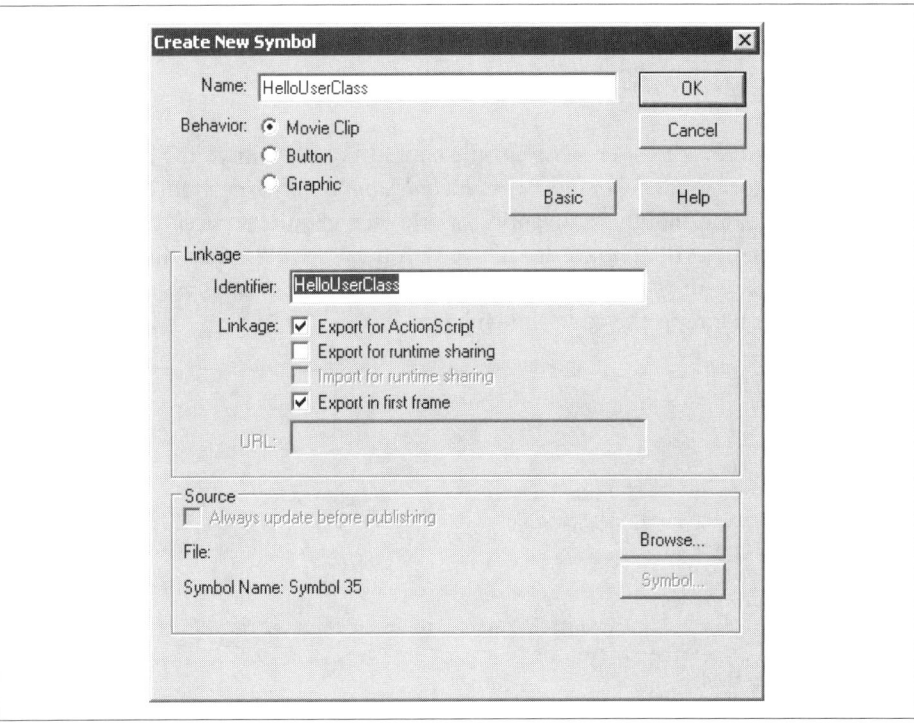

Figure 12-1. Creating a new MovieClip for HelloUser

Navigate back to the main movie and enter the following ActionScript into the *actions* layer of the main timeline. Notice the include file, *User.as*, which is a custom class that we'll set up for this application. The initialization code shown creates a *NetConnection* object upon loading (through the *HelloUserClass*), and creates a *User* object. From this code, you can see that the *User* object instance is calling three different methods: *setService( )*, *setName( )*, and *sayHello( )*. The submit_pb button has a private method, *displayMessage( )*, within the anonymous function built for the *onRelease* event. A reference to *displayMessage( )* is passed to the *User* object as a callback function:

```
#include "com/oreilly/frdg/User.as"

// Call the service when the user clicks the Submit button.
if (initialized == undefined) {
  initialized = true;
  _global.app = new HelloUserClass("http://localhost/flashservices/gateway");
  var servicePath = "com.oreilly.frdg.HelloUser";
  app.myUser = new User("User");
  app.myUser.setService(app._conn, servicePath);
}

submit_pb.onRelease = function () {
  displayMessage = function (message) {
```

```
      results_txt.text = message;
    }
    app.myUser.setName(userName_txt.text);
    app.myUser.sayHello(displayMessage, displayMessage);
};
```

7. Create the *User* class. The *User.as* file should be saved in your Flash configuration directory under *Configuration\Include\com\oreilly\frdg*. Our class files are using the same naming convention as the server-side services that have been used throughout the book. Alternatively, you can save the class files in the same directory as your *.fla* file—using the same subdirectories, *com\oreilly\frdg*. The *User.as* file contains the code shown here:

```
/*
User class

public User
  constructor:
    new User();      // Default user with no arguments
    new User(name);  // Set a default name property
      arguments:
        name: string
      properties:
        service: the remote service with which the user interacts
        name: the name of the user
      methods:
        getName: retrieve name property
        setName: set name property
          arguments:
            name: string
         getService: retrieve service object
         setService: set the remote service for the object
            arguments:
              connection: a NetConnection object
              servicePath: a path to a remote service
          sayHello: interface to remote method sayHello( )
            arguments:
              callback: function to handle results of the remote call
        Dependencies:
          com.oreilly.frdg.Result
*/
#include "com/oreilly/frdg/Result.as"

// Constructor takes one optional argument (name)
function User (name) {
  if (arguments)
    this.name = name;
}

User.prototype.getName = function () {
  return this.name;
};
```

```
// Set the name property only if the argument exists and is not blank
User.prototype.setName = function (name) {
  if (name != "" && name != undefined)
    this.name = name;
};

User.prototype.getService = function () {
  return this.service;
};

// Create remote service object as a property of User
User.prototype.setService = function (connection, servicePath) {
  this.service = connection.getService(servicePath);
};

// Interface to remote method, sayHello()
User.prototype.sayHello = function (callback, errorHandler) {
  this.getService().sayHello(new Result(callback, errorHandler), this.name);
};
```

The *User* class is extremely simple, with one argument in the constructor; two properties, each with getter/setter methods; and one public method that is used as an interface to the remote method, *sayHello( )*. The *User* class exists apart from the user interface code set up previously. The Flash UI that was set up will work with any *User* class that we implement in the future, as long as the API to the class remains the same (i.e., the same public properties, methods, and events).

8. You can see that the *User* class also requires one other class: the *Result* class. Create the *Result.as* file as follows, and save it to the same directory as the *User. as* file:

```
/*
public Result
  constructor:
    new Result(resultHandler, errorHandler); // Set result handler and error
                                                 handler properties

      arguments:
        resultHandler: function
        errorHandler: function (optional)
      properties:
        none
      methods:
        onResult: method to handle remote results
          arguments:
            myResult: argument returned from remote call
        onStatus: method to handle remote errors
          arguments:
            myError: argument returned from remote call in event of error
Dependencies:
    none
*/
```

```
function Result (resultHandler, errorHandler) {
  this.resultHandler = resultHandler;
  this.errorHandler = errorHandler;
}
// Set up onResult( ) and onStatus( ) handlers as methods of the Result class
Result.prototype.onResult = function (myResults) {
  this.resultHandler(myResults);
};

Result.prototype.onStatus = function (myError) {
  if (this.errorHandler == "undefined") {
    trace(myError.description);
  } else {
    this.errorHandler(myError.description);
  }
};
System.onStatus = Result.prototype.onStatus;
```

The *Result* class is a special responder object. The responder does not act on any of the results, and, as such, it can be used for any remote service call. You pass a callback function to the instance of the *Result* class when you instantiate it. In this case, we instantiated the object in the *User* object instance defined in Step 7:

```
User.prototype.sayHello = function (callback, errorHandler) {
  this.getService( ).sayHello(new Result(callback, errorHandler), this.name);
};
```

9. Save and test the movie. It should work exactly as the procedural example.

Objects communicating: that's what OOP is all about. The user interface knows nothing of the *Result* class. It knows only about the *User* object and how to communicate with it. It depends on the *User* object; however, any *User* object that provides the same properties, methods, and events could be substituted without a problem. You'll notice that the OOP code is much wordier than the simple procedural example that does the same thing. Even so, the initial time spent modeling your application and setting up your classes is regained when you implement the application and make modifications further down the road. Modifications come easy to an OOP application.

Broadcasters

A broadcaster is based on the Observer pattern, another standard design pattern in programming. A broadcaster is implemented in ActionScript using the undocumented *ASBroadcaster* class. With this class, you can create objects that broadcast custom events inside your movie. After an event is broadcast, a listener that is listening for that particular event will respond.

 *ASBroadcaster* is an undocumented class, and, as such, it may not remain in the language forever. You can implement the example here using *ASBroadcaster* or one of the numerous substitute broadcasters freely available on the Web.

Broadcasters fit right into the Flash Remoting framework because of the asynchronous nature of the technology. When you call a remote service, you don't wait for the response. The remote service method eventually returns a result to the responder function in the Flash client. The remote service is essentially a broadcaster, and your responder object is essentially a listener. This does not provide enough flexibility in handling results, however, so it makes sense to set up a custom broadcaster to convey the remote response to the part of your Flash movie that will benefit from it.

You can set up a broadcaster inside of your responder to broadcast a custom event to the movie. The advantage of this approach is that, once the event is broadcast, you can have one or more listeners acting on the remote response. To create a broadcaster, pass an instance of the generic *Object* class to the static *ASBroadcaster.initialize( )* method:

```
var myBroadcaster = new Object();
ASBroadcaster.initialize(myBroadcaster);
```

This converts myBroadcaster into an *ASBroadcaster* object capable of broadcasting. Specify the custom event to broadcast using the *broadcastMessage( )* method:

```
myBroadcaster.broadcastMessage("onMyCustomEvent", "Hello there");
```

Finally, set up a listener object to listen for the custom event. Here, we create an object, myListener, with an anonymous function assigned to the onMyCustomEvent property:

```
myListener = {
  onMyCustomEvent:function(message) {
    trace(message);
  }
}
```

Finally, add the listener to the object to myBroadcaster using the *addListener( )* method:

```
myBroadcaster.addListener(myListener);
```

Example 12-4 utilizes a broadcaster to broadcast the *onResult* event from the server, rather than using a callback function. It uses the same *HelloUserClass* class as shown earlier in *HelloUserOOP.fla*, with no changes. The only changes are in the ActionScript code in the movie, as well as the two classes that were set up.

Create a copy of the *User.as* file and rename it *UserBroadcaster.as*. Change the constructor and the *sayHello( )* method as show in Example 12-4 (changes shown in bold).

Example 12-4. UserBroadcaster class

```
/*
User class

* public UserBroadcaster
```

Example 12-4. UserBroadcaster class (continued)

```
      constructor:
        new UserBroadcaster( );     // Default user with no arguments
        new UserBroadcaster(name); // Set a default name property
      arguments:
        name: string
      properties:
        service: the remote service with which the user interacts
        name: the name of the user
      methods:
        getName: retrieve name property
        setName: set name property
          arguments:
            name: string
        getService: retrieve service object
        setService: set the remote service for the object
          arguments:
            connection: a NetConnection object
            servicePath: a path to a remote service
        sayHello:interface to remote method, sayHello( )
          arguments:
            none
    Dependencies:
      com.oreilly.frdg.BroadcasterResponder
*/

#include "com/oreilly/frdg/BroadcasterResponder.as"

function UserBroadcaster (name) {
  if (arguments)
    this.name = name;
  // Set this class up as a broadcaster
  ASBroadcaster.initialize(this);
}

UserBroadcaster.prototype.getName = function ( ) {
  return this.name;
};

// Set the name property only if the argument exists and is not blank
UserBroadcaster.prototype.setName = function (name) {
  if (name != "" && name != undefined)
    this.name = name;
};

UserBroadcaster.prototype.getService = function ( ) {
  return this.service;
};

// Create remote service object as a property of User
UserBroadcaster.prototype.setService = function (connection, servicePath) {
  this.service = connection.getService(servicePath);
};
```

Example 12-4. UserBroadcaster class (continued)

```
UserBroadcaster.prototype.sayHello = function () {
  this.getService().sayHello(new BroadcasterResponder("onSayHello", this),
                             this.name);
};
```

Let's compare the *UserBroadcaster* class in Example 12-4 with the *User* class from the earlier callback implementation. The main differences are the initialization of the class as an *ASBroadcaster* in the constructor and the fact that the *sayHello( )* method now uses a different responder object: *BroadcasterResponder*. You pass a custom event ("onSayHello") and the broadcaster object (this) to the responder function. The responder object notifies any listeners. The *BroadcasterResponder* responder function's definition is shown here:

```
/*
public BroadcasterResponder
  constructor:
    new BroadcasterResponder(event);
      arguments:
        event: the event that will be broadcast
      properties:
        none
      methods:
        onResult: method to handle remote results
          arguments:
            event: the event that will be broadcast
        onStatus: method to handle remote errors
          arguments:
            event: the event that the error occurred in
Dependencies:
    none
*/

function BroadcasterResponder (event, broadcaster) {
  this.event = event;
  this.broadcaster = broadcaster;
}
// Set up onResult() and onStatus() handlers as
// methods of the BroadcasterResponder class
BroadcasterResponder.prototype.onResult = function (myResults) {
  this.broadcaster.broadcastMessage(this.event, myResults);
};
BroadcasterResponder.prototype.onStatus = function (myError) {
  this.broadcaster.broadcastMessage(this.event + 'Error', myError);
};
System.onStatus = BroadcasterResponder.prototype.onStatus;
```

The *BroadcasterResponder* function accepts two arguments: the custom event that will fire when this responder is called, and the broadcaster that will broadcast the message (the *UserBroadcaster* object instance, in this case). The implementation is simple: when a successful result is returned from the server, the *onResult( )* method is called and the broadcaster broadcasts the event ("onSayHello" in this case) and the actual results from the remote call to the movie. If an error is received by the *onStatus( )* event handler, the name of the event becomes event + "Error", or "onSayHelloError" in this case. Next, listeners need to be set up in the main movie:

```
#include "com/oreilly/frdg/UserBroadcaster.as"

if (initialized == undefined) {
  initialized = true;
  _global.app = new HelloUserClass("http://localhost/flashservices/gateway");
  var servicePath = "com.oreilly.frdg.HelloUser";
  app.myUser = new UserBroadcaster("User");
  app.myUser.setService(app._conn, servicePath);
}

submit_pb.onRelease = function () {
  app.myUser.setName(userName_txt.text);
  app.myUser.sayHello();
};

// Listener object for the onSayHello event
results_txt.onSayHello = function (message) {
  this.text = message;
};

// Listener object for errors in onSayHello
results_txt.onSayHelloError = function (message) {
  this.text = message.description;
};

app.myUser.addListener(results_txt);
```

The listener object is the results_txt TextField. Any object can serve as a listener, but the object must have a function set up to respond to your custom event. We simply create the necessary event handlers on the object (by setting the onSayHello and onSayHelloError properties to anonymous functions) and then add it as a listener to receive events fired off by the *UserBroadcaster* instance (*app.myUser*).

Again, this technique is well suited to Flash Remoting. The Macromedia Pet Market blueprint application also uses custom broadcasters. One advantage, as mentioned earlier, is that you can add multiple listeners to the event. For example, you can add this code to create a built-in debugging listener:

```
var debug - true;
// var debug = false;  // Uncomment this line to turn off debugging
var debugListener = {onSayHello:function(message) {
  trace("User name: " + app.myUser.getName());
  trace("Results from server: " + message);
}}
if (debug) app.myUser.addListener(debugListener);
```

The listener is "turned on" when the debug flag is set to true. Doing this, you can add listeners to all of your remote calls without having to dig into your code to make changes and put *trace( )* statements all over the place. It can all be done from one place, because your listener is listening for the event.

Mixing Procedural and Object-Oriented Code

Another common way to build an application is to mix procedural style with some OOP concepts. ActionScript 1.0 makes it easy to program in this way by not forcing the rules of OOP on you, as some other languages, such as ActionScript 2.0, require. The procedural example shown earlier could easily benefit from some of the techniques shown in the sections about OOP. For example, the code could implement callback functions in a custom responder object or a broadcaster. Chapter 14 shows a complete Flash MX application that is built procedurally using OOP concepts.

ColdFusion RecordSets

ColdFusion programmers have a construct built into the *RecordSet* class on the client and server that can reduce the time it takes for the data to display. Chapter 5 went into detail about the technique of *RecordSet* paging. In many cases, this technique improves the apparent performance of your application; your users will see results on the screen even before the download of the entire recordset is complete. Improving the apparent performance of your application can often have as much of an impact on the end user as improving the actual performance of the application. Your user can judge the application only by what he sees.

Implementing Caching

Caching involves maintaining a piece of information in a store or cache to improve performance of an application. In Flash Remoting, you can create objects to hold the contents of a remote service call. This can be handy in many situations:

- An email program that retrieves email messages from a remote server, allowing you to read the messages by choosing a message header in a list. Upon moving to another message, the current message could be cached, so that if you were to return to that message, it would not have to be retrieved from the server again.

- A product listing that has master/detail pages of a product list. As you choose a product, the details page retrieves the product details from the remote server. Upon choosing another product, the current product is placed into a cache for easy access when the user returns to that product.

- A book review application, where a book review is retrieved from a remote service. As the user chooses another book, the current review is stored in a cache, in case the user returns to it. Each subsequent viewing of the book review comes from the cache rather than the remote service.

A cache is typically implemented as an object or an array of objects. Each object represents one item from the remote service. All items are not retrieved, but the cache is indexed in a way that each item that is placed in the cache can be easily retrieved, as in the following code snippet:

```
// Set up the custom object that holds the product information
MyCustomObject = function (productid, productname, productdesc) {
  this.ProductID = productid;
  this.ProductName = productname;
  this.ProductDesc = productdesc;
};

// Create the cache
var myCache = new Object();

// Set the first element of the cache as a new object with descriptive fields
// This can be displayed in the UI if there is no current product
myCache["0"] = new MyCustomObject(
          0,                      // ProductID
          "Product Name...",      // ProductName
          "Description...");      // ProductDesc

// findItem:  method for the cache array to find an
//            item with a ProductID that matches the specified item
function findItem (theArray, theItem) {
  for (i in theArray) {
    if (theArray[i].ProductID == theItem) {
     return true;
    }
  }
  return false;
}

// Change handler on a Tree component: user clicks an item, and the
//  corresponding detail page is populated
my_tree.setChangeHandler("displayProduct", _root);
displayProduct = function (tree) {
  var theNode = tree.getSelectedNode();
  var theProductId = theNode.data;
  if (findItem(myCache, theProductId)) {
      displayCacheItem(theProductId);
  } else {
      putProductInCacheAndDisplayIt(theProductId);
  }
};
```

The complete functionality of the preceding example is not implemented here, but similar functionality can be found in the application built in Chapter 14. When a user clicks an item in the Tree component, the *displayProduct( )* function fires off. We use a helper function, *findItem( )*, to pick the item out of the cache if the item exists. If so, the *displayCacheItem( )* function displays the item directly from the cache, rather than going to the remote service. If the item is not found, another function is called (*putProductInCacheAndDisplayIt( )*), which puts the current item into the cache before displaying it.

What to Walk Away With

I've isolated the sections in this chapter into 10 items that you should remember when building your Flash Remoting applications:

- Clearly separate the tasks for the application.
- Clearly separate and optimize the functionality between client, server, and database.
- Handle server downtime (lack of a connection) gracefully.
- Use components wisely.
- Maintain a clean API.
- Optimize your loops and other code blocks that are executed repeatedly.
- Use OOP or OOP concepts when possible.
- Use broadcasters or callback functions in your responder objects.
- Take advantage of incremental recordsets in ColdFusion.
- Cache objects from the server whenever possible—on the client using a cache object or on the server using cachedwithin in ColdFusion or whatever caching functionality is at your disposal.

Wrapping Up

In this chapter, you learned some new techniques that will improve your Flash Remoting application development. Following best practices in your applications can make both the time you spend coding and the time your user spends browsing much more productive. For more information on best coding practices, see the resources cited in Appendix B.

CHAPTER 13

Testing and Debugging

How often have you written an application or a Flash movie that worked as expected? Chances are, you have had to go through a thorough debugging process before finally reaching a point at which you could safely release the program into the world as a working application. Is the program bug-free? Probably not, but it is at a point where the usefulness of the functionality outweighs the number and severity of the bugs. This is the balance that most of us strive for in our software.

Testing and debugging are two completely separate processes, yet they are somehow intertwined throughout the application-building process. Generally, debugging occurs after the application is functional, but it is an integral part of the testing procedures throughout the development process. If everything worked right the first time, we wouldn't need to debug our programs. No program is bug-free, but the debugging process allows us to eliminate the bugs that are debilitating, the bugs that hamper the usefulness of the application, and the bugs that are just annoying.

Throughout this chapter, we will be using the *searchProducts.fla* example file from Chapter 3 as a reference point for the debugging discussion, as well as the *communitymx.fla* web service example from Chapter 10.

Debugging Flash Remoting Applications

Flash is a complex environment, and adding Flash Remoting to the equation only increases the complexity. You must contend not only with the visual aspects of your Flash movie and the underlying ActionScript, but also the server-side code, the database code, and the HTTP connections. There are quite a few pieces that make up the client/server environment of a Flash Remoting application, and quite a few places where your application can go wrong. Debugging a Flash Remoting application involves complex interaction between all of these environments, as well as the ability to separate the parts of the application so that they can be examined without the added burden of the sum of all the parts. Refer to the best practices offered in Chapter 12 for ways to isolate the various portions of your program to ease development and testing.

Types of Errors

Errors in any programming environment can be divided into several logical categories (although see "Error Types" in Chapter 3 for additional discussion of potential sources of errors):

Syntax errors

Errors caused by incorrect use of code. This could be a simple use of a programming construct in the wrong way, or using some programming construct that doesn't exist in ActionScript. These are usually caught at *compile time*. Previewing in Flash is considered compile time.

Typographical errors

Errors caused by simply mistyping a piece of code. Color coding is a big help in finding these types of errors; many times a misspelled keyword does not have the correct color coding on it, which is a dead giveaway that something is rotten. These errors are occasionally caught at compile time, but the more insidious ones can slip through if they are otherwise valid code.

Logical errors

Errors caused by improper logic in your code. These are often the insidious errors that don't cause a total failure of the application, but instead introduce errors in program results or introduce only occasional errors. Intermittent bugs are often the hardest to detect and solve. They are hard to detect because they happen only under certain conditions, which may be hard to reproduce. They are hard to solve because if you can't reliably reproduce a bug in the first place, you can't confirm that your fixes have solved the problem.

All of these errors can be tracked down through the debugging process. Many times, having someone else look at your code can help you more than hours spent debugging alone. The fresh set of eyes can spot a problem that you have missed or don't realize is a problem. You can use a coworker or post a problem piece of code to a support newsgroup or forum. Getting this far, however, means that you know where the problem lies. Many times, this is not the case.

Dissecting the Application

A Flash Remoting application flows through the following processes:

Flash client
  → ActionScript code
    → HTTP server
      → Application server
        → Flash Remoting gateway
          → Server-side code
            Database server
            Filesystem

Email system
Other server-side components
→ Server-side code
→ Application server
→ HTTP server
→ Flash Remoting gateway
→ ActionScript code
Flash client

A bug can occur in any of these areas, but to find the bug you have to know where to look and how to look for it. The Flash authoring environment provides many of the tools that will help you pinpoint a problem, but it is only the messenger; the error messages can help you determine where to look for the real problem.

Beginners often flounder with guesses and suppositions, while experienced developers rely on their debugging tools. For Flash Remoting applications, you can start you investigation with the NetConnection Debugger panel, as discussed in this chapter. Of course, to use any debugger effectively, you must have the foundational knowledge of the technology (which you should have after getting this far in the book) and you must have some knowledge of what component of the application performs a particular task. This might sound a bit simplistic, but people coming from Flash-only backgrounds often have trouble determining where a particular error is occurring, such as on the server. (This is doubly true if you are not the original developer of part or all of the application.) For example, a typical error message might look like this:

"Error connecting to Northwind"

What does it mean? The reason for the error could be, but is not limited to, one of the following:

- Bad username or password
- No database driver
- Wrong database driver
- Wrong format for connection string
- Bad server-side code calling the database
- No permission to access a database object, such as a table or stored procedure

Therefore, one of the keys to being able to pinpoint problems is knowing what does what. You must be able to track the logical progression of your code to determine where the error originates. As with most error messages, there are several different reasons why the error may be occurring. A little detective work may be involved:

- If your ActionScript code is passing anything to the database, you can start there.
- If not, look at your server-side code. The error could be a mistyped piece of code or connection string.

- You can also try logging on to your database directly and executing the code from there; many users log themselves on as an administrator when developing an application, only to find out that the permission levels they are using in an application are not working for all objects. Database servers like SQL Server allow you to set individual permission levels for each object. Make sure the permission levels are correct for the query you are running.

- If you are running a file-based database like Microsoft Access, make sure your web server has the appropriate permissions to access the database file.

All of these different error situations can be tracked down with a little bit of know-how and some digging. The Flash environment contains two debuggers to aid in this detective work—the Flash ActionScript interactive debugger and the NetConnection debugger. The ActionScript debugger is always available during authoring by choosing Ctrl → Debug Movie (or if you're already testing the movie, it's Window → Debugger). The NetConnection debugger is used for Flash Remoting. To activate the NetConnection debugger during authoring, include the *NetDebug.as* file in your Flash movie. This allows the NetConnection Debugger panel to become active and report problems as they arrive from the server.

Consistency

One of the best ways to avoid extensive debugging periods is to write your code with consistency. This includes such things as coding styles and conventions, variable naming conventions, comments and documentation, and readability. The important thing is not which convention you decide on, but that you stick to a convention. For example, some people prefer to format their loops like this:

```
for (i=0; i < 10; i++)
{
  print("something");
}
```

This is a perfectly acceptable convention, as is this (which we use in this book to save vertical space):

```
for (i=0; i < 10; i++) {
  print("something");
}
```

I find that the second approach makes it easier to spot bugs like this, in which the semicolon ends the *for* loop unintentionally:

```
for (i=0; i < 10; i++); {
  print("something");
}
```

I find such bugs harder to spot when code is formatted like this:

```
for (i=0; i < 10; i++);
{
```

```
    print("something");
  }
```

Consistency in variable naming is also important to debugging. If you have a convention of capitalizing the first letter in each word (except the first word), don't deviate from that in your code:

```
myFirstName = "Tom";
myLastName = "Muck";
myZIP = "22193";
```

The last variable does not follow my capitalization convention, so I might be prone to write it like this elsewhere in the code:

```
myZip = "22193";
```

In ActionScript 1.0 (when played in Flash Player 6), the case difference does not matter (at least with regard to variable names), and myZIP and myZip refer to the same variable. In other languages, like ActionScript 2.0, Server-Side ActionScript, ECMA-Script, Java, or C#, myZIP and myZip refer to different variables, which could be difficult to debug. ActionScript 1.0 is also strictly case-sensitive when developed in Flash 2004 or Flash Pro and exported in Flash Player 7 format. See Reference Guide → ActionScript Basics → Syntax → Case Sensitivity in the Flash 2004 and Flash Pro Help window for details.

Spacing is another key issue in writing code. Whitespace is in many ways just as important as the actual code; without whitespace, your code is unreadable. Consider this query:

```
SELECT c.CustomerID, c.CompanyName, c.ContactName FROM Customers c INNER JOIN Orders
o ON c.CustomerID = o.CustomerID INNER JOIN [Order Details] od ON o.OrderID = od.
OrderID WHERE c.Country = 'USA' GROUP BY c.CustomerID, c.CompanyName, c.ContactName
HAVING count(o.orderid) > 5
```

It's not very pretty, and it's not easy to spot where the bug is, or even if there is a bug. The query is supposed to retrieve all customers from the USA having at least five items in their order. When you run the query on the *Northwind* database, you get about 12 results. After reformatting the query with whitespace for readability, you spot the error more easily:

```
SELECT
  c.CustomerID
, c.CompanyName
, c.ContactName
FROM Customers c
  INNER JOIN Orders o
    ON
      c.CustomerID = o.CustomerID
  INNER JOIN [Order Details] od
    ON
      o.OrderID = od.OrderID
WHERE c.Country = 'USA'
GROUP BY
  c.CustomerID
```

```
, c.CompanyName
, c.ContactName

HAVING count(o.OrderID) > 5
```

The query should have been written with the `OrderID` column listed in the `GROUP BY` clause, as shown in bold (the initial portion of the query remains the same):

```
WHERE c.Country = 'USA'
GROUP BY
  o.OrderID
, c.CustomerID
, c.CompanyName
, c.ContactName

HAVING count(o.OrderID) > 5
```

Now the query returns three results, which is correct. Queries are much easier to debug when you write them clearly with whitespace. The first query might have taken a long time to debug, yet I have seen plenty of cases where people write their queries like this.

Commenting your code is extremely important as well. Sometimes, a well-placed comment can alert you to a bug in the code that you would normally not spot immediately. If the preceding query had included the following comment, containing the word "order," a trained developer would realize the order ID was missing from the `GROUP BY` clause:

```
-- Get all US orders that have more than 5 items
```

Feature Creep

Why is feature creep being discussed in a chapter about debugging and testing? Most projects have a plan in place that specifies exactly what the application will do and how it will do it. Feature creep happens when you don't stick to the plan. During the debugging and testing phase, adding a new feature increases the likelihood of new bugs being introduced into the application, causing delays in the entire process. For this reason it is usually best to note the new features and implement them in the next version of your software, rather than try to get them into the current version.

Trapping Errors

Error handling and error trapping are big parts of debugging. After all, a *bug* is a programming error that hasn't been fixed or can't be fixed. But not all errors are bugs. An error may simply reflect an operational condition, such as an attempt to divide by zero. The error is not in the programming logic, but in the data. An error message is a developer's way of saying "This is a condition that we couldn't prevent, but this is what happened and this is what you should do." It is the responsibility of the developer to fix errors caused by bugs and to handle errors caused by bad data or adverse runtime conditions (such as a loss of the connection).

try/catch Blocks

The *try/catch* construct gives server-side service developers an easy way to trap errors where they occur. (See "Handling Errors with try/catch" in Chapter 6, which covers Server-Side ActionScript; "Error Handling in Flash Remoting with .NET" in Chapter 8; or the related ColdFusion tags, `<cftry>` and `<cfcatch>`, in Chapter 5.)

 Remember, client-side ActionScript does not support *try/catch* constructs, so you should be diligent in handling possible error conditions in your Flash application.

To reiterate, the server-side *try/catch* construct works like this: the *try* block contains the code for which you want to trap any errors as it executes. You are saying "try to execute this code." If an error occurs, the *catch* block is executed. It can take whatever action is necessary to handle the error condition. For example, if the application is inserting data into a database, this might be as simple as not doing the insert. If the application is accessing a file, the *catch* block may have to close the open file and perform cleanup. Often, the *catch* block just passes an error message back to the user.

The main point of the *catch* block is that the application code handles the error, rather than allowing the language interpreter to throw an exception. Your code should handle errors in a way that allows the user to continue to work; otherwise, it should present an error message that makes sense to the user.

Some forms of *try/catch* blocks also have an optional *finally* block, which contains code to be executed whether or not an error occurs.

This is how it might look in practice:

```
function myFunction ( ) {
  try {
    // Do something here.
    // If there is an error, proceed to the catch block.
  } catch (e) {
    // Close files, do some cleanup, send an error message to the user, etc.
  } finally {
    // In either case, do this.
    return;
  }
}
```

The Flash Remoting adapter on the server also traps errors that can be handled in your client-side ActionScript.

The Flash Remoting adapter is, in effect, a large *try/catch* block around all of your server-side services. It handles any errors not handled by the server-side code. An error that occurs in a service on the server causes an *onStatus* event, rather than the *onResult* event, to be returned to your Flash movie.

You can implement an error-handling strategy that uses the best of both techniques: handling server errors from your ActionScript within the *onStatus( )* methods of the calls to the service. You can accomplish this with the *throw* construct, which allows you to generate custom errors. The benefit is that you can trap the actual error, perform your cleanup, and then throw a custom error message back to the Flash movie. The technique of throwing custom errors is shown throughout the examples in Chapters 5, 6, 7, and 8.

The Flash ActionScript Debugger

Debuggers have been around in other programming environments for years, but it is a necessary tool and a welcome addition to the Flash environment. We cover the Flash debugger only briefly, as it has been covered in depth elsewhere. The Flash debugger allows you to set up interactive debugging within the Flash movie. This allows you to interact with the code as it is executing—examining variables and stepping through the lines of code one by one to help you determine where a problem might exist. The debugger can also be used with a remote movie located on a web server. The movie will be retrieved and debugged locally in the Flash Player. More information on remote debugging can be found in the Flash online Help system under Help → Using Flash → Testing a Movie → Using the Debugger.

Using the Debugger

The Debugger panel becomes active when you choose Control → Debug Movie (Ctrl-Shift-Enter on Windows or Cmd-Shift-Enter on Macintosh). This effectively starts the movie in debug mode, allowing you to view the execution of code. The movie starts with the Debugger panel open at the first line of your script to await instructions, as shown in Figure 13-1.

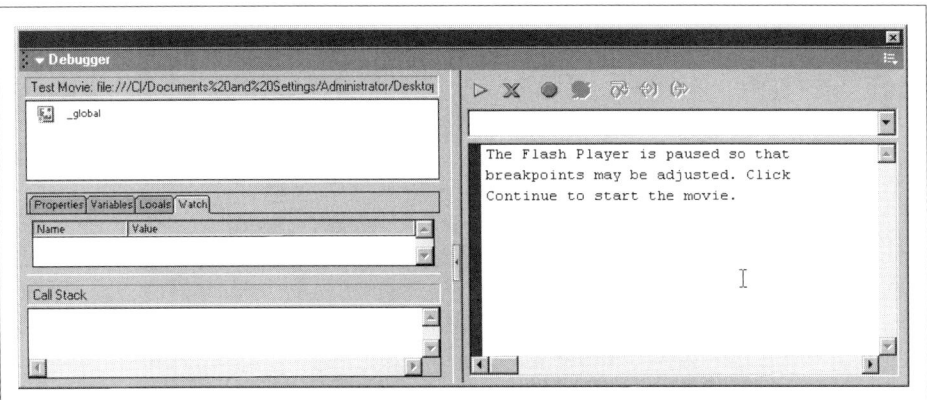

Figure 13-1. The interactive debugger of Flash MX

Having chosen the Debug Movie option, the first thing you'll need to do is to set up a breakpoint. Breakpoints make the code execution "stop here."

 The ActionScript interpreter executes the code up to the breakpoint and stops on the line that the breakpoint is on, *before* executing the line. Variables set on the current line won't update until you step past the line of code. Performing only one command per line (such as breaking *if* statements onto at least two lines) makes it easier to see which lines are executed and which are being skipped.

At that point in the code, you can examine any variables that are in use. It gives you a snapshot of your code, with live values for variables in that code. You are also able to step through your code line by line, examining the code execution and variable contents as you go.

You can set a breakpoint anywhere in your ActionScript code. You can navigate through the different sections of code in the debugger by using the code navigator drop-down box above the code window. You'll find that even simple movies have many areas of code that are superfluous to the debugging operation—built-in areas of Flash MX that you have no control over. You'll want to put your breakpoints into scripts that you have coded or areas that you want to track with the debugger. A good place to start for a Flash Remoting application is the main initialization script on the main timeline. In the examples for this book, the code can usually be found in the code navigator of the debugger as "Actions for Scene 1 Frame 1 for Layer named actions."

To set a breakpoint, click the Toggle Breakpoint button on the debugger control bar, or use the contextual menu in Code View on the debugger and choose Set Breakpoint. After setting the breakpoint, you can click the Continue button on the debugger to allow the movie to execute up to the breakpoint. That's where the fun begins. Once at the breakpoint, the movie stops again and allows you to interact with your code.

The Properties and Variables windows (accessed via tabs in the center pane on the left side as shown in Figure 13-2) give you editable lists of all properties and variables in a selected movie clip. The Watch and Locals windows (accessed via tabs in same pane) are more useful from a Flash Remoting perspective.

The Watch window

The Watch window allows you to examine certain variables of your own choosing. For example, if I want to determine the contents of my `results_rs` variable inside the *getSearchResult_Result( )* function, I add the `result_rs` variable to the Watch window. The variable shows as *undefined* until it comes into scope, at which point the variable's value is displayed in the Watch window.

The Locals window

The Locals window displays all local variables as they come into scope. It provides immediate feedback about relevant local variables, without requiring manual setup, as the Watch window does. For example, Figure 13-2 shows the Locals window when the debugger is paused at the *getSearchResult_Result( )* function. The nice thing about the debugger is that you have access to all properties of your Action-Script objects. The `result_rs` variable is a complex *RecordSet* object, and you can easily see the different properties of the object in the display, allowing you to determine if your script is retrieving the correct results or if your *RecordSet* object has the correct structure.

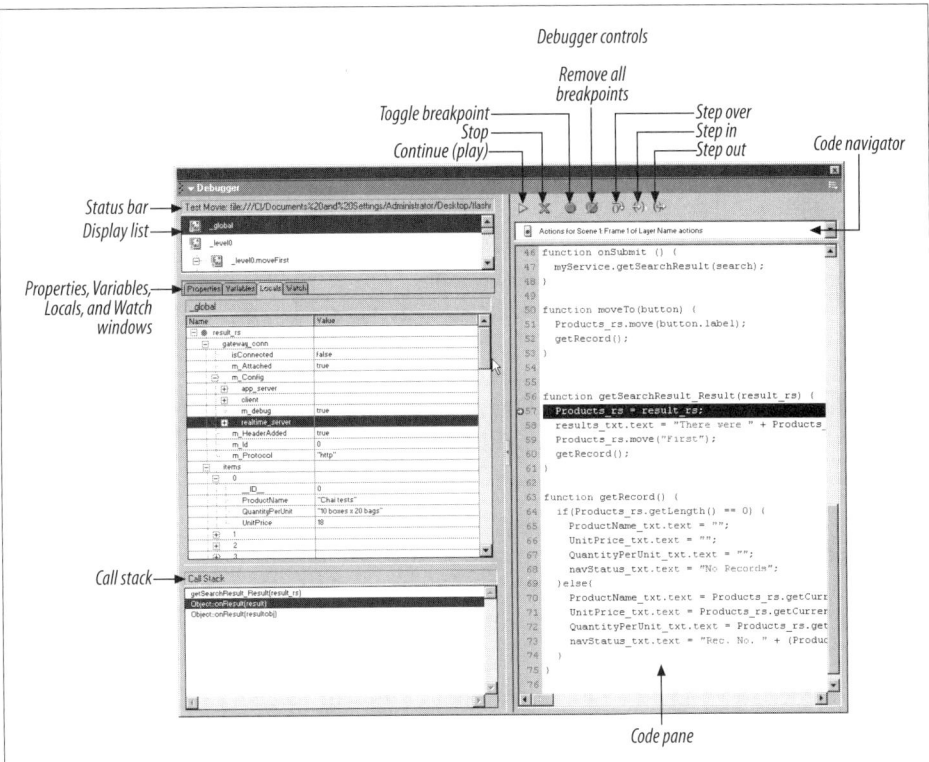

Figure 13-2. The Flash interactive debugger

Variables can also be modified from the debugger in any of these windows. Using this feature allows you to set different values to test different situations that might not be possible if you were relying only on values coming from a database, for example. What exactly would happen to your movie if a certain field contained a negative number? Using the debugger, you can test different situations such as these easily.

The Call Stack

The Call Stack gives you information about all functions that were called up to the current function. If you are debugging at the main timeline, the Call Stack will be empty. As you call functions, the Call Stack displays the function names in the stack. Functions called from within functions will appear in the Call Stack. Note that only user-defined functions show up in the Call Stack.

A Debugging Session

To fully appreciate the Flash interactive debugger, you need to use it. If you haven't tried it before, you can get your feet wet with it now. This section goes through a typical interactive debugging session using the *searchProducts.fla* file from Example 3-8. This section assumes that you have the sample file working and results successfully coming from the server. This exercise also allows you to see the order of execution of a typical Flash Remoting application.

 For this exercise, it is important that the *NetDebug.as* file is not included in the sample movie. The *NetDebug.as* file is required to use the NetConnection debugger to debug server-side service interaction, but it only adds unnecessary complexity to your client-side debugging with the Flash interactive debugger. Comment out the line #include "NetDebug.as" if you've previously included it.

Open the *searchProducts.fla* file and choose Ctrl → Debug Movie to begin a debugging session. Refer to Figure 13-2 for the location of the various controls within the Debugger panel. We'll set one breakpoint and then step through the code line by line:

1. Expand the Debugger panel so that it is large enough to examine the code easily. Move the vertical splitter in the center of the Debugger panel to the right to enlarge the left pane somewhat, but leave room for the Code pane on the right side.

2. Select the Locals tab in the center pane on the left. Expand the center pane by dragging the horizontal splitter downward.

3. Use the Code Navigator drop-down list to access "Actions for Scene 1:Frame 1 of Layer named actions."

4. Insert a breakpoint by clicking the Toggle Breakpoint button while the first executable line of code is highlighted:

    ```
    if (connected == null) {
    ```

5. Hit the Continue/Play button (green arrow) to begin debugging. The code should stop at your breakpoint.

6. Notice that the Locals window has a single entry, this, which represents the current timeline object. Expand the tree under it to show all associated properties.

7. Click the Step Over button once (it is the leftmost of the three stepping buttons), which takes you to the next line of code. The Locals window hasn't changed yet, because the code in the current line has not executed yet.

8. Click the Step Over button again, and the Locals window should change at this point. Now, the variable connected should have a value of true, as shown in Figure 13-3.

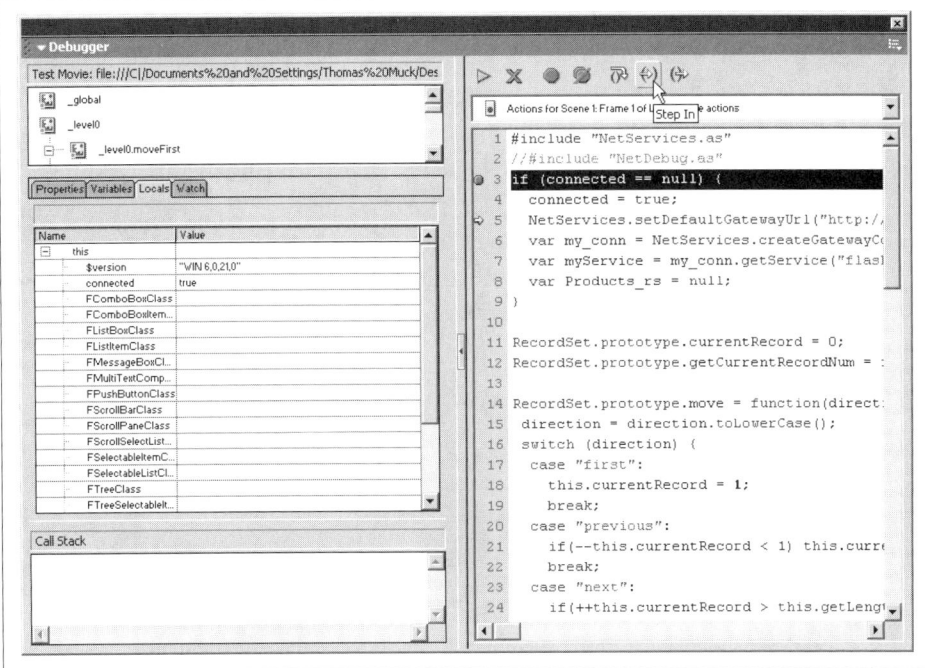

Figure 13-3. Stepping through code and examining variables

9. Click the Step In button (instead of the Step Over button), and the Code pane should show the *NetServices.as* file; this is where the *setDefaultGatewayUrl( )* method is being called. The Step In button "dives down" into any subroutine called on the current line (keep your eye on the Call Stack pane to see where you are in the code). The Locals window once again changes, but now the local variable this points to the *NetServices* object.

10. Keep clicking the Step In button slowly and keep track of where you are in the Code pane using the Call Stack pane for guidance. You should be stepping through the *createGatewayConnection( )* method, eventually ending up at this line:

```
var nc = new NetConnection( );
```

This is where the *NetConnection* object is created. You can see that at this point the URL is set up for the connection, but no connection has been made to the server yet. In fact, as you complete the *createGatewayConnection( )* method, the debugger will automatically step back (out) into the main timeline. There you will see that the my_conn variable is now populated with an isConnected property with the value false.

11. Step through the *getService( )* method next. You'll see from this section that you are creating a proxy to the service but still not connecting. As you step back to the main timeline, you now have the myService object created. The my_conn object still has the isConnected property set to false.

12. The rest of the inline code can now be stepped through quickly until the step buttons become grayed out.

13. Flash is *event-driven;* the movie is waiting for user interaction and your script is awaiting an event. Click the Submit button in the movie to continue the debugging.

14. If you've been single-stepping through the code, when you click the Submit button the debugger takes you inside the *onSubmit( )* function. If you look at the Call Stack window, you'll see that the *onSubmit( )* function was executed after *MovieClip::onRelease( )* and *MovieClip::executeCallBack( )*. This gives you some insight into the inner workings of Flash; the click handler function is actually executed in the *onRelease* event of the button.

15. If you are stepping through the code line by line, it might take a while to get through all the lines of code. Navigate to the *getSearchResult_Result( )* function using the Code pane and set a breakpoint there.

 While debugging, many of your interface elements won't work until the code that sets them up is executed. The Step Over button hastens stepping by executing the current line immediately, rather than stepping into any functions it calls line by line (as the Step In button does). The Step Out button immediately finishes the current function and continues step-debugging in the function that invoked it. Click the Continue/Play (a.k.a. Go) button to execute the code at full speed to the next breakpoint. Using the Go button requires that you set breakpoints in places where the code will be reached. Your understanding of Flash Remoting's event handling will help you anticipate which code will be executed next. You can always set multiple breakpoints and wait for any of them to be reached. If you've set them in the wrong place, the movie will simply run without activating the debugger.

Click the Go button, and the debugger should stop at the breakpoint set in *getSearchResult_Result( )*. (If not, there may have been an error, and you should set a breakpoint in *getSearchResult_Status( )* to examine that code.) Once inside *getSearchResult_Result( )*, the Locals window should contain the *RecordSet* object named result_rs, and you can examine its properties. You may recall that in Chapter 3 we enhanced the *RecordSet* object to include a currentRecord property, which should appear in the debugger, along with the fields and built-in properties of the recordset.

To demonstrate the usefulness of the Locals window, modify the `currentRecord` property by changing its value to 20 (simply edit the number in the Value column of the Locals window). As you step through your code, the movie should display the 20th record instead of the first record.

Unfortunately, the Flash MX Interactive Debugger doesn't remember your breakpoints between sessions. The next time you start the debugger, you will have to set any breakpoints again.

The Flash interactive debugger is useful for checking the client-side ActionScript code, including Flash Remoting code, as well as examining return objects and values from a remote service. The NetConnection debugger, on the other hand, gives you solid feedback on the Remoting process itself.

NetConnection Debugger

The NetConnection Debugger panel is a Flash movie itself. It is implemented as a Flash panel extension to Flash MX and is installed when you install the Flash Remoting components. The NetConnection debugger reports all connections, input, and output from the Flash movie to the server. Any arguments sent to the movie are exposed in the panel, and any response from the server is shown as well. This includes all error messages from the server.

The NetConnection debugger is available only during authoring time. Errors that occur in the application after the movie has been compiled and deployed will not be reported. It is up to you as the author of the Flash application to address the errors during authoring time so that the end user experience is without error.

The NetConnection Debugger panel must be opened from the Window menu in Flash before testing the movie for it to become active. To invoke it, open the NetConnection Debugger panel and choose Control → Test Movie. The Control → Debug Movie option invokes the Flash interactive debugger, not the NetConnection debugger, although the latter will also be active if it was previously open. Be sure to include the line `#include "NetDebug.as"` in your code if you've previously omitted it.

Parts of the Debugger

The NetConnection debugger, shown in Figure 13-4, consists of three panels in the main section of the debugger and two smaller panels below. The three main panels are:

Events
> Shows the client/server event that occurs, along with an icon representing the type of event (such as a Flash icon for an event from Flash), the event name, and brief summary of information about the event.

Summary

> Allows you to drill down from the Events panel to display a summary of a particular event, which usually includes the request and response information.

Details

> Allows you to drill down even farther to get more specific details about an event, including some header information.

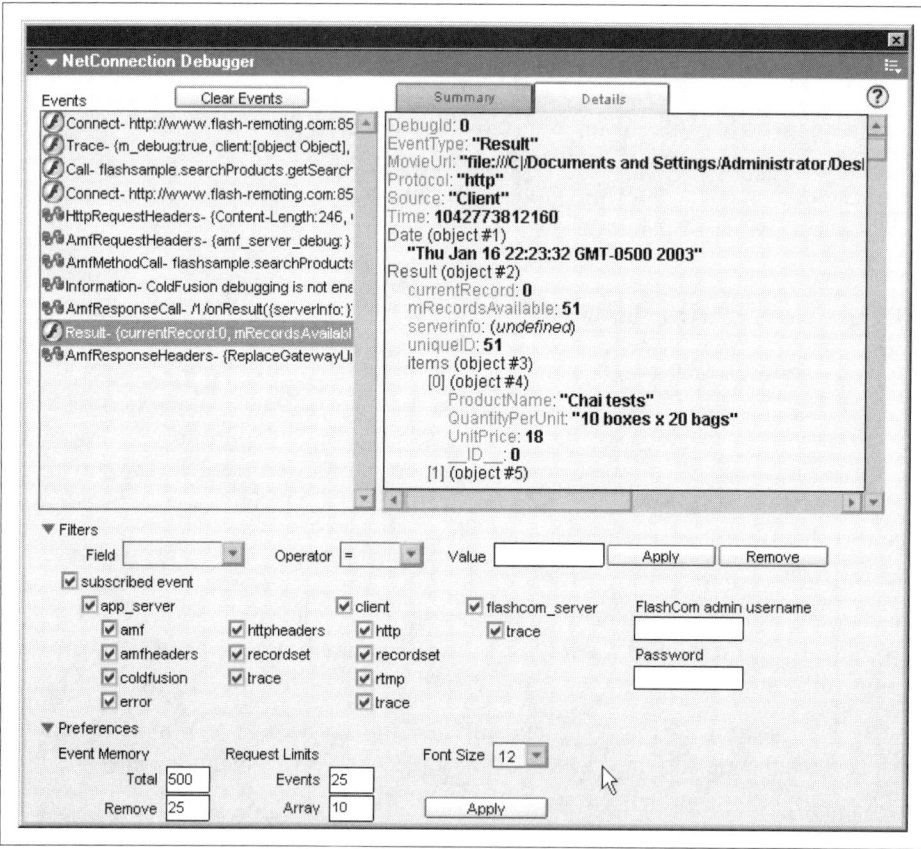

Figure 13-4. The NetConnection debugger for Flash Remoting

All events that occur between the client and the server are shown in this panel. A typical session consists of the following:

- A connection to the Flash Remoting gateway
- A call to a remote method
- The HTTP request headers
- The AMF request headers
- The AMF method call

- The AMF response upon a successful method call, or the AMF status upon failure
- The onResult or onStatus event
- The AMF response headers

All of this information is displayed in a formatted fashion in the NetConnection debugger. In addition, you can create your own events to display by using the methods of the NetDebug API, which will be discussed shortly.

If you are passing complex ActionScript objects to the server, the NetConnection debugger displays the object and its properties. Likewise, complex objects or recordsets returned from the server are also displayed in their entirety. If remote methods aren't returning the expected results, you can see exactly what is coming back from the server to help track down any errors in your code.

The bottom section of the NetConnection debugger contains the Filters and Preferences panes. The Filters pane allows you to set filters, which are used to limit the information that is displayed. By default, all events are subscribed to, but you can uncheck the events that you don't want to display. In most situations, the filter is not needed, but if you are calling many methods you may want to suppress some of the output.

The Preferences pane allows you to specify the number of events to display before old events are discarded. In addition, you can limit the length of arrays that will be displayed. Remember, the NetConnection Debugger panel is a Flash panel, so it is subject to the limitations of Flash. Large amounts of data will tend to drag down performance, so the panel defaults to displaying a maximum of 10 array elements, 25 events, and 500 total lines. The font size can also be adjusted.

To debug Flash Communication Server (FlashCom) applications, a username and password can be supplied. For more information on FlashCom, see *http://www.macromedia.com/desdev/mx/flashcom*.

Using the NetConnection Debugger

The following line adds the classes required to use the NetConnection debugger:

```
#include "NetDebug.as"
```

Simply add the preceding line to your Flash movie, and open the NetConnection Debugger panel using Window → NetConnection Debugger. If you commented out the #include statement during the earlier example using the Flash interactive debugger, uncomment it now to reactivate NetConnection debugging. For a ColdFusion Server, more debugging information is available if you turn on debugging in the ColdFusion Administrator. To do so, you need to know the IP address of the client machine where your Flash authoring environment is running from. If you are using a local ColdFusion Server, this is usually at the localhost IP address of 127.0.0.1. Figure 13-5 shows the debugging IP address settings of the ColdFusion Administrator.

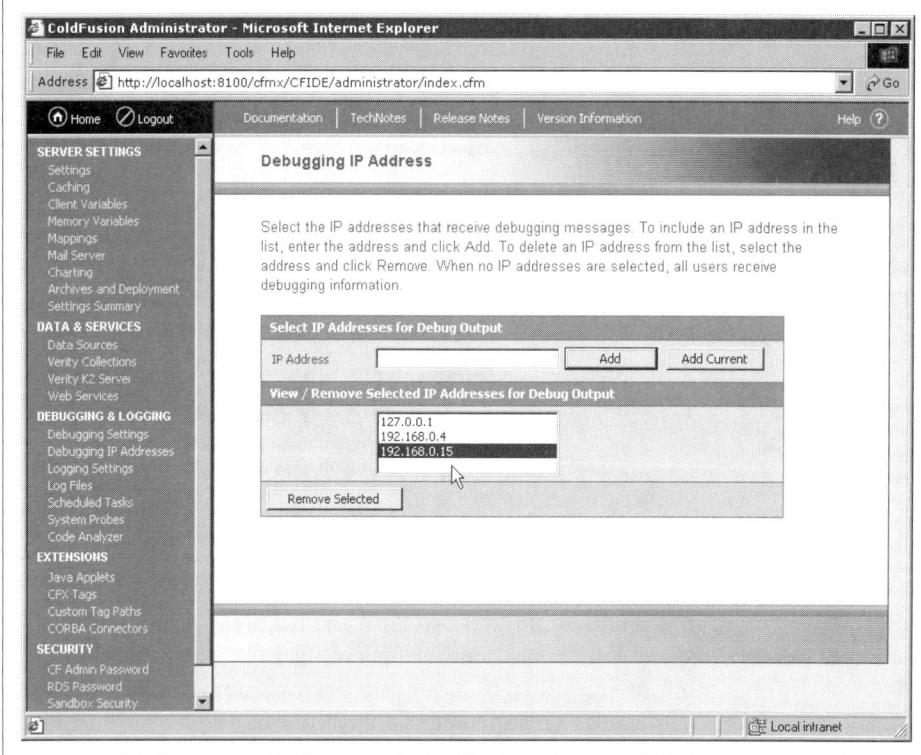

Figure 13-5. Setting up debugging IP addresses in the ColdFusion Administrator

We will go through a typical debugging session by testing a Flash Remoting application that was developed in an earlier chapter. A few key errors can be introduced so that you can see what effect they have on the debugging information presented in the NetConnection debugger.

Debugging a connection

The connection to the Flash Remoting adapter is one of the first things you might have to debug. If the connection to the adapter fails, you are dead in the water. This is also one of the areas that is not covered by the debugger. If the connection fails and you don't have error-handling code in your Flash movie, the movie will just appear to freeze and the NetConnection debugger will not show anything wrong.

The physical connection to Flash Remoting is not actually made until you call a remote method of your service. Only then can you track an error in the connection. Connection errors do not occur when the *NetConnection* object is instantiated, as you saw in the "A Debugging Session" exercise using the Flash interactive debugger earlier in the chapter. Errors also don't occur when the service is set up in your Flash movie.

Connection errors can be trapped in one of three locations:

- `_global.System.onStatus` event handler
- `NetConnection.onStatus` event handler
- `Your_connection.onStatus` event handler

A bad connection usually means that the URL is bad. It can also mean that a server is down temporarily. You can handle errors like these in one of the events shown previously, usually with a message box to the user or by redirecting the user to an error page. A typical *onStatus( )* method might look like this:

```
my_conn.onStatus = function (error) {
  _root.getURL("http://localhost/myConnectionErrorPage.html");
}
```

Try debugging the connection in *searchProducts.fla* by using this code. First, try the code with a working connection; then, stop the movie and change the URL to a non-existent URL. Try the movie again. You'll find that the *onStatus* event is triggered when you make the call to the service.

You can also check the URL of the Flash Remoting adapter from a browser. If you type the URL in a browser, you should see a blank page if the adapter is working at that URL. Connection errors can be more difficult to track down if they are sporadic. In such cases, there is little you can do other than trap the error and give the user a message or an alternative.

Debugging method calls

Each remote method call in your Flash Remoting application should have its own error-handling code. The *onStatus( )* handler for the method call can give you some information about an error, but in the debugging phase of application development you should use the NetConnection debugger to get more information about the errors. The debugger shows a full stack trace (a list of the functions or methods that are called) from the server, which can be extremely useful in tracking an error.

Debugging helps track logical or intermittent errors, as well as the more obvious connection errors. An application can seem to work fine but deliver erroneous results in certain situations. In these cases, the NetConnection debugger can help you to pinpoint the problems by showing all raw results as they come from the server. As you build your application, you should document exactly what each method does, what it requires, and what it returns. If something deviates from your plan, you can address it when debugging.

 Debugging is the systematic challenging of your assumptions. Instead of assuming something is working correctly, verify its operation by manually inspecting the information provided in the debugger. If something isn't working as expected, the problem often started earlier in your code. Examine the arguments submitted to each remote method call and the results passed back. Keep working backward in your application until you find where the errors originated. Depending on the point in your application at which failure occurs, it might be easier to start at the beginning and verify each step as you move forward than to follow the logic backward from the end.

Validating user data

Applications that depend on user-supplied data are frequently the hardest types of applications to debug, because you never know what a user might attempt to do with the application or when malicious users might prey on your application. Making the application bullet-proof to user input is one aspect of debugging. Sometimes, the best way to debug an application that requires user-supplied data is to test the application with various users, including users who don't know what they are doing. Ideally, you'll have a mix of skilled beta testers, clueless newbies, and some average users in between. If they can all use your application without errors, you are usually in good shape. Needless to say, validating all user-supplied data is essential.

Validation on the Flash client using ActionScript should be used only as a first line of defense against bad data. Your server methods should each contain validation routines to guard against bad user data or malicious attack as well.

System errors

Using the *onStatus* event of the connection object will trap connection errors, and *onStatus* events of your methods will trap errors in the methods, but there can be other types of general system errors that don't fall into these two categories. For example, this general error message occurred on an ASP.NET example and was not trapped by a connection error handler or a method error handler:

"Object reference not set to an instance of an object."

For this type of error, you can fall back on the generic system error trapping:

```
_global.System.onStatus = function(error) {
  _root.getURL("http://localhost/mySystemErrorPage.html");
}
```

Attempting to invoke a method that doesn't exist will throw a general system error.

NetDebug.as

The *NetDebug.as* file is not a required part of Flash Remoting, but it is required if you want to use the NetConnection debugger. The file can be included in your movie during debugging but should be removed from the code before deployment, as it adds considerable weight to the final movie.

If your application is complex, you can include a dummy *MyDebugFile.as* file in each of your *.fla* files as follows:

```
#include "MyDebugFile.as"
```

This dummy *MyDebugFile.as* file should contain one line:

```
// #include "NetDebug.as"
```

If the line is commented out (as indicated by the prepended slashes), the *NetDebug.as* file is not included. If you uncomment the line, the *NetDebug.as* file is included. This technique circumvents the lack of a conditional #include in ActionScript. It makes it easier to activate and deactivate NetConnection debugging in a single place, without the need to edit multiple *.fla* files.

By including the *NetDebug.as* file, you are also including the following files:

> *NetDebugHelpers.as*
> *NetDebugConfig.as*
> *NetDebugEvents.as*
> *NetDebugNetConnection.as*
> *NetDebugLocalConnection.as*
> *NetDebugImpl.as*

These files form the code base for the NetConnection debugger and the *NetDebug* class that you can utilize for debugging.

The *NetDebug* class exposes these methods, which can be called from an instance of the *NetConnection* object:

trace( )
> Displays an object to the NetConnection Debugger panel. This can be any ActionScript object.

getDebugConfig( )
> Gets the configuration object of *NetDebug* (*NetDebugConfig*).

getDebugID( )
> Gets the debugging identifier of the *NetConnection* object. This is an arbitrary number that can be changed by the developer.

setDebugID( )
> Set the internal debug ID of the *NetConnection* object, which can be useful for debugging multiple connections

The methods are called from the local connection object you've defined:

```
NetServices.setDefaultGatewayURL(myURL);
var my_conn = NetServices.createGatewayConnection();
var myService = myConnection_conn.getService(servicePath);
my_conn.trace(my_conn.getDebugConfig());
```

In the last line, the *NetConnection.trace( )* method is being used to trace (i.e., display the contents of) the *NetDebugConfig* object to the NetConnection debugger. The output looks something like Figure 13-6.

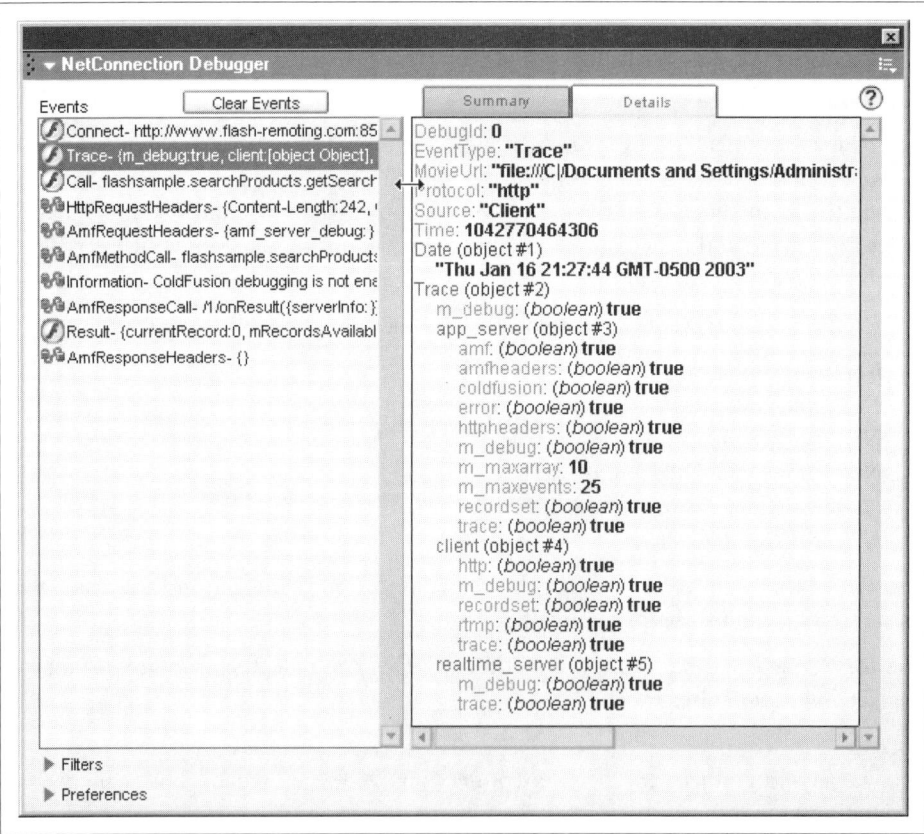

Figure 13-6. The NetConnection debugger showing the object returned by getDebugConfig( )

Trace Debugging

Trace debugging is sometimes the most useful way of debugging your applications, because it is quick to implement and offers immediate feedback. The Output window (a.k.a. *trace window*) in Flash's authoring environment provides instant feedback when you test a movie. By simply adding a *trace( )* statement to your movie, you are effectively adding debugging code.

In its simplest form, trace debugging involves tracing a value to the Output window:

```
trace(myVariable);
```

As you become more organized in your debugging and testing procedures, you will add more information so that the output is more readable and useful:

```
trace("myVariable: " + myVariable + " in function myFunction( )");
```

If your movie is complex and there are areas that demand constant debugging, you can put a debug flag in your script as a local variable and uncomment it when you want to debug:

```
// var myDebugFlag=true;
var myDebugFlag=false;
```

You can then sprinkle your code with *trace( )* statements. This one simply tells you that a particular function, *getSearchResult_Result( )*, was reached without requiring you to set a breakpoint in the debugger to verify it:

```
if (myDebugFlag) trace("debugging getSearchResult_Result( )");
```

This technique works well for routines called so frequently that it would be impractical to use a breakpoint, which would repeatedly stop the movie in the debugger. On the other hand, if frequently called routines display too much trace information, it becomes difficult to find other information in the Output window.

You can create some pretty complex and useful debugging tools using *trace( )*. For example, you can set up a more sophisticated trace-debugging system using a wrapper routine that accepts a priority number as a parameter:

```
function traceDebug (message, priority) {
  if (priority <= 3) {
    trace(message);
  }
}
```

and call it like this:

```
traceDebug("This is a priority 1 debugging message", 1);
traceDebug("This is a low-priority message", 5);
```

By adjusting the *if* statement in the *traceDebug( )* function or the priority of messages sent to it, you can display certain debugging messages while omitting others (or even suppress all messages).

Chapter 4 showed a client-side *RecordSetDebug.as* file that added custom methods to help debug your *RecordSet* objects on the client. The principles behind this class were based on trace debugging—building custom strings that contained descriptions and property values:

```
Recordset.prototype.showData = function () {
  var fields = this.getColumnNames();
  var i,j,tempfield="",temprow="",temprec="";
  trace("--Recordset Properties--");
```

```
    trace("Recordset length: " + this.getLength( ));
    trace("Fields: " + fields);
    trace("Begin records...");
    for (var i = 0; i<this.getLength( ); i++) {
      temprec = this.getItemAt(i);
      for (var j=0; j < fields.length; j++) {
        tempfield = fields[j];
        temprow += tempfield + ': "' + temprec[tempfield] + '"; ';
      }
      trace(temprow);
      temprow="";
    }
    trace("End records...");
    trace("--End Recordset Properties--");
  }
```

This code displays object properties in a way that is readable by you. By concatenating the descriptions of the properties with their values, you insure that the values in the properties are clearly labeled.

The Output window shows warnings and errors by default, but you can set the debug level to Verbose, which gives more detail in some situations. To do so, click on the Options menu in the upper-right corner of the Output window and choose the Debug Level option. Here, you will find the choices of None, Errors, Warnings, and Verbose.

There are built-in trace-debugging features that you should be aware of as well. While debugging your movie (Control → Debug Movie), the Debug menu contains two entries: List Variables and List Objects. These commands dump the current values of variables and objects in a hierarchical fashion to the Output window.

The *trace( )* statements have no effect in the final movie; they are displayed only in the authoring environment's Output window. However, it is best to disable them when publishing your movie, by using the Omit Trace Actions option under File → Publish Settings.

Trace debugging gives you a viable alternative to using a full-blown debugger, and it is often much quicker to get immediate feedback to a problem. Still, using the debugger will become more comfortable with time, and before long you'll wonder how you got along using only *trace( )* statements. The interactive debugger and *trace( )* statements are complementary tools, and you'd be well served to make use of them both as the situation demands.

Testing Server-Side Code

Your server-side code should be tested and debugged in isolation, by using your own server-side pages that you've set up for debugging purposes only—taking Flash and Flash Remoting completely out of the equation. You should be able to call your server-side methods from a basic page that contains calls to your remote methods

---

using test data. By doing this, the server-side logic can be verified (and debugged, if necessary) in a much more logical and structured manner. One of the advantages of using Flash Remoting is that you can separate your business logic from your presentation logic. The server-side methods can be viewed as if they were modules in your overall application. Debugging modules individually can often be more productive than trying to look at the whole picture. Let's look at some of the debugging tools available in the major server environments supported by Flash Remoting. This is not an exhaustive list, as you can use many different server-side development environments and each will have its own debugging tools.

Debugging in ColdFusion

ColdFusion MX allows debugging information to be displayed, including the following information:

- Execution times
- Database activity
- Exception information
- Variables (Application, CGI, Client, Cookie, Form, Request, Server, Session, and URL)

Debugging must be turned on from the ColdFusion Administrator, as shown in Figure 13-5. There are two modes of debugging: Classic and Dockable. The Classic mode of debugging simply lists the information at the bottom of the page when you execute a ColdFusion page. The Dockable style opens a separate window with the debugging information contained in a handy tree. The panel can also be docked with your page, as shown in Figure 13-7.

Flash Remoting allows you to work with ColdFusion Components (CFCs) from within Flash. As an example, look at the *searchProducts.fla* file that we've been examining in this chapter. The service that it calls is a CFC named *searchProducts.cfc*. ColdFusion Components can also be called from regular ColdFusion pages that use HTML for user interaction. This can be very helpful when debugging your Flash Remoting applications, because it allows you to verify your server-side code separate from your client-side code.

The best environment for building ColdFusion pages that utilize CFCs is Dreamweaver MX, which is part of Studio MX. Building a sample page that uses the *searchProducts.cfc* can be done in five simple steps:

1. Set up a sample site in Dreamweaver (using the Site → New Site option). Consult the Dreamweaver documentation for details on how to set up sites. Be sure to specify the server model as ColdFusion. If the site is set up correctly, Dreamweaver's Components panel will be populated with all the CFCs on your server.

2. Create a test page with a *.cfm* extension.

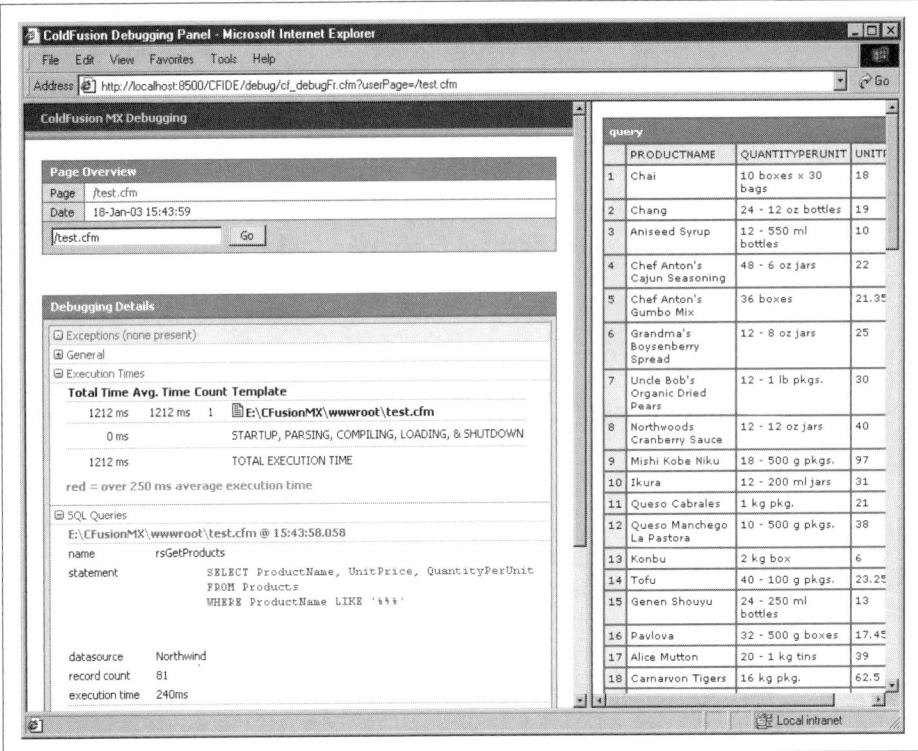

Figure 13-7. Dockable ColdFusion MX debugging

3. Drag the *getSearchResult( )* method from the Components panel to the Code view of your *.cfm* page. This will create a complete <cfinvoke> tag for calling the remote method.

4. Add a <cfdump> tag to the page below your component invocation. The tag should look like this:

```
<cfdump var=#getSearchResultRet# />
```

5. Press the F12 key to test the page in a browser.

The <cfinvoke> tag calls the method of the component, and the <cfdump> tag displays the result in the browser.

Returning momentarily to Flash, if debugging is turned on in the ColdFusion Administrator, you will be able to see all variables and error messages clearly in Flash's NetConnection debugger. For example, if the data source has not been set up yet, the NetConnection debugger would respond with an error message like this:

"Service threw an exception during method invocation: java.sql.SQLException: No such binding: Northwind"

With some experience, you will realize that this error most likely means that there is no data source set up in ColdFusion.

However, viewing the *.cfm* page that utilizes the same component in a browser gives you a much more descriptive error message than Flash's NetConnection debugger. As shown in Figure 13-8, the error message is much easier to decipher, gives line numbers for the error, and shows the actual code that caused the error. The actual error message on this page is:

"Data source Northwind could not be found."

It couldn't be any easier.

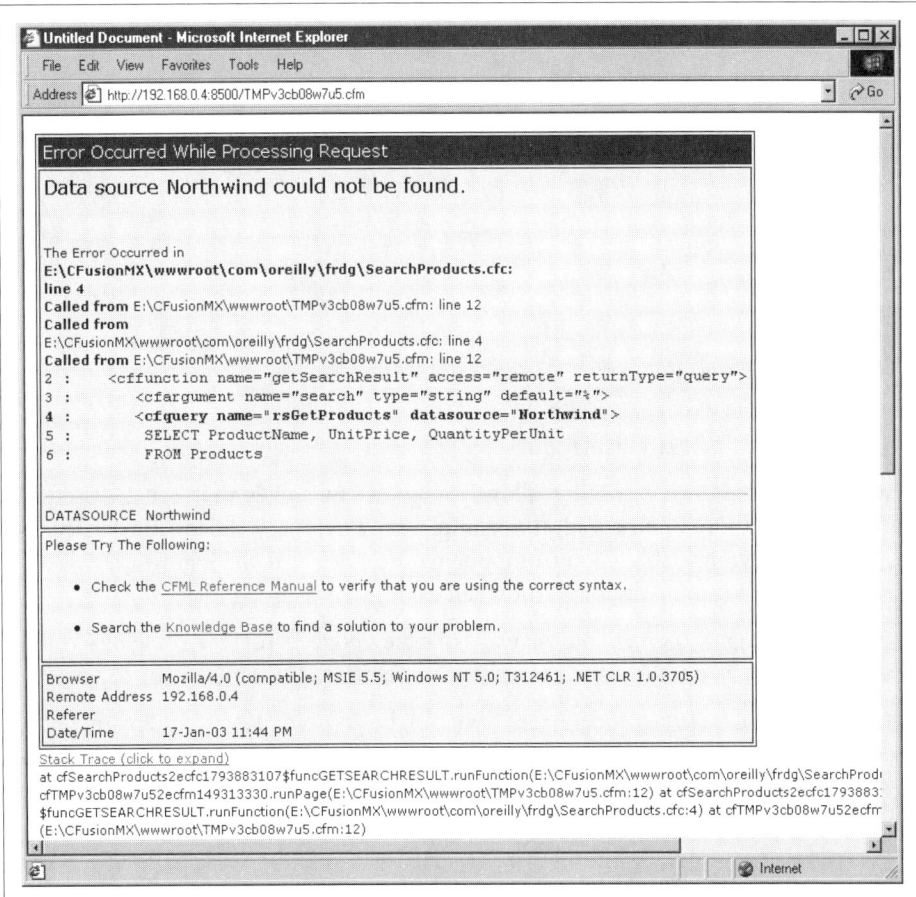

Figure 13-8. Error message in ColdFusion MX

Unfortunately, there is no debugging environment for ColdFusion MX coding, per se. In ColdFusion 5, you could do step-debugging with ColdFusion Studio, but the functionality was removed in the move to MX. Future generations of ColdFusion MX might contain step-debugging. For that reason, the `<cfdump>` tag is still the Cold-Fusion programmer's best friend. You can think of it as the ColdFusion cousin of

Flash's *trace( )* command. It dumps the contents of a variable or structure easily with one simple tag and attribute.

Along with the <cfdump> tag, you also have a <cftrace> tag at your disposal. You can use this tag in a fashion similar to <cfdump>, but it gives information that a simple dump of a variable won't, such as execution times. Also, <cftrace> tags are logged in the ColdFusion application logs, located in your *ColdFusion_root\logs* folder. If you use the <cftrace> tag in a page, the result will be written to the *cftrace.log* file.

The <cftrace> tag supports the following attributes:

abort
> Yes or no

category
> Any valid string

inline
> Yes or no

text
> Any valid string

type
> Information, warning, error, or fatal information

var
> Name of a variable to display

The category and text attributes allow you to set messages that can be useful in complex applications. You could, for example, set a category called "FlashRemoting" that you use in your ColdFusion Components. You can sort the log file on this category in the ColdFusion Administrator when examining your log files.

The <cftrace> tag also gives you the elapsed time between <cftrace> tag executions, so you can use it as a rudimentary timer as you debug and optimize your code.

The ColdFusion *IsDebugMode()* function can be used hand-in-hand with debugging. Using this function, you can sprinkle your code with <cfdump> and <cftrace> tags that are selectively called only when debugging is on. To do this, you can wrap the code in conditional logic, like this:

```
<cfif IsDebugMode( )>
  <cftrace category="TestingPhase2" var="rsGetProducts" />
</cfif>
```

This allows you to turn off debugging until you need it while you are in your testing phase. Having ColdFusion debugging turned on at all times increases the execution time of your pages and components substantially. For this reason, it is best not to use debugging until you need it.

Flash Remoting keeps its own log as well. In *ColdFusion_root\logs*, there is a *flash.log* file, which keeps all error messages that occurred through Flash Remoting—in other words, any *onStatus* event messages that were returned to the Flash movie. These can be useful in debugging, and they can also be useful after an application is deployed.

Dreamweaver MX also has a Server Debug mode, but it simply lists the same information in the Results panel in the Dreamweaver environment.

Debugging in Java

Java environments are varied and diverse, and they number in the dozens. If you are writing and compiling Java code to form your Flash Remoting services, you likely have all the tools necessary to debug the server-side code at your disposal. It is important to choose a Java IDE that has a capable debugger. Some of the best are Borland's JBuilder, the open source NetBeans, and IntelliJ Idea. Each of these environments contains the step-debugging functionality that you will need for debugging Java code.

One of the nice things about the Flash NetConnection debugger when using Java services is that the Java stack trace is sent to the debugger's Call Stack pane. You can examine exactly where the error might have occurred. In many cases, line numbers pinpoint the errors for you.

Server logs

Logs for Flash Remoting can be found in the *flashremoting-event.log* file in JRun 4, and in the individual server log folders for other J2EE servers. In the log file, you will find stack traces for the errors in a Flash Remoting call.

Debugging in ASP.NET

Building applications and services in ASP.NET can be done from a variety of different places, including Notepad and a command-line compiler. There are several more sophisticated tools available that can be used to create and deploy ASP.NET applications.

Visual Studio.NET

Visual Studio.NET (VS.NET) contains some of the most sophisticated debugging tools around, making it almost a pleasure to look for bugs in your code. The Visual Studio tools are similar to those in the Flash interactive debugger but much more responsive and versatile. For example, breakpoints are set and remembered by the program. There is an Immediate window that allows you to type in any variable or expression and have the current value printed to the screen. Also, hovering your cursor over a variable in the code while debugging will pop up a tooltip with the current value of that variable, as shown in Figure 13-9.

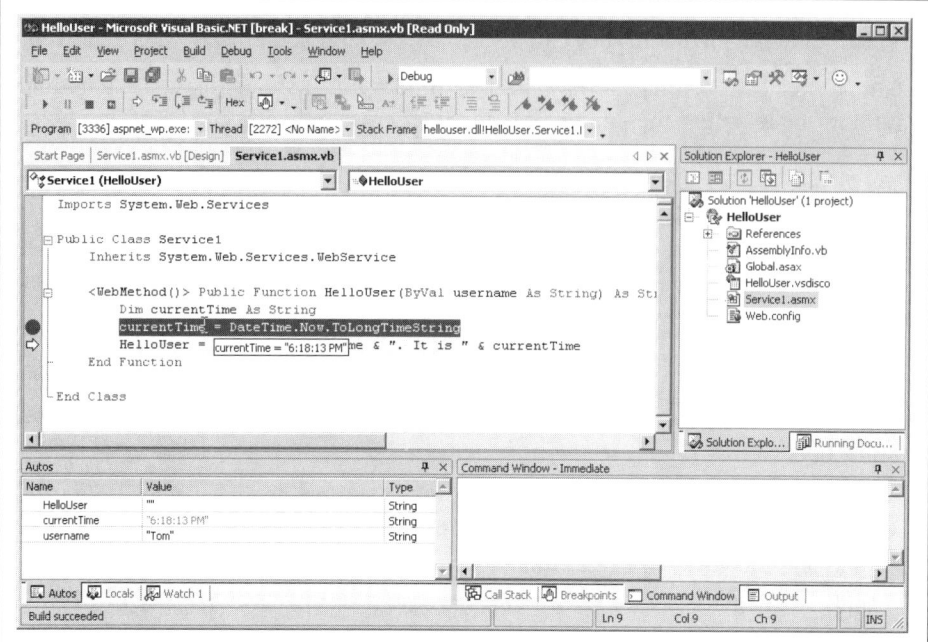

Figure 13-9. The Visual Studio debugging environment gives immediate feedback via tooltips

Some of the features available in Visual Studio include:

Immediate window
Allows you to type in an expression and display the resulting value.

Watches
Multiple watch windows allow you to watch several variables.

Locals
All local variables within a function are displayed here.

Call stack
See the tree of functions that got you to where you currently are in the code.

Threads
Breakdown of the threads that are currently active.

Breakpoints
Listing of all current breakpoints, with the ability to temporarily turn them on and off without removing them from your code.

Step Into, Step Over, and Step Out
Buttons act just like the Flash interactive debugger variants.

Show Next Statement
Allows you to preview the next statement before stepping into it.

Building SOAP-based web services for Flash Remoting is also easy to do in Visual Studio. While you are building your web service, you can test from a browser; Visual Studio creates HTML-based interfaces to your web service that also allow you to trigger the debugger while you build the web service. For example, the *HelloUser* web service shown earlier in this chapter takes one argument. Figure 13-10 shows the temporary test page that is generated by Visual Studio as you debug the web service. You can supply the argument and hit the Invoke button to transfer the focus back to Visual Studio to continue to step-debug your code.

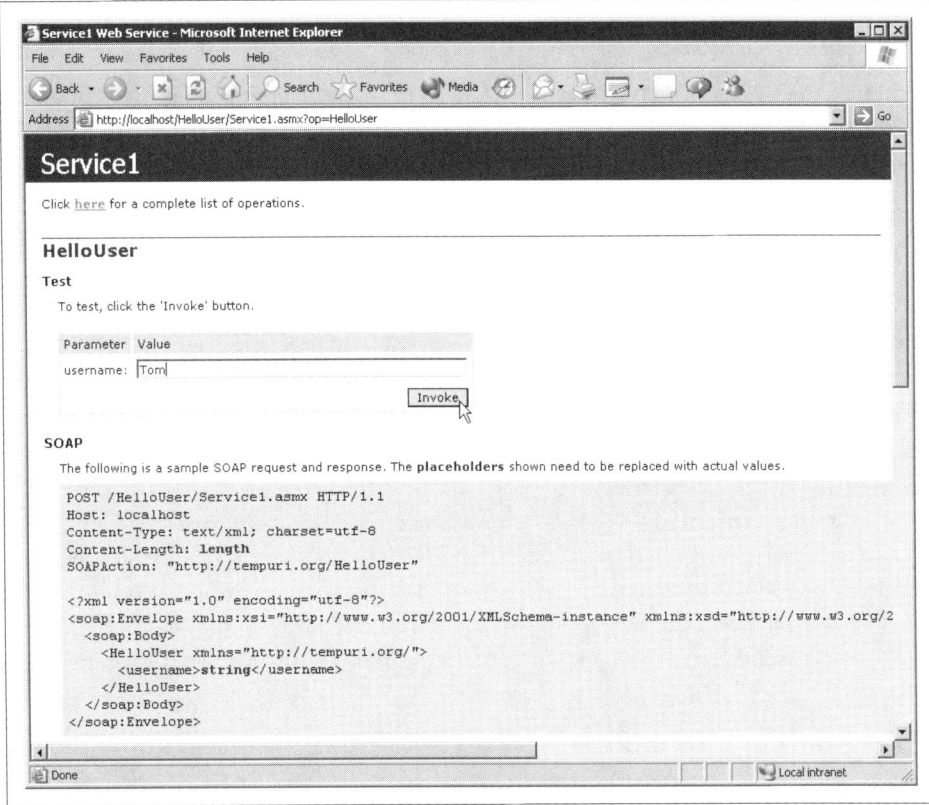

Figure 13-10. Web services can be debugged in Visual Studio

Of course, one of the best features is the ability to edit and change your code as you debug. If you come to an error while you are debugging, you can fix it on the spot and continue the debugging process from that point.

The temporary HTML files that are built by Visual Studio also contain all the SOAP packets that are used by the web service; both the request and response packets are shown in the browser.

If you are building DLLs, you can debug those as well, but Visual Studio generally requires that you set up test projects to be able to test and debug your DLLs.

ASP.NET Web Matrix

Visual Studio is a great programming environment, but it's not the only game in town for ASP.NET developers. Microsoft has also released a free IDE, called ASP.NET Web Matrix, that can be used to create ASP.NET pages, DLLs, and web services used in Flash Remoting, among other things. ASP.NET Web Matrix can be downloaded from:

> *http://www.asp.net*

Although the IDE is similar to Visual Studio in look and feel, it is a lightweight application that doesn't contain all the bells and whistles of Visual Studio. One of the major missing features is the integrated debugger. Still, for building simple services, the Web Matrix can be the perfect environment.

The one area where it truly shines is in the building of SOAP-based web services. When you create a service, you have the same previewing features that can be found in Visual Studio. Still, without the step-debugging features of Visual Studio, you have to do some detective work to find bugs in your applications.

Server logs

Flash Remoting keeps a log in the *bin* folder of your ASP.NET application. If you are having troubles tracking down an error, look in the server log called *flash.log*. One error that I had trouble tracking down, because I received no error message in the NetConnection debugger, was found in the *flash.log*; the trial version had expired and I had neglected to install the full version! Needless to say, when you don't have an error message to point you to an error, you often go around in circles looking for an answer. I could have saved a couple hours by going to the *flash.log* file right away.

Using a TCP Trace Utility

Have you wondered how you can view the HTTP headers going back and forth between Flash Remoting and your client movie? Or how you can view the AMF data that Flash Remoting uses to communicate? Or how to see the SOAP packets that are going back and forth from Flash Remoting to a web service? A TCP trace utility can be a good debugging tool when you are building applications that access web services or when you are having problems with client/server communication.

Basically, a TCP trace tool listens to a port and outputs any activity to a window so that you can examine it or save it to a file. For example, if you are sending a request to a web service and receiving a response that is inaccurate, you can examine the SOAP packet directly using a TCP trace utility.

TCP trace utilities can be used on the client and on the server. If your local machine is acting as client and server during debugging, you can open up two different sessions in the TCP trace utility and examine the requests and responses to HTTP requests.

We examine some of the popular TCP trace utilities in the following sections.

SOAP Trace Utility

Microsoft offers a SOAP toolkit that contains a trace utility called *MSSOAPT.exe*. You can find it at:

http://msdn.microsoft.com/downloads

Its usefulness as a tool does not stop with SOAP, however. It can also be used to examine your AMF headers to and from the Flash Remoting gateway, or any other HTTP packets.

 There are other utilities that work in a similar fashion, like the TCP-Tunnel utility that comes with the Apache SOAP Java package (*http:// xml.apache.org/soap*), but the Microsoft tool is easy to set up and use. If you are on a Macintosh, you might consider using the TCPTunnel utility in place of the MSSoapT tool.

The TCP trace tool must be able to intercept the HTTP call and then pass the call on to its final destination. To use it, set up a dummy port number, such as 81, and then pass the request to 81 rather than the actual destination. The trace utility then intercepts the call and outputs the text and/or binary code to the screen.

Testing Client Calls

To use MSSoapT to test the client-side code of a Flash Remoting application, set it up on the client machine (from which the movie is played) and run it. You will have to create a new Trace session using MSSoapT's File → New command. The Unformatted Trace is a better option to see the exact content that is being passed from the client to the server and back again. After choosing Formatted Trace or Unformatted Trace from the File menu, you'll have to set up the ports and the host address where the trace will be referred, as shown in Figure 13-11.

The "Local port #" should be set to a free port on the local machine. This allows the TCP trace utility to listen to the port. If the port is in use by another service, the trace utility will not be able to open a session.

The "Destination host" should be set to the IP address of the service that you are tracing. For example, if you want to trace the AMF headers going to the Flash Remoting gateway, put the IP address of the Flash Remoting gateway here.

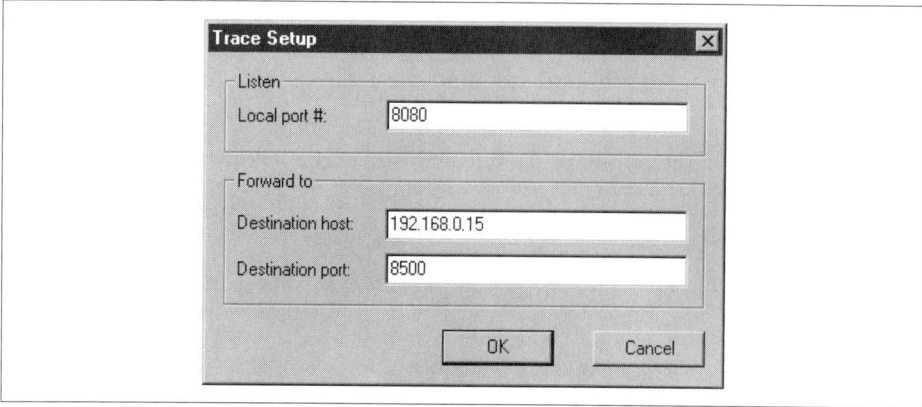

Figure 13-11. The MSSoapT TCP trace utility requires the port and host to be set up

The "Destination port" should be set to the port number of the service you are tracing. To test a Flash Remoting call to a server, this is the port number of the Flash Remoting gateway.

The last step is to set the IP address in your Flash movie for the Flash Remoting gateway to the IP address of the client machine.

For a typical example, let's say that the Flash Remoting gateway is at *http://192.168.0.15:8500/flashservices/gateway*. The local machine has a different IP address; in other words, you are building a Flash application on a machine other than the server you are calling. The local port number for the trace session could be set to 8080, assuming that port is not in use by something else. Any arbitrary port number will do (81, 82, etc). The destination host would be set to 192.168.0.15. The destination port would be set to 8500.

The Flash movie should be modified so that the Flash Remoting gateway URL is now *http://127.0.0.1/flashservices/gateway*. (This URL does not exist on the local machine but will force the Flash Remoting call to go through the TCP trace utility.) If you run the movie, the trace utility should display the call to the service and the result as well. You'll see the AMF headers and any other information that was passed in the HTTP call, as shown in Figure 13-12.

Tracing a Web Service

Web services can also be traced, and the MSSoapT trace utility will show you the SOAP headers going back and forth from client to server. In the case of web services, the client is the Flash Remoting adapter on the server. In other words, the client for the web service resides on the application server machine. For this reason, the tracing needs to take place entirely on the server.

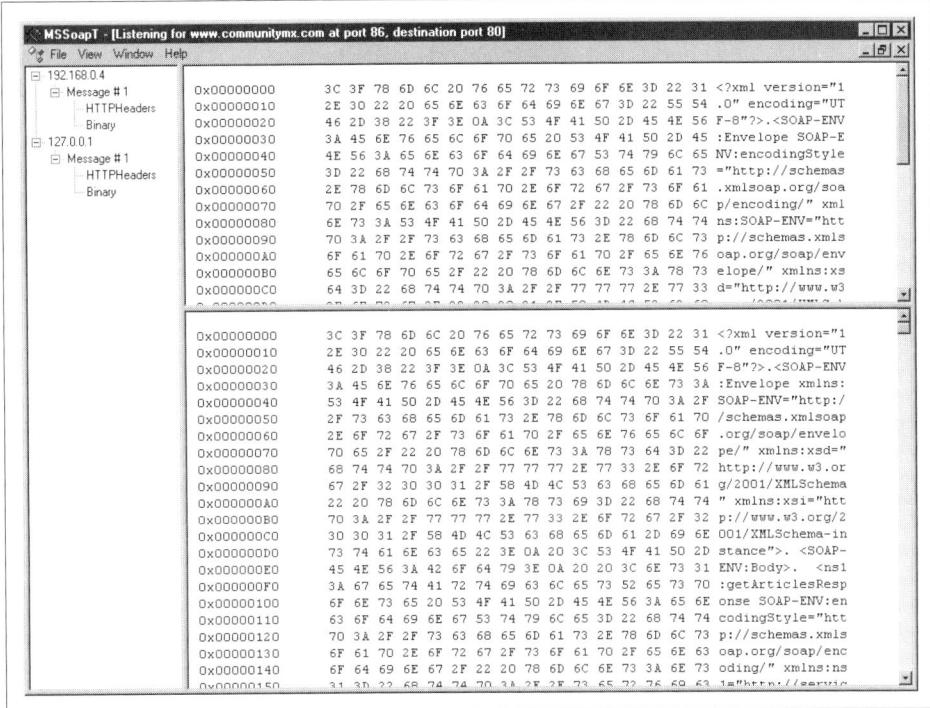

Figure 13-12. The MSSoapT utility displaying information from a Flash Remoting call

Tracing a web service generally requires you to modify the *.wsdl* file so that the URL points to your trace utility rather than the service. The technique is the same: you point your URL in the trace utility (the destination host) to the actual web service URL and set your port numbers accordingly. If the *.wsdl* file resides at a remote location, download the file to the server machine and save it in the web directory. Change the <wsdlsoap:address> tag so that the IP address and port number match your local machine and the port of the trace utility.

To demonstrate, we'll do a simple trace on the web service at:

http://www.communitymx.com/services/cmxfeed.wsdl

Assuming that you have the MSSoapT utility running on the same machine as your Flash Remoting adapter, the first step is to download the *.wsdl* file and save it to your local web root. Save the file as *cmxfeed.wsdl*.

Next, find the <wsdlsoap:address> tag in the file. Copy the address, because you'll need it in the trace utility. Change the IP address to your local *.wsdl* file (probably at *http://localhost:86/cmxfeed.wsdl*). The tag should now read like this:

```
<wsdlsoap:address location="http://localhost:86/services/cmxfeed.cfc" />
```

Notice that the path stays the same; only the IP address and port number change. Save the file.

Open the *communitymx.fla* file from Chapter 10. You will need to change the service path so that it matches the location of your new *.wsdl* file. Change the service path from:

```
var servicePath = "http://www.communitymx.com/services/cmxfeed.wsdl";
```

to:

```
var servicePath = "http://localhost:86/cmxfeed.wsdl";
```

Open up a new trace session and set the ports and host as follows:

Local port #: 86
Destination host: www.communitymx.com
Destination port: 80

Run the Flash movie, and you should see the SOAP packets on the server in the MSSoapT window, which will look very similar to the display shown in Figure 13-12.

This can be handy when building Flash interfaces to web services, because the Flash debuggers may not give you any indication of what might be going wrong with the call to the SOAP web service. The MSSoapT trace utility will show you the SOAP packets so that you can compare the results to the *.wsdl* file code and decide on a course of action.

Debugging SQL Code

Your Flash Remoting application may depend on calls made to a database, as the *searchProducts.fla* example does. If you have a database server such as Microsoft SQL Server, you will have all the tools at your disposal to properly test and debug SQL code. This means that you should have a workable copy of the database and database-programming environment available to you. It is unwise to debug database queries using a live server, so all debugging and optimization should be done locally or on a staging server before deploying your application.

Database Errors

Database errors can be difficult to track down from within Flash, so it is a good idea to try to track them down at the source: from within the database environment. Frequently, the error can be found in the syntax at the source, eliminating the guesswork when you execute the database code from Flash.

If the query runs successfully in the database environment, the next logical place to look for errors is in your server-side service. A successfully worded query can fail if you use a datatype that is not consistent. Frequent errors include forgetting the single quotes around character data or putting single quotes around numeric data improperly.

Another frequent error to watch out for is the improper use of NULL versus using an empty field. Often, a query result can be returned incorrectly if you are doing a search like this:

```
SELECT * FROM Customers WHERE Region = ''
```

You might be looking for Customers that don't have a Region column provided, but running this query on the *Northwind* database returns 0 records. If you look for NULL values instead, the query returns a handful of records:

```
SELECT * FROM Customers WHERE Region IS NULL
```

NULL values and empty values are two entirely different things to your database, and they must be treated differently when you build your queries. This can have some insidious consequences in your data results, especially when you are creating reports and doing aggregate queries.

Query Optimization

Debugging involves not only making the program run without errors but also optimizing the code to run as fast as possible. One of the bottlenecks in Flash Remoting can be your SQL code, if it is not properly optimized.

The SQL Server environment contains tools such as the Query Analyzer to help you optimize queries. It can help determine where to place indexes in your tables, by measuring the demands of a given SQL query and analyzing where the bottlenecks occur. Typically, when a SQL query takes a long time to run, that means the indexes are not set up properly.

There are a few key areas to look for in your queries. Columns that are joined in queries should be indexed, as in this query:

```
SELECT p.ProductID, p.ProductName, s.SupplierName
FROM Products p
INNER JOIN Suppliers s
ON p.SupplierID = s.SupplierID
```

In this case, an index on SupplierID in the Suppliers table will dramatically increase the speed of the query.

Columns referenced in ORDER BY clauses should be indexed. This is because data that is ordered frequently can be ordered more quickly if that column is indexed, as an index is an ordered list.

Columns that are searched frequently should be indexed, as in this query:

```
SELECT * FROM Products WHERE CategoryID = 7
```

On a small table, the savings might not be substantial, but as tables become increasingly large, query execution times become an important consideration. Imagine if you had to look up a phone number in a phone book, starting from page 1 and reading every name until you found the one you were looking for. This is the same principle as searching a database column that has no index on it. With the index, the database is able to narrow the search down to a few disk accesses, rather than scan the entire table.

There are a few things to watch out for in your queries. Queries that use LIKE with wildcards are slower than queries that use exact matches. In other words, this query is slower than a query that matches the field exactly:

```
SELECT * FROM Products WHERE ProductName LIKE '%sauce%'
```

Furthermore, queries that have a wildcard in the first character in the filter will not make use of an index on the column. The preceding query does not use an index. The following query can use an index on the ProductName field to speed up the search:

```
SELECT * FROM Products WHERE ProductName LIKE 'sauce%'
```

Database environments that don't contain tools like the Query Analyzer can be difficult to work with. MySQL contains an optimizer, but it is used from a command line. Regardless, you should make use of the tool and learn about query optimization. Flash Remoting calls can eat up precious seconds of Internet time, and a query that takes too long to execute is going to make restless users go elsewhere.

Wrapping Up

Testing and debugging are among the least glamorous aspects of programming, but they are necessary skills. All programs have bugs, and finding them can often be a challenge. Armed with the proper tools, debugging can be more of a game or a puzzle than a necessary evil to be endured. Flash Remoting makes debugging even harder because of all the different pieces of the puzzle, but by breaking the application into its component parts you can easily isolate and debug any issues you may be having.

In this book so far, you've learned all about what makes Flash Remoting tick. Chapter 14 brings it all together in a real-world application.

CHAPTER 14

Real-World Application

This book has presented many examples of Flash Remoting, but to tie it all together we'll build a complete application that draws on many of the concepts presented up to this point. We'll create a simple script repository application that allows a user to post a script to the server using a simple copy/paste, and then stores the script in a database and returns a script ID number and the URL from where the script can be downloaded. The application features several key elements of Flash Remoting, including application security with a user login framework, the passing of objects to and from the server, several screens utilizing different server-side services, and the seamless integration of client/server processes.

General Considerations

Above all else, building any substantial project requires organization. You can be the best coder in the world, but if the project is not well-organized, it will take longer to put together than it should. The longer you spend planning, the greater chance you will have of bringing a project in on time and under budget. With that in mind, we'll prepare for the coding first by laying out all the requirements, setting up a specification, creating a code skeleton framework, and finally getting down to some coding.

 The example application uses ColdFusion MX as the server model. Many of the concepts translate directly to other server models, and we've tried to leave the implementation as generic as possible to facilitate porting. Porting the example to other server models such as ASP.NET, Java, or PHP is left as an exercise for the reader.

The code shown in the examples uses `<cfquery>` tags for all databases queries. We've kept the query in the page purely to keep the implementation generic; these queries will work in SQL Server, as well as MS Access or MySQL, which do not support stored procedures. If your database supports stored procedures, you will want to move the queries into stored procedures.

When inserting records into a database, you'll often need to retrieve the primary key of the newly inserted record. There are various methods to do this in different Relational Database Management Systems (RDBMS), but the example application uses a generic method that will work in different databases. When a new user is inserted, you can use the username to retrieve the UserID; usernames are unique in the database. When inserting a script, we'll also insert a unique identifier that will aid in retrieving the ScriptID for a particular script.

Requirements

First, we need to create a list of the project requirements. We'll then flesh it out into a specification that we can use to generate the stub code. The stub code acts as an outline; just as a report outline can be laid out in advance to help create a report, the code outline helps guide the eventual coding. First, a mission statement:

> The Script Repository will provide a simple interface on the Web for authenticated users to post short ActionScript (or other) code snippets to a central database. The full list of categorized scripts will be made available to the general public for free download.

With that in place, we'll come up with a list of the main things that the application needs:

- Listing of scripts, ordered by category and clickable for download
- User registration and login section for uploading scripts
- Script upload form
- Repository for scripts
- Ability to upload new versions of scripts
- "Email this page to a friend" feature

Here are some of the minor features that are not essential but are desired:

- Email a forgotten username and password
- Contact form
- Search interface for scripts

The application is built using a client/server model in which the server-side services can be consumed by an HTML client or a Flash client, which offers greater usability. We'll create an interactive interface for the application, using simple sliding screens for registration, login, contact, and uploading/modifying files, and a button for downloading files.

Specifications

Now that we have the requirements, we can lay out the specifications. The specifications give a better understanding of what is necessary for the application. With a set of detailed specs, two programmers should be able to create almost identically functioning applications (although, admittedly, their internal implementations may differ markedly).

Users

The application should support two types of users: registered users and the general public. Since we are building a simple application, distinctions between the different user types will be clear-cut:

registered users
> Registered users have script upload privileges. They can add new scripts or modify their own scripts that are already in the system.

general public
> The general public has full access to scripts in the system, with the ability to download any of them. They cannot add, edit, or delete any scripts. They can send an email to any email address with a link to a specific script.

Scripts

Scripts are stored in a database. The application limits the size of each script; this script repository is intended for small scripts that implement one specific piece of functionality, not entire applications. Storing scripts in a database allows for easy access, change tracking, and download tracking.

Each stored script should have the following information:

author
> The author of the script, in the form of last name, first name. The author's name is available to the application because the user uploading the script is already logged in.

email
> The email address of the author of the script (an optional field that is verified as a valid-format email address). Again, the application has access to this information because the user must be logged in prior to uploading a new script.

date uploaded
> The date of the first upload of the script. This is automatically generated in the Flash movie based on the current date.

last modification
> The date of the last known modification to the script. This is automatically generated by the Flash movie upon updating the script.

version

Version number of the script. This is automatically generated by the application in the format of *major.minor.micro* (e.g., 1.0.0, 1.0.1, etc.). The author can override the default version number with a higher number.

description

A short description of how to use the script.

category

Chosen by the author from a predefined list of categories.

script

The body of the script. The author of the script must paste the text of the script into a text field. We are implementing it in this fashion because of some of the limitations of the Flash client in dealing with the file-upload process. There are workarounds, but we've decided to keep the first version of this application simple. Comments at the top of the script can include a URL pointing to a binary version of the file on the author's site, for example.

General

There are some other specifications that don't fall into the earlier categories. We can lump the rest of the specifications into a general category of site specifications:

about

The copyright notice, privacy notice, contact information, and other general information should be available to the end user. This could be hardcoded into the application, but as a rule these types of things are better suited to a database. An administrator can easily change the text of the general information from an administrative interface, rather than having to edit a *.fla* file and recompile a *.swf* file.

contact

All users should have a way to contact the site administrator. Rather than publish an email address in the application, the application has a button that triggers a contact form so that the email can be sent through the application itself.

The Modules

With the specifications in place, we can focus on the implementation. We'll document first and code later, and we'll use OOP techniques for much of the application. One advantage of this approach is that the specifications dictate how the coding takes place. For example, we have specified that we will have users and scripts; these elements can be implemented as objects. This makes the coding process more applicable to real-world situations. We know the different properties of a user and the different properties of a script (outlined in the specifications), so these will be the properties of our objects. Even though we are using some OOP techniques and some objects, the application is not strictly an object-oriented application.

Structure

We will build the overall structure before we set out to code the functionality of the application. I've found that this is often the best way to approach a problem. You can think of it like drawing a picture: if you draw the outline first, it is a lot easier to color in, rather than color the picture and then try to draw the outline around it after the fact. In this way, comments and function skeletons make up your outline, and the actual code is used to "color in" the program. This has the added benefit that the comments are finished when your code is finished, rather than requiring you to add comments at the end of the project.

The skeleton code should be fully working code. Even placeholder functions should include *return* statements so that the program works as you code.

Database

The database is the first physical structure to create. The database needs to be in place and functional before the application can be built. The database structure is shown in Tables 14-1 through 14-5. Table 14-1 shows the Users table, which is used to manage user login.

Table 14-1. Users table

Column name	Datatype	Length	Notes
UserID	integer	4	Auto-numbering, primary key
Username	text	16	
Password	text	12	
FirstName	text	60	
LastName	text	60	
EmailAddress	text	255	
HintQuestion	text	255	Prompt the user if password is forgotten
HintAnswer	text	20	Verify user response if password is forgotten

Table 14-2 shows the Categories table, which is used to group scripts into categories for easier searching and sorting once the repository grows larger.

Table 14-2. Categories table

Column name	Datatype	Length	Notes
CategoryID	integer	4	Autonumbering, primary key
CategoryDesc	text	60	

Table 14-3 shows the Scripts table, which is used to manage the contributed scripts.

Table 14-3. Scripts table

Column name	Datatype	Length	Notes
ScriptID	integer	4	Autonumbering, primary key
ScriptName	text	60	
ScriptDescription	text	255	
ScriptCode	text	4095	
LanguageID	integer	4	Foreign key to Languages table
CategoryID	integer	4	Foreign key to Categories table
UserID	integer	4	Foreign key to Users table
DateUploaded	date/time	8	Defaults to current date
DateModified	date/time	8	Defaults to current date
VersionMajor	integer	4	Defaults to 1
VersionMinor	integer	4	Defaults to 0
VersionMicro	integer	4	Defaults to 0
ScriptUniqueID	Unique identifier (UUID)	36	

Table 14-4 shows the Languages table, which is used to track the programming languages in which scripts are written.

Table 14-4. Languages table

Column name	Datatype	Length	Notes
LanguageID	integer	4	Autonumbering, primary key
LanguageName	text	50	

Table 14-5 shows the CompanyInfo table, which is used to provide contact information for contributors.

Table 14-5. CompanyInfo table

Column name	Datatype	Length
CompanyName	text	60
Address	text	127
City	text	60
State	text	2
Zip	text	9
Phone	text	50
Fax	text	50
ContactFirstName	text	50

Table 14-5. CompanyInfo table (continued)

Column name	Datatype	Length
ContactLastName	text	50
ContactEmail	text	127
PrivacyPolicy	text	1000
Description	text	1000

The database table specs have been shown in a generic fashion, to allow you to implement them in your own particular database. For example, the *text* datatypes are implemented as *varchar* or *nvarchar* fields in SQL Server or MySQL. Similarly, the DateUploaded field in the Scripts table is implemented as a *datetime* field, with a default value of *getdate( )* in SQL Server or *current_date( )* in MySQL. Other database implementations will vary.

The completed database diagram of table relationships is shown in Figure 14-1.

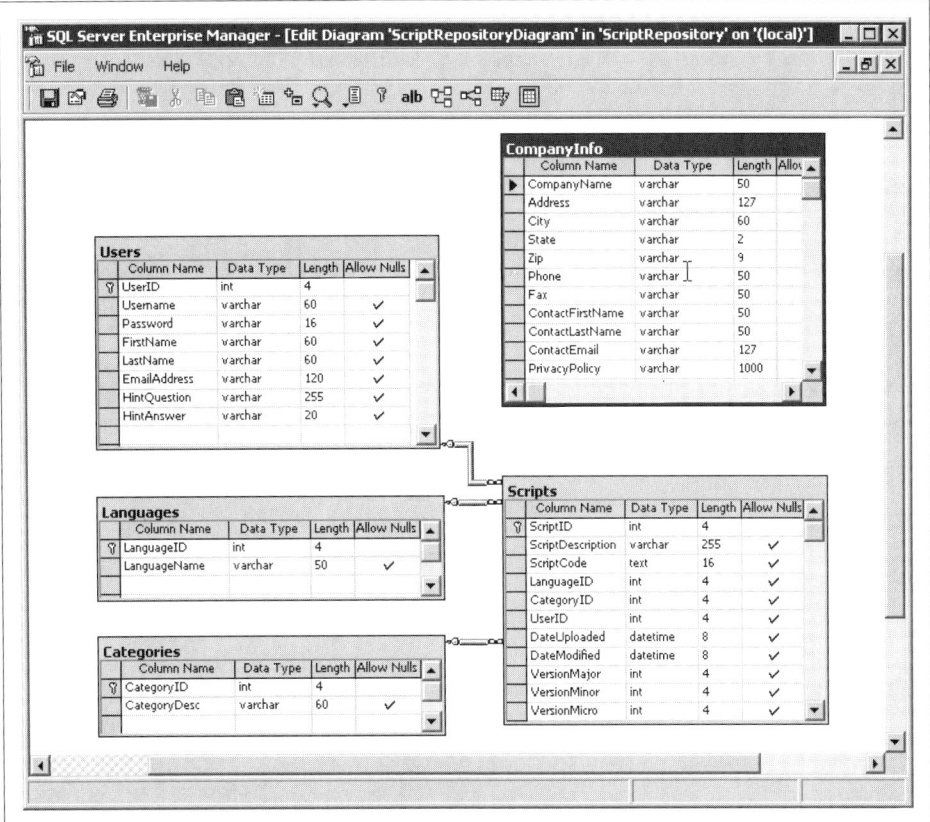

Figure 14-1. The completed database diagram shows table relationships

Defining Server-Side Services

The server-side services are implemented with ColdFusion Components. The required services are shown in Tables 14-6 through 14-8.

Table 14-6 lists the service methods of the *UserService* service.

Table 14-6. The UserService service

Service method	Description	Arguments	Returns
loginUser( )	Validates username and password against the database. Sets the session if the login is successful, and sets the user's access level.	Username (string), Password (string)	Userid (numeric)
addUser( )	Adds a new user to the database. If the registration is successful, the user is also automatically logged in.	UserObject	UserObject
emailPassword( )	Emails a password to a user if he forgets his password.	EmailAddress	True
createUserObj( )	Package method that creates an object of type UserObject for passing back to ActionScript.	FirstName, LastName, Email-Address, Username, Userpassword, HintQuestion, HintAnswer	UserObject
getEmail( )	Gets the user's hint question for retrieving a password.	EmailAddress	Hint question (string)
getScriptsForUser( )	Gets all scripts submitted by logged-in user.	UserID (numeric)	Recordset

Table 14-7 lists the service methods of the *ScriptService* service.

Table 14-7. The ScriptService service

Service method	Description	Arguments	Returns
addScript( )	Adds a script to the database.	ScriptObject	Script id (numeric)
updateScript( )	Updates an existing script in the database.	ScriptObject	ScriptObject
displayScript( )	Displays the script on the screen.	ScriptID (numeric)	ScriptObject
displayList( )	Displays a list of available scripts, with clickable links.	Search word (optional)	Recordset
getScript( )	Gets all information about a script to display.	ScriptID (numeric)	ScriptObject
createScriptObj( )	Package method that creates an object of type ScriptObject for passing back to ActionScript.	ScriptID, ScriptName, Script-Description, ScriptCode, LanguageID, CategoryID, UserID, DateUploaded, DateModified, VersionMajor, VersionMinor, VersionMicro, ScriptUniqueId	ScriptObject
DateTimeString( )	Package method that converts a Date object from ActionScript into a human-readable date/time string	Date object or string	Formatted date string

Table 14-8 lists the service methods of the *SiteService* service.

Table 14-8. The SiteService service

Service method	Description	Arguments	Returns
about( )	Returns a short paragraph about the company from the database.	None	RecordSet
contactForm( )	Contacts the site administrator by email through a standard form.	UserID (numeric), Comment (string)	true
sendPage( )	Sends the page information to a friend.	UserID (numeric), Email address (string), Script ID (numeric)	true
getCategories( )	Retrieves a list of all categories for drop-down list.	None	RecordSet
getLanguages( )	Retrieves a list of all languages for drop-down list.	None	RecordSet
getUsers( )	Retrieves a list of all users for drop-down list.	None	RecordSet

Using Dreamweaver MX, you can create skeletons for all of the services. Dreamweaver MX allows you to create CFCs using an interface (shown in Figure 14-2), with function skeletons in place.

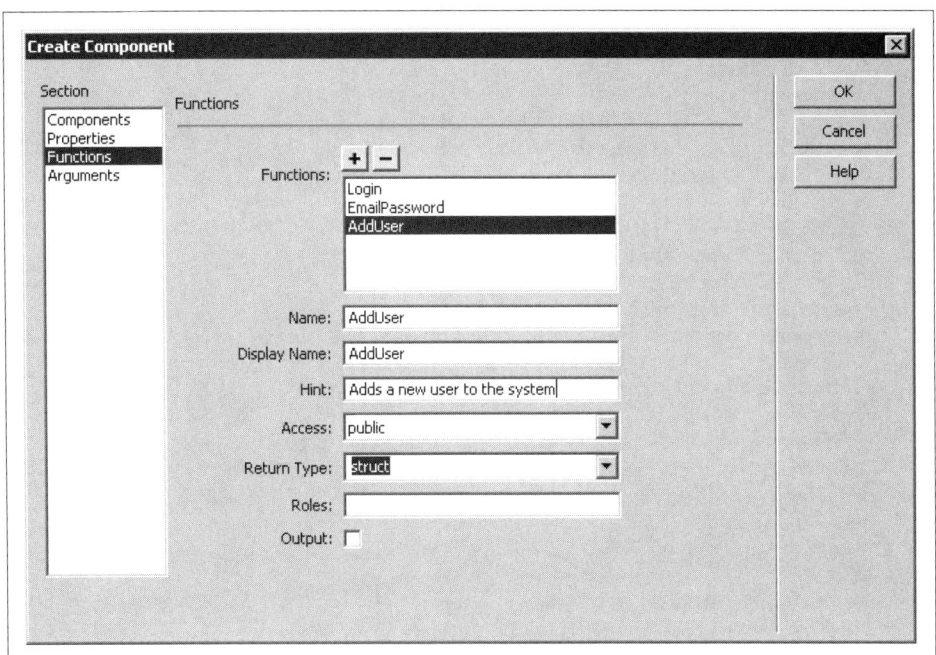

Figure 14-2. The Dreamweaver MX component interface

Example 14-1 lists the skeleton code for the *UserService* service.

Example 14-1. Autogenerated skeleton code for the UserService service

```
<!--- Generated by Dreamweaver MX 6.0.1722 [en] (Win32) - Wed Jan 29 19:07:39 GMT-0800
(Pacific Standard Time) 2003 --->

<cfcomponent displayName="UserService">
  <cffunction name="loginUser" displayName="loginUser"
    hint="Logs a user into the script repository"
    access="remote" returnType="string" output="false">
      <cfargument name="username" type="string" required="true">
      <cfargument name="password" type="string" required="true">
      <!--- loginUser body --->
      <cfreturn >
  </cffunction>
  <cffunction name="addUser" displayName="addUser"
    hint="Add a user to the database" access="remote"
    returnType="string" output="false">
      <cfargument name="Username" type="string" required="true">
      <cfargument name="FirstName" type="string" required="true">
      <cfargument name="LastName" type="string" required="true">
      <cfargument name="EmailAddress" type="string" required="true">
      <cfargument name="Password" type="string" required="true">
      <cfargument name="HintQuestion" type="string" required="false">
      <cfargument name="HintAnswer" type="string" required="false">
      <!--- addUser body --->
      <cfreturn >
  </cffunction>
  <cffunction name="emailPassword" displayName="emailPassword"
    hint="Email a password to a user, given the email address"
    access="remote" returnType="string" output="false">
      <cfargument name="EmailAddress" type="string" required="true">
      <cfargument name="HintQuestion" type="string" required="true">
      <!--- emailPassword body --->
      <cfreturn >
  </cffunction>
  <cffunction name="createUserObj" displayName="createUserObj"
    hint="Create ActionScript object to hold user information"
    access="package" returnType="struct" output="false">
      <cfargument name="Username" type="string" required="true">
      <cfargument name="FirstName" type="string" required="true">
      <cfargument name="LastName" type="string" required="true">
      <cfargument name="EmailAddress" type="string" required="true">
      <cfargument name="Password" type="string" required="true">
      <cfargument name="HintQuestion" type="string" required="false">
      <cfargument name="HintAnswer" type="string" required="false">
      <!--- createUserObj body --->
      <cfreturn >
  </cffunction>
  <cffunction name="getEmail" displayName="getEmail"
    hint="Retrieve the user's hint question given an email address"
    access="remote" returnType="string" output="false">
      <cfargument name="EmailAddress" type="string" required="true">
      <!--- getEmail body --->
      <cfreturn >
```

```
  </cffunction>
  <cffunction name="getScriptsForUser" displayName="getScriptsForUser"
    hint="Retrieve the user's scripts to feed a combo box"
    access="remote" returnType="recordset" output="false">
      <cfargument name="UserID" type="string" required="true">
      <!--- getEmail body --->
      <cfreturn >
  </cffunction>
</cfcomponent>
```

The methods of the CFC are each defined with all arguments and an empty return value. As you can see, the method bodies are empty, except for a comment. The code body will go there, but not yet. We'll fill in comments for each method, explaining what the method does, what is required, and what is returned. This will make it that much easier to write the methods afterwards, and the code will be fully commented. An example of a fully commented function skeleton is shown in Example 14-2. The component skeletons can be downloaded from the online Code Depot.

Example 14-2. The fully commented displayList() method skeleton

```
<cffunction name="displayList"
 access="remote"
 returnType="query"
 output="false">
<!---
    Method: displayList
    Version: 1.0.0
    Author: Tom Muck
    Arguments:
      search       Optional search criteria
    Return: query object of all script information. Properties are
      ScriptID    ID number of the script (primary key)
      Category    The category name
      CategoryID  The categoryID
      ScriptName  The name of the script
    Description:
      This service returns a complete list of scripts available or a list
      that meets the search criteria
--->
    <!--- displayList body --->
    <!--- End displayList body --->
    <cfreturn />
</cffunction>
```

Test mechanisms (also known as *test harnesses*) can be set up as plain ColdFusion pages to test that each service and each method is working. Inside of the Dreamweaver MX environment, simply drag the CFC from the Components panel onto a *.cfm* page and insert a form and conditional logic to test the form, as in the test page shown in Example 14-3.

Example 14-3. A test page for the UserService service

```
<cfparam name="form.test" default="" />
<html>
<head>
<title>User Service Test Page</title>
<meta http-equiv="Content-Type" content="text/html; charset=iso-8859-1">
</head>

<body>
<form name="form1" method="post" action="">
  <select name="test" id="test">
    <option value="addUser">addUser</option>
    <option value="emailPassword">emailPassword</option>
    <option value="loginUser">loginUser</option>
  </select>
  <input type="submit" name="Submit" value="Submit">
</form>
<cfif form.test EQ "addUser">
<cfinvoke
  component="com.oreilly.frdg.ScriptRepository.UserService"
  method="addUser"
  returnvariable="addUserRet">
    <cfinvokeargument name="Username" value="enter_value_here"/>
    <cfinvokeargument name="FirstName" value="enter_value_here"/>
    <cfinvokeargument name="LastName" value="enter_value_here"/>
    <cfinvokeargument name="EmailAddress" value="enter_value_here"/>
    <cfinvokeargument name="Password" value="enter_value_here"/>
    <cfinvokeargument name="HintQuestion" value="enter_value_here"/>
    <cfinvokeargument name="HintAnswer" value="enter_value_here"/>
</cfinvoke>
<cfoutput>#addUserRet#</cfoutput>
</cfif>

<cfif form.test eq "emailPassword">
<cfinvoke
  component="com.oreilly.frdg.ScriptRepository.UserService"
  method="emailPassword"
  returnvariable="emailPasswordRet">
    <cfinvokeargument name="EmailAddress" value="enter_value_here"/>
    <cfinvokeargument name="HintAnswer" value="enter_value_here"/>
</cfinvoke>
<cfoutput>#emailPasswordRet#</cfoutput>
</cfif>

<cfif form.test eq "loginUser"><cfinvoke
  component="com.oreilly.frdg.ScriptRepository.UserService"
  method="loginUser"
  returnvariable="loginUserRet">
    <cfinvokeargument name="username" value="enter_value_here"/>
    <cfinvokeargument name="password" value="enter_value_here"/>
</cfinvoke>
<cfoutput>#loginUserRet#</cfoutput>
</cfif>
```

Example 14-3. A test page for the UserService service (continued)

```
</body>
</html>
```

If you build pages like these to test each server-side service, they will be invaluable in determining where problems might occur before you begin to bring Flash into the equation. Using a page like this in ColdFusion gives you full access to ColdFusion debugging and also allows you to easily manipulate the parameters and return values to test different situations.

Implementing Server-Side Services

With the server-side service skeletons in place, you can begin to flesh out the services. If you have built ColdFusion test pages as recommended, you can test the services one by one as you build them.

> The services use a data source name called *ScriptRepository*, using the sample database available for download from *http://www.flash-remoting.com*. You must set this data source name up in your ColdFusion Administrator in order to create the server-side services.

The UserService service

The *UserService* service implements all methods that relate to users, such as logging in and retrieving passwords. You can easily add more methods to the service as the application becomes more advanced. In addition to the remote methods available to the Flash movie, there is a package method called *createUserObj( )* that is used internally by some of the methods to create an object of type *UserObject* to pass back to ActionScript.

The completed code for the *UserService* remote service is shown in Example 14-4. Refer to Table 14-6 for a summary of the service methods for this service.

Example 14-4. The UserService service, implemented as UserService.cfc

```
<!--- Generated by Dreamweaver MX 6.0.1722 [en] (Win32) - Wed Jan 29 19:07:39 GMT-0800
(Pacific Standard Time) 2003 --->

<cfcomponent displayName="UserService">
<!---
  Service:  UserService
  Package:   com/oreilly/frdg/ScriptRepository
  Description: Services to interact with Users from the
              ScriptRepository application
--->
  <cffunction name="createUserObj" displayName="createUserObj"
    hint="Create ActionScript object to hold user information"
    returnType="struct" access="package" output="false">
```

Example 14-4. The UserService service, implemented as UserService.cfc (continued)

```
  <!--- Create the ActionScript object --->
  <cfobject type="java"
    class="flashgateway.io.ASObject"
      name="UserObject"
      action="create" />
  <!--- Create an instance of the object --->
   <cfset o = UserObject.init( )>
  <!--- Set the type to our custom UserObjectClass for deserialization --->
   <cfset o.setType("UserObject")>

  <cfset o.put("UserID", arguments[1]) />
  <cfset o.put("Username", arguments[2]) />
  <cfset o.put("Userpassword", arguments[3]) />
  <cfset o.put("FirstName", arguments[4]) />
  <cfset o.put("LastName", arguments[5]) />
  <cfset o.put("Emailaddress", arguments[6]) />
  <cfset o.put("HintQuestion", arguments[7]) />
  <cfset o.put("isUserLogged", 1) />
  <cfset o.put("inited", 1) />
  <cfreturn o />
</cffunction>

<cffunction name="loginUser" displayName="loginUser"
  hint="Logs a user into the script repository"
  access="remote" returnType="any" output="false">
<!---
  Method: loginUser
  Version: 1.0.0
  Author: Tom Muck
  Arguments:
    username   string of up to 16 characters
    password   string of up to 12 characters

  Return: user object
  Description:
    This service allows the user to log in to the application by
    verifying the username/password in the database and returning
    all of the properties of the user to the Flash movie.
--->
  <cfargument name="username" type="string" required="true">
  <cfargument name="userpassword" type="string" required="true">
  <!--- loginUser body --->
  <cftry>
    <cfquery datasource="ScriptRepository"
      name="rsUserLogin">
      SELECT * FROM Users
      WHERE Username =
      <cfqueryparam cfsqltype="cf_sql_varchar" value="#username#">
       AND Password =
      <cfqueryparam cfsqltype="cf_sql_varchar" value="#userpassword#">
    </cfquery>
    <cfcatch type="Any">
```

```
        <cfthrow message="There was a database error" />
      </cfcatch>
    </cftry>

    <cfif rsUserLogin.RecordCount GT 0 >
      <cfset UserObj = createUserObj(rsUserLogin.UserID,
          rsUserLogin.Username,
          rsUserLogin.Password,
          rsUserLogin.FirstName,
          rsUserLogin.LastName,
          rsUserLogin.Emailaddress,
          rsUserLogin.HintQuestion
          ) />
    <cfelse>
      <cfthrow message="Not a valid user" />
    </cfif>
    <!--- end loginUser body --->

    <cfreturn UserObj />
  </cffunction>

  <cffunction name="addUser" displayName="addUser"
   hint="Add a user to the database" access="remote"
   returnType="any" output="false">
  <!---
    Method: addUser
    Version: 1.0.0
    Author: Tom Muck
    Arguments:
      FirstName   string of up to 60 characters
      LastName    string of up to 60 characters
      EmailAddress   string of up to 127 characters
      Username   string of up to 16 characters
      Userpassword   string of up to 12 characters
      HintQuestion   string of up to 255 characters
      HintAnswer   string of up to 20 characters
    Return: user object
    Description:
      This service allows a new user to be added to the database,
      and automatically to log in to the application by
      verifying the username/password in the database and returning
      all of the properties of the user to the Flash movie.
   --->
    <cfargument name="Username" type="string" required="true">
    <cfargument name="FirstName" type="string" required="true">
    <cfargument name="LastName" type="string" required="true">
    <cfargument name="EmailAddress" type="string" required="true">
    <cfargument name="Userpassword" type="string" required="true">
    <cfargument name="HintQuestion" type="string" required="false">
    <cfargument name="HintAnswer" type="string" required="false">
    <!--- addUser body --->
    <cftry>
```

```
    <cfquery datasource="ScriptRepository"
      name="rsDoesUserExist">
      SELECT * FROM Users
       WHERE Username =
      <cfqueryparam cfsqltype="cf_sql_varchar" value="#username#">
    </cfquery>
    <cfcatch type="Any">
      <cfthrow message="There was a database error" />
    </cfcatch>
  </cftry>
  <cfif rsDoesUserExist.RecordCount EQ 0>
    <cftry>
      <cfquery datasource="ScriptRepository"
       name="rsAddUser">
        INSERT INTO Users
        (Username, Password, FirstName, LastName,
        EmailAddress, HintQuestion, HintAnswer)
        VALUES (
      <cfqueryparam cfsqltype="cf_sql_varchar" value="#Username#">,
      <cfqueryparam cfsqltype="cf_sql_varchar" value="#Userpassword#">,
      <cfqueryparam cfsqltype="cf_sql_varchar" value="#FirstName#">,
      <cfqueryparam cfsqltype="cf_sql_varchar" value="#LastName#">,
      <cfqueryparam cfsqltype="cf_sql_varchar" value="#EmailAddress#">,
      <cfqueryparam cfsqltype="cf_sql_varchar"
        null="#HintQuestion EQ ''#" value="#HintQuestion#">,
      <cfqueryparam cfsqltype="cf_sql_varchar"
        null="#HintAnswer EQ ''#" value="#HintAnswer#">
        )
      </cfquery>
      <cfcatch type="Any">
        <cfthrow message="There was a database error" />
      </cfcatch>
    </cftry>
  <cfelse>
    <cfthrow message="Already a user with that username" />
  </cfif>

  <!--- End addUser body --->
  <cfreturn this.loginUser('#username#','#userpassword#') />
</cffunction>

<cffunction name="getEmail" displayName="getEmail"
  hint="Retrieve the user's hint question given an email address"
  access="remote" returnType="string" output="false">
<!---
  Method: getEmail
  Version: 1.0.0
  Author: Tom Muck
  Arguments:
    EmailAddress  string of up to 127 characters
  Return: Hint question (string)
  Description:
```

```
      This service retrieves the user's hint question given an email
      address
  --->
    <cfargument name="EmailAddress" type="string" required="true">
    <!--- getEmail body --->
     <cftry>
       <cfquery datasource="ScriptRepository"
        name="rsGetQuestion">
          SELECT HintQuestion FROM Users
          WHERE Emailaddress =
          <cfqueryparam cfsqltype="cf_sql_varchar" value="#EmailAddress#">
       </cfquery>
       <cfcatch type="Any">
         <cfthrow message="There was a database error" />
       </cfcatch>
     </cftry>

     <cfif rsGetQuestion.RecordCount NEQ 1>
       <cfthrow message="No match found in database" />
     </cfif>
     <!--- End getEmail body --->
     <cfreturn rsGetQuestion.HintQuestion />
  </cffunction>

  <cffunction name="emailPassword" displayName="emailPassword"
   hint="Email a password to a user, given the email address"
   access="remote" returnType="boolean" output="false">
  <!---
    Method: emailPassword
    Version: 1.0.0
    Author: Tom Muck
    Arguments:
      EmailAddress  string of up to 127 characters
      HintAnswer  string of up to 20 characters
    Return: boolean of successful email of the password
    Description:
      This service allows a user to have his password emailed to him,
      if the hint answer matches the user's hint in the database.
  --->
    <cfargument name="EmailAddress" type="string" required="true">
    <cfargument name="HintAnswer" type="string" required="true">
    <!--- emailPassword body --->
    <cftry>
      <cfquery datasource="ScriptRepository"
       name="rsGetUser">
        SELECT Username, Password FROM Users
        WHERE Emailaddress =
        <cfqueryparam cfsqltype="cf_sql_varchar" value="#EmailAddress#">
        AND HintAnswer =
        <cfqueryparam cfsqltype="cf_sql_varchar" value="#HintAnswer#">
      </cfquery>
       <cfcatch type="Any">
```

```
        <cfthrow message="There was a database error" />
      </cfcatch>
    </cftry>

    <cfif rsGetUser.RecordCount EQ 1>
    <!---Only send the email if there is a matching record in the database --->
      <cfmail from="admin@flash-remoting.com" to="#Emailaddress#"
      subject="Requested information">
Your username is: #rsGetUser.username#
Your password is: #rsGetUser.password#
Please respond to admin@flash-remoting.com if you have received
this message in error.

Administrator
      </cfmail>
    <cfelse>
      <cfreturn 0 />
    </cfif>
    <!--- End emailPassword body --->
    <cfreturn 1 />
  </cffunction>

  <cffunction name="getScriptsForUser" access="remote"
  returnType="query" output="false">
    <!---
    Method: getScriptsForUser
    Version: 1.0.0
    Author: Tom Muck
    Arguments:
      Username      username for currently logged-in user
      Userpassword      password for currently logged-in user
    Return:
      query object of scriptid and scriptname information.
    Description:
      This service returns a complete list of scripts available
      for the currently logged in user.
  --->
    <cfargument name="username" hint="Username of current user"
    type="string"  default="" />
    <cfargument name="userpassword" hint="Password of current user"
    type="string"  default="" />
    <!--- getScriptsForUser body --->
    <cftry>
      <cfquery name="rsScripts" datasource="ScriptRepository">
        SELECT s.ScriptID, s.ScriptName
        FROM Users u, Scripts s
        WHERE u.Username =
        <cfqueryparam cfsqltype="cf_sql_varchar" value="#username#">
        AND u.Password =
        <cfqueryparam cfsqltype="cf_sql_varchar" value="#userpassword#">
        AND s.UserID = u.UserID
        ORDER BY s.ScriptName
```

```
      </cfquery>
      <cfcatch type="any">
        <cfthrow message="There was a database error" />
      </cfcatch>
    </cftry>
    <!--- End getScriptsForUser body --->
    <cfreturn rsScripts />
  </cffunction>
</cfcomponent>
```

The *UserService* service interacts with the Flash movie using a *UserObject*, a custom object that we set up in ActionScript using *Object.registerClass*. As discussed in Chapter 4, this method of transferring objects allows for seamless passing of data between client and server. ColdFusion supports a <cfobject> tag, which allows you to set up the object as a Java object of type *flashgateway.io.ASObject*.

There are a few things of note in the code. All queries that contain user-supplied parameters are set up with a <cfqueryparam> tag. This tag guards the application against SQL injection attacks, in which a malicious user sends SQL statements in a URL to attempt to damage your data or even gain control of your database.

 Because we control the input from the Flash movie, you might think that the remote methods are safe, but that is not the case. A remote service that is set up for Flash Remoting is completely open to the outside world. A person can interact with your remote service if he knows the URL and the service name, which can easily be obtained from the Flash movie by decompiling it. A remote service can then be invoked through a URL, making all remote services that accept parameters open to attack.

The following query, from the *getEmail( )* method, demonstrates the use of the <cfqueryparam> tag:

```
<cfquery datasource="ScriptRepository"
  name="rsGetQuestion">
   SELECT HintQuestion FROM Users
   WHERE Emailaddress =
   <cfqueryparam cfsqltype="cf_sql_varchar" value="#EmailAddress#">
</cfquery>
```

The <cfqueryparam> tag takes the place of the parameter within the query and throws an error if the datatype is not right. Therefore, the parameter is usable only as a proper parameter; crackers cannot inject SQL statements into the query.

 The <cfqueryparam> tag has a counterpart if you are using stored procedures as well: <cfprocparam>. All queries and stored procedures that accept user-supplied parameters should use these tags.

Also, the queries in the page are all wrapped in *try/catch* blocks, in order to trap errors and simply throw them back to the Flash movie. We could put some other form of error handling within the block, such as writing to a log file or sending an email to a site administrator, but this method is the simplest.

The <cfmail> tag contains the body of the email message to be sent to the end user. For that reason, the text is aligned flush left, even though the code is nicely indented otherwise. The <cfmail> tag translates any spaces or line breaks within the body of the message literally, so the text format should be preserved inside the tag.

One last item deserves a mention: when a user is added to the database, the user is also automatically logged in, as shown in the following line from the *addUser( )* method:

```
<cfreturn this.loginUser('#username#','#userpassword#') />
```

Rather than simply return a Boolean value indicating whether the user was successfully added to the database, we log the user in using the *UserService.loginUser( )* method and return the *UserObject* to the Flash movie. This improves the end user's experience because she doesn't need to log in as a separate step after registering.

The ScriptService service

The *ScriptService* service includes methods that relate to the storing of the scripts. The service contains many of the same types of features that the *UserService.cfc* file had, such as the package method that creates a *ScriptObject* object type, and the use of the <cfqueryparam> tags to guard against malicious user input.

The completed *ScriptService* service is shown in Example 14-5. Refer to Table 14-7 for a summary of the service methods for this service.

Example 14-5. The ScriptService service, implemented as ScriptService.cfc

```
<!--- Generated by Dreamweaver MX 6.0.1722 [en] (Win32) - Wed Jan 29 19:32:00 GMT-0800
(Pacific Standard Time) 2003 --->
<cfcomponent displayName="ScriptService">
  <!---
  Service:  ScriptService
  Package:  com/oreilly/frdg/ScriptRepository
  Description: Utilizes a Script object to pass information back and forth
    from the Flash movie.
  --->
  <cffunction name="createScriptObj" hint="Create ActionScript object to
    hold script information" returnType="struct" access="package" output="false">
    <!--- Create the ActionScript object --->
    <cfobject type="java"
     class="flashgateway.io.ASObject"
     name="ScriptObject"
     action="create" />
    <!--- Create an instance of the object --->
    <cfset o = ScriptObject.init( )>
```

```
  <!--- Set the type to our custom UserObjectClass for deserialization --->
  <cfset o.setType("ScriptObject")>
  <cfset o.put("ScriptID", arguments[1]) />
  <cfset o.put("ScriptName", arguments[2]) />
  <cfset o.put("ScriptDescription", arguments[3]) />
  <cfset o.put("ScriptCode", arguments[4]) />
  <cfset o.put("LanguageID", arguments[5]) />
  <cfset o.put("CategoryID", arguments[6]) />
  <cfset o.put("UserID", arguments[7]) />
  <cfset o.put("DateUploaded", this.DateTimeString(arguments[8])) />
  <cfset o.put("DateModified", this.DateTimeString(arguments[9])) />
  <cfset o.put("VersionMajor", arguments[10]) />
  <cfset o.put("VersionMinor", arguments[11]) />
  <cfset o.put("VersionMicro", arguments[12]) />
  <cfset o.put("ScriptUniqueID", arguments[13]) />
  <cfset o.put("inited",1) />
  <cfreturn o />
</cffunction>

<cffunction name="addScript" access="remote" returnType="any" output="false">
  <!---
  Method: addScript
  Version: 1.0.0
  Author: Tom Muck
  Arguments:
    ScriptObj  a script object with all properties needed to add
    the script to the database. Properties are:
      ScriptName
      ScriptDescription
      ScriptCode
      LanguageID
      CategoryID
      UserID
      DateUploaded
      DateModified
      VersionMajor
      VersionMinor
      VersionMicro
  Return: scriptid
  Description:
    This service allows a registered user to upload a script
    to the database.
  --->
  <!--- <cfargument name="ScriptObj" type="struct" required="true"> --->
  <!--- AddScript body --->

<!--- Create a unique ID to aid in retrieving the primary key --->
<cfset scriptuniqueid = CreateUUID( ) />
<cfset ScriptObj = this.createScriptObj(
  0,
  arguments.ScriptName,
  arguments.ScriptDescription,
```

Example 14-5. The ScriptService service, implemented as ScriptService.cfc (continued)

```
        arguments.ScriptCode,
        arguments.LanguageID,
        arguments.CategoryID,
        arguments.UserID,
        arguments.DateUploaded,
        arguments.DateModified,
        arguments.VersionMajor,
        arguments.VersionMinor,
        arguments.VersionMicro,
        scriptuniqueid
        ) />
  <!--- Insert the script into the database --->
    <cftry>
    <cfquery name="insertScript" datasource="ScriptRepository">
    INSERT INTO Scripts (
       ScriptName,
     ScriptDescription,
     ScriptCode,
     LanguageID,
     CategoryID,
     UserID,
     DateUploaded,
     DateModified,
     VersionMajor,
     VersionMinor,
     VersionMicro,
     scriptuniqueid
    )
    VALUES (
    <cfqueryparam cfsqltype="cf_sql_varchar"
     null="#ScriptObj.ScriptName EQ ''#"
     value="#ScriptObj.ScriptName#">,
    <cfqueryparam cfsqltype="cf_sql_varchar"
     null="#ScriptObj.ScriptDescription EQ ''#"
     value="#ScriptObj.ScriptDescription#">,
    <cfqueryparam cfsqltype="cf_sql_varchar"
     null="#ScriptObj.ScriptCode EQ ''#"
     value="#ScriptObj.ScriptCode#">,
    <cfqueryparam cfsqltype="cf_sql_numeric"
     null="#ScriptObj.LanguageID EQ ''#"
     value="#ScriptObj.LanguageID#">,
    <cfqueryparam cfsqltype="cf_sql_numeric"
     null="#ScriptObj.CategoryID EQ ''#"
     value="#ScriptObj.CategoryID#">,
    <cfqueryparam cfsqltype="cf_sql_numeric"
     null="#ScriptObj.UserID EQ ''#"
     value="#ScriptObj.UserID#">,
    <cfqueryparam cfsqltype="cf_sql_timestamp"
     null="#ScriptObj.DateUploaded EQ ''#"
     value="#ScriptObj.DateUploaded#">,
    <cfqueryparam cfsqltype="cf_sql_timestamp"
     null="#ScriptObj.DateModified EQ ''#"
```

```
      value="#ScriptObj.DateModified#">,
    <cfqueryparam cfsqltype="cf_sql_numeric"
    null="#ScriptObj.VersionMajor EQ ''#"
    value="#ScriptObj.VersionMajor#">,
    <cfqueryparam cfsqltype="cf_sql_numeric"
    null="#ScriptObj.VersionMinor EQ ''#"
    value="#ScriptObj.VersionMinor#">,
    <cfqueryparam cfsqltype="cf_sql_numeric"
    null="#(ScriptObj.VersionMicro EQ '')#"
    value="#ScriptObj.VersionMicro#">,
    <cfqueryparam cfsqltype="cf_sql_varchar"
    null="no"
    value="#scriptuniqueid#">
  )
    </cfquery>
  <cfquery name="rsScript" datasource="ScriptRepository">
    SELECT ScriptID FROM Scripts
  WHERE ScriptUniqueID = '#scriptuniqueid#'
    </cfquery>
    <cfcatch type="any">
      <cfthrow message="There was a database error" />
    </cfcatch>
  </cftry>
  <!--- End AddScript body --->
  <cffile action="append" file="c:\log.txt" output=#this.objToString(ScriptObj)#>

  <cfreturn ScriptObj />
</cffunction>
<cffunction name="updateScript" access="remote" returnType="any" output="false">
  <!---
  Method: updateScript
  Version: 1.0.0
  Author: Tom Muck
  Arguments:
    ScriptObj  a script object with all properties needed to add
    the script to the database. Properties are:
      ScriptID
      ScriptDescription
      ScriptCode
      LanguageID
      CategoryID
      UserID
      DateUploaded
      DateModified
      VersionMajor
      VersionMinor
      VersionMicro
  Return: Updated ScriptObject
  Description:
    This service allows a registered user to change a script that
    exists in the database.
  --->
```

```
<!--- UpdateScript body --->
<cfset ScriptObj = this.createScriptObj(
  arguments.ScriptID,
  arguments.ScriptName,
  arguments.ScriptDescription,
  arguments.ScriptCode,
  arguments.LanguageID,
  arguments.CategoryID,
  arguments.UserID,
  arguments.DateUploaded,
  arguments.DateModified,
  arguments.VersionMajor,
  arguments.VersionMinor,
  arguments.VersionMicro,
  0
  ) />
<cftry>
  <cfquery name="updateScript" datasource="ScriptRepository">
      UPDATE Scripts SET ScriptName =
      <cfqueryparam cfsqltype="cf_sql_varchar"
       null="#ScriptObj.ScriptName EQ ''#"
       value="#ScriptObj.ScriptName#">,
      ScriptDescription =
      <cfqueryparam cfsqltype="cf_sql_varchar"
       null="#ScriptObj.ScriptDescription EQ ''#"
       value="#ScriptObj.ScriptDescription#">,
      ScriptCode =
      <cfqueryparam cfsqltype="cf_sql_varchar"
       null="#ScriptObj.ScriptCode EQ ''#"
       value="#ScriptObj.ScriptCode#">,
      LanguageID =
      <cfqueryparam cfsqltype="cf_sql_numeric"
       null="#ScriptObj.LanguageID EQ ''#"
       value="#ScriptObj.LanguageID#">,
      CategoryID =
      <cfqueryparam cfsqltype="cf_sql_numeric"
       null="#ScriptObj.CategoryID EQ ''#"
       value="#ScriptObj.CategoryID#">,
      UserID =
      <cfqueryparam cfsqltype="cf_sql_numeric"
       null="#ScriptObj.UserID EQ ''#"
       value="#ScriptObj.UserID#">,
      DateModified =
      <cfqueryparam cfsqltype="cf_sql_timestamp"
       null="#ScriptObj.DateModified EQ ''#"
       value="#ScriptObj.DateModified#">,
      VersionMajor =
      <cfqueryparam cfsqltype="cf_sql_numeric"
       null="#ScriptObj.VersionMajor EQ ''#"
       value="#ScriptObj.VersionMajor#">,
      VersionMinor =
      <cfqueryparam cfsqltype="cf_sql_numeric"
```

```
                 null="#ScriptObj.VersionMinor EQ ''#"
                 value="#ScriptObj.VersionMinor#">,
             VersionMicro =
             <cfqueryparam cfsqltype="cf_sql_numeric"
              null="#ScriptObj.VersionMicro EQ ''#"
              value="#ScriptObj.VersionMicro#">
             WHERE ScriptID   =
             <cfqueryparam cfsqltype="cf_sql_numeric"
              null="#ScriptObj.ScriptID EQ ''#"
              value="#ScriptObj.ScriptID#">
      </cfquery>
        <cfcatch type="any">
          <cfthrow message="There was a database error" />
        </cfcatch>
      </cftry>
      <!--- End UpdateScript body --->
      <cfreturn ScriptObj />
  </cffunction>
  <cffunction name="displayList" access="remote" returnType="query" output="false">
    <!---
    Method: displayList
    Version: 1.0.0
    Author: Tom Muck
    Arguments:
      search     Optional search criteria
    Return: query object of all script information. Properties are
      ScriptID  ID number of the script (primary key)
      Category  The category name
      CategoryID  The categoryID
      ScriptName  The name of the script
    Description:
      This service returns a complete list of scripts available or a list
      that meets the search criteria
    --->
  <cfargument name="search" hint="Search criteria for script listing"
   type="string"  default="" />
    <!--- DisplayList body --->
  <cftry>
      <cfquery name="rsScripts" datasource="ScriptRepository">
        SELECT c.CategoryDesc
        , c.CategoryID
        , s.ScriptID
        , s.ScriptName
        FROM Categories c
        INNER JOIN
        Scripts s ON
        c.CategoryID = s.CategoryID
        <cfif search neq "">
          WHERE s.ScriptDescription + s.ScriptName + c.CategoryDesc
          LIKE
          <cfqueryparam cfsqltype="cf_sql_varchar" value="%#search#%">
        </cfif>
```

Example 14-5. The ScriptService service, implemented as ScriptService.cfc (continued)

```
        ORDER BY c.CategoryDesc, s.ScriptID
      </cfquery>
      <cfcatch type="any">
        <cfthrow message="There was a database error" />
      </cfcatch>
    </cftry>
    <!--- End DisplayList body --->
    <cfreturn rsScripts />
  </cffunction>

  <cffunction name="getScript" access="remote" returnType="struct" output="false">
    <!---
    Method: getScript
    Version: 1.0.0
    Author: Tom Muck
    Arguments:
      ScriptID  ID number of the script to display
    Return: ScriptObj
    Description:
      This service returns a script object to be displayed in the
      Flash movie
    --->
    <cfargument name="ScriptID" type="any" required="true">
    <!--- DisplayScript body --->
  <cftry>
      <cfquery name="rsScripts" datasource="ScriptRepository">
    SELECT * FROM Scripts
    WHERE ScriptID =
    <cfqueryparam cfsqltype="cf_sql_numeric" value="#ScriptID#">
      </cfquery>
      <cfcatch type="any">
        <cfthrow message="There was a database error" />
      </cfcatch>
    </cftry>
  <cfif rsScripts.RecordCount EQ 1>
   <cfset ScriptObj = createScriptObj(rsScripts.ScriptID,
     rsScripts.ScriptName ,
     rsScripts.ScriptDescription ,
     rsScripts.ScriptCode,
     rsScripts.LanguageID,
     rsScripts.CategoryID,
     rsScripts.UserID,
     rsScripts.DateUploaded,
     rsScripts.DateModified,
     rsScripts.VersionMajor,
     rsScripts.VersionMinor,
     rsScripts.VersionMicro,
     rsScripts.ScriptUniqueID
     ) />
  <cfelse>
    <cfthrow message="No script with that ID" />
  </cfif>
```

```
    <!--- End getScript body --->
    <cfreturn ScriptObj />
  </cffunction>

  <cffunction name="DateTimeString" access="package" hint="Convert a date/time data to a
string for display" returntype="string" >
    <cfargument name="dateObj" type="any" required="false" />
  <cfif isdate(dateObj)>
    <cfset returnstring =
      "#DateFormat(dateObj,'mm/dd/yyyy')# #TimeFormat(dateObj, 'hh:mm:ss tt')#" />
  <cfelse>
    <cfset returnstring = dateObj />
  </cfif>
  <cfreturn returnstring />
  </cffunction>

</cfcomponent>
```

The SiteService service

The *SiteService* service contains methods to populate UI components, contact the site administrator, send messages to other users, and populate the About screen, as summarized in Table 14-8.

The complete server-side code for the service is shown in Example 14-6.

Example 14-6. The SiteService service, implemented as SiteService.cfc

```
<!--- Generated by Dreamweaver MX 6.0.1722 [en] (Win32) - Thu Jan 30 21:49:32 GMT-0800
(Pacific Standard Time) 2003 --->

<cfcomponent displayName="SiteService" hint="General service for site methods">
<!---
  Service:  SiteService
  Package:   com/oreilly/frdg/ScriptRepository
  Description: General utility methods for the site
--->
  <cffunction name="about" displayName="About"
  hint="Short paragraph and info about the company" access="remote"
  returnType="query" output="false">
  <!---
    Method: about
    Version: 1.0.0
    Author: Tom Muck
    Arguments:
      none
    Return: a query object with the information about the site
    Description:
      This service sends the information about the site back to the caller
  --->
```

```
    <!--- about body --->
    <cftry>
      <cfquery datasource="ScriptRepository"
         name="rsAbout">
         SELECT TOP 1 * FROM CompanyInfo
      </cfquery>
      <cfcatch type="Any">
        <cfthrow message="There was a database error" />
      </cfcatch>
    </cftry>

    <!--- End about body --->
    <cfreturn rsAbout />
  </cffunction>

  <cffunction name="contactForm" displayName="contactForm"
   hint="Contact the site administrator by email through a standard form"
   access="remote" returnType="string" output="false">
    <cfargument name="emailaddress" type="string" default="" />
    <cfargument name="userid" type="numeric" default=0 />
    <cfargument name="comment" type="string" default="" />
  <!---
    Method: contactForm
    Version: 1.0.0
    Author: Tom Muck
    Arguments:
      none
    Return: true
    Description:
      This service sends an email to the site administrator
  --->
    <!--- contactForm body --->
    <cfmail to="admin@flash-remoting.com" from=#emailaddress#
     subject="Comment: #left(comment,40)#..."
     >
UserID: #userid#
Emailaddress: #emailaddress#
Date/time: #DateFormat(now())# #TimeFormat(now())#

Comment:
#comment#
    </cfmail>
    <!--- End contactForm body --->
    <cfreturn 1 />
  </cffunction>

  <cffunction name="sendPage" displayName="sendPage" hint="Send the page
information to a friend" access="remote" returnType="string" output="false">
    <cfargument name="scriptid" required="true" type="numeric" />
    <cfargument name="emailto" required="true" type="string" />
    <cfargument name="emailfrom" required="true" type="string" />
  <!---
```

```
    Method: sendPage
    Version: 1.0.0
    Author: Tom Muck
    Arguments:
      none
    Return: true
    Description: This service sends an email to any email address with
                a link to a specific script
  --->
    <!--- sendPage body --->
    <cfset link = this.about().DownloadLink />
    <cfmail to=#emailto# from=#emailfrom#
     subject="#emailfrom# thought you might be interested in this page"
     bcc="emailrecord@flash-remoting.com">
This page was sent to you by #emailfrom#:
#link#?id=#scriptid#

Administrator, Flash-Remoting.com
    </cfmail>
    <!--- End sendPage body --->
    <cfreturn 1 />
  </cffunction>

  <cffunction name="getCategories" access="remote" returntype="query" >
  <!---
    Method: getCategories
    Version: 1.0.0
    Author: Tom Muck
    Arguments:
      none
    Return: recordset
    Description:
      This service returns a recordset for Categories to populate combo boxes
  --->
    <!--- getCategories body --->
    <cfquery name="rsCategories" datasource="ScriptRepository" >
     SELECT CategoryID, CategoryDesc FROM Categories
    </cfquery>
    <!--- END getCategories body --->
    <cfreturn rsCategories />
  </cffunction>

  <cffunction name="getLanguages" access="remote" returntype="query" >
  <!---
    Method: getCategories
    Version: 1.0.0
    Author: Tom Muck
    Arguments:
      none
    Return: recordset
    Description:
      This service returns a recordset for Categories to populate combo boxes
  --->
```

```
  <!--- getLanguages body --->
  <cfquery name="rsLanguages" datasource="ScriptRepository" >
   SELECT LanguageID, LanguageName FROM Languages
  </cfquery>
  <!--- End getLanguages body --->
  <cfreturn rsLanguages />
 </cffunction>

 <cffunction name="getUsers" access="remote" returntype="query" >
 <!---
  Method: getUsers
  Version: 1.0.0
  Author: Tom Muck
  Arguments:
    none
  Return: recordset
  Description:
    This service returns a recordset for Users to populate combo boxes
 --->
  <!--- getUsers body --->
  <cfquery name="rsUsers" datasource="ScriptRepository" >
   SELECT UserID, FirstName + ' ' + LastName as theName
   FROM Users
  </cfquery>
  <!--- END getUsers body --->
  <cfreturn rsUsers />
 </cffunction>
</cfcomponent>
```

After all server-side services are in full working order and have been tested, we can begin work on the Flash Remoting client-side code.

Client-Side ActionScript

The Flash user interface for the application was designed and implemented by a designer who worked from a short specification that described the interfaces needed and the fields needed in each interface. The design specification sheet can be seen in Appendix C. We won't concern ourselves with the actual design or implementation of the ActionScript code to make the interface work. The preliminary *.fla* (bare-bones interface) and completed Flash movies can be downloaded from the online Code Depot.

 My thanks to Edoardo "Edo" Zubler who created and implemented the interface design. Edo maintains a site at *http://www.aftershape.com*.

The ActionScript Flash Remoting code for the application features some of the techniques shown in Chapter 12 and is described here.

Objects

An object-based approach to building the interface makes it easier to expand the application in the future. It also makes it easier to reuse modules from the application in other applications. The objects we'll use are:

ScriptObject
> A *ScriptObject* object is a simple representation of a user's script, for both uploading and downloading. The *ScriptObject* class contains the methods for interacting with the *ScriptService* service. Methods correspond to the server-side methods of the *ScriptServices* service.

UserObject
> The *UserObject* object contains the properties of the currently logged-in user. The *UserObject* class contains all methods for interacting with the *UserService* service. Methods correspond to the server-side methods of the *UserServices* service.

Each object is self-contained and includes all code necessary to deal with the service, including the methods. If the object has to be sent to the server, Flash automatically takes care of stripping off the methods before sending the object.

Interface

The Flash movie contains several interfaces to implement all the functionality required of the application. The main interface is shown in Figure 14-3.

The following screen definitions resulted from the designer's feedback on the initial user interface specification (see Appendix C):

Main
> The main application screen, which lists the different options available and displays all scripts. Listing scripts in a Tree component allows all users to view available scripts and drill down to a description page for a particular script. The Search box allows a user to specify criteria to narrow the list of displayed scripts. A detail page appears to the right of the Tree on the same screen. Also present are a Download Script button to allow a script to be downloaded, and a send-to-a-friend feature to send the current detail page's link to an email address. The menu items always remain within reach via a sliding menu.

Login
> The login screen allows registered users to log in. It contains username and password fields and a button.

Register
> Allows a new user to register, with personal information and a username/password combination. If the registration is successful, the user is also automatically logged in.

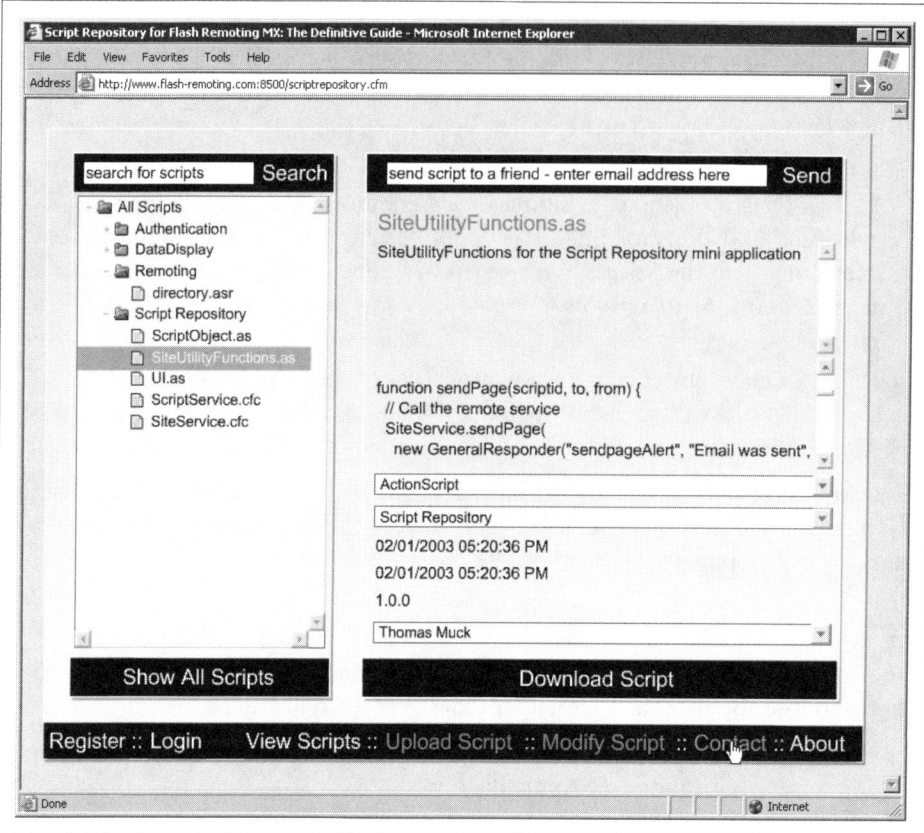

Figure 14-3. The Flash interface for the Script Repository

Upload Script

A blank form to allow a registered user to upload a script to the database.

Modify Script

A form that mimics the Upload Script form and is pre–filled in with information about a script that needs to be updated. A drop-down list of available scripts allows a user to view all scripts that he has uploaded, so he can choose which one to modify.

Contact Form

Allows a user to contact the site administrator.

About

A screen showing a short description of the site.

Alert Box

This page delivers messages to the user, with a simple OK button. The box allows an optional callback function to be executed upon clicking OK.

Retrieve Box

A general box that presents a label and a text field so that the user can enter a value and pass it to the application. The box allows an optional callback function to be executed upon clicking OK.

Working

A progress box that tells the user that the application is working.

The user interface has been designed independently of the server-side and Flash Remoting code. The user interface, as implemented by the designer, is entirely functional, with dummy methods to act as placeholders for eventual Flash Remoting methods. Fitting the Flash Remoting code into the existing interface will be a simple operation.

ActionScript code

The Flash Remoting code and ActionScript code not related to the user interface is placed into these include files:

ScriptRepository.as

Main ActionScript code file, which initializes the Flash Remoting connections and other objects needed for the application and includes all of the other necessary files.

RemotingInit.as

Initializes the Flash Remoting URL and the service objects.

UserObject.as

Class file that contains the *UserObject* class and all methods that interact with the *UserService* service.

ScriptObject.as

Class file that contains the *ScriptObject* class and all methods that interact with the *ScriptService* service.

SiteUtilityFunctions.as

ActionScript functions that implement some of the services for the site, such as emailing the site administrator.

NetServices.as

Flash Remoting file (included with Flash Remoting components from Macromedia).

UI.as

User interface utility functions and extensions to some basic Flash MX components.

Flash Remoting Code

The ActionScript code used to contact the remote services is contained in several files described in the following sections. One caveat when working with Flash Remoting is that the remote calls are asynchronous. This creates problems when you're trying to separate the logic in your applications, as discussed in Chapter 12. In our application, we decided to keep the logic simple by implementing the UI logic from within our responder objects. In other words, when a remote call returns a result, the responder object takes care of the details of updating the display.

RemotingInit.as

The *RemotingInit.as* file contains all of the Flash Remoting initialization code needed for the movie. The code is identical to the code you've seen throughout the book, but in this case we are creating three distinct service objects: one for the *UserService*, one for the *ScriptService*, and one for the *SiteService*. The code is shown in Example 14-7.

Example 14-7. Remoting initialization in the RemotingInit.as file

```
// Remoting initialization
if (initialized == null) {
  initialized = true;
  NetServices.setDefaultGatewayUrl("http://localhost/flashservices/gateway");
  my_conn = NetServices.createGatewayConnection();
  // Create the service objects
  UserService = my_conn.getService(
                    "com.oreilly.frdg.ScriptRepository.UserService");
  ScriptService = my_conn.getService(
                    "com.oreilly.frdg.ScriptRepository.ScriptService");
  SiteService = my_conn.getService(
                    "com.oreilly.frdg.ScriptRepository.SiteService");
}

// Major error handler, usually a connection is bad, so the movie will fail
System.onStatus = function (error) {
  errorHandler("There was a connection failure");
};

// General error handler for entire movie
function errorHandler (message, callbackFunction) {
    alertBox("errorHandlerAlert", message, callbackFunction);
};
```

The code also includes the general *System.onStatus( )* method to handle any catastrophic errors, such as a connection failure. Also, a general error handler is defined that will be used in all *onStatus( )* methods for responder objects in the movie. By centralizing the error handling we can easily customize the message presented to the user. During development, we are simply displaying the return message. During debugging, we might want to trace some debugging information. At some later point, we can change this function to present a more meaningful error to the user.

ScriptObject.as

The *ScriptObject.as* file contains the definition for the *ScriptObject* class. The complete *ScriptObject.as* file is shown in Example 14-8. As you can see, the client-side *ScriptObject* contains the same properties as the *ScriptObject* that was created in the server-side code in Example 14-5. The object is passed back and forth when necessary to simplify operations on both ends. When passed to the server, the properties become arguments of the ColdFusion function. When passed back to the client, the properties are copied to the current instance of the *ScriptObject* using the private *_copyProperties( )* method.

Example 14-8. The ScriptObject class

```
/*
ScriptObject  an object with all properties needed to add
the script to the database.
Properties:
  ScriptID
  ScriptName
  ScriptDescription
  ScriptCode
  LanguageID
  CategoryID
  UserID
  DateUploaded
  DateModified
  VersionMajor
  VersionMinor
  VersionMicro
  ScriptUniqueID
Methods:
  init         initialize the object.
  addScript    call the remote method to add a script to the DB
  updateScript call the remote method to update a script in the DB
  test         debugging method that is used to make sure object is returning
               from the remote method as an object of type ScriptObject
  onResult     Responder method for the object's remote calls
  onStatus     Responder error method for object's remote calls
  _copyProperties  "Private" method to copy the properties from remote call
               to the current instance of a ScriptObject
  toString     debugging method to display the current script's properties
*/

function ScriptObject (id) {
  if (!this.inited)
    this.init(arguments);
}
```

Example 14-8. The ScriptObject class (continued)

```
ScriptObject.prototype.init = function (args) {
  this.inited = true;      // Instance is initialized
  this.ScriptID            = (args[0] != undefined) ? Number(args[0]) : 0;
  this.ScriptName          = (args[1] != undefined) ? args[1] : "";
  this.ScriptDescription = (args[2] != undefined) ? args[2] : "";
  this.ScriptCode          = (args[3] != undefined) ? args[3] : "";
  this.LanguageID          = (args[4] != undefined) ? Number(args[4]) : 0;
  this.CategoryID          = (args[5] != undefined) ? Number(args[5]) : 0;
  this.UserID              = (args[6] != undefined) ? Number(args[6]) : 0;
  this.DateUploaded        = (args[7] != undefined) ? args[7] : "";
  this.DateModified        = (args[8] != undefined) ? args[8] : "";
  this.VersionMajor =
        (args[9] != undefined && args[9] != "") ? Number(args[9]) : 0;
  this.VersionMinor =
        (args[10] != undefined && args[10] != "") ? Number(args[10]) : 0;
  this.VersionMicro =
        (args[11] != undefined && args[11] != "") ? Number(args[11]) : 0;
  this.ScriptUniqueID = (args[12] != undefined) ? args[12] : "";
};

Object.registerClass("ScriptObject", ScriptObject);

// Define a toString() function for reading the object
ScriptObject.prototype.toString = function () {
  var temp = "inited: "        +  this.inited + '\n';
  temp += "ScriptID: "         +  this.ScriptID + '\n';
  temp += "ScriptName: "       +  this.ScriptName + '\n';
  temp += "ScriptDescription: " + this.ScriptDescription + '\n';
  temp += "ScriptCode: "       +  this.ScriptCode + '\n';
  temp += "LanguageID: "       +  this.LanguageID + '\n';
  temp += "CategoryID: "       +  this.CategoryID + '\n';
  temp += "UserID: "           +  this.UserID + '\n';
  temp += "DateUploaded: "     +  this.DateUploaded + '\n';
  temp += "DateModified: "     +  this.DateModified + '\n';
  temp += "VersionMajor: "     +  this.VersionMajor + '\n';
  temp += "VersionMinor: "     +  this.VersionMinor + '\n';
  temp += "VersionMicro: "     +  this.VersionMicro + '\n';
  temp += "ScriptUniqueID: "   +  this.ScriptUniqueID;
  return temp;
};

// Methods are simple interfaces to the remote methods
ScriptObject.prototype.addScript = function (service) {
  service.addScript(this, this);
};

ScriptObject.prototype.updateScript = function (service) {
  service.updateScript(this, this);
};

// Debugging function to let us know that the object returned from
// the server was registered properly. In responder function, do:
//    result.test()
```

Example 14-8. The ScriptObject class (continued)

```
ScriptObject.prototype.test = function () {
  trace("ScriptObject successful")
};

// Copy properties from an object to this (current instance of obj)
ScriptObject.prototype._copyProperties = function (from) {
  for (var prop in from) {
    if (this[prop] != from[prop]) this[prop] = from[prop];
  }
};

// Responder function
ScriptObject.prototype.onResult = function (result) {
  var exists = false;
  if (this.ScriptID) exists = true;  // If this is an update, ScriptID exists
    // Put all properties from the result into the instance of the ScriptObject
    this._copyProperties(result);
  alertBox("alertModify", "Successful.", scriptRepositoryRefresh(this, exists));
};

// Responder error handler
ScriptObject.prototype.onStatus = function (error) {
  errorHandler(error.description);
};

ScriptObject.prototype.validate = function () {
  var errorMsg = "";
  if (this.ScriptName == "")    errorMsg += "Script name must not be empty\n";
  if (this.ScriptDescription == "")
      errorMsg += "Script description must not be empty\n";
  if (this.ScriptCode == "")    errorMsg += "Script code must not be empty\n";
  if (this.LanguageID == 0)     errorMsg += "Must choose a script language\n";
  if (this.CategoryID == 0)     errorMsg += "Must choose a script category\n";
  if (this.DateUploaded == "") errorMsg += "Must choose date uploaded\n";
  if (this.DateModified == "") errorMsg += "Must include date modified\n";
  if (this.VersionMajor == "")
    errorMsg += "Script version must be in format x.x.x\n";
  if (this.VersionMinor == "")
    errorMsg += "Script version must be in format x.x.x\n";
  if (this.VersionMicro == "")
    errorMsg += "Script version must be in format x.x.x\n";
  return errorMsg;
}
```

The script is commented inline, but a few areas warrant further explanation. The calls to the remote service use a rather cryptic syntax, passing this as both the first and second parameters:

```
ScriptObject.prototype.addScript = function (service) {
  service.addScript(this, this);
};
```

This code passes the first argument of the current *ScriptObject* instance (this) as a responder object, because the object has *onResult( )* and *onStatus( )* methods declared on it. Flash will strip off the first argument to use as the responder, and the second argument (this) becomes the argument sent to the remote service. It is the current instance of the *ScriptObject* as well; all properties of the object are passed to the service.

The responder method, *onResult( )*, copies the properties of the result to the same instance of the *ScriptObject* that made the remote call. It then calls the *scriptRepositoryRefresh( )* function as a callback function that will add the script to the Tree component (and to the scriptCache property shown in Example 14-9). The exists variable tells the callback function that the current script is either a new script (exists is false) or an updated script (exists is true).

The *validate( )* method of the object is a general-purpose validation routine for the properties of the *ScriptObject*. Rather than validate the individual text fields, we wait until the call to the remote service to validate the text. By doing this, the complexities of validating various text fields and combo boxes throughout the application are eliminated; validation can be done all at once easily by invoking the *validate( )* method of the object.

The *init( )* method, as previously shown in Chapter 4, allows the object passed from the remote method to retain all of its properties upon instantiation, which occurs behind the scenes immediately upon return and before your ActionScript code can act on the object.

ScriptRepository.as

The *ScriptRepository.as* file is the only one included directly in our Flash movie. All other ActionScript documents are included from this file. The movie is initialized from here, and the user interface is populated from the remote methods.

The complete *ScriptRepository.as* file is shown in Example 14-9.

Example 14-9. The ScriptRepository.as file

```
// Flash Remoting include
#include "NetServices.as"
// NetDebug for debugging purposes
#include "NetDebug.as"
// Data provider for UI components
#include "DataGlue.as"
// Initialize Flash Remoting
#include "RemotingInit.as"
// Site utility functions
#include "SiteUtilityFunctions.as"
// UserObject class
#include "UserObject.as"
// ScriptObject class
```

Example 14-9. The ScriptRepository.as file (continued)

```
#include "ScriptObject.as"
// User interface stuff
#include "UI.as"

// Set up a cache for scripts to avoid hitting the remote service again
var scriptCache = new Object( );

// Initialize the user and some other globals
_global.currentUser = new UserObject( );
_global.currentScript = 0;    // If there is a current script shown, it will be here
_global.downloadLink = "http://www.flash-remoting.com";

// General responder object for methods that return nothing
//   onResult( ) method displays a message in an alert box
//   onStatus( ) method simply calls the error handler
function GeneralResponder (theName, theMessage, callbackFunction) {
  this.onResult = function (result) {
    alertBox(theName, theMessage, callbackFunction);
  };
  this.onStatus = function (error) {
    errorHandler(error.description);
  };
}

// Set up a default "script" that contains generic labels for the interface
scriptCache["0"] = new ScriptObject(
            0,                     // scriptid
            "Script name...",      // ScriptName
            "Description...",      // ScriptDescription
            "Code...",             // ScriptCode
            0,                     // LanguageID
            0,                     // CategoryID
            0,                     // UserID
            "Date uploaded...",    // DateUploaded
            "Date modified...",    // DateModified
            "",                    // Version major
            "",                    // Version minor
            "",                    // Version micro
            "");                   // ScriptUniqueID
// Display the dummy script
displayIt(0, cnt_main_mc.cnt_view_mc);

// Search the scripts database
function searchScripts (searchWord) {
  ScriptService.displayList(new ScriptListingResponder(
                            cnt_main_mc.cnt_view_mc.scripttree_tree,
                            'containing ' + searchWord),searchWord);
  workingAlert( );    // Display a "...working" box
}

// Get all of the scripts
function getAllScripts ( ) {
```

Example 14-9. The ScriptRepository.as file (continued)

```
  ScriptService.displayList(new ScriptListingResponder(
                          cnt_main_mc.cnt_view_mc.scripttree_tree));
  workingAlert( );    // Display a "...working" box
}

// Upon initialization, get all scripts for tree
// Tree control named scripttree_tree

// Call the remote service to display scripts
getAllScripts( );

// Responder object to populate tree with script names and IDs
function ScriptListingResponder (theTree, rootNode) {
  // Serves double duty for searches and all scripts.
  // Pass in the tree reference and a string containing the rootNode text.
  if (rootNode == undefined || rootNode == "") rootNode = "All Scripts";
  // Set a root node and open it
  var myRootNode = new FTreeNode(rootNode).setIsOpen(true);
  theTree.setRootNode(myRootNode);
  // Responder onResult() method lists the scripts and removes the "working" box.
  // The listScripts() function is defined within this object.
  this.onResult = function (result_rs) {
    listScripts(result_rs, theTree);
    theTree.refresh( );
    workingBox_mc.removeMovieClip( );
  };
  this.onStatus = function (error) {
    errorHandler(error.description)
  };

  function listScripts (my_rs, theTree) {      // Populate the tree
    // Set up a nested repeat using CategoryID.
    // CategoryIDs are in order, so when it changes, start a new node.
    var CatID = "";
    var catNode;
    var rootNode = theTree.getRootNode( );
    for (var i=0; i < my_rs.getLength( ); i++) {
      if (my_rs.getItemAt(i).CategoryID != CatID) {
        catNode = new FTreeNode(my_rs.getItemAt(i).CategoryDesc,
        my_rs.getItemAt(i).CategoryID);
        rootNode.addNode(catNode);
      }
      catNode.addNode(new FTreeNode(my_rs.getItemAt(i).ScriptName,
        my_rs.getItemAt(i).ScriptID));
      CatID = my_rs.getItemAt(i).CategoryID;
    }
  }
}

// Set up change handler for the Tree component
cnt_main_mc.cnt_view_mc.scripttree_tree.setChangeHandler("displayScript", _root);
```

Example 14-9. The ScriptRepository.as file (continued)

```
// Display the script in the interface
function displayScript (tree) {
  var theNode = tree.getSelectedNode( );
  var theScriptId = theNode.data;
  _global.currentScript = theScriptId;
  if (!theNode.isBranch( )) {
    if (findItem(scriptCache, theScriptId)) {
      displayIt(theScriptId, cnt_main_mc.cnt_view_mc);
    } else {
      putScriptInCacheAndDisplayIt(theScriptId, cnt_main_mc.cnt_view_mc);
    }
  } else {
    _global.currentScript = 0; // no current script
    // Display the dummy script
    displayIt(0, cnt_main_mc.cnt_view_mc);
  }
}

// Set up change handler for the scriptname_cb in
// cnt_main_mc.cnt_modify_mc (Modify screen)
cnt_main_mc.cnt_modify_mc.scriptname_cb.setChangeHandler(
                                         "displayScriptUpdate", _root);

// Display the script in the interface
function displayScriptUpdate (cb) {
  var theScript = cb.getSelectedItem( );
  var theScriptId = theScript.data;
  _global.currentScript = theScriptId;
  if (findItem(scriptCache, theScriptId)) {
    displayIt(theScriptId, cnt_main_mc.cnt_modify_mc);
  } else {
    putScriptInCacheAndDisplayIt(theScriptId, cnt_main_mc.cnt_modify_mc);
  }
}

// Display routines for scripts
// Scripts are cached the first time they are accessed from the remote DB

// Cache the script first, then display it
function putScriptInCacheAndDisplayIt (theScriptId, theMovieClip, refreshTree) {
  var temp = new ScriptObject(theScriptId);
  // Script is not cached, so get it from the remote service
  ScriptService.getScript(
      new ScriptDisplayResponder(theMovieClip,refreshTree), temp);
}

// Default responder for the remote method getScript( ).
// The movie clip is passed to the object so that
// the display will work in View and Modify screens
function ScriptDisplayResponder (theMovieClip, refreshTree) {
  this.onResult = function (result) {
    // Get the script from the remote method
    scriptCache[result.ScriptID] = result;
```

Example 14-9. The ScriptRepository.as file (continued)

```
    // Have to display from the responder function
    displayIt(result.ScriptId, theMovieClip);
    if (refreshTree)
      setTheScriptNode(cnt_main_mc.cnt_view_mc.scripttree_tree, result, true);
  };
}

function displayIt (theScriptId, theMovieClip) {
  // Set text fields
  theMovieClip.scriptname_txt.text = scriptCache[theScriptId].ScriptName;
  theMovieClip.scriptdesc_txt.text = scriptCache[theScriptId].ScriptDescription;
  theMovieClip.scriptcode_txt.text = scriptCache[theScriptId].ScriptCode;
  theMovieClip.scriptdateuploaded_txt.text =
                                  scriptCache[theScriptId].DateUploaded;
  theMovieClip.scriptdatemodified_txt.text =
                                  scriptCache[theScriptId].DateModified;
  theMovieClip.scriptversion_txt.text  =
                  scriptCache[theScriptId].VersionMajor + '.' +
                  scriptCache[theScriptId].VersionMinor + '.' +
                  scriptCache[theScriptId].VersionMicro;
  // Pick values in combo boxes
  theMovieClip.scriptlanguage_cb.pickValue(scriptCache[theScriptId].LanguageID);
  theMovieClip.scriptcategory_cb.pickValue(scriptCache[theScriptId].CategoryID);
  theMovieClip.scriptuser_cb.pickValue(scriptCache[theScriptId].UserID);
  return;
}

// Refresh the script tree
function scriptRepositoryRefresh (ScriptObj, exists) {
  scriptCache[ScriptObj.ScriptID] = ScriptObj;
  setTheScriptNode(cnt_main_mc.cnt_view_mc.scripttree_tree, ScriptObj, exists);
  displayScript(cnt_main_mc.cnt_view_mc.scripttree_tree);
}

// Open a specific node of the tree.
// If the node does not exist in the tree, add it.
function setTheScriptNode (theTree, theScript, exists) {
  var theParent = theTree.getRootNode();
  var theCategories = theParent.getChildNodes();
  var theParentNodeId = theScript.CategoryID;
  var theChildNodeId = theScript.ScriptID;
  for (var i=0; i < theCategories.length; i++) {
    if (theCategories[i].getData() == theParentNodeId) break;
  }
  if (!exists) {    // New script -- add the node to the main display tree
    theCategories[i].addNode(new FTreeNode(theScript.ScriptName,
                                      theScript.ScriptID));
  }
  theCategories[i].setIsOpen(true);
  theTree.refresh();
  var theNodes = theCategories[i].getChildNodes();
  for (var j=0; j < theNodes.length; j++) {
```

Example 14-9. The ScriptRepository.as file (continued)

```
    if (theNodes[j].getData( ) == theChildNodeId) break;
  }
  theTree.setSelectedNode(theNodes[j]);
}

// findItem:  method for the cache array to find an
//            item with a ScriptID that matches
function findItem (theArray, theItem) {
  for (var i in theArray) {
    if (theArray[i].ScriptID == theItem) {
      return true;
    }
  }
  return false;
}
```

The script is commented inline, but a few points are worth mentioning. A scriptCache property, which contains a generic *Object* instance, is set up as a cache for all displayed scripts. When a user clicks an item in the tree, the remote method is called and returns a *ScriptObject*. If the user clicks off the tree item and then back on again, further calls to the remote method are unnecessary, because the *ScriptObject* is stored in the cache. The zeroth element of the object become the descriptive label whenever a user has clicked on a folder in the tree; no script is shown. The code is written to be self-documenting (if it finds the items in the cache, it displays it; otherwise, it both adds it to the cache and displays it):

```
    if (findItem(scriptCache, theScriptId)) {
      displayIt(theScriptId, cnt_main_mc.cnt_modify_mc);
    } else {
      putScriptInCacheAndDisplayIt(theScriptId, cnt_main_mc.cnt_modify_mc);
    }
```

The *findItem( )* method is also declared in the *ScriptRepository.as* file. This function finds a script in the scriptCache object by iterating through the objects that are part of the scriptCache and comparing the theItem parameter (the second argument to the function) to the ScriptID property of each scriptCache element.

The *searchScripts( )* and *getAllScripts( )* methods utilize the same responder object. If searching for a phrase, the phrase is shown in the root of the tree ("scripts containing…"). If the user clicks the Show All Scripts button, "All Scripts" will be shown as the root node of the tree.

The *displayIt( )* function also serves double duty: the *displayScript( )* and *displayScriptUpdate( )* methods use it to refresh the main script and update script movie clips, respectively. User interface elements share the same names on the different movie clips, so we are able to reference them by passing the movie clip name to the function and using it as a prefix.

UserObject.as

The *UserObject*, like the *ScriptObject*, is a class definition that defines a class of an object that we will pass back and forth between client and server.

The complete *UserObject* class is shown in Example 14-10.

Example 14-10. The UserObject class definition

```
/*
UserObject
    Properties:
        UserID          numeric
        Username        string
        userpassword    string
        FirstName       string
        LastName        string
        Emailaddress    string
        HintQuestion    string
        HintAnswer      string
    Methods:
        init        initialize the object
        toString
        loginUser
        addUser
        emailPassword
        _copyProperties
        onResult
        onStatus
*/
function UserObject () {
  if (!this.inited)
    this.init(arguments);
}

UserObject.prototype.init = function (args) {
  this.inited = true; // Instance is initialized
  this.UserID          = (args[0] != undefined) ? args[0] : "";
  this.Username        = (args[1] != undefined) ? args[1] : "";
  this.Userpassword    = (args[2] != undefined) ? args[2] : "";
  this.FirstName       = (args[3] != undefined) ? args[3] : "";
  this.LastName        = (args[4] != undefined) ? args[4] : "";
  this.Emailaddress    = (args[5] != undefined) ? args[5] : "";
  this.HintQuestion    = (args[6] != undefined) ? args[6] : "";
  this.HintAnswer      = (args[7] != undefined) ? args[7] : "";
  this.PasswordConfirm = (args[8] != undefined) ? args[8] : "";
  this.isUserLogged    = (args[9] != undefined) ? args[9] : false;
};

// Register the object for use by Flash Remoting remote methods
Object.registerClass("UserObject", UserObject);

// Define a toString() function for reading the object
UserObject.prototype.toString = function () {
```

Example 14-10. The UserObject class definition (continued)

```
    var temp = "inited:    "      +  this.inited + '\n';
    temp += "UserID:    "         +  this.UserID + '\n';
    temp += "Username:    "       +  this.Username + '\n';
    temp += "Userpassword:    "   +  this.Userpassword + '\n';
    temp += "FirstName:    "      +  this.FirstName + '\n';
    temp += "LastName:    "       +  this.LastName + '\n';
    temp += "Emailaddress:    "   +  this.Emailaddress + '\n';
    temp += "HintQuestion:    "   +  this.HintQuestion + '\n';
    temp += "HintAnswer:    "     +  this.HintAnswer + '\n';
    temp += "PasswordConfirm:    " +  this.PasswordConfirm;
    temp += "isUserLogged:    "   +  this.isUserLogged;
    return temp;
};

// Call the remote loginUser( ) service
UserObject.prototype.loginUser = function (service) {
    service.loginUser(this, this);
};

// Call the remote addUser( ) service
UserObject.prototype.addUser = function (service) {
    if (this.Userpassword != this.PasswordConfirm) {
        errorHandler("Passwords don't match");
    this.isUserLogged = false;
    }
    service.addUser(this, this);
};

// Get scripts for user
UserObject.prototype.getScriptsForUser = function (service, box) {
    service.getScriptsForUser(new ComboBoxResponder(box), this);
};

// Debugging function to let us know that the object returned from
// the server was registered properly. In responder function, do:
//    result.test( )
UserObject.prototype.test = function ( ) {
    trace("UserObject successful")
};

// Copy properties from an object to this
UserObject.prototype._copyProperties = function (from) {
    for (var prop in from) {
        if (this[prop] != from[prop]) this[prop] = from[prop];
    }
};

// Responder method
UserObject.prototype.onResult = function (result) {
    if (result.isUserLogged == true) {
        // Put all properties from the result into the instance of the UserObject
        this._copyProperties(result);
        alertBox("userAlert", "Welcome " + result.FirstName);
```

Example 14-10. The UserObject class definition (continued)

```
    } else {
      trace("fail");
    }
};

// Call a global error handler for the movie
UserObject.prototype.onStatus = function (error) {
  errorHandler(error.description);
};

// Validation function for properties of the UserObject
UserObject.prototype.validate = function () {
  var errorMsg = "";
  if (this.Username == "")       errorMsg += "Username must not be empty\n";
  if (this.Userpassword == "") errorMsg += "Password must not be empty\n";
  if (this.FirstName == "")      errorMsg += "First name must not be empty\n";
  if (this.LastName == "")       errorMsg += "Last name must not be empty\n";
  if (!isValidEmail(this.Emailaddress))
      errorMsg += "Email address must be valid\n";
  if (this.HintQuestion == "") errorMsg += "Hint question must not be empty\n";
  if (this.HintAnswer == "")    errorMsg += "Hint answer must not be empty\n";
  if (this.PasswordConfirm == "")
      errorMsg += "Password confirmation must not be empty\n";
  return errorMsg;
};
```

You can see that the *UserObject* is constructed in a fashion similar to the *Script-Object*. The object contains an *init( )* method to allow objects returned from the server to retain their properties, a *_copyProperties( )* method to copy the properties from the object returned from the server to the current instance that called the remote service, *toString( )* and *test( )* methods for debugging, and *onResult( )* and *onStatus( )* methods that give it the ability to act as a responder object. The *validate( )* method of the *UserObject* works like its counterpart in the *ScriptObject*, with the exception that it calls a named function, *isValidEmail( )*, to validate an email address.

SiteUtilityFunctions.as

The calls to the site services are implemented as a set of named functions in the *SiteUtilityFunctions.as* file. The complete ActionScript code is shown in Example 14-11.

Example 14-11. The site utility functions

```
// General responder object for methods that return nothing:
//    onResult( ) method displays a message in an alert box
//    onStatus( ) method simply calls the error handler
function GeneralResponder (theName, theMessage, callbackFunction) {
  this.onResult = function (result) {
    alertBox(theName, theMessage, callbackFunction);
  };
```

Example 14-11. The site utility functions (continued)

```
  this.onStatus = function (error) {
    errorHandler(error.description);
  };
}

// Contact form event -- contactForm( ) calls remote method contactForm( )

function contactForm (from, userid, message) {
  if (message.length == 0) {
    errorHandler("Must enter a message");
    return;
  }
  // Call the remote service
  SiteService.contactForm(
    new GeneralResponder("contactAlert",
    "Email was sent: Thank you for contacting us"),
    from,      // Email from field
    userid,    // User ID
    message    // Message to send
  );
  workingAlert( );   // Display a "...working" box
  return;
}

// Send Page event -- sendPage( ) calls remote method sendPage( )
function sendPage (scriptid, to, from) {
  // Call the remote service
  SiteService.sendPage(
    new GeneralResponder("sendpageAlert", "Email was sent", setSendPageText),
      // Responder function fires alert
      scriptid,    // Script ID
      to,          // Email to field
      from         // Email from field
    );
  workingAlert( );  // Display a "...working" box
  return;
}

// Callback function to reset the text for the "send page to a friend" text field
function setSendPageText ( ) {
  cnt_main_mc.cnt_view_mc.sendto_txt.doDefault( );
}

// Set up About box on load
SiteService.about(new AboutResponder( ));

function AboutResponder ( ) {
  this.onResult = function (result_rs) {
    cnt_main_mc.cnt_about_mc.aboutname_txt.text =
      result_rs.getItemAt(0).CompanyName;
    cnt_main_mc.cnt_about_mc.aboutdesc_txt.text =
      result_rs.getItemAt(0).Description;
```

Example 14-11. The site utility functions (continued)

```
    // Set up the default download link for scripts stored in the remote database
    _global.downloadLink = result_rs.getItemAt(0).DownloadLink;
  };
  this.onStatus = function (error) {
    errorHandler(error.description);
  };
}

// Specialized responder object for retrieving the hint question
var GetEmailResponder = new Object( );
GetEmailResponder.onResult = function (result) {
  if ( _global.currentUser.HintQuestion == "")
    _global.currentUser.HintQuestion = result;
  retrieveBox("getHintAnswerBox", "Your hint Question", result,
            "Your answer", getAnswer);
};
GetEmailResponder.onStatus = function (error) {
  errorHandler(error.description);
};

// Callback function for getEmail( )
function getQuestion (theField) {
  _global.currentUser.Emailaddress = theField;
  UserService.getEmail(GetEmailResponder, theField);
  workingAlert( );    // Display a "...working" box
}


// Callback function for emailPassword( )
function getAnswer (theField) {
  var temp = SharedObject.getLocal("tries");
  if (temp.data.tries < temp.data.triesLimit &&
      temp.date.datetime < new Date( ).getMilliseconds( ) + temp.data.timeLimit) {
    UserService.emailPassword(EmailPasswordResponder,
                  _global.currentUser.Emailaddress,
                  theField);
    workingBox( );    // show the "...working" message
  } else {
    alertBox("badRetrieve",
      "You've tried more than " + temp.data.triesLimit + " times within " +
      temp.data.hours + " hours.\n" +
      "Try again later or contact the site administrator.");
  }
}

// Specialized responder object for emailPassword( )
var EmailPasswordResponder = new Object( );
EmailPasswordResponder.onResult = function (result) {
  if (result == true) {
    alertBox("goodRetrieveBox", "Your password has been sent");
  } else {
    retrieveBox("tryAgainBox", "Wrong answer. Try Again: ",
      _global.currentUser.HintQuestion, "", getAnswer);
```

Example 14-11. The site utility functions (continued)

```
      var temp = SharedObject.getLocal("tries");
      temp.data.tries ++;
  }
};

EmailPasswordResponder.onStatus = function (error) {
  errorHandler(error.description);
};

// Call the remote service emailPassword( ).
// This function interacts with alert boxes and message boxes in the main movie.
function emailPassword ( ) {
  // Set up limits for how many tries we will allow and store in SharedObject
  var hours = 24;
  var timeLimit = hours * 60 * 60 * 1000; // 1 day in milliseconds
  var triesLimit = 5;                     // triesLimit within the timeLimit specified

  var temp = SharedObject.getLocal("tries");
  // Set up the SharedObject if it hasn't been set up yet
  if (!temp.data.tries) {
    temp.data.tries      = 0;
    temp.data.triesLimit = triesLimit;
    temp.data.datetime   = new Date( );
    temp.data.timeLimit  = timeLimit;
    temp.data.hours      = hours;
  }
  // Step 1: Get email address
  retrieveBox("getEmail", "Enter your email address", "", "",getQuestion);
}

// Validate an email address (simple client-side validation): returns true or false
function isValidEmail (theString) {
  var isValid = (
   (theString.lastIndexOf('.') < theString.length - 2) &&   // must have dot
   (theString.indexOf('@') != -1) &&                        // must have @
   (theString.indexOf('@') == theString.lastIndexOf('@'))   // must not have two @@
   )
  return isValid;
}

// Put a Date object into human-readable date format (US format)
function doDateFormat (dateObj_date) {
  var d = dateObj_date.getDay( );
  var m = dateObj_date.getMonth( );
  var y = dateObj_date.getFullYear( );
  var h = dateObj_date.getHours( );
  var mn = dateObj_date.getMinutes( );
  mn = (mn < 10) ? '0' + mn : mn;
  var s = dateObj_date.getSeconds( );
  s = (s < 10) ? '0' + s : s;
  return m + '/' + d + '/' + y + ' ' + h + ':' + mn + ':' + s;
}
```

The *SiteUtilityFunctions.as* file takes care of calls to *contactForm( )*, *sendPage( )*, and *about( )* in the *SiteService* remote service. It also takes care of the email password functionality, which is one of the more complicated aspects of the application. In a typical HTML-based application, the steps can be followed like this:

1. User clicks the "email me my password" link and a page loads in with an email address box. User fills in email address and clicks Submit.

2. The remote service finds the user's email address in the database and returns a question. A new page loads in with a hint question and an answer box. User fills in answer and clicks Submit again.

3. The hint answer is checked in the database and, if correct, the username and password are mailed to the user. A new page loads, telling the user that the password has been mailed.

In the Flash Remoting application, we can't implement functionality that follows steps like this, but that is not a bad thing—it gives the application more of an immediate feel. Each call to the remote service is going to be handled by a responder object, but how do you call three remote services in a row that depend on the response from the previous call? You can't call them like this:

```
getQuestion(emailAddress);
getAnswer(hintAnswer);
emailPassword( );
```

If you were to execute this code, you would have an error because the three functions would fire immediately, even before the response was returned from the first function call.

Instead, we've created specialized responder objects that take care of calling the next remote method. It works like this:

1. The user clicks the email password link and the *emailPassword( )* function fires, displaying the dialog box that prompts the user for an email address.

2. The prompt box uses a callback function, *getQuestion( )*, which calls the remote method *getEmail( )* using the *GetEmailResponder* object.

3. The "...working" dialog box pops up while the question is being retrieved. Within the *GetEmailResponder.onResult( )* method, the hint question is shown in a second prompt box.

4. The prompt box (*retrieveBox( )*) function takes a callback function (*getAnswer( )*) as an argument. This way, when the user clicks OK, we can call another remote method: *emailPassword( )*.

5. If the hint answer matches the answer in the database, the username and password are mailed to the user. If not, *getAnswer( )* is called again, but a counter limits the number of attempts (for security reasons). After five unsuccessful attempts, the user is locked out for 24 hours. The number of tries and the length of lockout are variables that you can change.

Finally, the *SiteUtilityFunctions.as* file contains a few utility functions for email validation and date formatting.

UI.as

The *UI.as* file contains several additions to the built-in objects and components of Flash MX, and a responder object to simplify populating a combo box with a recordset result. The complete code for *UI.as* is shown in Example 14-12.

Example 14-12. The UI.as file contains code for GUI elements

```
// Set up a responder object to handle recordsets for ComboBoxes.
// This responder assumes that data is coming in with ID column
// in [0] position and description column in the [1] position.
// cbName is the fully-qualified name of the ComboBox.
// zeroElement is an optional argument that contains a zeroeth element
// of a descriptive label, like "--Categories--"

function ComboBoxResponder (cbName, zeroElement) {
  this.onResult = function (result_rs) {
    var fields = result_rs.getColumnNames( );
    // If there is a descriptive text to put in the Combo box
    // put it in the 0 position of the recordset.
    if (zeroElement != null) {
      var temp = {};
      result_rs.addItemAt(0, temp);
      result_rs.setField(0,fields[0], 0);
      result_rs.setField(0,fields[1],zeroElement);
    }
    var idField = '#' + fields[0] + '#';
    var descField = '#' + fields[1] + '#';
    DataGlue.bindFormatStrings(cbName, result_rs, descField, idField);
  };
  this.onStatus = errorHandler;
}

// Call the remote service to get all script IDs and names for scripts
// created by the current user.
function getUserScripts ( ) {
  ScriptService.getScriptsForUser(
    new ComboBoxResponder(
    cnt_main_mc.cnt_modify_mc.scriptname_cb, "-Scripts-"),
    _global.currentUser.username,
    _global.currentUser.password
  )
}

// pickValue( ): New method for ComboBoxes to be able to pick a value.
FComboBoxClass.prototype.pickValue = function (value) {
  for (var i=0; i<this.getLength( ); i++) {
    if (this.getItemAt(i).data == value) {
      this.setSelectedIndex(i);
```

Example 14-12. The UI.as file contains code for GUI elements (continued)

```
      break;
    }
  }
};

// setAutoBlank( ): New method for the TextField object.
// Set the field to blank when cursor is placed in field.
// NOTE: if passing false to the function to turn feature off,
// need to redefine any onSetFocus( ) functionality.
TextField.prototype.setAutoBlank = function (value) {
  if (value) {
    this.onSetFocus = function ( ) {this.text = "";}
  } else {
    this.onSetFocus = null;
  }
};

// defaultText: Allow for default text to be placed in a text field.
TextField.prototype.defaultText = null;

TextField.prototype.setDefaultText = function (value) {
  this.defaultText = value;
};

TextField.prototype.getDefaultText = function ( ) {
  return this.defaultText;
};

TextField.prototype.addProperty("defaultText",
                                this.getDefaultText,
                                this.setDefaultText);

// doDefault( ): Set the field text to defaultText.
TextField.prototype.doDefault = function ( ) {
  this.text = this.defaultText;
};
```

The *ComboBoxResponder* object is used by all combo boxes in the movie that are fed by remote recordsets. The recordsets are assumed to contain a number field and a description field. There are four combo boxes that use this responder object.

The *pickValue( )* method is added to the *FComboBox* class to add the functionality to all combo boxes in the movie. With this method, you can now pass a number to the combo box to have that particular record shown. For example, if you have a list of six categories in the Categories_cb combo box and you want the fourth item, you bring it into focus like this:

```
    Categories_cb.pickValue(3);
```

There are two additions to the *TextField* class as well. We've added an autoblank feature, which allows you to create a *TextField* that automatically becomes blank when you place your cursor in it. Turn on this functionality like this:

```
myTextfield.setAutoBlank(true);
```

We've also added a `defaultText` property to the *TextField* class. This property stores the default text for that particular field. Restore the default text for the text field using the custom *doDefault( )* method:

```
myTextField.doDefault( );
```

Flash User Interface Code

Many of the remote methods are called from the Flash interface. The ActionScript code for the interface is fairly elaborate and too long to reprint here in full, but a few of the key ActionScript snippets should be explained. (The full version can be downloaded from the online Code Depot.)

There are two custom message boxes that are built from movie clips rather than components, because one of the Macromedia components that would have been necessary is a commercial component (the Advanced Message Box). The message boxes are both set up to accept a callback function, which would be fired upon the user clicking the OK button. The *alertBox( )* function is shown in Example 14-13.

Example 14-13. Custom alert box movie clip is used extensively in the movie

```
// Display Alert Box
// Arguments:
//   theName:    name for the box
//   theMessage: text message to display
//   callback:   callback function when OK is clicked

function alertBox (theName, theMessage, callbackFunction, hideOK) {
  if (workingBox_mc)              // If there is a "...working" box, remove it
    workingBox_mc.removeMovieClip( );
  _root.attachMovie("alertbox_mc", theName, 1);
  var thisBox = _root[theName];
  thisBox._x = (Stage.width - thisBox._width)/2;
  thisBox._y = (Stage.height - thisBox._height)/2;
  thisBox.message_txt.text = theMessage;
  if (!hideOK) {
    // ok button
    thisBox.ok_btn.onRollOver = overState;
    thisBox.ok_btn.onRollOut = outState;
    thisBox.ok_btn.onPress = function () {
      thisBox.onUnload = callbackFunction;
      thisBox.removeMovieClip( );
    };
```

Example 14-13. Custom alert box movie clip is used extensively in the movie (continued)

```
  } else {
    thisBox.ok_btn._visible = false;
  }
};
```

The *workingAlert( )* function also shares this *alertBox( )* function and displays a "...working" message to the user. This is used by many remote methods in the application. The *retrieveBox( )* function displays a similar box, but it allows for user input, as shown in Figure 14-4.

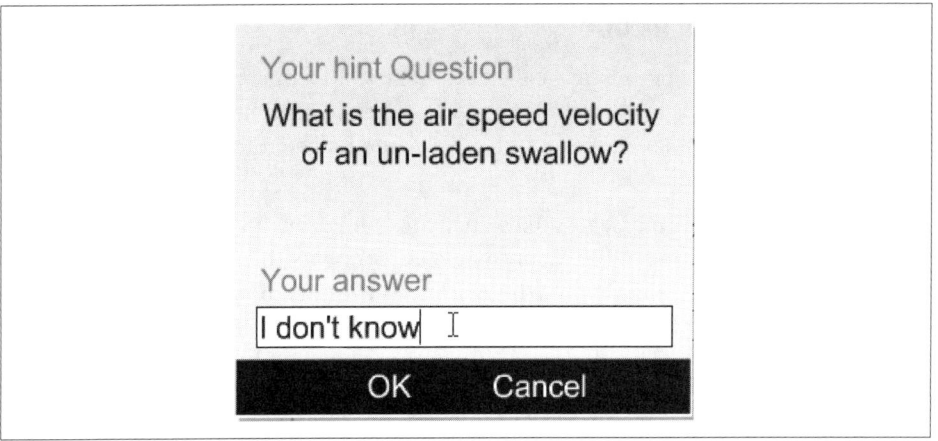

Figure 14-4. The retrieveBox( ) function calls a custom movie clip to retrieve information

Remote methods are called from the *onRelease* events of the buttons in the interface. Example 14-14 shows the code for the Upload Script button (scriptupload_btn).

Example 14-14. The Upload Script button calls

```
// scriptupload_btn
cnt_main_mc.cnt_upload_mc.scriptupload_btn.onRollOver = overState;
cnt_main_mc.cnt_upload_mc.scriptupload_btn.onRollOut = outState;
cnt_main_mc.cnt_upload_mc.scriptupload_btn.onRelease = function (mc) {
  var tempScript = new ScriptObject(null,
          cnt_main_mc.cnt_upload_mc.scriptname_txt.text,
          cnt_main_mc.cnt_upload_mc.scriptdesc_txt.text,
          cnt_main_mc.cnt_upload_mc.scriptcode_txt.text,
          cnt_main_mc.cnt_upload_mc.scriptlanguage_cb.getSelectedItem( ).data,
          cnt_main_mc.cnt_upload_mc.scriptcategory_cb.getSelectedItem( ).data,
          _global.currentUser.UserID,
          cnt_main_mc.cnt_upload_mc.scriptdateuploaded_txt.text,
          cnt_main_mc.cnt_upload_mc.scriptdatemodified_txt.text,
          1,
          0,
          0);
  // Make sure the script is filled in
  var errorMessage = tempScript.validate( );
```

Example 14-14. The Upload Script button calls (continued)

```
  if (errorMessage == "") {
    tempScript.addScript(ScriptService);
    workingAlert();
    mainScreen();
  } else {
    alertBox("validationError",errorMessage);
  }
};
```

In the scriptupload_btn button's *onRelease( )* event handler, a temporary *ScriptObject* is created using the text from the interface elements as the arguments to create the object. The tempScript variable contains the new *ScriptObject*, and the remote *addScript( )* method is called through this object. The "working" alert box is shown until it is removed by the appropriate responder function.

The "send this page to a friend" functionality is made possible by the use of the FlashVars attribute in the <object> and <embed> tags on the ColdFusion page that houses the movie. If an id variable is passed to the page, Flash will pick up the variable and execute the following code:

```
  if (scriptid != null && scriptid != "" && scriptid != "undefined") {
      putScriptInCacheAndDisplayIt(scriptid, cnt_main_mc.cnt_view_mc, true);
  }
```

We simply pass to the *putScriptInCacheAndDisplayIt( )* function the scriptid variable, the main display movie clip, and the value true to signal a refresh of the Tree component.

The HTML and ColdFusion code required for this functionality is shown in Example 14-15. The ColdFusion logic is highlighted in bold. Similar functionality can be created in PHP, ASP.NET, or Java pages as well.

Example 14-15. HTML and ColdFusion code to pass URL variables

```
<OBJECT classid="clsid:D27CDB6E-AE6D-11cf-96B8-444553540000"
codebase="http://download.macromedia.com/pub/shockwave/cabs/flash/
swflash.cab#version=6,0,65,0"
 WIDTH="100%" HEIGHT="100%" ALIGN="">
  <cfif isdefined("url.scriptid")><param name="flashvars"
    value="scriptid=<cfoutput>#url.scriptid</cfoutput>"></cfif>
<PARAM NAME=movie VALUE="ScriptRepository.swf">
<PARAM NAME=quality VALUE=high>
<PARAM NAME=bgcolor VALUE=#D9EFB4>
<EMBED src="ScriptRepository.swf" WIDTH="100%" HEIGHT="100%" ALIGN=""
quality=high bgcolor=#D9EFB4 TYPE="application/x-shockwave-flash"
PLUGINSPAGE="http://www.macromedia.com/go/getflashplayer"
<cfif isdefined("url.scriptid")>
flashvars="scriptid=<cfoutput>#url.scriptid#</cfoutput>"</cfif> ></EMBED>
</OBJECT>
```

You can also simply append variables to the end of the URL, but this technique is known to be buggy in several versions of the Player. Using FlashVars is a better approach when you can control the output of the HTML tags with server-side logic.

Testing and Debugging

With the first stages of the project completed and all parts in working order, the application should be tested. In the case of our *ScriptRepository.as* file, some built-in methods of the application and the objects used in the application make our life easier. We have defined *toString( )* methods of the two main objects, and also a *test( )* method to make sure that the object coming back from remote services has been cast to the correct datatype.

To use the *toString( )* method, simply sprinkle the code with the following, substituting the object name:

```
trace(myObject.toString());
```

This can even be used in the *init( )* method of your constructor to make sure your objects are being instantiated properly and at the right times:

```
trace(this.toString());
```

The *test( )* method is used in the responder *onResult( )* method. Simply call the *test( )* method on the result coming from the remote service. If the result has been cast to the correct object type, the *test( )* method will fire. If it hasn't been cast properly, the method will not fire:

```
ScriptObject.prototype.onResult = function (result) {
  result.test();
  // more code...
}
```

During testing we also set up a special server-side logging method to log each object that was being created on the server. The server-side code is shown in Example 14-16 and shows how easy it is to create a custom log file for a custom object.

Example 14-16. Server-side logging code

```
<cffunction access="remote" name="objToString"
 output="false" returntype="string" >
  <cfargument type="any" name="obj" />
  <cfloop collection = #obj# item = "i">
    <cfset temp = '#temp##1#. #obj.get(i)##chr(13)##chr(10)#'>
  </cfloop>

  <cfreturn temp />
</cffunction>
<cffunction name="logScript" access="remote" returntype="any">
  <cfargument name="scriptobj" type="any" />
  <cffile action="append" file="c:\log.txt"
   output=#this.objToString (ScriptObj)#>
</cffunction>
```

This method is called directly from another server-side service with a simple line, passing an object to the *logScript( )* method:

```
<cfset temp = logScript(scriptObj)>
```

Additionally, this logging routine will work with any *flashgateway.IO.ASObject* object.

The server-side services all contain *try/catch* blocks around the portions of the method that may throw an error. During debugging, you may want to comment out the *try/catch* blocks (using <!--- and ---> comment delimiters, as shown in bold) so that your errors are not captured; that way you can see the original error message as the server generated it:

```
<!---
<cftry>
--->
  <cfquery name="rsScripts" datasource="ScriptRepository">
    SELECT * FROM Scripts
    WHERE ScriptID =
    <cfqueryparam cfsqltype="cf_sql_numeric" value="#ScriptID#">
  </cfquery>
<!---
  <cfcatch type="any">
    <cfthrow message="There was a database error" />
  </cfcatch>
</cftry>
--->
```

Another good source of information while debugging can be found in the *flash.log* file created in the *ColdFusion_root\logs* directory.

Completed Application

The completed application can be viewed at *http://www.flash-remoting.com/scriptrepository/*. Files are also downloadable from the online Code Depot. The application can be used to compare against your own implementation if you are creating the examples on your own system.

Future Expansion

The application as it stands is workable, but it lacks a few key features that might be desirable. Following is a list of enhancements that you can add to the application if you feel the urge:

- Expand the CompanyInfo table to include more than one company by simply creating an autonumber field.
- Email notification to members if a new version of a script is uploaded.
- Add the ability to download multiple scripts in a *.zip* file.

- Add the ability to upload files from a filesystem rather than pasting into the application.
- Add an administrative interface and a new AccessGroup of "administrator".
- Add a "favorites" page that a user can go back to whenever he visits.

A common problem when building an application of this size is to allow feature creep to overtake you and prolong the application development time. By clearly setting out your specifications in advance, you can guard against feature creep by locking down the features that you will be implementing. Leave the other features for version 2.0.

Wrapping Up

In this chapter, you've seen the creation of a complete application that uses several key aspects of Flash Remoting, including database searches, inserting and updating a database, sending emails, passing variables from a URL to the Flash Remoting application, and passing objects from client to server and back again.

The next and final chapter, Chapter 15, is a Flash Remoting API reference.

Flash Remoting API

This chapter provides an alphabetical listing of ActionScript objects, methods, and events in the Flash Remoting API. It focuses on the Flash Remoting API as it is installed from the Flash Remoting components. This chapter complements the core ActionScript objects and classes found in *ActionScript for Flash MX: The Definitive Guide*, by Colin Moock (O'Reilly). Many more usage examples can be found in previous chapters, but this language reference consolidates the API calls in one place for easy reference.

Entry Headings

Each entry in this chapter is presented in the following basic format:

Entry   Availability

Purpose

Synopsis

The headings used to document each item in this chapter are described in Table 15-1.

Table 15-1. Flash Remoting API headings

Heading	Description
Availability	Indicates when the item was added to the Flash Remoting API. For this edition, the examples are all supported in Flash Player 6; however, if there are any API calls that became supported in a minor version of a Flash Player, the release version will be noted.
Synopsis	Shows the syntax used by the item. Anything that must be replaced by the user is shown in *constant-width italic* text. Optional arguments are noted in the *Arguments* section.
Methods	Applies to object and class entries. Simple listing of methods available to the object or class, further explained in their own API reference entries.

Table 15-1. Flash Remoting API headings (continued)

Heading	Description
Arguments	Applies to method entries only. Simple descriptions of all method arguments listed in the *Synopsis*.
Returns	Applies to method entries only. Describes the return value of the method (omitted if there is no return value).
Description	Explains how the item works, usually in a practical situation.
Bugs	Describes known problems associated with the item.
Example	Shows sample code associated with the item being described.
See Also	Lists cross-references to related entries within this API reference and other chapters.

DataGlue Object   Flash 6

allows data providers to be linked to data consumers

`DataGlue.methodName( )`

Methods

bindFormatFunction( )

> Binds a *RecordSet* object or other data provider to a UI component or other data consumer using a custom function that you create to format the data.

bindFormatStrings( )

> Binds a *RecordSet* object or other data provider to a UI component or other data consumer using special string replacements.

Description

The *DataGlue* object allows developers to easily bind *RecordSet* objects and other data providers to UI components. In most cases, the binding can be done with one line of code, which reduces the complexity of populating UI components with data.

To use the *DataGlue* object, you have to include the *DataGlue.as* file in the first frame of the Flash movie:

```
#include "DataGlue.as"
```

One advantage of using *DataGlue* over other techniques of populating UI components is that the data provider and the data consumer are bound together; changing one will change the other. If you delete a row in a recordset that is supplying a combo box, for example, the combo box will also have one of its items deleted.

For a component to work with *DataGlue*, it has to be *data-aware*. A data-aware component interacts with the *RSDataProviderClass* and includes the following methods:

> *addItem( )*
> *addItemAt( )*
> *getLength( )*
> *removeAll( )*
> *removeItemAt( )*

replaceItemAt( )
setDataProvider( )
sortItemsBy( )

See Also

The *RecordSet* class; Chapters 3 and 4

DataGlue.bindFormatFunction( ) Method

binds a data provider to a data consumer using a custom function

```
DataGlue.bindFormatFunction(dataConsumer, dataProvider, formatFunction)
```

Arguments

dataConsumer
> The UI component or other consumer of data to be bound to a data provider.

dataProvider
> A *RecordSet* object or other data provider to be bound to a data consumer.

formatFunction
> A custom function that you define that returns an object with the properties label and data. It must accept a single *RecordSet* object as a parameter.

Description

The *DataGlue* object is used to bind a data provider to a data consumer. The most common and useful application of this is to bind a *RecordSet* object to a ListBox, ComboBox, or other UI component that will display the data from the *RecordSet*. The *bindFormatFunction( )* method allows the developer to specify a function to format the appearance of the data in the UI component. If you don't need to format the data, using *DataGlue.bindFormatStrings( )* is more straightforward.

Example

The following example code assumes a combo box named allProducts_cb is present on the main timeline:

```
#include "NetServices.as"
#include "DataGlue.as"

// Initialize the connection and service objects.
if (connected == null) {
  connected = true;
  NetServices.setDefaultGatewayUrl("http://localhost/flashservices/gateway");
  var my_conn = NetServices.createGatewayConnection();
  var myService = my_conn.getService("com.oreilly.frdg.searchProducts", this);
}

// The remote getSearchResult( ) method (not shown) returns a recordset.
myService.getSearchResult();
```

```
// Display the product names in the combo box. Use the product IDs as the data.
// The product names are formatted in uppercase for display.
function formatDataForBox (theRecord) {
  var formatObj = new Object();
  formatObj.label = theRecord.ProductName.toUpperCase();
  formatObj.data  = theRecord.ProductID;
  return formatObj;
}

// The responder function binds the returned recordset to the combo box.
function getSearchResult_Result(result_rs) {
  DataGlue.bindFormatFunction(allProducts_cb, result_rs, formatDataForBox);
}
```

The *formatDataForBox( )* function creates an object with two properties: label and data. This function is called by the *bindFormatFunction( )* method for each row in the recordset. The recordset is bound to the combo box, which displays the recordset's capitalized product names in a list and uses the product IDs as the underlying data.

See Also

DataGlue.bindFormatStrings( ), the *RecordSet* class; Chapter 3

DataGlue.bindFormatStrings( ) Method   Flash 6

binds a data provider to a data consumer using string replacements

DataGlue.bindFormatStrings(*dataConsumer, dataProvider, labelString, dataString*)

Arguments

dataConsumer
> The field that you want to sort the *RecordSet* object by.

dataProvider
> The direction to sort the recordset. "DESC" specifies a descending sort; anything else is ascending.

labelString
> The label that will show in the UI component.

dataString
> The data that will correspond to the label in the UI component.

Description

The *DataGlue* object contains two methods for binding data to a UI component. The *bindFormatFunction( )* method is best used when the data coming from the recordset or other data provider has to be formatted in a particular way. If the data can be used directly, the *bindFormatStrings( )* method is easier to use because you don't have to define a custom function that formats the data. Simply specify the fields to use for the label and data properties of the data consumer in the method call.

Example

The following example code assumes a combo box named allProducts_cb is present on the main timeline:

```
#include "NetServices.as"
#include "DataGlue.as"

// Initialize the connection and service objects.
if (connected == null) {
  connected = true;
  NetServices.setDefaultGatewayUrl("http://localhost/flashservices/gateway");
  var my_conn = NetServices.createGatewayConnection();
  var myService = my_conn.getService("com.oreilly.frdg.searchProducts", this);
}
// The remote getSearchResult() method (not shown) returns a recordset.
myService.getSearchResult();

// Display the product names in the combo box. Use the product IDs as the data.
function getSearchResult_Result(result_rs) {
  DataGlue.bindFormatStrings(allProducts_cb, result_rs,
    '#ProductName#', '#ProductID#');
}
```

The fields that are utilized in the *bindFormatStrings( )* method (ProductName and ProductID) are surrounded by quotes and pound signs (#). The pound signs around the *RecordSet* fields denote that the field is to be replaced by a field from the data provider (the *RecordSet*, in this case).

See Also

DataGlue.bindFormatFunction( ), the *RecordSet* class; Chapters 3 and 4

NetConnection Class

Flash 6

enables a connection to a remote server

myNetConnectionObject.methodName(params)

Methods

addHeader( )
> Adds a header to every AMF packet in this connection.

call( )
> Invokes a service method on the remote server.

clone( )*
> Creates a clone of a *NetConnection* object, without headers.

---

* Added to the *NetConnection* object as a result of including *NetDebug.as*.

close( )
> Closes the *NetConnection* object.

connect( )
> Defines the URL used in a Flash Remoting connection.

getDebugConfig( )*
> Retrieves a *NetDebugConfig* object with all subscribed events.

getDebugId( )*
> Retrieves the *NetConnection* object's debug identifier.

getService( )*
> Creates a service object that acts as a proxy to a remote service method.

ReplaceGatewayUrl( )*
> Changes the gateway URL for the current connection.

RequestPersistentHeader( )*
> A method that can be initiated by a server-side service to add a header to the request packets.

setCredentials( )*
> Creates a credentials header that is attached to each AMF packet.

setDebugId( )*
> Creates a user-defined debug identifier.

trace( )*
> Sends output to the NetConnection Debugger panel.

Only the public methods of the *NetConnection* class are shown. Many of the methods require the inclusion of the *NetDebug.as* or *NetServices.as* file, as indicated in the footnotes.

Description

The *NetConnection* class is at the heart of Flash Remoting. The class is a core part of Flash MX after the installation of the Flash Remoting components; however, the *NetServices.as* and *NetDebug.as* files add several methods to the *NetConnection* class, as noted under the Methods heading.

A *NetConnection* object allows communication between the Flash movie and Flash Remoting on the server-side service. Methods of the *NetConnection* class allow the developer to call remote services and process the results within the Flash movie. A *NetConnection* object is typically created in the initialization phase of the Flash movie in the first frame on the main timeline (following any preloader) by calling *NetServices.createGatewayConnection( )*.

---

* Added to the *NetConnection* object as a result of including *NetServices.as*.

An important method of the *NetConnection* class is the *getService( )* method. The call to *NetConnection.getService( )* returns a service object (of the *NetServiceProxy* class), which acts as proxy to the remote service. Developers can invoke remote service functions as methods of the service object.

Examples

There are two ways of creating *NetConnection* objects in your Flash Remoting application. The first was demonstrated in most of the examples in this book. It involves the use of the *NetServices.as* file and the *NetServices.createGatewayConnection( )* method:

```
#include "NetServices.as"
if (connected == null) {
  // Initialize the variable, so this section is only called once
  connected = true;
  // Set the default URL, so the NetConnection object knows how to connect
  NetServices.setDefaultGatewayUrl("http://127.0.0.1/flashservices/gateway");
  // Create the NetConnection object
  var my_conn = NetServices.createGatewayConnection( );
}
```

A variation of this approach is to omit the call to *setDefaultGatewayUrl( )* and pass the gateway URL as a parameter to *createGatewayConnection( )* instead. See those methods under the *NetServices* class in this chapter for more information.

Including the *NetServices.as* file also adds other methods to the *NetConnection* class, such as *getService( )* and *setCredentials( )*.

The second way of creating a *NetConnection* object is to simply use the new keyword:

```
if (connected == null) {
  // Initialize the variable so this section is only called once
  connected = true;
  // Create the NetConnection object
  var my_conn = new NetConnection( );
  // Set the URL to the NetConnection object
  my_conn.connect("http://127.0.0.1/flashservices/gateway");
}
```

Using this technique, it is not necessary to include *NetServices.as*, but if you don't include it you will not have access to the methods of the *NetConnection* class contained in *NetServices.as*.

There are several private methods of the *NetConnection* class that are included when you include the *NetDebug.as* file in your Flash movie, in addition to those noted under the Methods heading. The NetConnection Debugger panel uses these methods internally: *attachDebug( )*, *sendDebugEvent( )*, *sendServerEvent( )*, *sendClientEvent( )*, *addNetDebugHeader( )*, *updateConfig( )*, *isRealTime( )*, *setupRecordset( )*, as well as several methods that take the place of actual *NetConnection* methods.

See Also

NetConnection.call( ), *NetConnection.connect( )*, the *NetDebug* class, the *NetDebug-Config* class, *NetServices.createGatewayConnection( )*, *NetServices.setDefaultGatewayUrl( )*; Chapter 4; the *NetServices.as*, *NetDebug.as*, *NetConnection.as*, and *RecordSet.as* files in your Flash *Includes* directory

NetConnection.addHeader( ) Method
Flash 6

adds a header to every AMF packet for a connection

myNetConnectionObject.addHeader(*name, mustUnderstand, object*)

Arguments

name
> An arbitrary header name that can be recognized by the server.

mustUnderstand
> A Boolean value that denotes whether the server must process the header before sending a result back to the Flash application.

object
> Any ActionScript object that becomes the header named in the *addHeader( )* call.

Description

The *addHeader( )* method is useful when you have a specific header that requires server processing, or an arbitrary piece of information that you want attached to every AMF packet, such as a user identification number or session ID.

After using *addHeader( )*, each subsequent AMF packet from the client will contain the header information. AMF calls returned from the server do not include this header, unless your server-side code processes the header and manually adds it to the return packet.

Example

The following code shows the basic syntax of the *addHeader( )* method:

```
if (connected == null) {
  connected = true;
  NetServices.setDefaultGatewayUrl("http://127.0.0.1/flashservices/gateway");
  var my_conn - NetServices.createGatewayConnection();
  var my_header = {user:'tom', password:'muck'};
  my_conn.addHeader('myLogin', false, my_header);
}
```

In this case, a header named myLogin is added to all AMF packets originating from the client on this connection. The my_header variable contains an ActionScript object that acts as the body of the myLogin header. The server must have the necessary code in place to process this information for it to be useful.

In most cases, you won't use *addHeader( )* directly, because the AMF packets are typically not manipulated by your server-side services. A notable exception is a Cold-Fusion or JRun 4 user-login framework, which uses the *setCredentials( )* method on the client. The *setCredentials( )* method, however, takes care of calling the *addHeader( )* method for you.

See Also

NetConnection.RequestPersistentHeader( ), *NetConnection.setCredentials( )*; Chapter 4

NetConnection.call( ) Method   Flash 6

invokes a server-side method from client-side ActionScript

myNetConnectionObject.call(*remoteMethod, resultObject, arg1,...argn*)

Arguments

remoteMethod

> The name of the server-side method to invoke, in the format *serviceName*. *methodName*. The syntax for calling the method varies with the server technology, as described in earlier chapters.

resultObject

> An ActionScript object with an *onResult( )* method to handle results from the call to the server-side method. You can also pass null, in which case no results are handled.

arg1, ...argn

> Zero or more arguments to be passed to the remote method. The third argument passed to the *call( )* method (i.e., arg1) is passed as the first argument to the remote method. The next argument, arg2, is passed as the second argument to the remote method, and so on.

Returns

Return value of the remote method is passed to the *onResult( )* handler of *resultObject*.

Description

The *call( )* method is used to invoke a remote method through the *NetConnection* object. The *call( )* method is not typically used directly by a developer. Instead, the developer typically uses the *getService( )* method, which is a wrapper around the *call( )* method that also adds more functionality. Using *call( )*, you have to create responder objects that contain *onResult( )* and *onStatus( )* methods; you can't use the named function *methodname_onResult( )* or *methodname_onStatus( )* techniques shown elsewhere in this book.

Because the *call( )* method is a core method of the *NetConnection* object, you don't have to include the *NetServices.as* file in your Flash application to use it.

Example

The following code shows the basic syntax of the *call( )* method:

```
// Create a responder object
var myResult = new Object( );
// Create an onResult( ) method to handle results from the call to the remote method
myResult.onResult = function (result) {
  display_txt.text = result;
};

// Create the connection
var my_conn = new NetConnection( );
// Attach a URL for the gateway
my_conn.connect("http://127.0.0.1/flashservices/gateway");
// Call the remote method
my_conn.call("com.oreilly.frdg.HelloUser.sayHello", myResult, firstname_txt.text);
// Nullify the connection
my_conn.close( );
```

In this case, a remote method named *sayHello( )* in the *com.oreilly.frdg.HelloUser* service is invoked with one argument: firstname_txt.text. A responder object is created before calling the remote method and is passed as the second argument to *call( )*. The *onResult( )* method of the responder object receives the response from the remote method call.

See Also

NetConnection.getService( ); Chapter 4

NetConnection.clone( ) Method   Flash 6

duplicates a connection object, without current headers

myNetConnectionObject.clone( )

Returns

A new *NetConnection* object with the same URL as the original *NetConnection* object, but without the headers of that object.

Description

The *clone( )* method is used when you need a new connection to the remote server that does not contain the headers of your existing connection, such as to call a method using a new authentication scheme.

Example

The following code shows the basic syntax of the *clone( )* method:

```
// NetServices.as is necessary to use clone( )
#include "NetServices.as"
```

```
// Set the URL for both connections
NetServices.setDefaultGatewayUrl("http://127.0.0.1/flashservices/gateway");
// Create the original connection
var my_conn = NetServices.createGatewayConnection();
// Set the credentials header for the first connection
my_conn.setCredentials('admin', '1234');
// Create the cloned connection without the headers (no credentials)
var my_cloneConnection = my_conn.clone();
```

See Also

NetServices.createGatewayConnection( ), *NetServices.setCredentials( )*; Chapter 4

NetConnection.close( ) Method   Flash 6

closes a connection to the Flash Remoting server

myNetConnectionObject.close( )

Description

The *close( )* method is used to close a connection to the Flash Remoting server. A *connection* is not a physical connection to the server, so this method does not physically close anything. It merely sets the URL of the *NetConnection* object to null, thereby causing any further attempts to connect to the server to fail.

Example

The following code shows the basic syntax of the *close( )* method:

```
if (connected == null) {
  connected = true;
  NetServices.setDefaultGatewayUrl("http://127.0.0.1/flashservices/gateway");
  var my_conn = NetServices.createGatewayConnection();
  var verified = myLoginService();
  if (!verified) my_conn.close();
}
```

In this case, another method named *myLoginService( )* is called. If the result of that service call is false, the connection to my_conn is closed at the ActionScript level, thereby nullifying any further attempts to connect to services using the my_conn connection. In practice, the *close( )* method is not used very often, as connections need not be closed in most situations.

See Also

NetConnection.connect( ); Chapter 4

NetConnection.connect( ) Method

defines the URL used in a Flash Remoting connection

myNetConnectionObject.connect(*targetURL*)

Arguments

targetURL

A URL of the Flash Remoting gateway that you wish to connect to. The URL can be prepended with an *http://* or *https://* protocol, but can also be used without any protocol, which defaults to *http://*.

Returns

true if the protocol is valid (*http://* or *https://*), and false otherwise.

Description

The *connect( )* method is used to connect to a Flash Remoting gateway. Using the *connect( )* method does not require the inclusion of the *NetServices.as* file. The word *connect* is something of a misnomer; at no time during this call does the *NetConnection* object connect to the remote server. The actual connection takes place when a service function call is made.

Example

The following code shows the basic syntax of the *connect( )* method:

```
// Create the connection
var my_conn = new NetConnection( );
// Attach a URL for the gateway
my_conn.connect("http://127.0.0.1/flashservices/gateway");
```

In most cases, you will not use this method directly but instead use the *createGatewayConnection( )* method, which instantiates a *NetConnection* object and connects to it as well.

See Also

NetConnection.ReplaceGatewayUrl( ), *NetServices.createGatewayConnection( )*, *NetServices.setDefaultGateway( )*; Chapter 4

NetConnection.getDebugConfig( ) Method

retrieves an object containing the subscribed debug events

myNetConnectionObject.getDebugConfig( )

Returns

A *NetDebugConfig* object containing the currently subscribed events.

Description

The *getDebugConfig( )* method is used to programmatically retrieve the currently subscribed events for the NetConnection Debugger panel.

Example

The following code shows the basic syntax of the *getDebugConfig( )* method and how it might be used:

```
#include "NetDebug.as"
#include "NetServices.as"
NetServices.setDefaultGatewayURL("http://localhost/flashservices/gateway");
var my_conn = NetServices.createGatewayConnection( );
var my_service = my_conn.getService("myService", this);
my_conn.trace("Service Object created.");

function onStatus (error) {
  // Show error message
  trace(error.description);
  // Get the NetDebugConfig object
  var debugConfig = my_conn.getDebugConfig( );
  // Iterate through the properties of the NetDebugObject
  for (i in debugConfig) {
    trace (i + ":" + debugConfig[i]);
    // If the property is an object itself, iterate through its properties
    for (j in debugConfig[i]) trace ("   " + j + ":" + debugConfig[i][j]);
  }
}
```

In the code, a *NetDebugConfig* object is created when a service call fails, and the properties of the object are written to the Output window. Note that some of the properties of the *NetDebugConfig* object are objects themselves, so they will be written to the Output window as [object Object]. The properties give you information about your current debug settings.

See Also

NetConnection.getDebugId( ), *NetConnection.setDebugId( )*, the *NetDebug* class, the *NetDebugConfig* class; Chapter 13

NetConnection.getDebugId( ) Method   Flash 6

retrieves a *NetDebugConfig* object's identifier

myNetConnectionObject.getDebugId( )

Returns

The identifier for the *NetDebugConfig* object.

Description

Each *NetDebugConfig* object has an associated ID, which is typically a sequential integer. However, you can set the identifier with *NetConnection.setDebugId( )*.

Example

The following code shows the basic syntax of the *getDebugId( )* method:

```
#include "NetDebug.as"
#include "NetServices.as"
NetServices.setDefaultGatewayURL("http://localhost/flashservices/gateway");
var my_conn = NetServices.createGatewayConnection( );
var my_service = my_conn.getService("myService", this);
trace(my_conn.getDebugId( ));
```

In this case, the *NetDebugConfig* object identifier is simply traced to the Output window.

See Also

NetConnection.setDebugId( ), *NetDebugConfig*; Chapter 13

NetConnection.getService( ) Method

Flash 6

creates a proxy to a remote service and optionally handles responses

myNetConnectionObject.getService(*serviceName, defaultResponder*)

Arguments

serviceName

> The name of the remote service whose methods you want to access. This varies according to the server model and the type of service you are accessing, as documented in earlier chapters.

defaultResponder

> An optional responder object that handles the responses and errors with defined *onResult( )* and *onStatus( )* methods. If you don't specify the *defaultResponder*, you must specify responders in your method calls.

Returns

A *NetServiceProxy* object.

Description

The *getService( )* method is used to create a proxy to a remote service and is one of the most frequently used *NetConnection* methods. The call to *getService( )* returns a *NetServiceProxy* object, which dispatches responses from the service to the client, as discussed in Chapter 4.

Example

The following code shows the basic syntax of the *getService( )* method:

```
#include "NetServices.as"
onResult = function (myResult) {
  results_txt.text = myResult;
};

onStatus = function (myError) {
  results_txt.text = myError.description;
};
var servicePath = "com.oreilly.frdg.HelloUser";
NetServices.setDefaultGatewayURL("http://localhost/flashservices/gateway");
var my_conn = NetServices.createGatewayConnection( );
var my_service = my_conn.getService(servicePath, this);
my_service.sayHello(firstname_txt.text);
```

The first parameter passed to *getService( )* must be the properly formed service name, as discussed at length in Chapters 1, 2, 5, 6, 7, 8, 9, and 10. In this case, the method is called with a second parameter, the keyword this, which acts as a responder object. The keyword this represents the current timeline object, and you can see from the code snippet that there are both *onResult( )* and *onStatus( )* methods defined in the timeline. You can also pass a custom responder object (one created for this express purpose), as shown throughout the book.

The *getService( )* method can also be called with no responder object. In that case, the responder object has to be passed in each remote method call, as in this code:

```
#include "NetServices.as"
function MyResult ( ) {
  this.onResult = function (myResult) {
    results_txt.text = myResult;
  };
  this.onStatus = function (myError) {
    results_txt.text = myError.description;
  };
}
var servicePath = "com.oreilly.frdg.HelloUser";
NetServices.setDefaultGatewayURL("http://localhost/flashservices/gateway");
var my_conn = NetServices.createGatewayConnection( );
var my_service = my_conn.getService(servicePath);
my_service.sayHello(new MyResult( ), firstname_txt.text);
```

In the code, which is almost identical in functionality to the previous example, the *getService( )* method call does not include a responder object (the second argument is omitted). For this to work without errors, each method call on the my_service object must include a responder object as the first argument. In this case, the first argument is stripped off by the *NetServiceProxy* object and used as the responder object.

See Also

NetConnection.call( ), the *NetServiceProxy* object; "Creating the Service Object" and "Creating Responder Functions" in Chapter 4

NetConnection.ReplaceGatewayUrl( ) Method

changes the gateway URL

myNetConnectionObject.ReplaceGatewayUrl(*targetURL*)

Arguments

targetURL

> A URL of the Flash Remoting gateway that you wish to connect to. The URL must be prepended with an *http://* or *https://* protocol.

Description

The *ReplaceGatewayUrl( )* method is used to change the Flash Remoting gateway URL previously specified via *NetConnection.connect( )*, *NetServices.createGatewayConnection( )*, or *NetServices.setDefaultGatewayUrl( )*. Using the *ReplaceGatewayUrl( )* method requires the inclusion of the *NetServices.as* file.

Example

The following code shows the basic syntax of the *ReplaceGatewayUrl( )* method:

```
#include "NetServices.as"
if (connected == null) {
  // Initialize the variable so this section is only called once
  connected = true;
  // Create the NetConnection object
  gatewayURL = "http://www.flash-remoting.com/flashservices/gateway";
  var my_conn = NetServices.createGatewayConnection(gatewayURL);
}
```

Then, at some later time:

```
newGatewayURL = "http://127.0.0.1/flashservices/gateway";
my_conn.ReplaceGatewayUrl(newGatewayURL);
```

Usage

You should not use this method directly, because it is reserved for use by the server, which can pass a ReplaceGatewayUrl header to the Flash movie.

See Also

NetConnection.close( ), *NetConnection.connect( )*, *NetServices.createGatewayConnection( )*, *NetServices.setDefaultGatewayUrl( )*; Chapter 4

NetConnection.RequestPersistentHeader( ) Method

requests a header in AMF packets sent to server

```
myNetConnectionObject.RequestPersistentHeader(name, object)
```

Arguments

name
> An arbitrary header name that can be recognized by the server.

object
> Any ActionScript object that becomes the header named in the *addHeader( )* call.

Description

RequestPersistentHeader( ) is a method that can be initiated by the server-side gateway to tell the Flash client to add a header to the request packets. It is equivalent to calling the *addHeader( )* method, but it can be triggered by the server-side gateway. It is useful when the server application desires that a specific header, such as a session ID, be attached to every AMF packet sent from the client to the server.

After the server invokes *RequestPersistentHeader( )*, each subsequent AMF packet from the client on the relevant connection will contain the specified header information. AMF packets returned from the server do not include this header, unless your server-side code manually adds it to the return packet.

Usage

You should not use this method directly, because it is reserved for future use by the gateway.

See Also

NetConnection.addHeader( ), *NetConnection.setCredentials( )*; Chapter 4

NetConnection.setCredentials( ) Method

authenticates a user with a credentials header

```
myNetConnectionObject.setCredentials(userid, password)
```

Arguments

userid
> A username to be used by the server for authentication.

password
> A password to be used by the server for authentication.

Description

The *setCredentials( )* method is used when you have an authentication routine on your server that works in tandem with a credentials header. After calling *setCredentials( )*, the credentials header is attached to every AMF packet generated by the client and going to the server.

As of this writing, only JRun 4 and ColdFusion MX support the credentials header. Calling *setCredentials( )* is the same thing as calling the *addHeader( )* method, like this:

```
my_conn.addHeader("Credentials", false, {userid: userid, password: password});
```

Example

The following code shows the basic syntax of the *setCredentials( )* method:

```
if (connected == null) {
  connected = true;
  NetServices.setDefaultGatewayUrl("http://127.0.0.1/flashservices/gateway");
  var my_conn = NetServices.createGatewayConnection( );
  my_conn.setCredentials(username_txt.text, password_text.text);
}
```

In this case, the credentials header is added to the AMF packet and every subsequent AMF packet going to the server.

See Also

NetConnection.addHeader( ); Chapter 4, "ColdFusion Security: Authenticating Users" in Chapter 5, Chapter 7

NetConnection.setDebugId( ) Method   Flash 6

assigns an arbitrary identifier to a *NetDebugConfig* object

myNetConnectionObject.setDebugId(*id*)

Arguments

id

An arbitrary header name that can be recognized by the server.

Description

The *setDebugId( )* method is used to specify an identifier for a *NetConnection* object. Each *NetConnection* object has an associated identifier that is typically a sequential integer. For example, if you call *getDebugId()* on a *NetConnection* object that is the only object in your movie, you will receive an ID of 0. To change this to a meaningful value, you can use the *setDebugId( )* method.

The code syntax completion of Flash Remoting, as well as the Flash Remoting documentation, lists the syntax as *setDebugID* (capital *I* and *D*), but the correct spelling is *setDebugId( )* (lowercase *d*).

Example

The following code shows the basic syntax of the *setDebugId( )* method:

```
if (connected == null) {
  connected = true;
  NetServices.setDefaultGatewayUrl("http://127.0.0.1/flashservices/gateway");
  var my_conn = NetServices.createGatewayConnection( );
  my_conn.setDebugId("Connection");
}
```

See Also

NetConnection.getDebugId( ), *NetConnection.setCredentials( )*; Chapter 13

NetConnection.trace( ) Method

displays a string or object in the NetConnection debugger

myNetConnectionObject.trace(*objectName*)

Arguments

objectName

  Any string or ActionScript object that is serializable as a string.

Description

The *trace( )* method is used during debugging to display a string, object, or other value in the NetConnection Debugger panel. This is useful during debugging for determining where a particular problem might be occurring.

The *NetDebug.as* file must be included in order to use the *trace( )* method, and the NetConnection Debugger panel must be open as well.

Example

The following code shows the basic syntax of the *trace( )* method:

```
#include "NetServices.as"
#include "NetDebug.as"

if (connected == null) {
  connected = true;
  NetServices.setDefaultGatewayUrl("http://127.0.0.1/flashservices/gateway");
  var my_conn = NetServices.createGatewayConnection( );
  my_conn.trace("URL established");
  var my_service = my_conn.getService("com.oreilly.frdg.searchProducts");
  my_conn.trace("Service object created");
}
```

The *trace( )* statements in this block of code merely alert the developer that a specific line in the code was reached. This is helpful for narrowing down problems in blocks of code. The output of the *NetConnection.trace( )* method is sent to the NetConnection debugger (don't confuse it with the global *trace( )* function, which displays text in the Flash authoring tool's Output window).

See Also

NetDebug.trace( ); Chapter 13

NetDebug Object

aids in debugging a Flash Remoting application

NetDebug.*methodName*(*params*)

Methods

trace( )
> Sends output to the NetConnection Debugger panel.

Description

The *NetDebug* object is the ActionScript object that powers the NetConnection Debugger panel, allowing a developer to view and trace output to and from the application server. The object is defined in the *NetDebugImpl.as* file, which is included automatically when *NetDebug.as* is included. Its one public method, *trace()*, is also duplicated in the *NetConnection* object, but the *NetDebug* object contains many private methods that can be put to use by the enterprising Flash Remoting developer. Because ActionScript 1.0 is not a strict OOP language, the public and private methods are all defined in the same way and accessible to programmers.

Private methods include *addNetConnection( )*, *removeNetConnection( )*, *sendDebugEvent( )*, *sendCommand( )*, *requestNewConfig( )*, *updateConfig( )*, *sendStatus( )*, *onEvent( )*, *onEventError( )*, *onReceiveCommand( )*, *onReceiveError( )*, and *traceNetServices( )*.

See Also

NetConnection.trace( ), the *NetDebugConfig* class; Chapter 13

NetDebug.trace( ) Method

displays a value in the NetConnection debugger

NetDebug.trace(*string_or_object*)

Arguments

string_or_object
> Any string or ActionScript object that is serializable as a string.

Description

The *trace( )* method is used during debugging to display a string, object, or other value in the NetConnection Debugger panel. This is useful during debugging for determining where a particular problem might be occurring.

The *NetDebug.as* file must be included in order to use the *trace( )* method, and the NetConnection Debugger panel must be open as well.

Example

The following code shows the basic syntax of the *trace( )* method:

```
#include "NetServices.as"
#include "NetDebug.as"

if (connected == null) {
  connected = true;
  NetServices.setDefaultGatewayUrl("http://127.0.0.1/flashservices/gateway");
  var my_conn = NetServices.createGatewayConnection( );
  NetDebug.trace("URL established");
  var my_service = my_conn.getService("com.oreilly.frdg.searchProducts");
  NetDebug.trace("Service object created");
}
```

The *trace( )* statements in this block of code merely alert the developer that a specific line in the code was reached. This is helpful for narrowing down problems in blocks of code. The output of the *NetDebug.trace( )* method is sent to the NetConnection debugger (don't confuse it with the global *trace( )* function, which displays text in the Flash authoring tool's Output window).

See Also

NetConnection.trace( ), the *NetDebugConfig* class; Chapter 13

NetDebugConfig Class   Flash 6

contains properties of the current debug settings

myNetDebugConfigObject.methodName(params)

myNetDebugConfigObject.propertyName

Methods

getDebug( )
    Returns the current state of debugging.

setDebug( )
    Allows you to set the state of debugging.

Properties

`app_server`

> Flash Remoting events that occur on the application server or in the Flash Gateway on the server.

`client`

> Flash Remoting activity from the client.

`flashcomm_server/realtime_server`

> Flash Communication Server MX events.

Description

The *NetDebugConfig* object is included when you include the *NetDebug.as* file in your Flash Remoting application. It holds the properties of your current NetConnection debugger configuration and also allows you to turn NetConnection debugging on and off for ActionScript objects. To use the *NetDebugConfig* object for your specific connection, retrieve it with the *NetConnection.getDebugConfig( )* method:

```
var myConfigObject = myConnection.getDebugConfig( );
```

You can then call methods on the *NetDebugConfig* object to turn debugging on and off programmatically and set the status of reporting for individual events. The events are associated with one of the properties of the object (`app_server`, `client`, or `flashcomm_server/realtime_server`), each of which are objects in their own right. Events for which debugging is active are logged in the NetConnection Debugger panel. The full listing of events is shown in Table 15-2.

Table 15-2. NetDebugConfig events of the NetConnection class

Event	Default	Description
app_server.amf	false	Server AMF events
app_server.amfheaders	false	AMF headers from the Flash Remoting gateway
app_server.coldfusion	true	ColdFusion debug events if ColdFusion Server debug mode is on
app_server.error	true	Any error that occurs on the server
app_server.httpheaders	false	HTTP headers from the server
app_server.recordset	true	Events from pageable recordsets
app_server.trace	true	Trace events on the server
client.http	true	Client-initiated HTTP events such as connections and service calls
client.recordset	true	Pageable recordset events
client.rtmp	true	Flash Communication Server client events which use Real Time Messaging Protocol (RTMP); not used by Flash Remoting
client.trace	true	Client *NetConnection.trace( )* events
flashcomm_server.trace realtime_server.trace	true	Flash Communication Server trace events

To retrieve individual settings of the *NetDebugConfig* object, use dot notation to address the event type and the event. Remember to retrieve the object using *NetConnection.getDebugConfig( )* first:

```
debugConfigObj = my_conn.getDebugConfig( )
trace(debugConfigObj.client.http);
```

The preceding code displays true in the Output window if the client.http debug setting is turned on. To turn it off, simply set the property to false:

```
debugConfigObj.client.http = false;
```

You can disable all debugging to the NetConnection debugger for the specified object using:

```
debugConfigObj.setDebug(false);
```

For more information on the NetConnection debugger and the *NetDebugConfig* object see:

*http://livedocs.macromedia.com/frdocs/Using_Flash_Remoting_MX/
DebugActionScript.jsp*

See Also

NetConnection.getDebugConfig( ), the *NetDebug* object; Chapter 13

NetDebugConfig.getDebug( ) Method   Flash 6

returns the current state of NetConnection debugging

myConnection.getDebugConfig(*id*).getDebug( )

Returns

A Boolean indicating the current state of debugging in the Flash Remoting application.

Description

The *getDebug( )* method returns the current state of debugging in Flash Remoting. Debugging can be on or off and can be set programmatically with the *setDebug( )* method. When debugging is on, the NetConnection debugger receives events and logs messages. When debugging is off, the NetConnection debugger is inactive.

The *NetDebug.as* file must be included in order to use the *getDebug( )* method.

Example

The following code shows the basic syntax of the *getDebug( )* method:

```
#include "NetServices.as"
#include "NetDebug.as"

if (connected == null) {
  connected = true;
```

```
NetServices.setDefaultGatewayUrl("http://127.0.0.1/flashservices/gateway");
var my_conn = NetServices.createGatewayConnection();
var my_service = my_conn.getService("com.oreilly.frdg.searchProducts");
trace(my_conn.getDebugConfig().getDebug());
}
```

The *trace( )* statement displays the current state of debugging in this particular application, which should be on because it has not been turned off in the code.

Bugs

At the time of this writing, this method returns 'undefined' in all cases. It has been removed from Macromedia's online documentation at *http://livedocs.macromedia.com/flashremoting/mx/Using_Flash_Remoting_MX/asDict4.htm#91933* and should be considered unsupported until Macromedia updates their documentation.

See Also

The *NetDebug* object, Table 15-2 under the *NetDebugConfig* object, *NetDebugConfig.setDebug( )*; Chapter 13

NetDebugConfig.setDebug( ) Method   Flash 6

sets the state of NetConnection debugging

myConnection.getDebugConfig( ).setDebug(*setting*)

Arguments
setting
    true or false value to turn debugging on or off.

Description

The *setDebug( )* method is used to turn debugging on or off programmatically. This can be useful if you are testing an application and need a way to turn debugging on only at certain times, such as when a problem occurs. This is a good way to limit logging so that errors aren't lost in a flood of status messages, although you can turn debugging on and off for individual events using the properties in Table 15-2.

The *NetDebug.as* file must be included in order to use the *setDebug( )* method.

Example

The following code shows the basic syntax of the *setDebug( )* method:

```
#include "NetServices.as"
#include "NetDebug.as"

if (connected == null) {
  connected = true;
  NetServices.setDefaultGatewayUrl("http://127.0.0.1/flashservices/gateway");
  var my_conn = NetServices.createGatewayConnection();
```

```
var my_service = my_conn.getService("com.oreilly.frdg.searchProducts");
my_conn.getDebugConfig( ).setDebug(true);
}
```

Bugs

At the time of this writing, this method has no effect on the debugging mode. It has been removed from Macromedia's online documentation at *http://livedocs.macromedia. com/flashremoting/mx/Using_Flash_Remoting_MX/asDict4.htm#91933* and should be considered unsupported until Macromedia updates their documentation.

See Also

The *NetDebug* object, Table 15-2 under the *NetDebugConfig* object, *NetDebugConfig.getDebug( )*; Chapter 13

NetServices Object   Flash 6

simplifies connection management

NetServices.*methodName*(*params*)

Methods
createGatewayConnection( )
> Creates a *NetConnection* object to allow connection to remote services through the Flash Remoting adapter on the server.

getVersion( )
> Returns the current version number of the *NetServices* object (currently 1.0).

setDefaultGateway( )
> Sets a default URL for a *NetConnection* object.

Description

The *NetServices* object abstracts some of the *NetConnection* class's functionality for easy access to the developer. Using the simple methods of the *NetServices* object, you can set up a gateway URL and create the *NetConnection* object. The *NetServices* object also aids in the creation of callback functions for remote services and creates proxies for the remote connections.

The *NetServices* object is included when you include the *NetServices.as* file in your Flash movie:

```
#include "NetServices.as"
```

You use the *NetServices* object directly; you don't construct an instance of the object. Typically, you use it to specify a default URL and create a *NetConnection* object:

```
NetServices.setDefaultGatewayUrl("http://127.0.0.1/flashservices/gateway");
var my_conn = NetServices.createGatewayConnection( );
```

Once you use the *NetServices* object to set up an instance of a *NetConnection* object, you should not have to use the *NetServices* object anymore. The benefit of using the *NetServices* object is that you have more control over your connection and responder objects. This is discussed in the individual method sections for *NetServices* in this chapter.

See Also

The *NetConnection* class; Chapter 4

NetServices.createGatewayConnection( ) Method

Flash 6

connects to the Flash Remoting gateway

```
NetServices.createGatewayConnection(url)
```

Arguments

url
> An optional string containing the URL of a Flash Remoting connection.

Returns

A *NetConnection* object.

Description

The *createGatewayConnection( )* method is the best way to create a new *NetConnection* object. You can set up a default URL in the ActionScript code and then override it with a URL passed from the HTML page that houses the Flash movie. The newly created *NetConnection* object is used connect to the Flash Remoting adapter on the server. You also call remote methods through the *NetConnection* object. The *NetConnection* object also handles the service results.

Example

The following code shows the basic syntax of the *createGatewayConnection( )* method:

```
#include "NetServices.as"

if (connected == null) {
  connected = true;
  theURL = "http://127.0.0.1/flashservices/gateway";
  var my_conn = NetServices.createGatewayConnection(theURL);
}
```

In this code, the gateway URL is passed to the *createGatewayConnection( )* method. If the URL is passed in this way, it overrides any other URLs that have been set up.

Here is a more flexible way to create a connection:

```
#include "NetServices.as"

if (connected == null) {
  connected = true;
  NetServices.setDefaultGateway("http://127.0.0.1/flashservices/gateway");
  var my_conn = NetServices.createGatewayConnection( );
}
```

In this case, the URL is passed to the *setDefaultGateway( )* method, which gives you more flexibility because the default gateway URL can be overridden by passing a URL from the HTML page. See the entry for *NetServices.setDefaultGateway( )* for more information.

See Also

The *NetConnection* class, *NetServices.setDefaultGateway( )*; Chapter 4

NetServices.getVersion( ) Method

Flash 6

returns the version of the *NetServices* object

```
NetServices.getVersion( )
```

Returns

A version number, currently 1.0.

Description

The *getVersion( )* method returns the current version number of the *NetServices* object (currently 1.0). It can be used to ensure backward compatibility and compatibility with future versions if the methods or properties of the object change in future implementations.

Example

The following code shows the basic syntax of the *getVersion( )* method:

```
#include "NetServices.as"
var netServ_version = NetServices.getVersion( );
trace("NetServices object version: " + netServ_version);
```

NetServices.setDefaultGateway( ) Method

Flash 6

sets a default URL for a gateway connection

```
NetServices.setDefaultGateway(url)
```

Arguments

url

A string containing the URL of a Flash Remoting gateway adapter.

Description

The *setDefaultGateway( )* method is a way that you can define a URL for your *NetConnection* object but allow it to be overridden by a URL passed from the HTML page that houses your Flash movie. In this way, a URL can be set up in the movie for testing or deployment, but if the URL has to change at any time in the future, the URL can be passed to the Flash movie using the gatewayURL variable.

After setting up the default URL using this method, the *createGatewayConnection( )* method can be called with no arguments to create a *NetConnection* object.

Example

The following code shows the basic syntax of the *setDefaultGateway( )* method:

```
#include "NetServices.as"

if (connected == null) {
  connected = true;
  NetServices.setDefaultGateway("http://127.0.0.1/flashservices/gateway");
  var my_conn = NetServices.createGatewayConnection( );
}
```

To override the default gateway URL, the gatewayURL variable can be passed to the movie using the FlashVars attribute in the HTML page that embeds the *.swf* file:

```
<OBJECT classid="clsid:D27CDB6E-AE6D-11cf-96B8-444553540000"
 codebase="http://download.macromedia.com/pub/shockwave/cabs/flash/
 swflash.cab#version=6,0,0,0" WIDTH="550" HEIGHT="400"
 id="mymovie" ALIGN="">
 <PARAM NAME=movie VALUE="mymovie.swf">
 <PARAM NAME=FlashVars
 VALUE="gatewayURL=http://www.flash-remoting.com/flashservices/gateway">
 <PARAM NAME=quality VALUE=high>
 <PARAM NAME=bgcolor VALUE=#FFFFFF>
 <EMBED src="mymovie.swf" quality=high bgcolor=#FFFFFF  WIDTH="550"
 HEIGHT="400" NAME="Untitled-2" ALIGN=""
 TYPE="application/x-shockwave-flash"
 FlashVars="gatewayURL=http://www.flash-remoting.com/flashservices/gateway"
 PLUGINSPAGE="http://www.macromedia.com/go/getflashplayer">
 </EMBED>
</OBJECT>
```

In this example, the FlashVars attribute contains the name/value pair of gatewayURL and the path to the Flash Remoting gateway on my server. You should update it for your server:

gatewayURL=http://www.flash-remoting.com/flashservices/gateway

The gatewayURL is a variable that the *NetConnection* object is expecting. It overrides any gateway URL set via *setDefaultGateway( )* but does not override a URL set via *createGatewayConnection( )*. Therefore, you should not pass a URL to *createGatewayConnection( )* when using the FlashVars approach.

See Also

The *NetConnection* class, *NetServices.createGatewayConnection( )*; Chapter 4

RecordSet Class

client-side resultset management

myRecordSet.methodName(params)

Methods

addItem( )
> Appends a row to the end of the recordset.

addItemAt( )
> Adds a row to the recordset at the specified index.

addView( )
> Used to notify an ActionScript object whenever a recordset changes.

filter( )
> Create a new recordset based on filtering an existing recordset.

getColumnNames( )
> Returns a list of column names in the recordset.

getItemAt( )
> Returns a specific row in the recordset.

getItemID( )
> Returns the internal item number of the recordset row.

getLength( )
> Returns the number of records in the recordset.

getNumberAvailable( )
> Returns the number of records that have been retrieved from the server.

isFullyPopulated( )
> Returns a Boolean value that tells if the recordset is populated entirely by the server yet.

isLocal( )
> Returns a flag that tells if a *RecordSet* object is associated with a server.

removeAll( )
> Removes all records from the recordset.

removeItemAt( )
> Removes a specified record from the recordset.

replaceItemAt( )
> Replaces the row at the specified index in the recordset.

setDeliveryMode( )

Sets the delivery mode for pageable recordsets ("ondemand", "fetchall", or "page").

setField( )

Replaces a single field in a row with a specified value.

sort( )

Sorts the recordset according to custom criteria.

sortItemsBy( )

Sorts the recordset by a specified field.

Description

The *RecordSet* class defines ActionScript objects that can be created on the client to create a multidimensional array that is indexed sequentially, starting with 0. A *RecordSet* object mimics the functionality of a server-side resultset. If you return a resultset from a Flash Remoting method on the server, it will automatically be cast into a *RecordSet* object in the Flash movie. Refer to Chapters 5 through 9 and Appendix A for datatype conversions on the various platforms.

The index of each row of the recordset is a sequential number from 0 to the length of the recordset minus one. In other words, a recordset containing 10 rows has index numbers from 0 to 9. There is also an internal identifier number, which should not be confused with the index number. The index number can change if you add or delete rows or sort the recordset. The internal identifier number is a sequential number that is assigned to each row and remains attached to that row. If a row is deleted, the internal identifying number is not used again and the internal ID numbers of remaining rows does not change (although their index numbers might). Similarly, if a recordset is sorted, the internal identifiers remain attached to each individual row. The internal identifier can be read with the *getItemId( )* method, or as a property of the recordset row:

```
myID = myRecordset_rs.getItemAt(0).__ID__
```

The *RecordSet* class is a subclass of the *RsDataProviderClass* class. Much of the *RecordSet* class's functionality comes from its superclass. The *RsDataProviderClass.as* file is included automatically when you include the *RecordSet.as* or *NetServices.as* files.

To utilize *RecordSet* objects, the *RecordSet.as* file must be included in the Flash movie. This file can be included on its own if you are not using Flash Remoting, but it is included automatically when you include the *NetServices.as* file. To create a client-side *RecordSet* object from scratch, instantiate it like so:

```
var myRecordset_rs = new RecordSet(["First", "Last", "Phone", "Fax", "Email"]);
```

The ActionScript naming convention for *RecordSet* objects is to use _rs at the end of your *RecordSet* object's variable name. This ensures that code hints work in the Flash and Dreamweaver authoring environments.

A typical *RecordSet* object is created by calling a method on the server that issues a SELECT statement against a database and returns a resultset. The resultset is returned to the Flash movie, and the resultset is automatically turned into a client-side *RecordSet* object. The field names in your database query become the field names in the *RecordSet* object. The object has many built-in methods that allow the developer to interact with the recordset as one would on an application server.

The *RecordSet* class is one of the cornerstones of Flash Remoting, because it allows the seamless integration of databases into a client-side Flash movie by allowing the developer to call remote services that return resultsets.

 Methods of the *RecordSet* class are discussed at length under "The RecordSet Object" in Chapter 4. This chapter provides a more formal discussion of each method's syntax, in alphabetical order. Consult Chapter 4 for a different perspective on each method covered here. For readability's sake, I use the informal term "recordset" interchangeably with the more formal "*RecordSet* object" where the distinction is obvious or irrelevant.

Bugs

The initial release of Flash Remoting had a problem with J2EE resultsets. The client-side *RecordSet* object did not automatically get created by Flash Remoting. Updater 1 fixes the problem.

See Also

Chapters 3 and 4 for general information and Chapters 5 through 9 for server-specific details

RecordSet.addItem( ) Method
Flash 6

appends a record to a recordset

myRecordSet.addItem(*record*)

Arguments

record
    An object with properties that match the fields of the existing *RecordSet* object.

Description

The *addItem( )* method is the easiest way to add a new record to a *RecordSet* object. The record is simply appended to the end of the recordset.

Example

The following code creates a recordset and adds one row to it using the *addItem( )*
method. The argument for *addItem( )* is a generic object with properties that match
the fields of the recordset:

```
#include "RecordSet.as"
var myRecordset_rs = new RecordSet(["First", "Last", "Email"]);
myRecordset_rs.addItem({First:"Tom", Last:"Muck", Email:"tom@tom-muck.com"});
```

In this case, the record is created on the fly and added to the *RecordSet* object named
myRecordset_rs. The new record is added at the end of the recordset and the length
of the recordset is increased by one.

The property names of the new record should match the field names of the existing
recordset. Only the properties that have matching field names will be added. If you
add this record to the myRecordset_rs object:

```
myRecordset_rs.addItem({First:"Biff", Last:"Bop", Phone:"555-555-5555"});
```

only the First and Last fields will be added to the new record in the recordset. The
Phone field will be lost.

See Also

RecordSet.addItemAt( ); Chapter 4

RecordSet.addItemAt( ) Method   Flash 6

adds a record at the specified index of a recordset

myRecordSet.addItemAt(*index, record*)

Arguments

index
> An integer from 0 to the length of the recordset minus one.

record
> An object with properties that match the fields of the existing *RecordSet* object.

Description

The *addItemAt( )* method inserts a record at a specified location by passing an index
number to the recordset along with the record being inserted. It differs from
addItem( ) in that the record need not be appended to the end of the recordset but
rather can be inserted at any valid index.

Example

The following code creates a *RecordSet* object, adds two rows using the *addItem( )*
method, then adds another row using *addItemAt( )*:

```
#include "RecordSet.as"
var myRecordset_rs = new RecordSet(["First", "Last", "Email"]);
```

```
myRecordset_rs.addItem({First:"Tom", Last:"Muck", Email:"tom@tom-muck.com"});
myRecordset_rs.addItem({First:"Jack", Last:"Splat", Email:"jack@tom-muck.com"});
myRecordset_rs.addItemAt(0,{First:"Biff", Last:"Bop", Email:"biff@tom-muck.com"});
```

At this point, the first record (at index 0) is the last one that was added, because the *addItemAt( )* method was used to insert the record at the 0 position within the recordset. However, the internal identifier of this record is 2 because it was added third:

```
trace(myRecordset_rs.getItemId(0));   // Returns 2
```

See Also

RecordSet.addItem( ); Chapter 4

RecordSet.addView( ) Method Flash 6

monitors RecordSet activity by watching certain events

myRecordSet.addView(*object*)

Arguments

object

> An object with a method named *modelChanged( )* that is notified of changes to the recordset.

Description

The *addView( )* method allows you to specify an object to be notified whenever changes occur to a *RecordSet* object. This allows you to perform certain actions in response to those changes. For example, if you want to implement a recordset logging feature, you can use an object that displays information about the recordset in the Output window whenever the recordset changes.

Typically *addView( )* is used during debugging to verify that certain events happened. Chapter 4 discusses the method in detail, and Example 4-3 creates a *RecordSetDebug.as* file containing methods to view recordsets for debugging purposes.

Table 15-3 shows the event information sent to the object specified in the *addView( )* method. It also indicates which operations generate each event.

Table 15-3. Events tracked in the addView( ) method

Event	Information object returned	Occurs when
addItem( ) and *addItemAt( )* methods	{event:"addRows", firstRow:*n*, lastRow:*nn*}	Row numbers between *n* and *nn* are added
onResult( ) method of responder object	{event:"allRows"}	The recordset is fully populated from the server
removeAll( ), *removeItemAt( )*	{event:"deleteRows", firstRow:*n*, lastRow:*nn*}	Row numbers between *n* and *nn* are deleted

Table 15-3. Events tracked in the addView( ) method (continued)

Event	Information object returned	Occurs when
onResult( ) method of responder object	{event:"fetchrows", firstRow:*n*, lastRow:*nn*}	Row numbers between *n* and *nn* are requested from the server, but have not yet arrived
sort( ) and *sortItemsBy( )* methods	{event: "sort"}	A recordset is sorted
Any change in the RecordSet	{event:"updateAll"}	A recordset changes in any way
replaceItemAt( ), *setField( )*	{event:"updateRows", firstRow:*n*, lastRow:*nn*}	Row numbers between *n* and *nn* change in any way

Example

First, create an ActionScript object that defines a *modelChanged( )* method, like this:

```
var myObject = new Object();
myObject.prototype.modelChanged = function (myInformationObject) {
  trace(myInformationObject.event);
};
```

Then call *addView( )*, passing myObject as a parameter:

```
myRecordset_rs.addView(myObject);
```

This causes myObject's *modelChanged( )* method to be invoked whenever the contents of myRecordset_rs change. When an event triggers the *modelChanged( )* method, it receives an information object (myInformationObject) as a parameter. This information object contains an event property, indicating the type of change that occurred to the recordset, as shown in Table 15-3. Some objects passed to *modelChanged( )* also contain firstRow and lastRow properties indicating the range or record numbers affected.

Here is a fleshed-out example that displays a message in the Output window whenever the recordset is sorted:

```
#include "RecordSet.as"
var myRecordset_rs = new RecordSet(["First","Last","Email"]);
// Create the generic object
var myObject = new Object();
// Add a modelChanged( ) event handler the object
myObject.modelChanged = function (myInformationObject) {
  if (myInformationObject.event == "sort") {
    trace("RecordSet was sorted");
  }
};
// Call addView( ) to set up the callback function (myObject.modelChanged)
myRecordset_rs.addView(myObject);
myRecordset_rs.addItem({First:"Tom",Last:"Muck",Email:"tom@tom-muck.com"});
myRecordset_rs.addItem({First:"Jack",Last:"Splat",Email:"jack@tom-muck.com"});

// Sort the recordset, triggering the modelChanged( ) method
myRecordset_rs.sortItemsBy("First");
```

At this point, the Output window should display "RecordSet was sorted."

See Also

Chapter 4 (especially Example 4-3)

RecordSet.filter( ) Method

filters records in a recordset

myRecordSet.filter(*filterFunction, context*)

Arguments

filterFunction
> A custom function that acts as a filter for the recordset.

context
> A parameter that can be passed to the filter function as an argument.

Returns

A filtered *RecordSet* object.

Description

The *filter( )* method creates a second recordset by filtering an existing recordset using a custom filter function. This function can filter the recordset on any kind of criteria you prefer. You could, for example, filter a recordset by date, returning only those records that contain a field that is within a certain date range. You can filter any other criteria, such as length of a field, first letter of a field, or a certain word within a field.

The filtered recordset does not contain any reference or association to the original server-side recordset, such as paging. However, the new *RecordSet* object created by the *filter( )* method contains references to rows in the original client-side *Recordset* object, not copies of that data. *The filter( )* method also consumes memory and processing time, so it should be used sparingly.

The filter function that you define can accept one or two arguments. The first argument is a record to examine, and the second, optional argument can be used in your filter criteria. Each record of the original *RecordSet* object is passed to the filter function; if the filter function returns true, the record is added to the new, filtered *RecordSet* object.

Example

The following code demonstrates the *filter( )* method:

```
#include "RecordSet.as"
var myRecordset_rs = new RecordSet(["First", "Last", "Email"]);
myRecordset_rs.addItem({First:"Tom", Last:"Muck", Email:"tom@tom-muck.com"});
```

```
myRecordset_rs.addItem({First:"Jack", Last:"Splat", Email:"jack@tom-muck.com"});
myRecordset_rs.addItem({First:"Biff", Last:"Bop", Email:""});

function filterOnEmail(aRecord) {
  return (aRecord.Email != "");
}
var filteredRecordset_rs = myRecordset_rs.filter(filterOnEmail);
trace(filteredRecordset_rs.getLength());
```

In this case, three records are added to the initial *RecordSet* object. The filter function removes records that don't have email addresses. The new *RecordSet* object contains the two records that have email addresses, as shown in the Output window.

See Also

RecordSet.sort( ), *RecordSet.sortItemsBy( )*; Chapters 3 and 4

RecordSet.getColumnNames( ) Method   Flash 6

retrieves column names of a recordset

myRecordSet.getColumnNames( )

Returns

A comma-separated list of column names in the *RecordSet*.

Description

The *getColumnNames( )* function provides an easy way to retrieve the column names in the recordset. If you think of the recordset as a two-dimensional array of rows and columns. The rows are records referenced by an index number. The columns are the recordset fields referenced by the column names that are contained in each record. The names returned in the *getColumnNames( )* method are listed in the order that they appear in the recordset.

Example

The following code gets the list of columns and converts it into an array before tracing each name in the Output window:

```
var myColumns = myRecordset.getColumnNames( );
var myColumnArray = myColumns.split(",");
for (var i=0; i < myColumnArray.length; i++) {
  trace(myColumnArray[i]);
}
```

See Also

RecordSet.getLength( ); Chapter 4

RecordSet.getItemAt( ) Method

returns the record at a given index number

myRecordSet.getItemAt(*index*)

Arguments

index

An integer between 0 and the length of the *RecordSet* object minus one.

Returns

A row (i.e., a single record) of the *RecordSet* object.

Description

The *getItemAt( )* method returns a full row of a recordset. The return value is a single record from the recordset, represented as an associative array whose keys correspond to the recordset's column names. You can retrieve individual fields by name from the row returned by this method.

Example

The following code returns a row of the recordset and then sets variables to the value of each field in the record:

```
var myRow = myRecordset.getItemAt(0);
var myFirstName = myRow.FirstName;
var myLastName = myRow.LastName;
myTextField.text = "Hello " + myFirstName + " " + myLastName;
```

Individual fields can also be accessed through associative array notation, as in this example:

```
var myRow = myRecordSet.getItemAt(0);
var myFirstName = myRow["FirstName"];
```

See Also

RecordSet.addItemAt( ), *RecordSet.getColumnNames( )*, *RecordSet.replaceItemAt( )*; Chapter 4

RecordSet.getItemID( ) Method

Flash 6

retrieves the internal ID number of a row

myRecordSet.getItemID(*index*)

Arguments

index

An integer between 0 and the length of the *RecordSet* object minus one.

Returns

The internal ID number that Flash assigns when the record is added to the recordset.

Description

The *getItemID( )* method returns an internal ID and is useful for determining the initial state of the *RecordSet* object (or the order in which records were added). If the order of the records in the recordset changes in some way, it can be restored or compared by using the original identifier that was given to each row when the recordset was created. Unlike the index of a record, which can change, the internal ID never changes and is destroyed if the row is deleted. The identifier of a deleted row is not reused again.

Example

The following code retrieves the original first row from the recordset, even after the sort changes the order of the rows:

```
#include "RecordSet.as"
var myRecordset_rs = new RecordSet(["First","Last","Email"]);
myRecordset_rs.addItem({First:"Tom", Last:"Muck", Email:"tom@tom-muck.com"});
myRecordset_rs.addItem({First:"Jack", Last:"Splat", Email:"jack@tom-muck.com"});
myRecordset_rs.addItem({First:"Biff", Last:"Bop", Email:"biff@tom-muck.com"});

// "Tom Muck" is the first item before the sort. After the sort, it is second.
myRecordset_rs.sortItemsBy("Last");

// Loop through the records looking for the one whose original ID is 0
for (var i; i < myRecordset_rs.getLength(); i++) {
  if (myRecordset_rs.getItemID(i) == 0) {
    trace(myRecordset_rs.getItemID(i));
    break;
  }
}
```

After the recordset is sorted, the first record is "Biff Bop", but its item ID is still 2. The second record in the sorted recordset is "Tom Muck", but its item ID is 0, telling us that it was the original first record. The *trace( )* statement displays Tom's record in the Output window.

See Also

RecordSet.addItemAt( ), *RecordSet.sortItemsBy( )*; Chapters 3 and 4

RecordSet.getLength( ) Method

returns the length of a recordset

myRecordSet.getLength( )

Returns

An integer specifying the number of rows in the *RecordSet* object.

Description

The *getLength( )* method returns an integer that contains the number of rows in the *RecordSet* object. This length is always be one more than the highest index number in the recordset. For example, a recordset that has 10 rows with index numbers from 0 to 9 has a length of 10.

Example

The following code gets the length of the *RecordSet* object and puts it into a variable:

```
var myRecordsetLength = myRecordset_rs.getLength();
```

The length is typically used to loop through all records in a recordset, such as:

```
var myRecordsetLength = myRecordset_rs.getLength();
for (var i; i < myRecordsetLength; i++) {
  trace(myRecordset_rs.getItemAt(i));
}
```

See Also

Chapter 4, "Loops and Repeated Operations" in Chapter 12

RecordSet.getNumberAvailable( ) Method

returns the number of records downloaded from the server

myRecordSet.getNumberAvailable( )

Returns

An integer specifying the number of records that have currently downloaded from the server.

Description

The *getNumberAvailable( )* method allows the developer to retrieve a count of how many records have been downloaded from the server when utilizing pageable result-sets from a ColdFusion MX Server. For example, if you are retrieving a resultset of 53 records in pages of 10, the *getNumberAvailable( )* method tells you how many records are available on the client upon calling the method. In this case, the method will return 10, 20, 30, 40, 50, or 53, depending on when it is called.

If the *getNumberAvailable( )* method returns the same number as the *getLength( )* method, the entire recordset is populated. You can also use the *isFullyPopulated( )* method to determine if the recordset is completely populated.

Example

The following code demonstrates the *getNumberAvailable( )* method:

```
trace(myRecordset_rs.getNumberAvailable( ));
```

As of this writing, the *getNumberAvailable( )* method works only in the ColdFusion implementation of Flash Remoting when employing pageable recordsets. It might typically be called within a handler that executes repeatedly, such as an *onEnter-Frame( )* handler. But you can use *addView( )* to be notified when all rows have downloaded (see the "allRows" event in Table 15-3).

Chapter 5 contains a more complete example in the context of a ColdFusion application.

See Also

RecordSet.addView( ), *RecordSet.getLength( )*, *RecordSet.isFullyPopulated( )*, *RecordSet.setDeliveryMode( )*; Chapters 4 and 5

RecordSet.isFullyPopulated( ) Method   Flash 6

determines whether a recordset is fully downloaded

myRecordSet.isFullyPopulated( )

Returns

The Boolean `true` if the *RecordSet* object is local or if a *RecordSet* object coming from a remote method has been fully received from the server.

Description

The *isFullyPopulated( )* method is used when you have a remote method that returns a resultset as a *RecordSet* object and you need to determine if it has been fully downloaded. This is often necessary, because the following methods work only with fully populated *RecordSet* objects:

> *addItem( )*
> *addItemAt( )*
> *filter( )*
> *removeAll( )*
> *removeItem( )*
> *replaceItemAt( )*
> *setField( )*
> *sort( )*

For a local *RecordSet* object, the *isFullyPopulated( )* method always returns true.

Example

The following code shows how the *isFullyPopulated( )* is called. In the example, if the *RecordSet* object is not fully populated, the button `last_pb` is disabled:

```
if (!myProducts_rs.isFullyPopulated()) last_pb.enabled = false;
```

As of this writing, the *isFullyPopulated( )* method works only in the ColdFusion implementation of Flash Remoting when employing pageable recordsets.

See Also

RecordSet.addView( ), *RecordSet.getLength( )*, *RecordSet.getNumberAvailable( )*, *RecordSet.setDeliveryMode( )*; Chapters 4 and 5

RecordSet.isLocal( ) Method

Flash 6

determines whether a recordset was created locally

myRecordSet.isLocal( )

Returns

The Boolean value true if the *RecordSet* did not come from a remote method; false if it did.

Description

The *isLocal( )* method allows you to test a given recordset to determine if it came from an application server as the result of a Flash Remoting call or if it was created locally.

Example

The following code displays true because it is a locally created recordset:

```
#include "RecordSet.as"
var myRecordset_rs = new RecordSet(["First", "Last", "Email"]);
myRecordset_rs.addItem({First:"Tom",Last:"Muck",Email:"tom@tom-muck.com"});
trace(myRecordset_rs.isLocal());
```

See Also

RecordSet.getNumberAvailable( ), *RecordSet.isFullyPopulated( )*

deletes all records in a recordset

myRecordSet.removeAll( )

Description

The *removeAll( )* method removes the entire contents of the *RecordSet* object. The structure (column names) of the *RecordSet* object remains intact, however, and the internal identifiers in use before calling the *removeAll( )* method are not reused.

Example

The following code removes the contents of the *RecordSet* object:

```
#include "RecordSet.as"
var myRecordset_rs = new RecordSet(["First", "Last", "Email"]);
myRecordset_rs.addItem({First:"Tom", Last:"Muck", Email:"tom@tom-muck.com"});
myRecordset_rs.addItem({First:"Jack", Last:"Splat", Email:"jack@tom-muck.com"});
myRecordset_rs.removeAll( );
trace(myRecordset_rs.getLength( ));
trace(myRecordset_rs.getColumnNames( ));
```

In this case, the Output window shows that the recordset has a length of 0, but it also shows that the field names are still in place. If we add a record to the *RecordSet* object now, the internal identifier of the row will be incremented from where it left off before; the internal identifier numbers of the two rows that existed previously are not reused:

```
myRecordset_rs.addItem({First:"Jack", Last:"Splat", Email:"jack@tom-muck.com"});
trace(myRecordset_rs.getItemId(0));
```

The Output window should show "2".

To completely delete the *RecordSet* object rather than simply empty the contents, you can set it to null:

```
myRecordset_rs = null;
```

See Also

RecordSet.getItemId( ), *RecordSet.removeItemAt( )*

RecordSet.removeItemAt( ) Method

Flash 6

removes a record from a recordset

myRecordSet.removeItemAt(*index*)

Arguments

index
    The index number of the record to be deleted.

Description

The *removeItemAt( )* method deletes a row in a *RecordSet* object. The internal identifier of the row is removed and not used again, and the length of the *RecordSet* object is reduced by one.

Example

The following code adds two records to the recordset, then deletes the first record (the record in the 0 position):

```
#include "RecordSet.as"
var myRecordset_rs = new RecordSet(["First", "Last", "Email"]);
myRecordset_rs.addItem({First:"Tom", Last:"Muck", Email:"tom@tom-muck.com"});
myRecordset_rs.addItem({First:"Jack", Last:"Splat", Email:"jack@tom-muck.com"});
myRecordset_rs.removeItemAt(0);
trace(myRecordset_rs.getLength());
```

In this case, the Output window displays "1" because one row has been deleted.

See Also

RecordSet.addItemAt( ), *RecordSet.getItemAt( )*, *RecordSet.getLength( )*, *RecordSet. getRemoveAll( )*, *RecordSet.replaceItemAt( )*

RecordSet.replaceItemAt( ) Method   Flash 6

replaces a row in a recordset

myRecordSet.replaceItemAt(*index*, *record*)

Arguments

index
> An integer that is between 0 and the length of the *RecordSet* object minus one.

record
> An object with properties that match the fields of the existing *RecordSet* object.

Description

The *replaceItemAt( )* method replaces the contents of an entire row in a *RecordSet* object. This allows for functionality similar to the SQL update statement. Typically, you use this method to update the contents of row of data in your *RecordSet* object that will be reflected in a display in the Flash movie, such as in a DataGrid.

Example

The following code shows the *replaceItemAt( )* method in use, replacing the contents of one row and tracing the *RecordSet* object's length to the Output window:

```
#include "RecordSet.as"
var myRecordset_rs = new RecordSet(["First","Last","Email"]);
myRecordset_rs.addItem({First:"",Last:"",Email:""});
```

```
var firstname = firstname_txt.text;
var lastname = lastname_txt.text;
var email = email_txt.text;
myRecordset_rs.replaceItemAt(0,{First:firstname,Last:lastname,Email:email});
trace(myRecordSet.getLength());
```

This code creates a recordset and adds one row. Then the first row (in the 0 position) is replaced. The Output window reports that the recordset still contains only one row.

See Also

RecordSet.addItemAt( ), *RecordSet.removeItemAt( )*, *RecordSet.setField( )*

RecordSet.setDeliveryMode( ) Method

returns paged resultsets from ColdFusion

myRecordSet.setDeliveryMode(*mode, pagesize, numPrefetchPages*)

Arguments

mode

> The mode to use in fetching pages from the server ("ondemand", "fetchall", or "page").

pagesize

> The number of records to return in each page (required in "fetchall" and "page" modes).

numPrefetchPages

> The number of pages to retrieve from the server (required in "page" mode).

Description

The *setDeliveryMode( )* method allows you to set the mode of pageable resultsets from a ColdFusion Server. The different modes are:

"ondemand"

> The delivery mode is "ondemand" by default. It simply means that the records are returned when they are requested. Use "ondemand" mode when each record is needed individually and at different times. Do not use this mode if you are iterating through the entire recordset at once, because it forces the client to make a separate request for each record, which is very inefficient. The mode is efficient only if you won't eventually load all the records and you want to limit network traffic to only those records that must be loaded. Also, it is fine for small recordsets where all records will download at once.

"fetchall"

> Using the "fetchall" parameter allows you to grab a page at a time, but in batches. The size of each batch is specified in the *pagesize* argument. Use "fetchall" mode when you know that you are going to load all the data but

would like to start displaying the data incrementally rather than having to wait for it all to load. For example, if you know you have 300 records to load, it makes sense to load them over the course of 10 requests, 30 records at a time, so that you can start displaying data as soon as possible.

"page"

Using "page" mode allows you to retrieve one page at a time. You must also specify the *pagesize* and *numPrefetchPages* arguments. The "page" mode lies somewhere between "ondemand" and "fetchall". Use "page" mode when you don't expect to need all the data in the recordset, but you don't want the overhead of loading each record individually. For example, you don't want to make the user wait for 10 pages of search results to load, because he will most likely find what he needs in the first two or three pages. Therefore, load the first two or three pages initially, then load the other pages as they are needed.

Example

The following code creates a pageable recordset and sets the delivery mode to "page":

```
#include "NetServices.as"

NetServices.setDefaultGatewayURL("http://localhost/flashservices/gateway");
var my_conn = NetServices.createGatewayConnection();
var customerService = my_conn.getService("com.oreilly.frdg.Customers", this);
// Set a global RecordSet variable
var myRS;
// Create the PushButton. Assumes FPushButtonSymbol is already in Library.
this.attachMovie("FPushButtonSymbol","submit_pb",4);
//Position and label the PushButton
with (submit_pb) {
  _x = 300;
  _y = 35;
  setLabel("Submit");
}
// Call the remote method once, retrieving 10 records
customerService.getCustomers({pagesize:10});

submit_pb.setClickHandler("getNext");
function getNext() {
  var recordNum = myRs.getNumberAvailable();
  // Attempt to get a record past the last record available.
  // This will cause the paging to kick in and retrieve another set of records.
  myRS.getItemAt(recordNum);
  trace(recordNum);
  // If the recordset is fully downloaded, display it in the Output window
  if (recordNum == myRS.getLength())
    for (var i=0; i<recordNum; i++)
      trace(myRS.getItemAt(i).ContactName);
}
```

```
function getCustomers_Result(result_rs) {
  myRS = result_rs;
  result_rs.setDeliveryMode("page", 10);
  // Trace the number of records available. This statement executes only once.
  trace("onresult: " + myRs.getNumberAvailable());
}
```

This self-contained code operates against the *Customers* service from Chapter 5. It demonstrates recordset paging using the "page" mode. Each time the user clicks a button, the *getNext( )* function attempts to retrieve a record that is beyond the end of the number of records available. When this happens, the next set of records is returned from the server. Note that when you click the button, the Output window displays the number of records from the *getNext( )* function, but the *getCustomers_Result( )* function is never called again; Flash Remoting takes care of the recordset paging, and the responder method *onResult* event is never triggered again.

Chapter 5 contains a complete example of recordset paging and demonstrates the *setDeliveryMode( )* method in greater detail.

See Also

RecordSet.getNumberAvailable( ), *RecordSet.isFullyPopulated( )*; Chapters 4 and 5

RecordSet.setField( ) Method   Flash 6

sets a field within a record

myRecordSet.setField(*index*, *fieldName*, *value*)

Arguments

index

> The index number of the recordset row that contains the field to be replaced.

fieldName

> The field name of the field that you want to replace the contents of.

value

> The value that you are setting the field to.

Description

The *setField( )* method replaces the contents of a single field within a row, with no effect on the other fields, allowing for finer control over updating than *replaceItemAt( )*.

Example

The following code creates a recordset and then replaces the email address in the first record:

```
#include "RecordSet.as"
var myRecordset_rs = new RecordSet(["First", "Last", "Email"]);
```

```
myRecordset_rs.addItem({First:"Tom", Last:"Muck", Email:"tom@tom-muck.com"});
var email = 'jacksplat@tom-muck.com';
myRecordset_rs.setField(0,"Email", email);
trace (myRecordset_rs.getItemAt(0).Email;
```

See Also

RecordSet.replaceItemAt( )

RecordSet.sort( ) Method

sorts a recordset

myRecordSet.sort(*compareFunction*)

Arguments

compareFunction
> A custom function that facilitates the sort of the recordset by comparing records.

Description

The *sort( )* method sorts a *RecordSet* object in place using a user-specified sort function. The compare function should compare two records (which are passed as two arguments to the function) and return a positive number if the first record is greater than the second record, a negative number if the second record is greater, and 0 otherwise.

Example

The following code demonstrates the *sort( )* method on a *RecordSet* object, sorting by last name and then first name using a custom *sortByFirstAndLast( )* function:

```
#include "RecordSet.as"
var myRecordset_rs = new RecordSet(["First", "Last", "Email"]);
myRecordset_rs.addItem({First:"Tom",  Last:"Muck"});
myRecordset_rs.addItem({First:"Jack", Last:"Splat"});
myRecordset_rs.addItem({First:"Bob",  Last:"Splat"});
myRecordset_rs.addItem({First:"Biff", Last:"Splat"});

function sortByFirstAndLast(rec1, rec2) {
  if (rec1.Last < rec2.Last) return -1;
  if (rec1.Last > rec2.Last) return 1;
  if (rec1.First < rec2.First) return -1;
  if (rec1.First > rec2.First) return 1;
  return 0;
}

myRecordset_rs.sort(sortByFirstAndLast);
for (var i=0; i < myRecordset_rs.getLength(); i++)
  trace(myRecordset_rs.getItemAt(i).Last + ", " +
    myRecordset_rs.getItemAt(i).First);
```

In this case, the records are sorted by last name and first name. If we want to sort by only one field, we can use the *sortItemsBy( )* method, which is about 10 times faster. After running the sort, the items are now in this order:

Muck, Tom
Splat, Biff
Splat, Bob
Splat, Jack

See Also

RecordSet.filter( ), *RecordSet.sortItemsBy( )*

RecordSet.sortItemsBy( ) Method

Flash 6

sorts a recordset by a field value

myRecordSet.sortItemsBy(*fieldName, direction*)

Arguments

fieldName

> The field that you want to sort the *RecordSet* object by.

direction

> The direction of the sort. "DESC" specifies a descending sort; anything else is ascending.

Description

The *sortItemsBy( )* method sorts a recordset by a specified field. This creates great flexibility for how you display your recordset. For example, a display might contain column headings that are clickable; clicking the column heading could trigger the *sortItemsBy( )* method.

The *sortItemsBy( )* method is defined in the *RsDataProviderClass* class.

Example

The following code adds two rows to a recordset and then sorts the recordset by last name:

```
#include "RecordSet.as"
var myRecordset_rs = new RecordSet(["First", "Last", "Email"]);
myRecordset_rs.addItem({First:"Jack", Last:"Splat", Email:"jack@tom-muck.com"});
myRecordset_rs.addItem({First:"Tom", Last:"Muck", Email:"tom@tom-muck.com"});
myRecordset_rs.sortItemsBy("Last");
```

See Also

RecordSet.filter( ), *RecordSet.sort( )*

PART IV

Appendixes

The appendixes include details on datatype conversion between ActionScript and various server-side languages, plus resources for further study on related topics. Appendix C details the specification for the real-world application implemented in Chapter 14.

- Appendix A, *ActionScript Datatype Conversion*
- Appendix B, *Books and Online Resources*
- Appendix C, *Specification and Implementation for a Real-World Application*

ActionScript Datatype Conversion

This appendix documents the conversion of native ActionScript datatypes to and from their nearest server-side equivalent in ColdFusion, Java, C#, Visual Basic, and SOAP.

ColdFusion Datatype Conversion

ActionScript 1.0 and CFML are both loosely typed languages. There is a close correlation between ActionScript datatypes and ColdFusion datatypes, but there are a few notable differences. Table A-1 shows the conversion from Flash ActionScript to ColdFusion.

Table A-1. Flash-to-ColdFusion datatype conversion

Flash (ActionScript)	ColdFusion (CFML)
ActionScript object	Struct (or ASObject)
ActionScript object (as only argument)	Named arguments
Array (indexed)	Array
Associative Array	Struct
Boolean	Boolean
Date Object	Date
Number	Number
RecordSet	-
String	String
Undefined	Null
XML Object	XML document
Null	Null

Table A-2 shows the conversion from ColdFusion to Flash ActionScript.

Table A-2. ColdFusion-to-Flash datatype conversion

ColdFusion (CFML)	Flash (ActionScript)
Struct	Associative array
Java object (flashgateway.IO.ASObject)	ActionScript object
Java object (flashgateway.IO.ASObject with `type` property set)	ActionScript object of that type
Array	Array (indexed)
Struct	Array (associative)
Boolean	String [a]
Date	Date object
Number	Number
Query object	RecordSet
String	String
XML document	XML object
Null	Null

[a] Booleans should be passed as numbers (1 or 0) from ColdFusion to Flash. A 1 will be passed as "true" to Flash, and anything else will pass as "false". For that reason, ColdFusion Booleans are not accurately returned to Flash.

Java Datatype Conversion

Java, unlike ActionScript 1.0, is a typed language. The Flash gateway on the server takes care of the datatype conversions back and forth between the Flash client and the Java server. Table A-3 shows the conversion from Flash ActionScript to Java. Refer also to the ASTranslator library, as discussed in Chapter 7. Chapter 7 also discusses intimate details of datatype conversion from ActionScript to Java and vice versa.

Table A-3. Flash-to-Java datatype conversion

Flash (ActionScript)	Java
ActionScript object	flashgateway.IO.ASObject (implements java.util.map)
Array (indexed)	ArrayList
Array (associative)	java.util.map
Boolean	Boolean
Date Object	Date
Number	Number
RecordSet	-
String	String
Undefined	Null

Table A-3. Flash-to-Java datatype conversion (continued)

Flash (ActionScript)	Java
XML Object	org.w3c.dom document
Null	Null

Table A-4 shows the conversion from Java to Flash ActionScript.

Table A-4. Java-to-Flash datatype conversion

Java	Flash (ActionScript)
Struct	Associative array
Java object (flashgateway.IO.ASObject)	ActionScript object
Java object (flashgateway.IO.ASObject with type property set)	ActionScript object of that type
Collection, Object[], array of primitive types	Array (indexed)
java.util.map	Array (associative)
Boolean	Boolean
Date	Date object
Number	Number
disconnected RowSet[a]	RecordSet
flashgateway.sql.PageableResultSet[a]	pageable RecordSet
String	String
org.w3c.dom document	XML object
flashgateway.io.ASXMLString	XML object
Null	Null

[a] Only with Flash Remoting MX Updater 1 and later.

C# Datatype Conversion

Unlike ActionScript 1.0, C# is a typed language. The Flash gateway on the server takes care of the datatype conversions back and forth between the Flash client and the ASP.NET server.

Table A-5 shows the conversion from Flash ActionScript to C#.

Table A-5. Flash-to-C# datatype conversion

Flash (ActionScript)	C#
ActionScript object	flashgateway.IO.ASObject (implements java.util.map)
Array (indexed)	System.Collections.ArrayList

Flash (ActionScript)	C#
Array (associative)	System.Collections.HashMap
Boolean	System.Boolean
Date object	System.DateTime
Number	any numeric type
RecordSet	-
String	System.String
Undefined	Null
XML object	System.Xml.XmlDocument
Null	Null

Table A-6 shows the conversion from C# to Flash ActionScript.

Table A-6. C#-to-Flash datatype conversion

C#	Flash (ActionScript)
FlashGateway.IO.ASObject	ActionScript Object
FlashGateway.IO.ASObject with `type` property set	ActionScript Object of that type
System.Collections.ICollection, object[]	Array (indexed)
System.Collections.HashTable, System.Collections.IDictionary	Array (associative)
System.Boolean, bool	Boolean
System.DateTime	Date object
Number	Number
System.Data.DataSet	Array of RecordSets
System.Data.DataTable	RecordSet
System.String, System.Char	String
System.Xml.XmlDocument	XML Object
Null	Null

Visual Basic Datatype Conversion

Like C#, Visual Basic is a typed language. C# and Visual Basic have a lot in common, but there are many differences as well. The Flash gateway on the server takes care of the datatype conversions back and forth between the Flash client and the ASP.NET server.

Table A-7 shows the conversion from Flash ActionScript to Visual Basic.

Table A-7. Flash-to-Visual Basic datatype conversion

Flash (ActionScript)	Visual Basic
ActionScript object	flashgateway.IO.ASObject (implements java.util.map)
Array (indexed)	System.Collections.ArrayList
Array (associative)	System.Collections.HashMap
Boolean	Boolean
Date object	Date
Number	any numeric type
RecordSet	–
String	System.String
Undefined	Nothing
XML Object	System.Xml.XmlDocument
Null	Nothing

Table A-8 shows the conversion from Visual Basic to Flash ActionScript.

Table A-8. Visual Basic-to-Flash datatype conversions

Visual Basic	Flash (ActionScript)
FlashGateway.IO.ASObject	ActionScript object
FlashGateway.IO.ASObject with `type` property set	ActionScript object of that type
System.Collections.ICollection, object[]	Array (indexed)
System.Collections.HashTable, System.Collections.IDictionary	Array (associative)
Boolean	Boolean
Date	Date object
Number	Number
System.Data.DataSet	Array of RecordSets
System.Data.DataTable	RecordSet
System.String, System.Char	String
System.Xml.XmlDocument	XML object
Nothing	Null

PHP Datatype Conversion

The conversion of datatypes between ActionScript and PHP is straightforward, as shown in Table A-9.

Table A-9. Flash-to-PHP datatype conversion

Flash (ActionScript)	PHP
Null	Null
Integer	Integer
Float	Double
String	String
Array	Array (associative)
Object	Object
Recordset	Resource[a]

[a] The only supported databases are MySQL, ODBC, and PostgreSQL.

The conversion of datatypes between PHP and ActionScript is shown in Table A-10. The one kind of conversion that can be a bit confusing has to do with PHP arrays. Refer to "Datatype Conversions" in Chapter 9 for details.

Table A-10. PHP-to-Flash datatype conversion

PHP	Flash (ActionScript)
Null	Null
Integer	Integer
Double	Float
String	String
Array (indexed)	Array
Array (associative)	Object
Object	Object
Resource[a]	Recordset

[a] The only supported databases are MySQL, ODBC, and PostgreSQL.

SOAP Datatype Conversion

Web services are varied but have a core set of datatypes that are readily converted by the Flash gateway. Table A-11 shows the datatype conversions from Flash Action-Script to SOAP.

Table A-11. Flash-to-SOAP datatype conversion

Flash (ActionScript)	SOAP
ActionScript object	complex type
Array (indexed)	array
Array (associative)	complex type
Boolean	boolean

Table A-11. Flash-to-SOAP datatype conversion (continued)

Flash (ActionScript)	SOAP
Date object	dateTime
Number	decimal, float, double, integer, int (depending on what the number is most readily converted to)
RecordSet	query object[a]
String	String
Undefined	null
XML Object	System.Xml.XmlDocument
Null	null

[a] ColdFusion only.

Table A-12 shows the datatype conversions from SOAP to Flash ActionScript.

Table A-12. SOAP-to-Flash datatype conversion

SOAP	Flash (ActionScript)
complex type	ActionScript object
complex type	ActionScript object of that type
array	Array (indexed)
complex type	Array (associative)
Boolean	Boolean
dateTime	Date object
decimal, float, double, integer, int	Number
complex type	Array of RecordSets
query object[a]	RecordSet
string	String
System.Xml.XmlDocument	XML object
nothing	Null

[a] ColdFusion only.

Books and Online Resources

This book has covered a lot of ground, but there are a number of other resources out there that will help you as you work with the various technologies that are part of Flash Remoting. Several books and web sites are listed in this appendix.

Flash Remoting Resources

Companion site for this book, with online examples and downloads (the Code Depot)
> *http://www.flash-remoting.com*

Macromedia Resources

Link to the Macromedia site where the Flash Remoting components are available
> *http://www.macromedia.com/software/flashremoting/downloads/*

Macromedia online forum for Flash Remoting using JRun
> *http://webforums.macromedia.com/jrun/categories.cfm?catid=252*

Macromedia's developer center for Flash Remoting
> *http://www.macromedia.com/desdev/mx/flashremoting*

Flash Remoting home page
> *http://www.macromedia.com/software/flashremoting*

Newsgroup that corresponds to the Flash Remoting forum at Macromedia
> *news://forums.macromedia.com/macromedia.flash.flash_remoting*

Online support forums at the Macromedia site for Flash Remoting
> *http://webforums.macromedia.com/flash/categories.cfm?catid=250*

Updater for Flash Remoting components, and Remoting gateway for ASP.NET and Java
> *http://www.macromedia.com/support/flash_remoting/releasenotes/mx/*
> *releasenotes_updater.html*

Documentation about integrating Java in ColdFusion applications (when registering ActionScript classes on the server)

>*http://livedocs.macromedia.com/cfmxdocs/Developing_ColdFusion_MX_Applications_with_CFML/Java.jsp*

Documentation for Flash Remoting

>*http://livedocs.macromedia.com/frdocs/Using_Flash_Remoting_MX/contents.htm*

Article on using Server-Side ActionScript in JRun 4

>*http://www.macromedia.com/support/flash/flashremoting/using_serverside_actions*

Macromedia Flash Exchange

>*http://www.macromedia.com/cfusion/exchange/index.cfm?view=sn110*

Best practice white papers and articles

>*http://www.macromedia.com/devnet/mx/blueprint/articles/flashbp.html*

>*http://www.macromedia.com/devnet/mx/flashremoting/white_papers.html*

Open Source Flash Remoting Projects

FLAP, an open source project adding Flash Remoting to Perl

>*http://www.simonf.com/flap*

AMFPHP, an open source project for Flash Remoting using PHP-based servers

>*http://www.amfphp.org*

OpenAMF, an open source project for Flash Remoting using Java

>*http://www.openamf.org*

Articles, Blogs, and Utilities

Andrew Muller has posted some good Flash Remoting tutorials in the Tips and Tricks section

>*http://www.daemon.com.au/index.cfm?objectid=615224B1-D0B7-4CD6-F9ED2333AA0EB068*

Blog from the Flash Community Manager, Mike Chambers

>*http://www.macromedia.com/go/blog_mchambers*

Connecting to the Amazon.com web service using ASP.NET

>*http://www.oreillynet.com/pub/a/javascript/2003/01/09/flash.html*

Documentation for the `<cflogin>` tag

>*http://livedocs.macromedia.com/cfmxdocs/Developing_ColdFusion_MX_Applications_with_CFML/appSecurity.jsp*

Good article on Flash Remoting for J2EE, including details on datatypes

>*http://www.onjava.com/pub/a/onjava/2003/02/26/flash_remoting.html*

Interesting weblog that deals with Java issues in Flash Remoting
http://radio.weblogs.com/0113514/

The ASTranslator utility, which aids in transferring Java objects to ActionScript
http://carbonfive.sourceforge.net/astranslator

Flash and ActionScript Resources

Books

ActionScript for Flash MX: The Definitive Guide, Second Edition
by Colin Moock (O'Reilly)

ActionScript Cookbook
by Joey Lott (O'Reilly)

Object-Oriented Programming with ActionScript
by Branden Hall and Samuel Wan (New Riders)

Links

Branden Hall's blog on ActionScript, Flash MX, and related stuff
http://www.waxpraxis.org

A community of developers focused on the MX family of products, including Flash
http://www.communitymx.com

Tutorials and more
http://www.flashguru.co.uk

Great place for Flash components
http://www.flashcomponents.net

Tutorial on building your own component
http://www.flashcomponents.net/tutorials/triangle/triangle.html

More component tutorials
http://www.macromedia.com/devnet/flashmx

Other Books of Interest

Dreamweaver

Dreamweaver MX: The Complete Reference
by Ray West and Tom Muck (McGraw-Hill Osborne Media)

Dreamweaver MX: The Missing Manual
by David McFarland (Pogue Press/O'Reilly)

ASP.NET

Programming ASP.NET
   by Dan Hurwitz and Jesse Liberty (O'Reilly)

ASP.NET in a Nutshell, Second Edition
   by G. Andrew Duthie and Matthew MacDonald (O'Reilly)

Programming C#, Third Edition
   by Jesse Liberty (O'Reilly)

Programming Visual Basic .NET, Second Edition
   by Dave Grundgeiger (O'Reilly)

Java

Head First Java
   by Kathy Sierra and Bert Bates (O'Reilly)

Learning Java, Second Edition
   by Patrick Niemeyer and Jonathan Knudsen (O'Reilly)

Java in a Nutshell, Fourth Edition
   by David Flanagan (O'Reilly)

Database Programming with JDBC and Java, Second Edition
   by George Reese (O'Reilly)

Java Web Services
   by David Chappell and Tyler Jewell (O'Reilly)

Java Servlet Programming, Second Edition
   by Jason Hunter with William Crawford (O'Reilly)

JavaServer Pages, Second Edition
   by Hans Bergsten (O'Reilly)

ColdFusion

Programming ColdFusion MX
   by Rob Brooks-Bilson (O'Reilly)

Macromedia ColdFusion MX: Web Application Construction Kit
   by Ben Forta, Nate Weiss, Leon Chalnick, and Angela Buraglia (Peachpit Press)

Web Services

Programming Web Services with SOAP
   by Pavel Kulchenko, James Snell, and Doug Tidwell (O'Reilly)

Web Services Essentials
   by Ethan Cerami (O'Reilly)

SQL

SQL in a Nutshell
  by Kevin Kline (O'Reilly)

Transact-SQL Cookbook
  by Jonathan Gennick and Ales Spetic (O'Reilly)

Sams Teach Yourself SQL in 10 Minutes
  by Ben Forta (Sams Publishing)

XML

XML in a Nutshell, Second Edition
  by Elliotte Rusty Harold and W. Scott Means (O'Reilly)

PHP

Programming PHP
  by Rasmus Lerdorf and Kevin Tatroe (O'Reilly)

Web Database Applications with PHP & MySQL
  by David Lane and Hugh E. Williams (O'Reilly)

Other Technologies

JavaScript: The Definitive Guide, Second Edition
  by David Flanagan (O'Reilly)

Mastering Regular Expressions, Fourth Edition
  by Jeffrey E. F. Friedl (O'Reilly)

Other Links of Interest

ASP.NET

Microsoft's main ASP.NET site, including downloads for the Web Matrix tool
  http://www.asp.net

O'Reilly's site for all things .NET
  http://dotnet.oreilly.com

Respected site for ASP and ASP.NET developers
  http://www.4guysfromrolla.com

Basics and more
  http://www.asp101.com

Microsoft's developer site
  http://msdn.microsoft.com

ColdFusion

Macromedia's developer site
http://www.macromedia.com/devnet

Publishers of *ColdFusion Developer's Journal*
http://www.sys-con.com/coldfusion

Community site full of tutorials and other content
http://www.communitymx.com

XML

O'Reilly's XML site
http://xml.oreilly.com

Web Services

O'Reilly's site for web services and SOAP
http://webservices.oreilly.com

PHP

Main PHP site, with downloads and documentation
http://www.php.net/

PHP tutorials and articles
http://www.phpbuilder.com

Java

Main Java site with Java downloads and information
http://java.sun.com

Sun's online documentation and tutorial
http://java.sun.com/docs/books/tutorial

O'Reilly's Java site
http://java.oreilly.com

Database Links

Microsoft SQL Server home page
http://www.microsoft.com/sql

Home page for Oracle's line of database products
http://www.oracle.com/ip/deploy/database/index.html

Official home page for MySQL
http://www.mysql.com/

Home page for PostgreSQL
http://www.postgresql.org/index.html

IBM DB2 information
http://www-4.ibm.com/software/data/db2

Other Technologies

Information on the Rhino parser, the basis of Server-Side ActionScript
http://www.mozilla.org/rhino

Specification and Implementation for a Real-World Application

This appendix includes details of the user interface specification and implementation of the real-world script repository application demonstrated in Chapter 14. It is instructive insofar as it shows how you might specify your application for the UI designer. It also shows how a good UI designer can improve the specification based on appropriate considerations and then implement it accordingly. Notes from the designer are shown in *italics*.

1. Screens

    The application is a Script Repository that allows users to paste scripts into a text field and stores them in a central repository database. Users can download scripts, and registered users can add scripts to the database.

    The UI should be one screen, with subscreens that pop up depending on the activity of the user. For example, if a user clicks Login, he is presented with a dialog box with a Submit button that asks for his username and password. If a user clicks Register, he is presented with a registration box.

    The Flash movie size should be about 800×600 so that it fills the entire browser window.

2. Main

    The main screen should always be in view and show all options available.

    The main screen is composed of two sections: the main area, where all the screens appear and which occupies 90% of the screen, and the navigation bar, at the bottom of the screen. The navigation bar is composed of an administrative section (on the left) and a main navigation section (which automatically disappears when not in use). When the application loads, the main navigation section appears for one second to catch user's attention.

    All the buttons (both in the content section and navigation) are displayed on a black background so they can be distinguished with ease.

    The whole application is made with vector graphics so that it can be easily scaled to any dimensions.

3. Login

(y pos: 1635 px) (y pos indicates position of movie clip symbol off stage; see designer notes at end of this appendix.)

Allows a user to log in.

The Login screen should have the following components and fields, or equivalents: username_txt, password_txt, login_btn

A fake login routine has been implemented. To activate the grayed-out buttons on the main navigation, you first have to log in on the login section.

4. Register

(y pos: 2180 px)

Allows a new user to register, with personal information and username/password combination.

The registration screen should have the following components and fields, or equivalents: firstname_txt, lastname_txt, email_txt, username_txt, password_txt, passwordconfirm_txt, hintquestion_txt, hintanswer_txt, register_btn.

5. Failed login

A simple message box that alerts a user if the login failed.

Implemented as custom message box.

6. Failed registration

A simple message box that alerts a user if the registration failed (username exists, etc.).

Implemented as custom message box.

7. About box

(y pos: 3270 px)

A simple screen that displays information about the company. The About screen should have the following components and fields, or equivalents:

- Company Name: aboutname_txt (single line)
- Company Description: aboutdesc_txt (multiline)

8. View Scripts

(y pos: 0 px)

A simple listing of scripts in a Tree component to allow all users to view the scripts available and drill down to a View Script page for a particular script. The View Scripts screen should have the following components and fields, or equivalents: search_txt, search_btn, scripttree_tree (Tree component).

9. View Script

(merged with previous item, "View Scripts")

A page with details of an individual script. This also contains a link to allow a script to be downloaded and a send-to-a-friend link to send this detail page link to an email address. The View Script screen should have the following components and fields, or equivalents:

- Name of the script: scriptname_txt (single line)
- Description: scriptdesc_txt (multiline) + scriptdesc_sb *(added ScrollBar component)*
- Code: scriptcode_txt (multiline) + scriptcode_sb *(added ScrollBar component)*
- Language: scriptlanguage_cb (ComboBox component)
- Category: scriptcategory_cb (ComboBox component)
- Date uploaded: scriptdateuploaded_txt (single line)
- Date modified: scriptdatemodified_txt (single line)
- Version number: scriptversion_txt (single line)
- Author of script: scriptuser_cb (ComboBox component)
- Download button: scriptdownload_btn

10. Send to a friend

   (merged with previous item, "View Script")

   Simple form to allow a user to send a View Script page to a friend. The Send to a friend screen should have the following components and fields, or equivalents:

   - Script URL: sendurl_txt *(Not implemented visually; should be hidden)*
   - Script Name: sendname_txt *(Not implemented visually; should be hidden)*
   - Send to: sendto_txt
   - Send button: send_btn

11. Upload Script

   (y pos: 545 px)

   A blank form to allow a registered user to upload a script to the database. Interface can be identical to the View Script interface, however all fields should allow user input.

   - Upload button: scriptupload_btn

   Note: User must be logged-in to see this page; therefore, the "Author of script" field from the View Script screen should be hidden on the Upload screen and has not been enclosed as dynamic field.

12. Modify Script

   (y pos: 1090 px)

   A form that mimics the Upload Script form that is pre-filled in with information about a script that needs to be updated.

   - Drop-down list of scripts: scriptname_cb (ComboBox component)
   - Modify button: scriptmodify_btn

Note: User must be logged to see this page; therefore, the "Author of script" field should be hidden and has not been enclosed as dynamic field.

13. Contact Form

(y pos: 2725 px)

Allow a user to contact the site administrator. The Contact form screen should have the following components and fields, or equivalents:

- Message to send: message_txt
- Submit button: contact_btn

Notes from the Designer

A fake login routine has been implemented. To activate the grayed-out buttons on the main navigation, you first have to log in on the login section.

All the content's movie clips are contained on the Library's content_main_mc symbol. If you need to change their instance names, first move them onto the visible area and, once renamed, move them again to their original position (all the positions are indicated on this document near the name of the section). If the Property inspector won't accept those pixel values, you should use the keyboard to return the movie clips to their original positions.

The following are the hexadecimal values of the tints used on the application:

- EEFDE1
- D9EFB4
- 8BB60A
- 618901

They have been added as swatches to the *.fla* source file and can be accessed from the Color Swatches panel.

The fonts used in the movie are the following:

- URW++ Neuzeit Grotesk T Regular
- URW++ Neuzeit Grotesk T Black

http://www.myfonts.com/fonts/urw/neuzeit-grotesk/

Note that all fonts have been embedded due to large use of masks (MM technote: *http://www.macromedia.com/support/flash/ts/documents/maskprintembed.htm*)

The following Flash components are used on the application:

- Tree—Flash UI Components Set 2
- ScrollBar—Flash UI Components Set 1
- ComboBox—Flash UI Components Set 1

Index

We'd like to hear your suggestions for improving our indexes. Send email to *index@oreilly.com*.

S

About the Author

Tom Muck is coauthor of six Macromedia-related books, including the bestseller *Dreamweaver UltraDev 4: The Complete Reference*. He is an extensibility expert focused on the integration of Macromedia products with ColdFusion, ASP, PHP, and other languages, applications, and technologies, and is a founding member of Community MX (*http://www.communitymx.com*). When not in front of the computer, Tom works on his Hong Kong movie collection. Once an aspiring heavy-metal musician, Tom is now content in his old age to sit on the porch playing the blues on his harmonica and banging out Robert Johnson songs on his beat-up acoustic guitar.

Contributors

Alon Salant, the author of Chapter 7, is an owner of Carbon Five (*http://www.carbonfive.com*), a premium services consultancy specializing in rich user experiences for Enterprise Java applications. He has been integrating Flash interfaces with server-side applications since 1998, is well-known as a developer of the ASTranslator project, and has contributed articles to the O'Reilly Network (*http://oreillynet.com*).

Joel Martinez, the author of Chapter 8, is a .NET developer based in Orlando, Florida. He is a partner at Community MX (*http://www.communitymx.com*) and founded the Orlando .NET User Group (*http://www.onetug.org*) to try and spread the .NET gospel.

Branden Hall, the author of Chapter 9, is a well-known ActionScript developer and instructor. He is a frequent speaker at industry conferences, including Flash Forward. He is the coauthor of *Object-Oriented Programming in ActionScript*. His personal site is at *http://www.waxpraxis.org*.

Colophon

Our look is the result of reader comments, our own experimentation, and feedback from distribution channels. Distinctive covers complement our distinctive approach to technical topics, breathing personality and life into potentially dry subjects.

The animal featured on the cover of *Flash Remoting: The Definitive Guide* is a cuttlefish. Cuttlefish (*Sepia officinalis*) are commonly found in the eastern Atlantic from England to North Africa and throughout the Mediterranean Sea. This soft-bodied marine creature belongs to the Cephalopoda class and, like all cephalopods, has a large head ringed by arms. Cuttlefish have eight arms, plus two long tentacles with suckers on their ends. Cuttlefish are usually about a foot long, and they move through the water by rippling a skirt of fins. They are sometimes called the chameleons of the sea because they can easily change their striped skin color to hide from predators or communicate with other cuttlefish.

In addition to the camouflage offered by their ability to change color, threatened cuttlefish use ink to defend themselves. Their ink glands produce a foul-smelling dark brown ink that distracts enemies such as sharks, larger fish, and even other cuttlefish. They can then fill the ink funnel with water, expel it, and propel themselves to safety. Cuttlefish ink (also called sepia) was once used to color photographs; however, they are no longer fished for this purpose, and cuttlefish caught in trawl nets usually wind up on a dinner table.

Cuttlefish are also well-known for the one bone in their body, called the cuttlebone. This bone is made up of porous calcium carbonate that allows the cuttlefish to control its buoyancy by changing the proportions of liquid to air within chambers of the bone. Cuttlebones often wash ashore and are the only remains of a cuttlefish after its death. These bones are often sold as bill-sharpeners for captive birds or are ground up and offered as a source of calcium for other pets.

Genevieve d'Entremont was the production editor for *Flash Remoting: The Definitive Guide*. Brian Sawyer proofread the book. Emily Quill and Claire Cloutier provided quality control. Mary Agner, Jamie Peppard, and James Quill provided production assistance. Octal Publishing, Inc. wrote the index.

Emma Colby designed the cover of this book, based on a series design by Edie Freedman. The cover image is a 19th-century engraving from *Cuvier's Animals*. Emma Colby produced the cover layout with QuarkXPress 4.1 using Adobe's ITC Garamond font.

David Futato designed the interior layout. This book was converted by Andrew Savikas and Julie Hawks to FrameMaker 5.5.6 with a format conversion tool created by Erik Ray, Jason McIntosh, Neil Walls, and Mike Sierra that uses Perl and XML technologies. The text font is Linotype Birka; the heading font is Adobe Myriad Condensed; and the code font is LucasFont's TheSans Mono Condensed. The illustrations that appear in the book were produced by Robert Romano and Jessamyn Read using Macromedia FreeHand 9 and Adobe Photoshop 6. The tip and warning icons were drawn by Christopher Bing. This colophon was written by Philip Dangler.